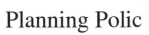
Planning Polic

Planning Policy

Richard Harwood QC

39 Essex Chambers and Bar Library, Belfast

and Victoria Hutton

Barrister

39 Essex Chambers

Bloomsbury Professional

Bloomsbury Professional

An imprint of Bloomsbury Publishing Plc

Bloomsbury Professional Ltd
41–43 Boltro Road
Haywards Heath
RH16 1BJ
UK

Bloomsbury Publishing Plc
50 Bedford Square
London
WC1B 3DP
UK

www.bloomsbury.com
BLOOMSBURY and the Diana logo are trademarks of
Bloomsbury Publishing Plc

British Library Cataloguing-in-Publication Data

A catalogue record for this book is available from the British Library.

ISBN: PB: 9781784516581
            ePDF: 9781784516604
            ePub: 9781784516598

Typeset by Phoenix Photosetting, Chatham, Kent
Printed and bound in Great Britain by CPI Group (UK) Ltd, Croydon, CR0 4YY

To find out more about our authors and books visit
www.bloomsburyprofessional.com. Here you will find extracts, author information,
details of forthcoming events and the option to sign up for our newsletters.

For James
&
Sebastian

Preface

Planning is as much about influence as it is about control – the ability of one public body to persuade other authorities and the private sector what development they should propose or resist. Traditionally, the Minister sits at the top of the tree, but the ability of the most energetic ministerial team to decide many cases has its limits. Similarly, in local authorities, councillors are in charge, yet the great majority of planning applications are decided by officers. Generally, planning applications come not from the planning authorities but in the main from the private sector and other public bodies. What development is needed, where it can go, and how it can be done, are matters that the planning authorities will want to set out before dealing with proposals on a case-by-case basis.

All of this is the realm of planning policy.

In this book we endeavour to do two things: to set out what the forms of planning policy are; and to explain how it is made. The first task is not as easy as it may seem. Beyond the obviously identified planning policies of ministers and local planning authorities, a wide range of public bodies have policies which are intended to influence planning decisions or which will necessarily do so. We have cast the net to catch the policies of other public authorities, such as the Environment Agency, which have distinct effects on land use planning and development. We look at the policy-making processes inevitably with lawyers' eyes (this is a law book after all) but also with a view to giving practical advice to plan-making authorities and interested parties on how to conduct the process. The meaning of particular planning policies and, in particular, the thankless task of trying to keep up with the myriad judgments on the meaning of the National Planning Policy Framework in England, let alone trying to reconcile them, we leave to others.

Law and practice is covered in England, Wales and Northern Ireland. The similarities in planning policy and its preparation across the three nations are greater than the differences, but they all have separate legislative bases and alterations in the guidance on the processes and their detail. We therefore set out general principles and practical advice which applies to all three: legal principles; strategic environmental assessment ('SEA') and habitats; examination practice; and legal challenges. These chapters will be useful in all contexts. The bulk of the case law and practical guidance has originated in England, but Northern Ireland has been a source of important SEA decisions. Planning policies and their processes are covered on a nation-by-nation basis, starting at the Ministerial level and moving down to the most local policies. Finally, we cover marine planning and a range of national and local policies, mainly from non-planning bodies. Some are parochial, whilst others are deployed across the UK.

We have sought to state the law as at 1 December 2017, but were able to make reference to later regulations.

As always, this book has benefited from our work and discussions with numerous colleagues in Chambers, other lawyers, planning officers, civil servants, consultants,

Preface

inspectors and judges. In particular, thanks are due to those officers and consultants with whom we have worked for long hours on local plan preparation. The chapters on Northern Ireland have drawn on Richard's practice as a member of the Bar Library in Belfast and training provided for the Planning Appeals Commission. The book draws generally on Richard's experience on the Local Plans Expert Group ('LPEG') which was appointed by the Housing and Planning Minister in 2015 to consider the local plan system in England. The thoughts of the multi-disciplinary members of the group, its civil service assistance and the representations made to it, have helped shape the practical advice. We draw shamelessly, and with approval, on LPEG's recommendations.

The Planning and Compulsory Purchase Act 2004 dramatically changed the process of plan-making with examinations into the plan rather than inquiries into objections, statutory and policy tests and binding reports. Whilst much of the Act has been amended, scrapped or supplemented and new plans have been devised, it caused a decisive shift in the case law. Few of the previous decisions are any longer of significance. Where they are, then they are picked up in the text. The bulk of the pertinent judgments have been delivered in the last ten years by new generations of judges.

Coming to the fore amongst these was Dame Frances Patterson. As one of the first judges of the Planning Court, and subsequently its lead judge, Frances delivered a series of judgments, including *IM Properties*, *JJ Gallagher* and *Stonegate*, which grappled with the workings of these new regimes. Her tragically early death has deprived those who work in planning of a valued colleague and friend.

As always, thanks are due to the team at Bloomsbury Professional. Leanne Barrett has given the right amount of encouragement as we have pondered the evolving mass of legislation, guidance and case law. Jenny Lank, Harriet Espin-Bradley and Jubriel Hanid have handled the design and marketing with charm and efficiency. Susan Ghaiwal turned around the proofs at great speed and saved us from a variety of mishaps.

Writing legal textbooks comes on top of working for clients. It does tend to get fitted into evenings and weekends. We therefore owe an immense debt to our families. Richard thanks Gráinne for everything in general and Cathan, James and Sophie in particular for allowing the book to be fitted around footballing commitments. For her part, Victoria thanks Matthew for everything, but in particular, his patience, Dad for setting the family trend for textbook writing, and Mum for providing the childcare for two-month old Sebastian which meant this book could finally be completed.

Richard Harwood OBE QC
Victoria Hutton

39 Essex Chambers
81 Chancery Lane
London
WC2A 1DD

December 2017

Contents

Contents

Table of statutes

Table of statutory instruments

Table of cases

Table of cases

Chapter 1

Introduction

1.1   A policy is a statement by a person or body of how they would or are likely to reach a decision or how they would like others to act in particular circumstances. It may set out general principles to be applied to a whole range of decisions or it may anticipate one individual decision. The classic example of the latter is a site allocation policy which sets out detailed criteria for an acceptable scheme. In either situation, policy is being used to guide the decision whether to authorise a particular proposal.

A need for policy arises because a public body makes a multitude of discretionary decisions. Both of these aspects are important. If decisions were few and far between then there would be too little experience to formulate policy and either sufficient differences between the proposals that any policy would be of little use or such similarities that the earlier decision could be repeated. The existence of discretion is required since if the decision maker merely applies rules then the sole question to ask is whether the particular proposal complies with the rules. What the rules are may be underpinned by policy, but that goes to the discretion in setting the rules.

The need for policy when numerous discretionary decisions are to be taken arises because of the importance attached to consistency and fairness. Everyone wants the right result to be reached in any individual decision which affects or interests them. The right result will depend upon the particular circumstances of that case. Those circumstances must be considered and cannot be disregarded. A small matter might change the outcome, and what is right in one case might not be appropriate two doors further down the road.

However, deciding a case on its merits does not sanction a free for all. An outcome which just depends upon what an individual or individuals happen to decide on for particular circumstances on a particular day generates numerous problems. Firstly, an applicant will have difficulty in knowing what to do to receive an approval. Beyond establishing what is legally capable of being relevant (and in planning that is an extremely wide category), a person will have little to tell them what is likely to be found to be acceptable. Other parties will struggle to know what the decision maker will see as important. Past decisions may provide some assistance – as even the most wilful decision maker is likely to feel that there is some consistency in their actions. The decision which was taken two doors down the road will have some bearing because of its effect on the reality on the ground and, if the decision is remembered, because the authority will want to be able to explain both outcomes, at least in its own mind. The explanation could be that the first conclusion was wrong and ought not to be repeated, but generally a public body will want to assert that it is both consistent and correct. For these reasons it is overly simplistic to assert that planning applications are determined on their own merits and have no precedent effect.

1.1 *Introduction*

Wildly unpredictable decision-making will tend to be seen as unfair. The householder will want to be able to understand why a different outcome was reached two doors down the road. If decision-making is seen as unpredictable then development might not be proposed or inefficient applications made – that is schemes which prove to be unacceptable or which are insufficiently ambitious.

However, evolving consistency through individual decisions is a slow process and would often be unsuccessful even if the decision maker does not change.

Lord Clyde explained in *R (on the application of Alconbury Developments Ltd) v Secretary of State for the Environment, Transport and the Regions*:[1]

> 'The formulation of policies is a perfectly proper course for the provision of guidance in the exercise of an administrative discretion. Indeed policies are an essential element in securing the coherent and consistent performance of administrative functions. There are advantages both to the public and the administrators in having such policies. Of course there are limits to be observed in the way policies are applied. Blanket decisions which leave no room for particular circumstances may be unreasonable. What is crucial is that the policy must not fetter the exercise of the discretion. The particular circumstances always require to be considered. Provided that the policy is not regarded as binding and the authority still retains a free exercise of discretion the policy may serve the useful purpose of giving a reasonable guidance both to applicants and decision makers.'

Policy is also a mechanism for one public authority to influence another. Indeed it is the principal means by which government Ministers influence local planning authority policies and decisions. Ministers can take over planning applications, and applications for some very major developments are made directly to central government. However, set against hundreds of Ministerial planning decisions a year, are hundreds of thousands of local authority decisions. Even planning appeals which put around 20,000 planning decisions into the hands of Ministers or their Inspectors are meant to be decided primarily on local policy. Ministers have power to take over or to direct changes to local policies, but that is rarely exercised. Legislation says very little about the substance of planning decisions, only occasionally ascribing weight to particular matters. So most of the influence that Ministers have on the outcome of planning decisions is attributable to their planning policies and the expectation that those will be carried out.

This illustrates one of the tensions in the policy-making process. How far is local policy a matter for local bodies and to what extent is it constrained by national policy? On one approach national policy could simply be a view which could be adopted or discarded as locals like. The alternative extreme is for local policy to be little more than the application and outworking of national policy in a particular area. Planning policy-making is therefore one example of the uncertain relationship between national and local government. Ministerial intervention powers are rarely used but plans at the local council level are examined by Inspectors or Commissioners who are civil servants. They seek to operate independently (and that independence is more formalised in Northern Ireland), but look at issues against a framework of national policy.

There has been a national reluctance, in all jurisdictions, to say in law that local policy should be in accordance with national policy. That has been seen as taking

---

[1]   [2001] UKHL 23, [2003] 2 AC 295, at para 143.

centralisation too far. In England the Planning and Compulsory Purchase Act 2004 had introduced a hierarchy of control, with local policies having to be in general conformity with regional spatial strategies which were prepared in the area but ultimately made by Ministers. This regional system was swept aside in the Localism Act 2011 because it resulted in too much national control. The development plan status being accorded to the new National Development Framework for Wales may be the first formal imposition of national supremacy. Instead of legal command, national policy has been used to expect consistency (in some form) with national policy. Since policy is only a relevant consideration and so does not have to be followed, a national policy that national policy should be followed is based on a certain amount of hope and circularity. Government-appointed examiners are sensitive both to the expectations of national government and their role in considering someone else's policy.

The other tension is between the policy makers and everyone else. A traditional view of policy-making is that it is for the public authority concerned to decide what its policy is. The more modern approach is to consult on policy before it is adopted because that should produce a more informed and so better policy and to allow those affected by policy to feel that they have had some opportunity to be involved in its making. Usually in government this is a written process, with the public body being the judge of its own policy, subject only to the law. Historically local planning policy has been an exception. Those interested have had the ability to challenge and propose to an independent person at an inquiry or examination.

That leads to a high level of scrutiny but again brings into relief the question of whose plan is it? An examination which will not lead to change, regardless of what the examiner thinks, is fruitless but the examiner has not been elected to write the plan. This leads to compromise. Before 2004, Inspector's reports were not binding upon local authorities and so Inspectors could take a relatively unfettered view of the merits of the plan, knowing that the council could, with reasons, disagree. That said, the great majority of recommendations were accepted. The Planning and Compulsory Purchase Act 2004 introduced binding Inspector's reports but introduced a statutory limit on the ability of Inspectors to act. They could only require changes if they were necessary to render the plan sound. So the local planning authority can prepare any plan it likes as long as it is sound. The limits of the Inspector's remit and indeed the meaning of 'sound' are explicitly or implicitly part of the debate at every examination.

These relationships, between central and local government, plan makers and other parties and examiners and form the key to the practices and procedures for planning policy-making at the strategic, local and neighbourhood level. There is no straightforward or obviously right answer to how they should interact and that helps explain the variations between different documents and nations.

POLICY AND GUIDANCE

1.2   A distinction is sometimes drawn between policy and guidance, with guidance being seen as more advisory than determinative.

In legal terms policy and guidance are the same. If relevant, they both have to be considered. Some documents do have a statutory status but some are non-statutory. The significance which the maker attaches to the document does depend upon its terms. It may be apparent from the document as a whole that a good practice guide is not to be applied with the same rigour as a policy. In England the Planning Practice Guidance ('PPG') is meant to sit below the National Planning Policy Framework ('NPPF'), but much of the PPG is policy which Ministers expect decision makers to adhere to. Indeed, some of it heavily qualifies parts of the NPPF.

Planning policy is a combination of documents adopted under statutory powers and policies which are non-statutory.

PLANNING POLICY IN ENGLAND

1.3   In England planning policy may be:

(i)   non-statutory national policy adopted by a Secretary of State usually on planning matters. This is now contained in the NPPF but until 2012 was in Planning Policy Statements ('PPSs'), Planning Policy Guidance Notes ('PPGs'), Mineral Planning Statements ('MPSs') and Mineral Policy Statements ('MPGs'). Further detail is contained in the Planning Practice Guidance, first published in March 2014 and revised on an ad hoc basis. Confusingly, this is also abbreviated to PPG;

(ii)   National Policy Statements, which are statutory policies on particular types of development;[2]

(iii)   other national policy. This may be specific to planning, often in the form of a Written Ministerial Statement to Parliament, or other national policy which explicitly or implicitly guides planning decisions. Other policy may have important effects, such as waste or air quality;

(iv)   remaining elements of regional strategies adopted by the Secretary of State under the Local Democracy, Economic Development and Construction Act 2009. These were mostly abolished under the Localism Act 2011;

(v)   the London Plan adopted by the Mayor of London;[3]

(vi)   non-statutory Supplementary Planning Guidance made by the Mayor of London;

(vii)   spatial development strategies made by combined authorities;

(vi)   local plans or development plan documents adopted by local planning authorities;[4]

(vii)   supplementary planning documents adopted by local planning authorities;[5]

(viii)   local development documents adopted by local planning authorities and which are not local plans, development plan documents or supplementary planning documents;

---

[2]   Adopted under the Planning Act 2008.
[3]   Adopted under the Greater London Authority Act 1999. See Chapter 9.
[4]   Government policy and the current regulations refer to local plans but the Planning and Compulsory Purchase Act 2004 calls them development plan documents.
[5]   Development plan documents and supplementary planning documents are adopted under the Planning and Compulsory Purchase Act 2004.

(ix) neighbourhood development plans prepared by town and parish councils or neighbourhood fora and made by local planning authorities following a referendum or draft plans which have been supported by referendum but which are not yet made.[6]

PLANNING POLICY IN WALES

1.4   In Wales planning policy may be:

(i) non-statutory national policy adopted by the Welsh Ministers in the form of Planning Policy (Wales)[7] and Technical Advice Notes (TANs) with older circulars and other documents;

(ii) the Wales Spatial Plan adopted under the Planning and Compulsory Purchase Act 2004;[8]

(iii) a National Development Framework for Wales to be introduced by the Planning (Wales) Act 2015 replacing the Wales Spatial Plan;

(iv) a strategic development plan to be introduced by the Planning (Wales) Act 2015;

(v) local development plans adopted by local planning authorities (which are due to replace unitary development plans);

(vi) non-statutory Supplementary Planning Guidance adopted by local planning authorities.

PLANNING POLICY IN NORTHERN IRELAND

1.5   In Northern Ireland there are:

(i) the Regional Development Strategy;

(ii) the Spatial Planning Policy Statement for Northern Ireland;

(iii) Planning Policy Statements;

(iv) Development Plan Practice Notes;

(v) Development Management Practice Notes;

(vi) departmental development plans;

(vii) local development plans; and

(viii) Supplementary Planning Guidance.

The first six types of Northern Irish documents are made by the Northern Ireland Executive (currently the Department for Infrastructure). Local development plans are adopted by councils, who may also prepare Supplementary Planning Guidance.

---

[6]   Made under the Planning and Compulsory Purchase Act 2004, as amended by the Localism Act 2011 and the Neighbourhood Planning Act 2017.

[7]   Currently the 9th edition (November 2016).

[8]   Adopted in 2004 and updated in 2008.

DRAFT POLICY AND OTHER SOURCES

1.6 In all cases draft policy may be relevant, although the weight to be attached to it will depend upon the degree of confidence as to whether it is likely to be adopted in that form.

In addition, in all nations there has been a mass of supporting material which may be relevant to decision-making, such as 'Companion Guides' or 'Good Practice Guides' to national policy guidance and letters to local authorities from the Chief Planner. Since 2010, there has been a concerted effort in England to cut down this further documentation.

There is also a variety of statutory policy documents which whilst not usually planning policies, may be relevant to particular planning issues. These include conservation area proposals or an area of outstanding natural beauty management plan.

Marine planning is now subject to a UK-wide Marine Policy Statement[9] and marine plans prepared for different areas.[10]

A range of non-statutory guidance documents from specialist government agencies might also be material.

THE DEVELOPMENT PLAN

1.7 The development plan is intended to be the primary planning policy for guiding development and determining planning applications in its particular area. Historically it has been the one matter singled out for consideration in any planning application.[11] In all three jurisdictions there is a presumption that planning decisions will be made in accordance with it. For England and Wales the Planning and Compulsory Purchase Act 2004, s 38(6) provides:

> 'If regard is to be had to the development plan for the purpose of any determination to be made under the planning Acts the determination must be made in accordance with the plan unless material considerations indicate otherwise.'

Similarly, the Planning Act (Northern Ireland) 2011, s 6(4) says:

> 'Where, in making any determination under this Act, regard is to be had to the local development plan, the determination must be made in accordance with the plan unless material considerations indicate otherwise.'

Whilst referred to in the singular, 'the development plan' may comprise a number of plans prepared by a variety of different authorities. There may be tensions between those documents, both in the course of preparation and in their use when determining planning applications.

---

9   Under the Marine and Coastal Access Act 2009, s 44.
10   Marine and Coastal Access Act 2009, Pt 3.
11   See the Town and Country Planning Act 1990, s 70(2): 'the provisions of the development plan, so far as material to the application'. See also the Planning Act (Northern Ireland) 2011, s 45(1). In England, local finance considerations were added to the Town and Country Planning Act 1990, s 70(2) by the Localism Act 2011.

Material considerations include anything other than the development plan which is relevant to the particular decision which is being taken. Part of these will be other policies. A further tension is the use of national planning policy to trump development plan policies when planning applications are being decided.

Traditionally, development plans have been prepared by local planning authorities and set out their policies and proposals for the development and use of land.[12] Although they have more recently been prepared by a wider range of bodies, development plans contain area-wide policies, site-specific designations and sites allocated for particular forms of development.

---

[12] The current local planning authority powers are in the Planning and Compulsory Purchase Act 2004, Pt 2 (for England) and Pt 6 (for Wales) and in the Planning Act (Northern Ireland) 2011, Pt 2.

Chapter 2

Legal Principles

2.1   There are many common legal principles which apply to policy making notwithstanding the multitude of differences between the individual processes. Before plunging into considering the individual regimes, it is useful to consider those requirements which arise on all or most planning policy making.

This chapter focuses on public law principles (so common law) and the operation of statutory processes which are used in various plans and duties on policy-makers to consider particular issues. It also considers some over-arching duties which arise in England, Wales and Northern Ireland. Chapter 3 addresses strategic environmental assessment and European habitats protection. Again keeping to common approaches, examination processes are considered in Chapter 21.

Legal duties derive either from statute (legislation made by Parliament, the Welsh Assembly, the Northern Ireland Assembly, the European Union ('EU') or Ministers making secondary legislation) or from judge-made law (the common law). The courts apply both. The law as it applies specifically to government decisions is known as public law. There is considerable overlap: a government decision is usually subject to duties imposed by statute and common law. The courts require compliance with statute and sometimes what common law might require is modified by legislation.

EU law binds government (and sometimes private persons) in the English and Welsh courts as it has been incorporated by Parliament's European Communities Act 1972. Other international law binds the UK government at an international level but not in this country's courts unless it has been incorporated by UK law.

THE POWER TO MAKE A POLICY

2.2   Decisions can only be taken by individuals or committees who are given the power to act. It is not simply a question of the body or person who is the relevant authority but may be who within that body is authorised to take the steps or who is able to act in that person's name. A decision taken by a person without authority is unlawful and liable to be quashed by the Court.

Policy-making powers are often conferred by statute, indeed, this book would be much shorter if plan-making was not authorised and controlled by legislation. However, the ability to create policy may also arise at common law or be implicit.

A public authority with a power to exercise a discretion may make a policy to guide how that discretion will be exercised: *British Oxygen*.[1] Such a policy may

---

[1]   *British Oxygen Co Ltd v Minster of Technology* [1971] AC 610 at 624 per Lord Reid.

be substantive such as setting out the factors to be considered, proposing tests to be applied or guiding outcomes in particular circumstances. A policy may also be procedural, explaining how a decision will be taken, explaining the steps leading up to or following the determination.

Policies might also be made by one public authority to influence the decision making of other public bodies. Mostly commonly, this is policy published by Ministers who wish local authorities to apply it. It is a view from one public body on how another should exercise its discretion. On *British Oxygen* principles there is no difficulty in the Minister setting out the policies which he will apply. However, few planning decisions are taken by Ministers and central government's ability to influence the planning system principally derives from issuing policy which it then followed. Absent express statutory power, the legal basis for issuing such policy has been uncertain.

In *R (on the application of West Berkshire Council) v Secretary of State for Communities and Local Government*[2] the Court of Appeal considered that Ministers in England had the power to issue planning policy as part of the Royal Prerogative. This view was disapproved by the Supreme Court in *Hopkins Homes Ltd v Secretary of State for Communities and Local Government.*[3] Lord Carnwath held that the Minister's 'powers derived, expressly or by implication, from the planning Acts which give him overall responsibility for oversight of the planning system'.[4]

Many planning policies adopted by other public bodies do have an express statutory basis, and where they do then the statutory processes must be followed. A significant number do lack explicit statutory authority, such as the Welsh Assembly Government's Planning Policy Wales and Technical Advice Notes or Supplementary Planning Guidance published by Welsh local authorities or the Mayor of London. In Northern Ireland, however, the Department for infrastructure is given a general policy-making power.[5]

Reviewing policy

2.3   If a public authority is able to establish a policy, then it is able to review and revise it. Whilst revising powers are often provided, the ability to change a policy is implicit. Carnwath LJ observed 'It is a trite proposition in administrative law that no policy can be set in stone. It must be open to reconsideration in the light of changing circumstances.'[6]

---

[2]   [2016] EWCA Civ 441, [2016] 1 WLR 3923, at para 12 per Laws and Treacy LJJ.
[3]   [2017] UKSC 37, [2017] 1 WLR 1865.
[4]   At paras 19 and 20. He had reached a similar view in *R (on the application of Hillingdon London Borough Council) v Secretary of State for Transport* [2010] EWHC 626 (Admin), [2010] JPL 976 that the Minister's publication of aviation policy was under the Civil Aviation Act 1982, s 1 of which charges the Secretary of State for Transport with the 'general duty of organising, carrying out and encouraging measures for... the development of civil aviation' (at para 46).
[5]   Planning Act (Northern Ireland) 2011, s 1(1): 'The Department must formulate and co-ordinate policy for securing the orderly and consistent development of land and the planning of that development'.
[6]   *R (on the application of Hillingdon London Borough Council) v Secretary of State for Transport* [2010] EWHC 626 (Admin), [2010] JPL 976, at para 51.

2.4 *Legal Principles*

Public law duties to be adequately informed

2.4   A public authority must have sufficient information before making a decision and in some circumstances must take steps to obtain that information. This is firstly a matter of good governance, essentially a political point that politicians will want to be properly informed and receive advice which is based on adequate material. Likewise the public and others affected by policy will want to know that it is based upon an understanding of what is happening or which might occur.

Having sufficient information is reflected in several public law duties, applied with varying degrees of exactitude. Firstly, there are matters which the decision maker must consider, whether anyone has raised them or not. These relevant considerations would usually be identified in legislation, although there may be cases where it is implicit that particular information is considered necessary to make a certain decision.

Sometimes the decision maker or a superior body will say or suggest in policy that matters should be considered or be examined by a particular method or reported in a certain way. In general, a public authority is only required to have regard to policy and is not obliged to follow it. In such cases the authority can choose not to do the work, but needs to have decided not to do so, having considered the policy. Legislation may sometimes give an enhanced status to policy, requiring decisions to be made in accordance with it or at least to be consistent with it.

Authorities will need to have regard to anything which is said to them, at least in accordance with consultation processes. It does not follow that they will then necessarily know enough to decide the matter. Responses may raise issues which require more work to be carried out.

Regard to relevant considerations

2.5   In exercising a discretion, a decision maker must have regard to relevant considerations and disregard irrelevant considerations. A relevant consideration is something which may affect the particular decision which is being taken. In principle what is or is not relevant is a matter for the Court whilst the weight to be attached to it is for the public authority concerned to decide.

A difficulty in practice is that the number of matters that might be legitimately considered is so substantial that a decision-maker can be swamped. For example, an authority might consider that an Inspector's report on a plan in another area is helpful in explaining how to deal with the assessment of housing need. However, it would be onerous for all Inspector's reports to be relevant considerations which every plan-making authority must diligently read through before putting finger to keyboard on its own plan. Whilst the public can expect relevant matters which they raise to be considered, they can also expect the authority to do a proper job and consider important issues even if they have not been raised.

Authorities therefore have to take this approach to relevant considerations:

(i)   Legislation may say that certain matters must be considered. That has to be done, whether or not these are raised by participants.

(ii)   If a matter is obviously important then it must be taken into account in any event.

(iii) A public body's policy or guidance may say that particular issues should be considered, policies made on certain topics or assessments carried out. The policy or guidance will itself be relevant (whether by legislation or being obvious) and so the policy-maker will need to consider it. Unless statute requires compliance with the policy, the policy-maker may choose not to follow it.

(iv) It must consider relevant matters contained in representations made pursuant to a right in legislation or policy.

(v) If representations are made without any right to do so (perhaps because they are late), the policy-maker will have to decide whether to consider them at all, which could be affected by the substance of the representation. If the representation is taken into account, then all relevant matters in it must be considered. In deciding to accept such representations the authority must act fairly to others who have or would have made non-statutory representations and to anyone who might have a view on the non-statutory representations which are considered.

(vi) Outside these categories, the policy-maker may choose to take any other relevant considerations into account. It ought not in principle be able to be criticised after the event for failing to address something which it could have, but did not, consider. However, it will need to decide what to consider reasonably, for example, it might be an error to consider merely one year's housing completions if other years might put a different complexion on housebuilding.

Whether to consult

2.6 A basis for consulting prior to adopting a policy may arise because:

(a) legislation requires consultation to be carried out;

(b) a promise to consult has been made either generally or in a particular case so that a legitimate expectation arises;

(c) a policy of consulting has been adopted;

(d) fairness might require consultation.

The source of the consultation proposal alters whether it needs to take place. A statutory obligation to consult must be complied with. A legitimate expectation may be departed from with good reason and a policy of consultation does not have to be followed, although some justification for not complying with the policy would be required. In the policy-making context, fairness will only require consultation if there are already some consultation requirements. Consultation might also be a means of ensuring that the decision maker is adequately informed.

How consultation is carried out

2.7 A decision to consult, whether or not required by law, imposes clear duties.

If consultation is carried out then public law imposes four basic requirements for consultations which were formulated by Stephen Sedley QC, as counsel, in *R v Brent*

London Borough Council ex p Gunning, and set out by Hodgson J.[7] Known as the Sedley requirements, they were distilled in the judgment of the Court of Appeal delivered by Lord Woolf MR in *R v North and East Devon Health Authority ex parte Coughlan*:[8]

> 'It is common ground that, whether or not consultation of interested parties and the public is a legal requirement, if it is embarked upon it must be carried out properly. To be proper, consultation must be undertaken at a time when proposals are still at a formative stage; it must include sufficient reasons for particular proposals to allow those consulted to give intelligent consideration and an intelligent response; adequate time must be given for this purpose; and the product of consultation must be conscientiously taken into account when the ultimate decision is taken.'

Whilst universally applied in the Administrative Court, the Sedley principles were finally adopted by the Supreme Court in *R (Moseley) v Haringey London Borough Council*:[9]

> 'First, that consultation must be at a time when proposals are still at a formative stage. Second, that the proposer must give sufficient reasons for any proposal to permit of intelligent consideration and response. Third … that adequate time must be given for consideration and response and, finally, fourth, that the product of consultation must be conscientiously taken into account in finalising any statutory proposals'.

How consultation is conducted will reflect who is being consulted. It must also be possible for a person who is neither a specialist nor prepared to devote hours of effort into understanding the policies, to make an informed response. But someone who is willing and able to delve into the detail must be able to do so.

Options being open

2.8   An essential part of consultation is that it takes place at a time when the responses are able to change the decision. The Sedley principles talk of 'a formative stage' whilst the Aarhus Convention requires 'early public participation, when all options are open'. That requirement is no more than that no option available under the decision-making process has been ruled in or ruled out and that the decision maker is willing to adopt any of those options after considering what has been said. Options might not be limitless: to take the most obvious example of a planning application, the authority can approve it, refuse it or approve it subject to conditions and planning obligations which control or modify the proposal to a limited degree. A plan or programme may be constrained by legal requirements or superior policies, plans or programmes. However, within the parameters of the plan the options must not have been prohibited. Similarly, whilst a decision-maker can be expected to have an open mind, in terms of a willingness to consider other views and a preparedness to change if persuaded to do so, an empty mind is not required, or even helpful. Politicians are expected to lead and governments to govern. Consultees who are offered a blank sheet may find that the final proposals are ones that they had not even thought of and on which they might have had a lot to say if they had appreciated the possibility.

---

[7]   (1985) 84 LGR 168 at 189.
[8]   [2001] QB 213, at para 108.
[9]   [2014] UKSC 56, [2014] 1 WLR 3947, at para 25 per Lord Wilson JSC.

Seeking comments when all options are open does not dictate whether the plan-maker should offer no suggestions, a list of possible approaches without a preference or their own preferred solution. However, either statutory procedures or published processes may require one or more consultations at particular points in the plan preparation.

The requirement that if consultation is to be undertaken then it should be carried out at a formative stage means that if consultation takes place it covers the principle of the proposal rather than merely the manner of its implementation. For example, in *Sadar v Watford Borough Council*[10] a local authority had decided to delimit the numbers of hackney car licences and then conducted a consultation which was inconsistent as to whether the principle had been settled. Quashing the decision, Wilkie J commented:[11]

> 'The fact that a Council may have come to a provisional view or have a preferred option does not prevent a consultation exercise being conducted in good faith at a stage when the policy is still formative in the sense that no final decision has yet been made. In my judgment, however, it is a difference in kind for it to have made a decision in principle to adopt a policy and, thereafter, to be concerned only with the timing of its implementation and other matters of detail. Whilst a consultation on the timing and manner of implementation may be a proper one on these issues it cannot, in my judgment, be said that such a consultation, insofar as it touches upon the question of principle, is conducted at a point at which policy on that issue is at a formative stage.
>
> On the crucial issue of principle the sequence has been – decision first, consultation later. It is a different matter to decide to reverse a previous decision rather than to take one in the first place and, in my judgment, the consultation exercise and its fruits went, on the issue of principle, to inform a decision of the first type rather than one of the second.'

In *R (on the application of Parents for Legal Action Ltd) v Northumberland County Council*,[12] there was a multi-stage consultation on schools reorganisation from three-tier to two-tier schooling where 'The Defendant acknowledges that at the conclusion of each stage a decision is made which "focuses the future consultation, which has become progressively more detailed and localised"'.[13] There was a statutory duty to consult on the future of individual schools, however, proposals for particular schools were only consulted upon after the decision had been made to adopt a two-tier system. It therefore excluded consideration as to whether individual schools should become part of a two-tier system or remain three-tier. This case demonstrates the importance of carefully structuring consultation if it is to be undertaken in stages.

The requirement to provide sufficient reasons when consulting on the proposals includes an obligation to provide adequate information in respect of the material lying behind the decision about which consultation is occurring, so as to enable a proper and intelligent response. *R (on the application of Greenpeace Ltd) v Secretary of State for Trade and Industry*[14] concerned the adoption of a policy in favour of nuclear power following a 2006 consultation document 'Our Energy Challenge'. The claimant relied on a legitimate expectation, criticising the consultation document in this way:[15]

---

[10] [2006] EWHC 1590.
[11] At paras 29 and 33.
[12] [2006] EWHC 1081, [2006] ELR 397.
[13] At para 8 per Munby J.
[14] [2007] EWHC 311 (Admin).
[15] At para 44 per Sullivan J.

'Two broad criticisms are made of the 2006 Consultation Document:

(i)   it either was or appeared to be in the nature of an issues paper, seeking consultees' views as to which issues should be examined by Government (and the manner in which they should be examined) when deciding whether or not the new nuclear build option, which had been left open, should now be taken up; rather than the consultation paper on the substantive issue itself: should the new nuclear build option be taken up? The decision in July 2006 "leapfrogged the stage of carrying out proper consultation on the substantive issue".

(ii)   if it was not simply an issues paper, but was intended to be a consultation paper on the substantive issue, it was inadequate, and the overall consultation process was unfair because:

(a)   consultees were not told in clear terms what the proposal was to which they were being invited to respond;

(b)   consultees were not provided with enough information to enable them to make an intelligent response; and

(c)   on many issues, including in particular the critical issues of the economics of new nuclear power and waste disposal, consultees were deprived of the opportunity to make any meaningful response because the relevant information on which the Government relied in making the decision that "nuclear has a role" was published after the consultation period had concluded.'

Sullivan J emphasised the need for the consultation to be fair and adopted the approach of asking whether 'something went "clearly and radically" wrong'.[16] He found that the consultation paper was simply an issues paper without an indication that the issue of principle would be decided and the fact that many consultees had responded on the issue of principle rather than just the questions asked did not salvage the process.[17] The Court observed that the less information that was available at an early stage the likelier it would be that consideration of further new information at a later stage would be unfair.[18]

A consultation will need to be carried out fairly, including as to whom to consult. Pill LJ has commented 'A fair consultation requires fairness in deciding whom to consult as well as fairness in deciding the subject matter of the consultation and its timing'[19]. Any consultation process must be carried out in a manner which is fair to all of the participants. It may be unfair to allow further comments from one person without allowing others to also comment.[20]

---

[16]   At paras 61 and 63.

[17]   At paras 81, 87–89.

[18]   At para 91. In this case 'It gave every appearance of being an issues paper, which was to be followed by a consultation paper containing proposals on which the public would be able to make informed comment. As an issues paper it was perfectly adequate. As *the* consultation paper on an issue of such importance and complexity it was manifestly inadequate. It contained no proposals as such, and even if it had, the information given to consultees was wholly insufficient to enable them to make "an intelligent response' (at para 116).

[19]   *R (on the application of Milton Keynes Council) v Secretary of State for Communities and Local Government* [2011] EWCA Civ 1575, [2012] JPL 728, at para 32. In that case Ministers were able representative bodies, rather than the public or local authorities at large, on the introduction of permitted development rights to change between C3 dwellings and C4 houses in multiple occupation, in circumstances where the decision was a 'macro-political' one and the previous government had consulted on the dwelling/HMO issue (albeit with an opposite intention): see paras 35–38.

[20]   *R (on the application of IM Properties Development Ltd) v Lichfield District Council* [2014] EWHC 2440 (Admin), [2014] PTSR 1484, at paras 35, 105 and 112 per Patterson J.

In *R (on the application of Edwards) v Environment Agency* [21] the House of Lords divided in relation to the extent of the duty to provide information as part of the consultation in respect of a decision to grant a permit under the Pollution Prevention and Control Regulations 2000 ('PPC Regulations').[22] Lord Hoffmann considered, *obiter*, that the common law did not add to duties of consultation under the PPC Regulations as 'the whole question of public involvement has been considered and dealt with in detail by the legislature' and the particular documents were 'part of the [Environment] Agency's decision-making process, prepared after a lengthy period of public consultation'. By contrast Lord Mance interpreted the PPC Regulations to require the provision of information obtained informally from the applicant as part of the consultation process.[23]

In *R(on the application of Bhatt Murphy) v Independent Assessor; R (Niazi) v Secretary of State for the Home Department*[24] Laws LJ identified the paradigm case of a procedural legitimate expectation where a public authority has provided an unequivocal assurance that it will give notice before changing a policy.

There may be circumstances in which a re-consultation will be required at common law, either because there is a fundamental change in the proposals or where a new factor emerges which needs to be consulted upon.[25] In *R (on the application of Stirling) v Haringey London Borough Council*, Sullivan LJ suggested that:[26]

'A holistic approach should be adopted, all relevant factors should be considered, and these may include, in addition to the nature and significance of the new material, such matters as the extent to which the new material is in the public domain, thereby affording consultees the opportunity to comment on its relevance to the proposal the subject of the consultation, and the practical implications, including cost and delay, of further consultation'.

Schiemann J warned in *R v Shropshire Health Authority ex p Duffus*:[27]

'A consultation procedure, if it is to be as full and fair as it ought to be, takes considerable time and meanwhile the underlying facts and projections are changing all the time. It is not just a question of an iterative process, which can speedily be run through a computer. Each consultation process if it produces any changes has the potential to give rise to an expectation in others, but they will be consulted about any changes. If the courts are to be too liberal in the use of their power of judicial review to compel consultation on any change, there is a danger that the process will prevent any change — either in the sense that the authority will be disinclined to make any change because of the repeated consultation process which this might engender, or in the sense that no decision gets taken because consultation never comes to an end. One must not forget there are those with legitimate expectations that decisions will be taken'.

---

[21] [2013] UKSC 78.

[22] SI 2000/1973.

[23] *Edwards*, at paras 78–81.

[24] [2008] EWCA Civ 755, at paras 29 and 30.

[25] *R (on the application of Stirling) v Haringey London Borough Council* [2013] EWCA Civ 116, [2013] PTSR 1285, overturned on the other ground of whether the original consultation was fair: *R (on the application of Moseley) v Haringey London Borough Council* [2014] UKSC 56, [2014] 1 WLR 3947. On planning applications, see *R (Holborn Studios) v London Borough of Hackney* [2017] EWHC 2823 (Admin).

[26] *Stirling*, at para 24.

[27] [1990] 1 Med LR 119.

ORAL HEARING

2.9   At common law there is no general right to an oral hearing in non-criminal cases before a decision is made affecting a person's interests.[28] Policy is removed from a decision which directly affects a person's rights and so no common law right to an oral hearing arises. Whilst a right to an oral hearing in non-criminal matters may also arise under Article 6(1) of the European Convention on Human Rights[29] any right to an oral hearing will depend upon the subject matter and circumstances of the particular case and the nature of the decision to be made.[30] The European Convention on Human Rights has little bearing on policy since a policy is not decisive of rights and would not enable a person to demand a hearing.[31]

A decision-maker must ensure that they are adequately informed. In some cases this may require the resolution of factual disputes which would need oral evidence.

Any right to an oral hearing has therefore to arise out a statutory right or a legitimate expectation created by a promise.

BIAS

2.10   Concerns of bias in decision-making cover a number of different legal grounds:

(i)   actual bias, which is that the decision-maker acted on a disposition for or against a person because of some personal favouritism or animosity, private interest or a public or political reason irrelevant to the purposes of the particular process, is an unlawful exercise of discretion by acting for an improper purpose or taking into account immaterial considerations;

(ii)   pre-determination or having a closed mind is when the decision-maker has decided how to act before being fully aware of all of the circumstances and arguments. That is again an unlawful exercise of discretion as a failure to have regard to material considerations or a failure to exercise the discretion at all;

(iii)   an appearance of bias because of the real possibility that the decision was influenced by an private or irrelevant interest;

(iv)   an appearance of bias because of the real possibility that the decision was pre-determined;

(v)   biased advice, such as a committee report which is skewed by the omission of material or officer opinions which are not motivated by a relevant consideration of the public interest.

---

[28]   Criminal matters and other decisions which concern the liberty of the individual, such as parole board cases are exceptions: *R (on the application of West) v Parole Board* [2005] UKHL 1, [2005] 1 WLR 350.

[29]   *Muyldermans v Belgium* (22 October 1991).

[30]   *R v Army Board of Defence Council ex p Anderson* [1992] QB 169 at 178 per Taylor LJ.

[31]   *Bovis Homes v New Forest District Council* [2002] EWHC 483 (Admin).

Pre-determination

2.11   The essence of pre-determination was set out by Ouseley J in the development plan case of *Bovis Homes v New Forest District Council:*[32]

'111. ... a Council acts unlawfully where its decision-making body has predetermined the outcome of the consideration which it is obliged to give to a matter, whether by the delegation of its decision to another body, or by the adoption of an inflexible policy, or as in effect is alleged here, by the closing of its mind to the consideration and weighing of the relevant factors because of a decision already reached or because of a determination to reach a particular decision. It is seen in a corporate determination to adhere to a particular view, regardless of the relevant factors or how they could be weighed. It is to be distinguished from a legitimate predisposition towards a particular point of view. I derive those principles from the *Kirkstall Valley Campaign Ltd*[33] case to which I have already referred, particularly at page 321G.

112. There is obviously an overlap between this requirement and the commonplace requirement to have rational regard to relevant considerations. But, in my judgment, the requirement to avoid predetermination goes further. The further vice of predetermination is that the very process of democratic decision making, weighing and balancing relevant factors and taking account of any other viewpoints, which may justify a different balance, is evaded. Even if all the considerations have passed through the predetermined mind, the weighing and balancing of them will not have been undertaken in the manner required. Additionally, where a view has been predetermined, the reasons given may support that view without actually being the true reasons. The decision-making process will not then have proceeded from reasoning to decision, but in the reverse order. In those circumstances, the reasons given would not be true reasons but a sham.'

The rule against bias

2.12   The rule against bias is a long-standing principle of natural justice. However, the formulation of the rule has been uncertain, with different camps preferring a 'reasonable likelihood' or 'real danger' as against a 'real possibility' of bias. The current formulation of the test, given by Lord Hope in *Porter v Magill* is:[34]

'The question is whether the fair-minded and informed observer, having considered the facts, would conclude that there was a real possibility that the tribunal was biased.'

The cases were pulled together by the Court of Appeal in *R (Lewis) v Redcar and Cleveland Borough Council*[35] where a contentious planning application, in which the Council had a development interest, was approved during a local election campaign. Pill LJ upheld the Council decision and pointed to:

'62. ... a more fundamental difference about the role of elected councillors in the planning process. There is no doubt that councillors who have a personal interest, as defined in the authorities, must not participate in council decisions. ... The committee which granted planning permission consisted of elected members who would be entitled, and indeed expected, to have and to have expressed views on planning issues. ... They are not, however, required to cast aside views on planning policy they will

---

[32]   [2002] EWHC 483 (Admin).
[33]   *R v Secretary of State for the Environment ex p Kirkstall Valley Campaign Ltd* [1996] 3 All ER 304.
[34]   [2001] UKHL 67, [2002] 2 AC 257 at 494, at para 103.
[35]   [2008] EWCA Civ 746, [2009] 1 WLR 83.

have formed when seeking election or when acting as councillors. The test is a very different one from that to be applied to those in a judicial or quasi-judicial position.

63 Councillors are elected to implement, amongst other things, planning policies. They can properly take part in the debates which lead to planning applications made by the council itself. It is common ground that in the case of some applications they are likely to have, and are entitled to have, a disposition in favour of granting permission. It is possible to infer a closed mind, or the real risk that a mind was closed, from the circumstances and evidence. Given the role of councillors, clear pointers are, in my view, required if the state of mind is to be held to have become a closed, or apparently closed, mind at the time of decision.'

The Court should make its own judgment whether there is a real risk that minds are closed, Pill LJ saying: [36]

'It is for the court to assess whether committee members did make the decision with closed minds or that the circumstances did give rise to such a real risk of closed minds that the decision ought not in the public interest to be upheld. The importance of appearances is, in my judgment, generally more limited in this context than in a judicial context.'

This question is entirely fact-specific, and turns upon whether a reasonable member of the public – neither complacent nor unduly sensitive or suspicious – would conclude that there was a real possibility that the tribunal was biased.[37]

The Court will examine whether pre-discussion commitments or pronouncements give rise to a perception that the decision maker has pre-determined the decision to be made through compliance with obligatory procedures.[38] Pill LJ reiterated that 'Central to such a consideration, however, must be a recognition that councillors are not in a judicial or quasi-judicial position but are elected to provide and pursue policies. Members of a planning committee would be entitled, and indeed expected, to have and to have expressed views on planning issues'.[39] Rix LJ noted that it was common ground that in the 'planning context a distinction has to be made between mere predisposition, which is legitimate, and the predetermination which comes with a closed mind which is illegitimate'.[40] There needed to be 'something which goes to the appearance of a predetermined, closed mind in the decision-making itself'.[41]

The Localism Act 2011

2.13 Reflecting the number of court cases on bias issues and some spectacularly over-cautious advice given to members in particular instances, the Localism Act 2011 sought to protect the position of councillors. By s 25(2):

'A decision-maker is not to be taken to have had, or to have appeared to have had, a closed mind when making the decision just because—

---

[36] *Lewis* at para 71 per Pill LJ. See also para 68.
[37] *Lawal v Northern Spirit* [2003] ICR 856 at 862 per Lord Steyn.
[38] *Bovis v New Forest District Council* [2002] EWHC 483 Admin at paras 111 and 112 per Ouseley J.
[39] At para 69, endorsing Woolf J in *R v Amber Valley DC ex p Jackson* [1985] 1 WLR 298.
[40] *Lewis*, at para 89. See also Longmore LJ at paras 105 to 107.
[41] *Lewis* at para 96 per Rix LJ. A court will weigh all such factors cumulatively to ascertain whether the requisite concern threshold is crossed, including a perusal of the actual decision making process, and any impression conveyed thereby: *Council for National Parks Ltd v Pembrokeshire Coast National Park Authority* [2004] EWHC 2907 (Admin) at para 60 per Jack J, and *Bovis*, at paras 113 and 114 per Ouseley J.

(a) the decision-maker had previously done anything that directly or indirectly indicated what view the decision-maker took, or would or might take, in relation to a matter, and

(b) the matter was relevant to the decision.'

A decision-maker is a member or co-opted member of an authority, but not an officer.[42] The critical point is that an actual or apparent bias by pre-determination cannot be found 'just because' of what a person did or said before the meeting. That reaches a similar outcome to *Lewis*. What happens at the meeting is critical, although earlier events may be relevant.

In *IM Properties* Patterson J held that the pre-meeting acts within s 25(2) include private statements (in that case an email to fellow councillors) as well as public statements.[43] The imposition of a party whip on the adoption of local plan modifications had not given rise to pre-determination.[44]

Can one person taint the committee?

2.14 There are differing views as to whether a real possibility of bias by one member taints the entire body. The whole committee may be more likely to be infected if the real possibility of bias is due to an interest rather than pre-determination.[45]

THE AARHUS CONVENTION

2.15 The UK is a party to the Convention on Access to Information, Public Participation in Decision-Making and Access to Justice in Environmental Matters ('Aarhus Convention'). This is relevant to the process of adopting policy on planning and other environmental matters.[46] Article 7 provides:

> '**PUBLIC PARTICIPATION CONCERNING PLANS, PROGRAMMES AND POLICIES RELATING TO THE ENVIRONMENT**
>
> Each Party shall make appropriate practical and/or other provisions for the public to participate during the preparation of plans and programmes relating to the environment, within a transparent and fair framework, having provided the necessary information to the public. Within this framework, article 6, paragraphs 3, 4 and 8, shall be applied. The public which may participate shall be identified by the relevant public authority, taking into account the objectives of this Convention. To the extent appropriate, each Party shall endeavour to provide opportunities for public participation in the preparation of policies relating to the environment.'

---

[42] See the Localism Act 2011, s 25(4).

[43] *R (on the application of IM Properties Development Ltd) v Lichfield District Council* [2014] EWHC 2440 (Admin), [2014] PTSR 1484, at para 85.

[44] *IM Properties*, at para 86. Whips being generally permitted in local authorities provided members make up their own minds and do not vote blindly in support of party policy: *R v Waltham Forest London Borough Council ex p Baxter* [1988] QB 419.

[45] For quashings on interest bias, see *Kirkstall Valley* at 328A; *Bovis*, at paras 104 and 105 and in the judicial context, *R v Bartle and Commissioner of Police ex p Pinochet* [1999] 2 WLR 827. Any risk of pre-determination bias by a single member on a committee might be insufficient without more evidence of them influencing the rest of the committee, see *R (Berky) v Newport City Council* [2012] EWCA Civ 378, [2012] Env LR 35 at para 30 per Carnwath LJ and Buxton LJ at paras 58 and 59.

[46] See *Greenpeace*, at paras 49 and 50.

The Article therefore draws a distinction between 'plans and programmes relating to the environment' which are subject to a transparent and fair framework and Articles 6(3), (4) and (8), and 'policies relating to the environment' which are subject to a more general obligation to 'endeavour to provide opportunities for public participation'. Article 6(3) itself refers back to Article 6(2).

Articles 6(2), (3), (4) and (8) provide:

'2. The public concerned shall be informed, either by public notice or individually as appropriate, early in an environmental decision-making procedure, and in an adequate, timely and effective manner, inter alia, of:

(i) the proposed activity and the application on which a decision will be taken;

(ii) the nature of possible decisions or the draft decision;

(iii) the public authority responsible for making the decision;

(iv) the envisaged procedure, including, as and when this information can be provided:

(a) The commencement of the procedure;

(b) The opportunities for the public to participate;

(c) The time and venue of any envisaged public hearing;

(d) An indication of the public authority from which relevant information can be obtained and where the relevant information has been deposited for examination by the public;

(e) An indication of the relevant public authority or any other official body to which comments or questions can be submitted and of the time schedule for transmittal of comments or questions; and

(f) An indication of what environmental information relevant to the proposed activity is available; and

(v) The fact that the activity is subject to a national or transboundary environmental impact assessment procedure.

3. The public participation procedures shall include reasonable time-frames for the different phases, allowing sufficient time for informing the public in accordance with paragraph 2 above and for the public to prepare and participate effectively during the environmental decision-making.

4. Each Party shall provide for early public participation, when all options are open and effective public participation can take place.

…

8. Each Party shall ensure that in the decision due account is taken of the outcome of the public participation."

The Aarhus Convention does not require that an oral hearing be available.

STATUTORY DUTIES TO CONSIDER VARIOUS MATTERS

2.16   Public authorities are subject to a variety of statutory duties to promote or consider various objectives and matters. Sometimes these duties apply to all public bodies and to all of their actions, insofar as relevant to the particular situation. Others apply to a range of planning or environmental functions of specific bodies. These two categories are addressed for convenience below. Obligations which arise on specific plans are discussed in the relevant chapters.

Sustainable development

2.17   Section 39 of the Planning and Compulsory Purchase Act 2004 imposes a duty on bodies exercising functions with respect to the Welsh Spatial Plan and local development documents in England or Wales[47] to 'exercise the function with the objective of contributing to the achievement of sustainable development'.[48] A similar duty is applied to local development plan-making in Northern Ireland.[49] The tortuous expression 'the objective of contributing to the achievement' distances the provision from a requirement that each decision is sustainable. Most obviously local planning authorities are subject to this duty. However, the function-exercising bodies include the Secretary of State, the Welsh Assembly Government, the Mayor of London (with respect to local policies), local authorities and planning inspectors.

The duty does not apply to other decisions under the Planning Acts, in particular development control.

The government resisted all attempts to define sustainable development during the Planning and Compulsory Purchase Act's passage. An amendment which came into force in 2010 did require in England that the person or body 'must (in particular) have regard to the desirability of achieving good design'.[50] In complying with the sustainable development duty bodies are required to have regard to national guidance and advice issued by the Secretary of State or the National Assembly for Wales, as appropriate.[51] In England this guidance is mainly contained in the National Planning Policy Framework ('NPPF').

The Mayor of London is under a separate duty to have regard to 'the effect which the proposed strategy or revision would have on … the achievement of sustainable development in the United Kingdom' when preparing or revising the London Plan (Spatial Development Strategy).[52] Additionally, the Mayor must 'include such of the available policies and proposals relating to the subject matter of the strategy as he considers best calculated' to contribute to this purpose.[53] These are part of the Mayor's general duties in relation to strategies.

All Northern Ireland Departments and councils are also required, when exercising their functions, to act in the way they consider best calculated to contribute to the achievement of sustainable development.[54] This is reinforced by requiring any local

---

[47]   That is, under the Planning and Compulsory Purchase Act 2004, Pts 2 and 6.
[48]   Planning and Compulsory Purchase Act 2004, s 39(2).
[49]   Planning Act (Northern Ireland) 2011, s 5(1).
[50]   Planning and Compulsory Purchase Act 2004, s 39(2A) inserted by the Local Democracy, Economic Development and Construction Act 2009, Sch 5, para 18(2)(b).
[51]   Planning and Compulsory Purchase Act 2004, s 39(3).
[52]   Greater London Authority Act 1999, s 41(4).
[53]   Greater London Authority Act 1999, s 41(7).
[54]   Northern Ireland (Miscellaneous Provisions) Act 2006, s 25.

development plan-making functions to be exercised with the objective of furthering sustainable development.[55]

CLIMATE CHANGE

2.18   The Secretary of State and the Welsh Ministers may issue guidance to any 'person or body within functions of a public nature',[56] so including local planning authorities, about:[57]

(a)   assessing the current and predicted impact of climate change in relation to the authorities' functions;

(b)   preparing proposals and policies for adapting to climate change in the exercise of their functions; and

(c)   co-operating with other such authorities.

No guidance has been issued on planning matters.

The Mayor of London is obliged to take action with a view to mitigation of, or adaptation to, climate change and to take into account any government policies with respect to climate change or the consequence of climate change when making any decisions. He must also have regard to any Ministerial guidance and comply with any direction on the Mayor's performance of these duties.[58]

Climate change measures reports in Wales

2.19   The Welsh Ministers publish a climate change measures report setting out what they consider local authorities can do to increase energy efficiency, microgeneration of energy and the use of various renewable technologies, to reduce greenhouse gas emissions, fuel poverty and address the impact of climate change.[59] Local authorities, comprising county and county borough councils as well as community councils,[60] must have regard to the current report when exercising any of their functions.[61] These functions will therefore include local development plan-making.

Marine planning

2.20   A public authority, including a local planning authority, must have regard to the appropriate marine policy documents in taking any decision which is capable of

---

[55]   Planning Act (Northern Ireland) 2011, s 5(1). In doing so they must have regard to any relevant policies and guidance issued by the Office of the First Minister and the deputy First Minister and by the Department for Regional Development: s 5(2).

[56]   Known as reporting authorities: Climate Change Act 2008, s 70(1).

[57]   Climate Change Act 2008, ss 61(1) and 66 respectively.

[58]   Greater London Authority Act 1999, s 361A(2).

[59]   Climate Change and Sustainable Energy Act 2006, s 3A(1), (3). The renewable technologies are listed in s 26(2) as biomass, biofuels, fuel cells, photovoltaics, water (including waves and tides), wind, solar power, geothermal sources, heat from air, water or the ground, combined heat and power systems.

[60]   Climate Change and Sustainable Energy Act 2006, s 3A(7).

[61]   Climate Change and Sustainable Energy Act 2006, s 3A(2).

affecting the whole or part of the UK marine area.[62] These include any marine plan in effect for the marine plan area affected by the decision.[63]

NATIONAL PARKS

2.21   National Parks are extensive tracts of country in England and Wales that are designated because their natural beauty and the opportunities they afford for open-air recreation, given their character and position in relation to population centres, make it desirable to take necessary measures for their purposes[64]. The purposes of designation are for 'conserving and enhancing the natural beauty, wildlife and cultural heritage' of those areas and promoting the understanding and enjoyment by the public of those special areas.[65] In this context natural beauty includes wildlife and cultural heritage.[66]

National Park authorities, which are the local planning authorities for their areas, 'shall seek to foster the economic and social well-being of local communities within the National Park'.[67] They will prepare the local planning policies for their areas, sometimes jointly with other planning authorities. Public bodies and statutory undertakers are required to have regard to the National Park purposes when exercising any functions which affect land in a National Park, giving greater weight to the purpose of conserving and enhancing the natural beauty, wildlife and cultural heritage of the National Park than promoting public understanding and enjoyment in the event of conflict.[68]

THE BROADS

2.22   Of similar status to the National Parks but with its own legal regime, is the Norfolk and Suffolk Broads. The Broads is defined by the Norfolk and Suffolk Broads Act 1988 as a particular area on the deposited map[69]. A Broads Authority is established with a general duty to manage the Broads for the purposes of:[70]

'(a) conserving and enhancing the natural beauty, wildlife and cultural heritage of the Broads;

(b) promoting opportunities for the understanding and enjoyment of the special qualities of the Broads by the public; and

(c) protecting the interests of navigation'.

The Broads Authority is the local planning authority for the Broads.[71] The authority is under a duty to have regard to[72]:

---

62 Marine and Coastal Access Act 2009, s 58(3). See the discussion of marine planning in Chapter 18 below.
63 Marine and Coastal Access Act 2009, s 59(3).
64 National Parks and Access to the Countryside Act 1949, s 5(2).
65 National Parks and Access to the Countryside Act 1949, s 5(1).
66 National Parks and Access to the Countryside Act 1949, s 5(2A).
67 National Parks and Access to the Countryside Act 1949, s 11A(1).
68 National Parks and Access to the Countryside Act 1949, s 11A(1), (2).
69 Norfolk and Suffolk Broads Act 1988, s 2(3), subject to any variations made by or under Sch 2 to that Act.
70 Norfolk and Suffolk Broads Act 1988, s 2(1).
71 Town and Country Planning Act 1990, s 5.
72 Norfolk and Suffolk Broads Act 1988, s 2(4).

'(a) the national importance of the Broads as an area of natural beauty and one which affords opportunities for open-air recreation;

(b) the desirability of protecting the natural resources of the Broads from damage; and

(c) the needs of agriculture and forestry and the economic and social interests of those who live or work in the Broads'.

Relevant authorities include neighbouring local planning authorities and the Secretary of State. By s 17A(1):[73]

'In exercising or performing any functions in relation to, or so as to affect, land in the Broads, a relevant authority shall have regard to the purposes of:

(a) conserving and enhancing the natural beauty, wildlife and cultural heritage of the Broads;

(b) promoting opportunities for the understanding and enjoyment of the special qualities of the Broads by the public; and

(c) protecting the interests of navigation'.

AREAS OF OUTSTANDING NATURAL BEAUTY

2.23 Areas of outstanding natural beauty ('AONBs') are designated as areas outside national parks but which are of such outstanding natural beauty that particular provisions of the Countryside and Rights of Way Act 2000 should apply to them 'for the purpose of conserving and enhancing the natural beauty of the area'.[74] Designation is carried out by Natural England or the Natural Resources Body for Wales, as appropriate. There are 38 AONBs in England and Wales having been originally created by the National Parks and Access to the Countryside Act 1949. Some AONBs consist of multiple separate areas.[75]

A duty to have regard applies to planning decisions by the Countryside and Rights of Way Act 2000, s 85(1):

'In exercising or performing any functions in relation to, or so as to affect, land in an area of outstanding natural beauty, a relevant authority shall have regard to the purpose of conserving and enhancing the natural beauty of the area of outstanding natural beauty'.

AONB management plans are prepared for each AONB and are considered in Chapter 20 below.

Safety and control of major accident hazards

2.24 Safety is relevant to planning decisions, albeit with due regard to other regulatory regimes. In practice, planning may be more concerned with whether vulnerable users should be put in proximity with dangerous sites than with the control of the dangerous sites themselves. For example, danger to the users or occupiers

---

[73] For consideration of the Norfolk and Suffolk Broads Act 1988, s 17A, see *Howell v Secretary of State for Communities and Local Government* [2014] EWHC 3627 (Admin), affirmed [2015] EWCA Civ 1189.
[74] Countryside and Rights of Way Act 2000, s 82.
[75] For example, the Cornwall AONB has 12 separate, non-contiguous parts.

of a proposed development from nearby installations will be relevant.[76] Advice on considering safety is given in England in the NPPF[77] and the Planning Practice Guidance ('PPG') (section 39) and in Wales in NAW Circular 20/01: *Planning Controls for Hazardous Substances.* The siting of vulnerable development, such as homes, close to installations is assessed using PADHI (Planning Advice for Developments near Hazardous Installations), addressing the risks of major accidents.[78] The PPG warns that 'advice from Health and Safety Executive that planning permission should be refused for development for, at or near to a hazardous installation or pipeline should not be overridden without the most careful consideration'.[79] Safety issues might therefore lead to protective zones being incorporated into plans or exclude the allocation of land for vulnerable development.

The EU has adopted a series of Directives on the control of major-accident hazards involving dangerous substances. The current Directive is 2012/18/EU (known as 'SEVESO III'). The Directive requires Member States to require operators to take all necessary measures to prevent major accidents and to limit their consequences. Article 13 of the SEVESO III Directive provides:

'1   Member States shall ensure that the objectives of preventing major accidents and limiting the consequences of such accidents for human health and the environment are taken into account in their land-use policies or other relevant policies. They shall pursue those objectives through controls on:

(a)   the siting of new establishments;

(b)   modifications to establishments covered by Article 11;

(c)   new developments including transport routes, locations of public use and residential areas in the vicinity of establishments, where the siting or developments may be the source of or increase the risk or consequences of a major accident.

2   Member States shall ensure that their land-use or other relevant policies and the procedures for implementing those policies take account of the need, in the long term:

(a)   to maintain appropriate safety distances between establishments covered by this Directive and residential areas, buildings and areas of public use, recreational areas, and, as far as possible, major transport routes;

(b)   to protect areas of particular natural sensitivity or interest in the vicinity of establishments, where appropriate through appropriate safety distances or other relevant measures;

(c)   in the case of existing establishments, to take additional technical measures in accordance with Article 5 so as not to increase the risks to human health and the environment.

3   Member States shall ensure that all competent authorities and planning authorities responsible for decisions in this area set up appropriate consultation procedures to facilitate implementation of the policies established under paragraph 1. The procedures shall be designed to ensure that operators provide sufficient information

---

[76]   *R (on the application of Health and Safety Executive) v Wolverhampton City Council* [2012] UKSC 34, [2012] 1 WLR 2264; *R (on the application of Saunders) v Tendring District Council* [2003] EWHC 2977 (Admin) is another example.

[77]   Paragraph 172: 'Planning policies should be based on up-to-date information on the location of major hazards and on the mitigation of the consequences of major accidents'.

[78]   More advice is on the HSE's Land Use Planning website.

[79]   ID 39-071-20140306. A similar point is made in the Welsh circular.

on the risks arising from the establishment and that technical advice on those risks is available, either on a case-by-case or on a generic basis, when decisions are taken.

Member States shall ensure that operators of lower-tier establishments provide, at the request of the competent authority, sufficient information on the risks arising from the establishment necessary for land-use planning purposes.'

Article 13 of the Directive is incorporated into domestic law in the three nations by regulations: the Planning (Hazardous Substances) Regulations 2015[80] in England; the Planning (Hazardous Substances) (Wales) Regulations 2015;[81] and the Planning (Hazardous Substances) (No 2) Regulations (Northern Ireland) 2015.[82] These impose similar responsibilities.

Firstly, in formulating a relevant policy Ministers must ensure that they take into account:[83]

(a)   the objectives of preventing major accidents and limiting the consequences of such accidents for human health and the environment; and

(b)   the matters referred to in Article 13(2) of the Directive.

For these purposes, relevant policies are:

(i)   for the Secretary of State, national policy statements (for England, Scotland or Wales) and national policies and advice contained in guidance issued by the Minister which is relevant to local development document making and which the Minister considers concerns matters affecting the risks or consequences of a major accident;[84]

(ii)   for the Welsh Ministers, the Wales Spatial Plan; and any current national land-use planning, transport routes or fishery harbour policy which in their opinion concerns matters affecting the risks or consequences of a major accident;[85]

(iii)   In Northern Ireland, any policy formulated by the Department and co-ordinate policy for securing the orderly and consistent development of land and the planning of that development or any policy or advice contained in guidance issued by the Department which is relevant to the preparation of a plan strategy or local policies plan.[86]

A 'general plan or programme' relating to planning for new establishments pursuant to Article 13 or new developments around establishments where the siting or developments may increase the risk or consequences of a major accident pursuant to Article 13 will be subject to public consultation requirements.[87] However, these provisions do not apply where strategic environmental assessment ('SEA') is carried

---

[80]   SI 2015/627.
[81]   WSI 2015/1597.
[82]   SR 2015/61.
[83]   Planning (Hazardous Substances) Regulations 2015, reg 24(1); Planning (Hazardous Substances) (Wales) Regulations 2015, reg 26(1); and the Planning (Hazardous Substances) (No 2) Regulations (Northern Ireland) 2015, reg 17(1).
[84]   Planning (Hazardous Substances) Regulations 2015, regs 1(3), 24(2).
[85]   Planning (Hazardous Substances) (Wales) Regulations 2015, reg 26(2).
[86]   Planning (Hazardous Substances) (No 2) Regulations (Northern Ireland) 2015, reg 17(2).
[87]   Planning (Hazardous Substances) Regulations 2015, reg 25; Planning (Hazardous Substances) (Wales) Regulations 2015, reg 27; and the Planning (Hazardous Substances) (No 2) Regulations (Northern Ireland) 2015, reg 18.

out, as the more detailed SEA requirements will have to be complied with.[88] The responsible authority (by which or on whose behalf a relevant plan or programme is prepared, so including a local authority) shall:[89]

> '(a) take such measures as it considers appropriate to ensure that public consultees are given early and effective opportunities to participate in the preparation, modification or review of the relevant plan or programme; and
>
> (b) in doing so, take such measures as it considers appropriate to ensure that—
>
>> (i) public consultees are informed of any proposals to prepare, modify or review a relevant plan or programme;
>>
>> (ii) relevant information about such proposals is made available to public consultees, including information about the right to participate in decision-making and about the authority to which comments or questions may be submitted;
>>
>> (iii) public consultees are entitled to express comments and opinions when all options are open before decisions on the relevant plan or programme are made; and
>>
>> (iv) any periods provided for public participation under this regulation allow public consultees sufficient time to prepare and participate in decision-making in relation to the relevant plan or programme;
>
> (c) take into account the results of the public participation in making those decisions; and
>
> (d) take such measures as it considers appropriate to inform the public consultees about the decisions taken and the reasons and considerations on which those decisions are based, including information about the public participation process.'

Public consultees are 'persons of whom the responsible authority is aware, including any non-governmental organisation promoting environmental protection, who are affected or likely to be affected by, or have an interest in, the relevant plan or programme in question'.[90]

Sites of special scientific interest

2.25 Local planning authorities, Ministers and Inspectors are 'section 28G authorities' for the purpose of decisions affecting sites of special scientific interest ('SSSIs') under the Wildlife and Countryside Act 1981.[91] In exercising their functions so far as their exercise is likely to affect the flora, fauna or geological or physiographical features by reason of which a site of SSI is of special interest, the authority is under a duty[92] to 'take reasonable steps, consistent with the proper exercise of the authority's functions, to further the conservation and enhancement of the flora, fauna or geological or physiographical features by reason of which the site is of

---

[88] Planning (Hazardous Substances) Regulations 2015, reg 25(3); Planning (Hazardous Substances) (Wales) Regulations 2015, reg 27(3); and the Planning (Hazardous Substances) (No 2) Regulations (Northern Ireland) 2015, reg 18(3).

[89] Planning (Hazardous Substances) Regulations 2015, reg 25(2); Planning (Hazardous Substances) (Wales) Regulations 2015, reg 27(2); and the Planning (Hazardous Substances) (No 2) Regulations (Northern Ireland) 2015, reg 18(2).

[90] Planning (Hazardous Substances) Regulations 2015, reg 25(6); Planning (Hazardous Substances) (Wales) Regulations 2015, reg 27(4); and the Planning (Hazardous Substances) (No 2) Regulations (Northern Ireland) 2015, reg 18(6).

[91] Wildlife and Countryside Act 1981, s 28G(1), (3).

[92] Wildlife and Countryside Act 1981, s 28G(1).

special scientific interest'.[93] In *R (on the application of Friends of the Earth England, Wales and Northern Ireland) v Welsh Ministers* Hickinbottom J distinguished this duty from the duty of 'special regard' to listed buildings when making development management decisions and said the question is 'not whether the Minister gave the desirability of conserving and enhancing these features particular enhanced weight, but whether she took reasonable steps to conserve and enhance those features'.[94]

Biodiversity

2.26 All public authorities are required to have regard to the purpose of conserving biodiversity insofar as it is consistent with the proper exercise of their functions.[95] This includes restoring or enhancing a population of a living organism or a type of habitat.[96]

CRIME AND DISORDER

2.27 Any local authority, as well as a National Park authority, the Broads Authority, the Greater London Authority and any combined authority are under an obligation to exercise their functions with due regard to their likely effect on, and the need to do all that they reasonably can to prevent crime and disorder (including anti-social and other behaviour adversely affecting the local environment), the misuse of drugs, alcohol and other substances and re-offending in their area.[97] *Planning Policy Wales* advises 'The aim should be to produce safe environments through good design'.[98]

ENERGY

2.28 Sometimes legislation provides a specific power which is then subject to restrictions which also constrain the general power. The Planning and Energy Act 2008 authorises local planning authorities and the Welsh strategic planning panels to include in development plans:[99]

> 'policies imposing reasonable requirements for—
>
> (a) a proportion of energy used in development in their area to be energy from renewable sources in the locality of the development;

---

[93] Wildlife and Countryside Act 1981, s 28G(2).

[94] [2015] EWHC 776 (Admin), [2016] Env LR 1, at para 133.

[95] Natural Environment and Rural Communities Act 2006, s 40(1). In doing so, Ministers, but not local authorities, are expressly required to have regard to the United Nations Environmental Programme Convention on Biological Diversity of 1992: s 40(2). The duty is discussed in *R (on the application of Buglife) v Thurrock Thames Gateway Development Corpn* [2008] EWHC 475 (Admin), [2008] Env LR 31 and see PPG, section 8.

[96] Natural Environment and Rural Communities Act 2006, s 40(3).

[97] Crime and Disorder Act 1998, s 17(1).

[98] *Planning Policy Wales* (Edition 9, November 2016), para 4.11.12.

[99] Planning and Energy Act 2008, s 1(1). Energy efficiency standards are those in regulations or national policy or guidance (of the Secretary of State or Welsh Ministers) and energy requirements, in the context of building regulations, are those relating to energy performance or the conservation of fuel and power: Planning and Energy Act 2008, s 1(2),(3).

(b) a proportion of energy used in development in their area to be low carbon energy from sources in the locality of the development;

(c) development in their area to comply with energy efficiency standards that exceed the energy requirements of building regulations.'

These policies could have been included in any event. The original policy requiring on-site renewable energy to be provided as part of a development was introduced in the London Borough of Merton's Unitary Development Plan without needing any specific legislative provision.[100] Known as the 'Merton Rule' it was widely adopted by other authorities and successfully applied in practice.

Whilst ostensibly a means of broadening the use of these policies, that existing ability to have renewable policies was restricted in England by the Planning and Energy Act 2008. Local plan policies could not be 'inconsistent with relevant national policies for England'.[101] As part of restricting energy efficiency standards to national provisions, the Deregulation Act 2015 proposes to exempt the 'construction or adaptation of buildings to provide dwellings or the carrying out of any work on dwellings' from those policies which could exceed the energy requirements in building regulations.[102]

HUMAN RIGHTS ACT 1998

2.29   The European Convention on Human Rights has some role in planning. It is most often relied upon in cases involving gypsies or travellers. Section 6(1) of the Human Rights Act 1998 imposes the general duty:

'It is unlawful for a public authority to act in a way which is incompatible with a Convention right'.

However, the Convention and the Human Rights Act 1998 only concern decisions which affect rights under the Convention. The preliminary question is therefore whether the adoption of a policy is capable of affecting such rights, or whether Convention rights are only engaged when decisions are taken having regard to the policy. Even if the adoption of policy does not interfere with rights, it would be desirable to have a policy which could be implemented in compliance with the Convention.

The adoption of planning policy is unlikely to affect rights under the European Convention on Human Rights and the Human Rights Act 1998, subject a possible exception if an allocation of land gives rise to a right to require its purchase under statutory blight procedures or a discretion for it to be acquired for non-statutory blight.[103]

---

[100] Merton's policy was introduced in the teeth of opposition from the Secretary of State's Government Office for London who said it was contrary to national policy. As one of the Merton councillors who voted to bring it in, Richard Harwood recalls that members supported it despite expecting Ministers to intervene.

[101] Planning and Energy Act 2008, s 1(5). In England and Wales they were also subject to the duty to have regard to national policies: s 1(4).

[102] Planning and Energy Act 2008, s 1(1A), prospectively inserted by the Deregulation Act 2015, s 43 (not yet in force).

[103] *Bovis Homes v New Forest District Council* [2002] EWHC 483 (Admin) at paras 300–320 per Ouseley J.

However, if a local plan allocation gives rise to automatic permission in principle, as may be introduced by the Housing and Planning Act 2016, then it will engage the human rights of the owners and occupiers of the allocated sites and (where the effect is sufficiently substantial) in the same way as for a planning application. In such cases the qualified rights to respect for family life and the home (Article 8) and property (Protocol 1, Article 1) and the right to a fair hearing within a reasonable time (Article 6) will apply. The practical effect on these rights on the planning process has been limited, but that compliance reflects the balancing of considerations and procedures in the UK planning application regime.

Convention rights which more usually arise in planning cases are Article 8 (right to respect for private and family life), Article 14 (prohibition on discrimination) and Article 1 of the First Protocol (protection of property). The procedural right to a fair trial under Article 6 applies, but in planning cases has added little to the common law, apart from a requirement to deal with cases within a reasonable time.[104]

'Article 8: Right to respect for private and family life

1   Everyone has the right to respect for his private and family life, his home and his correspondence.

2   There shall be no interference by a public authority with the exercise of this right except such as is in accordance with the law and is necessary in a democratic society in the interests of national security, public safety or the economic well-being of the country, for the prevention of disorder or crime, for the protection of health or morals, or for the protection of the rights and freedoms of others.

Article 14: Prohibition of discrimination

The enjoyment of the rights and freedoms set forth in this Convention shall be secured without discrimination on any ground such as sex, race, colour, language, religion, political or other opinion, national or social origin, association with a national minority, property, birth or other status.

Protocol 1, Article 1: Protection of property

Every natural or legal person is entitled to the peaceful enjoyment of his possessions. No one shall be deprived of his possessions except in the public interest and subject to the conditions provided for by law and by the general principles of international law.

The preceding provisions shall not, however, in any way impair the right of a State to enforce such laws as it deems necessary to control the use of property in accordance with the general interest or to secure the payment of taxes or other contributions or penalties'.

The substantive rights (Articles 8, 13, Protocol 1 art 1) which arise in planning cases are all qualified rights, in that a balance has to be struck between the right and the public interest. The Convention has been interpreted to give states a wide discretion in regulating planning matters.[105]

---

[104] See *Vergos v Greece* (2005) 41 EHRR 41.
[105] See *Sporrong and Lönroth v Sweden* (A/52) (1983) 5 EHRR 35 and *Hatton v United Kingdom* (36022/97) (2003) 37 EHRR 28.

PUBLIC SECTOR EQUALITY DUTY

2.30   For England and Wales, s 149 of the Equality Act 2010 provides:

'(1) A public authority must, in the exercise of its functions, have due regard to the need to:

(a) eliminate discrimination, harassment, victimisation and any other conduct that is prohibited by or under this Act;

(b) advance equality of opportunity between persons who share a relevant protected characteristic and persons who do not share it;

(c) foster good relations between persons who share a relevant protected characteristic and persons who do not share it.

(2) A person who is not a public authority but who exercises public functions must, in the exercise of those functions, have due regard to the matters mentioned in subsection (1).

(3) Having due regard to the need to advance equality of opportunity between persons who share a relevant protected characteristic and persons who do not share it involves having due regard, in particular, to the need to:

(a) remove or minimise disadvantages suffered by persons who share a relevant protected characteristic that are connected to that characteristic;

(b) take steps to meet the needs of persons who share a relevant protected characteristic that are different from the needs of persons who do not share it;

(c) encourage persons who share a relevant protected characteristic to participate in public life or in any other activity in which participation by such persons is disproportionately low.

(4) The steps involved in meeting the needs of disabled persons that are different from the needs of persons who are not disabled include, in particular, steps to take account of disabled persons' disabilities.

(5) Having due regard to the need to foster good relations between persons who share a relevant protected characteristic and persons who do not share it involves having due regard, in particular, to the need to:

(a) tackle prejudice, and

(b) promote understanding.

(6) Compliance with the duties in this section may involve treating some persons more favourably than others; but that is not to be taken as permitting conduct that would otherwise be prohibited by or under this Act.

(7) The relevant protected characteristics are: age;

disability;

gender reassignment;

pregnancy and maternity; race;

religion or belief; sex;

sexual orientation.

(8) A reference to conduct that is prohibited by or under this Act includes a reference to—

(a) a breach of an equality clause or rule;

(b) a breach of a non-discrimination rule'.

2.30 *Legal Principles*

Section 149 comprises nine needs: see *R (on the application of RB) v Devon County Council*:[106]

'They are

1) the need to eliminate discrimination;

2) the need to advance equality of opportunity between persons who share a relevant protected characteristic and persons who do not;

3) the need to remove or minimise disadvantages suffered by persons who share a relevant protected characteristic that are connected to that characteristic;

4) the need to take steps to meet needs of persons who share a relevant protected characteristic that are different from the needs from persons who do not share it;

5) in particular the need to take steps to take account of disabled person's disabilities;

6) the need to encourage persons who share any relevant protected characteristic to participate in public life or in any other activity in which participation by such persons is disproportionately low;

7) the need to foster good relations between persons who share a relevant protected characteristic and persons who do not;

8) the need to tackle prejudice, and

9) the need to promote understanding'.

There is a need to comply with the duty in substance, not in form – a failure to mention it is not in itself determinative. Conversely, it needs to be apparent how the duty has been addressed. The duty must be performed with vigour and an open mind. General awareness of the duty does not amount to the necessary due regard, being 'a proper and conscientious focus on the statutory criteria … In short, the decision-maker must be clear precisely what the equality implications are when he puts them in the balance, and he must recognise the desirability of achieving them, but ultimately it is for him to decide what weight they should be given in the light of all relevant factors'.[107] An equality impact assessment or equality statement may be produced to assess these matters. If a risk of adverse impact is identified, consideration should be given to measures to avoid that impact before fixing on a particular solution.[108] Such assessments may be required in policy formulation but does not require 'a precise mathematical exercise to be carried out in relation to particular affected groups or, for example, urban areas as opposed to rural areas'.[109]

Public authorities in Northern Ireland are also subject to equalities duties. When exercising their functions they are required to:[110]

'have due regard to the need to promote equality of opportunity—

(a) between persons of different religious belief, political opinion, racial group, age, marital status or sexual orientation;

---

[106] [2012] EWHC 3597 (Admin), [2013] Er LR 113, at para 20.
[107] *R (on the application of Bracking) v Secretary of State for Work and Pensions* [2014] Eq LR 60, at para 78 per McCombe LJ.
[108] *R (on the application of JM & NT) v Isle of Wight Council* [2011] EWHC 2911 (Admin), at paras 95–105.
[109] *R (on the application of West Berkshire Council) v Secretary of State for Communities and Local Government* [2016] EWCA Civ 441, [2016] 1 WLR 3923, at para 83 per Laws, Treacy LJJ.
[110] Northern Ireland Act 1998, s 75(1).

(b)   between men and women generally;

(c)   between persons with a disability and persons without; and

(d)   between persons with dependants and persons without.'

This includes having 'regard to the desirability of promoting good relations between persons of different religious belief, political opinion or racial group'.[111]

WASTE

2.31   Providing facilities for dealing with waste where it is generated and for subsequent processes and disposal is an essential role of the planning process. That has been overlain by obligations in European law.

Waste and Landfill Directives

2.32   The Waste Framework Directive 2008/98/EC requires Member States to take measures, which as relevant to planning policy are:[112]

'**Article 4 Waste hierarchy**

1   The following waste hierarchy shall apply as a priority order in waste prevention and management legislation and policy:

(a)   prevention;

(b)   preparing for re-use;

(c)   recycling;

(d)   other recovery, eg energy recovery; and

(e)   disposal.

2   When applying the waste hierarchy referred to in paragraph 1, Member States shall take measures to encourage the options that deliver the best overall environmental outcome. This may require specific waste streams departing from the hierarchy where this is justified by life-cycle thinking on the overall impacts of the generation and management of such waste.

Member States shall ensure that the development of waste legislation and policy is a fully transparent process, observing existing national rules about the consultation and involvement of citizens and stakeholders.

Member States shall take into account the general environmental protection principles of precaution and sustainability, technical feasibility and economic viability, protection of resources as well as the overall environmental, human health, economic and social impacts, in accordance with Articles 1 and 13.

Article 10 Recovery

1   Member States shall take the necessary measures to ensure that waste undergoes recovery operations, in accordance with Articles 4 and 13.

---

[111]   Northern Ireland Act 1998, s 75(2).
[112]   These terms are defined in Article 3.

Article 11 Re-use and recycling

1   Member States shall take measures, as appropriate, to promote the re-use of products and preparing for re-use activities, notably by encouraging the establishment and support of re-use and repair networks ...

Article 13 Protection of human health and the environment

Member States shall take the necessary measures to ensure that waste management is carried out without endangering human health, without harming the environment and, in particular:

(a)   without risk to water, air, soil, plants or animals;

(b)   without causing a nuisance through noise or odours; and

(c)   without adversely affecting the countryside or places of special interest.

Article 16 Principles of self-sufficiency and proximity

1   Member States shall take appropriate measures ... to establish an integrated and adequate network of waste disposal installations and of installations for the recovery of mixed municipal waste collected from private households, including where such collection also covers such waste from other producers, ...

2   The network shall be designed to enable the Community as a whole to become self-sufficient in waste disposal as well as in the recovery of waste referred to in paragraph 1, and to enable Member States to move towards that aim individually, taking into account geographical circumstances or the need for specialised installations for certain types of waste.

3   The network shall enable waste to be disposed of or waste referred to in paragraph 1 to be recovered in one of the nearest appropriate installations, by means of the most appropriate methods and technologies, in order to ensure a high level of protection for the environment and public health'.

These matters have to be considered by planning authorities and 'substantial weight' should be attached to them.[113] The Waste (England and Wales) Regulations 2011 require planning authorities to take into account the parts of Articles 13 and 16 quoted above when involved in local plan and local development plan making.[114] It is worth noting that Article 4 requires the development of waste policy to be 'a fully transparent process, observing existing national rules about the consultation and involvement of citizens and stakeholders'. Waste management plans have to be adopted[115] – in the UK this has been done for each nation. These plans must include the strategies for the reduction in biodegradable waste going to landfill which is required by the Landfill Directive 1999/31/EC.[116] Existing major disposal and recovery installations should be identified, along with locational criteria for new sites.[117]

---

[113]   *R (on the application of Blewett) v Derbyshire County Council* [2004] EWCA Civ 1508, [2005] JPL 620.

[114]   Waste (England and Wales) Regulations 2011, SI 2011/988, regs 17, 18. Regulation 19 requires planning authorities to carry out periodic inspections of waste disposal or recovery facilities.

[115]   Article 28. Public participation in the preparation of these plans in accordance with the Strategic Environmental Assessment Directive is required: see Article 31.

[116]   Waste Framework Directive, Art 28(5), Landfill Directive, Art 5.

[117]   Waste Framework Directive, Art 28(3)(b), (d).

Welsh language

2.33   In Wales the sustainability appraisal of a local development plan must include 'an assessment of the likely effects of the plan on the use of the Welsh language in the area of the authority'.[118]

PLACING POLICIES IN THE CORRECT DOCUMENTS

2.34   Legislation may prescribe types of policies or proposals which must be in certain documents, for example, a local planning authority's policies which allocate sites must be included in a local plan.[119] There is a consistent line of authority that local planning policies must be placed in the correct plan documents. The principle was set out by the House of Lords in *Westminster City Council v Great Portland Estates plc* by Lord Scarman:[120]

> 'The statute requires that a local plan shall formulate in such detail as the Council thinks appropriate their proposals for the development and use of land … If a local planning authority has proposals of policy for the development and use of land in its area which it chooses to exclude from the plan, it is, in my judgment, failing in its statutory duty. An attempt was made to suggest that the non-statutory guidance in this case went only to detail, as to which the council is given a discretion. …
>
> It was the duty of the council under Schedule 2 of the [Town and Country Planning] Act of 1971 to formulate in the plan its development and land use proposals. It deliberately omitted some. There was therefore a failure on the part of the council to meet the requirement of the Schedule. By excluding from the plan its proposals in respect of office development outside the central activities zone the council deprived persons such as the respondents from raising objections and securing a public inquiry into such objections.'

The *Great Portland Estates* principle was applied in various pre-2004 Act cases: *Kingsley v Secretary of State and Cheshire County Council*[121] (quashing of policy which was included in the explanatory memorandum of a structure plan rather than the plan itself); *Bloor Homes v Swindon Borough Council*[122] (whether allocation should be in structure plan or local plan) and *R (on the application of Pye (Oxford) Ltd) v Oxford City Council*[123] (whether contents of Supplementary Planning Guidance should be in a local plan).

All of these cases turn on the divisions laid down in statute as to the policies which must be in particular types of document. These issues have continued to arise in the various 2004 Act regimes, in particular the scope of supplementary planning documents in England.[124]

---

[118] Planning and Compulsory Purchase Act 2004, s 62(6A) inserted by the Planning (Wales) Act 2015, s 11(3) from 6 September 2015.

[119] Town and Country Planning (Local Planning) (England) Regulations 2012, SI 2012/767, regs 5, 6.

[120] [1985] AC 661 at 674.

[121] (2001) 82 P & CR 85.

[122] [2001] EWHC Admin 966.

[123] [2001] EWHC Admin 870, [2002] PLCR 330, [2002] EWCA Civ 1116.

[124] See *R (on the application of RWE Npower Renewables Ltd) v Milton Keynes Council* [2013] EWHC 751 (Admin) *R (on the application of William Davis Ltd) v Charnwood Borough Council* [2017] EWHC 3006 (Admin) and the discussion in Chapter 7.

Legislation may provide that policies dealing with certain matters must be in particular types of document, for example, what must be in a local plan.[125] Whether guidance should be included in a local plan or supplementary planning document/guidance is a matter of judgment, ultimately for the court, not a matter of discretion.[126] Whilst there may be a number of potential ways of addressing a particular issue (strategic, local or Supplementary Planning Guidance) the content of the guidance leads to a particular mechanism. In particular, the speed of one process against another is irrelevant.[127]

RELATIONS BETWEEN DOCUMENTS

2.35   Legislation may also set out a hierarchy of conformity between plans, for example, supplementary planning documents must not conflict with the development plan; a neighbourhood plan consistent with the strategic policies of the development plan; and a Northern Irish local policies plan consistent with the plan strategy. Whether a plan is compliant is a matter for the public authorities, subject to public law review, see *Persimmon Homes (Thames Valley) Ltd v Stevenage Borough Council*.[128]

REASONS

2.36   Policy-making powers tend to be littered with duties to give reasons for specific decisions. In addition to the particular plan-making provisions, reasons must be given for the adoption of plans which are the subject of strategic environmental assessment. There may also be circumstances in which reasons are required as a matter of fairness at common law or because of a legitimate expectation arising from a statement or practice. Even if there is no legal obligation to give reasons, the court may consider any reasons which are offered to decide whether the decision has been reached lawfully.

The most useful, and most often quoted, summary of the court's approach to the adequacy of reasons was given by Lord Brown of Eaton-under-Heywood in *South Buckinghamshire District Council v Porter (No 2)*:[129]

> 'The reasons for a decision must be intelligible and they must be adequate. They must enable the reader to understand why the matter was decided as it was and what conclusions were reached on the "principal important controversial issues", disclosing how any issue of law or fact was resolved. Reasons can be briefly stated, the degree of particularity required depending entirely on the nature of the issues falling for decision. The reasoning must not give rise to a substantial doubt as to whether the decision-maker erred in law, for example by misunderstanding some relevant policy or some other important matter or by failing to reach a rational decision on relevant grounds. But such adverse inference will not readily be drawn. The reasons need refer only to the main issues in the dispute, not to every material consideration. They should enable disappointed developers to assess their prospects of obtaining some alternative development permission, or, as the case may

---

[125] Town and Country Planning (Local Planning) (England) Regulations 2012.
[126] See on structure/local plans, *Bloor*, at paras 131 and 147.
[127] *Bloor*, at para 141.
[128] [2005] EWCA Civ 1365, [2006] 1 WLR 334, followed in *University of Bristol v North Somerset Council* [2013] EWHC 231 (Admin), [2013] JPL 940 and *Cooper Estates Strategic Land Ltd v Royal Tunbridge Wells Borough Council* [2017] EWHC 224 (Admin).
[129] [2004] UKHL 33, [2004] 1 WLR 1953, at para 36. See also *Uprichard v Scottish Ministers* [2013] UKSC 21.

be, their unsuccessful opponents to understand how the policy or approach underlying the grant of permission may impact upon future such applications. Decision letters must be read in a straightforward manner, recognising that they are addressed to parties well aware of the issues involved and the arguments advanced. A reasons challenge will only succeed if the party aggrieved can satisfy the court that he has genuinely been substantially prejudiced by the failure to provide an adequately reasoned decision'.

South Bucks concerned an Inspector's decision on a planning appeal and the standard of reasoning required will be affected by the type of decision reached and any particular statutory context. Policy-making tends to involve issues which can apply to a variety of situations and participants more often than individual cases, although the latter do arise in allocations and land designations. Examinations are into the plan rather than objections. So even though each individual representation made in response to a consultation must be considered, it will often be possible to address one issue from across a range of submissions. Any analysis does need to be comprehensible to the various participants and others who may also become interested in it, unlike a narrower, specific decision which might only need to be fully understood by a small number of persons. A policy decision can though be made easier to understand and so simpler to explain, by making the underlying submissions and evidence readily available online. The publication of material and the openness of the process is a critical feature of policy-making.

Chapter 3

Strategic Environmental Assessment and Habitats

3.1   This chapter considers the assessment regimes which are applied by European law to plans and programmes. These consist of strategic environmental assessment and what is generally referred to as the Habitats regime, but which encompasses protection under the Birds and Habitats Directives.

STRATEGIC ENVIRONMENTAL ASSESSMENT IN OUTLINE

3.2   Strategic environmental assessment ('SEA') is a procedure whereby environmental information is gathered and reported so that the environmental impacts of the adoption of certain 'plans and programmes' can be taken into account during their preparation and prior to their adoption.

The requirement for the SEA of certain plans and programmes comes from EU Directive 2001/42/EC on the assessment of the effects of certain plans and programmes on the environment ('SEA Directive'). This Directive has been transposed into law in England through the Environmental Assessment of Plans and Programmes Regulations 2004[1] ('SEA Regulations') and through the Environmental Assessment of Plans and Programmes (Wales) Regulations 2004[2] ('SEA Wales Regulations') and the Environmental Assessment of Plans and Programmes Regulations (Northern Ireland) 2004[3] ('SEA Regulations Northern Ireland'). The wording of the UK's SEA Regulations largely follows that of the SEA Directive. In interpreting these provisions it must be borne in mind that the word 'strategic' does not appear anywhere in the Directive[4] or the UK regulations.

The SEA Directive was adopted sixteen years after the original Environmental Impact Assessment Directive 85/337/EEC[5] ('EIA Directive') which legislates with regards to the assessment of the environmental effects on 'projects'. The objective of the SEA Directive and its interrelationship with the EIA Directive has been summarised by Advocate General Kokott as follows:[6]

---

[1]   SI 2004/1633.

[2]   WSI 2004/1656.

[3]   SR 2004/280.

[4]   A point made by Lord Carnwath JSC in *R (Buckinghamshire County Council) v Secretary of State for Transport* [2014] UKSC 3, [2014] 1 WLR 324, at para 35.

[5]   The version now in force is the consolidated Environmental Impact Assessment Directive 2011/92/EU as amended by Directive 2014/52/EU.

[6]   Her opinion in *Terre Wallonne ASBL v Région Wallonne* (Joined Cases C-105/09 and C-110/09) [2010] ECR I-5611, points 31 and 32 cited in *Walton v Scottish Ministers* [2012] UKSC 44, [2013] PTSR 51, at para 12 by Lord Reed JSC.

'31. The specific objective pursued by the assessment of plans and programmes is evident from the legislative background: the SEA Directive complements the EIA Directive, which is more than ten years older and concerns the consideration of effects on the environment when development consent is granted for projects.

32. The application of the EIA Directive revealed that, at the time of the assessment of projects, major effects on the environment are already established on the basis of earlier planning measures (Proposal for a Council Directive on the assessment of the effects of certain plans and programmes on the environment, COM (96) 511 final, p 6). Whilst it is true that those effects can thus be examined during the environmental impact assessment, they cannot be taken fully into account when development consent is given for the project. It is therefore appropriate for such effects on the environment to be examined at the time of preparatory measures and taken into account in that context.'

The broad purpose behind the SEA Directive is set out at Article 1 which is entitled 'objectives':

'The objective of this Directive is to provide for a high level of protection of the environment and to contribute to the integration of environmental considerations into the preparation and adoption of plans and programmes with a view to promoting sustainable development, by ensuring that, in accordance with this Directive, an environmental assessment is carried out of certain plans and programmes which are likely to have significant effects on the environment.'

At the time of writing, the UK voted in the 2016 referendum to exit the European Union, Article 50 has been triggered and the negotiations for exiting the European Union have begun. Prior to Brexit, the SEA and Habitats regimes remain in force.

THE NEED FOR SEA

3.3 Put simply, the SEA process involves the production of an environmental report which is prepared on an ongoing (or iterative) basis during the preparation of certain plans and programmes. The environmental report outlines the likely significant effects of the plan or programme on the environment and also the reasonable alternatives to it. The Directive (and the Regulations) mandate that the environmental report be subject to certain publicity and consultation requirements.

Plans and programmes

3.4 The requirement to carry out SEA applies to certain 'plans and programmes' (SEA Directive, Art 3). As was highlighted by Lord Reed in *Walton v Scottish Ministers*, the SEA Directive does not define these but instead qualifies them as those plans and programmes which fulfil certain criteria.[7]

---

[7] [2012] UKSC 44, [2013] PTSR 51, at para 19.

Article 2 of the SEA Directive defines plans and programmes as follows:[8]

> '(a) plans and programmes' shall mean plans and programmes, including those co-financed by the European Community, as well as any modifications to them:
>
> - which are subject to preparation and/or adoption by an authority at national, regional or local level or which are prepared by an authority for adoption, through a legislative procedure by Parliament or Government and,
>
> - which are required by legislative, regulatory or administrative provisions'.

The terms 'plans and programmes' are not to be interpreted narrowly. In *Walton* Lord Reed JSC said:

> '20   The terms "plan" and "programme" are not further defined. It is however clear from the case law of the Court of Justice of the European Union that they are not to be narrowly construed. As the court stated in *Inter-Environnement Bruxelles ASBL v Région de Bruxelles-Capitale* (Case C-567/10) [2012] 2 CMLR 909 , para 37: "the provisions which delimit the Directive's scope, in particular those setting out the definitions of the measures envisaged by the Directive, must be interpreted broadly". The interpretation of the Directive, in this respect as in others, has been based primarily upon its objective rather than upon its literal wording.
>
> 21   Adopting therefore a purposive approach, the complementary nature of the objectives of the SEA and EIA Directives has to be borne in mind. As Advocate General Kokott said in *Terre Wallonne* [2010] ECR I-5611, points 29–30:
>
> > "29. … According to article 1, the objective of the SEA Directive is to provide for a high level of protection of the environment and to contribute to the integration of environmental considerations into the preparation and adoption of plans and programmes by ensuring that an environmental assessment is carried out of certain plans and programmes which are likely to have significant effects on the environment.
> >
> > 30.   The interpretation of the pair of terms 'plans' and 'projects' should consequently ensure that measures likely to have significant effects on the environment undergo an environmental assessment."
>
> It is also necessary to bear in mind that the Directive is intended to be applied in member states with widely differing arrangements for the organisation of developments affecting the environment. Its provisions, including terms such as "plan" and "programme", have therefore to be interpreted and applied in a manner which will secure the objective of the Directive throughout the EU.'

Plans and programmes which are required

3.5   For a plan or programme to be caught by the SEA Directive, its adoption need not be compulsory. Due to the presence of the word 'required' in Article 2A of the SEA Directive, it had (unsurprisingly) been thought and argued by some that the SEA Directive would only apply to those plans or programmes which were

---

[8]   This is transposed with minor formatting alterations by the SEA Regulations, reg 2(1), the SEA (Wales) Regulations, reg 2(1) and the SEA Regulations (Northern Ireland), reg 2(2) as:
'plans and programmes, including those co-financed by the European Community, as well as any modifications to them, which–
(a)   are subject to preparation or adoption by an authority at national, regional or local level; or
(b)   are prepared by an authority for adoption, through a legislative procedure by Parliament or Government; and, in either case,
(c)   are required by legislative, regulatory or administrative provisions.'

required to be produced by legislation. However, in the case of *Inter-Environment Bruxelles ASBL v Region de Bruxelles-Capitale*[9] the European Court of Justice ('ECJ') disregarded the literal meaning of the word in favour of the purposive approach. That case concerned the repeal of a land use plan which a domestic Order had provided for but did not require to be produced. The Governments of Belgium, the Czech Republic and the UK argued that the wording of Article 2(a) meant that only plans or programmes which were required to be produced were covered by the Directive, a view supported by Advocate General Kokott. However the ECJ disagreed and held:

> '28 It must be stated that an interpretation which would result in excluding from the scope of Directive 2001/42 all plans and programmes, inter alia those concerning the development of land, whose adoption is, in the various national legal systems, regulated by rules of law, solely because their adoption is not compulsory in all circumstances, cannot be upheld.

> 29 The interpretation of art.2(a) of Directive 2001/42 that is relied upon by the abovementioned governments would have the consequence of restricting considerably the scope of the scrutiny, established by the directive, of the environmental effects of plans and programmes concerning town and country planning of the Member States.

> 30. Consequently, such an interpretation of art.2(a) of Directive 2001/42 , by appreciably restricting the directive's scope would compromise, in part, the practical effect of the directive, having regard to its objective, which consists in providing for a high level of protection of the environment (see, to this effect, *Valciukiene v Pakruojo rajono savivaldybe* (C-295/10) [2012] Env. L.R. 11 at [42]). That interpretation would thus run counter to the directive's aim of establishing a procedure for scrutinising measures likely to have significant effects on the environment, which define the criteria and the detailed rules for the development of land and normally concern a multiplicity of projects whose implementation is subject to compliance with the rules and procedures provided for by those measures.

> 31. It follows that plans and programmes whose adoption is regulated by national legislative or regulatory provisions, which determine the competent authorities for adopting them and the procedure for preparing them, must be regarded as "required" within the meaning, and for the application, of Directive 2001/42 and, accordingly, be subject to an assessment of their environmental effects in the circumstances which it lays down.'[10]

In *R (Buckinghamshire County Council) v Secretary of State for Transport*[11] the Supreme Court agreed, *obiter*, with the 'logical and impeccable analysis' of the Advocate General in *Inter-Environment Bruxelles.*[12] They also expressed doubt as to what the ECJ's approach in *Inter-Environment Bruxelles* actually meant:

> '184 If, instead of "required", one must read the word "regulated", the question arises what it means. Is it sufficient that legislative, regulatory or administrative provisions grant powers to some authority wide enough to permit a plan or programme to be prepared? Or must such provisions actually refer to a possibility that such a plan or programme will be prepared? Or must they specify points and/or conditions that such a plan or programme, if prepared, must address and/or fulfil? The Chamber referred to provisions which "determine the competent authorities for adopting them [i e the relevant plan or programme] and the procedure for preparing them": para 31.

---

9   (C-567/10) [2012] Env LR 30.
10   See the reliance of the Supreme Court on this case in *Walton v Scottish Ministers*, at para 22 per Lord Reed JSC.
11   [2014] UKSC 3, [2014] 1 WLR 324.
12   At paras 175–177 per Lords Neuberger and Mance.

185 If this is what is meant by "regulated", then not all plans and programmes can on any view be covered by the SEA Directive , and the desire for comprehensive regulation of plans and programmes "likely to have significant effects on the environment" cannot be met. In any event, it follows from the fact that the SEA Directive only applies to plans and programmes "which set the framework for future development consent of projects", that it is not exhaustive and does not cover every form of plan and programme simply because it could be said to be likely to have significant environmental effects: see Lord Carnwath and Lord Reed JJSC's judgments. The SEA Directive and its terms must be read as a whole.'

Lords Neuberger and Mance went on to state that had it been necessary the Court would have liked to have the matter referred back to the ECJ for it to consider whether its decision in *Inter-Environment Bruxelles* was correct.[13] The question has not been referred back to the ECJ and at the present time the principle in *Inter-Environment Bruxelles* remains good law.

Proposals, policies and projects

3.6   A 'proposal' as opposed to a plan will not be caught by the SEA Directive. In *R (on the application of Buckinghamshire County Council) v Secretary of State for Transport* the claimants challenged a Government Command Paper *High Speed Rail: Investing in Britain's Future—Decisions and Next Steps* issued under the Royal Prerogative in January 2012 wherein the government announced its decision to continue with a high speed rail link ('HS2') and set out the steps by which this would be realised ('the DNS'). The claimants judicially reviewed the DNS on the basis that the government should have conducted an SEA. The Supreme Court had to decide whether the DNS fell within the definition of Article 3(2) of the SEA Directive. In answering this question, Court placed significant emphasis on the evolution and general purpose of the Directive and its EIA counterpart.[14] The Court held that the Command Paper did not require environmental assessment under the SEA Directive and the decision was summarised by Lord Sumption JSC as follows:

'125 The main reason why the command paper cannot require an environmental assessment under the SEA is that it is nothing more than a proposal. Naturally, the fact that it is a Government proposal and appears in a command paper makes it influential in the broader sense that I have mentioned above. It means it is politically more likely to be accepted. But the command paper does not operate as a constraint on the discretion of Parliament. None of the factors which bear on the ultimate decision whether to pass the hybrid Bill into law have been pre-empted, even partially. I accept that this means that governments may in some cases be able to avoid the need for an environmental assessment by promoting specific legislation authorising development. But that is not because the SEA has no application to projects authorised in that way. It is because (i) the SEA Directive does not require member states to have plans or programmes which set the framework for future development consent, but only regulates the consequences if they do; (ii) where development consent is granted by specific legislation there are usually no plans or programmes which set the framework for that consent; and (iii) legislative grants of development consent are exempt from the EIA Directive by virtue of article 1(4), subject to conditions which replicate some of the benefits of a requirement for an environmental impact assessment, and which like every other member of the court, I consider to be satisfied by the proposed hybrid Bill procedure.'

---

[13]   At para 189.
[14]   See in particular the judgement of Lord Carnwarth JSC at 34-41.

The *Buckinghamshire* case also indicates that a distinction is to be drawn between some 'policies' and plans. In the context of the requirement that the plan 'sets the framework for future development consent', Lord Sumption highlighted that in England a range of planning policies existed whose legal effect may be weaker or stronger.[15] He went on to state:

> '123 None of this means that the only policy framework which counts is one which is determinative of the application for development consent, or of some question relevant to the application for development consent. What it means is that the policy framework must operate as a constraint on the discretion of the authority charged with making the subsequent decision about development consent. It must at least limit the range of discretionary factors which can be taken into account in making that decision, or affect the weight to be attached to them. Thus a development plan may set the framework for future development consent although the only obligation of the planning authority in dealing with development consent is to take account of it. In that sense the development plan may be described as influential rather than determinative. But it cannot be enough that a statement or rule is influential in some broader sense, for example because it presents a highly persuasive view of the merits of the project which the decision maker is perfectly free to ignore but likely in practice to accept. Nor can it be enough that it comes from a source such as a governmental proposal or a ministerial press statement, or a resolution at a party conference, or an editorial in a mass circulation newspaper which the decision-maker is at liberty to ignore but may in practice be reluctant to offend.

> 124 All of this is inherent in the concept of a "framework" and in the purpose of the Directive. It is consistent with the requirement of article 2(a) that the plan or programme must be regulated by legislative, regulatory or administrative provisions, for whatever may precisely be meant by that, it clearly indicates a degree of prescription ...'

The Court of Appeal of Northern Ireland has also considered the question of whether there is a distinction to be drawn between policies and plans when deciding whether SEA is required. In *Central Craigavon Ltd v The Department of the Environment for Northern Ireland*[16] the Court considered Draft Planning Policy Statement 5: Retailing, Town Centres and Commercial Leisure Developments ('PPS 5') which had been adopted by the Department of the Environment. PPS 5 included a policy (RPP2) which stated that individual applications within Sprucefield regional shopping centre would be judged on their own merits and set out some considerations which would be taken into account. A key issue for the Court was whether PPS 5 constituted a 'plan or programme providing a framework within Article 3.2(a)'. It decided that it did not, noting:

> '39. ... The travaux préparatoires of the formulation of the Directive forms part of the relevant matrix for arriving at the intent of the Directive. They indicate that the word policy was specifically omitted from the text. In many situations policy choices will be reached by Government in the exercise of governmental power rather than in the exercise of a specific duty, as we have noted in relation to draft PPS5 and such a policy thus does not qualify as a plan or programme within Article 2(a). A policy formulated on foot of a statutory duty could in certain circumstances constitute a plan giving rise to a framework depending upon its precise provisions and context. The label attached to the document would not be determinative of that issue for as the Commission Guidance points out "the name alone (plan, programme, strategy, guidelines etc) will not be a sufficiently reliable guide. Documents having all the

---

[15]   At para 121.
[16]   [2011] NICA 17, 2011 WL 5105533.

characteristics of a plan or programme as defined in the Directive may be found under a variety of names.'"

The Court went on to hold that a policy which merely points to relevant material considerations (as PPS 5 did) cannot be said to lay down a framework for development.[17]

It will therefore be necessary to examine the legal and practical effect of the policy in question in deciding whether it 'sets the framework for future development consent'. If it does not, then it will not require SEA.

As highlighted in the *Buckinghamshire* case and in *Walton v Scottish* Ministers the regulation of the plan or programme must be in legislative, regulatory or administrative provisions. In *Walton v Scottish Ministers* Lord Carnwath JSC said:[18]

'There may be some uncertainty as to what in the definition is meant by 'administrative', as opposed to 'legislative or regulatory', provisions. However, it seems that some level of formality is needed: the administrative provisions must be such as to identify both the competent authorities and the procedure for preparation and adoption.'

The SEA Directive does not cover decisions which approve projects and a key indicator that the scheme in question is not covered by the SEA Directive is that it is treated as a project under the EIA Directive. The interrelation (and indeed distinction) between, on the one hand, the definition of plans and programmes in the SEA Directive and the definition of projects in the EIA Directive was key in the *Walton v Scottish Ministers* case. The Supreme Court highlighted a number of indicators that the particular scheme in question (the 'fastlink' – a link of the city bypass around Aberdeen) was in fact a project rather than a plan or programme. These can be summarised as:

(a)   the Ministers' decision to go ahead with the 'fastlink' was taken in the course of executing a specific project and only affected that project;

(b)   the decision was not taken 'in the exercise of any power to modify the Modern Transport System strategy or otherwise set a legal or administrative framework for future development consent of projects' (para 67);

(c)   there were no national legislative or regulatory provisions which required the development in the Ministers' thinking about the project to be implemented by means of the adoption of a plan or programme (or the modification of such a plan or programme); and

(d)   the effects of the fastlink were capable of being fully assessed under the EIA Directive, giving effect to the purposive interpretation of the SEA Directive.

Modifications to plans and programmes

3.7   Article 2 of the SEA Directive explicitly states that the modification of plans and programmes will be caught by the Directive. The repeal of plans and

---

[17]   At para 43. Permission to appeal to the Supreme Court was granted, but the appeal was subsequently withdrawn.
[18]   At para 99.

programmes falls within the concept of modification of plans and programmes.[19] In *Inter-Environment Bruxelles* the ECJ held that although the Directive refers expressly to measures modifying plans and programmes and not measures repealing plans and programmes the possibility that such repealing measures might have a significant effects on the environment meant that the provisions delimiting the Directive's scope should be interpreted broadly. However, the ECJ went on to state that not all repealing measures will require SEA. It stated:

> '42 ... it must be made clear that, in principle, that is not the case if the repealed measure falls within a hierarchy of town and country planning measures, as long as those measures lay down sufficiently precise rules governing land use, they have themselves been subject of an assessment of their environmental effects and it may reasonably be considered that the interests which Directive 2001/42 is designed to protect have been taken into account sufficiently within that framework.'

Where the relevant modification is to a plan or programme which was prepared prior to the coming into force of the SEA Directive, the fact that the plan or programme pre-dated the Directive is irrelevant. This issue was addressed in *Walton v Scottish Ministers* where the Supreme Court rejected such an argument made by the Scottish Ministers. Lord Reed JSC stated:

> '63. ... Article 13(3) defines the temporal scope of application of the Directive: not what constitutes a plan or programme. It is based on the premise that there were plans and programmes of which the first formal preparatory act was before 21 July 2004: see the second sentence. The fact that article 4(1) does not apply to a plan or programme of which the first formal preparatory act was before that date, by virtue of article 13(3), does not therefore deprive such a plan or programme of its character as a plan or programme.'

Where a modification to a plan or programme is 'minor' it will only need to be subject to SEA where it has been determined as likely to have significant environmental effects.[20]

PLANS AND PROGRAMMES FALLING WITHIN ARTICLE 3

3.8   Only plans and programmes which fall within Article 3 must be subject to SEA. It states:

> '1.   An environmental assessment, in accordance with Articles 4 to 9, shall be carried out for plans and programmes referred to in paragraphs 2 to 4 which are likely to have significant environmental effects.
>
> 2.   Subject to paragraph 3, an environmental assessment shall be carried out for all plans and programmes,
>
>> (a)   which are prepared for agriculture, forestry, fisheries, energy, industry, transport, waste management, water management, telecommunications, tourism, town and country planning or land use and which set the framework for future development consent of projects listed in Annexes I and II to Directive 85/337/EEC, or

---

[19]   *Inter-Environment Bruxelles* [2012] 2 CMLR 909, at paras 38-40. The same conclusion had been reached by Sales J in the regional strategy revocation litigation: *R (on the application of Cala Homes (South) Ltd) v Secretary of State for Communities and Local Government* [2010] EWHC 2866 (Admin), at paras 54-67.

[20]   See Article 3(3), discussed below at 3.10 and 3.13.

(b)   which, in view of the likely effect on sites, have been determined to require an assessment pursuant to Article 6 or 7 of Directive 92/43/EEC.

3.   Plans and programmes referred to in paragraph 2 which determine the use of small areas at local level and minor modifications to plans and programmes referred to in paragraph 2 shall require an environmental assessment only where the Member States determine that they are likely to have significant environmental effects.

4.   Member States shall determine whether plans and programmes, other than those referred to in paragraph 2, which set the framework for future development consent of projects, are likely to have significant environmental effects.

5.   Member States shall determine whether plans or programmes referred to in paragraphs 3 and 4 are likely to have significant environmental effects either through case-by-case examination or by specifying types of plans and programmes or by combining both approaches. For this purpose Member States shall in all cases take into account relevant criteria set out in Annex II, in order to ensure that plans and programmes with likely significant effects on the environment are covered by this Directive.

6.   In this case-by-case examination and in specifying types of plans and programmes in accordance with paragraph 5, the authorities referred to in Article 6(3) shall be consulted.

7.   Member States shall ensure that their conclusions pursuant to paragraph 5, including the reasons for not requiring an environmental assessment pursuant to articles 4 and 9, are made available to the public.

8.   The following plans and programmes are not subject to this Directive:

●   plans and programmes the sole purpose of which is to serve national defence or civil emergency,

●   financial or budget plans and programmes.

9.   This Directive does not apply to plans and programmes co-financed under the current respective programming periods for Council Regulations (EC) No 1260/1999 and (EC) No 1257/999.'

Likely to have significant effects – ambiguity

3.9   As can be seen above, Article 3(1) specifically states that an environmental assessment should be carried out for all plans or programmes which are prepared for 'town and country planning or land use and which set the framework for future development consent of projects listed in Annex I or II to the Directive 85/337/ EEC' and which are likely to have significant environmental effects. However, that is simply a summary of the provision, with the applicable tests being contained in Article 3(2) to (4).

By Article 3(2) SEA must be carried out for all plans and programmes:

(a)   which are prepared for agriculture, forestry, fisheries, energy, industry, transport, waste management, water management, telecommunications, tourism, town and country planning or land use and which set the framework for future development consent of projects listed in the EIA Directive; or

(b)   which, in view of the likely effect on sites, have been determined to require an appropriate assessment under the Habitats or Birds Directive; but

(c)   if they determine the use of small areas at local level or are minor modifications to plans and programmes within Article 3(2) there must have been a determination that they are likely to have significant environmental effects.

By Article 3(4) a determination has to be made whether any other plan or programme which sets the framework for future development consent of projects, is likely to have significant environmental effects.

A plan or programme within Article 3(2) is therefore deemed to be likely to have significant effects on the environment and that conclusion can only be set aside in the limited circumstances in Article 3(3).

In the UK regulations the tests in Article 3(2) to (4) are applied,[21] without any separate approach based on Article 3(1).

Articles 3(2)(a) and 3(2)(b) and screening

3.10   When deciding whether a plan or programme should be subject to SEA it should first be considered whether the plan or programme in question is caught by Article 3(2)(a) or (b) of the SEA Directive. A plan or programme will fall within Article 3(2)(a) if it is prepared for 'agriculture, forestry, fisheries, energy, industry, transport, waste management, water management, telecommunications, tourism, town and country planning or land use and which set the framework for future development consent of projects listed in Annexes I and II to Directive 85/337/EEC (the "EIA Directive")' and must be subject to SEA. However, projects listed in Annexe II of the EIA Directive will only require EIA if they are determined to be likely to have significant effects on the environment. A plan or programme will fall into Article 3(2)(b) if it has been determined as requiring an appropriate assessment under the Habitats Directive as being likely to have a significant effect on a Special Area of Conservation or Special Protection Area designated under the Habitats or Birds Directives respectively.[22]

Where a plan or programme falls within Article 3(2)(a) or (b), it will require SEA unless it determines 'the use of small areas at local level' or is a minor modification to a plan or programme and a decision has been taken that it is not likely to have significant environmental effects (Article 3(3)).

If neither Article 3(2)(a) or (b) applies and the plan or programme sets the framework for future development consent of projects, then a decision should be made as to whether the plan or programme is likely to have significant environmental effects (Article 3(4)). Such a decision (often referred to as a screening decision) should be reached either on a case-by-case basis and/or through the Member State specifying types of plans or programmes which would meet the threshold.[23] Either way, the decision-maker must take into account the criteria in Annex II to the SEA Directive.[24] The criteria are:

---

[21]   SEA Regulations, SEA Wales Regulations, SEA Regulations Northern Ireland, reg 5(2) to (4).
[22]   See the comments of Advocate General Kokott on Article 3(2)(b) in *Region Wallonne ASBL v Region Wallonne* and *Inter-Environnement Wallonie ASBL v Region Wallonne* (C-105/09 and C-110/09) [2010] ECR I-5611, at paras 90–100.
[23]   SEA Directive, Art 3(5).
[24]   SEA Directive, Art 3(5).

'1. The characteristics of plans and programmes, having regard, in particular, to

- the degree to which the plan or programme sets a framework for projects and other activities, either with regard to the location, nature, size and operating conditions or by allocating resources,

- the degree to which the plan or programme influences other plans and programmes including those in a hierarchy,

- the relevance of the plan or programme for the integration of environmental considerations in particular with a view to promoting sustainable development,

- environmental problems relevant to the plan or programme,

- the relevance of the plan or programme for the implementation of Community legislation on the environment (e.g. plans and programmes linked to waste-management or water protection).

2. Characteristics of the effects and of the area likely to be affected, having regard, in particular, to

- the probability, duration, frequency and reversibility of the effects,

- the cumulative nature of the effects,

- the transboundary nature of the effects,

- the risks to human health or the environment (e.g. due to accidents),

- the magnitude and spatial extent of the effects (geographical area and size of the population likely to be affected),

- the value and vulnerability of the area likely to be affected due to:

  - special natural characteristics or cultural heritage,

  - exceeded environmental quality standards or limit values,

  - intensive land-use,

- the effects on areas or landscapes which have recognised national, Community or international protection status.'

Screening decisions and directions in the UK are governed by regs 9 and 10 of the SEA Regulations. The authority by which or on whose behalf the plan or programme is prepared is required to consult the consultation bodies when making a screening decision. These are Historic England, Natural England and the Environment Agency in England.[25] Under the Welsh SEA Regulations the relevant consultation bodies are the Natural Resources Body for Wales and Cadw.[26] In Northern Ireland, the Department of the Environment for Northern Ireland is the sole consultation body under the SEA Regulations.[27] A decision-maker cannot also be a consultation body.[28]

A screening decision must be made available to the public, including the reasons for not requiring an environmental assessment.[29]

---

[25] SEA Regulations, reg 4(1).

[26] SEA (Wales) Regulations, reg 4(1). If consultation takes place in Wales under the SEA Regulations for a plan which crosses national boundaries, then the National Assembly for Wales and the Natural Resources Body for Wales are consultation bodies: SEA Regulations, reg 4(4).

[27] SEA Regulations (Northern Ireland), reg 4(1). The function is delivered by the Northern Ireland Environment Agency.

[28] This is considered further below at 3.18.

[29] SEA Directive, Art 3(7) and SEA Regulations, reg 11(1) and (2).

The Secretary of State may require the authority by which or on whose behalf the plan or programme is prepared to send him a copy of a screening decision made under reg 9(1), a copy of the plan, programme or modification to which it relates and any statement prepared in accordance with that paragraph.[30] The Secretary of State may direct that a plan, programme or modification is likely to have significant environmental effects.[31] In reaching a decision he is required to take into account the criteria at Annex II to the Directive (also in Sch 1 of the SEA Regulations) and consult the relevant consultation bodies.[32] As soon as reasonably practicable, once the direction has been given, the Secretary of State must send a copy (together with a statement of reasons) to the authority by which or on whose behalf the plan or programme is prepared and each of the consultation bodies. Where a regulation 10 direction has been made in relation to a plan or programme, any regulation 9 screening decision will cease to have effect in relation to it.[33]

'Setting the framework'

3.11   In order for a plan or programme to be caught by Article 3(2)(a) or Article 3(4) it must 'set the framework for future development consent'. In the *Terre Wallone* case the ECJ considered whether programme for the management of nitrogen in agriculture was caught by the SEA Directive. Advocate General Kokott emphasised that the concept of setting a framework was very broad and should be construed flexibly. She said:

'64. Plans and programmes may, however, influence the development consent of individual projects in very different ways and, in so doing, prevent appropriate account from being taken of environmental effects. Consequently, the SEA Directive is based on a very broad concept of "framework".

65. This becomes particularly clear in a criterion taken into account by the member states when they appraise the likely significance of the environmental effects of plans or programmes in accordance with article 3(5): they are to take account of the degree to which the plan or programme sets a framework for projects and other activities, either with regard to the location, nature, size and operating conditions or by allocating resources (first indent of point 1 of Annex II). The term "framework" must therefore be construed flexibly. It does not require any conclusive determinations, but also covers forms of influence that leave room for some discretion.'[34]

Advocate General Kokott concluded that the action programmes were caught by the SEA Directive and the ECJ endorsed her reasoning.[35]

Exceptions

3.12   Article 3(8) of the SEA Directive states that the following plans are not subject to the SEA Directive:

---

[30] SEA Regulations, reg 10(1).
[31] SEA Regulations, reg 10(3).
[32] SEA Regulations, reg 10(4).
[33] SEA Regulations, reg 10(6).
[34] *Terre Wallonne ASBL v Region Wallonne* (C-105/9) and *Inter-Environment Wallone ASBL v Region Wallonne* (C-110/09) and cited in *Walton v Scottish Ministers*, at para 17.
[35] At para 52.

(i)   plans and programmes the sole purpose of which is to serve national defence or civil emergency,

(ii)   financial or budget plans and programmes.

The requirement for SEA in relation to planning policy documents

3.13   In September 2005, the Department for Communities and Local Government (DCLG) published 'A practical guide to the Strategic Environmental Assessment Directive', which remains extant guidance. Appendix 1 contains an indicative list of plans and programmes subject to the SEA Directive. It includes: local plans, the Mayor's Spatial Development Strategy (London), combined Minerals and Waste Local Plans, Areas of Outstanding Natural Beauty Management Plans and National Park Management Plans. Those which are planning policy documents will invariably require SEA. The other documents might, subject to their role in setting the framework for development consent decisions and the likelihood of significant effects.

Local development plans in Wales and Northern Ireland will invariably require SEA as setting the framework for projects within the SEA Directive.

Regional or national level plans and programmes will require SEA, the issues being primarily whether a particular document is a plan or programme and whether it is required (meaning regulated) by legislative, regulatory or administrative provisions.

The variety of types of policies which each neighbourhood plan may contain and the applicability of the small area exception[36] mean that some will require SEA whilst others will not. The Planning Practice Guidance intimates that it will only be in 'limited circumstances' where a neighbourhood plan will require strategic environmental assessment.[37] However, that does not mean that the requirement for SEA in relation to a neighbourhood plan is uncommon. The Planning Practice Guidance sets out some examples of where an SEA may be required:

> 'Whether a neighbourhood plan proposal requires a strategic environmental assessment, and (if so) the level of detail needed, will depend on what is proposed. A strategic environmental assessment may be required, for example, where:
>
> • a neighbourhood plan allocates sites for development
>
> • the neighbourhood area contains sensitive natural or heritage assets that may be affected by the proposals in the plan
>
> • the neighbourhood plan is likely to have significant environmental effects that have not already been considered and dealt with through a sustainability appraisal of the Local Plan'.[38]

Whilst there is no requirement for a neighbourhood plan to be subjected to a sustainability appraisal, there is a requirement to demonstrate how the neighbourhood

---

[36]   See *R (on the application of DLA) v Lewes District Council* [2017] EWCA Civ 58, [2017] Env LR 18 and *R (on the application of Crownhall Estates Ltd) v Chichester District Council* [2016] EWHC 73 (Admin).

[37]   Paragraph 27 Reference ID: 11-027-20150209.

[38]   Paragraph 046 Reference ID: 11-046-20150209.

plan will contribute to achieving sustainable development.[39] Practically, this is often done through the production of a report which is to all intents and purposes a sustainability appraisal. Where a neighbourhood plan is required to conduct an SEA, this assessment could be conducted as part of the sustainability appraisal/report.

Supplementary planning documents ('SPDs') and Supplementary Planning Guidance ('SPG') adopted by local planning authorities or the Mayor of London may require SEA. SPDs are regulated by legislative requirements. An issue may arise as to whether non-statutory SPG are regulated by regulatory or administrative provisions. Where published policy contains expectations as to their content or preparation process then these may fall within the SEA regime. A judgment then has to be made whether they set the framework for EIA Directive or other projects, whether the small area exception is applicable and, if appropriate, whether there are likely to be significant environmental effects.

THE ENVIRONMENTAL REPORT – CONTENT

Content and scoping

3.14   The SEA Directive specifies that an environmental assessment should contain an environmental report which describes and evaluates the likely significant environmental effects of implementing the plan or programme and also the reasonable alternatives which take into account the objectives and geographical scope of the plan or programme.[40] Annex I to the SEA Directive contains a list of the information to be included in an environmental report.

The list includes:

(a)   an outline of the contents, main objectives of the plan or programme and relationship with other relevant plans and programmes;

(b)   the relevant aspects of the current state of the environment and the likely evolution thereof without implementation of the plan or programme;

(c)   the environmental characteristics of areas likely to be significantly affected;

(d)   any existing environmental problems which are relevant to the plan or programme including, in particular, those relating to any areas of a particular environmental importance, such as areas designated pursuant to Directives 79/409/EEC and 92/43/EEC (Birds and Habitats Directives);

(e)   the environmental protection objectives, established at international, Community or Member State level, which are relevant to the plan or programme and the way those objectives and any environmental considerations have been taken into account during its preparation;

(f)   its likely significant effects on the environment, including on issues such as biodiversity, population, human health, fauna, flora, soil, water, air, climatic factors, material assets, cultural heritage including architectural and archaeological heritage, landscape and the interrelationship between the above factors;

---

[39]   Town and Country Planning Act 1990, Sch 4B, para 8(2) as applied to neighbourhood plans and modified by the Planning and Compulsory Purchase Act 2004, s 38C.

[40]   SEA Directive, Art 5(1).

(g)   the measures envisaged to prevent, reduce and as fully as possible offset any significant adverse effects on the environment of implementing the plan or programme;

(h)   an outline of the reasons for selecting the alternatives dealt with, and a description of how the assessment was undertaken including any difficulties (such as technical deficiencies or lack of know-how) encountered in compiling the required information;

(i)   a description of the measures envisaged concerning monitoring in accordance with Article 10;

(j)   a non-technical summary of the information provided under the above headings.'[41]

It should be noted that a footnote attached to (f) above specifically requires that the description of the likely significant effects should include 'secondary, cumulative, synergistic, short, medium and long-term permanent and temporary, positive and negative effects'.

The report should include the information 'that may reasonably be required taking into account current knowledge and methods of assessment, the contents and level of detail in the plan or programme, its stage in the decision-making process and the extent to which certain matters are more appropriately assessed at different levels in that process in order to avoid duplication of the assessment'.[42]

The requirement for a comparable assessment of the reasonable alternatives to the plan proposals should not be overlooked. The provisions of Annex 1 therefore apply to those reasonable alternatives as well.

Regulation 12 of the SEA Regulations governs the preparation of the environmental report; that it (together with Sch 2 to the Regulations) follows the wording of Annex I and Article 5(2) to the SEA Directive.[43]

Article 12(2) states that environmental reports must be 'of a sufficient quality to meet the requirements of' the Directive. In *Save Historic Newmarket*[44] Collins J stated:

> '... Quality involves ensuring that a report is based on proper information and expertise and covers all the potential effects of the plan or programme in question. In addition, since one of the purposes of the Directive is to allow members of the public to be consulted about plans or programmes which may affect them, the report should enable them to understand why the proposals are said to be environmentally sound. To that end, the report must not only be comprehensible but must contain the necessary information required by the Directive.' (para 12)

The environmental authorities must be consulted in deciding upon the scope and level of detail of information in any environmental report (SEA Directive, Art 5(4) and SEA Regulations, reg 12(4)). There is no requirement for a formal scoping report

---

[41]   SEA Directive, Annex I.
[42]   SEA Directive, Art 5(2).
[43]   As do the SEA (Wales) Regulations, reg 12 and the SEA Regulations Northern Ireland, reg 11.
[44]   *Save Historic Newmarket Ltd v Forest Heath District Council* [2011] EWHC 606 (Admin), [2011] JPL 1233.

to be prepared but it may prove a useful way of setting out the content of the SEA and the course which it is going to take.

In line with the wording of Article 5(2) of the SEA Directive and reg 12(3)(d) of the SEA Regulations, the courts have emphasised that the information required in an SEA is that which is 'reasonable'.[45] There has developed a tendency over recent years for bodies preparing local plans to commission lengthy reports; the usefulness of large parts of which is questionable. When setting out the scope for an SEA or SA the body concerned should carefully consider the legal requirements for the content of any such report and the views of any bodies consulted and, if necessary, question whether less voluminous (and no doubt expensive material) could fulfil the legal requirements and prove more useful to the plan-making authority.

Reasonable alternatives

3.15   A number of the challenges to the conduct of SEA processes have focused on the failure to identify reasonable alternatives.[46] The identification of reasonable alternatives is a matter for the decision-maker.[47] The decision-maker must turn its mind to those alternatives even if none are suggested by those consulted on the matter.[48]

Where a preferred option emerges during the plan-making process, the plan-making authority must give its reasons for selecting that preferred option. The failure to give reasons for the selection of the preferred option may equally be seen as a failure to give reasons for discounting alternative options and is therefore a breach of the Directive.[49]

The courts have also considered the level of assessment to which reasonable alternatives must be subjected. The European Commission's guidance was cited in the case of *Heard v Broadland District Council*.[50] It states:

> 'In requiring the likely significant environmental effects of reasonable alternatives to be identified, described and evaluated, the Directive makes no distinction between the assessment requirements for the drafted plan or programme and for the alternatives. The essential thing is that the likely significant effects of the plan or programme and the alternatives are identified, described and evaluated in a comparable way. The requirements in Article 5(2) concerning scope and level of detail for the information in the report apply to the assessment of alternatives as well. It is essential that the authority or parliament responsible for the adoption of the plan or programme as well as the authorities and the public consulted, are presented with an accurate picture of what reasonable alternatives

---

[45]   See, for example, *Shadwell Estates Ltd v Breckland District Council* [2013] EWHC 12 (Admin), at para 81, per Beatson J.

[46]   See, for example: *City and District Council of St Albans v Secretary of State for Communities and Local Government* [2009] EWHC 1280 (Admin), [2010] JPL 10; *Historic Newmarket Ltd v Forest Heath District Council* [2011] EWHC 606 (Admin), [2011] JPL 1233; *Heard v Broadland District Council* [2012] EWHC 344 (Admin), [2012] Env LR 23; and *R (on the application of Buckinghamshire County Council and Others) v Secretary of State for Transport*.

[47]   *Ashdown Forest Economic Development LLP v Secretary of State for Communities and Local Government* [2015] EWCA Civ 681, [2016] PTSR 78, at para 42, per Richards LJ.

[48]   *Ashdown Forest Economic Development LLP*, at para 50.

[49]   *Heard v Broadland District Council* [2012] EWHC 344 (Admin), [2012] Env LR 23, per Ouseley J at 66–71.

[50]   [2012] EWHC 344 (Admin), [2012] Env LR 23.

there are and why they are not considered to be the best option. The information referred to in Annex I should thus be provided for the alternatives chosen.'[51]

In *Heard* Mr Justice Ouseley expanded upon what is required:

'67   I accept that the plan-making process permits the broad options at stage one to be reduced or closed at the next stage, so that a preferred option or group of options emerges; there may then be a variety of narrower options about how they are progressed, and that that too may lead to a chosen course which may have itself further optional forms of implementation. It is not necessary to keep open all options for the same level of detailed examination at all stages. But if what I have adumbrated is the process adopted, an outline of the reasons for the selection of the options to be taken forward for assessment at each of those stages is required, even if that is left to the final SA, which for present purposes is the September 2009 SA

...

69   This is not an express requirement of the directive or regulations, and I do not regard European Commission guidance as a source of law. However, an outline of reasons for the selection of alternatives for examination is required, and alternatives have to be assessed, whether or not to the same degree as the preferred option, all for the purpose of carrying out, with public participation, a reasoned evaluative process of the environmental impact of plans or proposals. A teleological interpretation of the directive, to my mind, requires an outline of the reasons for the selection of a preferred option, if any, even where a number of alternatives are also still being considered. Indeed, it would normally require a sophisticated and artificial form of reasoning which explained why alternatives had been selected for examination but not why one of those at the same time had been preferred.

70   Even more so, where a series of stages leads to a preferred option for which alone an SA is being done, the reasons for the selection of this sole option for assessment at the final SA stage are not sensibly distinguishable from reasons for not selecting any other alternative for further examination at that final stage. The failure to give reasons for the selection of the preferred option is in reality a failure to give reasons why no other alternatives were selected for assessment or comparable assessment at that stage. This is what happened here. So this represents a breach of the directive on its express terms.

71   There is no express requirement in the directive either that alternatives be appraised to the same level as the preferred option. Mr Harwood again relies on the Commission guidance to evidence a legal obligation left unexpressed in the directive. Again, it seems to me that, although there is a case for the examination of a preferred option in greater detail, the aim of the directive, which may affect which alternatives it is reasonable to select, is more obviously met by, and it is best interpreted as requiring, an equal examination of the alternatives which it is reasonable to select for examination along side whatever, even at the outset, may be the preferred option. It is part of the purpose of this process to test whether what may start out as preferred should still end up as preferred after a fair and public analysis of what the authority regards as reasonable alternatives. I do not see that such an equal appraisal has been accorded to the alternatives referred to in the SA of September 2009. If that is because only one option had been selected, it rather highlights the need for and absence here of reasons for the selection of no alternatives as reasonable. Of course, an SA does not have to have a preferred option; it can emerge as the conclusion of the SEA process in which a number of options are considered, with an outline of the reasons for their selection being provided. But that is not the process adopted here.'

---

[51]   Cited at para 8 of the judgement.

A number of other case authorities have addressed the term 'reasonable alternatives'.[52] The principles deriving from these cases were analysed and summarised by Mr Justice Hickinbottom in *Friends of the Earth*[53] where he stated:

'i)   The authority's focus will be on the substantive plan, which will seek to attain particular policy objectives. The EIA Directive ensures that any particular project is subjected to an appropriate environmental assessment. The SEA Directive ensures that potentially environmentally-preferable options that will or may attain those policy objectives are not discarded as a result of earlier strategic decisions in respect of plans of which the development forms part. It does so by imposing process obligations upon the authority prior to the adoption of a particular plan.

ii)   The focus of the SEA process is therefore upon a particular plan—i.e. the authority's preferred plan—although that may have various options within it. A plan will be "preferred" because, in the judgment of the authority, it best meets the objectives it seeks to attain. In the sorts of plan falling within the scope of the SEA Directive, the objectives will be policy-based and almost certainly multi-stranded, reflecting different policies that are sought to be pursued. Those policies may well not all pull in the same direction. The choice of objectives, and the weight to be given to each, are essentially a matter for the authority subject to (a) a particular factor being afforded particular enhanced weight by statute or policy, and (b) challenge on conventional public law grounds.

iii)   In addition to the preferred plan, "reasonable alternatives" have to be identified, described and evaluated in the SEA Report; because, without this, there cannot be a proper environmental evaluation of the preferred plan.

iv)   "Reasonable alternatives" does not include all possible alternatives: the use of the word "reasonable" clearly and necessarily imports an evaluative judgment as to which alternatives should be included. That evaluation is a matter primarily for the decision-making authority, subject to challenge only on conventional public law grounds.

v)   Article 5(1) refers to "reasonable alternatives taking into account the objectives ... of the plan or programme ... " (emphasis added). "Reasonableness" in this context is informed by the objectives sought to be achieved. An option which does not achieve the objectives, even if it can properly be called an "alternative" to the preferred plan, is not a "reasonable alternative". An option which will, or sensibly may, achieve the objectives is a "reasonable alternative". The SEA Directive admits to the possibility of there being no such alternatives in a particular case: if only one option is assessed as meeting the objectives, there will be no "reasonable alternatives" to it.

vi)   The question of whether an option will achieve the objectives is also essentially a matter for the evaluative judgment of the authority, subject of course to challenge on conventional public law grounds. If the authority rationally determines that a particular option will not meet the objectives, that option is not a reasonable alternative and it does not have to be included in the SEA Report or process.

---

[52]   See *Save Historic Newmarket Ltd v Forest Heath District Council* [2011] EWHC 606 (Admin); *R (on the application of Buckinghamshire County Council) v Secretary of State for Transport* [2013] EWHC 481 (Admin); *R (on the application of Buckinghamshire County Council and Others) v Secretary of State for Transport* [2014] UKSC 3; *R (Chalfont St Peter Parish Council) v Chiltern District Council* [2013] EWHC 1877 (Admin), [2014] EWCA Civ 1397; *Ashdown Forest Economic Development LLP v Secretary of State for Communities and Local Government* [2014] EWHC 406 (Admin)

[53]   *R (on the application of Friends of the Earth England, Wales and Northern Ireland Ltd) v Welsh Ministers* [2015] EWHC 776 (Admin); [2016] Env LR 1 at para 88.

vii) However, as a result of the consultation which forms part of that process, new information may be forthcoming that might transform an option that was previously judged as meeting the objectives into one that is judged not to do so, and vice versa. In respect of a complex plan, after SEA consultation, it is likely that the authority will need to reassess, not only whether the preferred option is still preferred as best meeting the objectives, but whether any options that were reasonable alternatives have ceased to be such and (more importantly in practice) whether any option previously regarded as not meeting the objectives might be regarded as doing so now. That may be especially important where the process is iterative, i.e. a process whereby options are reduced in number following repeated appraisals of increased rigour. As time passes, a review of the objectives might also be necessary, which also might result in a reassessment of the "reasonable alternatives". But, once an option is discarded as not being a reasonable alternative, the authority does not have to consider it further, unless there is a material change in circumstances such as those I have described.

viii) Although the SEA Directive is focused on the preferred plan, it makes no distinction between the assessment requirements for that plan (including all options within it) and any reasonable alternatives to that plan. The potential significant effects of that plan, and any reasonable alternatives, have to be identified, described and evaluated in a comparable way.

ix) Particularly where the relevant plan sets a framework for future projects (e.g. a core planning strategy), it may be appropriate and indeed helpful to have an SEA process that is iterative. If so, the appraisal has to evaluate the extant options at each stage in a comparable way. As part of an iterative SEA process, options which may be capable of achieving the objectives may be discarded on the way; but such options cannot be discarded without being subjected to an SEA Directive -compliant assessment.

x) Although an SEA process that is iterative may be particular appropriate for some framework-setting plans and programmes, it is by no means mandatory. The authority may adopt a non-SEA process to identify those options which meet the objectives. That non-SEA process may itself be iterative.

xi) The objectives an authority sets for plans caught by the SEA Directive are likely to be particularly broad and high level, as well as multiple and varied. An assessment as to whether the objectives would be "met" by a particular option is therefore peculiarly evaluative; but an option will meet the objectives if, although it may not be (in the authority's judgment) the option that best meets the objectives overall (i.e. the preferred option), it is an option which is capable of sufficiently meeting the objectives such that that option could viably be adopted and implemented. That, again, is an evaluative judgment by the authority, which will only be challengeable on conventional public law grounds. However, whilst allowing the authority a due margin of discretion, the court will scrutinise the authority's choice of alternatives considered in the SEA process to ensure that it is not seeking to avoid its obligation to evaluate reasonable alternatives by improperly restricting the range options it has identified as such.

xii) The authority has an obligation to give outline reasons for selecting (i) its preferred option over the reasonable alternatives, and (ii) the alternatives "dealt with" in the SEA process. Alternatives "dealt with" include both (i) reasonable alternatives (which must be dealt with in the SEA process) and (ii) other alternatives (which need not, but may, be dealt with in that process). The reasons that are required are merely "outline". The authority need only give the main reasons, so that consultees and other interested parties are aware of why reasonable alternatives were chosen as such (including, in appropriate cases, why other options were not chosen as reasonable alternatives)—and, similarly, why the preferred option was chosen as such.'

The environmental report – timing

3.16   Where required to be undertaken, an environmental assessment is to 'be carried out during the preparation of a plan or programme and before its adoption or submission to the legislative procedure'.[54]

The SEA process is an iterative one[55]. This was explicitly stated by Collins J in *Save Historic Newmarket*:

> '16   The process adopted is in the planning jargon described as iterative. Thus it is open to an authority to reject alternatives at an early stage of the process and, provided that there is no change of circumstances, to decide that it is unnecessary to revisit them ...
>
> 17   It is clear from the terms of Article 5 of the Directive and the guidance from the Commission that the authority responsible for the adoption of the plan or programme as well as the authorities and public consulted must be presented with an accurate picture of what reasonable alternatives there are and why they are not considered to be the best option (See Commission Guidance Paragraphs 5.11 to 5.14). Equally, the environmental assessment and the draft plan must operate together so that consultees can consider each in the light of the other. That was the view of Weatherup J in the Northern Irish case *Re Seaport investments Ltd's Application for Judicial Review* [2008] Env. LR 23. However that does not mean that when the draft plan finally decided on by the authority and the accompanying environmental assessment are put out to consultation before the necessary examination is held there cannot have been during the iterative process a prior ruling out of alternatives. But this is subject to the important proviso that reasons have been given for the rejection of the alternatives, that those reasons are still valid if there has been any change in the proposals in the draft plan or any other material change of circumstances and that the consultees are able, whether by reference to the part of the earlier assessment giving the reasons or by summary of those reasons or, if necessary, by repeating them, to know from the assessment accompanying the draft plan what those reasons are. I do not think the Seaport case, which turned on its own facts including the lapse of time of over a year between the assessment and the draft plan, can provide any further assistance.'[56]

The result of this iterative process is that whilst the Directive and Regulations explicitly require only one round of reporting and consultation, the assessment is being carried out at the various stages of the plan-making process. This very often leads to the production of multiple interim environmental reports.

In practice the environmental report into a local development plan is often amalgamated with the sustainability appraisal which is required by domestic legislation. The Planning Practice Guidance states:

> 'Sustainability appraisals incorporate the requirements of the Environmental Assessment of Plans and Programmes Regulations 2004 (commonly referred to as the "Strategic Environmental Assessment Regulations") which implement the requirements of the European Directive 2001/42/EC ... on the assessment of the effects of certain plans and programmes on the environment. Sustainability appraisal ensures that potential environmental effects are given full consideration alongside social and economic issues.

---

[54]   SEA Directive, Art 4(1).
[55]   See *Seaport Investments Ltd's Application for Judicial Review* [2007] NIQB 62, [2008] Env LR 23.
[56]   For a further statement on the need for an iterative process, see Patterson J in *R (on the application of Stonegate Homes Ltd) v Horsham District Council* [2016] EWHC 2512 (Admin), [2017] Env LR 8, at para 88.

Strategic environmental assessment alone can be required in some limited situations where sustainability appraisal is not needed. This is usually only where either neighbourhood plans or supplementary planning documents could have significant environmental effects.'[57]

The environmental report – duplication

3.17 Paragraph 3 of Article 4 of the SEA Directive provides that:

> 'Where plans and programmes form part of a hierarchy, Member States shall, with a view to avoiding duplication of the assessment, take into account the fact that the assessment will be carried out, in accordance with this Directive, at different levels of the hierarchy. For the purpose of, inter alia, avoiding duplication of assessment, Member States shall apply Article 5(2) and (3).'

The carrying out of an environmental impact assessment under Directive 85/337 will not negate the need for SEA under the SEA Directive. However, it will be for the Court to decide whether the EIA in question already complies with the requirements of the SEA Directive such that there is no longer an obligation to conduct an SEA.[58]

In *Heard*[59] the claimant's second ground of challenge was that the SEA which accompanied the Joint Core Strategy had failed to assess the impact of a proposed new highway, the Northern Distributor Road ('NDR'), or alternatives to it. The Councils argued that the NDR had already been adequately assessed in documents prepared by the Highway Authority, Norfolk County Council. Mr Justice Ouseley held that the NDR was not within the remit of the Joint Core Strategy but was rather a piece of infrastructure promoted and planned by the Highways Authority and which had already been assessed in the Local Transport Plan. There was no need therefore to reassess the NDR as part of the Joint Core Strategy.

Consultation

3.18 The requirement to consult with regards to a strategic environmental assessment is contained within Article 6 of the SEA Directive. Paragraph 1 of that Article provides that the draft plan or programme together with the environmental report should be made available to both the public and those authorities who Member States have designated to be consulted by virtue of their specific environmental responsibilities.[60]

In UK law the requirement to consult is transposed by reg 13 of the SEA Regulations. Regulation 13(1) provides that 'Every draft plan or programme for which an environmental report has been prepared in accordance with regulation 12 and its accompanying environmental report ("the relevant documents") shall be made available for the purposes of consultation in accordance with the following provisions of this regulation'. The consultation period is not defined, but should be of 'such a

---

[57] Ref ID: 11-001-20140306.

[58] *Valčiukienė v Pakruojo rajono savivaldybe* (C-295/10) [2012] Env LR 11, at para 62.

[59] *Heard v Broadland District Council* [2012] EWHC 344 (Admin), [2012] Env LR 23.

[60] On the need for functional not legal separation between decision making and consultation bodies, see *Department of the Environment for Northern Ireland v Seaport (NI) Ltd* (C-474/10) [2012] Env LR 21.

length as will ensure that the consultation bodies and the public consultees are given an effective opportunity to express their opinion on the relevant documents'.[61]

The view of the High Court in Northern Ireland that the regulations were defective by failing to specify a consultation period was rejected by the ECJ in *Department of the Environment for Northern Ireland v Seaport (NI) Ltd*.[62] In practice, consultation arrangements will usually follow the legislation or guidance applicable to the particular plan-making process. However, plan makers should be careful to ensure that those processes, particularly the more informal ones, are sufficient for SEA purposes.

In circumstances where a Member State considers that the implementation of a plan or programme which is being prepared is likely to have significant effects on the environment within another Member State it is required to consult with that Member State before the adoption of that plan or programme.[63]

Decision-making

3.19   Article 8 of the SEA Directive provides that the environmental report, and consultation responses (both domestic and transboundary) must be taken into account during the preparation of the plan or programme and before its adoption or submission to the legislative procedure. It includes a requirement to consult the public and also the relevant consultation bodies.[64,65] There is no requirement for the decision-maker to choose the option which will engender the least environmental harm.[66]

The SEA Directive also contains a requirement that when a plan or programme is adopted, the consultees, the public and any other Member State who has previously been consulted under Article 7 should be informed and the following items should be made available to them: (a) the plan or programme as adopted; (b) a statement which summarises how environmental considerations have been integrated into the plan or programme and how the environmental report together with the consultation responses have been taken into account together with the reasons for choosing the adopted plan or programme in light of the other reasonable alternatives dealt with; and (c) the monitoring measures as decided on in accordance with Article 10 of the SEA Directive.

Monitoring

3.20   The requirements of the SEA Directive do not end with the adoption of the plan or programme. There is a continuing requirement to monitor the significant environmental effects which arise as the result of the implementation of a plan or

---

[61]   SEA Regulations, reg 13(3).
[62]   (C-474/10) [2012] Env LR 21.
[63]   The procedure for such consultation is contained within the SEA Directive, Art 7. Regulation 14 of the SEA Regulations deals with trans-boundary consultations for English plans and programmes. Regulation 15 deals with plans and programmes in other Member States which may affect the UK.
[64]   Defined in reg 4 as Historic England, Natural England and the Environment Agency in England and the National Assembly for Wales and the Natural Resources Body for Wales in Wales.
[65]   SEA Regulations, reg 13(2)(c) and (d).
[66]   *R (on the application of Friends of the Earth) v Welsh Ministers* at para 75 per Hikinbottom J.

programme in order to 'identify at an early stage unforeseen adverse effects, and to be able to undertake appropriate remedial action'.[67]

HABITATS ASSESSMENT – OVERVIEW

3.21   As with SEA discussed above, habitats assessments are a creature of European Law in particular, the Habitats Directive 92/43/EEC.

Two directives are relevant to the establishment of Special Protection Areas ('SPAs'): the Birds Directive 79/409/EEC (now codified as 2009/147/EC) and the Habitats Directive. Under the Birds Directive the EU established a network of SPAs which are the most suitable territories for the conservation of certain wild bird species. The Habitats Directive provided for the establishment of a European network of special areas of conservation ('SACs') under the title Natura 2000 as well as an assessment mechanism for projects affecting both types of area. Consequently, the process is referred to as habitats assessment. The Natura 2000 network also includes SPAs designated under the Birds Directive.[68]

Article 6(3) and 6(4)

3.22   The Habitats Directive places Member States a under a duty to protect SACs. One part of this duty is through the strict control of plans or projects which are likely to have a significant effect on an SAC. The Habitats Directive then applies the same duties to SPAs under the Birds Directive.[69] Article 6(3) states:

> 'Any plan or project not directly connected with or necessary to the management of the site but likely to have a significant effect thereon, either individually or in combination with other plans or projects, shall be subject to appropriate assessment of its implications for the site in view of the site's conservation objectives. In the light of the conclusions of the assessment of the implications for the site and subject to the provisions of paragraph 4, the competent national authorities shall agree to the plan or project only after having ascertained that it will not adversely affect the integrity of the site concerned and, if appropriate, after having obtained the opinion of the general public.'

There are some limited exceptions to Article 6(3) in Article 6(4) which states:

> 'If, in spite of a negative assessment of the implications for the site and in the absence of alternative solutions, a plan or programme must nevertheless be carried out for imperative reasons of overriding public interest, including those of a social or economic nature, the Member State shall take all compensatory measures necessary to ensure that the overall coherence of the Natura 2000 is protected. It shall inform the Commission of the compensatory measures adopted.

> Where the site concerned hosts a priority natural habitat type and/or a priority species, the only considerations which may be raised are those relating to human health or public safety, to beneficial consequences of primary importance for the environment or, further to an opinion from the Commission, to other imperative reasons of overriding public interest.'

---

[67]   SEA Directive, Art 10(1).
[68]   Habitats Directive, Art 3(1).
[69]   Habitats Directive, Art 7.

The Habitats Directive has been transposed into domestic law in the Conservation of Habitats and Species Regulations 2017[70] ('Habitats Regulations'). Regulations 63, 105 and 106 transpose the duty in Article 6(3). Regulation 105 applies to land use plans.[71] Paragraph (1) provides:

'(1) Where a land use plan –

    (a) is likely to have a significant effect on a European site or a European offshore marine site (either alone or in combination with other plans or projects), and

    (b) is not directly connected with or necessary to the management of the site,

the plan-making authority for that plan must, before the plan is given effect, make an appropriate assessment of the implications for the site in view of that site conservation objectives.'

Regulation 106 applies to neighbourhood plans. It requires that the qualifying body who submits a proposal for a neighbourhood plan should provide such information as the competent authority may reasonably require for the purpose of the appropriate assessment or to enable them to determine whether that assessment is required. Under subsection 3, where the competent authority decides to revoke or modify a neighbourhood plan they must make an appropriate assessment of the implications for any European site likely to be significantly affected in view of the site's conservation objectives. Regulations 105 and 106 apply to such revocations or modifications.

Marine policy statements and marine plans are covered by Chapter 8 of the Habitats Regulations by virtue of regs 112 and 113 respectively.[72] National policy statements are also covered by virtue of reg 106.

Regulation 107 transposes the limited exception in Article 6(4). Regulation 109 includes the requirement to take any necessary compensatory measures where a land use plan is given effect notwithstanding a negative assessment of the implications for a European site or a European offshore marine site.

Screening/threshold

3.23   Neither Article 6(3) and reg 105 explicitly require a screening assessment to be carried out. However, as the Court of Appeal pointed out in *No Adastral New Town v Suffolk Coastal District Council*:[73]

'If it is not obvious whether a plan or project is likely to have a significant effect on an SPA, it may be necessary in practice to carry out a screening assessment in order to ensure that the substantive requirements of the Directive are ultimately met.'[74]

---

[70] SI 2017/1012. These replaced the Conservation of Habitats and Species Regulations 2010, SI 2010/490 on 30 November 2017.

[71] Formerly the provisions were the Conservation of Habitats and Species Regulations 2010, regs 61, 102 and 102A.

[72] Formerly the Conservation of Habitats and Species Regulations 2010, regs 107A and 107B.

[73] [2015] EWCA Civ 88, [2015] Env LR 28.

[74] At para 68.

This 'screening stage' should not be overcomplicated and should not be conflated with screening in an environmental impact assessment context. As Lord Carnwath JSC put it in *R (Champion) v North Norfolk District Council*:[75]

> '… in cases where it is not obvious, the competent authority will consider whether the "trigger" for appropriate assessment is met (and see paras 41-43 of *Waddenzee*). But this informal threshold decision is not to be confused with a formal "screening opinion" in the EIA sense. The operative words are those of the Habitats Directive itself. All that is required is that, in a case where the authority has found there to be a risk of significant adverse effects to a protected site, there should be an "appropriate assessment".'[76]

The term 'likelihood' should be read as 'possibility'. In *Sweetman v An Bord Pleanala*[77] Advocate General Sharpston stated:

> '47. It follows that the possibility of there being a significant effect on the site will generate the need for an appropriate assessment for the purposes of art. 6(3). The requirement at this stage that the plan or project be likely to have a significant effect is thus a trigger for the obligation to carry out an appropriate assessment. There is no need to establish such an effect; it is … merely necessary to determine that there may be such an effect.
>
> 48. The requirement that the effect in question be "significant" exists in order to lay down a de minimis threshold …
>
> 49. The threshold at the first stage of art. 6(3) is thus a very low one. It operates merely as a trigger, in order to determine whether an appropriate assessment must be undertaken of the implications of the plan or project for the conservation objectives of the site. The purpose of that assessment is that the plan or project in question should be considered thoroughly, on the basis of what the Court has termed "the best scientific knowledge in the field" …[78]
>
> 50. The test which that expert assessment must determine is whether the plan or project in question has "an adverse effect on the integrity of the site", since that is the basis on which the competent authorities must reach their decision. The threshold at this (the second) stage is noticeably higher than that laid down at the first stage …'

Further, where there is doubt as to whether there will be significant effects on the site in question, then the precautionary principle means that an appropriate assessment should be carried out. This was highlighted by Ouseley J at first instance in *R (Buckinghamshire CC) v Secretary of State for Transport*:[79]

> '203 The circumstances requiring an "appropriate assessment" were considered in *Landelijke Vereniging tot Behoud van de Waddenzee v Staatssecretaris van Landbouw, Natuurbeheer en Visserij* Case C-127–02 [2005] 2 CMLR 31; CJEU; the Dutch cockle-pickers case. There had to be a "probability or a risk" that a plan or project would have significant effects on the site. But the precautionary principle meant that such a risk existed "if it cannot be excluded on the basis of objective information that the plan or project will have significant effects on the site concerned." This "implies that in case of doubt as to the absence of significant effects such an assessment must be carried out …" Hence, the first sentence of Article 6(3) "must be interpreted as meaning that any plan or project not directly connected with or necessary to the management of the site is to be subject to an appropriate assessment of its

---

[75] [2015] UKSC 52, [2015] 1 WLR 3710.
[76] At para 41.
[77] (C-258/11) [2013] 3 CMLR 16.
[78] Cited by Richards LJ in *Ashdown Forest Economic Development LLP*, at para 12.
[79] [2013] EWHC 481 (Admin), [2013] PTSR D25.

implications for the site in view of the site's conservation objectives if it cannot be excluded, on the basis of objective information, that it will have a significant effect on that site, either individually or in combination with other plans or projects'''.

A mere 'effect' on the site is not enough to trigger the need for an appropriate assessment. The effect in question must be likely to undermine that site's conservation objectives.[80] Equally, where a plan is likely to undermine the conservation objectives of the site concerned it will necessarily be considered to have a significant effect on the site.[81]

Where the plan includes measures to mitigate any harm to the protected site in question the plan-making authority is required to have regard to them in ascertaining whether the plan is likely to have a significant effect on the site.[82] Necessarily, the plan-making authority will need to be satisfied that the proposed mitigation is achievable.[83]

Although it is clearly desirable to carry out a screening assessment at an early stage in the plan's preparation, neither the Habitats Directive nor the Habitats Regulations specify the timing of such screening.[84]

The appropriate assessment

3.24   Where the plan in question is likely to have a significant effect on a European site or European offshore marine site the plan-making authority must conduct an appropriate assessment of the implications for the site in view of its conservation objectives.[85] The Habitats Directive does not prescribe any particular methodology for the carrying out of such an assessment. The ECJ has stated that the assessment must, however, take into account the cumulative effects of that plan or project with other plans or projects.[86] It should include the assessment of each aspect of the plan which can, either individually or in combination with other plans or protects, affect the conservation objectives of the site in light of the best scientific knowledge in that field.[87]

The Habitats Directive does not stipulate the time when the appropriate assessment must be undertaken. However, it must be undertaken before the plan is given effect.[88] Though it is clearly preferable for it to be undertaken at an early stage, 'a failure to conduct an appropriate assessment at the beginning of the process cannot vitiate the ultimate decision provided the assessment is carried out before the plan takes effect and the appropriate assessment does not demonstrate that there is likely to be any significant environmental effect'.[89]

---

[80]   *Waddenzee* (C-127–02) [2005] 2 CMLR 31, at para 47.
[81]   *Waddenzee*, at para 48.
[82]   *R (Hart District Council) v Secretary of State for Communities and Local Government* [2008] EWHC 1204, at para 76 per Sullivan J.
[83]   *No Adastral New Town v Suffolk Coastal District Council* [2015] EWCA Civ 88, [2015] Env LR 28, at para 72 per Richards LJ.
[84]   *No Adastral*, at para 68 per Richards LJ.
[85]   Habitats Directive, Art 6(3); Habitats Regulations, reg 105.
[86]   *Waddenzee*, at para 53.
[87]   *Waddenzee*, at para 54.
[88]   *No Adastral New Town v Suffolk Coastal District Council* [2014] EWHC 223 (Admin), [2015] Env LR 3, at para 142 per Patterson J.
[89]   *No Adastral New Town*, at para 142.

As with the threshold/screening stage discussed above, where mitigation measures are part of the project these may be taken into account. However, compensatory measures may not.[90]

The appropriate assessment enables the plan-making authority to ascertain whether the plan will adversely affect the integrity of the European Site. The Supreme Court has highlighted that 'appropriate' is not a technical term:[91]

> 'It indicates no more than the assessment should be appropriate to the task in hand: that task being to satisfy the responsible authority that the project "will not adversely affect the integrity of the site concerned" taking account of the matters set in the article. As the court itself indicated in Waddenzee the context implies a high standard of investigation. However, as Advocate General Kokott said in *Waddenzee* [2005] All ER (EC) 353, para 107:
>
> > "the necessary certainty cannot be construed as meaning absolute certainty since that is almost impossible to attain. Instead, it is clear from the second sentence of article 6(3) of the Habitats Directive that the competent authorities must take a decision having assessed all the relevant information which is set out in particular in the appropriate assessment. The conclusion of this assessment is, of necessity, subjective in nature. Therefore, the competent authorities can, from their point of view, be certain that there will be no adverse effects even though, from an objective point of view, there is no absolute certainty."
>
> In short, no special procedure is prescribed, and, while a high standard of investigation is demanded, the issue ultimately rests on the judgment of the authority.'

The plan-making authority may only give effect to the plan where it concludes that it will not adversely affect the integrity of the European site,[92] unless the plan in question falls into the Article 6(4) exception (see below).

The ECJ has stated that for the integrity of the site not to be adversely affected 'the site needs to be preserved at a favourable conservation status; this entails … the lasting preservation of the constitutive characteristics of the site concerned that are connected to the presence of a natural habitat type whose preservation was the objective justifying the designation of that site in the list of [sites of community importance], in accordance with the Directive'.[93]

Consultation and publicity

3.25   When making an appropriate assessment in relation to a land use plan, the plan-making authority is required to consult the appropriate nature conservation body.[94] It is required to have regard to any representations made by that body.[95]

Where the plan-making authority considers it appropriate they must take the opinion of the general public. The plan-making authority has a wide degree of discretion as to

---

[90]   *Briels v Minister van Infrastructuur en Milieu* (C-521/12) [2014] PTSR 1120.
[91]   *Champion* at para 41 per Lord Carnwarth JSC.
[92]   Habitats Regulations, reg 102(4).
[93]   *Sweetman* at para 39.
[94]   Habitats Regulations, reg 105(2).
[95]   Habitats Regulations, reg 105(2).

how the public are to be consulted as the regulations state 'they must take such steps for that purpose as they consider appropriate'.[96]

Article 6(4) exception

3.26   Article 6(4) of the Habitats Directive provides a limited exception to the prohibition of implementing plans or projects which might adversely affect the integrity of a European site. It states:

'If, in spite of a negative assessment of the implications for the site and in the absence of alternative solutions, a plan or programme must nevertheless be carried out for imperative reasons of overriding public interest, including those of a social or economic nature, the Member State shall take all compensatory measures necessary to ensure that the overall coherence of the Natura 2000 is protected. It shall inform the Commission of the compensatory measures adopted.

Where the site concerned hosts a priority natural habitat type and/or a priority species, the only considerations which may be raised are those relating to human health or public safety, to beneficial consequences of primary importance for the environment or, further to an opinion from the Commission, to other imperative reasons of overriding public interest.'

Article 6(4) has been transposed into domestic law for local plans by virtue of reg 106 of the Habitats Regulations. Material parts state:

'(1)   If the plan-making authority are satisfied that, there being no alternative solutions, the land use plan must be given effect for imperative reasons of overriding public interest (which, subject to paragraph (3), may be of a social or economic nature), they may give effect to the land use plan notwithstanding a negative assessment of the implications for the European site or the European offshore marine site (as the case may be).

(2)   In relation to a regional strategy, paragraph (1) applies to the Secretary of State as it applies to a plan-making authority in the case of any other land use.

(3)   Where the site concerned hosts a priority natural habitat type or a priority species, the reasons referred to in paragraph (1) must be either—

(a)   reasons relating to human health, public safety or beneficial consequences of primary importance to the environment; or

(b)   any other reasons which the plan-making authority, having due regard to the opinion of the European Commission, consider to be imperative reasons of overriding public interest.'

Only once the implications of a plan have been analysed in accordance with Article 6(3) (i.e. an appropriate assessment has been carried out) can Article 6(4) apply.[97] As the ECJ highlighted in *Solvay v Region Wallonne*:

'Knowledge of those implications in the light of the conservation objectives relating to the site in question is a necessary prerequisite for the application of art.6(4), since, in the absence of those elements, no condition for the application of that derogating provision can be assessed. The assessment of any imperative reasons of overriding public interest and that of the existence of less harmful alternatives require a weighing up against the

---

[96]   Habitats Regulations, reg 105(3)
[97]   *Solvay v Region Wallonne* [2012] Env LR 545, at paras 73 and 74.

damage caused to the site by the plan or project under consideration. In addition, in order to determine the nature of any compensatory measures, the damage to the site must be precisely identified (see *Commission v Italy* [2007] E.C.R. I-7495 at [83])'.[98]

In order for the Article 6(4) derogation to be met three 'tests' must be satisfied. First, there must be no feasible alternative solutions to the plan which are less damaging to European sites. Second, there must be 'imperative reasons of overriding public interest' ('IROPI'). Third, all necessary compensatory measures must be taken to ensure that the overall coherence of the Natura 2000 network is protected.

(1) No feasible alternatives

3.27 The Department for Environment, Food and Rural Affairs (DEFRA) guidance states:[99]

'Alternatives must be considered objectively and broadly. This could include options that would be delivered by someone other than the applicant, or at a different location, using different routes, scale, size, methods, means or timing. Alternatives can also involve different ways of operating a development facility.'

Note that the SEA Directive states that the alternatives considered must be 'feasible'. This can be taken to include options that are financially, legally and technically feasible.[100] Also, alternatives considered must involve less damage to the affected European site/s or to any other sites which could be affected by the given alternative.

(2) IROPI

3.28 The ECJ has made clear that the test of 'imperative reasons of overriding interest' ('IROPI') is to be strictly defined. In *Solvay v Region Wallone* the Court emphasised that the plan or project must be both 'public' and 'overriding' 'which means that it must be of such an importance that it can be weighed up against that directive's objective of the conservation of natural habitats and wild fauna and flora'.[101]

Note that for European sites designated under the Habitats Directive, the IROPI grounds on which a plan might proceed will depend upon the nature of the site affected. If the plan will negatively affect a European site which hosts a priority natural habitat type or priority species, the plan-making authority can only consider reasons relating to: human health, public safety or beneficial consequences of primary importance to the environment unless following an opinion from the European Commission other imperative reasons of overriding public interest may be taken into account.

Although IROPI sets a high bar, the test is not an insuperable one. In *Sweetman* Advocate General Sharpston stated:

---

[98] At para 74.
[99] 'Habitats and Wild Birds Directives: guidance on the application of article 6(4)' (December 2012), para 16.
[100] DCLG, 'A practical guide to the Strategic Environmental Assessment Directive' (September 2005), para 18.
[101] At para 75.

'66 Whilst the requirements laid down under article 6(4) are intentionally rigorous, it is important to point out that they are not insuperable obstacles to authorisation. The Commission indicated at the hearing that, of the 15 to 20 requests so far made to it for delivery of an opinion under that provision, only one has received a negative response.'

The domestic case law on what is likely to amount to IROPI is limited. However, the European Commission's guidance[102] together with their opinions, offer some idea of what sort of considerations are to be taken into account considering whether IROPI exist. The following section of the Commission's guidance is particularly relevant:

'The concept of "imperative reason of overriding public interest" is not defined in the Directive. However, Article 6 (4) second subparagraph mentions human health, public safety and beneficial consequences of primary importance for the environment as examples of such imperative reasons of overriding public interests. As regards the "other imperative reasons of overriding public interest" of social or economic nature, it is clear from the wording that only public interests, irrespective of whether they are promoted either by public or private bodies, can be balanced against the conservation aims of the Directive. Thus, projects developed by private bodies can only be considered where such public interests are served and demonstrated.' (p 7)

'Having regard to the structure of the provision, in the specific cases, the competent national authorities have to make their approval of the plans and projects in question subject to the condition that the balance of interests between the conservation objectives of the site affected by those initiatives and the above-mentioned imperative reasons weighs in favour of the latter. This should be determined according to the following considerations:

a)   the public interest must be overriding: it is therefore clear that not every kind of public interest of a social or economic nature is sufficient, in particular when seen against the particular weight of the interests protected by the Directive (see e.g. its 4th recital stating "Community's natural heritage") (see Annex I point 10).

b)   in this context, it seems also reasonable to assume that the public interest can only be overriding if it is a long-term interest; short term economic interests or other interests which would only yield short-term benefits for the society would not appear to be sufficient to outweigh the long-term conservation interests protected by the Directive.' (p 8)

The Commission Guidance lists specific instances which may be seen as potential IROPI cases (table at pp 8 and 9). They include:

•   Intersection of the Peene Valley (Germany) by the A20 motorway, the region suffers from exceptionally high unemployment and there was a need to connect the area to central regions of the Community;

•   Project Mainport Rotterdam, this is a harbour of Community importance and the works would allow the port to maintain its competitive position. Further, the development would assist modal shift of freight transport from road to water which would bring considerable environmental benefits;

•   The extension of the Daimler Chrysler Aerospace Airbus, this was of outstanding importance for Hamburg, North Germany and the European

---

[102] European Commission, 'Clarification of the concepts of: alternative solutions, imperative reasons of overriding public interest, compensatory measures, overall coherence, Opinion of the Commission' (2007/2012).

aerospace industry. It would have an economic and social impact on bordering regions.

In its opinion of 6 December 2011, the European Commission considered (at the request of Germany) a proposal to deepen and widen the river Elbe to the port of Hamburg. Four sites of community importance were assessed to be affected by the project and the appropriate assessment concluded that there would be significant impacts on the Natura 2000 sites. The German authorities assessed six potential alternatives to reach the objective together with the 'zero alternative' (ie doing nothing). Three options did not meet the objective or were unrealistic, the others would fail for economic reasons. The zero alternative meant that Hamburg would lose its competitiveness.

The Commission held that the imperative reasons of public importance were the economic importance of the Port's expansion for Hamburg and the whole country, hundreds and thousands of jobs were directly or indirectly dependent upon its prosperity. Some mitigation measures were confirmed by the German authorities to ensure some conservation objectives. The Commission concluded:

> '… the deepening and widening of the ship fairway Unter-and Außenelbe to the port of Hamburg is justified as an essential project of overriding public interest for which there are no viable alternatives.' (p 6)

(3) Compensatory measures

3.29   If a Member State is to rely upon the Article 6(4) exception it is to 'take all compensatory measures necessary to ensure that the overall coherence of the Natura 2000 is protected'.[103] Compensatory measures are not limited to the site in question but may concern other sites within the Natura 2000 network.[104] As the ECJ stated in *Briels*:[105]

> 'A compensatory measure differs from a measure of mitigation, minimisation or reduction by its nature, not by its geographical location. Although an adverse effect on the integrity of one site is unlikely to be mitigated by measures taken in another site, that logic does not apply where compensation is concerned. A compensatory measure is, by its nature, separate from that for which it seeks to compensate, whereas a mitigation measure is of necessity bound up with that which it is designed to mitigate. However, the fact that compensatory measures may be implemented elsewhere than in the affected site does not mean that they cannot be implemented within (possibly in another part of) that site. Nor is a measure any less likely to protect the overall coherence of Natura 2000 where it is implemented within the affected site than where it is implemented in another part of the Natura 2000 network (if anything, it may be more likely to do so).'

In England and Wales, where a competent authority[106] (other than the Secretary of State or Welsh Ministers) proposes to agree to a plan on the basis of the IROPI exception, it is required to notify the Secretary of State (in England) and the Welsh Ministers (in Wales) and must not agree to the plan before the end of the period of

---

[103]   Habitats Directive, Art 6(4).
[104]   *Briels*, at para 46. See also *Orleans v Vlaams Gewest* (C-387/15) [2017] Env LR 215.
[105]   Paragraph 46 of Advocate General Sharpston's Opinion and adopted by the Court in para 38 of the judgement.
[106]   As defined in Habitats Regulations, reg 7, the definition includes any public body.

21 days beginning with the day that their notification was received by the Secretary of State or Welsh Ministers, unless the Secretary of State or Welsh Ministers notifies them that they may adopt the plan at an earlier date.[107] The Secretary of State or Welsh Ministers may give directions to the competent authority in any such case prohibiting them from agreeing to the plan or project either indefinitely or during such a period as may be specified in the direction.[108]

Interrelationship with SEA

3.30   Habitats Regulations Assessments ('HRAs') and SEA should not be conflated. They are designed to do different things. The SEA is a process by which the environmental effects of a plan are identified as it is being prepared. It also requires the evaluation of reasonable alternatives (which are not required under an HRA);[109] whereas an HRA assesses whether the plan in question is likely to have a significant effect on a protected European site.

In *Commission v Ireland* (C-418/04)[110] the ECJ stressed that the appropriate assessment regime is separate from the SEA regime (and indeed the EIA regime). It stated:

> '230. Ireland adds that it implements the assessments pursuant to Council Directive 85/337/EEC of 27 June 1985 on the assessment of the effects of certain public and private projects on the environment (OJ 1985 L 175, p40) and to Directive 2001/42, also transposed by the European Communities (Environmental Assessment of Certain Plans and Programmes) Regulations 2004 and by the Planning and Development Strategic Environmental Assessment Regulations 2004.

> 231. Those two directives contain provisions relating to the deliberation procedure, without binding the Member States as to the decision, and relate to only certain projects and plans. By contrast, under the second sentence of Article 6(3) of the Habitats Directive, a plan or project can be authorised only after the national authorities have ascertained that it will not adversely affect the integrity of the site. Accordingly, assessments carried out pursuant to Directive 85/337 or Directive 2001/42 cannot replace the procedure provided for in Article 6(3) and (4) of the Habitats Directive.'

There is though an overlap in the material and the possible consequences. The PPG states that a sustainability appraisal should take into account the findings of any HRA.[111]

---

[107] Habitats Regulations, reg 62(5).
[108] Habitats Regulations, reg 62(6).
[109] As highlighted by Richards LJ in *Ashdown Forest*, at para 45.
[110] [2007] ECR I-10947.
[111] Paragraph 11, Reference ID: 11-011-20140306.

Chapter 4

National Planning Policy – England

THE NATIONAL PLANNING POLICY FRAMEWORK

Introduction

4.1   The government's principal planning policies for England are contained within the National Planning Policy Framework ('NPPF'). It was published in March 2012 and replaced a mass of Planning Policy Statements ('PPSs'), Planning Policy Guidance Notes ('PPGs'), Minerals Planning Statements ('MPSs'), Mineral Policy Statements ('MPGs'), circulars and letters to chief planning officers.[1] The NPPF is concerned with the approach to the formulation of local policy and the determination of planning applications. It also makes comment on process, such as the weight to be attached to emerging local plans.

4.2   The NPPF was originally accompanied by 'technical guidance to the National Planning Policy Framework' which provided further policy guidance on flood risk and minerals. However, this was withdrawn on 7 March 2014 and replaced by the Planning Practice Guidance which had been launched the day before.[2]

4.3   The NPPF was not enacted by legislation and does not form part of the development plan for the deciding of applications. It did, however, undergo some Parliamentary scrutiny as it was laid (in draft) before the Communities and Local Government Select Committee as a command paper. The Secretary of State's power to issue national policy is derived, expressly or by implication, from the Planning Acts which give him overall responsibility for oversight of the planning system.[3]

What the NPPF does not contain

4.4   The NPPF does not contain specific waste policies (see NPPF, para 3), as these are published as part of the National Waste Management Plan for England. Notwithstanding this, local authorities preparing waste plans are required to have regard to policies in the NPPF so far as they are relevant (NPPF, para 3).

---

[1]   Annex 3 to the NPPF contains a list of 44 separate documents which were replaced by the NPPF.
[2]   See *List of guidance documents cancelled by the planning practice guidance suite* (CLG, March 2014).
[3]   *Secretary of State for Communities and Local Government v Hopkins Homes; Richborough Estates Partnership LLP v Cheshire East BC* [2017] UKSC 37, [2017] 1 WLR 1865 at paras 19 and 20 per Lord Carnwarth.

4.5　　The NPPF does not contain specific policies for Nationally Significant Infrastructure Projects ('NSIPs').[4] These are covered by national policy statements ('NPSs') whose preparation and application is governed by the Planning Act 2008.

Simplicity and clarity?

4.6　　The headline purpose of the NPPF was to simplify planning. The foreword to the NPPF states:

> 'In part, people have been put off from getting involved because planning policy itself has become so elaborate and forbidding – the preserve of specialists, rather than people in communities.
>
> This National Planning Policy Framework changes that. By replacing over a thousand pages of national policy with around fifty, written simply and clearly, we are allowing people and communities back into planning.'[5]

4.7　　Of course, with the publication of the Planning Practice Guidance ('PPG') in 2014 the volume of national planning policy and guidance is more than the NPPF's fifty pages. However, the cancellation of previous policy and guidance on the publication of both documents is a considerable improvement on the previous mass of material in PPSs, PPGs, good practice guides, circulars and various miscellaneous publications. The PPG is discussed further below.

4.8　　The trumpeted simplicity and clarity of the NPPF has been somewhat belied by the volume of litigation which has been founded on the interpretation of the various policies contained therein. The principle that policy interpretation is a matter for the courts[6] has been applied to the provisions of the NPPF.[7] In examining the meaning of certain provisions contained within the NPPF, the courts have commented as follows:

> '[views] may differ as to whether simplicity and clarity have always been achieved but the policies are certainly shorter'[8]

> '... the process of simplification has in certain instances led to a diminution in clarity'[9]

> '... It was also common ground that policies in the Framework should be approached in the same way as those in a development plan. However, some concerns were expressed by the experienced counsel before us about the over-legalisation of the planning process, as illustrated by the proliferation of case law on paragraph 49 itself (see paras 27ff below). This is particularly unfortunate for what was intended as a simplification of national policy guidance, designed for the lay-reader. Some further comment from this court may therefore be appropriate.'[10]

---

[4]　NPPF, para 3.
[5]　National Planning Policy Framework (CLG, March 2012).
[6]　*Tesco Stores Ltd v Dundee City Council* [2012] UKSC 13, [2012] PTSR 983.
[7]　See *R (on the application of Hunston Properties Ltd) v Secretary of State for Communities and Local Government* [2013] EWCA Civ 1610, [2014] JPL 599.
[8]　*Redhill Aerodrome Ltd v Secretary of State for Communities and Local Government* [2014] EWCA Civ 1386; [2015] PTSR 274.
[9]　*R (on the application of Hunston Properties Ltd) v Secretary of State for Communities and Local Government* [2013] EWCA Civ 1610, [2014] JPL 599.
[10]　*Secretary of State for Communities and Local Government v Hopkins Homes; Richborough Estates Partnership LLP v Cheshire East Borough Council* [2017] UKSC 37, [2017] 1 WLR 1865, at para 23 per Lord Carnwath.

4.9　　In the *Hopkins Homes* decision, the Supreme Court did its best to discourage unnecessary litigation over the meaning of national planning policy. Lord Carnwarth stated:

> '24 In the first place, it is important that the role of the court is not overstated. Lord Reed's application of the principles in the particular case [*Tesco Stores Ltd v Dundee City Council* [2012] UKSC 13, 2012 SLT 739] (para 18) needs to be read in the context of the relatively specific policy there under consideration. Policy 45 of the local plan provided that new retail developments outside locations already identified in the plan would only be acceptable in accordance with five defined criteria, one of which depended on the absence of any "suitable site" within or linked to the existing centres (para 5). The short point was the meaning of the word "suitable" (para 13): suitable for the development proposed by the applicant, or for meeting the retail deficiencies in the area? It was that question which Lord Reed identified as one of textual interpretation, "logically prior" to the exercise of planning judgment (para 21). As he recognised (see para 19), some policies in the development plan may be expressed in much broader terms, and may not require, nor lend themselves to, the same level of legal analysis.
>
> 25 It must be remembered that, whether in a development plan or in a non-statutory statement such as the NPPF, these are statements of policy, not statutory texts, and must be read in that light. Even where there are disputes over interpretation, they may well not be determinative of the outcome. (As will appear, the present can be seen as such a case.) Furthermore, the courts should respect the expertise of the specialist planning inspectors, and start at least from the presumption that they will have understood the policy framework correctly. With the support and guidance of the Planning Inspectorate, they have primary responsibility for resolving disputes between planning authorities, developers and others, over the practical application of the policies, national or local. As I observed in the Court of Appeal (*Wychavon District Council v Secretary of State for Communities and Local Government* [2008] EWCA Civ 692; [2009] PTSR 19 , para 43) their position is in some ways analogous to that of expert tribunals, in respect of which the courts have cautioned against undue intervention by the courts in policy judgments within their areas of specialist competence (see *Secretary of State for the Home Department v AH (Sudan)* [2007] UKHL 49; [2008] 1 AC 678 , para 30 per Lady Hale.)
>
> 26 Recourse to the courts may sometimes be needed to resolve distinct issues of law, or to ensure consistency of interpretation in relation to specific policies, as in the *Tesco* case. In that exercise the specialist judges of the Planning Court have an important role. However, the judges are entitled to look to applicants, seeking to rely on matters of planning policy in applications to quash planning decisions (at local or appellate level), to distinguish clearly between issues of interpretation of policy, appropriate for judicial analysis, and issues of judgement in the application of that policy; and not to elide the two.'

The sustainable development conundrum

4.10　　The first sentence of the Ministerial forward to the NPPF states that '[T]he purpose of planning is to help achieve sustainable development'. A floating green box of text above paragraph 6 of the NPPF sets out the Bruntland Commission's[11] definition of sustainable development. It states:

> 'International and national bodies have set out broad principles of sustainable development. Resolution 42/187 of the United Nations General Assembly defined

---

[11]　World Commission on Environment and Development, which reported in 1987.

sustainable development as meeting the needs of the present without compromising the ability of future generations to meet their own needs. The UK Sustainable Development Strategy Securing the Future set out five "guiding principles" of sustainable development: living within the planet's environmental limits; ensuring a strong, healthy and just society; achieving a sustainable economy; promoting good governance; and using sound science responsibly.'

4.11   However, the NPPF does not refer to this definition again. Paragraph 6 states:

'The purpose of the planning system is to contribute to the achievement of sustainable development. The policies in paragraphs 18 to 219, taken as a whole, constitute the Government's view of what sustainable development in England means in practice for the planning system.'

4.12   Paragraph 7 of the NPPF goes on to explain that sustainable development is made up of three dimensions which gives rise to the need for planning to perform: an economic role, a social role and an environmental role. Paragraph 8 states that these roles are mutually dependent and should not be undertaken in isolation.

4.13   Paragraph 14 states that at the heart of the NPFF is a *presumption in favour of sustainable development*, which should be seen as a golden thread running through both plan-making and decision-taking.

The status of the NPPF

4.14   At paragraph 13, the NPPF seeks to explain its status. It states:

'The National Planning Policy Framework constitutes guidance for local planning authorities and decision-takers both in drawing up plans and as a material consideration in determining planning applications.'

The NPPF 'does not contain specific policies for nationally significant infrastructure projects' which are the subject of applications for development consent orders under the Planning Act 2008. However, it might be considered relevant to determining those applications.[12]

The status of the NPPF – plan-making

4.15   A local planning authority is required by statute to have regard to 'national policies and advice contained in guidance issued by the Secretary of State' when preparing a development plan document or any other local development document.[13] This therefore includes the NPPF.

4.16   Paragraphs 150–185 of the NPPF specifically cover plan-making. However, the whole of the NPPF is relevant as paragraph 151 states that local plan policies 'should be consistent with the principles and policies set out in this Framework, including the presumption in favour of sustainable development'.

---

[12]   NPPF, para 3.
[13]   Planning and Compulsory Purchase Act 2004, s 19(2)(a).

4.17   The NPPF contains guidance as to the format of Local Plans (para 153), the content of Local Plans (see paras 156 and 157 in particular), the preparation of Local Plans and the evidence supporting them (paras 158–177), the duty-to-co-operate (paras 178–181), the examination of Local Plans (para 182) and neighbourhood plans (paras 183–185).

4.18   When examining a Local Plan, an Inspector is required to consider (amongst other things) whether the plan is 'sound'. The four tests of soundness are found in paragraph 182. They include whether the plan is 'consistent with national policy'. In *Grand Union Investments Ltd v Dacorum Borough Council*[14] the High Court emphasised that the NPPF's guidance on 'soundness' is policy and not law and it should not be treated as law. The judgement cited (and endorsed in a post-NPPF world) the case of *Barratt Developments Plc v The City of Wakefield Metropolitan District Council*[15] where Carnwarth LJ stated:[16]

> '… so long as the inspector and the local planning authority reach a conclusion on soundness which is not "irrational (meaning perverse)", their decision cannot be questioned in the courts, and the mere fact that they have not followed relevant guidance in national policy in every respect does not make their conclusion unlawful. Soundness, he said (at paragraph 33) was "a matter to be judged by the inspector and the local planning authority, and raises no issue of law, unless their decision is shown to have been 'irrational', or they are shown to have ignored the relevant guidance or other considerations which were necessarily material in law".'

The status of the NPPF – decision-making

4.19   Planning decisions must be taken in accordance with the development plan unless material considerations indicate otherwise.[17] The NPPF is a material consideration in planning decisions (NPPF, para 2).

4.20   However, in practice, a significant amount of confusion has arisen as to the effect which the NPPF has on the consideration of development plan policies. This has promoted much litigation. Much of this has focused upon paragraph 14 of the NPPF which states:

> 'At the heart of the National Planning Policy Framework is a **presumption in favour of sustainable development,** which should be seen as a golden thread running through both plan-making and decision taking.
>
> …
>
> For **decision-taking** this means:
> - approving development proposals that accord with the development plan without delay; and
> - where the development plan is absent, silent or relevant policies are out-of-date, granting permission unless:
>   - any adverse impacts of doing so would significantly and demonstrably outweigh the benefits, when assessed against the policies in this Framework taken as a whole;
>   - specific policies in this Framework indicate that development should be restricted.'

---

14 [2014] EWHC 1894 (Admin), at para 58 per Lindblom J.
15 [2010] EWCA Civ 897, [2011] JPL 48.
16 Grand Union, at para 59.
17 Planning and Compulsory Purchase Act 2004, s 38(6).

4.21   The terms 'absent', 'silent' and 'out-of-date' are not defined in the NPPF. Paragraph 49 of the NPPF states that '[R]elevant policies for the supply of housing should not be considered up-to-date if the local planning authority cannot demonstrate a five-year supply of deliverable housing sites'.

4.22   Much legal ink has been spilt over the effect of paragraph 14 on extant development plan policies where it can be said that those policies are 'absent', 'silent' or 'out-of-date'. In *Secretary of State for Communities and Local Government v Hopkins Homes; Richborough Estates Partnership LLP v Cheshire East BC*[18] the Supreme Court examined the interrelationship between national policy and local development plans. Lord Carnwarth highlighted:

> '14. … Paragraph 14 cannot, and is clearly not intended to, detract from the priority given by statute to the development plan, as emphasised in the preceding paragraphs. Indeed, some of the references only make sense on that basis. For example, the reference to "Local Green Space" needs to be read with paragraph 76 dealing with that subject, which envisages local communities being able "through local and neighbourhood plans" to identify for "special protection green areas of particular importance to them", and so "rule out new development other than in very special circumstances …"'

> '21 Although planning inspectors, as persons appointed by the Secretary of State to determine appeals, are not acting as his delegates in any legal sense, but are required to exercise their own independent judgement, they are doing so within the framework of national policy as set by government. It is important, however, in assessing the effect of the Framework, not to overstate the scope of this policy-making role. The Framework itself makes clear that as respects the determination of planning applications (by contrast with plan-making in which it has statutory recognition), it is no more than "guidance" and as such a "material consideration" for the purposes of section 70(2) of the 1990 Act (see *R (Cala Homes (South) Ltd) v Secretary of State for Communities and Local Government* [2011] EWHC 97 (Admin); [2011] 1 P & CR 22 , para 50 per Lindblom J). It cannot, and does not purport to, displace the primacy given by the statute and policy to the statutory development plan. It must be exercised consistently with, and not so as to displace or distort, the statutory scheme.'

4.23   With regards to the interpretation of paragraphs 49 and 14 the Court held:[19]

> '54 The argument, here and below, has concentrated on the meaning of paragraph 49, rather than paragraph 14 and the interaction between the two. However, since the primary purpose of paragraph 49 is simply to act as a trigger to the operation of the "tilted balance" under paragraph 14, it is important to understand how that is intended to work in practice. The general effect is reasonably clear. In the absence of relevant or up-to-date development plan policies, the balance is tilted in favour of the grant of permission, except where the benefits are "significantly and demonstrably" outweighed by the adverse effects, or where "specific policies" indicate otherwise. (See also the helpful discussion by Lindblom J in *Bloor Homes East Midlands Ltd v Secretary of State for Communities and Local Government* [2014] EWHC 754 (Admin), paras 42ff.)

> 55 It has to be borne in mind also that paragraph 14 is not concerned solely with housing policy. It needs to work for other forms of development covered by the development plan, for example employment or transport. Thus, for example, there may be a relevant policy for the supply of employment land, but it may become out-of-date, perhaps because of the arrival of a major new source of employment in the area. Whether that is so, and with what consequence, is a matter of planning judgement,

---

[18]   [2017] UKSC 37, [2017] 1 WLR 1865.
[19]   Per Lord Carnwarth.

unrelated of course to paragraph 49 which deals only with housing supply. This may in turn have an effect on other related policies, for example for transport. The pressure for new land may mean in turn that other competing policies will need to be given less weight in accordance with the tilted balance. But again that is a matter of pure planning judgement, not dependent on issues of legal interpretation.

56   If that is the right reading of paragraph 14 in general, it should also apply to housing policies deemed "out-of-date" under paragraph 49, which must accordingly be read in that light. It also shows why it is not necessary to label other policies as "out-of-date" merely in order to determine the weight to be given to them under paragraph 14. As the Court of Appeal recognised, that will remain a matter of planning judgement for the decision-maker. Restrictive policies in the development plan (specific or not) are relevant, but their weight will need to be judged against the needs for development of different kinds (and housing in particular), subject where applicable to the "tilted balance".

Paragraph 49

57   Unaided by the legal arguments, I would have regarded the meaning of paragraph 49 itself, taken in context, as reasonably clear, and not susceptible to much legal analysis. It comes within a group of paragraphs dealing with delivery of housing. The context is given by paragraph 47 which sets the objective of boosting the supply of housing. In that context the words "policies for the supply of housing" appear to do no more than indicate the category of policies with which we are concerned, in other words "housing supply policies". The word "for" simply indicates the purpose of the policies in question, so distinguishing them from other familiar categories, such as policies for the supply of employment land, or for the protection of the countryside. I do not see any justification for substituting the word "affecting", which has a different emphasis. It is true that other groups of policies, positive or restrictive, may interact with the housing policies, and so affect their operation. But that does not make them policies for the supply of housing in the ordinary sense of that expression.

58   In so far as the paragraph 47 objectives are not met by the housing supply policies as they stand, it is quite natural to describe those policies as "out-of-date" to that extent. As already discussed, other categories of policies, for example those for employment land or transport, may also be found to be out-of-date for other reasons, so as to trigger the paragraph 14 presumption. The only difference is that in those cases there is no equivalent test to that of the five-year supply for housing. In neither case is there any reason to treat the shortfall in the particular policies as rendering out-of-date other parts of the plan which serve a different purpose.

59   This may be regarded as adopting the "narrow" meaning, contrary to the conclusion of the Court of Appeal. However, this should not be seen as leading, as the lower courts seem to have thought, to the need for a legalistic exercise to decide whether individual policies do or do not come within the expression. The important question is not how to define individual policies, but whether the result is a five-year supply in accordance with the objectives set by paragraph 47. If there is a failure in that respect, it matters not whether the failure is because of the inadequacies of the policies specifically concerned with housing provision, or because of the over-restrictive nature of other non-housing policies. The shortfall is enough to trigger the operation of the second part of paragraph 14. As the Court of Appeal recognised, it is that paragraph, not paragraph 49, which provides the substantive advice by reference to which the development plan policies and other material considerations relevant to the application are expected to be assessed.

60   The Court of Appeal was therefore right to look for an approach which shifted the emphasis to the exercise of planning judgement under paragraph 14. However, it was wrong, with respect, to think that to do so it was necessary to adopt a reading of

paragraph 49 which not only changes its language, but in doing so creates a form of non-statutory fiction. On that reading, a non-housing policy which may objectively be entirely up-to-date, in the sense of being recently adopted and in itself consistent with the Framework, may have to be treated as notionally "out-of-date" solely for the purpose of the operation of paragraph 14.

61   There is nothing in the statute which enables the Secretary of State to create such a fiction, nor to distort what would otherwise be the ordinary consideration of the policies in the statutory development plan; nor is there anything in the NPPF which suggests an intention to do so. Such an approach seems particularly inappropriate as applied to fundamental policies like those in relation to the Green Belt or Areas of Outstanding Natural Beauty. No-one would naturally describe a recently approved Green Belt policy in a local plan as "out of date", merely because the housing policies in another part of the plan fail to meet the NPPF objectives. Nor does it serve any purpose to do so, given that it is to be brought back into paragraph 14 as a specific policy under footnote 9. It is not "out of date", but the weight to be given to it alongside other material considerations, within the balance set by paragraph 14, remains a matter for the decision-maker in accordance with ordinary principles.'

4.24   Given the significant amount of litigation which the NPPF has engendered as to the meaning of its provisions, practitioners should ensure that they appraise themselves of the latest judicial decisions (if any) relating to individual provisions. The bulk of the relevant cases are not discussed in this book since we focus on policy-making.[20] The exception being the *Hopkins Homes* litigation which has been discussed at length due to its importance for the interrelationship between national planning policy and statutory development plan documents.

Amendments

4.25   Changes have been made to the meaning of the NPPF by Written Ministerial Statements ('WMS'), discussed further below (see 4.44 below).

4.26   In December 2015–January 2016 the government conducted a consultation into proposed changes to the NPPF. The consultation covered the following areas:

(i)   broadening the definition of affordable housing, to expand the range of low-cost housing opportunities;

(ii)   increasing the density of development around commuter hubs, to make more efficient use of land in suitable locations;

(iii)   supporting sustainable new settlements, development on brownfield land and small sites, and delivery of housing agreed in Local Plans;

(iv)   supporting delivery of starter homes; and

(v)   transitional arrangement.

4.27   In February 2017, the Department for Communities and Local Government published a White Paper entitled 'Fixing Our Broken Housing Market' this included proposals for amending the NPPF including an amendment to the definition of affordable housing (p 100), an amendment to the definition of 'sustainable

---

[20]   NPPF case law is considered from the development management perspective in Richard Harwood QC, *Planning Permission* (Bloomsbury, 2016), Ch 9.

development' within the NPPF (p 102), an amendment to the list of climate change factors to be considered during plan-making, to include reference to rising temperatures (p 102) and some amendments with regards to provisions on flood risk, noise and impacts on other developments and onshore wind energy.

4.28   It is currently unclear when and if changes to the NPPF will be made following these consultations.

PLANNING POLICY FOR TRAVELLER SITES

4.29   The Planning Policy for Traveller Sites ('PPTS') was originally published alongside the NPPF in March 2012 and has since been updated in (August 2015). It is to be read in conjunction with the NPPF.[21] Paragraph 4 of the NPPF states:

> 'This Framework should be read in conjunction with the Government's planning policy for traveller sites. Local planning authorities preparing plans for and taking decisions on travellers sites should also have regard to the policies in this Framework so far as relevant.'

4.30   It is the government's stated intention to review in the future whether PPTS should be incorporated within the NPPF.[22]

4.31   The PPTS applies to 'travellers' which includes 'gypsies and travellers' 'and 'travelling showpeople'.[23] Each term is defined in the glossary:

Gypsies and travellers: *'Persons of nomadic habit of life whatever their race or origin, including such persons who on grounds only of their own or their family's or dependants' educational or health needs or old age have ceased to travel temporarily, but excluding members of an organised group of travelling showpeople or circus people travelling together as such.'*

Travelling showpeople: *'Members of a group organised for the purposes of holding fairs, circuses or shows (whether or not travelling together as such). This includes such persons who on the grounds of their own or their family's or dependents' more localised pattern of trading, educational or health needs or old age have ceased to travel temporarily, but exclude Gypsies and Travellers as defined above.'*

Status

4.32   As with the NPPF, the PPTS is a material consideration in planning decisions and must be taken into account in the preparation of development plans.[24]

---

[21]   NPPF, para 4 and PPTS, para 1.
[22]   PPTS, para 6.
[23]   PPTS, Annex 1, para 4.
[24]   PPTS, para 2 and Planning and Compulsory Purchase Act 2004, s 19(2)(a).

PLANNING PRACTICE GUIDANCE

4.33   Between October and December 2012, Lord Taylor of Goss Moor led an external review of government Planning Practice Guidance ('PPG'). The panel conducting the review published their report on 21 December 2012. It highlighted:

> 'There is a clear understanding that the historic accumulation of out-of-date, contradictory and unmanageable material must be brought to an end, whittled down to an essential, coherent, accessible and well-managed suite of guidance that aids the delivery of good planning. It must then be maintained as such.'[25]

4.34   It concluded:

> 'Guidance should be cut to that which is essential and clearly defined and described as Government Planning Practice Guidance. This is not just a matter of eliminating some documents and updating others – it is about identifying the essential paragraphs, processes and pointers, and cutting the guidance suite down to these elements making sure they are in a form that is clear, concise, relevant, accessible and up-to-date.'[26]

4.35   Following public consultation and the testing of draft guidance on a Beta website, the PPG was eventually launched on 6 March 2014.

4.36   The PPG's website states:

> 'This guidance is intended to assist practitioners. Ultimately the interpretation of legislation is for the Courts but this guidance is an indication of the Secretary of State's views. The department seeks to ensure that the guidance is in plain English and easily understandable. Consequently it may sometimes be oversimplified and, as the law changes quickly, although we do our best, it may not always be up to date.'[27]

Format

4.37   The PPG is solely an online resource.[28] The PPG is currently divided into 48 separate chapters. They are: advertisements; air quality; appeals; before submitting an application; climate change; community infrastructure levy; conserving and enhancing the historic environment; consultation and pre-decision matters; crown development; design; determining a planning application; duty to cooperate; ensuring effective enforcement; ensuring the vitality of town centres; environmental impact assessments; fees for planning applications; flexible options for planning permissions; flood risk and coastal change; hazardous substances; health and wellbeing; housing and economic development needs assessments; housing and economic land availability assessment; housing – optional technical standards; land affected by contamination; land stability; lawful development certificates; light pollution; local plans; making an application; minerals; natural environment; neighbourhood planning; noise; open space, sports and recreation facilities, public rights of way and local greenspace; planning obligations; renewable and low carbon energy; rural housing; self-build and custom housebuilding; starter homes; strategic environmental assessment and sustainability appraisal; transport evidence bases in plan making and decision taking; travel plans, transport assessments

---

[25]   Lord Matthew Taylor of Goss Moor, 'External Review of Government Planning Practice Guidance' (DCLG, December 2012), p 6.

[26]   As above.

[27]   See: http://planningguidance.communities.gov.uk/about/.

[28]   It can be found at: http://planningguidance.communities.gov.uk/.

and statements in decision-taking; tree preservation orders and trees in conservation areas; use of planning conditions; viability; waste; water supply, waste water and water quality; and when is permission required?

4.38   Each chapter is divided into sections and presented in a question and answer format. Where there is related policy contained within the NPPF a link is provided to the relevant NPPF paragraph on the right-hand side of the PPG's text.

4.39   Portions of the PPG can be cited by using the chapter number and then the paragraph number which appears below each question and answer. Usefully, the reference ID also situated below the question and answer gives the date on which that section of the PPG was last amended.

Amendments

4.40   Being only available in an online format, the PPG is capable of constant amendment. It is therefore important to check the latest version of the text before it is used. Thus far, revisions or clarifications of the PPG have tended to be announced by Ministers in written statements to Parliament and then by alterations to the PPG.

4.41   One example of this is the Written Ministerial Statement ('WMS') dated 28 November 2014 which announced the government's new policy on affordable housing. This lead to an amendment of the PPG the same day and further revisions on 27 February and 26 March 2015. The WMS was the subject of an ultimately unsuccessful challenge in *R (on the application of West Berkshire District Council) v Secretary of State for Communities and Local Government.*[29]

Status

4.42   As with the NPPF and PPTS, the PPG is policy guidance to which a local planning authority must have regard when preparing a development plan document or any other local development document.[30]

4.43   The PPG is a material consideration in planning decisions. The fact that parts of it are written in trenchant terms does not mean that it is intended to frustrate or countermand development plan policies.[31] The weight to be given to it is a matter for the decision-maker.[32]

WRITTEN MINISTERIAL STATEMENTS

4.44   Despite the ease with which the PPG can be updated, the government has continued to use Written Ministerial Statements ('WMSs') to update policy guidance.

Some amendments/additions to the NPPF have been made by way of Written Ministerial Statements. For example, a written statement from Eric Pickles MP on various planning changes on 25 March 2015 said on parking:

---

[29] [2016] EWCA Civ 441, [2016] 1 WLR 3923, [2016] PTSR 982, reversing [2015] EWHC 2222 (Admin), [2016] PTSR 215.
[30] Planning and Compulsory Purchase Act 2004, s 19(2)(a).
[31] *West Berkshire District Council v Secretary of State for Communities and Local Government* [2016] EWCA Civ 441, [2016] 1 WLR3923, [2016] PTSR 982 at para 24 per Laws and Treacy LJJ.
[32] *West Berkshire*, at para 23.

'Following a consultation, we are now amending national planning policy to further support the provision of car parking spaces. Parking standards are covered in paragraph 39 of the National Planning Policy Framework. The following text now needs to be read alongside that paragraph: "Local planning authorities should only impose local parking standards for residential and non-residential development where there is clear and compelling justification that it is necessary to manage their local road network.'

Others state that they are to be read alongside the NPPF, for example, the Starter Homes WMS (2 March 2015) and the sustainable drainage systems WMS (18 December 2014). How far a statement amounts to a change can be debatable: the WMS of 1 July 2015 said that 'the single issue of unmet demand, whether for Traveller sites or for conventional housing' is unlikely to constitute very special circumstances outweighing harm to the green belt. This was viewed by the Court as a 'clarification' rather than a change of the policy.[33] A WMS on 12 December 2016 provided that most housing supply policies in neighbourhood plans would not be out of date unless there was a housing supply of less than three years:

'… relevant policies for the supply of housing in a neighbourhood plan, that is part of the development plan, should not be deemed to be "out-of-date" under paragraph 49 of the National Planning Policy Framework where all of the following circumstances arise at the time the decision is made:

- This written ministerial statement is less than 2 years old, or the neighbourhood plan has been part of the development plan for 2 years or less;

- the neighbourhood plan allocates sites for housing; and

- the local planning authority can demonstrate a three-year supply of deliverable housing sites.

This statement applies to decisions made on planning applications and appeals from today. This statement should be read in conjunction with the National Planning Policy Framework and is a material consideration in relevant planning decisions.'

Judicial review proceedings were brought against the statement, including against the absence of consultation on it.[34]

There exist some extant WMSs which pre-date the NPPF. One example is the 'Policy statement – planning for schools development' published by Department for Communities and Local Government ('DCLG') in August 2011. Other examples are the Secretary of States' policies applying to call-ins and the recovery of appeals. The policies relating to call-ins are comprised of the written answer of 12 December 2001 and the WMS of 26 October 2012 and the Secretary of State's recovery criteria can be found in the WMS of 30 June 2008.[35]

At least one WMS has been issued in response to a court judgement. In the case of *Wenman v Secretary of State for Communities and Local Government*[36] the High

---

[33] *Copas v Secretary of State for Communities and Local Government* [2014] EWHC 2634 (Admin), [2015] JPL 83, at paras 33 and 36, per Supperstone J.

[34] *R (on the application of Richborough Estates Ltd) v Secretary of State for Communities and Local Government* (case heard November 2017, judgment pending).

[35] These can all be found at: https://www.gov.uk/government/collections/planning-applications-called-in-decisions-and-recovered-appeals. Updated recovery criteria are in the Planning Practice Guidance para 16-005-20160713.

[36] [2015] EWHC 925 (Admin).

Court held that housing should not be interpreted narrowly as merely including bricks and mortar housing and included mobile homes. This meant that the provisions of the NPPF which deal with scenarios where a local planning authority cannot demonstrate a five-year supply of housing land (in particular paragraphs 49 and 14) could be brought into play in an application for mobile housing. In response the government issued a WMS on 22 July 2015 which stated:[37]

> 'Following a recent High Court Judgment (*Wenman –v– Secretary of State*), we are today making a technical adjustment to paragraphs 49 and 159 of the National Planning Policy Framework.
>
> Paragraph 49
>
> From today, those persons who fall within the definition of 'traveller' under the Planning Policy for Traveller Sites, cannot rely on the lack of a five year supply of deliverable housing sites under the National Planning Policy Framework to show that relevant policies for the supply of housing are not up-to-date. Such persons should have the lack of a five year supply of deliverable traveller sites considered in accordance with Planning Policy for Traveller Sites.
>
> Paragraph 159
>
> Planning Policy for Traveller Sites sets out how 'travellers' (as defined in Annex A of that document) accommodation needs should also be assessed. Those who do not fall under that definition should have their accommodation needs addressed under the provisions of the National Planning Policy Framework.
>
> This does not form part of the changes to planning policy for travellers, on which the Government consulted in 2014, and to which this Government intends to respond shortly.'

CIRCULARS

4.45   Circulars are issued by government departments on particular subjects and are used to expand upon relevant policy and legislation. They are capable of being material considerations in planning decisions. Historically, government planning policy had been set out in circulars. The introduction of PPGs in the 1980s saw a split between substantive advice on planning merits which tended to be in the PPGs or the later PPSs and guidance on the process which was still contained in circulars. The distinction was never hard and fast: advice on the local development framework process was contained in PPS12 rather than a circular.

A significant number of circulars were withdrawn by the introduction of the NPPF and then on publication of the PPG, however, some which were produced prior to 2012 remain. Some circulars have been issued post the adoption of the NPPF and PPG. A list of DCLG's planning circulars can be found at: https://www.gov.uk/government/collections/planning-circulars.

It is not only DCLG which issues circulars relevant to planning matters. Circulars relevant to planning are issued by other government departments. One example is the Department for Transport's Circular 02/2013 'The Strategic Road Network and the Delivery of Sustainable Development'.

---

[37]   Baroness Williams of Trafford, HL Deb, 22 July 2015, cWS.

Chapter 5

National Policy Statements

INTRODUCTION AND BACKGROUND

5.1   In May 2007, the Secretaries of State for Communities and Local Government, Environment Food and Rural Affairs, Trade and Industry and Transport presented a joint White Paper before Parliament. It identified a lack of clear policy frameworks for all areas of nationally significant infrastructure. It stated:

> 'The result is that fundamental issues such as whether there is a need for additional capacity or whether a technology is proven and safe are addressed from scratch in each individual application. This can make the process of preparing applications for individual project proposals more onerous and uncertain, and mean that many months have to be spent at the inquiries into these proposals debating high level issues such as need.'[1]

5.2   In order to address these (and other) issues, the White Paper proposed to put in place a new system to the multiple consent regimes which existed for key national infrastructure projects which would enable the government to 'take decisions on infrastructure in a way that is timely, efficient and predictable'.[2]

5.3   It proposed, as part of this new system, to produce National Policy Statements for key infrastructure areas. These would set out the national need for such infrastructure and explain how it fits with other policies and would give greater certainty and clarity to those involved in the planning process.[3]

5.4   The White Paper was followed by the Planning Act 2008 which gave the legislative framework for the production of the National Policy Statements ('NPSs').

The status of NPSs

5.5   NPSs regulate decisions in relation to Nationally Significant Infrastructure Projects ('NSIPs') for which Development Consent Orders ('DCOs') are required.

5.6   Section 14(1) of the Planning Act 2008 defines an NSIP as:

> '(1) In this Act "nationally significant infrastructure project" means a project which consists of any of the following—
>
> (a)   the construction or extension of a generating station;
>
> (b)   the installation of an electric line above ground;

---

[1]   White Paper, 'Planning for a Sustainable Future', para 1.7.
[2]   White Paper, para 1.36.
[3]   See White Paper, para 1.39.

(c)   development relating to underground gas storage facilities;

(d)   the construction or alteration of an LNG facility;

(e)   the construction or alteration of a gas reception facility;

(f)   the construction of a pipe-line by a gas transporter;

(g)   the construction of a pipe-line other than by a gas transporter;

(h)   highway-related development;

(i)   airport-related development;

(j)   the construction or alteration of harbour facilities;

(k)   the construction or alteration of a railway;

(l)   the construction or alteration of a rail freight interchange;

(m) the construction or alteration of a dam or reservoir;

(n)   development relating to the transfer of water resources;

(o)   the construction or alteration of a waste water treatment plant or of infrastructure for the transfer or storage of waste water;

(p)   the construction or alteration of a hazardous waste facility;

(q)   development relating to a radioactive waste geological disposal facility.'

5.7   Sections 15–30A of the Planning Act 1998 sets out further criteria which each type of development in the categories above must meet before they meet the definition of being an NSIP.

5.8   Section 31 of the Planning Act 2008 states that development consent is required 'for development to the extent that the development is or forms part of a nationally significant infrastructure project'. Under s 103 the Secretary of State has authority to decide applications for DCOs.

5.9   When taking a decision on whether to make a DCO where an NPS has effect in relation to that development the Secretary of State must have regard to any NPS which has effect in relation to development of the description to which the application relates along with:

(a)   the appropriate marine policy documents (if any), determined in accordance with s 59 of the Marine and Coastal Access Act 2009;

(b)   any local impact report;

(c)   any matters prescribed in relation to development of the description to which the application relates; and

(d)   any other matters which the Secretary of State thinks are both important and relevant to the Secretary of State's decision.[4]

5.10   However, the NPS is not merely one consideration amongst others and s 104(3) provides that the 'Secretary of State must decide the application in accordance with any relevant national policy statement, except to the extent that one or more of subsections (4) to (8) applies'. Subsections (4) to (8) provide:

---

[4]   Planning Act 2008, s 104(2).

'(4) This subsection applies if the Secretary of State is satisfied that deciding the application in accordance with any relevant national policy statement would lead to the United Kingdom being in breach of any of its international obligations.

(5) This subsection applies if the Secretary of State is satisfied that deciding the application in accordance with any relevant national policy statement would lead to the Secretary of State being in breach of any duty imposed on the Secretary of State by or under any enactment.

(6) This subsection applies if the Secretary of State is satisfied that deciding the application in accordance with any relevant national policy statement would be unlawful by virtue of any enactment.

(7) This subsection applies if the Secretary of State is satisfied that the adverse impact of the proposed development would outweigh its benefits.

(8) This subsection applies if the Secretary of State is satisfied that any condition prescribed for deciding an application otherwise than in accordance with a national policy statement is met.'

5.11   Further, under s 87(3) of the Planning Act 2008 when examining a DCO, the examining authority may disregard representations which relate to the merits of a policy set out in an NPS. Section 106 of the Planning Act 2008 contains a corresponding provision in relation to the Secretary of State who may also disregard representations if he considers them to relate to the merits of a policy set out within an NPS.

5.12   In a challenge to the Secretary of State's grant of a DCO for the Thames Tideway Tunnel ('TTT')[5] the claimants complained that the examining authority had not entertained representations designed to present strategic alternatives to the TTT but which were not advanced during the preparation of the NPS. The claimant relied upon s 104(7) of the Planning Act 2008 which states that where the Secretary of State is satisfied that the adverse impacts of a proposed development would outweigh its benefits he is entitled to decide the DCO otherwise than in accordance with the NPS.

5.13   Permission to apply for judicial review having been refused in the High Court, Sullivan LJ stated in his permission decision on the papers:

'Even though this application is still at the arguability stage the appeal does not have a real prospect of success. The two stage process was introduced by the 2008 Act in order to avoid precisely the outcome which this appeal seeks to achieve: the reopening at the second (examination by the panel) stage of the process, of alternatives to the option (in this case the tunnel) which has been adopted by the Government in the first (NPS) stage of the process. The provisions of the 2008 Act must be interpreted with the underlying objective of having a two-stage process for NSIPs in mind. Although the Claimant focuses upon the terminology of the final sentence of paragraph 16.25 of the panel's report (paragraphs 24 and 25 of the judgment), there was, in reality, no other way in which the panel could reasonably have exercised its discretion under section 87(3) given the statutory objective — to settle strategic alternatives at the first stage — and the flagrant conflict between the 'no alternatives to the tunnel' policy set out in the NPS (paragraphs 8 and 9 of the judgment) and the 'alternatives to the tunnel' put forward by the Claimant.'[6]

---

[5]   *R (on the application of Thames Blue Green Economy Ltd) v Secretary of State for Communities and Local Government* [2015] EWCA Civ 876, [2016] JPL 157; affirming [2015] EWHC 727 (Admin).
[6]   Cited at para 11.

5.14   At the oral permission stage, Sales LJ upheld this reasoning, and added in response to the argument that if new material comes forward regarding the strategic merits of a project then these new arguments must be taken into account:

> 'In my view, in a genuine case where new circumstances arise it would be open to a person to approach the Secretary of State to invite him to revisit the National Policy Statement. That would be the proper way in which such matters should be taken into account, since in revisiting the strategic need for a project the procedural protections which apply in relation to formation of a National Policy Statement would then again apply to ensure that proper consideration was given to the alleged change of circumstances and the impact they might have upon the National Policy Statement in question. There is no need to distort the interpretation of section 104(7) to take account of such a possibility: the statutory scheme allows for changes in circumstances to be catered for in a different and more appropriate way, as I have set out.'[7]

5.15   The significance of the NPSs does not only extend to DCO applications. Paragraph 3 of the National Planning Policy Framework ('NPPF') states: 'National policy statements form part of the overall framework of national planning policy, and are a material consideration in decisions on planning applications.'

The legislative framework

5.16   The preparation, adoption and legal challenges to NPSs are governed by Part 2 of the Planning Act 2008. This chapter is concerned with those NPSs which have been designated under s 5 of the Planning Act 2008. Section 5 states that the Secretary of State may designate an NPS if the statement is issued by him and sets out national policy in relation to one or more specified descriptions of development.[8] However, before designating a statement the Secretary of State must have: carried out a sustainability appraisal of it,[9] undertaken the consultation and publicity requirements in s 7 of the Planning Act 2008,[10] the Parliamentary requirements in s 9,[11] and:

(a)   21 sitting days[12] have expired without the House of Commons resolving during that period that the statement should not be proceeded with; or

(b)   the statement has been approved by resolution of the House of Commons –

    (i)   after being laid before Parliament under s 9(8); and

    (ii)   before the end of the consultation period.[13]

Content of NPSs

5.17   Section 5(5) of the Planning Act 2008 sets out what policy an NPS might contain. An NPS may:

---

7   At para 14.

8   Planning Act 2008, s 5(1).

9   Planning Act 2008, s 5(3).

10   Planning Act 2008, s 5(4).

11   Planning Act 2008, s 5(4).

12   This period may be extended by the Secretary of State by 21 sitting days or less under the Planning Act 2008, s 6B.

13   Planning Act 2008, s 5(4).

(a)   set out, in relation to a specified description of development, the amount, type or size of development of that description which is appropriate nationally or for a specified area;

(b)   set out criteria to be applied in deciding whether a location is suitable (or potentially suitable) for a specified description of development;

(c)   set out the relative weight to be given to specified criteria;

(d)   identify one or more locations as suitable (or potentially suitable) or unsuitable for a specified description of development;

(e)   identify one or more statutory undertakers as appropriate persons to carry out a specified description of development;

(f)   set out circumstances in which it is appropriate for a specified type of action to be taken to mitigate the impact of a specified description of development.

5.18   Where an NPS sets out policy in relation to a particular description of development, it must set out design criteria to be taken into account in designing development of that description.[14]

5.19   An NPS therefore contains one or two types of policy:

(i)   all contain some form of generic policy, explaining what the needs are for the infrastructure and the criteria to be applied in determining applications. As applications have to be determined in accordance with the relevant NPS, each NPS has tended to set out a full range of planning policies,[15] much of which will duplicate what is in the NPPF. No NPS has yet taken the simpler route of incorporating the NPPF policies on development management by reference and then setting out type-specific policy;

(ii)   an NPS might also promote a particular project or identify particular locations or sites which would be suitable for certain projects. The Waste Water Treatment NPS identified two projects which it said ought to happen, one of which being the Thames Tideway Tunnel. The Nuclear NPS identifies suitable locations for new nuclear plants and the draft Aviation NPS proposes the North West runway at Heathrow. Where specific projects are supported, it is important to understand how far that support goes (for example, a Thames Tunnel was supported to carry sewage but the route was left to the application). Specific criteria for those projects will also be set out, in addition to the generic policies in the NPS.

5.20   An NPS must give reasons for its policy.[16] Those reasons must include an explanation of how the policy takes account of government policy relating to the mitigation of and adaptation to climate change.[17]

---

[14]   Planning Act 2008, s 5(6).
[15]   Energy decisions rely on a generic 'over-arching' energy NPS and particular NPSs for certain types of generator or supply.
[16]   Planning Act 2008, s 5(7).
[17]   Planning Act 2008, s 5(8).

Sustainability

5.21   In drawing up, designating and reviewing NPSs the Secretary of State is required to exercise his functions with the objective of contributing to the achievement of sustainable development. The Secretary of State is required in particular to have regard to the desirability of mitigating and adapting to climate change and achieving good design.[18]

Consultation and publicity

5.22   The Secretary of State is required to conduct 'such consultation, and arrange for such publicity, as the Secretary of State thinks appropriate'[19] in relation to a decision to designate a statement as an NPS under s 5 of the Planning Act 2008 or any proposed amendment.

5.23   The Infrastructure Planning (National Policy Statement Consultation) Regulations 2009[20] did prescribe, for the purposes of s 7 of the Planning Act 2008, the persons to be consulted by the Secretary of State. However, those Regulations were revoked on 13 April 2014.[21] The change was explained this way:[22]

> 'The requirements in the regulations can be achieved through non-regulatory means. Once the regulations are revoked the Department for Communities and Local Government will make it clear to all Government Departments preparing National Policy Statements that they should continue to consult the bodies that were previously set out in regulations. The general duty to consult set out in the Planning Act 2008 will remain in place.'

5.24   If the policy set out in the statement or amendment identifies one or more locations as suitable or potentially suitable for a specified description of development then the Secretary of State is required to ensure that 'appropriate steps are taken to publicise the proposal'.[23] In deciding what steps are appropriate, the Secretary of State is required to consult each of the following local authorities:

(a)   a local authority in whose area any of the locations fall;

(b)   a local authority who borders a local authority who is a unitary council or a lower-tier district council and in whose area any of the locations fall;

(c)   a local authority who borders an upper-tier County Council within whose area any of the locations fall that local authority is not a lower-tier district council;

(d)   the Greater London Authority where any of the locations concerned is in the authority's area.[24]

5.25   For the purposes of s 8 of the Planning Act 2008, a local authority means: a county council or district council in England, a London borough council, the Common Council of the City of London, the Council of the Isles of Scilly, a county

---

18   Planning Act 2008, s 10.
19   Planning Act 2008, s 7(2).
20   SI 2009/1302.
21   By the Town and Country Planning (Revocations) Regulations 2014, SI 2014/692, Sch 1.
22   Explanatory Memorandum to the Town and Country Planning (Revocations) Regulations 2014, para 7.13.
23   Planning Act 2008, s 7(5).
24   Planning Act 2008, s 8(2)–(3A).

council or county borough council in Wales, a Scottish council, a National Park Authority and the Broads Authority.[25]

5.26   The statute requires the Secretary of State to have regard to responses to consultation and publicity in deciding whether to designate a statement or amend an NPS.[26]

Parliamentary requirements

5.27   The Parliamentary requirements are two-fold: firstly an opportunity for Parliament to comment on the draft NPS or amendment; secondly the final draft being put before Parliament for approval (or at least, non-resistance) by the House of Commons.

5.28   As originally enacted, the Planning Act 2008 merely provided the first stage: that Parliament should be consulted and Ministers should reply to what it says. The Localism Act 2011 introduced the second stage Parliamentary veto.[27]

5.29   Section 9 of the Planning Act 2008 sets out the parliamentary requirements which are required to be met before an NPS is designated under s 5 or an amendment to an NPS is made. The Secretary of State is required to lay the NPS or amendment before Parliament.[28] There is then a period (the 'relevant period' specified by the Secretary of State for this particular statement) within which either House of Parliament may make a resolution on the NPS or amendment or a committee of either House may make recommendations with regards to the NPS or amendment.[29] If such a resolution or recommendation is made, then the Secretary of State must lay a statement before Parliament which sets out his response to the resolution or recommendation.[30]

5.30   After the consultation stage and any response to a Parliamentary resolution or committee, the Secretary of State has to lay the final version of NPS or amendment before Parliament under s 9(8).

5.31   The statement may only be designated if it has been approved by resolution of the House of Commons or the consideration period on the final version has passed without the Commons resolving that the statement should not be proceeded with.[31] The consideration period is 21 sitting days beginning with the first sitting day after the day on which the final version of the statement is laid before Parliament.[32] A 'sitting day' means a day on which the House of Commons sits, bearing in mind that each House does not necessarily sit on the same days.

---

[25]   Planning Act 2008, s 8(4).
[26]   Planning Act 2008, s 7(6).
[27]   It gave effect to Opposition amendments tabled during the Bill's passage and the desire in the Conservative Green Paper, 'Open Source Planning' that there should be 'proper Parliamentary ratification of the National Policy Statements'.
[28]   Planning Act 2008, s 9(2).
[29]   Planning Act 2008, s 9(4).
[30]   Planning Act 2008, s 9(5).
[31]   Planning Act 2008, s 5(4).
[32]   Planning Act 2008, s 5(4A). The Secretary of State may extend the period by up to 21 sitting days, one or more times: Planning Act 2008, s 6B.

5.32   Whilst the NPS will be laid before both Houses, the House of Lords is not able to veto its designation. That said, significant opposition from the Lords, and certainly a vote against an NPS, is likely to give Ministers pause for thought.

Review

5.33   The Secretary of State is required to review each NPS whenever he thinks it appropriate to do so.[33] A review might be of whole or part of an NPS.[34] When deciding whether to review an NPS (or part thereof), the Secretary of State is required to take certain factors into account, as follows:

(a)   whether since the time when the statement (or part thereof) was first published or (if later) last reviewed, there has been a significant change in any circumstances on the basis of which any of the policy set out in the statement was decided;

(b)   the change was not anticipated at that time; and

(c)   if the change had been anticipated at that time, any of the policy set out in the statement would have been materially different.[35]

5.34   Having completed a review of all or part of an NPS, the Secretary of State must amend the statement, withdraw its designation or leave the statement as it is.[36] However, if the NPS is to be amended in such a way which materially affects the policy, then the Secretary of State must first conduct a sustainability appraisal of the policy in the proposed amendment[37] and comply with the consultation and publicity requirements in s 7 and the Parliamentary requirements in s 9.[38] Finally, as with the adoption of a new NPS the following must have occurred:

(a)   21 sitting days[39] have expired without the House of Commons resolving during that period that the statement should not be proceeded with; or

(b)   the statement has been approved by resolution of the House of Commons –

(i)   after being laid before Parliament under s 9(8); and

(ii)   before the end of the consultation period.[40]

Suspension pending review

5.35   If since an NPS (or part thereof) was first published or (if later) last reviewed, the Secretary of State considers that there has been a significant change in circumstances on the basis of which any policy in the statement was decided, the change was not anticipated at that time and had the change been anticipated any policy in the NPS (or part thereof) would have been materially different, then the Secretary of State may suspend the operation of all or any part of the NPS until a review of it or that part has been completed.[41]

---

[33]   Planning Act 2008, s 6(1).
[34]   Planning Act 2008, s 6(2).
[35]   Planning Act 2008, s 6(3) and (4).
[36]   Planning Act 2008, s6(5).
[37]   Planning Act 2008, s 6(6).
[38]   Planning Act 2008, s 6(7).
[39]   This period may be extended by the Secretary of State under the Planning Act 2008, s 6B.
[40]   Planning Act 2008, s 6(7) and (7A).
[41]   Planning Act 2008, s 11(1)–(4).

5.36   If the Secretary of State suspends the operation of an NPS or part thereof then it is treated as having been withdrawn until the Secretary of State has either amended the statement, withdrawn the statement's designation as an NPS or decided to leave the statement as it is under s 5(5) of the Planning Act 2008.[42]

5.37   In circumstances where an application is made for a DCO of a description where an NPS has effect and the Secretary of State is of the view that as a result of a change in circumstances since the NPS was first published or (if later) the statement or part thereof was last reviewed that all or part of the NPS should be reviewed before the application is decided, the Secretary of State may direct that until the review has been completed the examination of the DCO is suspended.[43]

The National Policy Statements ('NPSs')

5.38   The NPSs are presently in three categories: energy, transport and water:

Energy NPSs (designated by the Secretary of State for Energy and Climate Change on 19 July 2011):

- EN-1 Overarching Energy NPS;
- EN-2 Fossil Fuel Electricity Generating Infrastructure NPS;
- EN-3 Renewable Energy Infrastructure NPS;
- EN-4 Gas Supply Infrastructure & Gas and Oil Pipelines NPS;
- EN-5 Electricity Networks Infrastructure NPS;
- EN-6 Nuclear Power Generation NPS – Volumes I and II.

Transport:

- Ports (designated by the Secretary of State for Transport on 26 January 2012);
- National networks (designated by the Secretary of State for Transport on 14 January 2015).

Water:

- Hazardous Waste (published 6 June 2013);
- Waste Water Treatment (published 9 February 2012).

Two additional NPSs are proposed:

(1)   Airports NPS: On 1 July 2015, the Airports Commission reported to the Secretary of State for Transport on the need for additional UK airport capacity. It concluded the strongest case for providing additional capacity was the addition of a new northwest runway at Heathrow Airport.[44] On 25 October 2016, the Secretary of State for Transport announced his support for a new runway at

---

[42]   Planning Act 2008, s 11(5).
[43]   Planning Act 2008, s 108.
[44]   Airports Commission final report and supporting documents (1 July 2015).

Heathrow and said that a draft NPS would be published in 2017.[45] The 'Draft Airports National Policy Statement: new runway capacity and infrastructure at airports in the South East of England' was published for consultation on 2 February 2017, with a revised draft being issued for consultation on 24 October 2017.

(2)   Water Supply NPS: However, it is unclear when this will come forward.

Guidance and advice notes

5.39   The Department for Communities and Local Government ('DCLG') has published a number of guidance documents on the operation of the Planning Act 2008. Further, there are a series of 'advice notes' published by the Planning Inspectorate which address matters regarding the Planning Act 2008 process. The guidance and advice notes are non-statutory and do not have policy status.

---

[45]   Government Heathrow Airport announcement (25 October 2016) available at: https://www.gov.uk/government/news/government-decides-on-new-runway-at-heathrow.

Chapter 6

National Waste and Air Quality Policies and Strategies

INTRODUCTION

6.1   This chapter deals with national policies and strategies which address waste and air quality. Much of the policy in this area has been developed/accumulated as a result of European law directives. With regards to waste this is as a result of the Waste Framework Directive 2008/98/EC and with regards to air quality this is a result of the Air Quality Directive 2008/50/EC.

WASTE

Introduction

6.2   This part of the chapter deals with national policy relevant to waste. It discusses: waste management plans, waste prevention programmes and the National Planning Policy for Waste. The preparation of the first two of these is required by European law. The third is the government's national policy on waste whose preparation is not required by either European law or statute.

The European dimension

6.3   The first Waste Framework Directive was brought into force in 1975 (Directive 75/442/EEC).[1] It was substantially amended in 1991 (Directive 91/156/EEC). The current Directive (2008/98/EC) was enacted on 17 June 2008. It provides a common definition of waste and lays down basic principles of waste management. A key tenet of its policy is the principle of the waste management hierarchy which is:

(a)   Prevention;

(b)   Preparing for Re-use;

(c)   Recycling;

(d)   Recovery; and

(e)   Disposal.

6.4   In terms of planning, the Waste Framework Directive requires Member States to adopt waste management plans and waste prevention programmes. These are discussed further below.

---

[1]   Legal obligations which arise generally under this Directive are also discussed in Chapter 2 above, at 2.32.

WASTE MANAGEMENT PLANS AND WASTE PREVENTION PROGRAMMES

The European requirement

6.5   Article 28 of the Waste Framework Directive requires Member States to establish (in accordance with Articles 1, 4, 13 and 16) one or more waste management plans. The plans must, alone or in combination with each other, cover the whole geographic territory of the state concerned. Paragraphs 2–5 of Article 28 dictate the required content of the waste management plans (together with some matters which Member States may include). They state:

'2.   The waste management plans shall set out an analysis of the current waste management situation in the geographical entity concerned, as well as the measures to be taken to improve environmentally sound preparing for re-use, recycling, recovery and disposal of waste and an evaluation of how the plan will support the implementation of the objectives and provisions of this Directive.

3.   The waste management plans shall contain, as appropriate and taking into account the geographical level and coverage of the planning area, at least the following:

(a)   the type, quantity and source of waste generated within the territory, the waste likely to be shipped from or to the national territory, and an evaluation of the development of waste streams in the future;

(b)   existing waste collection schemes and major disposal and recovery installations, including any special arrangements for waste oils, hazardous waste or waste streams addressed by specific Community legislation;

(c)   an assessment of the need for new collection schemes, the closure of existing waste installations, additional waste installation infrastructure in accordance with Article 16, and, if necessary, the investments related thereto;

(d)   sufficient information on the location criteria for site identification and on the capacity of future disposal or major recovery installations, if necessary;

(e)   general waste management policies, including planned waste management technologies and methods, or policies for waste posting specific management problems.

4.   The waste management plan may contain, taking into account the geographical level and coverage of the planning area, the following:

(a)   organisational aspects related to waste management including a description of the allocation of responsibilities between public and private actors carrying out the waste management;

(b)   an evaluation of the usefulness and suitability of the use of economic and other instruments in tackling various waste problems, taking into account the need to maintain the smooth functioning of the internal market;

(c)   the use of awareness campaigns and information provision directed at the general public or at a specific set of consumers;

(d)   historical contaminated waste disposal sites and measures for their rehabilitation.

5.   Waste management plans shall conform to the waste planning requirements laid down in Article 14 of Directive 94/62/EC and the strategy for the implementation of the reduction of biodegradable waste going into landfills, referred to in Article 5 of Directive 1999/31/EC.'

6.6   Further, Article 29 of the Waste Framework Directive requires Member States to establish (in accordance with Articles 1 and 4) waste prevention programmes. The Article states:

> '1   ... Such programmes shall be integrated either into the waste management plans provided for in Article 28 or into other environmental policy programmes, as appropriate, or shall function as separate programmes. If any such programme is integrated into the waste management plan or into other programmes, the waste prevention measures shall be clearly identified.
>
> 2.   The programmes provided for in paragraph 1 shall set out the waste prevention objectives. Member States shall describe the existing prevention measures and evaluate the usefulness of the examples of measures indicated in Annex IV or other appropriate measures.
>
> The aim of such objectives and measures shall be to break the link between economic growth and the environmental impacts associated with the generation of waste.
>
> 3.   Member States shall determine appropriate specific qualitative or quantitative benchmarks for waste prevention measures adopted in order to monitor and assess the progress of the measures and may determine specific qualitative or quantitative targets and indicators, other than those referred to in paragraph 4, for the same purpose.
>
> 4.   Indicators for waste prevention measures may be adopted in accordance with the regulatory procedure referred to in Article 39(3).
>
> 5.   The Commission shall create a system for sharing information on best practice regarding waste prevention and shall develop guidelines in order to assist the Member States in the preparation of the Programmes.'

6.7   Article 30 of the Waste Framework Directive requires Member States to ensure that their waste management plans and waste prevention programmes are evaluated every six years and revised as appropriate.

6.8   Article 31 of the Waste Framework Directive provides that Member States must ensure that 'relevant stakeholders and authorities and the general public have the opportunity to participate in the elaboration of the waste management plans and waste prevention programmes, and have access to them once elaborated ...'.

Domestic law – waste prevention programmes and waste management plans

6.9   Under reg 4 of the Waste (England and Wales) Regulations 2011[2] ('Waste Regulations') the Secretary of State was required (by 12 December 2013) to establish one or more programmes of waste prevention measures having evaluated the usefulness of the waste prevention measures set out in Annex IV of the Waste Framework Directive. Waste prevention measures are defined as measures taken before a substance, material or product has become waste and that reduce: (a) the quantity of waste, including through the re-use of products or the extension of the life span of products; (b) the adverse impacts of generated waste on the environment and human health; or (c) the content of harmful substances in materials and products.[3]

---

[2]   SI 2011/988.
[3]   Waste Regulations, reg 4(3).

6.10   The Waste Regulations require that any waste prevention programme is compatible with the following objectives:

'1.   To protect the environment and human health by preventing or reducing the adverse impacts of the generation and management of waste and by reducing overall impacts of resource use and improving the efficiency of such use.'[4]

2.(1) To apply the following waste hierarchy as a priority order in waste prevention and management policy –

    (a) prevention;

    (b) preparing for re-use;

    (c) recycling;

    (d) other recovery (for example energy recovery);

    (e) disposal.

(2) When applying the waste hierarchy in sub-paragraph (1), the appropriate authority must ensure that it –

    (a) encourages the options that deliver the best overall environmental outcome, which may require specific waste streams to depart from the hierarchy where this is justified by life-cycle thinking on the overall impacts of the generation and management of such waste;

    (b) takes into account –

        (i)   the general environmental protection principles of precaution and sustainability,

        (ii) technical feasibility and economic viability,

        (iii) protection of resources, and

        (iv) the overall environmental, human health, economic and social impacts.'[5]

6.11   Further, any waste prevention programme must have as its purpose a contribution towards breaking the link between economic growth and the environmental impacts associated with the generation of waste. The programmes must be expressed in writing, set out the objectives of the programme and a description of existing waste prevention measures and, if integrated into a waste management plan or other programme must clearly identify the programme's waste prevention measures.[6]

6.12   In order to monitor and evaluate waste prevention programmes, the appropriate authority (in England, the Secretary of State, in Wales, the Welsh Ministers[7]) is required to establish qualitative or quantitative benchmarks and may also establish qualitative and quantitative targets and indicators against which to assess the programmes. These must be published.[8]

6.13   The appropriate authority is further required to ensure that there are one or more plans containing policies in relation to waste management in England or Wales[9],

---

[4]   Waste Regulations, Sch 1, Pt 1, para 1 read with reg 5(a).
[5]   Waste Regulations, Sch 1, Pt 1, para 2 read with reg 5(a).
[6]   Waste Regulations, reg 5.
[7]   Waste Regulations, reg 3(1).
[8]   Waste Regulations, reg 6.
[9]   Note that these definitions include the sea adjacent to England or Wales as the case may be as far out as the seaward boundary of the territorial sea (Waste Regulations, reg 7(3)).

as the case may be.[10] These are called waste management plans. The appropriate authority must ensure that their waste management plans, when taken together, cover the whole of England or Wales as the case may be.[11]

6.14   The appropriate authorities are required to ensure that the waste management plans include a statement of the policies for attaining the following objectives:

(a)   the overall objective to protect the environment and human health by preventing or reducing the adverse impacts of the generation and management of waste and by reducing overall impacts of resource use and improving the efficiency of such use;

(b)   to apply the waste hierarchy as a priority order in waste prevention and management policy: prevention, preparing for re-use, recycling, other recovery (for example, energy recovery), disposal;

(c)   to ensure that waste management is carried out without endangering human health, without harming the environment and in particular (a) without risk to water, air, soil, plants or animals; (b) without causing a nuisance through noise or odours; and (c) without adversely affecting the countryside or places of special interest;

(d)   to establish an integrated and adequate network of waste disposal installations and of installations for the recovery of mixed municipal waste collected from private households, including where such collection also covers such waste from other producers, taking into account best available techniques[12,13].

6.15   The appropriate authorities must ensure that the waste management plans include policies in relation to:

(a)   an analysis of the current waste management situation in England or Wales as the case may be, the measures to be taken to improve environmentally sound preparing for re-use, recycling, recovery and disposal of waste and an evaluation of how the plan will support the implementation of the objectives and the provisions of the Waste Framework Directive;

(b)   as appropriate: (i) the type, quantity and source of waste generated within the territory, the waste likely to be shipped from or to the UK, and an evaluation of the development of waste streams in the future; (ii) existing waste collection schemes and major disposal and recovery installations, including any special arrangements for waste oils, hazardous waste or waste streams addressed by specific European Union legislation; (iii) an assessment of the need for new collection schemes, the closure of existing waste installations, additional waste installation infrastructure and if necessary the related investments; (iv) sufficient information on the location criteria for site identification and on the capacity of future disposal or major recovery installations, if necessary; (v) general waste management policies, including planned waste management technologies and methods, or policies for waste posing specific management problems;

---

[10]   Waste Regulations, reg 7(1).
[11]   Waste Regulations, reg 8(1).
[12]   See para 4 of Sch 1 to the Waste Regulations for further requirements for the network of waste disposal operations.
[13]   Waste Regulations, reg 8(2)(a) and Sch 1, Pt 1.

(c)   in pursuance of objectives and measures in Directive 94/62/EC of the European Parliament and of the Council on packaging and packaging waste, a chapter on the management of packaging and packaging waste, including measures taken pursuant to Articles 4 and 5 of that Directive;

(d)   measures to promote high quality recycling including the setting up of separate collections of waste where technically, environmentally and economically practicable and appropriate to meet the necessary quality standards for the relevant recycling sectors;

(e)   as appropriate, measures to encourage the separate collection of bio-waste with a view to the composting and digestion of bio-waste;

(f)   as appropriate, measures to be taken to promote the re-use of products and preparing for re-use activities, in particular:(i) measures to encourage the establishment and support of re-use and repair networks; (ii) the use of economic instruments; (iii) the use of procurement criteria; (iv) the setting of quantitative objectives;

(g)   measures to be taken to ensure that, by 2020, at least 50% by weight of waste from households is prepared for re-use or recycled; measures to be taken to ensure that, by 2020, at least 70% by weight of the waste mentioned in paragraph (3) is subjected to material recovery; (3) that waste is construction and demolition waste excluding: (i) hazardous waste; (ii) naturally occurring material falling within the description of code 17 05 04 in the List of Wastes.[14]

6.16   The Waste Regulations also include matters which may be included in a waste management plan. These are:

(a)   organisational aspects related to waste management including a description of the allocation of responsibilities between public and private actors carrying out waste management;

(b)   an evaluation of the usefulness and suitability of the use of economic and other instruments in tackling various waste problems, taking into account the need to maintain the smooth functioning of the internal market;

(c)   the use of awareness campaigns and information provision directed at the general public or at a specific set of consumers; and

(d)   historical contaminated waste disposal sites and measures for their rehabilitation.[15]

6.17   Waste management plans must conform to the strategy for the reduction of biodegradable waste going to landfill (as required in England by s 17(1) of the Waste and Emissions Trading Act 2003, and in Wales by s 19(1) of that Act).[16]

Review

6.18   The appropriate authorities are required to review each waste prevention programme and national waste management plan at least every six years.[17] During

---

[14]   Waste Regulations, reg 8(2)(b) and Sch 1, Pt 2.
[15]   Waste Regulations, reg 8(2)(b) and Sch 1, Pt 3.
[16]   Waste Regulations, reg 8(4).
[17]   Waste Regulations, reg 10(1).

the preparation of proposals for a waste prevention programme or national waste management plan or proposals to modify such, the appropriate authorities must consult with such bodies or persons as appear to be representative of the interests of local government and the interests of industry as the authority considers appropriate.[18]

Public participation and consultation

6.19   The Waste Regulations also contain provisions with regard to the inclusion of public participation in programmes and plans.[19] The publicity provisions do not apply to: plans which are designed for the sole purpose of serving national defence or taken in cases of civil emergencies, plans which are subjected to strategic environmental assessment[20] or those plans or programmes containing only provision relating to paras 8 (policies in relation to separate collection of waste), 9 (policies in relation to bio-waste), 10 (policies in relation to re-use) or 11 (preparing for re-use, recovery and recycling targets) of Sch 1.

6.20   Where the publicity provisions of the Waste Regulations apply, as soon as reasonably practicable after preparing proposals for a waste prevention programme or a national waste management plan or for its modification, the appropriate authority must send a copy to the consultation bodies.[21] The consultation bodies in England are: Natural England and Historic England. In Wales, the consultation body is the Natural Resources Body for Wales.[22] It must also take such steps as it considers appropriate to bring the proposals to the attention of the persons who, in the authority's opinion, are or are likely to be affected by the plan or programme or have an interest in the plan or programme.[23] It must inform those persons, termed the 'public consultees' of the address at which a copy of the proposals may be viewed and from which a copy can be obtained (which may be a website) and invite both the consultation bodies and public consultees to express their opinions on the proposals.[24] The period of consultation must be 'of such a length as will ensure that the consultation bodies and the public consultees are given an effective opportunity to express their opinion on the proposals.'[25]

6.21   The appropriate authorities are required to take into account any opinion which has been expressed by a consultation body or public consultee.[26] As soon as reasonably practicable after making decisions on a waste prevention programme or national waste management plan, the appropriate authority must inform the consultation bodies and public consultees of: the decisions made, the reasons and considerations on which those decisions were based and information about the public participation procedure.[27] The appropriate authority must also take such steps as it considers appropriate to bring those matters to the public's attention and if it has

---

[18]   Waste Regulations, reg 10(3).
[19]   Waste Regulations, reg 11 and Sch 1, Pt 4, arising from Article 31 of the Waste Framework Directive.
[20]   Under Pt 3 of the Environmental Assessment of Plans and Programmes Regulations 2004, SI 2004/1633, or Pt 3 of the Environmental Assessment of Plans and Programmes (Wales) Regulations 2004, WSI 2004/1656.
[21]   Waste Regulations, Sch 1, para 14.
[22]   Waste Regulations, Sch 1, para 13.
[23]   Waste Regulations, Sch 1, para 14(1)(b).
[24]   Waste Regulations, Sch 1, para 14(1)(c).
[25]   Waste Regulations, Sch 1, Pt 5, para 14(2).
[26]   Waste Regulations, Sch 1, para 15(1).
[27]   Waste Regulations, Sch 1, para 15(2) and (3).

adopted the plan or programme must make a copy available for inspection at its principal office at all reasonable times and free of charge.[28]

6.22   Whether or not the publicity provisions in Part 4 of Sch 1 apply to a particular plan or programme, the appropriate authorities must ensure that all other waste prevention programmes and national waste management plans are available on a publicly available website.[29]

The Waste Management Plan for England

6.23   In December 2013, the Department for the Environment, Food and Rural Affairs published the Waste Management Plan for England in order to comply with Article 28 of the Waste Framework Directive. The plan did not set out new policies but brought together pre-existing waste management policies into a single national plan.

6.24   It is a high level document which is not site-specific. The plan provides an overview of the current waste management situation in England. It then sets out how it will implement the provisions of the revised Waste Framework Directive.

The Waste Prevention Programme for England

6.25   In December 2013, HM Government published 'Prevention is better than cure. The role of waste prevention in moving to a more resource efficient economy' as the Waste Prevention Programme for England. The executive summary states the aim of the programme as being:

> 'to improve the environment and protect human health by supporting a resource efficient economy, reducing the quantity and impact of waste produced whilst promoting sustainable economic growth.'

NATIONAL PLANNING POLICY FOR WASTE

6.26   The National Planning Policy for Waste ('NPPW') was adopted on 16 October 2014. It sets out detailed waste planning policies. Its introduction states that it is to be read in conjunction with the NPPF, the Waste Management Plan for England and National Policy Statements for Waste Water and Hazardous Waste or any successor documents. It replaced Planning Policy Statement 10: *Planning for Sustainable Waste Management*, which had been published in July 2005 and revised in March 2011.[30]

6.27   Unlike the Waste Management Plan for England or the Waste Prevention Programme for England, the Secretary of State was not required by statute to prepare the NPPW. Rather, like the NPPF it is a policy document which is to be taken into account as a material consideration in decision-making. The introduction states that '[A]ll local planning authorities should have regard to its policies when discharging their responsibilities to the extent that they are appropriate to waste management'.

---

[28] Waste Regulations, Sch 1, para 15(2)(b) and (c).
[29] Waste Regulations, reg 11(2).
[30] Written Ministerial Statement by Eric Pickles MP, 16 October 2014.

Those responsibilities include the preparation of the waste aspects of local plans and the taking of decisions on waste projects.

6.28   Further, although its production is not required by European law, its policies draw upon the Waste Framework Directive. For example, Appendix A sets out the waste hierarchy, a creature of European law as discussed above and includes a footnote which directs the reader of the full definition of each level of the waste hierarchy as being set out in Article 3 of the Waste Framework Directive.

6.29   With regards to local plan preparation, the NPPW requires waste planning authorities to: use a proportionate evidence base,[31] identify the need for waste management facilities (including a requirement to drive waste management up the waste hierarchy),[32] identify suitable sites and areas.[33] Paragraphs 7 and 8 contain provisions pertaining to the determination of planning applications by waste planning authorities.

6.30   NPPW also includes a requirement for local planning authorities to monitor and report: the take-up in allocated sites and areas, existing stock of waste management facilities and their capacity, waste arisings and the amounts of waste recycled, recovered or going for disposal.[34]

Other relevant national policy/guidance on Waste

6.31   The National Policy Planning Framework ('NPPF') and Planning Practice Guidance contain provisions which are relevant to waste plans and decision taking on waste applications. Paragraph 5 of the NPPF states:

> 'This Framework does not contain specific waste policies, since national waste planning policy will be published as part of the National Waste Management Plan for England. However, local authorities preparing waste plans and taking decisions on waste applications should have regard to policies in this Framework so far as relevant.'

6.32   The Planning Practice Guidance contains a chapter which deals with waste (chapter 16) which was issued alongside the National Planning Policy for Waste. It contains guidance on a range of matters including: implementing the waste hierarchy, preparing local plans, regulatory regimes and inspections and monitoring.

6.33   On occasion the government publishes plans and strategies which are relevant to particular types of waste or aspects of dealing with waste. Currently in force are documents such as:

(a)   The Anaerobic Digestion Strategy and Action Plan (June 2011, DEFRA);

(b)   The UK Plan for Shipments of Waste (May 2012, DEFRA);

(c)   A Strategy for Hazardous Waste Management in England (March 2010, DEFRA);

---

[31]   NPPW, para 2.
[32]   NPPW, para 3.
[33]   NPPW, paras 4–6 and Appendix B.
[34]   NPPW, para 9.

(d)   Quality Action Plan: Proposals to promote high quality recycling of dry recyclates (February 2013, DEFRA).

6.34   There are two National Policy Statements which are relevant to waste. These are: the National Policy Statement for Hazardous Waste and the National Policy Statement for Waste Water. National Policy Statements are dealt with in Chapter 5 of this book. However, it should be noted that NPPW specifically states that it should be read in conjunction with these national policy statements.[35]

AIR QUALITY

The European dimension

6.35   Directive 2008/50 'the Air Quality Directive' imposes limits on ambient nitrogen dioxide and other pollutants in the territories of Member States. Where those limits are exceeded, it requires Member States to publish Air Quality Plans which are aimed at reducing exposure to ambient nitrogen dioxide.

6.36   The Air Quality Directive was preceded by two other Directives: 96/62/EC and 1999/30/EC (which it repealed and replaced). The aim of Directive 96/62/EC was described in *R (on the application of ClientEarth) v DEFRA*[36] as: 'to define and establish objectives for ambient air quality, to facilitate the assessment of ambient air quality in Member States, to obtain information on ambient air quality and to maintain or improve ambient air quality. It introduced concepts, such as "Air Quality Plans", "limit value, and "target value", devised for the measurement and management of air quality, which concepts were adopted in subsequent Directives.'[37] Directive 1999/30/EC imposed limit values for specific pollutants including nitrogen dioxide.

6.37   Article 1 of the Air Quality Directive sets out the measures which the Directive seeks to achieve. It states:

'This Directive lays down measures aimed at the following:

1.   defining and establishing objectives for ambient air quality designed to avoid, prevent or reduce harmful effects on human health and the environment as a whole;

2.   assessing the ambient air quality in Member States on the basis of common methods and criteria;

3.   obtaining information on ambient air quality in order to help combat air pollution and nuisance and to monitor long-term trends and improvements resulting from national and Community measures;

4.   ensuring that such information on ambient air quality is made available to the public;

5.   maintaining air quality where it is good and improving it in other cases;

6.   promoting increased cooperation between the Member States in reducing air pollution.'

6.38   Article 4 of the Air Quality Directive requires Member State to establish 'zones and agglomerations' throughout their territories and that air quality assessments and air quality management should be carried out in all zones and agglomerations.

---

[35]   NPPW, introduction.
[36]   [2016] EWHC 2740 (Admin).
[37]   At para 6.

6.39   Article 13 of the Air Quality Directive imposes limit values and alert thresholds for certain pollutants for the protection of human health. It states:

> '1.   Member States shall ensure that, throughout their zones and agglomerations, levels of sulphur dioxide, PM10, lead, and carbon monoxide in ambient air do not exceed the limit values laid down in Annex XI.
>
> In respect of nitrogen dioxide and benzene, the limit values specified in Annex XI may not be exceeded from the dates specified therein.
>
> Compliance with these requirements shall be assessed in accordance with Annex III.
>
> The margins of tolerance laid down in Annex XI shall apply in accordance with Article 22(3) and Article 23(1).
>
> 2.   The alert thresholds for concentrations of sulphur dioxide and nitrogen dioxide in ambient air shall be those laid down in Section A of Annex XII.'

6.40   Article 23 of the Air Quality Directive provides that in circumstances where in a given zone or agglomeration the levels of pollutants in ambient air exceeds the limit value or target value then Member States must ensure that Air Quality Plans are drawn up for those areas in order to achieve the relevant limit or target value. It further states:

> '1.   … In the event of exceedances of those limit values for which the attainment deadline is already expired, the Air Quality Plans shall set out appropriate measures, so that the exceedance period can be kept as short as possible. The air quality plans may additionally include specific measures aiming at the protection of sensitive population groups, including children.
>
> Those air quality plans shall incorporate at least the information listed in Section A of Annex XV and may include measures pursuant to Article 24. Those plans shall be communicated to the Commission without delay, but no later than two years after the end of the year the first exceedance was observed.
>
> Where air quality plans must be prepared or implemented in respect of several pollutants, Member States shall, where appropriate, prepare and implement integrated air quality plans covering all pollutants concerned.
>
> 2.   Member States shall, to the extent feasible, ensure consistency with other plans required under Directive 2001/80/EC, Directive 2001/81/EC or Directive 2002/49/EC in order to achieve the relevant environmental objectives.'

6.41   Article 24 of the Air Quality Directive requires the production of short-term action plans '[W]here, in a given zone or agglomeration, there is a risk that the levels of pollutants will exceed one or more of the alert threshold specified in Annex XII.'[38]

6.42   Article 22 of the Air Quality Directive allows for the postponement of attainment deadlines and exemptions from the obligation to apply certain limit values. It states:

> '1.   Where, in a given zone or agglomeration, conformity with the limit values for nitrogen dioxide or benzene cannot be achieved by the deadlines specified in Annex XI, a Member State may postpone those deadlines by a maximum of five years for that particular zone or agglomeration, on condition that an air quality plan is established in accordance with Article 23 for the zone or agglomeration to which the postponement would apply; such air quality plan shall be supplemented by the

---

[38]   Different considerations for ozone in Section B of Annex XIII can be found at Article 24(1).

information listed in Section B of Annex XV related to the pollutants concerned and shall demonstrate how conformity will be achieved with the limit values before the new deadline.

2.   Where, in a given zone or agglomeration, conformity with the limit values for PM10 as specified in Annex XI cannot be achieved because of site-specific dispersion characteristics, adverse climatic conditions or transboundary contributions, a Member State shall be exempt from the obligation to apply those limit values until 11 June 2011 provided that the conditions laid down in paragraph 1 are fulfilled and that the Member State shows that all appropriate measures have been taken at national, regional and local level to meet the deadlines.

3.   Where a Member State applies paragraphs 1 or 2, it shall ensure that the limit value for each pollutant is not exceeded by more than the maximum margin of tolerance specified in Annex XI for each of the pollutants concerned.

4.   Member States shall notify the Commission where, in their view, paragraphs 1 or 2 are applicable, and shall communicate the air quality plan referred to in paragraph 1 including all relevant information necessary for the Commission to assess whether or not the relevant conditions are satisfied. In its assessment, the Commission shall take into account estimated effects on ambient air quality in the Member States, at present and in the future, of measures that have been taken by the Member States as well as estimated effects on ambient air quality of current Community measures and planned Community measures to be proposed by the Commission.

Where the Commission has raised no objections within nine months of receipt of that notification, the relevant conditions for the application of paragraphs 1 or 2 shall be deemed to be satisfied.'

If objections are raised, the Commission may require Member States to adjust or provide new air quality plans.

6.43   Annex XI to the Air Quality Directive sets out limit values for the protection of human health. Limit values are provided for: sulphur dioxide, nitrogen dioxide, benzene, carbon monoxide, lead and PM10.

6.44   Annex XV to the Air Quality Directive sets out information to be included in the local, regional or national Air Quality Plans for improvement in ambient air quality. It provides that Air Quality Plans prepared in accordance with Article 23 must contain the following information:

'1.   Localisation of excess pollution

(a)   region;

(b)   city (map);

(c)   measuring station (map, geographical coordinates).

2.   General information

(a)   type of zone (city, industrial or rural area);

(b)   estimate of the polluted area (km2) and of the population exposed to the pollution;

(c)   useful climatic data;

(d)   relevant data on topography;

(e)   sufficient information on the type of targets requiring protection in the zone.

3. Responsible authorities

   Names and addresses of persons responsible for the development and implementation of improvement plans.

4. Nature and assessment of pollution

   (a) concentrations observed over previous years (before the implementation of the improvement measures);

   (b) concentrations measured since the beginning of the project;

   (c) techniques used for the assessment.

5. Origin of pollution

   (a) list of the main emission sources responsible for pollution (map);

   (b) total quantity of emissions from these sources (tonnes/year);

   (c) information on pollution imported from other regions.

6. Analysis of the situation

   (a) details of those factors responsible for the exceedance (e.g. transport, including cross-border transport, formation of secondary pollutants in the atmosphere);

   (b) details of possible measures for the improvement of air quality.

7. Details of those measures or projects for improvement which existed prior to 11 June 2008, i.e:

   (a) local, regional, national, international measures;

   (b) observed effects of these measures.

8. Details of those measures or projects adopted with a view to reducing pollution following the entry into force of this Directive:

   (a) listing and description of all the measures set out in the project;

   (b) timetable for implementation;

   (c) estimate of the improvement of air quality planned and of the expected time required to attain these objectives.

9. Details of the measures or projects planned or being researched for the long term.

10. List of the publications, documents, work, etc., used to supplement information required under this Annex.'

Domestic law – Air Quality Strategy

6.45   By virtue of s 80(1) of the Environment Act 1995 ('EA 1995') the Secretary of State was required 'as soon as possible to prepare and publish a statement … containing policies with respect to the assessment or management of the quality of air'.[39] The strategy must contain policies for implementing the obligations of the UK under EU Treaties or international agreements to which the UK is a party.[40] The format of the strategy is prescribed by s 80(3) which provides that the strategy must consist of a statement relating to the whole of Great Britain and two or more statements relating to every part of Great Britain. The strategy must include statements with respect to: (a) standards relating to the quality of air (b) objectives

---

[39]   EA 1995, s 80(1).
[40]   EA 1995, s 80(2).

for the restriction of the levels at which particular substances are present in the air and (c) measures which are to be taken by local authorities and other persons for the purpose of achieving those objectives.[41]

6.46   In preparing the strategy or any modification to it, the Secretary of State is required to consult: (a) the appropriate agency (the Environment Agency in England and Natural Resources Wales in Wales) (b) such bodies or persons who appear to him to be representative of the interests of local government as he may consider appropriate (c) such bodies or persons who appear to him to be representative of the interests of industry as he may consider appropriate (d) such other bodies or persons as he may consider appropriate.[42] The statute includes the duty to consult upon pre-publication drafts of the strategy or modifications to it.[43]

6.47   The first National Air Quality Strategy was published in 1997. It included commitments to achieve certain air quality objectives by 2005. A subsequent review of the Strategy led to the preparation and publication of the Air Quality Strategy for England, Scotland, Wales and Northern Ireland in January 2000. This was followed by the publication of an Addendum on February 2003. The Air Quality Strategy 2000 and its addendum were subsequently reviewed and this review led to the publication of a revised strategy in 2007.[44]

Status of the Air Quality Strategy

6.48   Strategic highways companies (ie Highways England) and local authorities upon whom functions are conferred under the Road Traffic Regulation Act 1984 are required to exercise their functions having regard to the National Air Quality Strategy prepared under s 80 of EA 1995 (so far as practicable).[45]

6.49   In exercising their pollution control functions under Part 1 of the Environmental Protection Act 1990, local authorities in England and Wales are required to have regard to the National Air Quality Strategy published under s 80 of EA 1995.[46]

The Air Quality Standards Regulations 2010 – Air Quality Plans

6.50   In England the Air Quality Standards Regulations 2010[47] implement the Air Quality Directive together with Directive 2004/107/EC relating to arsenic, cadmium, mercury, nickel and polycyclic aromatic hydrocarbons in ambient air. Part 5 of those Regulations govern Air Quality Plans. Regulation 26 states:

'(1) Where the levels of sulphur dioxide, nitrogen dioxide, benzene, carbon monoxide, lead and PM_{10} in ambient air exceed any of the limit values in Schedule 2 or the level of $PM_{2.5}$ exceeds the target value in Schedule 3, the Secretary of State must draw up and implement an air quality plan so as to achieve that limit value or target value.

---

[41]   EA 1995, s 80(5).
[42]   EA 1995, s 80(6).
[43]   EA 1995, s 80(7).
[44]   The Air Quality Strategy for England, Scotland, Wales and Northern Ireland, 2007.
[45]   Road Traffic Regulation Act 1984, s 122.
[46]   Environmental Protection Act 1990, s 4(4).
[47]   SI 2010/1001.

(2) The air quality plan must include measures intended to ensure compliance with any relevant limit value within the shortest possible time.

(3) Between the date when these Regulations come into force and 31st December 2014, the Secretary of State must draw up and implement an air quality plan if levels of $PM_{2.5}$ in ambient air exceed a level calculated by applying the margin of tolerance set out in Schedule 2 to the limit value.

(4) Air quality plans must include the information listed in Schedule 8.

(5) Wherever possible, air quality plans must be consistent with other plans drawn up in accordance with obligations imposed under Council Directive 2001/80/EC on the limitation of emissions of certain pollutants into the air from large combustion plants, Council Directive 2001/81/EC on national emission ceilings for certain atmospheric pollutants, and Council Directive 2002/49/EC on assessment and management of environmental noise.

(6) Where an air quality plan is required in relation to more than one pollutant, the Secretary of State must, where appropriate, draw up and implement an integrated plan in relation to all pollutants concerned.

(7) Where the level of ozone in a zone exceeds the target value in Schedule 3, the Secretary of State must draw up and implement an air quality plan unless the measures necessary to achieve the target value would entail disproportionate cost.'

6.51   The Regulations governing other areas of the UK are: the Air Quality Standards Regulations (Northern Ireland) 2010,[48] the Air Quality Standards (Scotland) Regulations 2010[49] and the Air Quality Standards (Wales) Regulations 2010.[50]

The ClientEarth litigation

6.52   The UK has been divided into 48 zones and agglomerations.[51] In 2010, 40 of those zones and agglomerations were in breach of one or more of the limit values for nitrogen dioxide.[52] The Secretary of State submitted Air Quality Plans and applications for time extensions (under Article 22) in respect of 24 zones. Nine of those applications were approved unconditionally by the European Commission, three were accepted subject to conditions being fulfilled.[53]

6.53   In July 2011, ClientEarth commenced judicial review proceedings in the High Court, seeking a declaration that the UK was in breach of its obligations to comply with the nitrogen dioxide limits in Article 13 of the Air Quality Directive. The challenge was unsuccessful before the High Court and the Court of Appeal. However, it succeeded in the Supreme Court. The Supreme Court concluded that the breach of Article 13 was 'clearly established' and that it ought to grant the declarations sought. However, it decided to ask a number of questions of the European Court of Justice ('ECJ') on other issues.[54] The questions were reformulated by the ECJ and answered as follows:

---

[48]   SR 2010/188.

[49]   SSI 2010/204.

[50]   WSI 2010/1433.

[51]   The division into zones and agglomerations is a requirement of Article 4 of the Air Quality Directive.

[52]   *R (ClientEarth) v Secretary of State for the Environment, Food and Rural Affairs* [2015] UKSC 28, [2015] PTSR 909, at para 16.

[53]   *ClientEarth,* at para 17.

[54]   *R (on the application of ClientEarth) v The Secretary of State for the Environment, Food and Rural Affairs* [2013] UKSC 25, [2013] 3 CMLR 29, at para 39.

'1. Article 22(1) of Directive 2008/50/EC of the European Parliament and of the Council of 21 May 2008 on ambient air quality and cleaner air for Europe must be interpreted as meaning that, in order to be able to postpone by a maximum of five years the deadline specified by the Directive for achieving conformity with the limit values for nitrogen dioxide specified in annex XI thereto, a Member State is required to make an application for postponement and to establish an air quality plan when it is objectively apparent, having regard to existing data, and notwithstanding the implementation by that Member State of appropriate pollution abatement measures, that conformity with those values cannot be achieved in a given zone or agglomeration by the specified deadline. Directive 2008/50 does not contain any exception to the obligation flowing from article 22(1).

2. Where it is apparent that conformity with the limit values for nitrogen dioxide established in annex XI to Directive 2008/50 cannot be achieved in a given zone or agglomeration of a member state by 1 January 2010, the date specified in that annex, and that Member State has not applied for postponement of that deadline under article 22(1) of Directive 2008/50 , the fact that an air quality plan which complies with the second subparagraph of article 23(1) of the Directive has been drawn up, does not, in itself, permit the view to be taken that that Member State has nevertheless met its obligations under article 13 of the Directive.

3. Where a Member State has failed to comply with the requirements of the second subparagraph of article 13(1) of Directive 2008/50 and has not applied for a postponement of the deadline as provided for by article 22 of the Directive, it is for the national court having jurisdiction, should a case be brought before it, to take, with regard to the national authority, any necessary measure, such as an order in the appropriate terms, so that the authority establishes the plan required by the Directive in accordance with the conditions laid down by the latter.'[55]

6.54   Following the reference to the ECJ the Supreme Court remarked that the ECJ's reformulation of the first two questions had unfortunately led to a 'degree of ambiguity'.[56] However, the Court concluded that it would not be necessary to make a ruling on the ambiguity or make a further reference.[57]

6.55   The UK government presented evidence which showed a significant deterioration in air quality since the case had last been before the Supreme Court.[58] The Secretary of State accepted that the Air Quality Plans which were previously before the Court would need to be revised in order to take account of the new information and of new measures to address the problems.[59]

6.56   The Supreme Court concluded that the government had failed to meet its obligations under Article 13 of the Directive. The government accepted this and also accepted that it was required to devise a new Air Quality Plan in accordance with Article 23 and to publish it by December 2015. The Court noted:

'30 Furthermore, during the five years of breach the prospects of early compliance have become worse, not better. It is rightly accepted by the Secretary of State that new measures have to be considered and a new plan prepared. In those circumstances, we clearly have jurisdiction to make an order. Further, without doubting the good faith of the Secretary of State's intentions, we would in my view be failing in our

---

[55] *R (on the application of ClientEarth) v Secretary of State for the Environment, Food and Rural Affairs* (C-404/13) [2015] 1 CMLR 55; [2015] ENV LR 17.
[56] [2015] UKSC 28, [2015] PTSR 909, at para 6. See also paras 26 and 27 for discussion of the ambiguity.
[57] At para 6.
[58] At para 20.
[59] At para 23.

duty if we simply accepted her assurances without any legal underpinning. It may be said that such additional relief was not spelled out in the original application for judicial review. But the delay and the consequent change of circumstances are not the fault of the claimant. That is at most a pleading point which cannot debar the claimant from seeking the appropriate remedy in the circumstances as they now are, nor relieve the court of its own responsibility in the public interest to provide it.

31 In normal circumstances, where a responsible public authority is in admitted breach of a legal obligation, but is willing to take appropriate steps to comply, the court may think it right to accept a suitable undertaking, rather than impose a mandatory order. However, Miss Smith candidly accepts that this course is not open to her, given the restrictions imposed on Government business during the current election period. The court can also take notice of the fact that formation of a new Government following the election may take a little time. The new Government, whatever its political complexion, should be left in no doubt as to the need for immediate action to address this issue. *The only realistic way to achieve this is a mandatory order requiring new plans complying with article 23(1) to be prepared within a defined timetable.'*

6.57 In response to the judgement of the Supreme Court (and the mandatory order) DEFRA published its Air Quality Plan (on 17 December 2015) entitled 'Improving Air Quality in the UK – Tackling Nitrogen Dioxide in our Towns and Cities'. The plan was comprised of a UK overview document, a technical report, a list of UK and national measures and individual zone plans for 38 air quality zones which were still to meet the nitrogen dioxide limit. The plan projected emissions at five-yearly intervals and gave 2020 as a compliance date for regional zones and 2025 as the compliance date for London.

6.58 In response to this Air Quality Plan, ClientEarth brought a second round of litigation.[60] ClientEarth alleged that the UK remained in breach of the Air Quality Directive in that the government had erred in its approach to Article 23(1) of that Directive. Article 23 states that periods of exceedance should be kept 'as short as possible'. ClientEarth argued that the compliance dates breached this requirement. It was further argued that the government had given disproportionate weight to considerations of cost, political sensitivity and administrative difficulties and that the government's modelling method for emissions was erroneous.[61]

6.59 Mr Justice Garnham upheld the challenge and issued a declaration that the UK was in breach of Article 23(1) and the corresponding domestic regulation (Air Quality Standards Regulations 2010, reg 26(2)). In doing so he held that although Article 23 gives Member States some discretion as to the necessary measures for compliance, that discretion was narrow.[62] With regards to the cost of various measures and proportionality, Mr Justice Garnham held:

'50 … In my judgement, there can be no objection to a Member State having regard to cost when choosing between two equally effective measures, or when deciding which organ of government (whether a department of central government or a local government authority) should pay. But I reject any suggestion that the state can have any regard to cost in fixing the target date for compliance or in determining the route by which the compliance can be achieved where one route produces results

---

[60] *ClientEarth v Secretary of State for the Environment, Food and Rural Affairs* [2016] EWHC 2740 (Admin), [2017] PTSR 203.
[61] At para 38.
[62] Applying *Janeck* [2008] ECR I-622, at paras 46 and 49.

quicker than another. In those respects the determining consideration has to be the efficacy of the measure in question and not their cost. That, it seems to me, flows inevitably from the requirements in the Article to keep the exceedance period as short as possible.

51   In my view, the measures a Member State may adopt should indeed be "proportionate", but they must be proportionate in the sense of being no more than is required to meet the target. To do more than is required, especially in the field of environmental protection, may well impact adversely on other, entirely proper and reasonable interests. So, for example, compliance with the nitrogen dioxide limits might well be achieved by denying access to all vehicles in all city centres forthwith. But such a measure would have wholly undesirable economic consequences for the public in general. And such extreme measures would be unnecessary when better targeted efforts would equally well achieve compliance with the requirements of the Directive. That is the sense in which, I apprehend, the Commission used the word "proportionate" in this context and that is the sense in which, in my judgement, the concept is properly applicable here.

52   It follows that I accept Ms Lieven's first submission that the Secretary of State must aim to achieve compliance by the soonest date possible and Mr Tromans' submission that she must choose a route to that objective which reduces exposure as quickly as possible.'

6.60   Garnham J set out his ultimate conclusions as follows:

'95   For the reasons set out above I conclude:

i)   that the proper construction of Article 23 means that the Secretary of State must aim to achieve compliance by the soonest date possible, that she must choose a route to that objective which reduces exposure as quickly as possible, and that she must take steps which mean meeting the value limits is not just possible, but likely.

ii)   that the Secretary of State fell into error in fixing on a projected compliance date of 2020 (and 2025 for London);

iii)   that the Secretary of State fell into error by adopting too optimistic a model for future emissions; and

iv)   that it would be appropriate to make a declaration that the 2015 AQP fails to comply with Article 23(1) of the Directive and Regulation 26(2) of the Air Quality Standards Regulations 2010 , and an order quashing the plan.'

6.61   In a separate decision,[63] Garnham J ordered the Secretary of State to publish a draft modified Air Quality Plan by 24 April 2017 and a final Air Quality Plan by 31 July 2017. This decision was not appealed by DEFRA. However, DEFRA did apply for an extension of time and the Court agreed to extend time for the publication of the draft plan but not the final version.[64]

---

[63]   *R (on the application of ClientEarth) v Secretary of State for Environment, Food and Rural Affairs* [2016] EWHC 3613 (Admin).

[64]   *R (on the application of ClientEarth) v Secretary of State for Environment, Food and Rural Affairs* [2017] EWHC 1618 (Admin).

Chapter 7

Local Plans

7.1 Local plans are the parts of the development plan which contain policies and proposals of English local planning authorities. They are usually the most important component of the development plan. A local planning authority will have a local plan, although it might consist of several documents.

Policy-making by local planning authorities is set out in Pt 2 of the Planning and Compulsory Purchase Act 2004, with some still relevant transitional provisions in Sch 8. The detailed provisions are contained within the Town and Country Planning (Local Planning) (England) Regulations 2012[1] ('Local Planning Regulations 2012'). These Regulations replaced the Town and Country Planning (Local Development) (England) Regulations 2004[2] ('Local Development Regulations 2004') which had themselves been heavily amended in 2008.[3] The 2012 Regulations apply to all plans in the course of preparation as at 6 April 2012[4] and so the earlier provisions are only of historic interest. Local authorities are under statutory duties to have regard to any guidance issued by the Secretary of State.[5] Extensive guidance is contained in the National Planning Policy Framework, supported by the Planning Practice Guidance.[6]

LOCAL PLANS AND THEIR PREDECESSORS

7.2 There is no reference to local plans in Acts of Parliament, although they are described as such in the Local Planning Regulations 2012 and the National Planning Policy Framework. The legislation has used a plethora of terms for local plans and related documents. One consequence is that several different titles appear and it is worth tracing what these are.[7]

Firstly, a variety of documents fall under the rubric of 'local plan' and are part of the development plan.

Prior to 2004, the development plan system was contained in the Town and Country Planning Act 1990, having been heavily amended by the Planning and Compensation Act 1991. In areas with two tiers of local authorities (counties and district or borough councils) the development plans were:

---

[1] SI 2012/767.
[2] SI 2004/2204.
[3] Following the consultation paper, 'Streamlining Local Development Frameworks' (November 2007).
[4] Local Planning Regulations, regs 1, 37, 38.
[5] Planning and Compulsory Purchase Act 2004, ss 19(2)(a), 34.
[6] Previously guidance had been contained in *Planning Policy Statement 12: Local Development Frameworks* ('PPS12') and *Creating Local Development Frameworks: A Companion Guide to PPS12*.
[7] The various species of development plan which existed before the 1991 legislation are (we think) no longer in force.

- structure plans adopted by county councils, which set out the strategic policies for their area;

- a single local plan for each district or borough council, containing its policies, along with local plans for minerals and waste matters, adopted by the respective county council for its area.

In the London boroughs and the former metropolitan counties, the unitary authorities each had a unitary development plan which fulfilled the functions of the structure plan and local plan.

In the 1990s a number of unitary authorities were formed in some shire counties, often based on cities. Practice varied as to whether they made unitary development plans or prepared a joint structure plan with neighbouring authorities and their own local plan.

When the Planning and Compulsory Purchase Act 2004 proposed to establish a new set of policy documents, transitional provisions allowed those draft plans which had been deposited prior to 28 September 2004 to be adopted.[8] Such plans could remain in effect for up to three years from their adoption. Additionally those plans which had been adopted before 28 September 2004 would stay in force for a further three years unless they were cancelled or specific policies replaced by a new development plan document at an earlier time.[9] However, the preparation of development plan documents took much longer than the government had anticipated and so the Secretary of State had to make directions saving numerous policies.[10] Those saved policies remain in force until replaced or cancelled by new documents.

The Planning and Compulsory Purchase Act 2004 required authorities to establish a suite of documents which were given the general and non-statutory heading of the Local Development Framework ('LDF'). Within this framework, the authority's policies for the development and use of land would be contained in local development documents ('LDDs'). Some LDDs would be part of the development plan and be called development plan documents ('DPDs'). Those LDDs outside the development plan would be supplementary planning documents ('SPDs').

DPDs were required to include:[11]

(a)   core strategies;

(b)   any area action plans;

(c)   any other document which included a site allocation policy.

The local planning authority could make other documents DPDs as these categories were not exclusive.[12]

Core strategies were intended to deal with strategic policies: the authority's spatial approach, the numbers required, key policies and strategic sites. However, the 2004

---

[8]   Planning and Compulsory Purchase Act 2004, Sch 8.
[9]   Planning and Compulsory Purchase Act 2004, Sch 8, para 1(1), (2).
[10]   Under the Planning and Compulsory Purchase Act 2004, Sch 8, para 1(3).
[11]   Local Development Regulations 2004, reg 7.
[12]   Planning and Compulsory Purchase Act 2004, s 15(2)(c).

Local Development Regulations 2004 contained a wide definition of core strategy as any document containing statements of:[13]

(i)   the development and use of land which the local planning authority wish to encourage during any specified period;

(ii)   objectives relating to design and access which the local planning authority wish to encourage during any specified period;

(iii)   any environmental, social and economic objectives which are relevant to the attainment of the development and use of land mentioned in paragraph (i);

(iii)   the authority's general policies in respect of the matters referred to in paragraphs (i) to (iii).

The scope of this is explored below in respect of the current provisions[14] but it would tend to encompass all development policies and much of what is now in Supplementary Planning Documents. Leaving aside therefore the possibility that several documents would be classified as core strategies under the legislation, authorities tended to start their LDFs with a genuinely strategic core strategy.[15]

An area action plan ('AAP') was any document which:[16]

(i)   related to part of the area of the local planning authority;

(ii)   identified that area as an area of significant change or special conservation; and

(iii)   contained the authority's policies relevant to areas of significant change or special conservation.

AAPs were relatively rare.

Local planning authorities did though prepare other DPDs, including site allocations DPDs and development management DPDs, the latter containing detailed policies for determining planning applications.

The result was that by the early 2010s, authorities could have a mix of DPDs and old local plan, structure plan or unitary development plan policies comprising their part of the development plan. They would be at different stages of plan preparation or review.

---

13   Local Development Regulations 2004, reg 6(1)(a), (3).

14   See 7.6 and 7.7 below.

15   The profusion of documents raised questions as to what matters should be dealt with in which documents and the order in which they should be produced. In *Associated British Ports v Hampshire County Council* [2008] EWHC 1540 (Admin) at paras 23, 50, 53 Keith J held that the Hampshire Minerals and Waste Core Strategy should have decided whether a new wharf was needed for crushed rock imports rather than deal with this matter in a later document. The Court relied heavily on the need to make 'tough strategic decisions' in core strategies, but the word 'tough' did not appear in PPS12 (2004) at all and was based on the Planning Inspectorate's paper *Lessons Learnt*. In fairness to the Inspector that conclusion did not follow from the legislation, which merely required a later document to be in conformity with the Core Strategy. Once the language of 'tough decisions' is left out of policy, it is difficult to characterise the deferral of a particular matter as perverse. In *Capel Parish Council v Surrey County Council* [2009] EWHC 350 (Admin), [2009] JPL 1302, at para 13 Collins J agreed with the argument that it was implicit in PPS12 (2004), para 2.9 that a core strategy should become before other development plan documents.

16   Local Development Regulations 2004, reg 6(2)(a), (4). Significant change was viewed as growth or regeneration: see the now-cancelled PPS12 (2004), para 2.17.

7.3 *Local Plans*

The Coalition government re-introduced the concept of a local plan. Whilst the National Planning Policy Framework envisaged this as a single document,[17] practice was more mixed. In part this reflected the state which local authorities had reached with their documents: some might have a recently adopted core strategy but needed a site allocations document. Neighbourhood plans have taken over much of the role of identifying development proposals and detailed planning policies from rural district councils, justifying a pause in creating district wide site allocation plans. A more relaxed approach to whether there were one or more documents in the local plan was called for by the Local Plans Expert Group. Some local plans will be called core strategy or sites local plans. However, legislation has not fully caught up with the reintroduction of local plans. Whilst the regulations and guidance talk of local plans, the 2004 Act still refers to DPDs.

Policies are also contained in SPDs and a residual and unnamed category of LDDs. Prior to the 2004 Act, non-statutory Supplementary Planning Guidance ('SPG') was often made. These categories of documents are not part of the development plan.[18]

A variety of other documents are contained within the LDF:

- the adopted policies map shows development proposals and designations in the development plan;

- the submitted policies map shows those proposals and designations contained in a submission draft local plan;

- the local development scheme ('LDS') sets out the local plan documents which the local planning authority has prepared or intends to prepare, with a timetable;

- the statement of community involvement ('SCI') contains the authority's policies for involving interested persons in the preparation of local plans and in considering planning applications.

The result is an alphabet soup of acronyms to join others in the planning process,[19] such that examination inspectors' reports often start with a two-page list of abbreviations.

THE PRESENT LOCAL PLANNING DOCUMENTS

7.3 The concept of the Local Development Framework ('LDF') as a suite of documents has fallen into disuse. There is though an extensive array of material which local planning authorities have to produce.

The local plan

7.4 The local planning authority's LDDs must set out their 'policies relating to the development and use of land in their area'.[20] The local plan is only one type of

---

[17] NPPF, para 154.
[18] SPDs, other local development documents and SPGs are considered in Chapter 11 below.
[19] Neatly parodied by Baroness Hanham during the passage of the 2004 Act: *Hansard,* 24 February 2004, Col. 209.
[20] Planning and Compulsory Purchase Act 2004, s 17(3).

LDD. Consequently, not all of those policies have to be in the local plan, some can be in SPDs or other LDDs. Certain policies, however, have to be in the local plan.

The comprehensive nature of local development documents

7.5 The authority's land use and development policies must be contained within the LDDs. Section 17(3) of the 2004 Act provides that: 'The local planning authority's local development documents must (taken as a whole) set out the authority's policies (however expressed) relating to the development and use of land in their area'. A similar duty applies on county councils for their policies in relation to county matters.[21]

Consequently, policies cannot be contained in non-statutory documents. The force of this provision has though diminished with later changes to the secondary legislation. The Local Development Regulations 2004 required the policies to be in DPDs or SPDs, each having their own statutory processes. This not only replaced the power to make non-statutory Supplementary Planning Guidance ('SPG') but also the variety of notes, guidance, interim policy and moratoria prepared by authorities whenever they felt like it. All of the LDDs had to be in the LDS. The Local Planning Regulations 2012 create a third, lower tier of LDDs containing policy which does not fall within reg 5 of those Regulations and so have to be in a local plan or SPDs. These documents are not subject to any requirements in the Regulations as to form or preparation, although in making them, the authority is required to comply with its SCI.[22]

The flexibility of the LDD process means that a proposal for a new document, for example, a planning brief on a windfall site, can be made and given effect to with reasonable despatch provided that it is suitable for that level of document. It does though exclude the use of non-statutory processes to bypass the consultation and conformity requirements placed on the various tiers of documents. This approach is consistent with the approach of the House of Lords in *Westminster City Council v Great Portland Estates Plc*[23] to the omission of policies from a local plan.

Each LDD is not expected to deal with all the authority's policies, which is why the obligation is that the documents as a whole set out the policies.

The section 17(3) duty to have all policies in LDDs creates difficulties for SPG in existence when Pt 2 was brought into effect.[24] Plans or documents relating to an old policy are DPDs.[25] This appears simply to be the statutory development plans, as SPG would otherwise be converted to development plan status. There was no other saving provision for the (non-statutory) SPG. Planning Policy Statement 12 ('PPS12') assumed that SPG could be retained by reference in the LDS, but SPG is

21 Planning and Compulsory Purchase Act 2004, s 17(4).
22 Planning and Compulsory Purchase Act 2004, s 19(3). These documents are discussed further in Chapter 11.
23 [1985] AC 661. See also *Kingsley v Secretary of State and Cheshire County Council* (2001) 82 P & CR 85 and *R (on the application of Pye (Oxford) Ltd) v Oxford City Council* [2001] EWHC Admin 870, [2002] PLCR 330; confirmed [2002] EWCA Civ 1116, [2003] JPL 45. This issue is discussed in para 2.34 above.
24 28 September 2004.
25 Planning and Compulsory Purchase Act 2004, Sch 8, para 15.

not an LDD, and so cannot meet the requirement that all policies are in LDDs. In practice, some pre-2004 SPGs remain in use.

THE CONTENT OF LOCAL PLANS AND OTHER LOCAL DEVELOPMENT DOCUMENTS

7.6   As mentioned above, an authority's LDDs must (taken as a whole) set out their policies relating to the development and use of land in their area.[26] When preparing local plans the Neighbourhood Planning Act 2017 will introduce a duty on local planning authorities to identify the strategic priorities for the development and use of land in the authority's area.[27] They will then have to include policies to address those priorities in their local plan[28] unless the authority are satisfied that sufficient policies to address these priorities are contained in a spatial development strategy in Greater London or a combined authority's area.[29]

The local plan must also include policies designed to secure that the development and use of land in the local planning authority's area contribute to the mitigation of, and adaptation to, climate change.[30]

There is distinction between those policies which must, if made, be part of the development plan and matters which can be left to other documents. Given the enhanced status of the development plan and the independent examination it goes through, the distinction is important.[31] The issue tends to arise when an SPD is challenged on the basis that it should be prepared and adopted as part of the development plan, but it is helpful to consider it when identifying the scope of local plans.

Any document containing statements on the following matters set out in reg 5(1)(a) must be a local plan:[32]

'(i) the development and use of land which the local planning authority wish to encourage during any specified period;

(ii) the allocation of sites for a particular type of development or use;

...

(iv) development management and site allocation policies, which are intended to guide the determination of applications for planning permission.'

The other subparagraph in reg 5(1)(a) is (iii) which concerns statements regarding 'any environmental, social, design and economic objectives which are relevant to the

---

[26]   Planning and Compulsory Purchase Act 2004, s 17(3).
[27]   Planning and Compulsory Purchase Act 2004, s 19(1B), to be inserted by Neighbourhood Planning Act 2017, s 8(1).
[28]   Planning and Compulsory Purchase Act 2004, s 19(1C), to be inserted by Neighbourhood Planning Act 2017, s 8(1).
[29]   Planning and Compulsory Purchase Act 2004, s 19(1D), (1E), to be inserted by Neighbourhood Planning Act 2017, s 8(1).
[30]   Planning and Compulsory Purchase Act 2004, s 19(1A).
[31]   See the litigation on the issue generally, discussed in Chapter 2 above.
[32]   Listed in the Local Planning Regulations, reg 5(1)(a)(i), (ii), (iv) and required to be in a local plan by reg 6.

attainment of the development and use of land mentioned in paragraph (i)'. These must be contained in an LDD but this may be an SPD rather than the local plan.[33]

Additionally the following documents, if prepared, must be a local plan under reg 5(2):[34]

> '(a) any document which–
>
>> (i) relates only to part of the area of the local planning authority;
>>
>> (ii) identifies that area as an area of significant change or special conservation; and
>>
>> (iii) contains the local planning authority's policies in relation to the area; and
>
> (b) any other document which contains a site allocation policy.'

The meaning of these provisions is unduly complex. Jay J observed in *Skipton Properties* 'the quest for the true construction and meaning of regulation 5(1)(a) is unnecessarily challenging. Frankly, those responsible for these regulations should consider redrafting them'.[35] In considering whether a document falls with the categories in reg 5 which must be in a local plan, those policies which are already contained in the local plan but which are repeated by way of background or clarity should be disregarded. The question is the nature of any new policies.[36]

Reg 5(1)(a)(iii) objectives

7.7   Sub-paragraph (iii) concerns:

> 'any environmental, social, design and economic objectives which are relevant to the attainment of the development and use of land mentioned in paragraph (i)'

A document which contains such objectives but does not otherwise come within reg 5 will be an SPD.[37] This is a change from the Local Development Regulations 2004 which had required such objectives to be in a DPD. The possibly unintentional effect of the Local Planning Regulations 2012 is that SPDs would now be made for matters that had previously been for the development plan and those topics previously covered by an SPD were now left to a residual category of LDDs.[38]

Sense therefore needs to be made of policies which are objectives under sub-paragraph (iii) and policies which fall under other sub-paragraphs and so have to be in the local plan.

Taking sub-paragraph (iii) with (i), the objectives must be 'relevant to the attainment of the development and use of land which the local planning authority wish to encourage during any specified period'. Since the authority's policies on the development and use of land must be in an LDD, the development and use of land which the authority wishes to encourage will be in a local plan. The objectives in

---

33   Local Planning Regulations, regs 2(1), 5(1)(a)(iii).
34   Local Planning Regulations, reg 5(2) and to be in a local plan by reg 6.
35   *R (on the application of Skipton Properties Ltd) v Craven District Council* [2017] EWHC 534 (Admin), at para 60.
36   *R (on the application of RWE Npower Renewables Ltd) v Milton Keynes Council* [2013] EWHC 751 (Admin), at paras 67–69 per John Howell QC, approved by Jay J in *Skipton*, at para 67.
37   Local Planning Regulations, regs 2(1), 5, 6.
38   See *RWE Npower*, at para 53, 54, 60 per John Howell QC.

the supplementary document must therefore be in respect of development which the local plan is encouraging. Jay J said in *Skipton*:[39]

> 'The purpose of regulation 5(1)(a)(iii) is to make clear that a local planning authority may introduce policies which are supplementary to a DPD subject only to these policies fulfilling the regulatory criteria. The Defendant has made clear that it may introduce an SPD, supplementary to its new local plan, which sets out additional guidance in relation to affordable housing'.

It is also necessary to consider only what the SPD adds beyond what is in the development plan. It will be inevitable that an SPD will make reference to existing development plan policies and those matters which are repeated cannot mean that it must be a local plan.[40]

The ability to hang objectives in an SPD off the encouragement of particular development and uses in a local plan is critical. Detailed criteria on wind energy were legitimately a matter for the SPD in *RWE Npower* because the development plan contained policies on wind energy.[41] However, in *Skipton* affordable housing policies could not be contained in an SPD when there was no local plan policy on affordable housing [42] and the detailed mix of house types and size was excluded from an SPD in R (on the application of *William Davis Ltd*) v *Charnwood Borough Council*[43] despite a general local plan policy requiring a mix.

Reg 5(1)(a)(iv) development management and site allocation policies

7.8   Sub-paragraph (iv) includes within those matters which must be in local plans 'development management and site allocation policies, which are intended to guide the determination of applications for planning permission'. Development management and site allocation policies are to be considered disjunctively ('or').[44] The sub-paragraph does not extend to any policy relevant to the determination of a planning application because otherwise it would render the rest of the regulation otiose and prevent there ever being an SPD. As was said in *RWE Npower* 'That would be a result contrary to the manifest intention of the 2012 Regulations'.[45]

Reg 5(2) areas and site allocation policies

7.9   Regulation 5(2)(a) contains what were area action plans under the 2004 Regulations.[46]

A 'site allocation policy' in sub-paragraph (b) is 'a policy which allocates a site for a particular use or development'.[47] It is concerned with particular proposals on

---

[39]   At para 90. See also para 94.
[40]   *RWE Npower*, at para 67, 69 per John Howell QC; *Skipton*, at para 67 per Jay J.
[41]   *RWE Npower*, at paras 79–82 per John Howell QC.
[42]   *Skipton*, at paras 5, 91, 92 per Jay J. It may be debatable whether the local plan support for housing was sufficient to allow an SPD on affordable housing, without having an affordable housing policy in the development plan.
[43]   [2017] EWHC 3006 (Admin).
[44]   *RWE Npower*, at para 72; *Skipton*, at para 93(2),(3).
[45]   At para 74 per John Howell QC.
[46]   Local Development Regulations 2004, reg 6(2)(a), (4).
[47]   Local Planning Regulations, reg 2(1).

particular sites, rather than a general support for particular types of development in certain areas (such as the common policy that further residential development is acceptable in what are shown as residential areas). It is usual though for allocated sites to be given their own designation in a plan.

Documents comprising the local plan

7.10   There may be more than one local plan (or document within a local plan). The Regulations require documents containing spatial and strategic policies, site allocations and development management policies to be local plans, so in statutory terms a local plan is defined by what it contains rather than what it is called. The National Planning Policy Framework envisaged that there would one local plan for an area and 'any additional development plan documents should only be used where clearly justified'.[48] The legal definition is, however, distinct from the more casual use of the expression in policy. There has also been the practical reality that local planning authorities have had different parts of the development plan in place and so have often produced partial plans, such as on strategy or sites rather than a single, comprehensive plan.

Supplementary planning documents and other local development documents

7.11   A supplementary planning document ('SPD') means an LDD within reg 5 which is not a local plan, adopted policies map or SCI.[49] Regulation 5 sets out various matters and reg 6 identifies which of those must be in local plans. That leaves only one category within SPDs which are statements regarding:[50]

> 'any environmental, social, design and economic objectives which are relevant to the attainment of the development and use of land mentioned in paragraph (i)'

Paragraph (i) is that development and use of land which the authority wishes to encourage in a specified period. Prior to the 2012 Regulations, statements on these objectives had to be included in the development plan. The 2012 amendments not only transferred some of the development plan content to SPDs but left the previous content of SPDs out of the definition of SPDs. There is therefore a residual category of LDDs which are not part of the local plan, SPDs, statements of community involvement and policies maps. This appears to be entirely inadvertent. These documents are considered in Chapter 11.

Form and content of a local plan

7.12   All local plans must contain a reasoned justification of the policies contained within them.[51] As a matter of good practice it ought to be clear what are the policies and what is the reasoned justification. Policies should be labelled (eg ENV1) and shown in a different typeface (such as being emboldened). However, whilst policy ought to be separate from reasoned justification, the understanding of the meaning

---

[48]   NPPF, para 153.
[49]   Local Planning Regulations, reg 2(1).
[50]   Local Planning Regulations, reg 5(1)(a)(iii).
[51]   Local Planning Regulations, reg 8(2).

and application of policy will be informed by the reasoned justification. The reasoned justification will be part of the LDD and will often be relevant to a planning decision.[52]

More formulaically an adopted local plan must contain the date of adoption and say that it is a local plan.[53]

The statutory requirements on local plans do not explain their frequently considerable length.[54] In part this is due to the number of matters that the National Planning Policy Framework expects them to address.

Local plan drafters should remember that whilst there is a need to set out their policies and explain why they are adopted, a local plan is a practical, day-to-day, decision-making tool which is used by planning officers, councillors, developers, consultants and the public. A lengthy document tends to make it harder to identify what is important and to generate rather than avoid disputes.

The Local Plans Expert Group ('LPEG') considered that plans should be more concise, addressing matters more efficiently and proportionately. In particular they said that 'there is no need for local plans to replicate the policies of the NPPF – instead, plans should contain a statement that the authority adopts and will apply the NPPF in determining planning applications'.[55] LPEG discussed good practice in plan content.[56]

CONFORMITY

The general conformity obligation with the London Plan, combined authorities' Spatial Development Strategies or Regional Strategy

7.13   Under s 24 of the Planning and Compulsory Purchase Act 2004 LDDs within the areas of the published London Plan, a spatial development strategy published by a combined authority or a remaining Regional Strategy, must be in general conformity with it.[57] The obligation previously existed with respect to unitary development plans and the London Plan.[58] However, the requirement to be in general conformity with regional policy was entirely new. It also made a fundamental change in the relationship between local and central government. The previous general conformity requirement was between different tiers of local government (county structure plans and district local plans, the London Plan and London unitary development plans). The requirement on non-London authorities became one of general conformity with the Minister's policy as expressed in the Regional Spatial Strategies (later Regional Strategies).

---

52   See *R (on the application of Cherkley Campaign Ltd) v Mole Valley DC* [2014] EWCA Civ 567, [2014] EGLR 98 for the lawful approach to reasoned justifications as opposed to policies in decision-taking.
53   Local Planning Regulations, reg 8(1).
54   Plans range from less than 100 pages to sometimes more than 300 or even 400 pages: Local Plans Expert Group ('LPEG'), 'Local Plans Expert Group: report to the Secretary of State' (March 2016), para 12.3.
55   LPEG report, para 10.2(iv).
56   LPEG report, Chs 10 and 12; LPEG Discussion Paper No 5, *Local Plan Content*.
57   Planning and Compulsory Purchase Act 2004, s 24(1).
58   Town and Country Planning Act 1990, s 12 inserted by the Greater London Authority Act 1999, s 344.

With the revocation of all regional strategies other than limited parts of those strategies for the South East and Yorkshire and Humber[59] the need for general conformity with regional policy has become unimportant. General conformity will be required with the spatial development strategies within the areas of the Manchester City, Liverpool City and West of England combined authorities.[60]

There is no requirement to be in general conformity with a draft of the London Plan.

The general conformity obligation is applied when the plan is submitted for examination.[61]

Opinions on general conformity with the London Plan

7.14   A London borough or Mayoral development corporation must ask the Mayor for an opinion as to general conformity of a local plan with the published London Plan, as must a local planning authority under a combined authority's spatial development strategy.[62] This request should be made at the same time as the submission local plan is made available for consultation under reg 19 of the Local Planning Regulations 2012.[63] The Mayor is required to give his opinion on conformity to the local planning authority and the Secretary of State within six weeks from the date of the request.[64] The local planning authority may also request an opinion from the Mayor with respect to any other LDD.[65] However, the Mayor is not required to respond on non-DPDs. He is though able to give an opinion as to the general conformity of any LDDs whether or not he has been asked to do so.[66]

If the Mayor is of the opinion that the document is not in general conformity then he is taken as having made representations seeking a change in the document.[67]

Ultimately though, whether a plan is in general conformity is a matter for the Inspector conducting the examination,[68] who is not bound by the Mayor's opinion.

Consistency within the development plan

7.15   The policies in a local plan must be consistent with the adopted development plan[69] except for any policy that is intended to supersede another policy in the adopted

---

[59] See Regional Strategy for the South East (Partial Revocation) Order 2013 (which revokes all except Policy NRM6: Thames Basin Heaths Special Protection Area) and Regional Strategy for Yorkshire and Humber (Partial Revocation) Order 2013 (leaving only the policies on the York Green Belt).
[60] See Chapter 10 below.
[61] *R (on the application of Stevenage Borough Council) v Secretary of State for Communities and Local Government* [2011] EWHC 3136 (Admin), at para 33 per Ouseley J.
[62] Planning and Compulsory Purchase Act 2004, s 24(4)(a).
[63] Local Planning Regulations, reg 21(1).
[64] Local Planning Regulations, reg 21(2).
[65] Planning and Compulsory Purchase Act 2004, s 24(4)(b).
[66] Planning and Compulsory Purchase Act 2004, s 24(5).
[67] Planning and Compulsory Purchase Act 2004, s 24(7).
[68] Planning and Compulsory Purchase Act 2004, s 20(5)(a).
[69] Local Planning Regulations, reg 8(4).

development plan.[70] In that latter case, the plan must state that fact and identify the superseded policy.[71]

The adopted development plan extends beyond the local plan to encompass the London Plan or any spatial development strategy, any other authority's local plan and any neighbourhood development plan applying to all or part of the area. Potentially therefore there are a significant number of other bodies' plans which might constrain a local plan. In particular conflicts may arise between county council minerals and waste policies and district level local plans if there are different intentions for the same site.

If different documents within the development plan are in conflict, then the latest plan prevails.[72]

Prohibition on conflict by supplementary planning documents

7.16 Any policies in an SPD must not conflict with the policies in the adopted development plan.[73] This is considered further in Chapter 11 below.

The meaning of general conformity, consistent and conflict

7.17 Whether a plan meets requirements of 'general conformity', 'consistent' and 'conflict' is a matter for the individual decision-maker, subject only to public law review. Any departures may be a matter of black letter meaning of policies, such that on any application of the plan there is a conflict. Other departures may involve differences in the practical effect of the policies: when operated they would tend to depart. Lack of conformity or consistency is affected by the nature and importance of the departure. These latter aspects are pre-eminently a matter of planning judgment.

Care needs to be taken in considering what is to be compared with the superior document. LDDs must be in general conformity with the London Plan,[74] a test which concerns the document as a whole. However, the policies in a local plan must be consistent with the adopted development plan,[75] putting the focus on the policies although not necessarily each individual policy.[76]

The issues are longstanding. Local plans used to have to be in 'general conformity' with structure plans and allow some departure from the overall policy. During the passage of the 2004 Act the Minister explained 'it is the Government's policy that it is only where a LDD would cause significant harm to the implementation of the regional spatial strategy that the local development document should be considered not to be in general conformity'.[77]

---

[70] Local Planning Regulations, reg 8(5).
[71] Local Planning Regulations, reg 8(5).
[72] Planning and Compulsory Purchase Act 2004, s 38(5).
[73] Local Planning Regulations, reg 8(3).
[74] Planning and Compulsory Purchase Act 2004, s 24(1).
[75] Local Planning Regulations, reg 8(4).
[76] By contrast 'any policies' in an SPD must not conflict with the development plan: Local Planning Regulations, reg 8(3).
[77] Lord Rooker, *Hansard*, 27 January 2004, Col. 155.

In *University of Bristol v North Somerset Council*[78] the Court followed *Persimmon Homes (Thames Valley) Ltd v Stevenage Borough Council*[79] in treating the question of general conformity as a matter for the public authorities, subject to public law review. That same approach was taken by the High Court in *R (on the application of RWE Npower Renewables Ltd) v Milton Keynes Council*[80] in respect of an SPD not conflicting with the development plan. Consistency does allow for some departures, the significance of which is a matter for the examination.[81]

The hierarchy of conformity

7.18   Consequently the following rules apply:

(i)   any LDDs must be in general conformity with any London Plan, Regional Strategy or combined authority spatial development strategy applicable to their area;

(ii)   any local plan must be consistent with the existing development plan unless it supersedes existing policies;

(iii)   the policies in SPDs must not be in conflict with the development plan.

STATEMENT OF COMMUNITY INVOLVEMENT

7.19   Local planning authorities, including county councils, are required to prepare statements of community involvement ('SCI').[82] The SCI is defined in s 18(2) of the Planning and Compulsory Purchase Act 2004 as a 'statement of the authority's policy as to the involvement in the exercise of the authority's functions under sections 13, 15, 19, 26 and 28 of this Act and Part 3 of the principal Act of persons who appear to the authority to have an interest in matters relating to development in their area'. Section 19 concerns the preparation of local plans and s 26 their revision. Section 28 is the preparation of joint local plan documents. The Neighbourhood Planning Act 2017 added ss 13 and 15 to the list of provisions, so encompassing the survey of the authority's area and its LDS.

When originally enacted, the preparation of SCIs required a formal consultation process and examination by a planning Inspector. This was abandoned by the Planning Act 2008 once those examinations had little real effect on the statements which had been produced. Presently, SCIs are LDDs[83] but not DPDs.[84] However, whilst being local document documents, they are not subject to the requirements to have regard

---

[78]   [2013] EWHC 231 (Admin).

[79]   [2006] 1 WLR 334.

[80]   [2013] EWHC 751 (Admin).

[81]   *Cooper Estates Strategic Land Ltd v Royal Tunbridge Wells Borough Council* [2017] EWHC 224 (Admin), at para 70 per Ouseley J.

[82]   Planning and Compulsory Purchase Act 2004, s 18(1). Whilst county councils in two-tier areas are not local planning authorities under the Act (see s 37(4)) they are required to prepare SCIs as their mineral and waste development schemes are subject to most of the same provisions as LDSs (s 16(3)) including the duty to specify the SCI as a local development document: s 17(1). In practice, county councils have prepared and maintain statements of community involvement.

[83]   Planning and Compulsory Purchase Act 2004, s 18(3).

[84]   Planning and Compulsory Purchase Act 2004, s 18(3A).

to various policies and strategies in s 19(2) nor to be in general conformity with the London Plan or other strategic plans.[85]

An SCI is not an SPD.[86] In consequence there are no procedural requirements for adopting or revising an SCI beyond the need for it to be adopted by resolution of the local planning authority or approved by the Secretary of State.[87] An SCI might say how it would be revised and that could create a legitimate expectation that the proposed procedure would be followed, although the statement's statutory role does not include its own preparation under s 18.[88]

The Neighbourhood Planning Act 2017 introduces a requirement for the statement to set out the local planning authority's policies for giving advice or assistance on proposals for making or modifying neighbourhood plans and making neighbourhood development orders.[89] It also allows the Secretary of State to prescribe additional matters that an SCI must address.[90]

SCIs conventionally contain separate sections on policy-making and development management. At the very least they ought to explain correctly the statutory procedures, including who is to be notified or consulted. The statements should though go further and set out the local approach, bearing in mind any particular local characteristics or sensitivities. The purpose of an SCI is to add, in a local context, to what has to be done. Authorities should take care to distinguish between what further steps they will take in certain circumstances and what they might carry out. A promise to carry out non-statutory consultation or publicity has to be followed, under statute for LDD-making[91] or as a legitimate expectation in development management.[92] The duty though is to comply with the statement: the requirement to have a statement does not impose an obligation to achieve a certain level of public involvement beyond that already contained in statute.[93]

Lindblom J has observed 'the essential purpose of the council's statement of community involvement … is to set in place a workable strategy for consultation … As a strategy for consultation it is framed in deliberately broad terms'.[94]

When the 2004 Act was being passed, the Minister explained that regulations were proposed that would set out minimum standards for community engagement,

---

[85]   Planning and Compulsory Purchase Act 2004, s 18(3).

[86]   Falling outside the definition of SPD in the Local Planning Regulations, reg 2(1), (5).

[87]   Planning and Compulsory Purchase Act 2004, s 17(8).

[88]   Planning and Compulsory Purchase Act 2004, s 19(3) says that when preparing the SCI, authorities do not have to comply with their SCI, but that might be because it would not, at that stage, be in place.

[89]   Planning and Compulsory Purchase Act 2004, s 18(2B), (2C), to be inserted by the Neighbourhood Planning Act 2017, s 6. The duty applies irrespective of whether the authority has neighbourhood areas or qualifying bodies in its area (s 18(2D)) since the intention is to encourage neighbourhood planning.

[90]   Planning and Compulsory Purchase Act 2004, s 18(3B), to be inserted by the Neighbourhood Planning Act 2017, s 13(3). The SCI provisions in the Neighbourhood Planning Bill were changed repeatedly during its passage. Originally they had allowed the Minister to require a review of a statement but that was abandoned.

[91]   Planning and Compulsory Purchase Act 2004, s 19(3).

[92]   *R (on the application of Majed) v London Borough of Camden* [2009] EWCA Civ 1029, [2010] JPL 621, at para 14 per Sullivan LJ.

[93]   *Kendall v Rochford District Council* [2014] EWHC 3866 (Admin), [2015] Env LR 21, at para 56 per Lindblom J.

[94]   *Kendall*, at para 57.

in respect of both LDD preparation and development control functions.[95] These standards would apply to all local planning authorities and would be based on current good practice. To the extent that has been done, it is in the Local Planning Regulations 2012 and the various statutory procedures for planning applications. Local planning authorities are free to set additional standards, to be defined in the SCI.

The SCI is meant to be about the exercise of the local planning authority's functions rather than imposing obligations on applicants for permission. When the 2004 Act was being passed the Minister said:[96]

> 'The point I must make is that the statement of community involvement is a statement of the local authority's policy. That is what it is about—the local authority's policy. The provisions of the Bill do not place any direct obligations on developers or other persons who wish to take part in the planning process. It is not a backdoor route to placing unnecessary burdens on those interested in the planning process. It is not intended to do that.'

Adopted policies map

7.20 A plan without a map of some sort will not be a great deal of use. It could set out numbers and criteria, but not clearly identify which land was subject to which policies or where allocated sites were. Plans have always therefore been accompanied by maps or diagrams.

The adopted policies map is produced by the district local planning authority which shows geographically the application of the policies in all parts of the adopted development plan.[97] This should include policies in the local plan but also in any county minerals and waste plans,[98] neighbourhood development plans or in the surviving remnants of the regional strategies. Whilst an increasingly complex task as the development plan may consist of several documents from different bodies, the policies map is intended to be a single compilation of the designations, proposals and policy areas contained in all of the plans. The intention is to show which land is subject to policies which have a limited geographical application, for example, site allocations, areas where particular forms of development are acceptable (such as residential areas, town centres), areas of restriction (for example, Green Belt, countryside, landscape designations) and safeguarding zones.

These entries on the adopted policies map have to derive from submission policies maps which are produced through the local plan process or maps in published regional strategies or made neighbourhood plans. There is no independent process of deciding which land is subject to a policy and adding it to the map.

Designations which arise outside the development plan making process do not have to be included in the map, such as conservation areas and sites of special scientific interest. It may be convenient to add them, but the policies map has no legal status for

---

[95] Standing Committee G, *Official Report,* col 232; 16 January 2003.
[96] Hansard, 27 January 2004, Col.115-116. The PPS12 Companion Guide said that statements could not require developers to carry out consultation: para 7.
[97] Local Planning Regulations, reg 9(1).
[98] The inclusion of county policies on the district map was recognised in 2004 by PPS12, para 2.22. A county council in a two-tier area does not have its own adopted policies map, but will produce submission policies maps with its local plans.

non-development plan notifications and is not definitive. The designation documents made under other powers show legally where the site is.

The adopted policies map must be comprised of, or contain, a map of the local planning authority's area reproduced from, or be based on, an Ordnance Survey map.[99] This might include inset maps of areas shown separately on a larger scale (such as town centres or villages),[100] although the introduction of electronic mapping has made these less common in practice.

The map will have a key, explaining the symbols or notations which it uses.

Where the adopted policies map consists of text and maps, the text prevails if the map and text conflict,[101] although it is not obvious when this is likely to occur as the maps are simply maps.

Prior to the 2004 Act, each plan had its own map or key diagram. Structure plans would have key diagrams which generally indicated proposals and constraints by symbols, lines and shading. Key diagrams are sketch maps of the plan area designed to point in general terms to locations. They are not drawn on a map base and are not intended to show precise sites or boundaries. Local plans and unitary development plans had proposals maps which would show allocations and designations contained in the local plan. Each plan had its own proposals map, so a two-tier area, with the county council as the minerals and waste planning authority, could have three local plans with three proposals maps and the structure plan's key diagram.

The Local Development Regulations 2004 introduced adopted proposals maps. When first adopted such a map would show the geographical extent of any DPDs adopted at the same time and any old policies which remained current.[102] Those proposals maps, as updated, became policies maps under the Local Planning Regulations 2012.

Other maps and diagrams may be contained within a local plan itself. The general spatial approach may be indicated on a key diagram, showing the general location of development and areas of restrictions.[103]

Submission policies map

7.21   A submission policies map is produced alongside the draft of the local plan which is to be submitted to the Secretary of State showing any amendments which would be made to the adopted policies map by the accompanying local plan, if it

---

[99]   Local Planning Regulations, reg 9(1).
[100] The Local Development Regulations 2004 referred to inset maps (reg 14) but they are not mentioned in the Local Planning Regulations 2012.
[101] Local Planning Regulations 2012, reg 9(2).
[102] Local Development Regulations 2004, reg 14(4).
[103] Such a key diagram or other sketch map may be an aid to the interpretation of a policy, such as where a policy applies, in the absence of a defined boundary in the adopted policies map: see *Tiviot Way Investments Ltd v Secretary of State for Communities and Local Government* [2015] EWHC 2489 (Admin), [2016] JPL 171, at para 45 per Patterson J.

were adopted.[104] It would be published with the draft of the local plan which goes for regulation 19 consultation[105] and then submitted to the Minister with the plan.[106]

It has been suggested that this map will be an SPD.[107]

SURVEY OF THE AREA

Duties on local planning authorities

7.22   Section 13 of the Planning and Compulsory Purchase Act 2004 places a local planning authority under a duty to 'keep under review the matters which may be expected to affect the development of their area or the planning of its development'.[108] This is based on a longstanding obligation in the Town and Country Planning Acts. However, the obligation is confined to district councils, unitaries (including those county councils which are unitaries) and London Boroughs.[109] The review need not be in any particular form and in the past has been dealt with by authorities as an obligation to be alert to the social, economic and physical environment rather than a requirement to produce a report on a periodic or any other basis. Monitoring reports are now required under s 35 on the implementation of the LDS and some material relevant to the survey may be contained in that report.

The matters to be reviewed include:[110]

'(a) the principal physical, economic, social and environmental characteristics of the area of the authority;

(b) the principal purposes for which land is used in the area;

(c) the size, composition and distribution of the population of the area;

(d) the communications, transport system and traffic of the area;

(e) any other considerations which may be expected to affect those matters;'

Section 13(3) then provides that the authority should also consider any changes which they think may occur 'in relation to any other matter' and 'the effect such changes are likely to have on the development of the authority's area or the planning of such development'. The wording of this sub-section obscures its purpose of requiring authorities to consider the future as well as the present. The use of 'other' appears to be superfluous as the section requires consideration of changes to the sub-section

---

[104] Local Planning Regulations, regs 2(1), 5(1)(b). If the local plan document would not alter the adopted policies map then no submission policies map is required: reg 17, 22(1)(b).

[105] As a proposed submission document: Local Planning Regulations, regs 17, 19.

[106] Local Planning Regulations, reg 22(1)(b).

[107] *Skipton*, at para 23(2) per Jay J. The Court's analysis was that a map showing how the adopted policies map will be changed is identified in Local Planning Regulations, reg 5(1)(b) (but is not a local plan by reason of reg 6) and those documents described in reg 5 which are not a local plan are defined as SPDs under reg 2(1). Whilst revealing a further problem in the drafting of the regulations, such a map is parasitic on the draft local plan and only has effect to change the adopted policies map when the new local plan is adopted. It does not go through the separate adoption procedure for SPDs. The definition of SPDs needs to be read as not including such submission policies maps.

[108] Planning and Compulsory Purchase Act 2004, s 13(1).

[109] Planning and Compulsory Purchase Act 2004, s 37(4), (5). An order may make a Mayoral development corporation a local planning authority for these purposes: Planning and Compulsory Purchase Act 2004, s 37(5ZA).

[110] Planning and Compulsory Purchase Act 2004, s 13(2).

(2) matters. The requirement to consider the effect of the changes is also unnecessary as the effect of any matters on development and planning must be considered under s 13(1).

An authority may also keep under review and examine these matters within a neighbouring area if those matters might affect its area but must consult the relevant local planning authority.[111] This is the first requirement for authorities to look beyond their borders.

The Secretary of State is able to prescribe or direct other matters to be considered in the survey,[112] but has not done so.

Duties on county councils

7.23   County councils in two-tier areas have two survey responsibilities.[113] Firstly they are required by s 14(1) of the Planning and Compulsory Purchase Act 2004 to review the matters which may affect development or the planning of development which is a county matter (that is minerals or waste sites).[114] These duties apply in the same way as for district planning authorities under s 13 and so include the power to consider relevant matters in other authorities' areas.[115]

By regulations or, in a particular case, a direction, the Secretary of State may require counties to keep under review section 13 matters which districts are also monitoring.[116] The original 2004 Regulations imposed this duty,[117] but it is absent from the Local Planning Regulations 2012.

THE LOCAL DEVELOPMENT SCHEME

Introduction

7.24   Local planning authorities are required to prepare and maintain a local development scheme ('LDS')[118] setting out their proposed local plan documents and the timetable for their preparation. As introduced in 2004 the LDS would describe all of the LDDs proposed by the authority. Its role was confined to DPDs by the Localism Act 2011. Whilst approved by the local planning authority, changes to the LDS may be required by the Secretary of State or the Mayor of London.

---

[111] Planning and Compulsory Purchase Act 2004, s 13(4), (5), (6).
[112] Planning and Compulsory Purchase Act 2004, s 13(2)(f).
[113] County councils which are unitary authorities also perform the functions of district councils and are local planning authorities for the purpose of s 13.
[114] County matters are defined in the Town and Country Planning Act 1990, Sch 1, para 1, but exclude for the purposes of this section matters partly in and partly out of National Parks: Planning and Compulsory Purchase Act 2004, s 14(6).
[115] Planning and Compulsory Purchase Act 2004, s 14(2).
[116] Planning and Compulsory Purchase Act 2004, s 14(3).
[117] Local Development Regulations 2004, reg 5.
[118] Planning and Compulsory Purchase Act 2004, s 15(1).

Contents of the local development scheme

7.25   The LDS will specify:[119]

'(aa) the local development documents which are to be development plan documents;

(b) the subject matter and the geographical area to which each development plan document is to relate;

(d) which development plan documents (if any) are to be prepared jointly with one or more other local planning authorities;

(e) any matter or area in respect of which the authority have agreed (or proposed to agree) to the constitution of a joint committee under section 29;

(f) the timetable for their preparation and revision of the development plan documents.'

Further requirements for the LDS could be prescribed by regulations.[120] The Local Development Regulations 2004 required greater details of the content and timing of the documents[121] but no such obligations are contained in the Local Planning Regulations 2012.

The LDS will encompass the particular authority's planning responsibilities, so unitary authorities will include waste and mineral planning policies in their LDSs.

The initial preparation of local development schemes

7.26   When first prepared, LDSs had to be submitted to the Secretary of State and the relevant regional planning body or the Mayor of London.[122] The deadline for submission of LDSs to the Secretary of State was 28 March 2005, six months after Pt 2 came into force.[123]

The Minister was then empowered to direct the local planning authority to amend the scheme.[124] Following the adoption of an LDS, the Minister was able to direct the authority to revise the scheme.[125]

The revision of a local development scheme

7.27   All local planning authorities now have their LDS in place.[126] There will then be a need, from time to time, to revise the LDS. The LDS legislation has been revised several times since 2004. In part this has reduced the scope of such schemes by omitting SPDs and cutting back on the detail required in them. However, the

---

[119] Planning and Compulsory Purchase Act 2004, s 15(2).
[120] Planning and Compulsory Purchase Act 2004, s 14(2)(g).
[121] Local Development Regulations 2004, regs 8, 9.
[122] Planning and Compulsory Purchase Act 2004, s 15(3), as originally enacted.
[123] Local Development Regulations 2004, reg 10(1).
[124] Planning and Compulsory Purchase Act 2004, s 15(4), as originally enacted.
[125] Planning and Compulsory Purchase Act 2004, s 15(8), as originally enacted.
[126] Whilst of relevance only to newly formed local planning authorities, if no LDS has been prepared then the Secretary of State or the Mayor of London may prepare one and direct the authority to bring it into effect: Planning and Compulsory Purchase Act 2004, s 15(3A).

Mayor of London has been given powers of direction[127] over London boroughs' schemes and Ministerial powers have been altered several times.

The local planning authority must revise the LDS when they consider it appropriate or when directed to do so by the Secretary of State or the Mayor of London (subject to any counter-direction by the Secretary of State). As local plan documents must be prepared in accordance with the LDS,[128] it has to be revised if the authority wishes to add, delete or alter proposed local plans or change their subject matter or geographical area.

Procedures for making and revising LDSs have been changed since 2004. No consultation procedures are set out: there is no longer a duty to send a draft to the Secretary of State. The scheme (or revised scheme) is brought into effect by a resolution of the local planning authority which sets out the date on which it would take effect.[129] Where the council operates executive arrangements the approval of the scheme is an executive function, so usually taken by the cabinet or a cabinet member, unless the full council decide to determine it.[130]

The Secretary of State and the Mayor of London's powers of direction

7.28   The Secretary of State and the Mayor of London are given powers of direction in respect of the preparation, amendment and revision of LDSs.

Where a local planning authority does not have an LDS, then the Minister or the Mayor may prepare a scheme themselves and direct the authority to bring it into effect.[131]

The Secretary of State and the Mayor of London are each able to 'direct the local planning authority to make such amendments to the scheme as he thinks appropriate for the purpose of ensuring full and effective coverage (both geographically and with regard to subject matter) of the authority's area by the development plan documents (taken as a whole) for that area'.[132] The power of direction is therefore not unlimited: it must be for the specified purpose. However, it is difficult to see why a direction would have been made unless the scheme was considered not to be effective. Lack of effectiveness may involve a failure to update an existing local plan.

Both the Secretary of State and the Mayor of London are able to direct an authority to revise its LDS.[133] A direction may only be made if he thinks that 'revision of the scheme is necessary for the purpose of ensuring full and effective coverage (both

---

[127]   In amendments introduced by the Greater London Authority Act 2007, s 30. The Mayor's powers are limited to the schemes of London boroughs: Planning and Compulsory Purchase Act 2004, s 15(4A), (8A).

[128]   Planning and Compulsory Purchase Act 2004, s 19(1).

[129]   Planning and Compulsory Purchase Act 2004, s 15(7).

[130]   Local Government Act 2000, s 9D(2). It would seem to be a plan or strategy under the Local Authorities (Functions and Responsibilities) (England) Regulations 2000, SI 2000/2853, Sch 4, para 1 and so could be taken over for approval by the full council.

[131]   Planning and Compulsory Purchase Act 2004, s 15(3). These powers have not been given to combined authorities.

[132]   Planning and Compulsory Purchase Act 2004, s 15(4).

[133]   Planning and Compulsory Purchase Act 2004, s 15(8).

geographically and with regard to subject matter) of the authority's area by the development plan documents (taken as a whole) for that area'.[134]

A direction to prepare or to amend an LDS must contain the Minister's or the Mayor's reasons for giving it.[135] There is no statutory duty to give reasons for requiring the revision of a scheme,[136] but it is likely that some reason would be given.

The Secretary of State (but not the Mayor of London) is also able to direct two or more local planning authorities to prepare a joint local plan.[137] At the same time the authorities may be directed to amend their LDSs to cover the joint plan.[138] Whilst there will be a statutory duty to give reasons for directing the preparation of a joint local plan, no duty to give reasons arises for an obviously consequential direction on the scheme.

The procedure for Mayoral directions

7.29   The Secretary of State and the Mayor may have different views about a London borough's scheme. A procedure is in place for resolving such disputes, unsurprisingly in favour of the Minister.

When making a direction the Mayor must have regard to any guidance issued by the Secretary of State.[139]

Copies of the direction must be sent to the Secretary of State at the same time as it is given to the local planning authority.[140] An electronic copy must be sent along with two copies in paper form.[141] The Secretary of State may direct the London borough to disregard the direction or alternatively to make a scheme or amendments as modified by the minister.[142] The Ministerial direction must be made within three weeks, starting on the day of the Mayoral direction and the local planning authority may not act on the Mayor's direction until the end of that period.[143]

Availability of the local development scheme

7.30   The local planning authority must make available to the public the up-to-date text of the scheme and a copy of any amendments made to it.[144] Since that text will incorporate the amendments, those amendments have to be separately

---

[134] Planning and Compulsory Purchase Act 2004, s 15(8AA).
[135] Planning and Compulsory Purchase Act 2004, s 15(5).
[136] There is no obvious explanation for the differences in respect of the giving of reasons and it appears to be a quirk of drafting.
[137] Planning and Compulsory Purchase Act 2004, s 28A, inserted by the Neighbourhood Planning Act 2017, s 9 from 15 January 2018.
[138] Planning and Compulsory Purchase Act 2004, s 28A(6), inserted by the Neighbourhood Planning Act 2017, s 9.
[139] Planning and Compulsory Purchase Act 2004, s 15(4A)(8A). There does not appear to be any current guidance.
[140] Planning and Compulsory Purchase Act 2004, s 15(6A)(a), (8B)(a).
[141] Local Planning Regulations, reg 7(1).
[142] Planning and Compulsory Purchase Act 2004, s 15(6B), (8C).
[143] Planning and Compulsory Purchase Act 2004, s 15(6B), (8B), (8C(b)) and the three-week period is in the Local Planning Regulations, reg 7(2).
[144] Planning and Compulsory Purchase Act 2004, s 15(9A)(a), (b).

identifiable, whether as discrete copies of the changes or as tracked changes to the scheme, referenced with their date. Additionally up-to-date information showing the state of the authority's compliance (or, pessimistically, non-compliance) with the scheme's timetable is similarly to be made available.[145]

There is no requirement as to how this material is made available. A document is taken to be made available for the purposes of the Local Planning Regulations when it is available for inspection at the local planning authority's principal office and any places within their area which they consider appropriate as well as on their website.[146] That approach can be taken to making the LDS available for the purposes of the Act.

The county council minerals and waste development scheme

7.31 A county council for an area which includes a district council will not prepare an LDS[147] but will prepare and maintain a minerals and waste development scheme.[148] The LDS provisions in the Act and Regulations apply to production of the minerals and waste development scheme, except it is not subject to the joint committee provisions[149] and (as a matter of geography) the Mayor of London's jurisdiction does not apply.[150]

THE PREPARATION OF LOCAL PLANS

Introduction

7.32 The procedure for preparing and adopting a local plan is principally set out in ss 19 to 24 of the Planning and Compulsory Purchase Act 2004 and Pt 6 of the Local Planning Regulations 2012.

Matters to be considered in preparation

7.33 The material that must be considered when formulating a local plan is considerable.[151] A good starting point is that in preparing a local plan the local planning authority must have regard to the documents set out in s 19(2) of the 2004 Act:

- national policies and advice contained in guidance issued by the Secretary of State;

---

[145] Planning and Compulsory Purchase Act 2004, s 15(9A)(c).
[146] Local Planning Regulations, reg 35(1). The Local Development Regulations 2004 had provided that an LDS brought into effect had to be available for inspection at the authority's principal office and placed on the council website: reg 12(1).
[147] Since it is not a local planning authority for the purposes of Pt II: Planning and Compulsory Purchase Act 2004, s 37(4). Unitary county councils will prepare an LDS including minerals and waste matters.
[148] Planning and Compulsory Purchase Act 2004, s 16(1).
[149] Planning and Compulsory Purchase Act 2004, s 16(2).
[150] In part because the Mayor's powers are limited to London boroughs and certain general conformity provision are disapplied in any event: Planning and Compulsory Purchase Act 2004, s 16(4)(b), (c).
[151] It is tabulated in the LPEG report, Appendix 10A.

- the regional strategy for the region or for any region which adjoins the area of the authority;[152]

- the London Plan if the authority are a London borough or adjoin Greater London;

- any combined authority spatial development strategy for their area;[153]

- the Wales Spatial Plan if the for their region or for any adjoining region;

- other LDDs adopted by the authority; and

- the resources likely to be available for implementing the proposals in the document.

A variety of other statutory duties to have regard to Ministerial guidance are also imposed. When exercising any powers under Pt 2 of the 2004 Act there is a general duty to have regard to any guidance issued by the Secretary of State.[154] Where the duty to co-operate applies, the authority must also consider any guidance issued by the Secretary of State about how that is to be complied with.[155] When exercising the plan-making function with the objective of contributing to the achievement of sustainable development, local planning authorities must also have regard to national policies and advice contained in guidance issued by the Secretary of State for these purposes.[156] All in all, this amounts to unnecessary legislative duplication.

The Neighbourhood Planning Act 2017 will introduce a duty on the Secretary of State to issue guidance on how LDDs should address housing needs that result from old age or disability.[157]

Several other statutory duties to have regard to documents arise. The local planning authority must consider the Self-build and Custom Housebuilding register for its area.[158] Also in complying with the duty to co-operate, the authority must have regard to the activities of local enterprise partnerships and local nature partnerships insofar as they are relevant.[159]

Since a local plan must be consistent with the adopted development plan,[160] the other parts of the development plan for the area which are not mentioned in s 19(2) must also be taken into account: local plans adopted by other tiers (such as minerals and waste plans) and neighbourhood plans.

---

[152] The authority's area must adjoin the other region: it is not enough that the region adjoins the region which the authority is in.

[153] Planning and Compulsory Purchase Act 2004, s 19(2) is modified in those cases by the relevant combined authority order. See Chapter 10 below.

[154] Planning and Compulsory Purchase Act 2004, s 34.

[155] Planning and Compulsory Purchase Act 2004, s 33A(7). This guidance is in the NPPF, paras 178–181.

[156] Planning and Compulsory Purchase Act 2004, s 39(3).

[157] Planning and Compulsory Purchase Act 2004, s 34(2) to be inserted by Neighbourhood Planning Act 2017, s 8(2).

[158] Self-build and Custom Housebuilding Act 2015, s 2.

[159] Planning and Compulsory Purchase Act 2004, s 33A(2)(b); Local Planning Regulations, reg 4(2).

[160] Local Planning Regulations, reg 8(4).

7.33 *Local Plans*

General duties are also relevant including to national parks,[161] the Norfolk and Suffolk Broads,[162] areas of outstanding natural beauty[163], sites of special scientific interest, the conservation of biodiversity,[164] renewable and low carbon energy and energy efficiency,[165] the public sector equality duty[166] and, where relevant, human rights. These are discussed further in Chapter 2 above.

Additionally, the Secretary of State has prescribed that regard must be had to the following:[167]

- policies developed by a local transport authority in accordance with the Transport Act 2000, s 108 (which is the local transport plan);[168]

- the requirements of Articles 5 and 13 of the European Union Council Directive 2012/18/EU on the control of major accident hazards involving dangerous substances (known as 'SEVESO III');

- the national waste management plan;[169]

- if the authority's area is adjacent to Wales, the *Planning Policy Wales* ('PPW');[170]

- the National Planning Framework for Scotland, if the authority's area is adjacent to Scotland.[171]

The National Planning Policy Framework ('NPPF') sets out a considerable number of matters which the government considers ought to be addressed in local plans. Authorities dealing with housing policies are expected to:[172]

- prepare a Strategic Housing Market Assessment to assess their full housing needs, working with neighbouring authorities where housing market areas cross administrative boundaries. The Strategic Housing Market Assessment should identify the scale and mix of housing and the range of tenures that the local population is likely to need over the plan period which:

  - meets household and population projections, taking account of migration and demographic change;

  - addresses the need for all types of housing, including affordable housing and the needs of different groups in the community (such as, but not limited to, families with children, older people, people with disabilities, service families and people wishing to build their own homes); and

  - caters for housing demand and the scale of housing supply necessary to meet this demand;

---

[161] National Parks and Access to the Countryside Act 1949, s 11A(1), (2).
[162] Norfolk and Suffolk Broads Act 1988, s 17A.
[163] Countryside and Rights of Way Act 2000, s 85(1).
[164] Natural Environment and Rural Communities Act 2006, s 40(3).
[165] Planning and Energy Act 2008, s1.
[166] Equality Act 2010, s 149.
[167] Local Planning Regulations, reg 10(1).
[168] The local transport plan is prepared by the county council, unitary authority or passenger transport authority under s 108 of the Transport Act 2000.
[169] Defined in the Waste (England and Wales) Regulations 2011 (SI 2011/988).
[170] The 2012 Regulations refer to the 2011 PPW but the current version (presently 9th Editions 2016) should be considered.
[171] The 2012 Regulations refer to the 2009 version but again the current version should be considered.
[172] NPPF, para 159.

• prepare a Strategic Housing Land Availability Assessment to establish realistic assumptions about the availability, suitability and the likely economic viability of land to meet the identified need for housing over the plan period.'

The NPPF also advises that local planning authorities should set out their policy on local standards in the local plan, including requirements for affordable housing. An assessment of the likely cumulative impacts on development in their area of all existing and proposed local standards, SPDs and policies that support the development plan, when added to nationally required standards, should also be carried out.[173]

Authorities are also expected to deal in their evidence base with business needs and likely changes in the market, assess land and floor space requirements and supply, town centre roles, functions and capacity, locations of deprivation and the needs of the 'food production industry'.[174]

The NPPF advises local planning authorities to:

• assess the quality and capacity of infrastructure for transport, water supply, wastewater and its treatment, energy (including heat), telecommunications, utilities, waste, health, social care, education, flood risk and coastal change management, and its ability to meet forecast demands;[175]

• take account of the need for strategic infrastructure including nationally significant infrastructure within their areas;[176]

• liaise with the Ministry of Defence's Strategic Planning Team to address defence and security needs;[177]

• in co-operation with others, take into account the most up-to-date information about higher risk sites in their area for malicious threats and natural hazards, including steps that can be taken to reduce vulnerability and increase resilience;[178]

• base planning policies and decisions on up-to-date information on the 'natural environment and other characteristics of the area', for example, ecological networks and River Basin Management Plans.[179]

The NPPF says that a strategic flood risk assessment ('SFRA') may be required.[180] In practice an SFRA will probably be essential. Flood risks affect the spatial strategy and the location of sites.

In coastal areas, shoreline management plans should be considered as part of the evidence base.[181] The authority's historic environment record will give indications of likely undesignated heritage assets and archaeological remains.[182] Landscape

---

[173] NPPF, para 174.
[174] NPPF, para 161.
[175] NPPF, para 162
[176] NPPF, para 162.
[177] NPPF, para 164.
[178] NPPF, para 164.
[179] NPPF, para 165.
[180] NPPF, para 166.
[181] NPPF, para 168.
[182] NPPF, para 169.

work which may need to be considered will include available landscape character assessments, including historic landscape characteristics.

In preparing a local plan the authority must also comply with their SCI.[183]

Minerals planning authorities are expected to work with other organisations to understand the extent and location of mineral resource in their areas and the projected demand. The use of secondary and other sources of materials (that is, reused or recycled) is encouraged.[184]

Sustainability appraisal

7.34   In preparing a local plan the local planning authority must: [185]

'(a) carry out an appraisal of the sustainability of the proposals in each development plan document;

(b)   publish a report of the findings of the appraisal'.

This report is referred to in the Regulations as a sustainability appraisal report.[186] The report must be provided with the proposed submission documents as part of the reg 19 consultation on the draft local plan.[187] It is then sent to the Minister with the submitted plan.[188]

Sustainability appraisal is not explained further in the Act or Regulations although sustainable development is identified as an objective of plan-making.[189] A tripartite approach to sustainability appraisals was urged by *Planning Policy Statement 12* which said 'the purpose of sustainability appraisal is to appraise the social, environmental and economic effects of the strategies and policies in a local development document from the outset of the preparation process'.[190] This included consideration of sustainable development principles as required by s 39 of the 2004 Act.[191]

The Planning Practice Guidance ('PPG') says:[192]

'A sustainability appraisal is a systematic process that must be carried out during the preparation of a Local Plan. Its role is to promote sustainable development by assessing the extent to which the emerging plan, when judged against reasonable alternatives, will help to achieve relevant environmental, economic and social objectives.'

Sustainability appraisal is a separate requirement from any need for strategic environmental assessment, although there has been encouragement to deal with both

---

[183] Planning and Compulsory Purchase Act 2004, s 19(3). This duty only applies once the statement has been adopted: s 19(4).
[184] NPPF, para 163.
[185] Planning and Compulsory Purchase Act 2004, s 19(5). This obligation was confined to DPDs by the Planning Act 2008, having originally applied to all local development documents.
[186] Local Planning Regulations, reg 2(1).
[187] Local Planning Regulations, reg 17,
[188] Local Planning Regulations, 22(1)(a).
[189] Planning and Compulsory Purchase Act 2004, s 39.
[190] PPS12 (2004), para 3.17.
[191] Considered in Chapter 2 above.
[192] PPG, para 11-001-20140306.

exercises in the same document.[193] Going beyond the requirements of the statute, guidance sees sustainability appraisal as an ongoing process:[194]

'Sustainability appraisal is integral to the preparation and development of a Local Plan, to identify how sustainable development is being addressed, so work should start at the same time that work starts on developing the plan.'

The PPG treats it as the equivalent of a strategic environmental assessment, but spread across economic, social as well as environmental objectives.[195] As to the level of detail required in sustainability appraisals, the PPG now advises:[196]

'The sustainability appraisal should only focus on what is needed to assess the likely significant effects of the Local Plan ... It should focus on the environmental, economic and social impacts that are likely to be significant. It does not need to be done in any more detail, or using more resources, than is considered to be appropriate for the content and level of detail in the Local Plan.'

The LPEG considered that the sustainability appraisal process had become lengthy but not useful to decision-making. It ought to be confined to a single report at the submission stage explaining how the plan compared to the expectations of sustainable development and separated from strategic environmental assessment.[197]

Strategic environmental assessment

7.35   LDDs will require strategic environmental assessment ('SEA') under the Environmental Assessment of Plans and Programmes Regulations 2004[198] ('SEA Regulations') where they:

(i)   set the framework for future development consent of projects which are listed in Annex I or II of the Environmental Impact Assessment Directive[199] ('EIA Directive');

(ii)   require appropriate assessment under the Birds or Habitats Directive; or

(iii) set the framework for future development consent of projects and the plan or programme is likely to have significant environmental effects;

subject in the first two cases to limited exceptions.[200]

The EIA Directive projects do not take account of the thresholds and criteria in Sch 2 of the Town and Country Planning (Environmental Impact Assessment)

---

[193] PPG, para 11-001-20140306, 11-011-20140306.
[194] PPG, para 11-006-20140306 and see the chart at para 11-013-20140306. Scoping, development and testing of alternatives and assessing effects are proposed alongside the earlier stages of the local plan process.
[195] See PPG, para 11-018-20140306 including 'The sustainability appraisal needs to compare all reasonable alternatives including the preferred approach and assess these against the baseline environmental, economic and social characteristics of the area and the likely situation if the Local Plan'.
[196] PPG, para 11-008-20140306.
[197] LPEG report, para 9.24, 9.25; Appendix 10, para 52-57.
[198] SI 2004/1633.
[199] Directive 85/337/EEC as amended by Council Directive 97/11/EC.
[200] SEA Regulations, reg 5. For more consideration of SEA, see Chapter 3 above.

Regulations 2017,[201] however, smaller plans may be excepted under reg 5(6) of the SEA Regulations.

The reg 5(6) exception applies to plans:

(i)   in the EIA Directive categories or which require appropriate assessment; which

(ii)   determine the use of a small area at a local level or are for a minor modification of a plan or programme in the EIA Directive/appropriate assessment categories; and

(iii)   have been determined not to be likely to have significant environmental effects.[202]

In those cases SEA will only be required if the project is likely to have significant effects on the environment.

A district-wide local plan will invariably require SEA. However a local plan document which relates to part of a plan area might not do so. The size of a 'small area' is undefined will be a matter of judgment for the decision-maker, subject to correctly understanding the law and reaching a rational view.[203] Partial reviews of local plans might also not have significant effects on the environment, for example if they are concerned with small scale development or are limited in their effect.[204]

The SEA process requires the preparation of an environmental report, which is sent to statutory consultees and made available to the public, the receipt of responses and their evaluation in a reasoned fashion. The SEA Regulations apply to all plans and programmes subject to the EIA Directive and so impose obligations in a generalist fashion. The sequence of steps required ought not to conflict with the Local Planning Regulations 2012. The detail of assessment is, however, greater and local authorities will need to ensure that their processes are carried out in accordance with both Regulations.

The duty to co-operate

7.36   Plan-making authorities and other public bodies must co-operate together on strategic matters arising on local plans, other LDDs and marine plans.[205]

The duty to co-operate[206] was introduced by the Localism Act 2011 and was an attempt to address the need for policy co-ordination beyond an authority's boundary as well as fully engaging the myriad of bodies involved in delivering development. Historically, strategic planning policy had been dealt with by structure plans but that was then supplemented and, from 2004, supplanted by regional policy. In scrapping regional policy but not restoring structure plans, local planning authorities (outside

---

[201] SI 2017/571.

[202] The determination is either that of the responsible authority under reg 9(1) or the Secretary of State under reg 10(3).

[203] *R (on the application of Goodman) v London Borough of Lewisham* [2003] EWCA Civ 130, [2003] JPL 1309.

[204] The LPEG drew attention to the possibility that SEA would not be needed in such cases: LPEG report, para 26; Appendix 10, para 49.

[205] Planning and Compulsory Purchase Act 2004, s 33A.

[206] Sometimes known as 'DTC'.

London) were charged with resolving those matters themselves. To encourage that to be done, they were put under a new duty to co-operate with other interested authorities.

When the duty to co-operate arises

7.37   The duty, in s 33A of the Planning and Compulsory Purchase Act 2004, is concerned with the preparation of DPDs, other LDDs, marine plans and activities that can reasonably be considered to prepare the way for any of these activities which are or could be contemplated or which support the preparation of any of these plans.[207] In all cases the duty only applies 'so far as relating to a strategic matter'.[208]

The following are strategic matters:[209]

'(a) sustainable development or use of land that has or would have a significant impact on at least two planning areas, including (in particular) sustainable development or use of land for or in connection with infrastructure that is strategic and has or would have a significant impact on at least two planning areas;

(b) sustainable development or use of land in a two-tier area if the development or use-

(i) is a county matter, or

(ii) has or would have a significant impact on a county matter.'

This list is not exclusive[210] but tends to be the approach taken to determining what are strategic matters. In the first limb, a planning area is the area of a district or unitary council, National Park, the Broads or English inshore or offshore region.[211] Whether an impact on two or more planning areas would be significant is a matter of planning judgment.[212] Setting out the spatial strategy for growth, identifying housing and employment requirements or major sites or infrastructure are likely to have significant impacts beyond the plan-making authority's area.[213] A proposal which significantly increases or restricts an area's capacity to accommodate development is also likely to be strategic, such as a major change to the green belt. Routine development management policies or small sites are unlikely to be strategic, although a tall buildings policy is capable of having a significant impact.

The second limb is directed towards the relationship between county councils and their districts and boroughs. County matters are concerned with minerals or waste, including former mineral sites.[214] The minerals and waste local plans and supporting SPDs and LDDs of county councils in two-tier areas will therefore be subject to the duty to co-operate. A proposal in another authority's document which would have a

---

[207] Planning and Compulsory Purchase Act 2004, s 33A(3).

[208] Planning and Compulsory Purchase Act 2004, s 33A(3).

[209] Planning and Compulsory Purchase Act 2004, s 33A(4).

[210] It might be thought that it is even more important that the duty apply to unsustainable development.

[211] Planning and Compulsory Purchase Act 2004, s 33A(5).

[212] *Zurich Assurance Ltd v Winchester City Council* [2014] EWHC 758 (Admin), at para 109 per Sales J.

[213] The PPG emphasises the strategic priorities in NPPF, para 159 and infrastructure as potentially strategic matters for the purposes of the duty to co-operate: para 9-013-20140306.

[214] Planning and Compulsory Purchase Act 2004, s 33A(5) applying the Town and Country Planning Act 1990, Sch 1 para 1 (except sub-paragraph 1(1)(i) (applications crossing national park boundaries)) and the Town and Country Planning (Prescription of County Matters) (England) Regulations 2003, SI 2003/1033. These are set out in Richard Harwood, *Planning Permission* (Bloomsbury, 2016), at para 6.17.

significant impact on a county matter is also subject to the duty. An example would be an allocation which is likely to frustrate a minerals or waste site.

The persons subject to the duty to co-operate

7.38   The duty to co-operate applies to local planning authorities, county councils in England which are not local planning authorities and the following prescribed list of bodies:[215]

(a)   the Environment Agency;

(b)   Historic England (formally the Historic Buildings and Monuments Commission for England);

(c)   Natural England;

(d)   the Mayor of London;

(e)   the Civil Aviation Authority;

(f)   the Homes and Communities Agency;

(g)   each National Health Service clinical commissioning group established under s 14D of the National Health Service Act 2006;

(ga)   the National Health Service Commissioning Board;

(h)   the Office of Rail and Road;

(i)   Transport for London;

(j)   each Integrated Transport Authority;

(k)   each highway authority, including Highways England and the Secretary of State;[216] and

(l)   the Marine Management Organisation.

The duty is to co-operate with every other person on the list 'in maximising the effectiveness' with which the plan preparation activities on strategic matters are undertaken.[217] They are required to 'engage constructively, actively and on an ongoing basis in any process' by which this plan preparation is carried out.[218] This engagement includes:[219]

(a)   considering whether to consult on and prepare, and enter into and publish, agreements on joint approaches to undertaking these activities, and

(b)   if the person is a local planning authority, considering whether to agree prepare joint LDDs.

In addition, the bodies are required to co-operate with the local enterprise partnership and local nature partnerships, but those partnerships are not required to co-operate

---

[215] Planning and Compulsory Purchase Act 2004, s 33A(1). The prescribed list is in Local Planning Regulations, reg 4(1).
[216] See Highways Act 1980, s 1.
[217] Planning and Compulsory Purchase Act 2004, s 33A(1).
[218] Planning and Compulsory Purchase Act 2004, s 33A(2).
[219] Planning and Compulsory Purchase Act 2004, s 33A(6).

with the other bodies under s 33A.[220] The other bodies are also required to have regard to the partnerships' activities as far as relevant to the duty.[221]

The legislation does not explicitly limit the geographical scope of the duty but it must be confined to bodies who are interested in the particular strategic matter arising on that plan.[222] The PPG points out that different strategic matters may require co-operation between different groupings in the same plan.[223]

The duty to co-operate bodies (with the exception of the local enterprise and nature partnerships) must have regard to the Secretary of State's guidance on the duty to co-operate.[224] This guidance is in the NPPF and the PPG.[225]

The duty to co-operate was introduced on 15 November 2011 so is only concerned with steps taken from that date.[226] It also deals with the preparation of the plan and therefore concludes when the plan is submitted to the Secretary of State.[227] In practical terms this does not remove the need for other authorities to co-operate in the examination process to explain agreed positions or try to resolve disputes.

What the duty involves in any particular case is a matter of judgment, initially for the local planning authority and then for the examination inspector. Engaging constructively, actively and on an ongoing basis does go beyond the mere formality of consultation. There needs to be a dialogue and that may involve considerable joint working, for example in calculating needs beyond a single local authority area. Authorities have to consider whether joint local plans are appropriate but there is no presumption in favour of taking that approach. Any dialogue involves two or more active participants. A plan making authority simply has to proceed if the authorities it deals with have nothing to say, but should carefully document the steps taken.[228]

It is sensible for the plan-making authority to produce a statement setting out how it has complied with the duty to co-operate and documenting the various communications and meetings. This ought to accompany the submitted plan and if necessary be supplemented during the examination.

The duty is to co-operate but is not a duty to agree.[229] A council may have complied with the duty to co-operate but be at loggerheads with neighbouring authorities. That may be a reflection of the democratic process in different councils. In such cases the duty may be complied with even if the results are unproductive. The more

---

[220] As the partnerships are brought into the duty by the Planning and Compulsory Purchase Act 2004, s 33A(9) and the Local Planning Regulations, reg 4(2) rather than by the principal provisions under s 33A(1). See also PPG, para 9-006-20160519.
[221] Planning and Compulsory Purchase Act 2004, s 33A(2)(b).
[222] It would otherwise be absurd for local planning authorities at other ends of the country to discuss matters that do not affect each other, or for a council in Buckinghamshire to have to deal with the Marine Management Organisation.
[223] PPG, para 9-015-20140306.
[224] Planning and Compulsory Purchase Act 2004, s 33A(7).
[225] NPPF, paras 178–181; PPG, para 9-001-20140306 to 9-023-20140306.
[226] *University of Bristol v North Somerset Council* [2013] EWHC 231 (Admin), at para 67–69 per Judge Alice Robinson.
[227] *University of Bristol*, at paras 58, 62 per Judge Alice Robinson; *Samuel Smith Old Brewery (Tadcaster) v Selby District Council* [2014] EWHC 3441 (Admin), [2015] PTSR 719, at para 28-41 per Ouseley J.
[228] See PPG, para 9-019-20140306.
[229] A point made by the PPG, para 9-003-20140306.

141

fundamental problem which may arise between neighbouring authorities is whether the plan is sound. The soundness tests involve seeking to meet an authority's own needs and unmet needs from other authorities as well as having effective joint working on cross-boundary strategic priorities.[230] The LPEG reported concerns that these needs were not being met even where the duty was complied with.[231] An authority will though need to prepare a plan which takes account of the position adopted by its neighbours even if that sharply conflicts with its own approach.[232]

The Housing White Paper seeks to address concerns about the effectiveness of the duty to co-operate by consulting on amendments to the NPPF 'so that authorities are expected to prepare a Statement of Common Ground, setting out how they will work together to meet housing requirements and other issues that cut across authority boundaries'.[233]

In *Zurich Assurance Ltd v Winchester City Council* Sales J emphasised that whether there was compliance with the duty was a matter for the inspector subject only to public law review:[234]

> 'Deciding what ought to be done to maximise effectiveness and what measures of constructive engagement should be taken requires evaluative judgments to be made by the person subject to the duty regarding planning issues and use of limited resources available to them. The nature of the decisions to be taken indicates that a substantial margin of appreciation or discretion should be allowed by a court when reviewing those decisions.'

The development plan document process

7.39   Part 6 of the Local Planning Regulations 2012 provides further procedural requirements for local plans. Where an SCI is in place, the process must comply with its requirements in addition to those of the Regulations.

The current preparation stages which are required by the Local Planning Regulations 2012 are:

- consultation with public bodies on what the local plan should contain (regulation 18 consultation);[235]

- publication of the draft local plan for representations (regulation 19 consultation);[236]

- submission of the draft local plan to the Secretary of State for examination;[237]

---

[230] NPPF, para 182.
[231] LPEG report, paras 5.3–5.12.
[232] *R (on the application of Stevenage Borough Council) v Secretary of State for Communities and Local Government* [2011] EWHC 3136 (Admin), at paras 41–44 per Ouseley J is an illustration of a plan being unsound because the strategy was critically dependent upon a neighbouring local authority which was opposed to the strategy.
[233] 'Fixing our broken housing market' (2017), para 1.9.
[234] [2014] EWHC 758 (Admin), at para 110; followed in *Trustees of the Barker Mill Estates v Test Valley Borough Council* [2016] EWHC 3028 (Admin), [2017] PTSR 408 at para 55 per Holgate J.
[235] Local Planning Regulations, reg 18.
[236] Local Planning Regulations, reg 19, 20.
[237] Local Planning Regulations, reg 22.

- independent examination (in practice by a planning inspector);[238]

- publication of the examiner's recommendations including any modifications;[239]

- adoption of the plan.[240]

Pre-submission consultation (regulation 18)

7.40   The first statutory stage is for the local planning authority to consult various public and voluntary bodies.[241] The authority must consult those of the 'specific consultation bodies' which the authority considers may have an interest in subject of the proposed local plan.[242] These specific bodies are the Coal Authority, the Environment Agency, Historic England, the Marine Management Organisation, Natural England, Network Rail Infrastructure Limited, any strategic highways company whose area is in or adjoins the authority's area, Highways England, the Secretary of State for Transport if he is the highways authority for a road in the area, any other local planning authority, county council, parish council, neighbourhood forum or local policing body whose area is in or adjoins the authority's area, the Homes and Communities Agency, the Mayor of London (for London planning authorities only) and any electronic communications code operators, electricity and gas licensees, sewerage and water undertakers and clinical commissioning group or the National Health Service Commissioning Board who act in the area.[243]

The authority must also consult such of the 'general consultation bodies' it considers appropriate.[244] These are voluntary bodies with activities benefiting the authority's area, bodies representing the interests of different racial, ethnic or national groups, religious groups or disabled persons in the area and those representing the interests of businesses in the area.[245]

The requirements of reg 18 are that at this stage the various bodies are simply invited to make representations as to what a local plan with the proposed subject should contain.[246] In those terms the local planning authority does no more than offer a few words to some other public bodies and await replies. In practice the regulation 18 stage is far more extensive.[247] Consultation has usually taken place on a detailed paper canvassing potential issues or sometimes what is effectively a draft plan, setting out its preferred options. A draft of the sustainability report, or a scoping document explaining what it will cover, is often produced alongside the consultation paper. The documents would be published and the public invited to make comments along with the consultation bodies.

No consultation period is prescribed, but it is usual to use the same six-week period as for the later submission draft.

---

[238] Planning and Compulsory Purchase Act 2004, s 20; Local Planning Regulations, reg 23, 24.
[239] Local Planning Regulations, reg 25.
[240] Planning and Compulsory Purchase Act 2004, s 23; Local Planning Regulations, reg 26.
[241] Local Planning Regulations, reg 18.
[242] Local Planning Regulations, reg 18(2)(a).
[243] Local Planning Regulations, reg 2(1).
[244] Local Planning Regulations, reg 18(2)(b).
[245] Local Planning Regulations, reg 2(1).
[246] Local Planning Regulations, reg 18(1)(b).
[247] As the LPEG pointed out: LPEG report, Appendix 10, paras 10, 12, 25.

Consideration of representations on the regulation 18 consultation

7.41   The local planning authority will need to consider the representations made in response to the invitation issued.[248] When submitting the local plan to the Secretary of State in due course the authority has to provide a statement of who was consulted and how that was done under reg 18, with a summary of the main issues raised and how they were taken into account.[249]

Further non-statutory consultation

7.42   The Local Development Regulations 2004 had required a further consultation on proposals for the DPD.[250] In practice this would be a preferred options draft, which might also outline rejected options. This pre-submission public participation stage was removed by the 2008 amendments to the Regulations in an attempt to speed up the process.

There has been a tendency to carry out non-statutory rounds of consultation when preparing local plans. This has been criticised by the LPEG as damaging the plan-making process, creating uncertainty and increasing the risk of error.[251]

Publication of a local plan (regulation 19)

7.43   Having considered the regulation 18 representations, the authority must then prepare the local plan itself. This is consulted upon prior to submission to the Secretary of State.[252] At this stage the document is referred to in the legislation as the DPD or the local plan[253] even though it is not adopted. For these reasons it is common to refer to it as the draft or submission local plan.

This will be a complete draft of the local plan. It will not contain consultation questions or rejected options although those could be set out separately.

The 'proposed submission documents' which are published are the submission local plan, a submission policies map (but only if adoption of the local plan would change the adopted policies map), the sustainability appraisal report, a statement on the regulation 18 consultation and 'such supporting documents as in the opinion of the local planning authority are relevant to the preparation of the local plan'.[254] The statement on the earlier consultation will set out:[255]

'(i)   which bodies and persons were invited to make representations under regulation 18,

(ii)   how those bodies and persons were invited to make such representations,

(iii)   a summary of the main issues raised by those representations, and

(iv)   how those main issues have been addressed in the local plan.'

---

[248] Local Planning Regulations, reg 18(3).
[249] Local Planning Regulations, reg 22(1)(c).
[250] Local Development Regulations 2004, reg 26 and see PPS12 (2004), para 4.13.
[251] LPEG report, Appendix 10, paras 13, 14, 26.
[252] This is a change introduced in 2008. As originally made, the Local Development Regulations 2004 required consultation to start when the plan was submitted to the Minister: reg 29(1).
[253] Planning and Compulsory Purchase Act 2004, s 20(1); Local Planning Regulations, reg 19.
[254] Local Development Regulations 2004, reg 17.
[255] Local Development Regulations 2004, reg 17.

No list of likely supporting documents is provided in statute or policy, but it is the evidence base for the plan. Policy in the NPPF and the PPG sets out a large number of documents which are expected to be produced.[256] Documentation which has been produced for the local plan process, bearing on the examination issue and which the authority consider should be referred to ought to be in, such as evidence on compliance with the duty to co-operate. Any further explanatory papers, often called topic papers, ought to be provided at this stage. More caution can be taken with other documents published by the authority and other public bodies. Many will not be of more than tangential importance and they are often readily available. The LPEG expressed concern at the scale of material produced and recommended that the PPG say it should be confined to that which is 'strictly necessary to show whether the plan is legally compliant, sound and in compliance with the duty to co-operate'.[257]

All of these documents are made available by inspection during normal office hours at the authority's principal office and any other place in their area they consider appropriate and by publication on the authority's website.[258] Copies of these documents must be provided as soon as reasonably practicable following any request and subject to any reasonable charge.[259]

A statement of the representations procedure will similarly be made available, setting out the local plan's title, subject matter and geographical area covered, the date by which representations about the local plan must be received, the address for written or electronic representations to be set to, and that representations may be accompanied by a request to be notified of the plan's submission, adoption and the publication of the inspector's report.[260] This statement is also sent to those specific and general consultation bodies who were consulted at the regulation 18 stage. Newspaper advertisement is no longer required for this process, although it will usually be a matter of sufficient importance for the authority to seek local media coverage.

The consultation period is not less than six weeks from the day on which the statement of the representations procedure is published.[261] There is no prescribed form for representations, although a model is provided in the Planning Inspectorate's *Procedural Practice in the Examination of Local Plans*.[262] Whilst not in the model but pertinent for data protection, the form should say that the representations will be published and made available for inspection, with personal email addresses, telephone number and signatures redacted from the online version.[263] Any person may make representations:[264] there is no need to have a property or even local interest.

The Local Development Regulations 2004 introduced a counter-representation stage allowing all persons interested in a site which was proposed in another's representation to make comments. This was removed in the 2008 amendments.

---

[256] See the LPEG report, Appendix 10A.
[257] LPEG report, para 9.22. The group commented 'Inspectors literally receive a van load of evidence when they are instructed on a local plan but, in reality, only a handful of documents are strictly central to the issues to be examined': para 9.18.
[258] Local Development Regulations 2004, reg 35(1).
[259] Local Development Regulations 2004, reg 36.
[260] Local Development Regulations 2004, reg 17.
[261] Local Planning Regulations, reg 17. Making representations is considered further in Chapter 21 below.
[262] Annex 1, June 2016 (4th Edition v.1).
[263] Removing those personal contact details does not obscure the representation or the information necessary to evaluate it.
[264] Local Planning Regulations, reg 20(1).

The local planning authority will need to collate the representations and summarise the main issues raised in them for the Secretary of State.[265] In practice, it will wish to consider whether they have merit. There is though no statutory process for changing the plan between the regulation 19 stage and its submission. If following the publication of the regulation 19 plan, the authority wish to make material changes to it, they have two options:

(i) withdraw the submission draft and produce a new regulation 19 plan, conducting a further full consultation on it in accordance with reg 20;

(ii) propose modifications to the plan.

Material modifications to a submission plan may only be made if recommended by the examination inspector or required by the Secretary of State. A modification proposed before the plan is submitted is treated in the same way as a modification raised in the course of the examination. Consequently, the submitted plan is the original regulation 19 draft and the proposed changes can only be made if the examiner finds that the submitted plan is unsound and the changes are considered by the examiner to be appropriate solutions to the soundness issue. The authority may consult on the proposed modifications, limiting comments to them or any alternative or consequential changes.

If the authority wishes to make pre-submission material changes to a sound plan, or to have control over the changes, then it would need to publish a new regulation 19 plan and re-consult. Otherwise the authority may propose changes in advance of submission and consult on them, but such changes would just be proposed modifications to the draft plan. If they amount to main modifications then the Inspector must be persuaded that the original draft plan is unsound and should be remedied by those proposals.

Checking general conformity with the London Plan

7.44 London boroughs are required to ask the Mayor for his opinion whether the proposed local plan is in general conformity with the London Plan on the same day as they make the submission draft available for inspection.[266] The Mayor must send his opinion to the Secretary of State and the local planning authority within six weeks from the day of the request.[267]

Submission of the local plan to the Secretary of State

7.45 Following the regulation 19 consultation, the local plan is then sent to the Secretary of State[268] along with the sustainability appraisal report, any submissions policies map, the statement on the regulation 18 consultation, a further statement on the number of representations made on the regulation 19 consultation and the main issues raised by them, copies of those representations and the supporting documents relevant to the preparation of the plan.[269] From 15 January 2018, there is

---

[265] Local Planning Regulations, reg 22(1).
[266] Local Planning Regulations, reg 21(1).
[267] Local Planning Regulations, reg 21(2).
[268] Planning and Compulsory Purchase Act 2004, s 20(1).
[269] Local Planning Regulations, reg 22(1).

no longer a requirement to provide a paper and electronic copy of each document to the Minister.[270]

The submitted documents must be made available for inspection at the authority's principal offices and any other place they chose and published online as soon as reasonably practicable following submission.[271] A statement that these are available for inspection and of the places and times at which they can be inspected is also to be published.[272] Notice of this is to be sent to the general and specific consultation bodies who were consulted at the regulation 18 stage.[273] Additionally the authority must give notice of the submission of the plan to anyone who asked in their representations to be told of that.[274]

A summary of the issues raised by representations on the submission draft has to be sent to the Minister but in practice the local planning authority will want to consider the merits of those representations. There is no duty to express a view on them, either before submission or during the examination, but the representations will contribute to most of the issues which will arise. The authority should consider whether the representations prompt a need for modifications to be proposed to the plan, further evidence to be produced or submission to be delayed whilst problems are resolved.

When submitting the plan, the authority must think that it is ready for the examination.[275]

The examination

7.46   Section 20 of the Planning and Compulsory Purchase Act 2004 provides that each DPD has to be submitted to the Secretary of State for independent examination by a person appointed by him.[276] In practice the examiner will be a planning inspector.

The then Labour government originally proposed that the right to be heard, which had been enjoyed by objectors in unitary development plan and local plan inquiries, should not apply to development plan examinations under the 2004 regime.[277] In July 2002, ministers bowed to public and Parliamentary opposition, giving all objectors a right to be heard.[278] Section 20(6) provides that a person who makes representations seeking to change a DPD must, if he so requests, be given the opportunity to appear before and be heard by the person carrying out the examination. The Act and Regulations[279] refer to a person requesting an opportunity to be heard, leaving the

---

[270] Local Planning Regulations, reg 22(2), revoked by the Town and Country Planning (Local Planning) (England) (Amendment) Regulations 2017, SI 2017/1244, reg 5.

[271] Local Planning Regulations, reg 22(3), in accordance with reg 35. Representations and supporting documents only need to be available as far as it is practicable to do so (reg 22(3)(a)(iii)) but it is difficult to see how it would be practicable to send a copy to the Minister but not to have one for inspection in the council's offices.

[272] Local Planning Regulations, reg 22(3)(a)(iv).

[273] Local Planning Regulations, reg 22(3)(b).

[274] Local Planning Regulations, reg 22(3)(c).

[275] Planning and Compulsory Purchase Act 2004, s 20(2).

[276] An examination is a statutory inquiry under the Tribunals and Inquiries Act 1992 and so subject to the supervisory jurisdiction of the Council on Tribunals: Planning and Compulsory Purchase Act 2004, s 114.

[277] Planning Green Paper, 'Fundamental Change' (2001).

[278] 'Sustainable Communities: Delivering through Planning' (2002), para 38.

[279] Local Planning Regulations, reg 24(1).

possibility that the opportunity is not automatically offered. It is therefore prudent for people who may want to be heard to request an opportunity when making their initial representations.

The Planning Inspectorate guidance says:[280]

> 'Hearing sessions will be inquisitorial, with the Inspector probing the issues as opposed to an adversarial approach. Those who have sought modifications to the plan and asked to be heard must be invited to the hearings by the Inspector. If essential, additional parties who did not ask to be heard may be invited by the Inspector to contribute specialist expertise and knowledge.'

The Inspectorate also explains that for these hearings:[281]

> 'The most common format will be hearing sessions to which a number of participants who have made representations on the same issue are invited.'

Broadly speaking the discussion will follow an agenda prepared by the Inspector to address the soundness and any other issues which he has to address on that topic.[282] A more formal hearing might be required in some circumstances:[283]

> 'It may be appropriate that part of the hearing session allows for formal presentation of evidence followed by cross-examination and re-examination. This will only happen in very exceptional instances where the Inspector is convinced that a formal approach is essential for adequate testing of the evidence.'

Four procedures for considering representations had been contained in the 2004 PPS12: written representations; round table discussions; informal hearing sessions and formal hearing sessions.[284]

Procedural Practice in the Examination of Local Plans is useful guidance for the conduct of all forms of examination and so it is considered further along with examination practice generally in Chapter 21 below.

The examination tests – lawfulness and soundness

7.47   The independent examination considers whether:[285]

(a)   the requirements of the Planning and Compulsory Purchase Act 2004 and the Local Planning Regulations 2012 have been complied with;

(b)   the plan is sound;

(c)   the duty to co-operate has been complied with (if applicable).

The plan may only be adopted if:

(a)   the Inspector finds all of these requirements are met; or

---

[280]   *Procedural Practice in the Examination of Local Plans* June 2016 (4th Edition v.1), para 10.
[281]   *Procedural Practice in the Examination of Local Plans,* para 5.10.
[282]   *Procedural Practice in the Examination of Local Plans,* para 5.15 to 5.17.
[283]   *Procedural Practice in the Examination of Local Plans,* para 5.12.
[284]   PPS12 (2004), para D15.
[285]   Planning and Compulsory Purchase Act 2004, s 20(5).

(b)	any applicable duty to co-operate has been satisfied and whilst there has been a failure of legislative compliance or soundness, that is cured by 'main modifications' recommended by the Inspector at the local planning authority's request.

A plan may only be adopted as submitted, or with modifications recommended by the Inspector, subject to any intervention by Ministers.

INSPECTOR TO CURE ANY LEGAL OR SOUNDNESS FAILURES

7.48	The paragraph (a) legal requirements are those in s 17 (plan content), s 19 (preparation in accordance with the LDS, regard to particular policies, compliance with the SCI, sustainability appraisal), s 24(1) (general conformity with the Regional Strategy, London Plan or spatial development strategy) of the Planning and Compulsory Purchase Act 2004 and the Local Planning Regulations 2012.[286] The examination is not confined, as local plan inquiries were, to considering objections to the plan. The inspector must give a judgment on the document as a whole, even on parts where representations have not been made.

'Sound' is not defined in the Act or Regulations. It has though been expanded upon considerably in policy, currently in the NPPF. Lindblom J has emphasised that the guidance on soundness in the NPPF 'was policy, not law, and it should not be treated as law' and it was not unlawful or unsound for a plan not to follow national policy in every respect.[287] However, the practice of examinations is to consider whether a plan is sound by reference to the policy definitions rather than any separate legal meaning it might have.

PPS12 had initially set out nine tests which mixed matters of procedural compliance and soundness.[288] The 2008 version of PPS12 re-wrote these tests, separating the legal requirements from soundness.[289] In summary it said:[290]

> 'To be "sound" a core strategy should be JUSTIFIED, EFFECTIVE and consistent with NATIONAL POLICY.
>
> "Justified" means that the document must be:
>
> •	founded on a robust and credible evidence base
>
> •	the most appropriate strategy when considered against the reasonable alternatives

---

[286]	Planning and Compulsory Purchase Act 2004, s 20(5).

[287]	*Grand Union Investments Ltd v Dacorum Borough Council* [2014] EWHC 1894 (Admin), at para 59. Commenting on the earlier PPS12, Carnwath LJ said in *Barratt Developments v Wakefield Metropolitan District Council* [2010] EWCA Civ 897, [2011] JPL 48, at para 11:
'this guidance, useful though it may be, is advisory only. Generally it appears to indicate the Department's view of what is required to make a strategy "sound", as required by the statute. Authorities and inspectors must have regard to it, but it is not prescriptive.'

[288]	PPS12 (2004), para 4.24. Whilst of only historic interest in England, they are the basis of the soundness test in Northern Ireland, see Development Plan Practice Note 6 and Chapter 17 below.

[289]	See PPS12 (2008), para 4.49.

[290]	PPS12 (2008), para 4.52. The shouty use of capital letters was the original emphasis. The concepts of justification and effectiveness were expanded at paragraphs 4.36–4.38 and 4.44–4.47. The same principles were applied to non-core strategy development plan documents: PPS12 (2008), para 5.2.

7.49 *Local Plans*

"Effective" means that the document must be:

- deliverable
- flexible
- able to be monitored'

This text was replaced by the NPPF, para 182 which says a plan is sound if it is:

- **Positively prepared** – the plan should be prepared based on a strategy which seeks to meet objectively assessed development and infrastructure requirements, including unmet requirements from neighbouring authorities where it is reasonable to do so and consistent with achieving sustainable development;

- **Justified** – the plan should be the most appropriate strategy, when considered against the reasonable alternatives, based on proportionate evidence;

- **Effective** – the plan should be deliverable over its period and based on effective joint working on cross-boundary strategic priorities; and

- **Consistent with national policy** – the plan should enable the delivery of sustainable development in accordance with the policies in the Framework.'

Whether a plan is sound is a matter of planning judgment, reviewable by the courts on the basis of general public law principles.[291]

Whilst non-statutory, these are the tests considered by Inspectors. The elaborating text provides useful guidance although some parts of it are more suited to the strategic elements in plans.

Positively prepared

7.49   A positively prepared plan sets out what the local planning authority wants to see happen in its area. A local plan should not be a purely reactive document, setting out criteria to apply to planning applications which come in.

Meeting objectively assessed needs ('OANs') in local plans is also part of the presumption in favour of sustainable development in paragraph 14 of the NPPF:

- local planning authorities should positively seek opportunities to meet the development needs of their area;

- Local Plans should meet objectively assessed needs, with sufficient flexibility to adapt to rapid change, unless:

    – any adverse impacts of doing so would significantly and demonstrably outweigh the benefits, when assessed against the policies in this Framework taken as a whole; or

    – specific policies in this Framework indicate development should be restricted.'

Footnote 9 gives examples of policies which indicate that development should be restricted:

---

[291]   *Oxted Residential Ltd v Tandridge District Council* [2016] EWCA Civ 414; *Barratt Developments v Wakefield Metropolitan District Council* [2010] EWCA Civ 897, [2011] JPL 48, at para 11 per Carnwath LJ.

150

'For example, those policies relating to sites protected under the Birds and Habitats Directives (see paragraph 119) and/or designated as Sites of Special Scientific Interest; land designated as Green Belt, Local Green Space, an Area of Outstanding Natural Beauty, Heritage Coast or within a National Park (or the Broads Authority); designated heritage assets; and locations at risk of flooding or coastal erosion.'

The aim therefore is to meet an area's OANs unless the harm caused by doing so will outweigh the benefits. This approach is reiterated for housing in paragraph 47 expecting local planning authorities to:

'ensure that their Local Plan meets the full, objectively assessed needs for market and affordable housing in the housing market area, as far as is consistent with the policies set out in this Framework'

Housing needs are calculated across housing market areas, reflecting geographical rather than administrative areas. A Strategic Housing Market Assessment should be produced to identify needs.[292] Concern at the costs, delays and uncertainties in producing an OAN figure for housing led the LPEG to propose a simplified method calculation. Essentially this starts with the government's household projections with standard adjustments for the affordability of market housing and needs for affordable housing.[293] In September 2017, Ministers consulted on a standard methodology for calculating OAN in 'Planning for the right homes in the right places: consultation proposals', drawing on LPEG's proposals.

Justified

7.50   The LPEG commented on 'the most appropriate strategy':[294]

'Whilst this may suggest that the Inspector decides upon the best approach for the authority, in practice examinations have considered whether the plan is justifiable rather than necessarily the best. We support this approach which reflects localism: local planning policy is primarily a matter for the local planning authorities representing local people and the role of the examination is to ensure that the policy is sound. It is for the local authority to decide what the appropriate strategy is.'

Accordingly LPEG considered that the text should be changed to 'an appropriate strategy' to cut down on debate at examinations.[295] That proposal was adopted by the Housing White Paper.[296] As Ouseley J has emphasised, 'A plan may be sound, even if other approaches could also have been sound'.[297]

All of this reflects one of the cardinal points in the 2004 regime: that whilst the Inspector's views are binding, it is the local planning authority's plan not the Inspector's. The Inspector is not deciding whether the authority's proposals are right or saying how he would write the plan but reviewing whether the authority's plan is defensible.[298]

---

[292] NPPF, para 159. High-level guidance on how to produce an SHMA is contained in the PPG, section 2a. The NPPF is discussed further in Chapter 4 above.

[293] LPEG report, paras 3.12–3.24 and Appendix 6.

[294] LPEG report, Appendix 10, para 76.

[295] LPEG report, para 9.34. LPEG viewed the change as reflecting current examination practice in any event.

[296] Housing White Paper, 'Fixing our broken housing market' (2017), para A.18.

[297] *Cooper Estates Strategic Land Ltd v Royal Tunbridge Wells Borough Council* [2017] EWHC 224 (Admin), at para 61.

[298] The consequences of this approach for examinations is discussed in Chapter 21 below.

7.51 *Local Plans*

The authority does though need to explain how it has arrived at the plan, considering other plausible options. Any strategic environmental assessment would assist, as the reasonable alternatives have to be assessed in its environmental report. Whilst not simply substituting his own opinion, the Inspector should look carefully at the alternatives considered and the justification for their rejection. In *Capel* Collins J considered that there needed to be a 'rigorous examination of any suggested alternative sites' and criticised what he viewed as the Inspectors' failure to look behind the County Council's rejection of one alternative site (Copyhold at Redhill) in particular.[299]

Effective

7.51 Deliverability over the plan period involves going beyond asking what is desirable in planning terms to addressing what is likely to happen. A plan which is based on schemes which would not be carried out is not an effective plan. Consideration may therefore be required of a number of factors:

- Market demand for the project – is anyone likely to want to buy or occupy the development?

- If the project is to be publicly funded, what is the likelihood of that funding coming forward?

- Would the scheme be economically viable, now or in the foreseeable future?

- Whether there are any infrastructure constraints (such as roads or water) and what is the likelihood that they can be overcome? Where would the infrastructure funding come from?

- Are the relevant landowners willing or likely to be willing to promote the site? Any allocations should be supported by evidence of the owners' intentions. However that an owner is not promoting a site does not mean that it is necessarily unavailable or that it will not become available within the plan period.[300]

Consistent with national policy

7.52 The NPPF expects local plans to be consistent with national policy; however, consistency is not a legal obligation. The expectation is only contained in policy and whilst local planning authorities are required to have regard to national policy,[301] a decision-maker is not under a duty to follow its own or another's policy in the absence of a statutory requirement. National policy cannot therefore insist that local authorities' plans are consistent with national policy.

Deficiencies in plans can sometimes be cured by the promise of an early review. In *Grand Union Investments Ltd v Dacorum Borough Council*[302] the Inspector had found that the Council had failed to undertake a proper assessment of the housing needs of its area[303] and not done what it should to establish whether and how much of the

---

[299] *Capel Parish Council v Surrey County Council* [2009] EWHC 350 (Admin), [2009] JPL 1302, at paras 17, 29.
[300] *R (on the application of the Manydown Company Ltd) v Basingstoke and Deane Borough Council* [2012] EWHC 977 (Admin), [2012] JPL 1188, at para 127 per Lindblom J.
[301] Planning and Compulsory Purchase Act 2004, s 19(2)(a).
[302] [2014] EWHC 1894 (Admin).
[303] Contrary to the NPPF, para 47.

OAN for market and affordable housing could be met. He found that the unsoundness of the core strategy as a result of these errors could be cured by main modifications providing for a partial review. The Court agreed this was a pragmatic, rational and justified approach.[304] An early review may also be a sensible means of dealing with changes to government policy or other material considerations which arise late on in the plan-making process.[305] There is no value in delaying local policy until national policy stops changing, because it never stops changing.

Where a plan does not supersede existing plans, it is entitled to rely on them even if there is a case for a review of the earlier policy. In *Gladman Developments Ltd v Wokingham Borough Council*[306] it had been lawful to find a site allocations plan sound where it relied upon the core strategy's figure which had been derived from the then-revoked South East Plan and had not been revised following the National Planning Policy Framework's OAN approach. The soundness of a plan has to be judged by reference to its scope and what it sets out to do.[307] That may be particularly important when the plan operates at the second tier, below strategic policies in a spatial development strategy, the London Plan or strategic level local plan.

In 2004, the original PPS12 had said 'The presumption will be that the development plan document is sound unless it is shown to be otherwise as a result of evidence considered at the examination'. In *Persimmon Homes (Northern) Ltd v Blyth Valley Borough Council*[308] the Court of Appeal found that an Inspector had been misled by this wording. There was no presumption (such as the presumption in favour of the development plan in s 38(6) of the Planning and Compulsory Purchase Act 2004), which meant that evidence from objectors had to show that the plan was unsound. The proper exercise was neutral, in the sense of being an evaluation of the soundness of the plan in the light of all the evidence.

The binding inspector's report

7.53   The person carrying out the examination will make recommendations and give reasons.[309] These include reasons for any modifications which the Inspector recommends.[310] The term 'recommendations' is a linguistic hangover from the previous regime, as the report is binding on the local planning authority. Reporting is considered in Chapter 21 below.

Prior to the 2004 Act, inspectors conducting development plan inquiries only made recommendations which the local planning authority was able to reject. Reasons would have to be given for such a decision and the great majority of recommendations

---

[304] At para 63 to 69 per Lindblom J.
[305] *Persimmon Homes (North East) Ltd v Blyth Valley Borough Council* [2008] EWCA Civ 861, [2009] JPL 335, at paras 32, 33 per Keene LJ.
[306] [2014] EWHC 2320 (Admin), at para 182 per Lewis J, approved in *Oxted Residential Ltd v Tandridge District Council* [2016] EWCA Civ 414, at paras 29–36 per Lindblom LJ.
[307] *Cooper Estates*, at para 75 per Ouseley J.
[308] [2008] EWCA Civ 861, [2009] JPL 335, at para 40 per Keene LJ; followed in *Capel Parish Council v Surrey County Council* [2009] EWHC 350 (Admin), [2009] JPL 1302, at para 16 per Collins J.
[309] Planning and Compulsory Purchase Act, s 20(7).
[310] *University of Bristol v North Somerset Council* [2013] EWHC 231 (Admin), [2013] JPL 940, at paras 72–75 per Judge Alice Robinson, followed in *Cooper Estates Strategic Land Ltd v Royal Tunbridge Wells Borough Council* [2017] EWHC 224 (Admin), at para 23 per Ouseley J.

would be accepted, but ultimately the plan would be adopted in the form which the authority wished.

One of the most controversial aspects of the 2004 changes was to make the Inspector's report binding. As originally enacted an authority could only adopt a DPD as originally prepared if the inspector recommended it was adopted in that form.[311] Similarly, they could only adopt a DPD with modifications if those modifications are recommended by the inspector.[312]

Following the Localism Act 2011 amendments, the purpose of the examination is to consider whether the local plan met various statutory requirements, is sound and, if applicable, the local planning authority has complied with the duty to co-operate.[313]

If the Inspector considers it would be reasonable to conclude that all of these requirements have been met then the recommendation must be that the plan is adopted.[314]

If there has been a failure to comply with the duty of co-operation then this cannot be remedied by modifications.[315] The Inspector must recommend 'non-adoption' of the plan,[316] in practice, its withdrawal. Otherwise, if the Inspector does not consider that, in all the circumstances, it would be reasonable to conclude that the document satisfies the legal requirements[317] and is sound, then the plan can only be adopted if those defects are cured. On the request of the local planning authority the Inspector must recommend modifications of the plan which mean that it satisfies the legal and soundness tests.[318] The local planning authority does not have to request any particular modification. Under s 20(7C) of the Planning and Compulsory Purchase Act 2004 the request is for the Inspector to recommend modifications, not a provision that the Inspector may only recommend modifications put forward by the local planning authority. In practice if the authority is told that the Inspector will recommend that the document is not adopted for particular reasons, they will usually have a preferred form of modification. As structured, the Act appears to envisage the request for modifications being made following receipt of the Inspector's report.

In practice though the Inspector will usually indicate during the course of the examination where findings of unsoundness are likely to be made and encourage the authority to propose modifications to address them. In such cases the local planning authority's request for the Inspector to recommend modifications would be made whilst the examination is ongoing. There would then be an opportunity to consult, if necessary, on the authority's proposed modifications and any amendments

---

[311] Planning and Compulsory Purchase Act 2004, a 23(2), (4) (as originally enacted).
[312] Planning and Compulsory Purchase Act 2004, s 23(3), (4) (as originally enacted). For an early discussion of the extent of the changes that an Inspector could propose, see *Inspectors' Changes to Development Plan Documents – Exploding Some Myths* [2007] JPL 1423.
[313] Planning and Compulsory Purchase Act 2004, s 20(5).
[314] Planning and Compulsory Purchase Act 2004, s 20(7)
[315] Planning and Compulsory Purchase Act 2004, s 20(7A) to (7C).
[316] Planning and Compulsory Purchase Act 2004, s 20(7A).
[317] Under Planning and Compulsory Purchase Act 2004, s 20(5)(a).
[318] Planning and Compulsory Purchase Act 2004, s 20(7B), (7C). The Inspector may only recommend main modifications if asked to do so, although there is no reason why the Inspector cannot indicate what modifications are likely to overcome the problem.

to the sustainability appraisal or SEA environmental report[319] prior to the Inspector reporting.[320] The Inspector could still make further adverse findings in the report, but usually these would be on small points or give rise to straightforward deletions. If modifications had not already been requested then the authority could ask the Inspector to propose changes following the report, but ordinarily the recommended modifications would be in the report.

The legislation assumes that a soundness or legal error can be corrected by a modification, although that will not always be the case. An Inspector will still, in some cases, have to recommend that the plan is withdrawn.

A plan may be adopted with the Inspector's modifications and additionally modifications proposed by the authority that (taken together) do not materially affect the policies set out in the document.[321] Although often raised in the examination, those non-material modifications are not strictly a matter for the Inspector who is concerned solely with modifications which are required to meet the legal or soundness tests. Whilst it might be useful to publish immaterial modifications as they occur to the authority there is no need to consult on them.

The Inspector's report will be peer reviewed in draft by one or more other planning Inspectors to seek to ensure consistency.[322] The conclusions in the report will still be those of the examining Inspector(s) and reviewing inspectors will assist with the clarity and rigour of the report.

The fact check of the report

7.54   The Inspector's report will be provided in draft to the local planning authority to allow them to identify errors and suggest corrections. This is not intended to be an exercise in persuading the Inspector to change the recommendations, but is concerned with factual errors and omissions. If parts of the report or recommendations are unclear then clarity can be sought.[323] It may of course be that factual corrections necessitate changes to the recommendations, although those will usually be minor. If the authority has concerns about the lawfulness of the report then this is an opportunity to raise them, however, care needs to be taken in case the report is not amended to fully address those matters.

Publication of the report

7.55   Following the fact check, the examiner's final report will be sent to the local planning authority. It must publish the report as soon as reasonably practicable after receipt of the report or after receipt of any direction by the Minister.[324] The report

---

[319] These documents might need updating in the light of proposed modifications: see *R (on the application of IM Properties Development Ltd) v Lichfield District Council* [2014] EWHC 2440 (Admin), [2014] PTSR 1484, at paras 110, 111 per Patterson J.

[320] This is considered in Chapter 21 below.

[321] Planning and Compulsory Purchase Act 2004, s 23(2), (3).

[322] *Procedural Practice in the Examination of Local Plans*, June 2016 (4th Edition v.1), para 12.

[323] *Procedural Practice in the Examination of Local Plans*, June 2016 (4th Edition v.1), para 7.1.

[324] Local Planning Regulations, reg 25(1). The duty is to publish the recommendations and reasons (Planning and Compulsory Purchase Act 2004, s 20(8)) but even if it was possible to distinguish that from the totality of the report, no distinction has ever been drawn.

will be made available for inspection at the authority's principal offices, at any other locations they wish in the area and online.[325] Additionally, notice is given to anyone who requested to be informed when the report became available.[326]

The Secretary of State's powers during the preparation of a plan

7.56   The Secretary of State has powers to direct the local planning authority or the examiner prior to the adoption of a plan which is being prepared. The authority may be directed to change the plan, withdraw it or submit it to the Minister for approval. They may also be required to pause the process whilst the Minister decides whether to act. Additionally the examiner may be directed to take certain steps. These powers only arise once the proposed consultation or submission draft of the document exists.

Further powers which are given to the Minister if a plan is not being prepared or preparation is at an earlier stage are considered below.[327]

If the Minister thinks that an LDD[328] is unsatisfactory he may direct the local planning authority to modify the document in accordance with the direction at any time prior to adoption.[329] The authority then has to comply with the direction and must not adopt the document until the Secretary of State gives notice that he is satisfied that they have complied[330] or the direction is withdrawn.[331]

At any time after a local plan has been submitted for independent examination, but prior to adoption, the Secretary of State may direct the local planning authority to withdraw it.[332] The Minister does not have to wait until the Inspector reports and can simply on civil service advice. In practice the power is more likely to be exercised if the Inspector has said that the plan should be withdrawn and the local planning authority is not following that advice.

Prior to adoption the Secretary of State may direct that the local plan,[333] or any part of it, is submitted to him for approval.[334] The local planning authority then has no power to act until the Minister decides whether to approve the document, approve it subject to specified modifications or reject it in whole or in part or withdraws the direction.[335] Unless the direction is withdrawn the plan (or part of it) then proceeds under the Minister's control. Any part of the plan which is not subject to a direction can be progressed by the authority.

---

[325]   Local Planning Regulations, reg 25(2), applying reg 35.
[326]   Local Planning Regulations, reg 25(2).
[327]   See at 7.62 below.
[328]   Including SPDs and residual LDDs as well as the local plan.
[329]   Planning and Compulsory Purchase Act 2004, s 21(1). Reasons must be given for making the direction: s 21(1)(a).
[330]   Planning and Compulsory Purchase Act 2004, s 21(2).
[331]   Planning and Compulsory Purchase Act 2004, s 21(3).
[332]   Planning and Compulsory Purchase Act 2004, s 21(9A).
[333]   This power is confined to local plans (DPDs) and unlike the power to direct modifications, cannot be used on other local development documents.
[334]   Planning and Compulsory Purchase Act 2004, s 21(4). Various procedural changes are made by the Local Planning Regulations, Sched 1.
[335]   Planning and Compulsory Purchase Act 2004, s 21(5)(a), (9)(a).

If the direction is given before the plan has been submitted to the Secretary of State then the Minister must hold an independent examination.[336] This is to prevent the plan being approved without participants being able to appear before an Inspector but also stops the Minister from peremptorily rejecting a plan or part of it.

Where the Minister takes over the plan during the examination the Inspector will report to him.[337] Since the plan goes to the Minister for approval it is implicit that where the Secretary of State has made a direction before submission and then held an examination, the Inspector reports to the Minister rather than the local planning authority. Where the Secretary of State holds an independent examination, the Inspector will consider the duty to co-operate, the legal tests and soundness in the usual way, although requests for modifications would come from the Minister rather than the authority.[338]

However, the Minister is not bound by the Inspector's recommendations nor does he have to judge the plan by the tests in s 20. The Secretary of State can just decide to disagree with the plan. However in doing so, he will need to act on sufficient evidence and fairly. The Local Planning Regulations 2012 require notice to be given to the plan-making authority of any proposed changes which depart from the Inspector's recommendations[339] and any person may make representations on them.[340]

The Secretary of State is able to make a holding direction in relation to any LDD whilst he considers whether to exercise any of his section 21 powers. Such a section 21A direction will prevent the local planning authority from taking any step in connection with the document's adoption until the direction is withdrawn or expires under any time limit in it.[341] A direction will apply to the whole of the document, even though the intervention powers are capable of being applied to it in part. By s 21A(2) 'A document to which a direction under this section relates has no effect while the direction is in force'. Since the holding direction power applies to documents which are not yet adopted, this appears to mean that the document will not be able to be a material consideration.

The Minister may by notice require the local planning authority to reimburse his costs incurred under any of the section 21 powers, to the sum specified in a notice.[342] Where the powers are exercised on a joint LDD or joint local plan, the Neighbourhood Planning Act 2017 introduces a power for the Secretary of State to apportion his costs between the authorities involved as he thinks just.[343]

Sometimes the Ministerial concern is about the Inspector's approach. Whilst being civil servants and appointed by Ministers, Inspectors have operated independently. Ministers have had the power to override an Inspector's recommendation and so

---

[336] Planning and Compulsory Purchase Act 2004, s 21(5)(b).
[337] Planning and Compulsory Purchase Act 2004, s 21(5)(c).
[338] Planning and Compulsory Purchase Act 2004, s 20(4)–(7C) as applied by s 21(5A).
[339] Local Planning Regulations, Sch 1, para 4.
[340] Local Planning Regulations, Sch 1, para 5.
[341] Planning and Compulsory Purchase Act 2004, s 21A(1). The holding direction would cease to have effect if a section 21 direction is made (s 21A(3)), but that latter direction would then prevent the authority from acting. The first holding direction was made on the Birmingham Development Plan prompted by concerns by a local MP about development in the Green Belt.
[342] Planning and Compulsory Purchase Act 2004, s 21(11).
[343] Planning and Compulsory Purchase Act 2004, s 21(12), to be inserted by the Neighbourhood Planning Act 2017, s 9(3).

correct any perceived error at a later stage. This has been seen as insufficient and the Housing and Planning Act 2016 introduced a power to give directions to the examining inspector.

The Secretary of State may by notice to the Inspector:[344]

(a)   direct the Inspector not to take any step, or any further step, in connection with the examination of the local plan, or of a specified part of it, until a specified time or until the direction is withdrawn;

(b)   require the Inspector—

    (i)   to consider any specified matters;

    (ii)   to give an opportunity, or further opportunity, to specified persons to appear before and be heard by the person;

    (iii)   to take any specified procedural step in connection with the examination.

Consequently, if there is serious concern about how the examination is being conducted then the Minister could be asked to intervene.

Adoption of a local plan

7.57   To come into force a local plan has to be adopted by a resolution of the local planning authority.[345] Where the authority is a council, this decision will be taken by a meeting of all of the councillors: the full council.[346] Usually the local plan will be reported to the next scheduled meeting of the full council.[347]

Whilst going to the most important meeting of councillors, members do have limited choices. Their options are:

•   adopt the plan with any main modifications recommended by the Inspector and any non-material modifications they wish;

•   defer adoption of the plan whilst asking the Secretary of State to intervene under s 21 and so overrule the Inspector;

•   bring judicial review proceedings against the Inspector's report;

•   withdraw the plan.

Withdrawal of local development documents

7.58   An LDD can be withdrawn by the local planning authority at any time before adoption.[348] It had always been implicit that a draft plan could be withdrawn

---

[344] Planning and Compulsory Purchase Act 2004, s 20(6A), inserted by the Housing and Planning Act 2016, s 144.

[345] Planning and Compulsory Purchase Act 2004, s 23(5)

[346] See at para 7.59 (on functions and responsibilities).

[347] These tend to be held every six weeks to two months. For these reasons the average period between receipt of the Inspector's report and adoption is around 55 days: see LPEG report, p 13.

[348] Planning and Compulsory Purchase Act 2004, s 22(1).

or abandoned.[349] However, by the original 2004 Act provisions, an authority was not allowed withdraw a DPD once it had been submitted for independent examination unless either the inspector recommended withdrawal (and the Secretary of State did not overrule him) or the Secretary of State directed that it be withdrawn.[350] Consequently, a local planning authority could not unilaterally withdraw a DPD because it did not agree with the Inspector's recommendations.

The Localism Act 2011 lifted that restriction. A local plan document may be withdrawn by the local planning authority prior to adoption at any time. However, an authority would rarely withdraw a plan towards the end of an examination unless urged to do so by the Inspector. Withdrawal would abandon the entire plan or revision and require the authority to start again. It might therefore lose more good policies than the recommendations which it seeks to avoid. Jettisoning a plan may lead to government intervention or difficulties in planning appeals. If the issue arises from late changes in circumstances or government policy it may be better to adopt the plan and conduct an immediate and limited review.

As soon as reasonably practicable following the withdrawal of a local plan, notice must be given by making a statement available,[351] notifying the general consultation bodies and those specific consultation bodies who were invited to make representations and withdrawing the other available documents.[352] Removing the published documentation does not usually (and fortunately) occur. Whilst that is no longer part of a draft policy it is likely to be useful evidence for future planning policy and decisions.

The allocation of responsibilities within councils

7.59   Most English principal councils[353] operate executive arrangements whereby certain decisions have to be taken by the authority's executive (comprising a cabinet and, sometimes, an elected mayor) rather than by committees of councillors who are not on the executive.[354] The making of planning policy is an executive function.[355] However, certain steps in formulating or preparing a local plan or alterations to it are not to be the sole responsibility of the executive.[356] Such steps require a decision from all the council members siting together, what is known as full council.[357] The

---

[349] *R (on the application of Persimmon Homes (Thames Valley) Ltd) v North Hertfordshire DC* [2001] EWHC Admin 565, [2001] 1 WLR 2393, at para 23 per Collins J; approved by *R (on the application of Martin Grant Homes Ltd) v Wealden District Council* [2005] EWCA Civ 1221, [2006] JPL 583, at para 5, judgment of the Court, delivered by Mummery LJ.

[350] Planning and Compulsory Purchase Act 2004, s 22(2) (as originally enacted).

[351] In accordance with the Local Planning Regulations, reg 35.

[352] Local Planning Regulations, reg 27.

[353] That is, county, district and borough authorities.

[354] Local Government Act 2000, Pt 1A.

[355] It is not one of the planning functions which are prescribed as not being executive matters: Local Authorities (Functions and Responsibilities) (England) Regulations 2000, SI 2000/2853, Sch 1.

[356] Local Authorities (Functions and Responsibilities) (England) Regulations 2000, reg 4(1)(a), Sch 3.

[357] These responsibilities of the council (as distinct from the executive) may not be delegated to committees or officers under the Local Government Act 1972, s 101: see Local Authorities (Functions and Responsibilities) (England) Regulations 2000, reg 4(8).

approval of a local plan for submission to the Secretary of State[358] and its adoption are matters for the full council.[359]

The withdrawal or modification of a local plan is a matter for the executive if this is required by a ministerial direction or a recommendation of the examination inspector.[360] Otherwise it is a matter for the full council.[361]

Revocation of adopted documents

7.60   A local plan may only be revoked by the Secretary of State at the request of the local planning authority.[362] An authority may though revise the local plan or adopt a new plan which supersedes the existing plan.

If a local plan is revoked then the local planning authority must as soon as reasonably practical after the revocation:[363]

(a)   make a statement of the revocation available;

(b)   cease to have any other documents relating to the revoked local plan available; and

(c)   take any other steps they consider necessary to draw the revocation of the local plan to the attention of persons living or working in their area.

Revision of adopted documents

7.61   Authorities are under a general duty to keep their LDDs under review having regard to their surveying of their area.[364] The Neighbourhood Planning Act 2017 enables regulations to be made requiring local planning authorities to review LDDs at prescribed times.[365] Reviews are to be completed every five years from the adoption of the local plan or statement of community involvement.[366] As with the similar provisions in Wales and Northern Ireland,[367] a review is a consideration of whether the document should be changed. An authority might decide that no revisions are required, but otherwise it would have to start the revision process.

Section 26 of the Planning and Compulsory Purchase Act 2004 provides that a local planning authority may revise an LDD at any time.[368] However, the revision of a document is treated in the same way for the purpose of Pt 2 of the Act as its

---

[358]   Under the Planning and Compulsory Purchase Act 200, s 20.
[359]   Local Authorities (Functions and Responsibilities) (England) Regulations 2000, reg 4(1), (3)(ca), (d). Again, these powers cannot be delegated to officers or a committee: see reg 4(8), disapplying Local Government Act 1972, s 101.
[360]   Local Authorities (Functions and Responsibilities) (England) Regulations 2000, reg 4(4)(a).
[361]   Local Authorities (Functions and Responsibilities) (England) Regulations 2000, reg 4(4)(b).
[362]   Planning and Compulsory Purchase Act 2004, s 25.
[363]   Local Planning Regulations, reg 28. Availability in these provisions refers to making available in accordance with reg 35.
[364]   Planning and Compulsory Purchase Act 2004, s 17(6).
[365]   Planning and Compulsory Purchase Act 2004, s 17(6A)–(6C), inserted by the Neighbourhood Planning Act 2017, s 12.
[366]   Local Planning Regulations, reg 10A, inserted by the Town and Country Planning (Local Planning) (England) (Amendment) Regulations 2017, reg 4, from 6 April 2018.
[367]   See Chapters 14 and 17 below.
[368]   Planning and Compulsory Purchase Act 2004, s 26(1).

original preparation.[369] The preparation of the revision must therefore take place in accordance with the LDS.[370] An authority which proposes a revision should therefore amend its LDS to accommodate the change.

The Secretary of State may direct that an LDD is revised in accordance with a timetable which he directs.[371]

The local planning authority is also obliged to review every LDD if an enterprise zone scheme is made and prepare modifications as required.[372]

Secretary of State's default powers

7.62   The Secretary of State has several powers if he considers that a local planning authority is failing or omitting to do anything it is necessary for them to do in connection with the preparation, revision or adoption of a local plan.[373] The Minister may:

- prepare or revise the plan himself;

- give directions to the authority on what it must do;

- if there is a higher tier authority for the authority's area, invite it to prepare or revise the plan. This would be the Mayor of London, a combined authority or upper-tier county council.

Default powers had been included in s 27 when the 2004 Act was passed but there was some question whether they were workable. The section was comprehensively substituted by the Housing and Planning Act 2016 and the Minister enabled to authorise the Mayor of London and combined authorities to make the plans. This ability to have another authority for the area take over the plan was extended to county councils in the Neighbourhood Planning Act 2017.

In all cases these powers arise if the Minister considers that a local planning authority are 'failing or omitting to do anything it is necessary for them to do in connection with the preparation, revision or adoption of a development plan document'.[374]

If the Minister chooses to he may prepare or revise the local plan himself, holding an independent examination and publishing the recommendations and reasons of the examining Inspector.[375] Alternatively the Secretary of State may direct the local planning authority in relation to preparing or revising the plan and if so, must direct it to submit the plan for examination and publish the Inspector's recommendations and reasons.[376] Whether the plan has been prepared or revised by the Minister or the local planning authority under a direction, the Minister is able to approve the document (with or without modifications) or direct the authority 'to consider' adopting it.[377] The

---

[369] Planning and Compulsory Purchase Act 2004, s 26(3).
[370] Planning and Compulsory Purchase Act 2004, s 19(1).
[371] Planning and Compulsory Purchase Act 2004, s 26 (2).
[372] Planning and Compulsory Purchase Act 2004, s 26(4)–(7).
[373] These powers do not apply to SPDs and residual local development documents.
[374] Planning and Compulsory Purchase Act 2004, s 27(1).
[375] Planning and Compulsory Purchase Act 2004, s 27(2)(a), (3)(a), (4)(a).
[376] Planning and Compulsory Purchase Act 2004, s 27(2)(b), (3)(b), (4)(b).
[377] Planning and Compulsory Purchase Act 2004, s 27(5)(a), (b).

Secretary of State may also reject the plan if it was prepared by the local planning authority.[378] The Inspector will report on the plan's compliance with the legal and soundness tests, but without considering the duty to co-operate.[379]

The Minister must give reasons for any steps he takes under s 27.[380]

The local planning authority must reimburse the Secretary of State's costs incurred in connection with anything done in preparing or revising the local plan and which the authority had failed to do.[381]

The Secretary of State may invite the Mayor of London or a combined authority to prepare or revise the local plan within their area if he considers that the local planning authority 'are failing or omitting to do anything it is necessary for them to do in connection with the preparation, revision or adoption of a development plan document'.[382] The power is extended to upper tier county councils.[383] The appointed authority must hold an independent examination, publish the report and approve the document (with or without modifications) or direct the local planning authority to publish the report and consider adopting the plan.[384] The role of the examination in considering the legal compliance and soundness of the plan is unchanged, but leaves out consideration of the duty to co-operate.[385] The authority taking over the plan must give reasons when preparing or approving the plan.[386]

The costs of the exercise fall on the local planning authorities.[387]

Whilst the Secretary of State will have invited the Mayor of London, the combined authority or county council to sort out the failures of the local planning authority, the intervening bodies are not wholly trusted. The Minister has the usual array of powers to intervene on the default plans which they are preparing.[388]

Where the Secretary of State prepares a local plan under s 27 or the Mayor of London or a combined authority prepare a local plan under Sch A1, then various consequential

---

[378] Planning and Compulsory Purchase Act 2004, s 27(5)(c).
[379] Planning and Compulsory Purchase Act 2004, s 20(4)–(7C) as modified by s 27(6), (7).
[380] Planning and Compulsory Purchase Act 2004, s 27(8).
[381] Planning and Compulsory Purchase Act 2004, s 27(9). The Neighbourhood Planning Act 2017, s 9(4) will introduce a power to apportion these costs between authorities in the case of a joint plan: Planning and Compulsory Purchase Act 2004, s 27(10). In referring to a 'joint local development document or joint development plan document' in new sub-section (10) the former reference is superfluous as s 27 only applies to DPDs: s 27(1).
[382] Planning and Compulsory Purchase Act 2004, Sch A1, para 1 and 4 respectively.
[383] Planning and Compulsory Purchase Act 2004, Sch A1, para 7B, inserted by the Neighbourhood Planning Act 2017, Sch 2, para 4, from 15 January 2018. Consequential amendments are made to the Local Planning Regulations, regs 29, 31.
[384] Planning and Compulsory Purchase Act 2004, Sch A1, paras 2, 6 and para 7C for the Mayor, combined authority or county council respectively.
[385] Planning and Compulsory Purchase Act 2004, Sch A1, paras 3(1), 7(1) and para 7D(1).
[386] Planning and Compulsory Purchase Act 2004, Sch A1, paras 3(2), 7(2) and para 7D(2).
[387] Planning and Compulsory Purchase Act 2004, Sch A1, paras 3(3), (4), 7(3),(4) and para 7D(3), (4).
[388] Planning and Compulsory Purchase Act 2004, Sch A1, paras 8–12, amended by the Neighbourhood Planning Act 2017, Sch 2, paras 5–7. The Secretary of State may make a holding direction if he is considering intervening on these plans: Planning and Compulsory Purchase Act 2004, Sch A1, para 13, amended by the Neighbourhood Planning Act 2017, Sch 2, para 8.

amendments are made to the plan making power by the Local Planning Regulations 2012, Schs 1 and 2. These provisions were further amended when the default powers were extended to county councils.

STRATEGIC PLANNING AND JOINT LOCAL PLANS

7.63   Some issues cross local authority boundaries and merit a joint approach. For example, a housing market (reflecting where people seek to live and work) may include all or part of several district areas. Strategic planning – planning wider than individual districts – has a long and political history. The latest versions began with the 2004 which abolished structure plans (adopted by county councils, sometimes jointly with unitary authorities) and introduced statutory regional spatial strategies made by the Secretary of State drawing on the work of regional planning bodies. Those regional policies would often contain sub-regional policies. Greater London, by then, had the Mayor's London Plan. The 2004 Act also included various provisions allowing local planning authorities to prepare joint documents. The case for joint working was accentuated by the abolition of regional strategies by the Localism Act 2011. As part of those changes the duty to co-operate encouraged authorities to work together and consider joint plans. The joint planning mechanisms have been strengthened in later changes.

At the heart of this is strategic planning: the notation that there are some issues which benefit from a common approach by geographically and functionally linked local authorities. The relevant areas and issues will vary immensely across the country. One common grouping is the city-region where a historic city has long expanded into suburbs in other council areas and works with a wider hinterland of residents who work and shop in the city.

A strategic approach might be agreed between authorities in a non-plan document and then promoted by each participant in its own local plan process. An example would be a group of authorities agreeing a total housing requirement and how it is divided amongst them. With that concordat they would then prepare their local plans. Alternatively the group of authorities could prepare a joint local plan to address those issues, leaving detailed policies and smaller sites to individual district wide local plans. In London and some combined authorities the strategic approach will be set out in spatial development strategies.

Joint local development documents

7.64   Two or more local planning authorities may prepare joint LDDs under the Planning and Compulsory Purchase Act 2004, s 28. There are two means of preparing such documents, with different legal and decision making consequences. The first is for the authorities to prepare a joint document where decisions are taken by each authority. Subject to certain requirements the result has been treated as the adoption of identical, but legally separate, plans for each of the authority areas. The second method is available only in two-tier areas and is the making of a joint plan by a joint committee (including the county council). The joint committee will become the local planning authority for those purposes. That does produce a single document.

In the former case the authorities will need to agree to prepare one or more joint documents.[389] The provisions of the 2004 Act apply for any step which may be or is required to be taken for a joint document as it applies to a single-authority document.[390] Additionally 'anything which must be done by or in relation to a local planning authority in connection with a LDD must be done by or in relation to each of the authorities'.[391] So a joint local plan will need to be specified in each authority's LDS.[392]

However, each authority will carry out the steps in relation to its own area in conjunction, but with separate legal effects. For example, resolutions to adopt a joint local plan will be passed at separate meetings by each authority. The likelihood is the meetings will be on different days.[393] Unless each authority's resolution is conditional upon the others or defers the adoption, the joint plan will be adopted at different times in the particular areas. Consequently, the periods for bringing High Court challenges will not expire on the same date.[394] This issue arose in *Wealden District Council v Secretary of State for Communities and Local Government*[395] where a joint core strategy had been adopted on different dates by two authorities, Lewes District Council and the South Downs National Park Authority. Jay J held that adoption was not step which must be undertaken because it is a matter of discretion so each decision could operate separately.[396] He considered that:[397]

> 'The whole structure of Part 2 of the 2004 Act is predicated on a development plan document being the development plan for the relevant local planning authority, which means that authority's geographical area. In the present case, the JCS became the development plan document for LDC's area once adopted by LDC; it did not become the development plan document for SDNPA's area until it was adopted by SDNPA. Conceptually and juridically, therefore, the JCS had a separate status before it was adopted by both authorities; and, I would add, thereafter – it continues to apply to each authority's area on a discrete basis.'

For example, an action area plan or SPD could be prepared for a development area which crosses administrative boundaries or all district councils within a county could prepare common policies on housing design.

Joint committees

7.65 However, s 28 does not permit the involvement of non-unitary county councils. The counties can only be involved in a joint committee under s 29. A joint

---

[389] Planning and Compulsory Purchase Act 2004, s 28(1). In local authorities, the agreement must be reached by the full councils not by the executive, a committee or officers: see Local Authorities (Functions and Responsibilities) (England) Regulations 2000, reg 4(1), (4A), (4C(a)), (7).
[390] Planning and Compulsory Purchase Act 2004, s 28(2).
[391] Planning and Compulsory Purchase Act 2004, s 28(3).
[392] *Wealden District Council v Secretary of State for Communities and Local Government* [2017] EWHC 351 (Admin), [2017] Env LR 31, at para 78 per Jay J.
[393] Councils adopt plans at meetings of the full council and it is unlikely that special meetings will be called (let alone held simultaneously) for that purpose.
[394] This was treated as being the case in *Calverton Parish Council v Nottingham City Council* [2015] EWHC 503 (Admin), [2015] PTSR 1130, at paras 12–15 per Lewis J where the issue was whether a challenge to a joint local plan was out of time in respect of the earliest authority to adopt it.
[395] [2017] EWHC 351 (Admin), [2017] Env LR 31.
[396] And so was within s 28(2) rather than 28(3): see paras 78–81.
[397] At para 82. Consequently, the proceedings were brought in time against one authority and out of time in respect of the other so the Court only had power to quash the plan for the 'in time' area: para 121.

committee may be formed under s 29 in areas which are two tier: having both a county and a district council. The committee must include the county council (or county councils if the area straddles a county boundary) and the local planning authorities for the area.[398] The agreement must specify the matters that the committee is responsible for.[399] If agreement is reached, the Secretary of State may by order constitute the joint committee as the local planning authority.[400] The Secretary of State still has discretion whether to make the order and it is subject to the negative resolution procedure in Parliament.

Six orders have been made, establishing joint committees in parts of Bedfordshire, Cambridgeshire, Lincolnshire and Northamptonshire.[401] The committees consist of a small number of councillors from each authority, which has included county councils, and are able to co-opt non-voting members.

The only means of creating a joint committee to submit or adopt a local plan is under this provision. These are non-executive functions, which are reserved to the full council and cannot be exercised jointly with another authority or by a committee or joint committee.[402]

Section 29 is the only means of including non-unitary councils amongst those making non-minerals and waste plans. They are not included in local planning authorities for the purpose of s 28.[403]

Having secured the order, the constituent authorities can extend the joint committee's geographical and subject remit by agreement.[404] Implicitly the additional area must be within the areas of the local authorities. It is a curiosity of what are obscurely drafted provisions that an order appears to be required to set up the local planning authority for a particular area and matters, but its geographical remit can be extended by agreement without any further order.[405] However, the rules governing the joint committee, such as composition are prescribed in the order and further authorities cannot be added to the joint committee by agreement alone. Any enlargement of area or matter comes into force once all of the constituent authorities and the joint committee have revised their LDS in accordance with the agreement.[406]

The Secretary of State may revoke the order constituting the joint committee at the request of a constituent authority either generally or for any matter.[407] The local planning authorities will then revert to the original authorities or any new joint committee made by order.

---

[398] See Planning and Compulsory Purchase Act 2004, s 29(1).
[399] Planning and Compulsory Purchase Act 2004, s 29(1).
[400] Planning and Compulsory Purchase Act 2004, s 29(2).
[401] North Northamptonshire Joint Committee Order 2005, Luton and South Bedfordshire Joint Committee Order 2007, West Northamptonshire Joint Committee Order 2008, Cambridge City Fringes Joint Committee Order 2009, Central Lincolnshire Joint Strategic Planning Committee Order 2009, South East Lincolnshire Joint Strategic Planning Committee Order 2011.
[402] See Local Authorities (Functions and Responsibilities) (England) Regulations 2000, reg 4(1), (3), (7) which disapplies the Local Government Act 1972, s 101 in respect of such decisions.
[403] See Planning and Compulsory Purchase Act 2004, s 37(4).
[404] Planning and Compulsory Purchase Act 2004, s 30.
[405] The extension power in s 30 is entitled 'additional functions' and the legislation says that the order constitutes the joint committee: Planning and Compulsory Purchase Act 2004, ss 29(2), 31(1).
[406] Planning and Compulsory Purchase Act 2004, s 30(2), (3).
[407] Planning and Compulsory Purchase Act 2004, s 31(1).

In some circumstances steps in the preparation of LDDs or LDSs will be counted towards the preparation of new documents or schemes by successor authorities.[408] To be able to be applied such a new document must not relate to the area of any local planning authority which had requested the revocation of the order.[409] Previous steps on a joint committee local plan or SPD can count as steps for a new document in a 'remainer' area if the new document has substantially the same effect on that area as the original document did.[410]

Any independent examination which is underway at the time of revocation will be suspended,[411] but the Secretary of State may direct that it is resumed to consider the corresponding document if a local planning authority (but not a new joint committee) request.[412] Resumption of the examination must be requested within three months of the revocation.[413]

In local authorities operating executive arrangements, any agreement to establish a joint committee or to extend its area or scope or any request for the revocation of a joint committee order has to be determined by the full council.[414]

Transitional provisions

7.66   Many development plans were in the process of review or alteration when the 2004 Act came into force. Schedule 8 allowed the adoption of deposited plans, although some of the new Act's procedures were applied.

If proposals for a structure plan replacement or alteration were deposited[415] before 28 September 2004 the Town and Country Planning Act 1990 continued to apply and they could be adopted. The report of the examination in public was not binding on the local planning authority. Any proposals at an earlier stage could not be adopted and would have 'have no effect'.[416]

Unitary development plan or local plan proposals which had not been placed on deposit by 28 September 2004 could not be adopted and again had no effect.[417] Where these proposals had been placed on deposit and there were no objections or an inspector had been appointed to hold an inquiry prior to 28 September 2004 the unitary development plan or local plan could proceed to adoption in accordance with the 1990 Act.[418]

Where unitary development plans or local plans have reached first deposit stage but either there were objections or no Inspector had been appointed, the plans could

---

[408] Planning and Compulsory Purchase Act 2004, s 31(3). Successor authorities are local planning authorities or a new joint committee.

[409] Local Planning Regulations, reg 33(2)(a).

[410] Local Planning Regulations, reg 33(2)(b).

[411] Planning and Compulsory Purchase Act 2004, s 31(5)

[412] Planning and Compulsory Purchase Act 2004, s 31(6).

[413] Local Planning Regulations, reg 33(1).

[414] Local Authorities (Functions and Responsibilities) (England) Regulations 2000, reg 4(1), (4A), (4C) (b)–(d), (7) which disapply the Local Government Act 1972, s 101.

[415] Under the Town and Country Planning Act 1990, s 33(2).

[416] Planning and Compulsory Purchase Act 2004, Sch 8, para 2.

[417] Planning and Compulsory Purchase Act 2004, Sch 8, paras 3 and 8 respectively.

[418] Planning and Compulsory Purchase Act 2004, Sch 8, paras 4 and 9 respectively.

proceed under the revised 1990 Act procedures.[419] The plan would be re-deposited before proceeding to an inquiry. The local planning authority was required to follow the recommendations of the inspector and may not promote changes after the inquiry.[420]

A transitional period was introduced for existing development plan policies with the intention of giving local planning authorities a limited time to prepare new plans. This period was three years from the commencement of the new regime on 28 September 2004 or, if earlier, when existing 'old' policies were expressly replaced by new policies.[421] Old style plans which were adopted after 28 September 2004 would have a life of three years from the date of adoption.[422] The consequence was that at the end of the period the old policies would cease to be part of the development plan. They would be treated at that point as expired.

In case new plans were not in place by 2007, the Secretary of State was empowered to 'direct that for the purposes of such policies as are specified in the direction [the three-year period] does not apply'.[423] However few DPDs had been adopted by September 2007 and even then they did not entirely replace the existing plans. Consequently, numerous saving directions were made, some of which are still relevant as a full set of 2004 Act documents is not in place in every area.

The Ministerial directions have referred only to particular saved policies (rather than saving a plan in its entirety) but also save the reasoned justification for those policies.

In *R (on the application of Cherkley Campaign Ltd) v Mole Valley District Council*[424] the Secretary of State's direction saving a policy in a 2000 local plan also saved the reasoned justification associated with that policy. Richards LJ held:[425]

> 'To blue-pencil the supporting text would risk altering the meaning of the policy, which cannot have been the legislative intention. It seems to me that the true effect of the statutory provisions was to save not just the bare words of the policy but also any supporting text relevant to the interpretation of the policy, so that the policy would continue with unchanged meaning and effect until replaced by a new policy.'

A saving direction will also preserve any parts of the adopted policies map which relate to the saved policies.[426]

[419] Planning and Compulsory Purchase Act 2004, Sch 8, paras 5(1) and 10(1) respectively. Local planning authorities retained their implicit power to withdraw a proposed development plan: *R (on the application of Martin Grant Homes Ltd) v Wealden District Council* [2005] EWCA Civ 1221, at para 38 judgment of the Court, delivered by Mummery LJ.
[420] Planning and Compulsory Purchase Act 2004, Sch 8, paras 5(4), (5) and 10(4), (5) respectively.
[421] Planning and Compulsory Purchase Act 2004, Sch 8, para 1(2).
[422] Planning and Compulsory Purchase Act 2004, Sch 8, paras 2(4), 6, 12 and see *Martin Grant*, at para 52. The Court of Appeal was concerned that the wording of Sch 8, para 1 meant that such old style but post-September 2004 plans would not cease to have effect when new style policies were adopted: see paras 51–53.
[423] Planning and Compulsory Purchase Act 2004, Sch 8, para 1(3).
[424] [2014] EWCA Civ 567, [2014] 2 EGLR 98.
[425] At para 18.
[426] *Fox Land and Property Ltd v Secretary of State for Communities and Local Government* [2015] EWCA Civ 298, at paras 27–30 per Richards LJ.

Urban Development Corporations

7.67   Urban Development Corporations ('UDCs') have in the past been given development control powers but not powers to prepare development plans. This distinction was maintained in the 2004 Act. The local authorities remain responsible for preparing the LDF. However, the Secretary of State may direct under s 33 that Pt 2 of the 2004 Act does not apply to the area of an UDC.[427] In those cases, the local planning authorities will not be able to produce LDDs for those areas.

In 2004, Opposition amendments proposed that UDCs have to prepare SCIs for the exercise of their development control functions.[428] The government resisted those proposals. The minister explained that Planning Policy Statements would expect UDCs to apply relevant community involvement principles and that UDCs would be expected by government to follow the relevant local authority's SCI for consulting on planning applications.[429]

Monitoring reports

7.68   Section 35 requires each local planning authority[430] to prepare monitoring reports on the implementation of their LDS and the extent to which the policies in their LDDs are being achieved.[431]

As originally enacted these required an annual report to be made to the Secretary of State but this was repealed by the Localism Act 2011.[432] The report must still be produced as prescribed, but at least every 12 months.[433]

The report will set out the documents in the LDS, the LDS's timetable for their adoption and the stage reached. If documents are behind the timetable an explanation of the reasons must be given and a timetable, which may be revised, given for the remaining steps in the process, and the title and date of any adopted or approved document.[434] The regulations require these details to be given of both local plans and SPDs, however, the latter requirement appears to be an error as SPDs no longer need to be specified in LDSs.[435]

If the local planning authority 'are not implementing a policy' in a local plan they should say so in the report, give reasons why not and the steps (if any) they intend to take to secure that the policy is implemented.[436] As the local planning authority has no power to simply disapply or ignore the development plan, non-implementation would seem to relate to positive policies of steps the authority will take and possibly to whether targets are being met. The language is obscure.

---

[427] Planning and Compulsory Purchase Act 2004, s 33.
[428] See Lords Hansard, 24 February 2004, Col. 220-223.
[429] Letter from Rt Hon Jeff Rooker to Baroness Hanham, 22 March 2004. A copy is in the House of Lords Library.
[430] Including county councils with respect to their waste and minerals responsibilities: Planning and Compulsory Purchase Act 2004, s 16(3).
[431] Planning and Compulsory Purchase Act 2004, s 35.
[432] Localism Act 2011, s 113 and Sch 25(17), para 1.
[433] Planning and Compulsory Purchase Act 2004, s 35(2)(a).
[434] Local Planning Regulations, reg 34(1).
[435] Planning and Compulsory Purchase Act 2004, s 15(2).
[436] Local Planning Regulations, reg 34(2).

Where the local planning authority have determined that policies to address their strategic priorities are set out in the London Plan or a combined authority's spatial development strategy then the report will identify where in those documents the policies are.[437]

Local planning authorities are required to report on compliance with any local plan figures for net additional dwellings or net additional affordable dwellings in the authority's area or any part of it.[438] The monitoring report will specify the number provided in the period of the report and since the plan's adoption.[439]

In terms of plan preparation or revision, the report must give details of any actions they have taken to work with other authorities under the duty to co-operate during the period of the report.[440] This includes co-operation in respect of other authorities' plans.

Any neighbourhood development plan or neighbourhood development order made by the authority must be detailed in the report.[441] The Local Planning Regulations 2012 have dropped the requirement to set out title of any local development order adopted, with the reasons for making the order and a statement of the effect of the order.[442]

A charging authority for community infrastructure levy ('CIL') purposes[443] is required to produce a report each financial year in which it collects CIL. CIL is collected on its behalf or it has CIL which has not been spent.[444] The mandatory parts of the report have to be included in the monitoring report prepared under the Local Planning Regulations 2012.[445] The Regulations seem to envisage that there will still be two separate reports, although they could be combined. The CIL material which must be in the monitoring report is:[446]

- the total CIL receipts for the reported year;

- the total CIL expenditure for the reported year;

- summary details of CIL expenditure during the reported year (other CIL repaid by local councils or retained by the charging authority because there was no local council) including—

   (i) the items of infrastructure to which CIL (including land payments) has been applied,

---

[437] Planning and Compulsory Purchase Act 2004, s 35(3A)–(3C), inserted by the Neighbourhood Planning Act 2017, s 8(3).
[438] Local Planning Regulations, reg 34(3).
[439] Local Planning Regulations, reg 34(3)(a),(b).
[440] Local Planning Regulations, reg 34(6). This includes co-operation in respect of other authorities' plans.
[441] Local Planning Regulations, reg 34(4). The Regulations do not say whether this is simply those plans or orders made in the report period, but it is helpful to have a comprehensive list of such documents in any event.
[442] Cf Local Development Regulations 2004, reg 48(3)(e), (f).
[443] Usually the district local planning authority and the Mayor of London: Planning Act 2008, s 206(5)(a), applying with modifications the Planning and Compulsory Purchase Act 2004, s 37.
[444] Community Infrastructure Levy Regulations 2010, SI 2010/948, reg 62(1).
[445] Local Planning Regulations, reg 35(5).
[446] Community Infrastructure Levy Regulations, reg 62(4).

(ii)   the amount of CIL expenditure on each item,

(iii)   the amount of CIL applied to repay money borrowed, including any interest, with details of the infrastructure items which that money was used to provide (wholly or in part),

(iv)   the amount of CIL applied to administrative expenses, including as a percentage of CIL collected in that year;

- the amount of CIL passed to any local council and any person for the purpose of providing infrastructure;

- summary details of the receipt and expenditure of CIL repaid by local councils or retained by the charging authority because there was no local council[447] during the reported year including the total CIL receipts, the items they have been spent on and the expenditure on each item;

- summary details of any notices served requiring repayments from local councils for not spending the receipts, including the total value of CIL receipts requested from each local council and any sums not recovered;

- the total amount of CIL receipts retained at the end of the year, distinguishing between those received in the current and previous years and those repaid by local councils or retained by the charging authority because there was no local council and all other receipts; and

- the items of infrastructure to which the infrastructure payments accepted by the charging authority relate and their amount.

The authority must make the monitoring report available to the public.[448] There is no requirement as to how this is made available, but it would usually be put on the authority's website.[449]

Monitoring reports must be considered in a wider context. The authority is required to keep under review matters which may affect the planning of its area.[450] Where the local plan or other LDD was subject to strategic environmental assessment then the local planning authority must 'monitor the significant environmental effects of the implementation of each plan or programme with the purpose of identifying unforeseen adverse effects at an early stage and being able to undertake appropriate remedial action'.[451] The local plan will include monitoring requirements to judge how its policies are being implemented and to determine whether further action should be taken, such as releasing reserve sites and being a plan review. That information has to be assembled and ought to be published.

Local planning authorities should therefore consider what information they need to have to guide the planning of their area, what legislation requires them to have and what can be collected in a practical and proportional way.

---

[447]   Community Infrastructure Levy Regulations, regs 59E, 59F.
[448]   Planning and Compulsory Purchase Act 2004, s 35(4).
[449]   Publication on the website was the single requirement of the Local Development Regulations 2004, reg 48(8).
[450]   Planning and Compulsory Purchase Act 2004, ss 13, 14, see 7.22 above.
[451]   SEA Regulations, reg 17(1).

A separate obligation on local planning authorities is to make available 'any up-to-date information, which they have collected for monitoring purposes',[452] such as housing and employment provision data. This must be published on their website and be open for inspection at the authority's principal offices and any other locations they choose.[453]

---

[452] Local Planning Regulations, reg 34(7).
[453] Local Planning Regulations, reg 34(7), applying reg 35.

Chapter 8

Brownfield Land Registers

8.1   A brownfield land register is kept by a local planning authority in England and shows previously developed land which it considers to be suitable for housing development. The register is in two parts: Part 1 lists all sites; whilst Part 2 gives planning consent 'permission in principle' for development of identified sites. Whilst referred to as a register, there is a considerable amount of judgment left to the local planning authority as to whether land should be included on the register and a further discretion whether to grant permission in principle.

The origin of the brownfield register is in the Housing and Planning Act 2016 which introduced a new form of planning permission as 'permission in principle'. This would be granted either automatically upon the inclusion of proposals in particular planning documents or by an application to the local planning authority in respect of particular sites and uses identified in planning policy. In bringing forward the 2016 Act the government's intention was that the planning documents which could grant permission in principle would be a new brownfield land register, local plans and neighbourhood development plans. So far, the power has just been included in brownfield land registers and it is not apparent whether it will be extended to parts of the development plan.

Brownfield land registers are provided for by the Planning and Compulsory Purchase Act 2004, s 14A and the Town and Country Planning (Brownfield Land Register) Regulations 2017[1] ('Brownfield Land Register Regulations'). Permission in principle is granted for land in Part 2 of the brownfield land register by the Town and Country Planning (Permission in Principle) Order 2017 ('Permission in Principle Order'). The current Ministerial guidance is *Brownfield registers and permission in principle: frequently asked questions.*[2]

On 16 April 2017, the duty to establish brownfield land registers was introduced[3] and local planning authorities[4] are required to publish their registers by 31 December 2017.[5]

---

[1]   SI 2017/403.
[2]   21 April 2017.
[3]   Brownfield Land Register Regulations, reg 1.
[4]   Local planning authorities have the same meaning as in the remainder of Pt 2 of the Planning and Compulsory Purchase Act 2004: district and London borough councils, unitary county councils, the Broads Authority, any National Park authority and any orders making a Mayoral development corporation or the Homes and Communities Agency a local planning authority: Planning and Compulsory Purchase Act 2004, s 37(4)–(5B).
[5]   Brownfield Land Register Regulations, reg 3(2).

Grant of permission in principle by development order

8.2   Permission in principle could derive from two routes: grant by a development order or grant on application to the local planning authority. Permission in principle would be followed by a 'technical details consent' which together would be the equivalent of a full planning permission. Planning conditions would be imposed at the technical details consent stage.

The first route is for permission in principle to be granted by a development order in relation to land which is allocated for development in a qualifying document.[6] A 'qualifying document' is a 'plan, register or other document … made, maintained or adopted' by a local planning authority, of a prescribed description, which 'indicates that the land in question is allocated for development for the purposes of this section' and which contains 'prescribed particulars in relation to the land allocated and the kind of development for which it is allocated'.[7] 'Adopted' can encompass a local plan, whilst neighbourhood development plans are 'made' by the local planning authority. 'Maintained' is intended for registers of land (now brownfield land registers) required by the Planning and Compulsory Purchase Act 2004, s 14A. Permission in principle is granted for land allocated in Part 2 of the brownfield land register.[8]

In addition to the brownfield land register, it was anticipated that permission in principle would be granted to allocations within particular categories in local plans or neighbourhood development plans. Those powers have not yet been brought into force. Such a document would have to allocate the land for the purposes of permission in principle,[9] so existing allocations will not have that effect.

The second route is intended to be by an application for permission in principle for certain categories and sizes of development. These are envisaged as being for residential development of up to 10 units, the intention being to make it less expensive for small site developers to obtain planning certainty for funding purposes.

So far the power has solely been used for brownfield land registers.

Permission in principle takes effect when Part 2 of the register takes effect or the land is subsequently allocated there[10] unless the local planning authority directs that it takes effect on another date.[11] Permission in principle granted by a development order, such as following inclusion in the register, ceases to have effect after five years beginning with the date of the entry or any other period directed by the local planning authority.[12]

BROWNFIELD LAND REGISTERS

8.3   Under s 14A of the Planning and Compulsory Purchase Act 2004 local planning authorities are required to prepare, maintain and publish a register of

---

[6]   See the Town and Country Planning Act 1990, s 59A(1)(a).
[7]   Town and Country Planning Act 1990, s 59A(2).
[8]   Town and Country Planning (Permission in Principle) Order 2017, SI 2017/402, art 4.
[9]   Town and Country Planning Act 1990, s 59A(2).
[10]   Town and Country Planning Act 1990, s 59A(4).
[11]   Town and Country Planning (Permission in Principle) Order 2017, art 5.
[12]   Town and Country Planning Act 1990, s 59A(7).

land which is of a prescribed description or which satisfies prescribed criteria.[13] Regulations would prescribe when land has to be included and also where local planning authorities have a discretion whether to include it, or indeed any power to exclude land which would otherwise be included.[14] In exercising its functions under the Brownfield Land Register Regulations, the local planning authority must have regard to the development plan and national policies and advice issued by the Secretary of State and any other guidance issued by the Minister for the purpose of the register.[15]

Whilst s 14A has been drafted in very wide times, it was always envisaged that the registration duty would require the creation of a brownfield register of previously developed land which was suitable for housing development.[16]

Each local planning authority is required to prepare and maintain a brownfield land register. The register shows previously developed land within the authority's area[17] which meets all of the following criteria:[18]

(a)   the land has an area of at least 0.25 hectares or is capable of supporting at least five dwellings;

(b)   the land is suitable for residential development;

(c)   the land is available for residential development; and

(d)   residential development of the land is achievable.

There is a discretion to add sites to Part 1 of the register if they are below the 0.25 hectare and five dwelling thresholds.[19]

Sites are added to Part 2 (and so receive permission in principle) if they meet these criteria (or the smaller sites discretion is exercised in their favour) and the authority decide to allocate the land for development in that Part.[20]

The meaning of previously developed land and the terms in the criteria can be considered in turn.

Previously developed land

8.4   Previously developed land is as defined in the National Planning Policy Framework ('NPPF') 'as it has effect from time to time'.[21] It is therefore in the relatively unusual, but not unique, position of being a statutory test which can be

---

13   Planning and Compulsory Purchase Act 2004, s 14A(1).
14   Planning and Compulsory Purchase Act 2004, s 14A(4).
15   Planning and Compulsory Purchase Act 2004, s 14A(7),(8). The presumption in the Planning and Compulsory Purchase Act 2004, s 38(6) that where regard is to be had to the development plan when making determinations under the planning Acts then decisions will be taken in accordance with that plan unless material considerations indicate otherwise does not apply as those Acts are the 1990 legislation and do not include the 2004 Act: Planning and Compulsory Purchase Act 2004, s 117.
16   Explanatory Notes to Housing and Planning Bill 2015, First Reading, House of Commons, para 262.
17   Brownfield Land Register Regulations, reg 3(1).
18   Brownfield Land Register Regulations, reg 4(1).
19   Brownfield Land Register Regulations, reg 5(3).
20   Brownfield Land Register Regulations, reg 5(2), (4).
21   Brownfield Land Register Regulations, reg 2(1).

changed by government policy. The NPPF's definition of previously developed land is:[22]

'Land which is or was occupied by a permanent structure, including the curtilage of the developed land (although it should not be assumed that the whole of the curtilage should be developed) and any associated fixed surface infrastructure. This excludes: land that is or has been occupied by agricultural or forestry buildings; land that has been developed for minerals extraction or waste disposal by landfill purposes where provision for restoration has been made through development control procedures; land in built-up areas such as private residential gardens, parks, recreation grounds and allotments; and land that was previously-developed but where the remains of the permanent structure or fixed surface structure have blended into the landscape in the process of time.'

The term 'curtilage' covers land and buildings which are 'part and parcel' of the land comprised with a building.[23] The critical point is that curtilage land is associated with a building. Curtilage is not necessarily confined to a small area around a building.[24] However, the curtilage of the buildings on a large open site, such as a former airfield, may be a limited part of the space.

The exclusion of 'is or has been occupied by agricultural or forestry buildings' does not include former agricultural or forestry buildings which have been put in another lawful use.[25] If land in 'private residential gardens, parks, recreation grounds and allotments' would otherwise be previously developed as containing structures or being within their curtilage, then it is only excluded if it is within a built up area.[26] Whilst literally correct, treating a rural domestic garden as previously developed land when an urban garden is not encourages significantly increased built development in the countryside and that wording is ripe for revision.

It must be implicit that the factors which make land previously developed must be lawfully present, otherwise a person may benefit from an unlawful and reversible state of affairs.

An area of at least 0.25 hectares or capable of supporting at least five dwellings

8.5   The register is not concerned with the smallest sites but in this criterion the net is thrown wide. A 20 dwellings per hectare capacity is low density so many sub-0.25 hectare sites are able to be included. The five dwellings[27] would appear to be the final figure following redevelopment, rather than net additional dwellings as the question at this point is the capacity of the land.

---

[22] NPPF, Annex 2: Glossary.
[23] *Methuen-Campbell v Walters* [1979] QB 525, at 543 per Buckley LJ.
[24] *Skerritts of Nottingham Ltd v Secretary of State for the Environment, Transport and the Regions* [2001] QB 59.
[25] *R (on the application of Lee Valley Regional Park Authority) v Broxbourne Borough Council* [2015] EWHC 185 (Admin), at para 38 per Ouseley J.
[26] *Dartford Borough Council v Secretary of State for Communities and Local Government* [2017] EWCA Civ 141, [2017] PTSR 737, at para 9 per Lewison LJ.
[27] Dwellings include flats: Brownfield Land Register Regulations, reg 2(1).

8.6   *Brownfield Land Registers*

Suitable for residential development

8.6   Residential development means 'development the main purpose of which is housing development'.[28] Housing development is 'development for the provision of dwellings'.[29]

Suitability covers sites which have already been supported for residential development or alternatively a judgment made by the local planning authority in compiling the register. In the former category, land is suitable if it is allocated in a local development plan document for residential development or has planning permission or permission in principle for such development.[30] Allocations do not therefore include sites allocated in neighbourhood development plans or spatial development strategies.[31] To maintain the rigour of the planning process, allocation must mean allocation in an adopted local plan, rather than being in a draft. Similarly 'has' permission requires a current planning permission is which is capable lawfully of being carried out, subject to the grant of any further approvals under conditions. Where planning permission was previously granted for residential development, but the time limits for carrying it out have expired, then it would be incorrect to say that it 'has' permission. Such a site may now be profoundly unsuitable for housing and ought to be considered afresh. Where development has been completed under a planning permission it would again be incorrect to say that the land has planning permission for residential development. The register is looking forward to the carrying out of development, not merely noting what has happened.

Alternatively land is suitable if the local planning authority consider it is appropriate for residential development. The authority is required to have regard to any adverse impact on the natural environment, the local built environment, including in particular on heritage assets,[32] and any adverse impact on local amenity which the development might cause for intended occupiers of the development or occupiers of neighbouring properties.[33] Appropriateness is not confined to consideration of these factors but would include all relevant planning considerations. This would include other planning impacts (such as the loss of employment land) as well as any benefits of residential development and housing requirements and supply. A judgement is to be reached having regard to the development plan and national policy, applying the statutory presumption in favour of the plan.[34] The brownfield land register is intended to be a speedy means of identifying and sometimes approving land for housing development, not a mechanism to bypass proper and conventional planning judgment.

The authority is required to have regard to relevant representations, which are those received in the statutory consultation period and which are relevant to the definition, which includes in the present criterion whether it is appropriate for residential development.

---

[28]   Brownfield Land Register Regulations, reg 2(1).
[29]   Brownfield Land Register Regulations, reg 2(1).
[30]   Brownfield Land Register Regulations, reg 4(2).
[31]   Planning and Compulsory Purchase Act 2004, s 37(2).
[32]   Heritage assets are World Heritage Sites, scheduled monuments, listed buildings, conservation areas, registered parks or gardens, conservation areas and any 'building, monument, site, place, area or landscape which has been identified by the local planning authority as having heritage interest': Brownfield Land Register Regulations, reg 4(2). The local built environment is wider than heritage interests.
[33]   Brownfield Land Register Regulations, reg 4(2).
[34]   Planning and Compulsory Purchase Act 2004, s 14A(7),(8).

Available for residential development

8.7   A site is available for residential development where all of the owners or the developer of the site have demonstrated an intention to carry out residential development on it or the local planning authority considers that there are no ownership or legal impediments to residential development.

An owner is a person who is the estate owner in fee simple (usually the freeholder) or who has a tenancy with at least 15 years remaining.[35] The developer is the developer in control of the land.[36] Usually that control will be demonstrated by an option or conditional contract for the freehold or long leasehold acquisition of the site. The requisite intention is for the owners to sell or develop the land and for a developer to develop the land. Implicitly the intended development must be for residential development.

Whether someone is an owner or developer is determined 42 days before the date on which the land is added to Part 1 of the register.[37]

The owners or the developer must have expressed the requisite intention not more than 21 days before the register entry is made. In practice that requires a written statement has to be sent to the local planning authority as part of preparing the register. As well as the expressed intention, there must be 'no evidence indicating a change to that intention', having regard to information publicly available or relevant representations received.[38] That concerns evidence about the intention rather than scepticism about whether the site could or would be developed which arises under the achievability of residential development criterion. Of course, evidence may or may not be persuasive. To shut a site out of the register, the evidence would need to be cogent. It may be that the issue of intention is to be determined on the balance of probabilities if there is a conflict between an expressed intention and other evidence.

The other basis for finding land available is the local planning authority's assessment of whether there are 'no issues relating to the ownership of the land or other legal impediments which might prevent residential development'.[39] In reaching a conclusion the authority will have to consider representations made and also Land Registry information not just on ownership but also other interests, including easements and covenants affecting the land. Unless the land is inalienable[40] a person with the benefit of a property right may agree to transfer or dispose of it to allow a development to proceed. The local planning authority has therefore to consider the likelihood of those persons agreeing. This will include any representations which they have made but also making an objective assessment of the likelihood of the site being made available. A broadbrush viability exercise may indicate whether it makes economic sense to redevelop it for housing.

---

[35]   Brownfield Land Register Regulations, reg 4(2). Whether persons with the benefit of easements or covenants support the development of the site is not relevant to this test of availability.
[36]   Brownfield Land Register Regulations, reg 4(2).
[37]   See Brownfield Land Register Regulations, regs 2(1), 4(2).
[38]   Brownfield Land Register Regulations, reg 4(2). Consideration of other information is not prohibited, but would need to be handled fairly.
[39]   Brownfield Land Register Regulations, reg 4(2).
[40]   As some National Trust property is. National Trust Act 1907, s 21; National Trust Act 1939, s 8.

The authority has to consider whether residential development 'might' be prevented. That does not involve a certainty that it will not happen, but conversely there cannot be certainty that ownership issues will allow a residential development to take place. Might suggests a chance which is less than a probability.

Whether residential development is achievable

8.8   Achievable means that in the opinion of the local planning authority 'the development is likely to take place within 15 years of the entry date'.[41] Since suitability is considered in another criterion, this will involve a judgment as to the likelihood of a developer wishing to and being able to bring forward whatever housing development is acceptable given the viability of such development, any infrastructure constraints and the possibility of overcoming any such obstacles. As with 'might' under the availability test, the percentage chance involved in a development being 'likely' is unclear. However, it will not go down to the small prospects which are 'likely' in environmental impact assessment.[42]

Both the availability and achievability tests illustrate that the role of the brownfield land register is to identify suitable developments which are likely to come forward rather than cluttering up planning with purely theoretical sites.

THE DETAILS ON THE REGISTER

8.9   The information included in the register sets out what the Part 1 entry describes or what a Part 2 entry grants permission in principle for.[43] The preparation of the register has to be carried out in an adequate manner to determine those matters.

In addition to the basic details including a plan which identifies the land (so showing its boundaries), the register must show for Part 1 land:

- the size of the site in hectares;

- whether it is in public authority ownership, mixed (public/private) ownership, not owned by a public authority or all or part of the ownership is unknown;

- whether the land is permissioned (and if so the type of permission[44]), not permissioned or pending decision;[45]

---

[41]   Brownfield Land Register Regulations, reg 4(2).
[42]   More than a bare possibility: *R (on the application of Bateman) v South Cambridgeshire District Council* [2011] EWCA Civ 157, at para 17 per Moore-Bick LJ.
[43]   Brownfield Land Register Regulations, reg 15, Sch 2.
[44]   Permissions may be full planning permission, outline planning permission, reserved matters approval, permission in principle, technical details consent, planning permission granted under a local development order, a mayoral development order or a neighbourhood development order or 'other': Brownfield Land Register Regulations, Sch 1, para 1(l). Other is any other grant of planning permission or deemed planning permission (see Brownfield Land Register Regulations, Sch 2, para 5), the most common example of which would be having gone through the prior approval process to change to residential use under the Town and Country Planning (General Permitted Development) (England) Order 2015, SI 2015/596, Sch 2, Pt 3.
[45]   An application is pending if it has not been finally determined by the local planning authority, the Secretary of State or in subsequent court proceedings, any right of appeal has not expired and it has not been withdrawn.

- a description of any proposed housing development *or* the minimum and maximum net number of dwellings which the authority considers the site is capable of supporting;

- in any event, the minimum net number of dwellings which, in the authority's opinion, the land is capable of supporting; and

- the scale and proposed use of any non-housing development.

The net numbers of dwellings are those in the proposed development less the number of dwellings on the land immediately prior to the entry being made on the register.[46] The figures are therefore for the net increase in dwellings on the site.

In addition the Part 1 entry must note if the site is deliverable, that is, there is a reasonable prospect that residential development will take place on the land within five years beginning with the entry date.[47]

For a Part 2 entry, the register must contain:[48]

'(a) the minimum net number of dwellings, and the maximum net number of dwellings, given as a range, which, in the authority's opinion, the land is capable of supporting; and

(b) where the development includes non-housing development, the scale of any such development and the use to which it is to be put.'

Part 2 must also contain the statement that the land within it is 'allocated for residential development for the purposes of section 59A of the Town and Country Planning Act 1990 (permission in principle)'.[49]

ENTERING LAND ON THE REGISTER

8.10   The processes for entering land on the register must be sufficient to resolve whether the criteria for inclusion apply and the details which would be included on the register. Since the intention is to find and identify sites, the authority must in practice conduct some searches itself and invite proposals for sites.

No procedure is laid down for the entry of land in Part 1. The local planning authority 'may carry out procedures (including consultation) as they see fit'. If consultation is carried out then a period for representations must be specified and the authority must consider any representations received within that period.[50]

As Part 2 grants permission in principle for development the process is prescribed in detail.[51] It is closely based on planning application procedures in the Town and Country Planning (Development Management Procedure) (England) Order 2015.[52]

---

46   Brownfield Land Register Regulations, reg 2(1).
47   Brownfield Land Register Regulations, Sch 2, paras 1(j), 5.
48   Brownfield Land Register Regulations, Sch 2, para 2.
49   Brownfield Land Register Regulations, Sch 2, para 4.
50   Brownfield Land Register Regulations, regs 4(2), 5(6).
51   Brownfield Land Register Regulations, reg 5(7) requiring compliance with regs 6–13.
52   SI 2015/595. For detailed consideration of planning application procedures, see Chapter 6 of Richard Harwood, *Planning Permission* (Bloomsbury Professional, 2016).

8.10 *Brownfield Land Registers*

Where the local planning authority proposes to enter a site in Part 2 it must:

- display a site notice[53] for not less than 21 days[54] on or near the land giving details of the minimum and maximum net number of dwellings that the land is capable of supporting along with the description of any non-housing development and how and when to make representations;

- publish on the authority's website details of each site including a plan, site area, permission status, maximum and minimum number of dwellings and the scale and use of a non-housing development, along with how and by when representations should be made.[55] If consultation would be required with the Health and Safety Executive, the Office for Nuclear Regulation or the Control of Major Accident Hazards competent authority because of the proximity of the proposed residential use to a dangerous site[56] then the website must refer to this and provide further information under the Planning (Hazardous Substances) Regulations 2015;[57]

- if the land is already entered in Part 1 and that Part has been published, the statement that the land is 'proposed for residential development (permission in principle)' should be added to Part 1 within seven days of notice being given of the authority's intention to add the land to Part 2;[58]

- if the land is within 10 metres of an operational railway (or land authorised for the purposes of an operational railway),[59] serve the notice on the infrastructure manager of the relevant railway land;[60]

- serve the notice on any parish council or neighbourhood forum for the area which has requested the local planning authority to notify it of proposed entries on Part 2 within its area;[61]

- consult the county planning authority (if different) if residential development of the land would materially conflict with county minerals or waste policy, affect minerals or waste sites or land which the county wish to develop themselves;[62]

- consult the Mayor of London if the residential development would be of potential strategic importance under the Town and Country Planning (Mayor

---

[53] In the form in Sch 1 or substantially to the same effect: Brownfield Land Register Regulations, reg 2(1).

[54] Brownfield Land Register Regulations, reg 6(1).

[55] Brownfield Land Register Regulations, reg 6(4).

[56] These requirements are set out in the Town and Country Planning (Development Management Procedure) (England) Order 2015, Sch 4, Table, paras (e), (f), (zb) applied by the Planning (Hazardous Substances) Regulations 2015, SI 2015/627, reg 26(5).

[57] The information required is in Planning (Hazardous Substances) Regulations 2015, reg 26(2).

[58] Brownfield Land Register Regulations, Sch 2, para 1(2).

[59] See the definition of 'relevant railway land' in the Brownfield Land Register Regulations, reg 2(1). Authorisation is by a planning permission, development consent order or Act of Parliament.

[60] Brownfield Land Register Regulations, reg 7(1). Notice should be served unless the infrastructure manager has previously given a written instruction (which has not been withdrawn) that notice is not required for that land or geographical area: Brownfield Land Register Regulations, reg 7(2), (3).

[61] Brownfield Land Register Regulations, reg 8. This mirrors the provisions for planning applications in the Town and Country Planning Act 1990, Sch 1 paras 8, 8A. It is an unnecessary complication, and risks error, for parish councils and neighbourhood forums to have to ask to be notified.

[62] Town and Country Planning Act 1990, Sch 1, para 7(4). These provisions are set out fully and discussed in Richard Harwood, *Planning Permission* (Bloomsbury Professional, 2016), at paras 6.131–6.132. Notice does not have to be given if the county planning authority has previously indicated that it does not wish to be notified of Part 2 applications within particular areas: Brownfield Land Register Regulations, reg 10(2).

of London) Order 2008.[63],[64] At present the Mayor is though only a consultee on these sites. Whilst the Town and Country Planning Act 1990 allows a development order to be made allowing the Mayor to take over proposals or direct the refusal of permission in principle,[65] the Mayor of London Order 2008 has not yet been amended to allow this to be done;

- consult those persons who would have been consulted on a planning application for residential development of the land. These are the persons or bodies who would have been consulted under the Town and Country Planning (Development Management Procedure) Order 2015[66] and any other person who the authority would have been required to consult.[67] Where there is a requirement to consult has to be judged against the potential effects of the scale of residential and any other development contemplated. Consultation is not required if the person has said it does not wish to be consulted on Part 2 applications or has issued standing advice within the last two years on that potential development.[68]

The periods for making representations are the later of:

- 21 days beginning with the date the site notice is first displayed;[69]

- the date specified in the website announcement, which is a minimum of 14 days beginning with the date of publication;[70]

- 42 days beginning with service of the notice on a railway infrastructure manager, parish council or neighbourhood forum if this is before the first publication of Part 2 of the register, or 21 days if it has already been published;[71]

- similarly, 42 days beginning with the giving on notice on a person required to be consulted under the Brownfield Land Register Regulations, or 21 days if the Part 2 register has already been published.[72]

Representations made within these periods are to be taken into account even if they are not made by the person consulted under the particular provision to which the period applies.[73]

DECISION-MAKING WITHIN THE LOCAL PLANNING AUTHORITY

8.11   Where a local planning authority is a council which operates executive arrangements then the responsibility for preparing the register is split. The inclusion

---

[63]   SI 2008/580.
[64]   Brownfield Land Register Regulations, reg 11. These are the categories of planning application which have to be referred to the Mayor. For details of the categories and the Mayor of London's role in planning, see Chapter 10 of Richard Harwood, *Planning Permission* (Bloomsbury Professional, 2016).
[65]   Town and Country Planning Act 1990, ss 2A, 74(1B).
[66]   Brownfield Land Register Regulations, reg 12(1) applying the Town and Country Planning (Development Management Procedure) (England) Order 2015, Sch 4.
[67]   Brownfield Land Register Regulations, reg 12(2). The requirement to consult may be in Acts of Parliament, orders or regulations or in directions made by the Secretary of State. These are set out in Richard Harwood, *Planning Permission* (Bloomsbury Professional, 2016), at paras 6.125–6.129.
[68]   Brownfield Land Register Regulations, reg 12(3), (4).
[69]   Brownfield Land Register Regulations, reg 9(2).
[70]   Brownfield Land Register Regulations, regs 6(4)(d), 9(3).
[71]   Brownfield Land Register Regulations, reg 9(4).
[72]   Brownfield Land Register Regulations, reg 13.
[73]   See the definition of relevant representations: Brownfield Land Register Regulations, reg 2(1).

of sites in Part 1 is an executive matter, whilst the duty to enter land in Part 2 (and so grant permission in principle) is a regulatory function for the council's planning committee.[74] In this respect it reflects the distinction between planning policy (which is executive) and the non-executive function of determining planning applications. It does though add several complications to the issues of who should make decisions on the register and how the process is carried out.

Considering land for Part 1 involves a mixture of administrative action, professional judgement and planning or political judgement. Whether land has planning permission or is allocated in the local plan is a purely administrative matter, involving no exercise of discretion. Deciding whether residential development is achievable and the site is available is a matter for judgment about owners' intentions, viability and infrastructure requirements. Councillors are able to reach views on these issues, but they can be left to officers. The suitability of a site which does not have an existing allocation or permission is a matter of planning judgement, which depending upon the size and circumstances of the site may usually be for councillors, whether in the cabinet (for policy) or planning committee (for planning permission). Even where a site is already consented or allocated, the Part 1 register entry may specify a maximum scale of development which is greater than has been approved. That involves an element of planning judgement which might be for members. It may be appropriate therefore to split Part 1 decisions between officers and executive members or simply to seek approval from the executive to all, noting that some require an exercise of judgement.

As with planning applications, Part 2 decisions could be taken by officers, the non-executive planning committee of the council or conceivably by the full council meeting. The obvious course is to deal with them in the same way as those planning applications which raise the same issues of scale, policy compliance and representations.

The separation of decision makers between Parts 1 and 2 raise important matters of process. In councils with executive arrangements, different councillors would have to deal with the Parts on different occasions. That points in practice towards a two-stage process of entering sites in Part 1 and then consulting on any proposals to allocate sites for development under Part 2. Regulation 3 does not require land to be entered in Part 1 before it is entered in Part 2, except that small sites below the 0.25 hectare and five units thresholds can only be in Part 2 if the discretion has already been exercised to add them to Part 1.[75] As discussed above, land can only be added to Part 2 if the local planning authority propose it and then carry out statutory consultation. The authority needs therefore to be sufficiently informed to start the process, confident that the site will come forward and able to persuade its own planning committee to grant permission in principle for it.

---

[74] Local Authorities (Functions and Responsibilities) Regulations 2000, SI 2000/2853, Sch 1, Pt A, para 32.
[75] Brownfield Land Register Regulations, reg 5(4). In theory a planning committee could add other sites to Part 2 even if the executive thought that they did not meet the Part 1 criteria but that would involve the council reaching two contradictory decisions: see reg 5(2).

DECISIONS ON ADDING LAND TO PART 2

8.12   For land to be allocated under Part 2 it must meet the criteria to be entered under Part 1 (or if under 0.25 hectares or 5 dwellings, the authority must have decided to include it in Part 1) and the authority must have decided to add it to that Part.[76] An issue may arise as to whether the Part 2 decision maker can or should consider the merits of any Part 1 entry. A council planning committee cannot alter the Part 1 entry, but might not be bound by it.[77] Whether the land meets the criteria is put in the present tense, so is judged when the Part 2 decision is taken. Circumstances may have changed since the Part 1 entry was made and may have to be taken into account.[78] It remains to be resolved whether the committee can contradict the Part 1 decision without a change in circumstances. Potentially the most contentious issue is the significance of a Part 1 decision that the site is appropriate for residential development and so suitable. That conclusion would be relevant to whether to allocate the land under Part 2.

The decision-maker must have regard to the development plan and national policy and guidance.[79] The authority must also have special regard to 'the desirability of preserving the building or its setting or any features of special architectural or historic interest which it possesses'[80] along with the other duties which are generally applicable to public authorities.[81]

As well as what is proposed, a decision whether to permit a development may require regard to what is lost. Careful consideration is required as to whether the permission in principle will authorise demolition, whether certain existing uses are protected and regard to designated heritage assets, such as listed buildings and conservation areas, and undesignated assets such as locally listed buildings and assets of community value.

If the Planning (Hazardous Substances) Regulations 2015 apply to the proposal because of its proximity to certain dangerous sites, then a reasoned decision must be made available.[82]

ENVIRONMENTAL REGIMES: STRATEGIC ENVIRONMENTAL ASSESSMENT, ENVIRONMENTAL IMPACT ASSESSMENT AND THE HABITATS REGULATIONS

8.13   The various European regimes on environmental effects would apply in different ways to both Parts 1 and 2 of the brownfield land register. In summary, Part 1 of the register may be subject to strategic environmental assessment and Habitats

---

[76] Brownfield Land Register Regulations, reg 5(2), (4).
[77] Unless the land was added as a sub-threshold site where the Part 2 criterion is whether it is in Part 1: Brownfield Land Register Regulations, reg 5(4).
[78] However, certain of the achievable and available tests relate to the entry date, which is fixed as the date the land is entered in Part 1: Brownfield Land Register Regulations, regs 2(1), 4(2).
[79] Planning and Compulsory Purchase Act 2004, s 14A(7), (8).
[80] Planning (Listed Buildings and Conservation Areas) Act 1990, s 66(1), as amended for permission in principle. The statutory duty in s 72 to pay special attention to conservation areas does not apply, as the Planning and Compulsory Purchase Act 2004 is not amongst the provisions identified in that section.
[81] See Chapter 4 above.
[82] Planning (Hazardous Substances) Regulations 2015, reg 26(3).

Regulations assessment whilst entries cannot be made in Part 2 if they require environmental impact assessment or Habitats Regulations assessment.

Strategic environmental assessment

8.14   Strategic environmental assessment ('SEA') is of plans and programmes for town and country planning purposes (amongst others) which set the framework for development consent for projects listed within Annexes I or II of the Environmental Impact Assessment Directive 2011/92/EU ('EIA Directive').[83] These include urban development projects.[84] Part 1 of a brownfield land register will be part of setting the framework for development consent (usually planning permission). Consequently, the inclusion of land for residential development within Part 1 of a brownfield land register might require SEA.[85]

However, SEA is not required of a particular plan if it 'determines the use of a small area of land at a local level' and it is considered not to be likely to have significant effects on the environment.[86] The effect of the plan does depend upon how far it adds to existing plans or authorisations.[87] Any screening decision should focus on land which does not already benefit from a development plan allocation or planning permission. The register will merely record rather than provide a framework for existing allocations and consents (unless perhaps a substantial increase in size is proposed). Those existing sites will bear on the screening decision only insofar as they have a cumulative effect with new sites contained in the register.

SEA is not required to add a site to Part 2, since that allocation will grant development consent (which might require environmental impact assessment) rather than set the framework for a future development consent decision.

Habitats Regulations assessment of Part 1

8.15   Part 1 of a brownfield land register will be a plan and an appropriate assessment will have to be carried out under the Conservation of Habitats and Species Regulations 2010[88] if its proposals are likely to have a significant effect on a European site (Special Area of Conservation, a Special Protection Area or a proposal for such an area) and are not directly connected with or necessary to its management.[89] If any of the proposals may adversely affect the integrity of the European site then strict tests apply before they can be included.[90]

---

[83] Environmental Assessment of Plans and Programmes Regulations 2004, SI 2004/1633 ('SEA Regulations'), reg 5(2)(b). See Chapter 3 above for greater consideration of SEA.

[84] EIA Directive, Annex II, point 10(b).

[85] A point confirmed by the *Brownfield registers and permission in principle: frequently asked questions*, para 16.

[86] SEA Regulations, reg 5(6)(a), 9.

[87] See SEA Regulations, Sch 1, para 1(a) 'the degree to which the plan or programme sets a framework for projects and other activities'.

[88] SI 2010/490.

[89] Conservation of Habitats and Species Regulations 2010, reg 61. The specific land use plan provisions in the Conservation of Habitats and Species Regulations 2010, regs 102–107 do not apply to brownfield land registers, see the definition of land use plan in reg 107(1).

[90] See Chapter 3 above.

Environmental impact assessment ('EIA')

8.16   The automatic grant of permission in principle by reason of the status of land in a document means that the document itself is a development consent under the EIA Directive. It authorises the developer to proceed, as part of a multi-stage consent process.[91] Part 2 entries will therefore be development consents. If the projects, individually or cumulatively, are likely to have significant effects on the environment then EIA is required. An EIA would be a far more involved and expensive process than is envisaged for Part 2.

The Brownfield Land Register Regulations therefore take the approach of preventing land being added to Part 2 if the proposal would require EIA.

Land may not be entered in Part 2 of the register if its residential development could be Schedule 1 development,[92] that is, within the categories which always require EIA. None of these categories include residential development (where the main purpose is housing development) in any event. Where residential development of the land could be Schedule 2 development under the Environmental Impact Assessment Regulations then it cannot be added to Part 2 unless a screening decision has been made that EIA is not required. Schedule 2 development includes urban development projects[93] which include more than 150 dwellings, have an overall area of more than 5 hectares or include more than 1 hectare of urban development which is not dwellinghouse development or which are in a sensitive area.[94]

To undertake the screening exercise, the local planning authority must have a plan identifying the land; a description of the development, including in particular, a description of the physical characteristics of the development and, where relevant, of demolition works; the location of the development, with particular regard to the environmental sensitivity of geographical areas likely to be affected; and the aspects of the environment likely to be significantly affected by the development.[95] The maximum net number of dwellings which the site is capable of supporting must be identified.[96] Taken with any other information, the authority must have sufficient

---

[91] EIA Directive, Art 1(2).

[92] Brownfield Land Register Regulations, reg 14(1). Schedule 1 development is that in Sch 1 of the Town and Country Planning (Environmental Impact Assessment) Regulations 2017, SI 2017/571 derived from Annex I to the EIA Directive.

[93] Even without the reference to dwellings in the threshold, urban development projects have been held to include residential development: *R (on the application of Loader) v Secretary of State for Communities and Local Government* [2012] EWCA Civ 869, [2013] PTSR 406.

[94] Town and Country Planning (Environmental Impact Assessment) Regulations 2017, reg 2(1) and Sch 2, table, point 10(b). A sensitive area is a site of special scientific interest, National Park, the Broads, World Heritage Site, scheduled monument, area of outstanding natural beauty, Special Protection Area or Special Area of Conservation: Town and Country Planning (Environmental Impact Assessment) Regulations 2017, reg 2(1).

[95] Town and Country Planning (Environmental Impact Assessment) Regulations 2017, reg 2(a), (b), (c). The Brownfield Land Register Regulations, reg 14(2)(a)(i) refers to the previous provision in the Town and Country Planning (Environmental Impact Assessment) Regulations 2011, SI 2011/1824 reg 5(2) (a),(b), but the replacement provision in the Town and Country Planning (Environmental Impact Assessment) Regulations 2017 applies with the modifications made in it: Interpretation Act 1978, ss 17(2)(a), 23.

[96] Brownfield Land Register Regulations, reg 14(2)(a)(ii). This might be adjusted downwards to avoid requiring EIA. Unlike the handling of planning applications, the Secretary of State has no power to direct EIA of projects which are below the thresholds and outside sensitive areas.

information to adopt a screening opinion, identifying whether the proposal would be likely to have a significant effect on the environment.[97]

If the proposal is Schedule 2 development then the land may only be added to Part 2 if the local planning authority adopts a screening opinion that EIA is not required, the Secretary of State makes a screening direction to that effect or the Minister takes the exceptional step of exempting the project from EIA.[98]

Habitats Regulations assessment and Part 2 entries

8.17   A proposal cannot be added to Part 2 if appropriate assessment has to be carried out of it under the habitats regime because of its potential effect on European designated sites.

Excluded from inclusion in Part 2 is land whose residential development up to a maximum level would be habitats development.[99] Habitats development is likely to have a significant effect on a Special Area of Conservation, a Special Protection Area or a proposal for such an area and is not directly connected with or necessary to its management and so would require appropriate assessment.[100]

TECHNICAL DETAILS CONSENT

8.18   If planning permission in principle is granted, whether automatically or following an application, then a full planning permission is achieved by the approval of a technical details consent. Any application for technical details consent must be within the matters approved by the permission in principle and contain sufficient details to be a full, but not outline, planning application:[101]

'An application for technical details consent is an application for planning permission that—

(a) relates to land in respect of which permission in principle is in force,

(b) proposes development all of which falls within the terms of the permission in principle, and

(c) particularises all matters necessary to enable planning permission to be granted without any reservations of the kind referred to in section 92.'

Unless the permission in principle is out of date, the local planning authority has to determine the application in accordance with it:[102]

'The authority must determine an application for technical details consent in accordance with the relevant permission in principle.'

---

[97]   On the adequacy of information to screen, see *Younger Homes (Northern) Ltd v First Secretary of State* [2003] EWHC 3058 (Admin), [2004] JPL 950, at paras 55–65 per Ouseley J.

[98]   Brownfield Land Register Regulations, reg 14(2).

[99]   Brownfield Land Register Regulations, reg 14(4). The habitats regime is discussed in Chapter 3 above.

[100] Brownfield Land Register Regulations, reg 14(5). The categories of sites are listed in the Offshore Marine Conservation (Natural Habitats, &c.) Regulations 2007, SI 2007/1842, reg 15 and Conservation of Habitats and Species Regulations 2010, reg 8.

[101] Town and Country Planning Act 1990, s 70(2ZZB).

[102] Town and Country Planning Act 1990, s 70(2ZZA). The period is prescribed by the Town and Country Planning (Permission in Principle) Order 2017, art 7.

A permission would be out of date if it has been in force for longer than the prescribed period of five years and there has been a material change in circumstances since it came into force.[103]

The requirements that the technical details application accords with the permission in principle and that the authority cannot go back on the principle which has been established when determining it reflects the case law on reserved matters and the approval of details under conditions.[104] A technical details application could relate to only part of the site of a permission in principle, although it could be refused if a more comprehensive application was considered necessary or it would prejudice the development of the remainder of the site.

REVIEW OF THE BROWNFIELD LAND REGISTER

8.19   The entries in each Part within the register must be reviewed at least once a year.[105] The review procedure is relatively informal and is concerned solely with existing entries. Adding entries to the register is carried out in accordance with the procedures above. Since a change to a Part 2 entry would have the effect of granting permission in principle, this cannot be done under a review. Any Part 2 entry which requires changing is simply deleted and the statutory consultation process will have to be followed to introduce a different entry.

In the review, if the land no longer meets the criteria of being at least 0.25 hectares or capable of accommodating five or more dwellings, suitable and available for residential development and such development being achievable on it then it must be removed from Part 1 and, if applicable, removed from Part 2.[106] Entries in Part 1 must also be updated, if necessary, in that process, for example, if a different view is taken as to the maximum or minimum number of units. Reasons for removal may include a demonstrated lack of interest in developing the site, an existing planning permission expiring and its suitability being reassessed or residential development being carried out.

Whilst land can be removed from Part 2, this does not alter the effect of the permission in principle which has already been granted in accordance with the original entry.[107] If the local planning authority changes the description of the proposed housing development, the maximum or minimum number of dwellings or the scale and use of any non-housing development in the Part 1 entry for a site, then any Part 2 entry for it will be removed.[108] Any new Part 2 entry (whether for a greater or lesser quantum of development) will have to go through the allocation procedures in regs 6 to 13.

---

[103] Town and Country Planning Act 1990, s 70(2ZZC).
[104] See the discussion of approval of reserved matters and details under conditions in Chapter 16 of Richard Harwood, *Planning Permission* (Bloomsbury Professional, 2016).
[105] Brownfield Land Register Regulations, reg 17(1). A review must take place within each register year, which is by the anniversary of the publication of that particular part of the register: reg 17(10).
[106] Brownfield Land Register Regulations, reg 17(2), (3). If the land was added as a sub-threshold site then the size criteria do not apply to its review: Brownfield Land Register Regulations, reg 17(3).
[107] Town and Country Planning Act 1990, s 59A(6).
[108] Brownfield Land Register Regulations, reg 17(6). The Part 2 entry cannot be updated: reg 17(5).

If the grant of permission in principle for a particular site has expired then the authority must remove that Part 2 entry,[109] but can proceed to allocate the land again under Part 2.

In making any other revision to the register, by removing entries in either Part or changing Part 1 entries, the authority has a discretion as to the process it follows, including whether to carry out consultation.[110] If it does consult then then any representations received within the period it specifies must be considered.[111]

---

[109]   Brownfield Land Register Regulations, reg 17(8).
[110]   Brownfield Land Register Regulations, reg 17(7)(a).
[111]   Brownfield Land Register Regulations, reg 17(7)(b).

Chapter 9

London and Devolved City Regions

9.1   A perennial issue is the exercise of power, including the adoption of planning policy, above the level of an individual local authority. Strategic planning functions are exercised by the Mayor of London who has adopted a spatial development strategy, universally referred to as the London Plan.[1] These spatial development plan powers have also been given to some combined authorities which have been recently established, principally in city regions.[2]

LONDON

Introduction

9.2   In London the development plan is made up of the spatial development strategy ('the London Plan') which is published by the Mayor of London, development plan documents which have been adopted by the individual Boroughs and any neighbourhood development plan documents which have been made in relation to an area.[3]

Strategic planning – The London Plan

9.3   Strategic planning within Greater London is the responsibility of the Mayor of London, the London Boroughs (32 in total) and the Corporation of the City of London. The preparation and publication of a spatial development strategy ('SDS') (or alterations thereto) for London is governed by Pt VIII of the Greater London Authority Act 1999 and the Town and Country Planning (London Spatial Development Strategy) Regulations 2000.[4]

Section 334 of the Greater London Authority Act 1999 requires the Mayor of London to produce an SDS for London. Unusually, the power is vested solely in the Mayor, rather than being shared with the Greater London Assembly or a statutory board. The current SDS is the London Plan.

The first London Plan was published by the then Mayor Ken Livingstone in 2004. A full replacement London Plan was published by then Mayor Boris Johnson in 2011

---

[1]   For an early consideration of the Mayor of London's planning powers, see Richard Harwood, 'Planning London' [2002] JPL 520. The Mayor's development management powers are considered in Richard Harwood, *Planning Permission* (Bloomsbury Professional, 2016), Ch 10.
[2]   The preparation of joint local plans and other working between local authorities is discussed in Chapter 7 above.
[3]   Planning and Compulsory Purchase Act 2004, s 38(1).
[4]   SI 2000/1491. The Regulations are made under the Greater London Authority Act 1999, s 343.

which has been subject to a number of alterations. This is the version in force at the time of writing.

Three sets of alterations have been made to the current London Plan:

(i)   revised early minor alterations ('REMA') which were made to the Plan to ensure it reflected the National Planning Policy Framework (published March 2012) and the government's approach to affordable housing (published 11 October 2013);

(ii)   further alterations to the London Plan ('FALP') in order to reflect Mayoral priorities (published on 10 March 2015); and

(iii)   minor alterations to the London Plan ('MALPs') were published on 14 March 2016. These were prepared in order to bring the London Plan in line with national housing standards and car parking policy.

At present, the Mayor of London Sadiq Kahn is in the process of preparing a new London Plan. The projected publication date is Autumn 2019.

Content

9.4   The SDS for London may only deal with matters which are of strategic importance to Greater London.[5] However, those matters do not have to affect the whole area of Greater London[6] and the statute specifically enables the SDS to 'make different provision for different cases or for different parts of Greater London'.[7] It therefore sets out a strategic framework within which the London Boroughs are to draft their more detailed local planning policies.

Along with the SDS, the Mayor is required to prepare a number of other strategies. These are: a transport strategy,[8] an economic development strategy,[9] a health inequalities strategy,[10] a housing strategy,[11] an environment strategy[12] and a culture strategy.[13] Each of these strategies (together with the SDS) is required to be consistent with each other.[14] Further, the Mayor is required in the SDS to include statements dealing with the general spatial development aspects of those other strategies.[15]

The statute requires the Mayor to have regard to a number of factors in preparing or revising the London Plan. These are:

(a)   the principal purposes of the Authority (promoting economic development and wealth creation in Greater London, promoting social development in Greater London and promoting the improvement of the environment in Greater London);[16]

---

[5]   Greater London Authority Act 1999, s 334(5).
[6]   Greater London Authority Act 1999, s 334(6).
[7]   Greater London Authority Act 1999, s 334(8).
[8]   Prepared and published under the Greater London Authority Act 1999, s 142.
[9]   Prepared and published under the Greater London Authority Act 1999, s 333F.
[10] Prepared and published under the Greater London Authority Act 1999, Pt VIII.
[11] Prepared and published under the Greater London Authority Act 1999, s 333A.
[12] Prepared and publish in accordance with the Greater London Authority Act 1999, Pt IX.
[13] Prepared and published under the Greater London Authority Act 1999, s 376.
[14] Greater London Authority Act 1999, s 41(5)(b).
[15] Greater London Authority Act 1999, s 334(4)(a).
[16] Greater London Authority Act 1999, s 41(4)(a) and the principal purposes listed at s 30(2).

(b)   the effect which the proposed strategy or revision would have on:

    (i)   the health of persons in Greater London;[17]

    (ii)   health inequalities between persons living in Greater London;[18]

    (iii)   the achievement of sustainable development in the United Kingdom;[19]

    (iv)   climate change, and the consequences of climate change;[20]

(c)   the need to ensure that the strategy is consistent with national policies, with the EU obligations of the UK and with such other international obligations of the UK as the Secretary of State may notify to the Mayor;[21]

(d)   the need to ensure that the strategy is consistent with other strategies prepared by the Mayor. These are the transport strategy, the economic development strategy, the health inequalities strategy, the London housing strategy, the London environment strategy and the culture strategy;[22]

(e)   the resources available for the implementation of the strategy;[23] and

(f)   the desirability of promoting and encouraging the use of the River Thames safely, in particular for the provision of passenger transport services and for the transportation of freight.[24]

Further, in exercising his functions in preparing and publishing an SDS the Mayor is required to have regard to any regional strategy made for a region adjoining Greater London[25] and:[26]

(a)   the national waste management plan (within the meaning of the Waste (England and Wales) Regulations 2011;[27]

(b)   the objectives of preventing major accidents and limiting the consequences of such accidents for human health and the environment;

(c)   the need in the long term –

    (i)   to maintain appropriate safety distances between establishments and residential areas, buildings and areas of public use, recreational areas, and, as far as possible, major transport routes;

    (ii)   to protect areas of particular natural sensitivity or interest in the vicinity of establishments, where appropriate through appropriate safety distances or other relevant measures;

---

[17]   Greater London Authority Act 1999, s 41(4)(b)(i).
[18]   Greater London Authority Act 1999, s 41(4)(b)(ia).
[19]   Greater London Authority Act 1999, s 41(4)(b)(ii).
[20]   Greater London Authority Act 1999, s 41(4)(b)(iii).
[21]   Greater London Authority Act 1999, s 41(5)(a). Legislation for local planning authorities does not seek consistency with national policy so the provision is anomalous, particularly given the electoral mandate of the Mayor. It is tempered by the requirement being to have regard to the need to ensure consistency, rather than a duty to be consistent.
[22]   Greater London Authority Act 1999, s 41(5)(b).
[23]   Greater London Authority Act 1999, s 41(5)(c).
[24]   Greater London Authority Act 1999, s 41(5)(d).
[25]   All that remains of the South East Plan, which was the regional strategy under Pt 5 of the Local Democracy, Economic Development and Construction Act 2009, is the Thames Basin Heaths Special Protection Area policy.
[26]   Greater London Authority Act 1999, s 342(1) and the Town and Country Planning (London Spatial Development Strategy) Regulations 2000, reg 6(1).
[27]   SI 2011/988.

(iii)   in the case of existing establishments, to take additional technical measures, in accordance with Article 5 of the Control of Major Accident Hazards involving Dangerous Substances Directive 2012/18/EU, so as not to increase the risks to human health and the environment.

The Regulations require that the SDS contains a reasoned justification for the Mayor's strategy for spatial development in Greater London.[28] The reasoned justification must contain a statement of the regard the Mayor has had to these matters in formulating the SDS.[29]

The SDS must also contain a diagram (called the key diagram) which illustrates the Mayor's strategy for spatial development in Greater London.[30] It may also contain a diagram (called an inset diagram) which illustrates the application of the Mayor's general policies to part of the area covered by the SDS.[31] Where such an inset diagram is included, the area covered by it must be identified on the key diagram and the application of the general policies to that area should be illustrated on the only on the inset diagram.[32]

Public participation

9.5   Before determining the content of the SDS, the Mayor is required to:

(a)   prepare a draft plan;

(b)   make copies of the draft available for inspection at the principal office of the Greater London Authority and such other places within Greater London as the Mayor considers appropriate;[33]

(c)   send a copy to each of the following bodies:

(i)   the Secretary of State

(ii)   the Assembly and the functional bodies;[34]

(iii)   every London borough council;

(iv)   the council of any county or district whose area adjoins Greater London and is affected by the proposed SDS;

(v)   Natural England, the Environment Agency and Historic England;[35]

(vi)   any other body to which, or person to whom, the Mayor considers it appropriate to send a copy.[36] These bodies must include:

---

[28] Town and Country Planning (London Spatial Development Strategy) Regulations 2000, reg 4(1).

[29] That is, those specified in ss 41 and 342(1)(a) of the Greater London Authority Act 1999 and reg 6(1) of the Town and Country Planning (London Spatial Development Strategy) Regulations 2000: see reg 6(3).

[30] Town and Country Planning (London Spatial Development Strategy) Regulations 2000, reg 5(1).

[31] Town and Country Planning (London Spatial Development Strategy) Regulations 2000, reg 5(2).

[32] Town and Country Planning (London Spatial Development Strategy) Regulations 2000, reg 5(3).

[33] Town and Country Planning (London Spatial Development Strategy) Regulations 2000, reg 7(1).

[34] The functional bodies are Transport for London, any Mayoral development corporation, the Mayor's Office for Policing and Crime and the London Fire and Emergency Planning Authority: Greater London Authority Act 1999, s 424(1).

[35] Town and Country Planning (London Spatial Development Strategy) Regulations 2000, reg 7(5).

[36] Greater London Authority Act 1999, s 335(3).

- voluntary bodies some or all of whose activities benefit the whole or part of Greater London;

- bodies which represent the interests of different racial, ethnic or national groups in Greater London;

- bodies which represent the interests of different religious groups in Greater London;

- bodies which represent the interests of persons carrying on business in Greater London;[37] and

(d)   consider any representations made in accordance with the Regulations. These are defined as representations made in writing and addressed to the Mayor at the address indicated in the published notice.[38,39]

The draft SDS must be accompanied by a sustainability appraisal which sets out how the SDS contributes towards the achievement of sustainable development.[40] It will also be subject to the requirements of strategic environmental assessment.

Once the Mayor has made copies of the draft SDS and sustainability appraisal available for inspection, he must as soon as is reasonably practicable give notice by advertisement. That notice shall specify a period not less than 12 weeks within which representations may be made and thereafter considered by the Mayor.[41] However, where in the Mayor's opinion the proposed alterations to the SDS are minor then the minimum period is reduced to not less than six weeks.[42] In each case, the period begins with the date on which the notice is first published in a newspaper and ends on the date specified in the notice.[43] During that period, the local planning authority for each London borough must make available for inspection at its principal office a copy of the proposed SDS and sustainability appraisal.[44]

Examination in public

9.6   Before publishing a plan, the Mayor is required to arrange for an examination in public ('EIP') to be held (unless the Secretary of State directs otherwise).[45] The legislation does use the expression 'examination in public', rather than the 2004 regime's 'examination' and in this context means a public hearing rather than the totality of the examination process. The EIP is conducted by a person or persons appointed by the Secretary of State (hereinafter termed 'the panel').[46] The remit of the panel appointed by the Secretary of State at the EIP is broad. The statute states that the 'matters examined at an examination in public shall be such matters affecting the

---

[37]   Greater London Authority Act 1999, s 32(3) read with s 335(4).
[38]   Town and Country Planning (London Spatial Development Strategy) Regulations 2000, reg 7(9).
[39]   Greater London Authority Act 1999, s 335(2).
[40]   Town and Country Planning (London Spatial Development Strategy) Regulations 2000, reg 7(2).
[41]   Town and Country Planning (London Spatial Development Strategy) Regulations 2000, reg 7(6) read with the Greater London Authority Act 1999, s 335(7)
[42]   Town and Country Planning (London Spatial Development Strategy) Regulations 2000, reg 7(7). The Notice must be in the form in the regulations.
[43]   Town and Country Planning (London Spatial Development Strategy) Regulations 2000, reg 7(8).
[44]   Town and Country Planning (London Spatial Development Strategy) Regulations 2000, reg 7(3).
[45]   Greater London Authority Act 1999, s 338(1).
[46]   Greater London Authority Act 1999, s 338(3).

consideration of the spatial development strategy as the person or persons conducting the examination in public may consider ought to be so examined'.[47]

As soon as is reasonably practicable, after the panel has been appointed to conduct the EPP, the Mayor shall send the panel a copy of all representations made in accordance with the Regulations.[48] At least 12 weeks before the EIP is opened the panel is required (after consulting the Mayor) to make available for inspection a draft list of: the matters to be examined in public and the persons who will be invited to take part in the EIP. Representations may be made on the draft list in writing within 28 days that notice of the draft list is given by advertisement.[49]

No person has a right to be heard at the EIP and only the Mayor and those invited to take part in the EIP by the panel may take part.[50] Taking part concerns actual appearance at the examination hearings and anyone may make written submissions in accordance with the regulations. The panel is required to make a report to the Mayor.[51]

At least six weeks before the opening of the EIP the panel is required (again after consulting with the Mayor) to notify those persons who are invited to take part of the matters to be examined, make available for inspection the list of matters to be considered at the EIP and of the persons who will be invited to take part and give notice of certain details of the EIP in an advertisement.[52] Written submissions may be made on the matters to be examined, however, the panel is only required to consider a written submission where: it concerns one or more matters to be examined at the EIP; it is shorter than 2000 words; and the panel receives (no later than three weeks before the EIP's opening) the number of copies reasonably required by the panel to ensure that a copy can be sent to each person taking part in the EIP.[53] This is an unusual case of a word limit being in placed in legislation rather than guidance.

The panel's report is made in writing and a copy sent to the Mayor and Secretary of State.[54] Within eight weeks of receiving the report the Mayor must make it available for inspection and send a copy of the report to the Council of each borough.[55] The Mayor is prohibited from publishing the SDS unless:

(a)   he has sent to the Secretary of State –

   (i)   a statement of his intention to publish the SDS;

   (ii)   a copy of the SDS; and

   (iii) where he proposes not to accept a panel recommendation, a statement of the reasons for not doing so; and

---

[47]   Greater London Authority Act 1999, s 338(4).
[48]   Town and Country Planning (London Spatial Development Strategy) Regulations 2000, reg 8(1).
[49]   Town and Country Planning (London Spatial Development Strategy) Regulations 2000, reg 8(2) and (3).
[50]   Greater London Authority Act 1999, s 338(6) and (7).
[51]   Greater London Authority Act 1999, s 338(5).
[52]   Town and Country Planning (London Spatial Development Strategy) Regulations 2000, reg 8(4).
[53]   Town and Country Planning (London Spatial Development Strategy) Regulations 2000, reg 8(5).
[54]   Town and Country Planning (London Spatial Development Strategy) Regulations 2000, reg 8(7), (8).
[55]   Town and Country Planning (London Spatial Development Strategy) Regulations 2000, reg 8(9). The Mayor has an unnecessarily generous eight-week period in which to send the report out and start making it available.

(b)   a period of six weeks, or such longer period as the Secretary of State in writing requires, have elapsed beginning with the date notified to the Mayor in writing that the Secretary of State as the date he received the latest of the above statements and copy of the SDS.[56]

The Mayor is not required to accept the panel's conclusions/recommendations; rather to take them into account. In *Islington London Borough Council v Mayor of London*[57] the Mayor had rejected certain recommendations of the Examining Inspector regarding the removal of a prohibition of rent caps. In one ground of challenge the claimants (which included a number of the London Boroughs) argued that the Mayor had erred in refusing to accept the Inspector's recommendation. The Court considered the reasoning given by the Mayor for not accepting those recommendations and concluded that having given proper consideration to those recommendations the Mayor was entitled to reject them.[58]

Publication

9.7   The SDS becomes operative from the date of publication.[59]

The Mayor may withdraw a draft SDS (including a draft modification) at any time before it is published.[60] If not withdrawn, the Mayor may publish the SDS after:

(a)   he has considered any representations made in accordance with the regulations or, if no such representations are made, the expiry of the prescribed period;[61]

(b)   he has sent to the Secretary of State, a statement of his intention to publish the SDS, a copy of the SDS, where he proposes not to accept a recommendation contained in a report of the panel a statement of reasons for not accepting that recommendation and a period of six weeks (or such longer period as the Secretary of State in writing requires) have elapsed since the date notified in writing to the Mayor by the Secretary of State as the date he received the latest of those statements and copy.[62]

The published version of the SDS will be published either as originally prepared or as modified taking into account representations made in accordance with the Regulations, any direction given under s 337(7) (see below), any examiner's report and any other material considerations.[63]

A section 337(7) direction is a direction given by the Secretary of State to the Mayor not to publish the SDS except in a form which includes modifications in order to remove any inconsistency with current national policies (or the regional spatial strategy for a region adjoining Greater London) or any detriment to the interests of an area outside Greater London.[64] Where such a direction is given, the Mayor may

---

[56]   Town and Country Planning (London Spatial Development Strategy) Regulations 2000, reg 9(2).
[57]   [2014] EWHC 751 (Admin).
[58]   At para 34 per Lang J.
[59]   Greater London Authority Act 1999, s 337(9).
[60]   Greater London Authority Act 1999, s 336(1).
[61]   Greater London Authority Act 1999, s 337(4).
[62]   Town and Country Planning (London Spatial Development Strategy) Regulations 2000, reg 9(2).
[63]   Greater London Authority Act 1999, s 337(2).
[64]   Greater London Authority Act 1999, s 337(6) and (7).

not publish the SDS unless he has satisfied the Secretary of State that the necessary modifications have been made or the direction has been withdrawn.[65]

When the Mayor publishes the SDS he is required to:

(a)   give notice by advertisement in Form 3;

(b)   serve notice in a similar form on the council of any county or district whose area adjoins Greater London and is affected by the proposed SDS;[66]

(c)   make available for inspection the SDS, a copy of any direction given by the Secretary of State under s 337(7), a copy of any written statement of the Secretary of State indicating that he is satisfied that the Mayor has made the necessary modifications to the SDS to comply with any such direction and where the Mayor has not accepted any recommendation contained in the report of the panel, a statement of his reasons for not accepting that recommendation available for inspection at the places where the proposed SDS was made available for public inspection; and

(d)   send to the Secretary of State and the council of each London borough a copy of the SDS, the notice published by advertisement and any statement of reasons for not accepting a panel's recommendation.[67]

Continuing review and monitoring

9.8   The Mayor is required to keep matters which may be expected to affect the development of Greater London or the planning of its development or which are otherwise relevant to the content of the SDS under review and to consult the local planning authorities whose areas to which those matters relate.[68] The Mayor must also review the SDS from time to time.[69] A review may also be directed by the Secretary of State.[70]

The Mayor is further required to monitor the SDS' implementation, to monitor the local development documents of each London borough council and to monitor and collect information about matters relevant to the preparation, review, alteration, replacement or implementation of the SDS.[71]

The Mayor is empowered to prepare and publish alterations to the SDS or a new SDS at any time.[72] The Secretary of State may direct the Mayor to prepare and publish such alterations or the preparation and publication of a new SDS.[73] The procedure followed for alterations or a new SDS is the same as the original SDS.[74]

---

[65]   Greater London Authority Act 1999, s 337(8).
[66]   Regulations could require other persons to be served but those powers have not been exercised.
[67]   Town and Country Planning (London Spatial Development Strategy) Regulations 2000, reg 9(3).
[68]   Greater London Authority Act 1999, s 339.
[69]   Greater London Authority Act 1999, s 340(1).
[70]   Greater London Authority Act 1999, s 340(2).
[71]   Greater London Authority Act 1999, s 346.
[72]   Greater London Authority Act 1999, s 341(1).
[73]   Greater London Authority Act 1999, s 341(2).
[74]   See the Greater London Authority Act 1999, s 341(3).

London boroughs' development plan documents

9.9   In preparing their local development documents the local planning authorities in Greater London (and those adjoining Greater London) must have regard to the SDS.[75] Any local development documents produced by those London planning authorities must be consistent with the London Plan.[76] Consistency is not merely a matter of planning judgement for the individual boroughs. Rather, a local planning authority which is a London borough (or a Mayoral corporation) is required to request an opinion in writing from the Mayor as to the general conformity of any development plan document with the SDS. The local planning authority may request such an opinion with regards to any other local development document.[77] Absent any request, the Mayor is empowered to give such an opinion unprompted.[78] Where the Mayor is of the opinion that a document is not in general conformity with the SDS the Mayor is taken to have 'made representations seeking a change to the document'.[79]

In *Islington London Borough Council v Mayor of London*[80] it was said that the general conformity requirement meant that the London Plan takes precedence over local development documents on matters of strategic importance. Where there is policy conflict between the London Plan and a local development document on a strategic matter, the London Plan can lawfully prevail.[81]

Schedule A1 to the Planning and Compulsory Purchase Act 2004 sets out default powers to prepare a borough's local plan which are exercisable by the Mayor of London at the request of the Minister. Under para 1 of that Schedule, if the Secretary of State thinks that a London borough council, in their capacity as local planning authority, are failing or omitting to do anything necessary in conjunction with the preparation, revision or adoption of a development plan document and invites the Mayor of London to prepare or refused the document, the Mayor may prepare or revise that development plan document. Paragraph 2 regulates the preparation and revision of such development plan documents by the Mayor. It requires that an independent examination must be held. Once the examination has been held, the Mayor is required to publish the recommendations and reasons of the person conducting the examination and give directions to the particular council with regards to those recommendations and reasons. The Mayor may then approve the document (as it is or subject to specified modifications) or direct the Council to consider adopting the document by resolution.

The Minister still has a power to intervene. Where a development plan document has been prepared or revised by the Mayor of London under para 1 of Sch 1A to the Planning and Compulsory Purchase Act 2004 and the Secretary of State is of the view that the document is unsatisfactory he may (prior to its adoption or approval) direct the Mayor of London to modify the document in accordance with his direction. Any such direction must be accompanied by reasons.[82] The Mayor is required to comply with the direction (unless withdrawn) and the development plan document

---

[75]   Planning and Compulsory Purchase Act 2004, s 19(2)(c).
[76]   Planning and Compulsory Purchase Act 2004, s 24.
[77]   Planning and Compulsory Purchase Act 2004, s 24(4).
[78]   Planning and Compulsory Purchase Act 2004, s 24(5).
[79]   Planning and Compulsory Purchase Act 2004, s 24(7).
[80]   [2013] EWHC 4142 (Admin).
[81]   At para 26.
[82]   Planning and Compulsory Purchase Act 2004, Sch A1, para 8(3).

must not be adopted or approved unless the Secretary of State gives notice that the direction has been complied with.[83]

Alternatively the Minister may direct the Mayor to withdraw such a plan at any time after a local plan after it has been submitted for independent examination but before it is adopted or approved.[84]

MAYORAL SUPPLEMENTARY PLANNING GUIDANCE

9.10   The Mayor of London also produces Supplementary Planning Guidance ('SPG'). This has no explicit statutory basis, although it can be drawn from the Mayor's planning functions. Consultation is carried out on draft SPG, normally with a six-week public consultation period.

The London Plan identifies the role of the Mayor's SPG:[85]

'An SPG (sometimes called supplementary guidance) gives guidance on policies in the London Plan. It does not form a part of the statutory plan. It can take the form of design guides or area development briefs, or supplement other specific policies in the plan. However it must be consistent with national and regional planning guidance, as well as the policies set out in the adopted plan. It should be clearly cross-referenced to the relevant plan policy or proposal that it supplements. Public consultation should be undertaken and SPGs should be regularly reviewed. While only the policies in the London Plan can have the status that the GLA Act 1999 provides in considering planning applications, SPGs may be taken into account as a further material consideration.'

The current SPG consists of:

- Affordable Housing & Viability (August 2017);
- Crossrail Funding (March 2016);
- Housing (March 2016);
- Central Activities Zone (March 2016);
- Social Infrastructure (May 2015);
- Accessible London: Achieving an Inclusive Environment (October 2014);
- The control of dust and emissions during construction and demolition (July 2014);
- Town Centres (July 2014);
- Character and Context (June 2014);
- London Planning Statement (May 2014);
- Sustainable Design and Construction (April 2014);
- Safeguarded Wharves Review (March 2013);
- Preparing Borough Tree and Woodland Strategies (February 2013);

---

[83]   Planning and Compulsory Purchase Act 2004, Sch A1, para 8(3).
[84]   Planning and Compulsory Purchase Act 2004, Sch A1, para 8(7).
[85]   London Plan, March 2016, Annex 6 Glossary, p 426.

- Use of planning obligations in the funding of Crossrail, and the Mayoral Community Infrastructure Levy (April 2013);

- Land for Industry and Transport (September 2012);

- Play and Informal Recreation (September 2012);

- Olympic Legacy (July 2012);

- All London Green Grid (March 2012);

- London View Management Framework (March 2012);

- London's Foundations (March 2012);

- London World Heritage Sites (March 2012);

- Planning for Equality and Diversity in London (October 2007);

A draft Culture and Night Time Economy SPG was published for consultation in April 2017.

THE DEVOLVED CITY REGIONS

9.11   A key part of Conservative government policy over the past eight years or so has been to devolve certain powers away from central government. This agenda has been pursued both through legislative measures (in particular the establishment of combined authorities with directly elected mayors upon whom certain functions are bestowed) and the reaching of more informal 'devolution deals'.

Part 6 of the Local Democracy, Economic Development and Construction Act 2009 ('the 2009 Act'), under the previous Labour government, enables the Secretary of State to make an order establishing combined authorities for areas which meet certain conditions.[86] A combined authority is a corporate body which enables local authorities to work jointly to deliver improvements in economic development, regeneration and transport across a functional economic area.

The 2009 Act enabled the Secretary of State to transfer certain local authority functions to a combined authority.[87] In 2016, Parliament enacted the Cities and Local Government Devolution Act 2016. This broadened the powers which may be conferred upon a combined authority and on all other local authorities, in particular through the addition of s 105A to the 2009 Act.[88] It also inserted s 107A into the 2009 Act which enables the Secretary of State to, by order, provide for there to be a mayor for a combined authority and s 107D which provides for the functions of mayors.

Put simply, the combined effect of ss105A and 107D is that the Secretary of State may by order provide for a Mayor of a combined authority to exercise powers which correspond to those which are exercisable by another public authority. Therefore, because the Mayor of London has a strategic planning function (see above) the Secretary of State can provide for the Mayor of a combined authority also to exercise

---

[86]   See the Local Democracy, Economic Development and Construction Act 2009, s 103 for the conditions.
[87]   Local Democracy, Economic Development and Construction Act 2009, ss 104 and 105.
[88]   See the Cities and Local Government Devolution Act 2016, s 7 which inserts s 105A into the 2009 Act.

a strategic planning function. The procedure for making such an order is set out in s105B.

The following combined authorities with directly elected mayors have thus far been established: Greater Manchester, West Midlands, Tees Valley, West of England, Liverpool City Region, Cambridgeshire and Peterborough and Sheffield City Region. Further, two combined authorities have been established without provision for directly elected mayors: North East Combined Authority and West Yorkshire Combined Authority. One region, Cornwall, has reached a devolution deal with central government but statute has not provided for the establishment of a combined authority covering the area or indeed a directly elected mayor. Not all of the combined authorities have been given strategic planning powers, the establishment of each combined authority and its strategic planning powers are discussed below.

Manchester

9.12 The Greater Manchester Combined Authority ('GMCA') was established on 1 April 2011 by the Greater Manchester Combined Authority Order.[89] It is made up of the constituent councils of: Bolton, Bury, Manchester, Oldham, Rochdale, Salford, Stockport, Tameside, Trafford and Wigan.

The first devolution deal agreement was reached in this region in November 2014. The 'deal' was subsequently expanded in July 2015, November 2015 and March 2016. Part of the original deal (November 2014) was the devolution of strategic planning powers to the directly elected Mayor of Greater Manchester including the power to create a statutory spatial framework for Greater Manchester. It provides a good example of strategic planning policy powers being given to a combined authority.

The agreed planning functions were given a statutory basis through art 3 of the Greater Manchester Combined Authority (Functions and Amendment) Order 2016[90] which bestows on the GMCA the Mayor of London's powers to make, alter and replace an SDS. The approval of an SDS for consultation or publication, or its withdrawal, alteration or replacement requires a unanimous vote by all of the members of the combined authority who are appointed by the constituent councils.[91] Various consequential modifications are made to apply the Greater London Authority Act 1999 and the Planning and Compulsory Purchase Act 2004.[92]

The GMCA is currently in the process of producing the Greater Manchester Spatial Framework pursuant to the planning powers conferred on it by the Greater Manchester Combined Authority (Functions and Amendment) Order 2016.

In preparing their own local development documents, local planning authorities within the GMCA or adjoining Greater Manchester will be required to have regard to the Greater Manchester SDS.[93] The local development documents of the constituent

---

[89] SI 2011/908.
[90] SI 2016/1267.
[91] Greater Manchester Combined Authority (Functions and Amendment) Order 2016, art 3(2).
[92] Greater Manchester Combined Authority (Functions and Amendment) Order 2016, art 4, Sch 1.
[93] Planning and Compulsory Purchase Act 2004, s 19(2)(c) as substituted by the Greater Manchester Combined Authority (Functions and Amendment) Order 2016, Sch 1, Pt 2, para 2(2).

local authorities must be in general conformity with that SDS.[94] As with the Mayor of London, the GMCA's view on general conformity must be sought in respect of local plans.[95]

Liverpool

9.13   The Liverpool City Region Combined Authority ('LCRCA') was established on 1 April 2014 by the Halton, Knowsley, Liverpool, St Helens, Sefton and Wirral Combined Authority Order 2014.[96] Its constituent councils are those mentioned in the title of the 2014 Order.

A devolution deal for the city region was agreed in November 2015 and expanded in March 2016. It includes provision for the devolution of powers over strategic planning, including the responsibility to create a Single Statutory City Region Framework to support the delivery of strategic employment and housing sites throughout the city region.

The LCRCA has since been given statutory powers to prepare and publish its own SDS. This is by virtue of arts 3 and 4 and Sch 1 to the Liverpool City Region Combined Authority (Functions and Amendment) Order 2017.[97] As with the corresponding Order for the Greater Manchester Combined Authority, the Order amends certain sections of the Greater London Authority Act 1999 and the Planning and Compulsory Purchase Act 2004 in order to facilitate this planning function.

Tees Valley

9.14   A devolution deal was reached in this region in October 2015. The Tees Valley Combined Authority ('TVCA') was established on 1 April 2016 by the Tees Valley Combined Authority Order 2016.[98] It is made up of the following constituent councils: Darlington, Hartlepool, Middlesbrough, Redcar and Cleveland and Stockton-on-Tees.

On 3 March 2017, the TVCA was empowered to set up mayoral development corporations. These could become the local planning authority for their area, but only if the affected local planning authorities consent.[99] The TVCA does not have the power to develop its own SDS.

West Midlands

9.15   A devolution deal for the West Midlands was reached in November 2016. It states that planning powers will be conferred on the Mayor to drive housing delivery

---

[94]   Planning and Compulsory Purchase Act 2004, s 24(1) as substituted by the Greater Manchester Combined Authority (Functions and Amendment) Order 2016, Sch 1, Pt 2, para 2(3)(a).
[95]   Planning and Compulsory Purchase Act 2004, s 24(4A) as inserted by the Greater Manchester Combined Authority (Functions and Amendment) Order 2016, Sch 1, Pt 2, para 2(3)(b).
[96]   SI 2014/865.
[97]   SI 2017/430.
[98]   SI 2016/449.
[99]   Tees Valley Combined Authority (Functions) Order 2017, art 3, applying the Localism Act 2011, ss 202, 204.

and improvements in housing stock. The deal stops short of promising to bestow strategic planning functions on the Mayor.

The West Midlands Combined Authority ('WMCA') was established on 17 June 2016 by the West Midlands Combined Authority Order 2016.[100] It is comprised of the constituent councils: Birmingham, Coventry, Dudley, Sandwell, Solihull, Walsall and Wolverhampton. It has not, as yet, been granted powers to develop its own SDS.

West of England

9.16   A devolution deal for the West of England was reached in March 2016. It provided for the West of England Combined Authority Mayor to exercise strategic planning functions which include the power to adopt a statutory SDS.

The West of England Combined Authority ('WECA') was established on 9 February 2017 by the West of England Combined Authority Order 2017.[101] It is made up of the following constituent councils: Bath and North East Somerset, Bristol City and South Gloucestershire.

From 8 May 2018, the WECA will have statutory planning powers to develop its own SDS by virtue of the coming into force of arts 10 and 11 of the 2017 Order.

Cambridgeshire and Peterborough

9.17   A devolution deal was reached in this region in June 2016 between the government, seven local authorities covering Cambridgeshire and Peterborough and the Greater Cambridge Greater Peterborough Local Enterprise Partnership. With regards to planning powers it provides:

'21. The Mayor will exercise strategic planning powers to support and accelerate these ambitions. These will include the power to:

a.   Create a non-statutory spatial framework, which will act as the framework for planning across the Combined Authority area, and for the future development of Local Plans. The spatial framework will need to be approved by unanimous vote of the members appointed by constituent councils of the mayoral Combined Authority. This approach must not delay the production of Local Plans.

b.   Create supplementary planning documents, that can act as material considerations in the determination of planning applications within the Combined Authority area, subject to the approval process.

c.   Create Mayoral Development Corporations or similar rural vehicles, with planning and land assembly powers, which will support delivery of strategic sites in the Combined Authority area. This power will be exercised with the consent of the cabinet member in which the development corporation is to be used.'

The Cambridgeshire and Peterborough Combined Authority was established on 3 March 2017 by the Cambridgeshire and Peterborough Combined Authority

---

[100]   SI 2016/653.
[101]   SI 2017/126.

Order 2017.[102] It is comprised of the following constituent councils: Cambridge, Cambridgeshire, East Cambridgeshire, Fenland, Huntingdonshire, Peterborough and South Cambridgeshire. It has not been granted statutory planning powers to develop its own SDS or supplementary planning documents.

Sheffield City Region

9.18   On 1 April 2014, a combined authority for the Sheffield City Region was established by the Barnsley, Doncaster, Rotherham and Sheffield Combined Authority Order 2014.[103] The constituent councils are those listed in the 2014 Order.

A devolution deal was reached for this region in December 2014 and was expanded in October 2015. The expanded deal gives the Mayor strategic planning powers which include the ability create a spatial framework to manage planning across the city region. These powers have not yet been given a statutory footing.

North East

9.19   The North East Combined Authority was established on 15 April 2015 by the Durham, Gateshead, Newcastle Upon Tyne, North Tyneside, Northumberland, South Tyneside and Sunderland Combined Authority Order 2014.[104] As yet, no devolution deal has been reached for this region and there is no statutory provision for a directly elected mayor or for the exercise of planning powers.

West Yorkshire

9.20   The West Yorkshire Combined Authority was established on 1 April 2014 by the West Yorkshire Combined Authority Order 2014.[105] The constituent councils are: Bradford, Calderdale, Kirklees, Leeds and Wakefield. No devolution deal has been reached for this region and there is no statutory provision for a directly elected mayor or for the exercise of planning powers.

Cornwall

9.21   Although a combined authority has not been established in Cornwall, a devolution deal was reached for the region in July 2015 between the government, Cornwall Council and Cornwall and Isles of Scilly Local Enterprise Partnership. The deal does not include provision for the devolution of strategic planning powers.

---

[102] SI 2017/251.
[103] SI 2014/863.
[104] SI 2014/1012.
[105] SI 2014/864.

Chapter 10

Neighbourhood Development Plans

10.1   Neighbourhood planning was introduced by Pt 6, Ch 3 of the Localism Act 2011. In essence, it is the devolution of planning powers below the district or borough council level and comprises the following elements:

(a)   the establishment of neighbourhood areas;

(b)   the giving of certain planning powers to the parish council or a neighbourhood forum;

(c)   the making of a neighbourhood development plan;

(d)   the granting of planning permission by development orders or community right to build orders.[1]

10.2   These plans and orders are prepared by parish councils and neighbourhood forums, subjected to examination and then made by the local planning authority.

10.3   Section 38A(2) of the Planning and Compulsory Purchase Act 2004 defines a neighbourhood development plan as:

'a plan which sets out policies (however expressed) in relation to the development and use of the land in the whole or any part of a particular neighbourhood area specified in the plan.'

10.4   The plans are usually in practice just referred to as neighbourhood plans.

10.5   The key legislation comprises: ss 61E to 61Q and Sch 4B of the Town and Country Planning Act 1990, ss 38A to 38C of the Planning and Compulsory Purchase Act 2004, the Neighbourhood Planning (General) Regulations 2012[2] and the Neighbourhood Planning (Referendums) Regulations 2012.[3] The Town and Country Planning Act 1990 provisions establish neighbourhood areas and the bodies who exercise planning powers in them, but are then concerned with the grant of planning permission by neighbourhood development order. The neighbourhood development order provisions are then applied with various additions, omissions and modifications to neighbourhood plans by the Planning and Compulsory Purchase Act 2004. At the time of writing, there are some relevant legislative amendments in the Neighbourhood Planning Act 2017 which are being progressively brought into force. They amend sections of both the Town and Country Planning Act 1990 and the Planning and Compulsory Purchase Act 2004.

---

[1]   The grant of planning permission by these orders is considered in Richard Harwood, *Planning Permission* (Bloomsbury, 2016), at 26.24–26.45. The process for making these orders is similar to that for neighbourhood plans.

[2]   SI 2012/637.

[3]   SI 2012/2031.

10.6   The statutory scheme relating to neighbourhood plans is relatively complex and practitioners will often need to cross-refer between various provisions in order to ascertain their application to neighbourhood planning. The detail of neighbourhood planning is set out in the Town and Country Planning Act 1990 for neighbourhood development orders. Neighbourhood plans are then authorised by ss 38A to 38C of the Planning and Compulsory Purchase Act 2004 which applies the order making provisions with various modifications.

10.7   Local planning authorities must have regard to any guidance issued by the Secretary of State in the exercise of any function relating to neighbourhood development plans.[4] The Planning Practice Guidance contains a chapter entitled 'Neighbourhood Plans'. Practitioners should therefore be familiar with this guidance when advising in relation to neighbourhood plans.

THE STATUS OF NEIGHBOURHOOD PLANS AND THEIR RELATIONSHIP WITH LOCAL PLANS

10.8   The neighbourhood development plan is part of the development plan. It therefore benefits from the presumption that when legislation requires regard to be had to the development plan then decisions must be taken in accordance with it unless material considerations indicate otherwise.[5]

10.9   A neighbourhood plan had become part of the development plan from the point at which it is finally made by the local planning authority.[6] Following amendments by the Neighbourhood Planning Act 2017 the development plan now includes neighbourhood plans which have been approved by referendum but which have not yet been made. This brings forward the acquisition of development plan status by a month or so.[7]

10.10   A draft neighbourhood plan is part of the development plan if:[8]

(a)   a majority of those voting in the referendum (or each referendum) have approved the plan;

(b)   the local planning authority have not yet made the plan.

10.11   The neighbourhood plan will cease to be part of the development plan if the authority decide not to make it.[9] If two referendums are held (for residents and business interests), with one approving the plan and the other rejecting it, then the local planning authority have a discretion whether to make the plan.[10] In such

---

[4]   Town and Country Planning Act 1990, s 61O as applied to neighbourhood development plans by the Planning and Compulsory Purchase Act 2004, s 38C.

[5]   Planning and Compulsory Purchase Act 2004, s 38(6).

[6]   Planning and Compulsory Purchase Act 2004, s 38(3)(c). Section 38(10) provides that the term 'neighbourhood development plan' must be construed in accordance with s 38A.

[7]   A neater solution would have been for the neighbourhood plan to be made by approval in the referendum (or referendums), with the local planning authority only having to make the plan if two referendums produced a split result.

[8]   Planning and Compulsory Purchase Act 2004, s 38(3A), inserted by the Neighbourhood Planning Act 2017, s 3 from 19 July 2017.

[9]   Planning and Compulsory Purchase Act 2004, s 38(3B), inserted by the Neighbourhood Planning Act 2017, s 3 from 19 July 2017.

[10]   Planning and Compulsory Purchase Act 2004, s 38A(5).

circumstances the neighbourhood plan will not become part of the development plan unless and until it is made by the authority.

10.12   As with any other emerging plan, a draft neighbourhood plan will be a material consideration in the determination of a planning application with the weight to be given to it affected by how advanced it is, the degree of opposition to particular elements and any apparent conflict with other policies. Unnecessarily therefore, the Neighbourhood Planning Act 2017 has amended s 70 of the Town and Country Planning Act 1990 so that in dealing with an application for planning permission or permission in principle the local planning authority shall have regard to 'a post-examination draft neighbourhood development plan, so far as material to the application'.[11] A 'post-examination draft neighbourhood development plan' is one where the local planning authority has decided or the Secretary of State has directed that a referendum or referendums should be held or an examiner has recommended that an existing plan should be modified.[12] A plan will cease to be a post-examination draft if it is approved by referendum or made, or it is decided not to make the plan.[13]

The relationship with other parts of the development plan

10.13   Further, s 38(5) of the Planning and Compulsory Purchase Act 2004 states that 'If to any extent a policy contained in a development plan for an area conflicts with another policy in the development plan the conflict must be resolved in favour of the policy which is contained in the last document to become part of the development plan'. Therefore, where a neighbourhood development plan has been made after a local plan and the provisions of it are inconsistent with that development plan document then the conflict must be resolved in favour of the neighbourhood plan.

10.14   Neighbourhood plans must comply with various basic conditions, one of which is that the plan 'is in general conformity with the strategic policies contained in the development plan for the area of the authority (or any part of that area)'.[14] The development plan is defined in s 38 of the Planning and Compulsory Purchase Act 2004 and comprises any regional strategy, development plan documents (taken as a whole) which have been adopted or approved in relation to the area and any neighbourhood development plan. However, this is qualified by para 17(a) of Sch 4B to the Town and Country Planning Act 1990 which provides that the reference to 'development plan' in Sch 4B 'does not include so much of a development plan as consists of a neighbourhood development plan'. Neighbourhood plan preparation is therefore not bound by an existing neighbourhood plan. The statute does not define 'strategic policies' or 'general conformity'. This 'basic condition' (see 10.103) has been the subject of considerable litigation.

---

[11]   Town and Country Planning Act 1990, s 70(2)(aza), inserted by the Neighbourhood Planning Act 2017, s 1(2) from 19 July 2017.

[12]   Town and Country Planning Act 1990, s 70(3B), inserted by the Neighbourhood Planning Act 2017, s 1(3) from 19 July 2017. Where an examiner considering a modification to an existing plan recommends that the plan is made with further modifications then the relevant plan is in that final modified form: s 70(3C).

[13]   Town and Country Planning Act 1990, s 70(3D), (3E), inserted by the Neighbourhood Planning Act 2017, s 1(3) from 19 July 2017.

[14]   Town and Country Planning Act 1990, Sch 4B, para 8(2)(e). See also National Planning Policy Framework ('NPPF'), para 184.

10.15   In *R (on the application of DLA Delivery Ltd) v Lewes District Council*[15] the appellants challenged the Newick Neighbourhood Plan ('NNP') on the basis that it was not in general conformity with the strategic policies of the Local Plan as the adopted Local Plan only addressed development needs up to 2011 and therefore did not contain any relevant strategic content as regards contemporary housing needs for the area. It further argued that the evidence demonstrated that the NNP was not intended to be in conformity with the adopted Local Plan but rather the emerging Local Plan.[16]

10.16   Previous High Court decisions had established that a neighbourhood plan could be 'made' before a Local Plan had been adopted, ie the lack of strategic policies for housing in an up-to-date Local Plan did not prevent the making of a neighbourhood development plan.[17] Lord Justice Lindblom approved the first instance decisions in this regard and went on to state:

'22   ... The provisions of Part 2 of the 2004 Act envisage a "local development scheme" comprising "development plan documents", which will together form the statutory development plan for the local planning authority's area (section 17(3) of the 2004 Act). A neighbourhood development plan, once made, will be a constituent part of the development plan (section 38A(2) of the 2004 Act). As one would expect, the statutory scheme seeks to ensure an appropriate degree of consistency between a neighbourhood development plan and the strategy of the extant, statutorily adopted development plan. That is the essential purpose of the "basic condition" in paragraph 8(2)(e). Section 13 of the 1990 Act requires local planning authorities to keep their development plan documents under review. If a neighbourhood development plan has been made and the local planning authority later produces a development plan document containing new "strategic policies", that development plan document will, under section 38(5) of the 2004 Act, prevail over any inconsistent policies in the neighbourhood development plan. And if a policy in a neighbourhood development plan is not, or ceases to be, up-to-date, this will be a material consideration in a development control decision, and may justify departing from that policy.

23   Nor, in my view, does the language of paragraph 8(2)(e) bear the interpretation urged upon us by Mr Young. The true sense of the expression "in general conformity with the strategic policies contained in the development plan" is simply that if there are relevant "strategic policies" contained in the adopted development plan for the local planning authority's area, or part of that area, the neighbourhood development plan must not be otherwise than in "general conformity" with those "strategic policies". The degree of conformity required is "general" conformity with "strategic" policies. Whether there is or is not sufficient conformity to satisfy that requirement will be a matter of fact and planning judgment (see the judgment of Laws L.J. in *Persimmon Homes and others v Stevenage Borough Council* [2006] 1 W.L.R. 334, at pp.344D-345D and pp.347F-348F).

24   ... Housing allocations made in a neighbourhood development plan for a plan period which does not coincide or even overlap with the period of an adopted local plan cannot logically be said to lack "general conformity" in this respect with the strategic housing policies of that local plan for that local plan period. In those circumstances the two plans will have been planning for the provision of housing

15   [2017] EWCA Civ 58, [2017] JPL 721.
16   See para 115 of Foskett J's judgement at first instance cited by the Court of Appeal at para 13.
17   See *R (on the application of Gladman Developments Ltd) v Aylesbury Vale District Council* [2014] EWHC 4323 (Admin), [2015] JPL 656; *Woodcock Holdings Ltd v Secretary of State for Communities and Local Government* [2015] EWHC 1173 (Admin), [2015] JPL 1151; *R (on the application of Crownhall Estates Ltd) v Chichester District Council* [2016] EWHC 73 (Admin).

in wholly different periods. In this case – as in *Gladman Developments v Aylesbury Vale District Council* (see paragraphs 27 and 31 of the judgment), but in contrast, for example, to the situation in Crane (see paragraph 7 of the judgment in that case) – the period for which the 2003 local plan had planned had elapsed before the preparation of the NNP was begun, and some four years before it was made. As Mr Young himself submitted in reply, the NNP does not align itself with the housing requirement in the 2003 local plan, and the NNP could not possibly do that because its period runs from 2015 to 2030, whereas the period of the 2003 local plan ran from 1991 to 2011.

25   Paragraph 8(2)(e) does not require the making of a neighbourhood development plan to await the adoption of any other development plan document. It does not prevent a neighbourhood development plan from addressing housing needs unless or until there is an adopted development plan document in place setting a housing requirement for a period coinciding, wholly or partly, with the period of the neighbourhood development plan. A neighbourhood development plan may include, for example, policies allocating land for particular purposes, including housing development, even when there are no "strategic policies" in the statutorily adopted development plan to which such policies in the neighbourhood development plan can sensibly relate. This may be either because there are no relevant "strategic policies" at all or because the relevant strategy itself is now effectively redundant, its period having expired. The neighbourhood development plan may also conform with the strategy of an emerging local plan. It may, for example, anticipate the strategy for housing development in that emerging plan and still not lack "general conformity" with the "strategic policies" of the existing development plan.'

Lindblom LJ considered that the approach in the National Planning Policy Framework and Planning Practice Guidance was consistent with this.[18]

10.17   General conformity is assessed against the neighbourhood plan as a whole.[19] Dove J has observed:[20]

'exercising the planning judgment in relation to general conformity there is sufficient elasticity in the evaluation to accommodate some conflict with strategic policies as well as the prospect of strategic policies being reviewed. But that elasticity has limits, and the extent of the limit will be part and parcel of the planning judgment.'

NEIGHBOURHOOD AREAS, PARISH COUNCILS AND NEIGHBOURHOOD FORUMS

10.18   Two separate, but related, processes are the designation of a neighbourhood area and, in the absence of a parish council, the identification of the body to exercise planning powers in respect of it. Determining the neighbourhood area logically comes first, but since they are proposed by the bodies who intend to run them, they are closely aligned.

---

[18]   At para 26, approving Foskett J at para 129 and citing the NPPF, paras 184, 185.
[19]   *R (on the application of Crownhall Estates Ltd) v Chichester District Council*, at para 29(ii) per Holgate J; *R (on the application of Swan Quay LLP) v Swale Borough Council* [2017] EWHC 420 (Admin), at para 29 per Dove J.
[20]   *Swan Quay*, at para 32, after citing *Persimmon Homes (Thames Valley) Ltd v Stevenage Borough Council* [2005] EWCA Civ 1365, [2006] 1 WLR 334; followed in *R (on the application of Bewley Homes plc) v Waverley Borough Council* [2017] EWHC 1776 (Admin), [2017] 2 P & CR 19, at para 37 per Lang J.

Parish councils

10.19   A parish council is authorised to act in relation to a neighbourhood area if that area consists of or includes the whole or any part of the parish council's area.[21] Where a neighbourhood area also includes the whole or any part of the area of another parish council, a parish council will only be authorised to act for neighbourhood plan purposes if the other parish council gives its consent.[22] Where the neighbourhood area (or part of that area) falls within the area of a parish council then no other organisation or body may be designated for that neighbourhood area.[23]

10.20   One consequence of neighbourhood plan preparation is to increase the consultation rights of parish councils on planning applications. The Neighbourhood Planning Act 2017 proposes to require the local planning authority to notify[24] the parish council of any planning application or reserved matters application or alteration to such an application relating to land within the area of a made or post-examination neighbourhood plan,[25] unless the parish council has said it does not want to be notified.[26] Where there is no neighbourhood plan (or only an earlier draft), the parish council has only to be notified if it has asked to be informed of applications generally or a specific description of application.[27] These provisions could be simplified by requiring parish councils to be automatically notified of applications with their area.

Neighbourhood forum

10.21   Whilst a parish council is automatically authorised to act for a neighbourhood area, any other body may only act if they are designated by the local planning authority as a neighbourhood forum.[28]

10.22   The decision to designate an organisation or body as a neighbourhood forum may only be made in response to an application by that body.[29] The application must include: the name of the proposed neighbourhood forum; a copy of its written constitution; the name of the neighbourhood area to which the application relates (together with a map identifying that area); the contact details of one member of the proposed neighbourhood forum and a statement of how the proposed neighbourhood forum meets the conditions as set out in s 61F(5) of the Town and Country Planning Act 1990.[30]

---

[21]   Town and Country Planning Act 1990, s 61F(1) as applied by the Planning and Compulsory Purchase Act 2004, s 38C.
[22]   Town and Country Planning Act 1990, s 61F(2) as applied by the Planning and Compulsory Purchase Act 2004, s 38C.
[23]   Town and Country Planning Act 1990, s 61F(4) as applied by the Planning and Compulsory Purchase Act 2004, s 38C.
[24]   Town and Country Planning Act 1990, Sch 1, para 8(3B), prospectively inserted by the Neighbourhood Planning Act 2017, s 2 and not yet in force.
[25]   A post-examination neighbourhood development plan is broadly one which is being put to a referendum: see Town and Country Planning Act 1990, s 70(3B)–(3F) and 10.10 and 10.11 above.
[26]   A parish council can say that it does not want to be notified of any planning applications or only be informed of applications of a particular description: Town and Country Planning Act 1990, Sch 1, para 8(3C), (3D).
[27]   Town and Country Planning Act 1990, Sch 1, para 8(1)–(3).
[28]   Town and Country Planning Act 1990, s 61F(3) as applied to neighbourhood plans by the Planning and Compulsory Purchase Act 2004, s 38C.
[29]   Town and Country Planning Act 1990, s 61F(7)(c) as applied to neighbourhood plans by the Planning and Compulsory Purchase Act 2004, s 38C.
[30]   Neighbourhood Planning (General) Regulations 2012, reg 8.

10.23   The local planning authority may decline to determine an application for a new neighbourhood forum if a forum has already been designated for that area and the designation has not expired or been withdrawn.[31]

10.24   Section 61F(5) of the Town and Country Planning Act 1990 states that a local authority may designate an organisation or body as a neighbourhood forum if it meets certain conditions. Those conditions are as follows.

> '(a) it is established for the express purpose of promoting or improving the social, economic and environmental well-being of an area that consists of or includes the neighbourhood area concerned (whether or not it is also established for the express purpose of promoting the carrying on of trades, professions or other businesses in such an area);'

A neighbourhood forum can be an existing organisation, such as a local amenity society or a business organisation, or it may be formed for the purpose of being a neighbourhood forum. Either route has advantages and disadvantages. An established body may have the membership and infrastructure to put together a plan with wide involvement, yet it may also have a reputation and policy approach which puts off potential participants. A new organisation will lack that historical baggage but may have to work harder to become well-known and representative.

> '(b) its membership is open to –
>
> > (i) individuals who live in the neighbourhood area concerned,
> >
> > (ii) individuals who work there (whether for business carried on there or otherwise), and
> >
> > (iii) individuals who are elected members of a country council, district council or London borough council any of whose area falls within the neighbourhood area concerned,'

Membership has to be genuinely open. A neighbourhood forum is a public body, exercising statutory powers in the public interest. It is not a private members' club. Paragraph (b) sets out those who must be allowed to join. No further explanation is given on the categories, but living in the area is straightforward and should be given a wide meaning. It will include part-time residents such as students and second-home occupiers. Working in the area will include someone whose place of employment or business is based in the area. A person whose regular 'beat' is in the area could also work there even if their physical base is elsewhere, such as a postal worker or police officer. Councillors are entitled to be members if the neighbourhood forum is in the council area: it does not have to include part of their ward or division.

> '(c) its membership includes a minimum of 21 individuals each of whom –
>
> > (i) lives in the neighbourhood area concerned,
> >
> > (ii) works there (whether for a business carried on there or otherwise), or
> >
> > (iii) is an elected member of a county council, district council or London borough council any of whose area falls within the neighbourhood area concerned,'

One way the legislation seeks to ensure local credibility is having a minimum number of members with a local qualification.

> '(d) it has a written constitution, and'

---

[31] Neighbourhood Planning (General) Regulations, reg 11.

No requirements had been set out for a written constitution. However, it would need to cover membership, the election of officers, decision-making, recording of meetings and decisions, and interests of officers and those actively involved in preparing the plan.

'(e)   such other conditions as may be prescribed.'[32]

No further conditions have thus far been prescribed.

10.25   Section 61F(5) confers a discretion to designate and the local planning authority are not obliged to do so even if all of the criteria are satisfied. It could, for example, refuse to designate a body which was advancing repeated applications for neighbourhood areas which the authority was seeking to refuse.[33]

10.26   Section 61F(6) allows the Secretary of State to prescribe criteria for a body to be designated which are different and an alternative to those in s 61F(5).[34] However, no such prescribed conditions have been set.

10.27   Ideally a neighbourhood forum should be representative of its area. The local planning authority must have regard to the desirability of designating an organisation or body:[35]

(i)   which has secured (or taken reasonable steps to attempt to secure) that its membership includes at least one individual falling within category of living, working and being an elected member for the area on a principal council;

(ii)   whose membership is drawn from different places in the neighbourhood area concerned and from different sections of the community in that area; and

(iii) whose purpose reflects (in general terms) the character of that area.

10.28   The local planning authority must publish the application on its website and in other ways likely to bring it to the attention of people who live, work or carry on business in the area along with a statement that if a designation is made no other organisation or body may be designated for that neighbourhood area until that designation expires or is withdrawn; details of how to make representations; and the closing date for those representations.[36] The consultation period is a minimum of six weeks from first publication of the application.[37] The Neighbourhood Planning (General) Regulations 2012 prescribe the date by which the local planning authority must reach a decision on any neighbourhood forum application.[38] Two different deadlines apply depending on where the neighbourhood area is located:

(a)   in a case where the neighbourhood area to which the application relates falls within the area of two or more local planning authorities, the authority must determine the application by the last day of the expiry of 20 weeks beginning with the day following that when the application is first publicised in accordance with reg 9 of the Neighbourhood Planning (General) Regulations 2012; and

---

[32]   Town and Country Planning Act 1990, s 61F(5).
[33]   *R (on the application of Daws Hill Neighbourhood Forum) v Wycombe District Council* [2014] EWCA Civ 228, [2014] 1 WLR 1362, at paras 12, 18 per Sullivan LJ.
[34]   As the local planning authority 'may also designate' a body which meets those conditions.
[35]   Town and Country Planning Act 1990, s 61F(7)(a).
[36]   Neighbourhood Planning (General) Regulations 2012, reg 9.
[37]   Neighbourhood Planning (General) Regulations 2012, reg 9.
[38]   Neighbourhood Planning (General) Regulations 2012, reg 9A.

(b)   in all other cases, the authority must determine the application by the last day of the expiry of 13 weeks beginning with the day following that when the application is first publicised in accordance with reg 9 Neighbourhood Planning (General) Regulations 2012.[39]

10.29   A local authority cannot designate more than one organisation or body as a neighbourhood forum for each neighbourhood area.[40] Where a neighbourhood forum has been designated in relation to a neighbourhood area, and that designation has not expired or been withdrawn,[41] the local planning authority may decline to consider any other neighbourhood forum application which relates to that neighbourhood area.[42]

10.30   If a neighbourhood forum is designated, the authority must as soon as possible publicise on its website and by any other means to bring to local attention:[43]

(a)   the name of the neighbourhood forum;

(b)   a copy of the written constitution of the neighbourhood forum;

(c)   the name of the neighbourhood area to which the designation relates; and

(d)   contact details for at least one member of the neighbourhood forum.

10.31   Where an application by an organisation or body to be designated as a neighbourhood forum is refused, a local planning authority must give reasons for its decision.[44] These are to be set out in a refusal statement, published on its website by any other way to bring to local attention, and available for inspection.[45]

10.32   Where a designation is made by a local planning authority it will have effect for a period of five years beginning with the day on which the designation is made. The expiry of a designation will not affect the validity of any proposal for a neighbourhood development plan made before the end of that period.[46] It is proposed that a forum's designation will cease to have effect if all or part of the neighbourhood area is incorporated into a new or amended parish council area.[47]

---

[39] Note that these dates do not apply where, on that date, the authority is considering another neighbourhood forum application and that other application relates to an area which consists of or includes some or all of the neighbourhood area to which the application relates (reg 9A(3)).

[40] Town and Country Planning Act 1990, s 61F(7)(b) as applied to neighbourhood plans by the Planning and Compulsory Purchase Act 2004, s 38C.

[41] See Town and Country Planning Act 1990, s 61F(9) and the Neighbourhood Planning (General) Regulations 2012, reg 12, discussed at 10.36 below.

[42] Neighbourhood Planning (General) Regulations 2012, reg 11. It will not then need to publicise the application: reg 9.

[43] Neighbourhood Planning (General) Regulations 2012, reg 10(1).

[44] Town and Country Planning Act 1990, s 61F(7)(d) as applied to neighbourhood plans by the Planning and Compulsory Purchase Act 2004, s 38C.

[45] Neighbourhood Planning (General) Regulations 2012, reg 10(2).

[46] Town and Country Planning Act 1990, s 61F(8)(a) as applied to neighbourhood plans by the Planning and Compulsory Purchase Act 2004, s 38C.

[47] Town and Country Planning Act 1990, s 61F(8A), as proposed to be inserted by the Neighbourhood Planning Act 2017, s 5(2) and applied by the Planning and Compulsory Purchase Act 2004, s 38C(2). The validity of a proposal for a neighbourhood plan will be unaffected by the forum's designation ceasing to have effect: Town and Country Planning Act 1990, s 61F(8B), as proposed to be inserted by the Neighbourhood Planning Act 2017, s 5(2).

10.33   Where an unincorporated body is designated as a neighbourhood forum, a change in its membership will not affect the designation.[48]

10.34   A parish council or neighbourhood forum may only make one proposal for a neighbourhood plan in relation to a neighbourhood area at a time.[49] This reflects the nature of neighbourhood plans as single documents for their area.

10.35   A neighbourhood forum has rights to be consulted on planning applications. From the point that it is designated it may make a written request to be informed of any application for planning permission, reserved matters approval or permission in principle in its area, or any alteration of such application and it will then be notified.[50] Additionally, the local planning authority will be under a duty to notify[51] the neighbourhood forum of any planning application or reserved matters application or alteration to such an application relating to land within the area of a made or post-examination neighbourhood plan,[52] unless the forum has said it does not want to be notified.[53] As with parish council notification, these provisions are unnecessarily complicated.

10.36   A neighbourhood forum's designation may be withdrawn by a local planning authority if it considers that it is no longer meeting the designation conditions[54] or any other criteria that the authority had to have regard to. If a neighbourhood forum gives notice that it wishes to cease that role then the authority must withdraw its designation.[55] Reasons must be given to a forum for the withdrawal of its designation[56] and a withdrawal statement published on the authority's website and locally.[57]

Neighbourhood area

10.37   The meaning of 'neighbourhood area' and their designation is governed by s 61G(1) of the Town and Country Planning Act 1990. It states:

---

[48] Town and Country Planning Act 1990, s 61F(8)(b) as applied to neighbourhood plans by the Planning and Compulsory Purchase Act 2004, s 38C.

[49] Town and Country Planning Act 1990, s 61F(10) as applied to neighbourhood plans by the Planning and Compulsory Purchase Act 2004, s 38C.

[50] Town and Country Planning Act 1990, Sch 1, para 8(1). The duty arose from 1 October 2016, inserted by the Housing and Planning Act 2016, s 142. When informed of an application, the forum must notify the local planning authority as soon as practicable whether it intends to make representations and send those in within 21 days: Town and Country Planning (Development Management Procedure) (England) Order 2015, SI 2015/595, art 25(a). The authority must take any such representations into account and inform the forum of its decision on the application, any referral to the Secretary of State and the Minister's decision on any referral: Town and Country Planning (Development Management Procedure) (England) Order 2015, art 25(2),(3) applied by art 25A(b).

[51] Town and Country Planning Act 1990, Sch 1, para 8A(1B), prospectively inserted by the Neighbourhood Planning Act 2017, s 2 and not yet in force.

[52] A post-examination neighbourhood development plan is broadly one which is being put to a referendum: see Town and Country Planning Act 1990, s 70(3B)–(3F) and 10.10 and 10.11 above.

[53] A neighbourhood forum will be able to say that it does not want to be notified of any planning applications or only be informed of applications of a particular description: Town and Country Planning Act 1990, Sch 1, para 8A(1C), (1D).

[54] Withdrawal is under the Town and Country Planning Act 1990, s 61(9); the conditions are in s 61F(5) and the reference to other criteria appears to be to s 61F(7), all as applied to neighbourhood plans by the Planning and Compulsory Purchase Act 2004, s 38C.

[55] Neighbourhood Planning (General) Regulations 2012, reg 12(1).

[56] Town and Country Planning Act 1990, s 61F(9) as applied to neighbourhood plans by the Planning and Compulsory Purchase Act 2004, s 38C.

[57] Neighbourhood Planning (General) Regulations 2012, reg 12(2).

10.38 *Neighbourhood Development Plans*

'A "neighbourhood area" means an area within the area of a local planning authority in England which has been designated by the authority as a neighbourhood area; but that power to designate is exercisable only where –

(a) a relevant body has applied to the authority for an area specified in the application to be designated by the authority as a neighbourhood area, and

(b) the authority are determining the application (but see sub-section 5)).'

10.38   Therefore a neighbourhood area is simply an area which has been designated by the local planning authority on an application by a body who could exercise planning powers in the area.

10.39   It is clear that there is considerable flexibility in what will amount to a 'neighbourhood area'. This sentiment was elucidated by Greg Clark MP, Minister of State, Department for Communities and Local Government before the Public Bill Committee on the Localism Bill.[58] He stated:

'I understand the hon. Gentleman's point. It illustrates a theme in our drafting of this section of the Bill, which is not to prescribe from the centre exactly what a neighbourhood should look like. I was going to say that that was fraught with difficulties, but it is actually impossible. He is absolutely right that all neighbourhoods differ, so the only people who can make such an assessment are those on the ground, who know the natural set of connections between people locally. It is impossible to design that in the Bill or to say that every neighbourhood is a local authority ward, for example, or a county division. That is why we have allowed flexibility for the determination of what a neighbourhood should be, and we have given a crucial role to the local authority in determining that. The question of whether a neighbourhood is right for the purposes of a neighbourhood forum is vested in the local authority. It will have the final decision, and the Bill refers in various ways to related requirements. It requires that the local authority has the final say on designating the appropriate area, which will be subject to criteria for what local authorities should take into account. Those criteria will be set out and as the Bill progresses, we will share what we have in mind with Parliament. It is clear, however, that local planning authorities will have the final say in designating the areas. That is absolutely right, because such bodies are the most consistent and democratically accountable organisations to determine that, and proposed new section 61G to the Town and Country Planning Act 1990 makes it clear that the local planning authority has the final say in designating neighbourhood areas.'

10.40   The authority can decline to designate the specified area if they consider it is not 'an appropriate area to be designated' by virtue of the Town and Country Planning Act 1990, s 61G(5) which provides:

'If –

(a) a valid application is made to the authority,

(b) some or all of the specified area has not been designated as a neighbourhood area, and

(c) the authority refuse the application because they consider that the specified area is not an appropriate area to be designated as a neighbourhood area,

the authority must exercise their power of designation so as to secure that some or all of the specified area forms part of one or more areas designated (or to be designated) as neighbourhood areas.'

---

[58]   Localism Bill, Public Bill Committee, 1 March 2011, col 684.

10.41 The case of *R (on the application of Daws Hill Neighbourhood Forum) v Wycombe District Council*[59] concerned a challenge brought by a residents association who had applied to the district council for designation of a neighbourhood area and to be its neighbourhood forum under ss 61F and 61G of the Town and Country Planning Act 1990. After the district council decided to designate only part of the area applied for (which excluded two strategic development sites) the claimants brought a judicial review against that decision. Upholding the decisions, the High Court found that a local planning authority has a broad discretion under s 61G(5) which is to be exercised having regard to the factual and policy matrix which pertains in relation to the individual case at the time of the determination.[60] The Court of Appeal upheld that judgment confirming that broad discretion upon a local planning authority. Lord Justice Sullivan stated:[61]

'7 … On the face of it, a power given to a local planning authority to decide whether a specified area is "an appropriate area" to be designated as a neighbourhood area necessarily confers a broad discretion. The designation of an area as a neighbourhood area is not an end in itself. The purpose of designating an area as a neighbourhood area is to define the area within which a neighbourhood forum (outside the area of a parish council) is authorised to exercise certain planning powers: the making of a neighbourhood plan and/or a neighbourhood development order. When determining the issue of appropriateness it may, therefore, be necessary to have regard to a wide range of planning considerations.'

Sullivan LJ held that the authority could reject part of the applied for area and leave it outside any neighbourhood area:

'8 … When imposing the duty on the manner in which the designation power must be exercised under section 61G(5), Parliament clearly envisaged that a local planning authority might exercise the power so as to designate a smaller area as a neighbourhood area leaving part or parts of the specified area outwith any neighbourhood area.'

10.42 The authority had been entitled to have regard to the factual and policy circumstances at the time and exclude the two strategic sites from the neighbourhood area where their planning processes were well advanced.[62]

10.43 A parish council may make an application as a relevant body[63] but only for an area which includes (and so may extend beyond) part or all of the parish.[64]

An organisation or body which is, or is capable of being, designated as a neighbourhood forum for the proposed area may apply.[65] Sullivan LJ suggested in *Daws Hill* that a body could not make an application for a neighbourhood area if an application by it to be a neighbourhood forum had been refused.[66] Since the body for a parish's area is the parish council, no other person may apply for the designation of a neighbourhood area which includes a parish.[67]

---

[59] [2014] EWCA Civ 228, [2014] 1 WLR 1362.
[60] [2013] EWHC 513 (Admin), [2013] PTSR 970, at para 57 and also see para 42 per Supperstone J.
[61] At para 7.
[62] *Daws Hill*, at paras 20 and 22 per Sullivan LJ.
[63] Town and Country Planning Act 1990, s 61G(2)(a).
[64] Town and Country Planning Act 1990, s 61G(3)(a).
[65] Town and Country Planning Act 1990, s 61G(2)(b).
[66] At para 18 per Sullivan LJ.
[67] Town and Country Planning Act 1990, s 61G(3)(b).

10.44 There is a presumption in favour of neighbourhood areas covering entire parishes, as the authority must have regard to:

> 'the desirability of designating the whole of the area of a parish council as a neighbourhood area'.[68]

It is also seen as desirable to maintain the existing boundaries of areas already designated as neighbourhood areas.[69]

10.45 There is otherwise no explanation of what can or cannot be a neighbourhood area. Some force must be given to its description as a neighbourhood area – it should be based around something that can be described as a neighbourhood but need not include all of any such area. An entire district, borough or county council area could not be designated as a neighbourhood, on rationality grounds and because, given the intention to create a planning layer below those principal authorities, it would not be a neighbourhood.[70]

10.46 One or more existing neighbourhood areas may be modified when an application for a new or altered area is made. However, a parish council's neighbourhood area can only be modified with its consent.[71]

10.47 The power to make a modification on an application is to be significantly amended by the Neighbourhood Planning Act 2017. This will explicitly include power:[72]

(a)   to change the boundary of an existing neighbourhood area;

(b)   to replace an existing neighbourhood area with two or more separate neighbourhood areas; and

(c)   to replace two or more existing neighbourhood areas with a single neighbourhood area.

10.48 The boundaries of the new area or areas may include additional land which was previously outside any neighbourhood area.[73] A neighbourhood plan will survive the modification of its neighbourhood area even if more than one such plan has effect for that area.[74] Of course, in the event of conflict between the plans, the most recent one will prevail.[75] A new neighbourhood plan may amend or revoke an existing

---

[68]   Town and Country Planning Act 1990, s 61G(4)(a). However, the local planning authority is not obliged to agree a parish council's request for the whole of their area to be a neighbourhood area: *Daws Hill*, at para 8 per Sullivan LJ.

[69]   Town and Country Planning Act 1990, s 61G(4)(b).

[70]   The complexities as to what is a locality in village and town green legislation should be avoided.

[71]   Town and Country Planning Act 1990, s 61G(6).

[72]   Town and Country Planning Act 1990, s 61G(6A), proposed to be inserted by the Neighbourhood Planning Act 2017, s 5(3).

[73]   Town and Country Planning Act 1990, s 61G(6B), (6C), proposed to be inserted by the Neighbourhood Planning Act 2017, s 5(3).

[74]   Planning and Compulsory Purchase Act 2004, s 38C(5A) as proposed to be inserted by the Neighbourhood Planning Act 2017, s 5(8), applying the Town and Country Planning Act 1990, s 61G(6D), proposed to be inserted by the Neighbourhood Planning Act 2017, s 5(3). This will be an exception to the normal rule that there may only be one neighbourhood plan for an area: Planning and Compulsory Purchase Act 2004, s 38(2A), proposed to be inserted by the Neighbourhood Planning Act 2017, s 5(7), as an exception to s38(1)(c),(2).

[75]   Planning and Compulsory Purchase Act 2004, s 38(5).

plan. If the area boundaries have changed in the meantime then the alteration or replacement will only have effect in relation to the area for which the change is made. The original plan will continue to have effect on other land.[76]

10.49 There can only be one neighbourhood area for any piece of land: designated neighbourhood areas must not overlap with each other.[77]

10.50 A local planning authority must publish a map setting out the areas that are for the time being designated as neighbourhood areas.[78]

10.51 Reasons must be given to the applicant if the application is refused.[79]

10.52 When a neighbourhood area is designated or modified the local planning authority must consider whether they should designate it as a business area.[80] They may only exercise this power if they consider the area is 'wholly or predominantly business in nature'.[81] Even so, designating a business area appears to be discretionary – there is no duty to designate. The significance of such designation is that two referendums will be held in business areas with electors and non-domestic ratepayers voting separately.

10.53 Where a neighbourhood area falls within two or more local planning authorities the power to designate such an area is exercisable by those planning authorities.[82]

10.54 An application to the local planning authority for designation of a neighbourhood area must include: a map which identifies the area to which the area application relates; a statement explaining why that area is considered appropriate to be designated as a neighbourhood area; and a statement that the organisation or body making the area application is a relevant body for the purposes of s 61G.[83] A local planning authority may decline to consider an area application if the relevant body has already made an area application and a decision has not been made on that application.[84]

10.55 Once a local planning authority has received such an application it must publicise a copy of the application, details of how to make representations and the date by which representations must be received[85] on its website and in such manner as it considers is likely to bring the application to the attention of people who live, work or carry on business in the area to which the application relates.[86]

---

[76] This is because a parish council or neighbourhood forum cannot initiate a change in policy outside its neighbourhood area. The point will be made explicitly for the replacement of a plan in part of its previous area by the Planning and Compulsory Purchase Act 2004, s 38A(11B), (11C), proposed to be inserted by the Neighbourhood Planning Act 2017, s 5(6).

[77] Town and Country Planning Act 1990, s 61G(7).

[78] Town and Country Planning Act 1990, s 61G(8).

[79] Town and Country Planning Act 1990, s 61G(9).

[80] Town and Country Planning Act 1990, s 61H(1),(2).

[81] Town and Country Planning Act 1990, s 61H(3).

[82] Town and Country Planning Act 1990, s 61I.

[83] Neighbourhood Planning (General) Regulations 2012, reg 5(1).

[84] Neighbourhood Planning (General) Regulations 2012, reg 5(2).

[85] This is not less than six weeks from the date on which the area application is first published: Neighbourhood Planning (General) Regulations 2012, reg 6(c).

[86] Neighbourhood Planning (General) Regulations 2012, , reg 6.

10.56   An application by a parish council for the entirety of its area, no land outside it and not including part of a neighbourhood area which crosses the boundary must be approved by the local planning authority.[87]

10.57   If the neighbourhood area proposed in the applications falls within the areas of two planning authorities then they have 20 weeks from the day after publication of the application to decide it; and a single authority has 13 weeks from the day after publication in all other cases.[88] Where the local planning authority fails to make a decision in time it is required to designate the whole of the application area as the neighbourhood area unless on that date: (a) some or all of the specified area has been designated as a neighbourhood area; or (b) some or all of the specified area is specified in another area application and that other area application has not been determined.[89]

10.58   As soon as possible following designation the local planning authority must publish on its website and by other means to bring to the attention of those who live, work and carry on business in the area, the name of the neighbourhood area, a map showing it and the relevant body who made the application.[90] If an application is refused then the authority must similarly publish a 'decision document' setting out the refusal and the reasons for it.[91]

THE CONTENT OF NEIGHBOURHOOD PLANS

10.59   Neighbourhood plans must specify the period for which they are to have effect.[92] A plan may only relate to one neighbourhood area[93] and each neighbourhood area may only have one neighbourhood plan which relates to it.[94]

10.60   Neighbourhood plans may not contain provisions about development which is 'excluded development'.[95] Excluded development is defined in s 61K of the Town and Country Planning Act 1990 as:[96]

(a)   minerals development amounting to county matters, including development affecting approved restoration schemes;[97]

(b)   development which consists of the carrying out of any operation wholly or mainly for the purposes of recovering, treating, storing, processing, sorting, transferring or depositing of waste or the use of land or the carrying out of operations for any purposes ancillary to any such use or operations, including

---

[87]   Neighbourhood Planning (General) Regulations 2012, reg 5A(1). The application does not then have to be publicised: reg 5A(2).
[88]   Neighbourhood Planning (General) Regulations 2012, reg 6A(2).
[89]   Neighbourhood Planning (General) Regulations 2012, reg 6A(3).
[90]   Neighbourhood Planning (General) Regulations 2012, reg 7(1).
[91]   Neighbourhood Planning (General) Regulations 2012, reg 7(2).
[92]   Planning and Compulsory Purchase Act 2004, s 38B(1)(a).
[93]   Planning and Compulsory Purchase Act 2004, s 38B(1)(c).
[94]   Planning and Compulsory Purchase Act 2004, s 38B(2).
[95]   Planning and Compulsory Purchase Act 2004, s 38(1)(b).
[96]   Applies to neighbourhood plans by the Planning and Compulsory Purchase Act 2004, s 38B(6).
[97]   Town and Country Planning Act 1990, Sch 1, para 1(1)(a)–(h).

the formation, laying out, construction or alteration of a vehicular access to any public highway;[98]

(c) development which automatically requires environmental impact assessment under Annex 1 of the Environmental Impact Assessment Directive 85/337/EEC; and

(d) development that consists (whether wholly or partly) of a nationally significant infrastructure project.[99]

10.61 The approved restoration scheme exclusion is 'the carrying out of operations in, on, over or under land, or a use of land, where the land is or forms part of a site used or formerly used for the winning and working of minerals and where the operations or use would conflict with or prejudice compliance with a restoration condition or an aftercare condition'.[100] In *R (on the application of Hoare) v Vale of White Horse District Council* a former quarry was subject to a planning permission requiring restoration to agriculture by September 2016 and then a five-year aftercare period.[101] The neighbourhood plan policy safeguarded the land for employment uses 'following the completion of quarrying and restoration activities'. John Howell QC considered that 'restoration activities' would be complete at the end of the aftercare period and so the plan did not relate to excluded development.[102]

10.62 Although it may appear obvious, the Planning and Compulsory Purchase Act 2004 specifically provides that where a policy set out in a neighbourhood plan conflicts with another statement or other information in the plan the conflict must be resolved in favour of the policy.[103]

10.63 The courts have confirmed that neighbourhood development plans can include site allocations.[104] However, where a neighbourhood development plan does contain policies for the use of land for housing or indeed housing allocations it does not need to contain strategic policies to meet objectively assessed needs across a local plan area.[105]

THE PREPARATION OF A NEIGHBOURHOOD PLAN

10.64 Neighbourhood plans go through the following stages in their preparation:

(i) formulation of the proposals;

(ii) consultation by the parish council or neighbourhood forum on the plan proposal;

---

[98] Town and Country Planning Act 1990, Sch 1, para 1(1)(j) and the Town and Country Planning (Prescription of County Matters) (England) Regulations 2003, SI 2003/1033. Categories of waste development can be excluded from this restriction by regulation (Town and Country Planning Act 1990, s 61K(b)) but this has not been done.

[99] As defined in the Planning Act 2008.

[100] Town and Country Planning Act 1990, Sch 1, para 1(1)(h). Restoration and aftercare conditions are defined in the Town and Country Planning Act 1990, Sch 5, paras 2, 3.

[101] [2017] EWHC 1711 (Admin), at para 26 per John Howell QC.

[102] See paras 32, 52, 53. A neighbourhood plan which did support employment uses in the restoration or aftercare periods would conflict: para 54.

[103] Planning and Compulsory Purchase Act 2004, s 38B(3).

[104] See *R (on the application of Larkfleet Homes Ltd) v Rutland County Council* [2015] EWCA Civ 597, [2015] PTSR 589.

[105] *R (on the application of Crownhall Estates) v Chichester District Council* [2016] EWHC 73 (Admin).

(iii)   the final draft being sent to the local planning authority;

(iv)   the local planning authority deciding to seek representations on it and send it to examination;

(v)   the examination;

(vi)   consideration of the plan and the examiner's report by the local planning authority;

(vii)   consultation where the authority departs from the examiner's report; and

(viii)   the holding of one or more referendums.

Formulation of the plan

10.65   The responsibility for preparing the plan proposal rests with the qualifying body, whether a parish council or neighbourhood forum.

10.66   Local planning authorities are required to give 'such advice or assistance' to qualifying bodies as, in all the circumstances, they consider appropriate for the purpose of or in connection with, facilitating the making of proposals for neighbourhood development plans or orders in relation to neighbourhood areas within their area.[106] This statutory requirement does not require the giving of financial assistance[107] and instead funding is available from central government. A number of local authorities have published general guidance to those wishing to prepare a neighbourhood plan. This is well worth consulting before a parish council or neighbourhood forum commences the process of plan preparation. The Neighbourhood Planning Act 2017 will require local planning authorities to include policies for giving such advice or assistance in their statement of community involvement.[108]

10.67   The Planning Practice Guidance section on neighbourhood planning also contains some guidance as to the preparation of neighbourhood plans. However, what is clear is that aside from the prescribed documents which must be submitted with the neighbourhood plan (see 10.79, 10.80) and the completion of mandatory consultation prior to submission (also see 10.72 below) there is no prescribed route to the formation of a neighbourhood plan.

10.68   Parish councils and neighbourhood forums tend to engage consultants to assist with the neighbourhood plan process. The input of professionals can be extremely valuable, especially given the environmental issues which may arise and the complex legal provisions surrounding plan preparation and particularly where a neighbourhood plan needs to comply with the law surrounding strategic environmental assessment (see Chapter 3). The demands upon the parish council or neighbourhood forum when preparing a plan are considerable. They must assemble the evidence

---

[106] Town and Country Planning Act 1990, Sch 4B, para 3(1) as applied to neighbourhood plans by the Planning and Compulsory Purchase Act 2004, s 38C.

[107] Town and Country Planning Act 1990, Sch 4B, para 3(2) as applied to neighbourhood plans by the Planning and Compulsory Purchase Act 2004, s 38C.

[108] Planning and Compulsory Purchase Act 2004, s 18(2B)–(2D), as proposed to be inserted by the Neighbourhood Planning Act 2017, s 6. To encourage neighbourhood planning, the duty arises even if the local planning authority's area does not contain neighbourhood areas or qualifying bodies: proposed Planning and Compulsory Purchase Act 2004, s 18(2D). For discussion of statements of community involvement, see Chapter 7, at 7.17.

base. Some of that may be readily available, such as census data and a strategic housing land availability assessment. Other material may need to be commissioned and produced. Existing local plan policies will be important, particularly where they are strategic.

10.69   New survey work or assessments are likely to be required. Such exercises should be based on criteria justified in the light of planning policy and any standards, accurate data, carried out openly and properly recorded. In *Crownhall* the Court saw force in criticisms that the parish council's site selection exercise was defective because it scored sites against a settlement boundary which had been redrawn around the parish council's preferred sites and mischaracterised a conifer nursery as previously developed land.[109]

10.70   Even with professional assistance, a substantial amount of work will fall on volunteers in the qualifying body. They might want to have the following questions in mind:

- What decisions does the neighbourhood need to make?

- How does the plan add to current planning policies – it is not worth producing otherwise?

- Does the plan go with the grain of national and local planning policy? Departures can take place and innovation often happens at the most local level, but what is the justification for it?

- How do the proposals fare against the basic conditions?

- What useful information is available to support the plan-making process?

- To the extent that rational and objective comparisons help, are they done properly?

- Will the process be seen as being open and fair?

- Will the plan be helpful and clear when deciding planning applications?

- Is it no longer useful?

10.71   Strategic environmental assessment ('SEA') will be required unless the local planning authority decides that the plan 'determines the use of a small area at local level' and is not likely to have a significant effect on the environment.[110] Authorities must ensure that the planning officer who makes such screening decisions has authority to do so for neighbourhood plans.[111]

---

[109] *Crownhall,* at paras 74–78 per Holgate J, although the decision was ultimately not quashed on the basis that any error did not affect the outcome.

[110] Environmental Assessment of Plans and Programmes Regulations 2004, SI 2004/1633, regs 5(6) (a), 9(1). The local planning authority is the responsible authority (reg 2(1)) as 'the authority by which or on whose behalf it is prepared' since it does ultimately make the plan. The application of SEA to neighbourhood development plans was confirmed in *R (on the application of DLA) v Lewes District Council* [2017] EWCA Civ 58, [2017] Env LR 18, at para 58 per Lindblom LJ and *R (on the application of Larkfleet Homes Ltd) v Rutland County Council* [2015] EWCA Civ 597, at para 24 per Richards LJ. In *DLA* whilst the reasons given for deciding that SEA was not required were inadequate, the decision was not quashed.

[111] In the first case of *R (on the application of Crownhall Estates Ltd) v Chichester District Council* a decision to make a plan following a referendum was quashed because authority to decide not to have SEA had not been delegated to officers: see the later judgment in *R (on the application of Crownhall Estates Ltd) v Chichester District Council* [2016] EWHC 73 (Admin), at para 4 per Holgate J.

Pre-submission consultation and publicity on a plan proposal

10.72   Before submitting its neighbourhood plan proposal to a local planning authority, a qualifying body must publicise it in a manner that is likely to bring it to the attention of people who live, work or carry on business in the neighbourhood area.[112] They must send a copy to the local planning authority.[113] They must also consult any of the consultation bodies whose interests the qualifying body considers may be affected by the proposals for a neighbourhood development plan.[114] The consultation bodies are:[115]

'(a) where the local planning authority is a London borough council, the Mayor of London;

(b) a local planning authority, county council or parish council any part of whose area is in or adjoins the area of the local planning authority;

(c) the Coal Authority;

(d) the Homes and Communities Agency;

(e) Natural England;

(f) the Environment Agency;

(g) Historic England;

(h) Network Rail Infrastructure Limited;

(i) a strategic highways company (Highways England) any part of whose area is in or adjoins the neighbourhood area;

(ia) where the Secretary of State is the highway authority for any road in the area of a local planning authority any part of whose area is in or adjoins the neighbourhood area, the Secretary of State for Transport;

(j) the Marine Management Organisation;

(k) any electronic communications code operator who owns or controls electronic communications apparatus situated in any part of the area of the local planning authority;

(l) where it exercises functions in any part of the neighbourhood area—

(i) a clinical commissioning group established under section 14D of the National Health Service Act 2006;

(ia) the National Health Service Commissioning Board;

(ii) a person to whom a licence has been granted under section 6(1)(b) and (c) of the Electricity Act 1989;

(iii) a person to whom a licence has been granted under section 7(2) of the Gas Act 1986;

(iv) a sewerage undertaker; and

(v) a water undertaker;

(m) voluntary bodies some or all of whose activities benefit all or any part of the neighbourhood area;

---

[112] Neighbourhood Planning (General) Regulations 2012, reg 14(a).
[113] Neighbourhood Planning (General) Regulations 2012, reg 14(c).
[114] Neighbourhood Planning (General) Regulations 2012, reg 14(b).
[115] Neighbourhood Planning (General) Regulations 2012, Sch 1, para 1.

(n) bodies which represent the interests of different racial, ethnic or national groups in the neighbourhood area;

(o) bodies which represent the interests of different religious groups in the neighbourhood area;

(p) bodies which represent the interests of persons carrying on business in the neighbourhood area; and

(q) bodies which represent the interests of disabled persons in the neighbourhood area.'

10.73   The categories are drawn widely and some relate to bodies in or adjoining the area of the local planning authority (which could mean the other end of Cornwall), whilst the scope of voluntary and representational bodies concerns involvement with the neighbourhood area.

10.74   This consultation stage is the practical opportunity to review the merits of the plan as the later stages are concerned with whether it complies with the basic conditions. Interested parties should ensure that they are fully engaged at this point, even if they have not already been involved. It is much harder to change the plan once it has been submitted to the local planning authority.

10.75   The parish council or neighbourhood forum will need to consider those representations and decide whether to make changes to the proposed plan. They will subsequently have to produce a consultation statement which explains what main issues were raised, and how they were then dealt with.[116] Decision-making should therefore be public, transparent and, within the expectations of the consultation statement, reasoned.

Consultation and electronic communication

10.76   The Neighbourhood Plan (General) Regulations 2012 make specific provision for the use of electronic communication in the consultation processes required under those Regulations. Regulation 4 provides that where a person is required to consult or seek representations from another person or body who has an address for the purpose of electronic communications, the document, copy, notice or notification may be sent by way of electronic communication.[117]

10.77   Representations made in response to any matter or document may be made either in writing or by electronic communication.[118]

10.78   Where methods of electronic communication are used either to consult or to respond to a consultation response, and the communication is received outside of 'normal working hours' it shall be taken to be received on the next working day.[119]

---

[116] Neighbourhood Planning (General) Regulations 2012, reg 15(2).
[117] Neighbourhood Plan (General) Regulations 2012, reg 4(1).
[118] Neighbourhood Plan (General) Regulations 2012, reg 4(2).
[119] Neighbourhood Plan (General) Regulations 2012, reg 4(3). 'Working day' for the purposes of reg 4 means a day which is not a Saturday, Sunday, bank holiday under the Banking and Financial Dealings Act 1971 or other public holiday in England: reg 4(4).

Submission to the local planning authority

10.79   A qualifying body may submit a proposal for a neighbourhood plan to the local planning authority within which the neighbourhood area is situated.[120] The plan proposal must be accompanied by the following documents:[121]

(a)   a map or statement which identifies the area to which the proposed neighbourhood development plan relates;

(b)   a consultation statement;

(c)   the proposed neighbourhood development plan;

(d)   a statement explaining how the proposed neighbourhood development plan meets the basic conditions;[122]

(e)   an environmental report prepared in accordance with the Environmental Assessment of Plans and Programmes Regulations 2004, reg 12(2), (3), or where it has been determined under reg 9(1) of those Regulations that the plan proposal is unlikely to have significant environmental effects (and therefore does not require an SEA), a statement of reasons for that determination; and

(f)   a statement containing a summary of the proposals and reasons why the plan should be made in the proposed terms.

10.80   A consultation statement:[123]

(a)   contains details of the persons and bodies who were consulted about the proposed neighbourhood development plan;

(b)   explains how they were consulted;

(c)   summarises the main issues and concerns raised by the persons consulted; and

(d)   describes how these issues and concerns have been considered and, where relevant, addressed in the proposed neighbourhood development plan.

10.81   There is no requirement on the qualifying body to send to the authority copies of representations which it has received: only a statement summarising the main issues raised. So unless voluntarily submitted by the parish council or neighbourhood forum, the initial consultation comments will only reach the examiner if they are resubmitted when representations are invited by the local planning authority.

Post-submission representations and publicity

10.82   As soon as possible after receipt of the plan proposal, the local planning authority must publicise the neighbourhood plan proposal on its website and by other means likely to bring it to the attention of people who live, work or carry on business in the neighbourhood area. The publicity must set out:[124]

---

[120] Town and Country Planning Act 1990, Sch 4B, para 1(1) as applied to neighbourhood plans by the Planning and Compulsory Purchase Act 2004, s 38C.

[121] Town and Country Planning Act 1990, Sch 4B, para 1(2), as applied to neighbourhood plans by the Planning and Compulsory Purchase Act 2004, s 38C and the Neighbourhood Planning (General) Regulations 2012, reg 15.

[122] Town and Country Planning Act 1990, Sch 48, para 8.

[123] Neighbourhood Planning (General) Regulations 2012, reg 15(2).

[124] Neighbourhood Planning (General) Regulations 2012, reg 16(a).

(i)   details of the plan proposal;

(ii)   details of where and when the plan proposal may be inspected;

(iii)   details of how to make representations;

(iv)   a statement that any representations may include a request to be notified of the local planning authority's decision on the examiner's report; and

(v)   the date by which those representations must be received, being not less than six weeks from the date on which the plan proposal is first publicised.

10.83   The local planning authority must further notify any consultation body referred to in the consultation statement that the proposal has been received.[125]

10.84   Representations can be made on whether the plan proposal complies with the requirements for submission to examination as well as the examination tests, in particular the basic conditions. These representations will all be submitted to the examination[126] and will be the principal source of third party comment on the plan.

Withdrawal

10.85   A qualifying body may withdraw a proposal at any time before the local authority makes a decision whether to submit it to a referendum.[127] If the designation of the qualifying body is withdrawn before the proposal is submitted by the local planning authority for independent examination, then the proposal also is treated as withdrawn.[128] However, if the withdrawal of the designation occurs after the proposal has gone to the examiner then this will not affect the validity of the draft plan.[129]

Consideration of proposals by local planning authorities

10.86   The local planning authority's ability to consider the plan prior to the examination is limited to matters of formal compliance and process.

10.87   The first, but hopefully usually unnecessary exercise is to consider whether it is a repeat proposal and, if so, whether to decline to consider it. A local planning authority may decline to consider a proposal if it considers that it is a 'repeat proposal'.[130] Where a local authority declines to consider a repeat proposal it must give its reasons for doing so.[131]

10.88   A repeat proposal is defined as a proposal which meets both conditions A and B. Condition A is that in the period of two years ending with the date on which

---

[125] Neighbourhood Planning (General) Regulations 2012, reg 16(b).
[126] Neighbourhood Planning (General) Regulations 2012, reg 17(d).
[127] Town and Country Planning Act 1990, Sch 4B, para 2(1) as applied to neighbourhood plans by the Planning and Compulsory Purchase Act 2004, s 38C.
[128] Town and Country Planning Act 1990, Sch 4B, para 2(2) as applied to neighbourhood plans by the Planning and Compulsory Purchase Act 2004, s 38C.
[129] Town and Country Planning Act 1990, Sch 4B, para 2(3) as applied to neighbourhood plans by the Planning and Compulsory Purchase Act 2004, s 38C.
[130] Town and Country Planning Act 1990, Sch 4B, para 5(1) as applied to neighbourhood plans by the Planning and Compulsory Purchase Act 2004, s 38C.
[131] Town and Country Planning Act 1990, Sch 4B, para 5(6) as applied to neighbourhood plans by the Planning and Compulsory Purchase Act 2004, s 38C.

the proposal is received the authority has refused a proposal following an examiner's report or on European Union or human rights grounds following a referendum[132] that is the same or similar to the proposal in question or a referendum relating to a proposal for a neighbourhood plan has been held under Sch 4B and half or less than half of those voting voted in favour of the plan. Condition B is that the local planning authority considers that there has been no significant change in relevant considerations since the refusal of the proposal or the holding of the referendum.[133] For these purposes relevant considerations mean national policies and advice contained in guidance issued by the Secretary of State which is relevant to neighbourhood development plans and strategic policies contained within the development plan for the area of that authority.[134] If a plan is a repeat proposal then the authority will need to act reasonably declining to consider it.

10.89   Where a plan proposal is made to a local planning authority it is required to consider the following matters:[135]

(a)   whether the qualifying body is authorised to act in relation to the neighbourhood area;

(b)   whether there is no other outstanding proposal in relation to that area[136] and any provisions made under that section;

(c)   whether the proposal and the information and documents accompanying it (including the draft neighbourhood plan) comply with the legal requirements;[137]

(d)   whether the body has complied with the publicity and consultation requirements in the Neighbourhood Planning (General) Regulations 2012;[138]

(e)   whether the draft neighbourhood plan complies with ss 38A and 38B of the Planning and Compulsory Purchase Act 2004.[139]

10.90   This exercise will usually be carried out following the representation period, since the authority would then submit a successful plan to examination. However, a local planning authority might find the plan defective or a repeat on first receipt and it would be a waste of effort to invite representations on the plan.

---

[132] So under the Town and Country Planning Act 1990, Sch 4B, para 12 or the Planning and Compulsory Purchase Act 2004, s 38A(6); see the Town and Country Planning Act 1990, Sch 4B, para 5(3) as modified by the Planning and Compulsory Purchase Act 2004, s 38C(5)(a). A second plan put forward after the original was defeated in a referendum or withdrawn would not be a repeat proposal.

[133] Town and Country Planning Act 1990, Sch 4B, para 5(2) as applied to neighbourhood plans by the Planning and Compulsory Purchase Act 2004, s 38C.

[134] Town and Country Planning Act 1990, Sch 4B, para 5(4) as applied to neighbourhood plans by the Planning and Compulsory Purchase Act 2004, s 38C.

[135] Town and Country Planning Act 1990, Sch 4B, para 5(4) and (3) as applied to neighbourhood plans by the Planning and Compulsory Purchase Act 2004, s 38C(5).

[136] The plan must comply with any provision made by s 61F (see Sch 4B, para 6(2)(b)) and the outstanding proposal provision is the only apparently relevant one.

[137] In the Town and Country Planning Act 1990, Sch 4B, para 1 and the Neighbourhood Planning (General) Regulations 2012, reg 15, discussed in 10.75, 10.79, 10.80 above.

[138] See the Neighbourhood Planning (General) Regulations 2012, reg 14, made under the Town and Country Planning Act 1990, Sch 4B, para 4.

[139] Town and Country Planning Act 1990, Sch 4B, para 6(3) as modified by the Planning and Compulsory Purchase Act 2004, s 38C(5)(b) requires compliance with the Planning and Compulsory Purchase Act 2004, ss 38A, 38B. These requirements would be setting out policies for the development and use of land in the whole or part of the area (s 38A(2)), specifying its period, not including excluded development or relating to more than one neighbourhood area (s 38B(1)).

10.91   Where the authority is not satisfied that the above requirements have been complied with they must refuse the proposal and notify the qualifying body of their reasons for the refusal.[140]

10.92   Conversely, where the authority is satisfied that the above requirements have been met the authority must submit the draft neighbourhood plan (together with any other prescribed documents) for independent examination.[141]

EXAMINATION

10.93   An 'independent examination' of a draft neighbourhood plan is organised by the local planning authority.[142] It provides external scrutiny of the plan, although against defined tests. The procedure is primarily written, with hearings being discretionary, although the Neighbourhood Planning Act 2017 allows the introduction of a right to a hearing.

The examiner

10.94   The local planning authority's responsibilities include the appointment of the examiner. That appointment must be consented to by the qualifying body.[143] However, where it appears to the Secretary of State that the local planning authority and the qualifying body are incapable of agreeing on an examiner, the Secretary of State may appoint one himself if he considers it expedient to do so.[144]

10.95   The person appointed must be someone who: is independent of the qualifying body and the local planning authority, does not have any interest in land which may be affected by the draft neighbourhood plan, and has appropriate qualifications and experience.[145] An examiner may be an employee of the Secretary of State (usually a planning inspector) or of another local planning authority,[146] but obviously not of the local planning authority who is making the plan. The examiner must also not have any interests which could give rise to apparent bias at common law, such as being a director or employee of a person who has made representations on the plan. The test for bias was formulated in *Porter v Magill* by Lord Hope at para 103:[147]

> 'The question is whether the fair-minded and informed observer, having considered the facts, would conclude that there was a real possibility that the tribunal was biased.'

---

[140] Town and Country Planning Act 1990, Sch 4B, para 6(4) as applied to neighbourhood plans by the Planning and Compulsory Purchase Act 2004, s 38C.
[141] Town and Country Planning Act 1990, Sch 4B, para 7(1), (2) as applied to neighbourhood plans by the Planning and Compulsory Purchase Act 2004, s 38C.
[142] Town and Country Planning Act 1990, Sch 4B, para 7(3) as applied to neighbourhood plans by the Planning and Compulsory Purchase Act 2004, s 38C.
[143] Town and Country Planning Act 1990, Sch 4B, para 7(4) as applied to neighbourhood plans by the Planning and Compulsory Purchase Act 2004, s 38C.
[144] Town and Country Planning Act 1990, Sch 4B para 7(5) as applied to neighbourhood plans by the Planning and Compulsory Purchase Act 2004, s 38C.
[145] Town and Country Planning Act 1990, Sch 4B, para 7(6) as applied to neighbourhood plans by the Planning and Compulsory Purchase Act 2004, s 38C.
[146] Town and Country Planning Act 1990, Sch 4B, para 7(7).
[147] *Porter v Magill* [2002] 2 AC 357, at para 103.

Such bias can arise either from an interest held by a participant or because of an appearance of pre-determination – having made a decision before knowing all of the relevant facts. In respect of interests the Planning Inspectorate Conflict of Interest policy[148] is a useful standard to apply. Several neighbourhood plans have been challenged because of their examiners' interests. In *R (on the application of BDW Trading Ltd) v Cheshire West and Chester Borough Council*[149] the examiner was a non-executive director of a strategic land company which was promoting a sustainable urban extension of 1,300 dwellings as a Green Belt release within the local planning authority area and some five miles from the boundary of the Tattenhall Neighbourhood Plan which was being examined. Recognising the fact-sensitive nature of the exercise, Supperstone J concluded that the planning and market positions of relevant sites were different and there was no risk of bias.[150]

10.96 The Neighbourhood Planning Independent Examiner Referral Service[151] keeps a list of examiners but others may be chosen.

10.97 In *R (on the application of DLA Delivery Ltd) v Lewes District Council* Lindblom LJ rejected the submission that it was structurally unfair that the local planning authority was able to choose the examiner in consultation with the qualifying body.[152] It was also not relevant that the particular examiner had approved all (or nearly all) of the plans he had examined.[153] It is though important that the selection of the examiner is seen to be fair since one set of participants (the public authorities) are able to choose their own judge.[154] There should be no attempt to sound out potential examiners on their views on issues in the neighbourhood plan.

Examination procedure

10.98 As soon as possible after an examiner has been appointed, the local planning authority must send the plan proposal, the documents submitted with the plan proposal, any appropriate assessment (if required under the Conservation of Habitats and Species Regulations 2017[155]) and a copy of any representations made by way of the regulation 16 consultation to that person.[156]

10.99 The examiner has a discretion as to how to conduct the examination. However, the legislation provides that 'the general rule' is that the examination takes place by written representations.[157] A written procedure requires a fair opportunity to participate and openness. At the very least, those who commented on the submission plan should be invited to make written representations. Examiner's questions and all

---

[148] February 2017.
[149] [2014] EWHC 1470 (Admin).
[150] At paras 101–104.
[151] The service was set up by the Royal Institute of Chartered Surveyors, the Royal Town Planning Institute, the Planning Officers Society, Action with Communities in Rural England and Locality.
[152] [2017] EWCA Civ 58, [2017] 2 P & CR 7, at para 79.
[153] *DLA*, at para 79 per Lindblom LJ.
[154] The examiner appointment process is an issue in *R (on the application of Legard) v Royal Borough of Kensington and Chelsea* CO/399/2016 (judgment pending).
[155] SI 2017/1012 which revoked and replaced the Conservation of Habitats and Species Regulations 2010, SI 2010/490 from 30 November 2017.
[156] Neighbourhood Planning (General) Regulations 2012, reg 17.
[157] Town and Country Planning Act 1990, Sch 4B, para 9(1) as applied to neighbourhood plans by the Planning and Compulsory Purchase Act 2004, s 38C.

correspondence should be put on an examination website.[158] However, the examiner must hold a hearing on a particular issue where the examiner concludes that the consideration of oral representations is necessary to ensure adequate examination of the issue or a person has a fair chance to put their case, or in such other cases as may be prescribed.[159] A fair chance may be needed not only for objectors who seek to change the plan but also for parish councils and neighbourhood forums who might find the examiner recommending changes.[160] Any hearing must be in public.[161] The examiner has control over how the hearing is to be conducted. This includes whether to allow cross-examination or not and also how much time is to be given for representations/questions.[162] However, in general the questioning should be done by the examiner, except where the examiner considers that questioning by another is necessary to ensure adequate examination of a particular issue or that a person has a fair chance to put their case.[163]

10.100   Where a hearing is held, the qualifying body, the local planning authority, and any person who is to be given a fair chance to put their case have the right to make oral representations.[164] Other persons may be invited to be heard at the examiner's discretion, but the fact that one person is being heard may make it unfair not to allow other persons to appear, whether on the same or a different topic.

Draft reports and meetings

10.101   Reflecting concerns that even the parish council or neighbourhood forum have no right to be heard by the examiner, the Neighbourhood Planning Act 2017 allows regulations to require the examiner to provide draft reports or other information and to enable bodies to insist on meeting with the examiner.[165] Regulations would be able to require the examiner to provide prescribed information to the qualifying body, the local planning authority and prescribed persons.[166] The regulations may also provide for those persons to be invited to meetings with the examiner at particular points in the examination process.[167] Much will turn on the text of the regulations, but this appears to introduce a right to be heard for at least some participants. In holding meetings the examiner must act fairly. Meetings will need to be held in public and

---

[158]   The openness of communications by the local planning authority and the neighbourhood forum with the examiner is also an issue in *R (on the application of Legard) v Royal Borough of Kensington and Chelsea* CO/399/2016 (judgment pending).

[159]   Town and Country Planning Act 1990, Sch 4B, para 9(1) and (2) as applied to neighbourhood plans by the Planning and Compulsory Purchase Act 2004, s 38C.

[160]   The qualifying body can feel hard done by if there is no hearing. Baroness Cumberlege said of her own village's plan 'In our case, this was a paper exercise. Our examiner saw no one and spoke to no one. He devastated the plan ...' (Hansard, 17 January 2017, col 163).

[161]   Town and Country Planning Act 1990, Sch 4B, para 9(4) as applied to neighbourhood plans by the Planning and Compulsory Purchase Act 2004, s 38C.

[162]   Town and Country Planning Act 1990, Sch 4B, para 9(5) as applied to neighbourhood plans by the Planning and Compulsory Purchase Act 2004, s 38C.

[163]   Town and Country Planning Act 1990, Sch 4B, para 9(6) as applied to neighbourhood plans by the Planning and Compulsory Purchase Act 2004, s 38C.

[164]   Town and Country Planning Act 1990, Sch 4B, para 9(3) as applied to neighbourhood plans by the Planning and Compulsory Purchase Act 2004, s 38C. Regulations may prescribe other persons who are entitled to be heard if a hearing is held, but that has not been done.

[165]   Neighbourhood Planning Act 2017, s 7.

[166]   Town and Country Planning Act 1990, Sch 4B, para 11(3),(4), proposed to be added by the Neighbourhood Planning Act 2017, s 7.

[167]   Town and Country Planning Act 1990, Sch 4B, para 11(3)(c), (d), (4), proposed to be added by the Neighbourhood Planning Act 2017, s 7.

fairness might require other persons to be able to take part. If, for example, a meeting must be held at the insistence of the parish council if the examiner proposes to recommend changes following a written procedure, then it may be unfair to allow the qualifying body to appear but not those who had sought the particular changes. The examiner may also be required to publish a draft report.[168]

10.102 In addressing the draft plan the examiner must consider:

(a) whether the draft neighbourhood plan meets the basic conditions;

(b) whether the draft neighbourhood plan complies with ss 38A and 38B of the Planning and Compulsory Purchase Act 2004 or any provision made thereunder (that is, the Neighbourhood Planning (General) Regulations 2012);

(c) whether the area for any referendum should be extended beyond the neighbourhood area to which the draft order relates; and

(d) such other matters as may be prescribed (although none have been prescribed).[169]

10.103 A neighbourhood plan meets the basic conditions if:[170]

'(a) having regard to national policies and advice contained in guidance issued by the Secretary of State, it is appropriate to make the order;

...

(d) the making of the order contributes to the achievement of sustainable development;

(e) the making of the order is in general conformity with the strategic policies contained in the development plan for the area of the authority (or any part of that area);[171]

(f) the making of the order does not breach, and is otherwise compatible with, EU obligations,'

The following basic condition ('(g)') is added by the Neighbourhood Planning (General) Regulations 2012:[172]

'The making of the neighbourhood development plan is not likely to have a significant effect on a European site (as defined in the Conservation of Habitats and Species Regulations 2010) or a European offshore marine site (as defined in the Offshore Marine Conservation (Natural Habitats, &c.) Regulations 2007) (either alone or in combination with other plans or projects).'

---

[168] Town and Country Planning Act 1990, Sch 4B, para 11(3)(b), proposed to be added by the Neighbourhood Planning Act 2017, s 7.

[169] Town and Country Planning Act 1990, Sch 4B, para 8(1) as applied to neighbourhood plans by the Planning and Compulsory Purchase Act 2004, s 38C.

[170] Town and Country Planning Act 1990, Sch 4B, para 8(2) as applied to neighbourhood plans and modified by the Planning and Compulsory Purchase Act 2004, s 38C. Sub-paragraphs (b) and (c), relating to listed buildings and conservation areas, are omitted for the purpose of neighbourhood plans.

[171] 'Development plan' for the purposes of Sch 4B includes a pre-2004 Act development plan (see Planning and Compulsory Purchase Act 2004, s 38 and Sch 8, para 1) but does not include a neighbourhood plan (Town and Country Planning Act 1990, Sch 4B, para 17 as applied to neighbourhood plans by the Planning and Compulsory Purchase Act 2004, s 38C).

[172] Town and Country Planning Act 1990, Sch 4B, para 8(2) as applied to neighbourhood plans by the Planning and Compulsory Purchase Act 2004, s 38C and the Neighbourhood Planning (General) Regulations 2012, Sch 2, para 1.

10.104 The examiner is expressly prohibited from considering any matter which does not fall into those listed above (apart from considering whether the draft neighbourhood plan is compatible with human rights)[173] but is able to recommend the correction of errors and this may have the effect of broadening the exercise. Since the neighbourhood plan is only policy and does not itself determine individual rights, it is difficult to envisage a situation where a plan could contravene rights under the European Convention on Human Rights. In the sole neighbourhood plan human rights case so far, the claim was that carrying out the policy (to prevent part time occupation or holiday letting of new homes in a Cornish town) would contravene Convention rights and so, in essence, the policy was unworkable and ought not to have been adopted.[174]

10.105 The examiner must report on the draft neighbourhood plan and that report may contain the following recommendations: that the draft neighbourhood plan be submitted to a referendum, that modifications are made to the draft neighbourhood plan and that the modified draft is submitted to referendum, or that the proposal is refused.[175] The report must give reasons for each of its recommendations and must also include a summary of its main findings.[176]

10.106 The examiner is limited to recommending the following modifications: those which the examiner considers necessary to ensure compliance with the 'basic conditions', modifications which the examiner considers necessary to secure that the draft is compatible with Convention rights, modifications which the examiner considers necessary to secure compliance with ss 38A and 38B of the Planning and Compulsory Purchase Act 2004, and modifications for the correction of errors.[177]

10.107 The power to correct errors may well widen the examiner's role. Some errors are indisputable but also have no effect on the substance of the plan. However, other claimed errors might be matters of judgment or rely on correctly interpreting the plan. They might be intensely controversial. For example, in the case of *R (on the application of Maynard) v Chiltern District Council*[178] the examiner examining the Chalfont St Peter neighbourhood plan recommended the deletion of a nightclub from the list of community facilities in the draft plan. The local authority rejected this recommendation and their decision was to do so was quashed on the basis that the authority had failed to have regard to whether the club provided insufficient benefits to the local community to qualify as a community facility.

10.108 Where the examiner considers that the draft plan (including if modified as recommended) does not meet the basic conditions or comply with ss 38A and 38B of

---

[173] Town and Country Planning Act 1990, Sch 4B, para 8(6) as applied to neighbourhood plans by the Planning and Compulsory Purchase Act 2004, s 38C. There is though, a tension between this provision and the examiner's power to correct errors in the plan: para 10(6).

[174] *R (on the application of RLT Built Environment Ltd) v Cornwall Council* [2016] EWHC 2817 (Admin), [2017] JPL 378, [2017] ACD 16.

[175] Town and Country Planning Act 1990, Sch 4B, para 10(2) as applied to neighbourhood plans by the Planning and Compulsory Purchase Act 2004, s 38C.

[176] Town and Country Planning Act 1990, Sch 4B, para 10(6) as applied to neighbourhood plans by the Planning and Compulsory Purchase Act 2004, s 38C.

[177] Town and Country Planning Act 1990, Sch 4B, para 10(3) as applied to neighbourhood plans by the Planning and Compulsory Purchase Act 2004, s 38C.

[178] [2015] EWHC 3817 (Admin).

the Planning and Compulsory Purchase Act 2004, the examiner may not recommend that the draft plan is submitted to referendum.[179]

10.109 Where the examiner's report recommends that a neighbourhood plan is submitted to a referendum, the report must also recommend whether the area for the referendum should extend beyond the neighbourhood area to which the draft plan relates. Where an extended area is recommended, the examiner must recommend what that area must be.[180]

10.110 The examiner's power to correct errors in the neighbourhood plan has the potential to broaden the scope of the examination, since an alleged error can be considered whether or not it goes to compliance with the basic conditions.

10.111 The examiner must send a copy of their report to the local planning authority and the qualifying body.[181]

10.112 The basic conditions should be recognised as quite separate tests to the soundness tests applied to local plans.

10.113 The courts have confirmed the different role of the examiner in the neighbourhood plan process. In *Woodcock Holdings Ltd v Secretary of State for Communities and Local Government*[182] Holgate J held:

'132 Apart from any issues as to compatibility with convention rights, the examination of a draft neighbourhood plan may only consider whether the "basic conditions" are met … The basic conditions do not include the issue of whether the plan is "sound" in the sense in which that term is used when dealing with development plan documents (sections 20 (5)(b) of the 2004 Act and paragraph 182 of the NPPF). Therefore, where a neighbourhood plan precedes a local plan, the effect of paragraph 8 of Schedule 4B of the 1990 Act is that the examination of a neighbourhood plan cannot consider whether it is based upon a strategy to meet objectively assessed housing needs. Nor can the examination consider whether the proposed strategy is the most appropriate or justified by a proportionate evidence base (paragraphs 57, 62 and 63 above).

133 The Secretary of State's PPG also explains how the examination of a neighbourhood plan is very different from that of a local plan. The Examiner is limited to testing whether the neighbourhood plan meets the "basic conditions" and "is not testing the soundness of a neighbourhood plan or examining other material considerations" (paragraph 055 with emphasis added). Although the Examiner has a discretion as to whether to conduct the examination by way of a public hearing, paragraphs 056 of the PPG "expects" that the examination will proceed by considering written representations and not a hearing. The statutory scheme for the preparation of neighbourhood plans has been designed so as to make the evidential and procedural

---

[179] Town and Country Planning Act 1990, Sch 4B, para 10(4) as applied to neighbourhood plans by the Planning and Compulsory Purchase Act 2004, s 38C. Whilst sub-paragraph (4) talks about not recommending a referendum on the plan (with or without modifications) if the plan does not comply, there is power to recommend modifications to ensure compliance (para 10(3)) so it is only if modifications cannot rescue the plan that it cannot be put to referendum.
[180] Town and Country Planning Act 1990, Sch 4B, para 10(5) as applied to neighbourhood plans by the Planning and Compulsory Purchase Act 2004, s 38C.
[181] Town and Country Planning Act 1990, Sch 4B, para 10(7) as applied to neighbourhood plans by the Planning and Compulsory Purchase Act 2004, s 38C.
[182] [2015] EWHC 1173 (Admin), [2015] JPL 1151.

requirements, and the intensity of independent examination, less onerous for the promoting body than in the case of a local plan.'[183]

Consideration of the examiner's report

10.114   On receipt of the report the local planning authority must consider the recommendations and what action should be taken in response.[184] It has to consider the same tests as the examiner and whilst it must take into account the examiner's report, is not bound by it. Where the local planning authority is satisfied that the draft neighbourhood plan meets the basic conditions, is compatible with Convention rights and complies with ss 38A and 38B of the Planning and Compulsory Purchase Act 2004 or any provision made thereunder or that the draft neighbourhood plan would meet those requirements if modifications were made to the draft order, it must hold a referendum or referendums.[185] Where the local authority considers that modifications should be made to a draft neighbourhood plan, it is the draft as modified which is to be submitted to referendum.[186]

10.115   The local planning authority is limited in the changes which it can make. It can only make the following modifications: those which the local planning authority consider necessary to ensure the draft meets the basic conditions, those it considers necessary to ensure that it is compatible with Convention rights; those which are necessary to ensure compliance with ss 38A and 38B of the Planning and Compulsory Purchase Act 2004 or provisions made thereunder, modifications for the purpose of correcting errors.[187]

10.116   Where a local planning authority considers that the draft neighbourhood plan does not meet the basic conditions, is not compatible with Convention rights or does not comply with ss 38A and 38B of the Planning and Compulsory Purchase Act 2004 and would not meet those requirements even where modified, then it must refuse the draft neighbourhood plan proposal.[188]

10.117   The local planning authority must publish the examiner's report.[189] However, it is only obliged to publish once it has decided what action to take on the recommendations. At that point it must publish a statement of its decision on the plan, with reasons, along with the examiner's report.[190] It is though good practice to publish the report as soon as the final version is received. Additionally, if the report

---

[183]   See also judgment of Supperstone J in *R (on the application of BDW Trading) v Cheshire West and Chester Borough Council* [2014] EWHC 1470 (Admin).

[184]   Town and Country Planning Act 1990, Sch 4B, para 12(2) as applied to neighbourhood plans by the Planning and Compulsory Purchase Act 2004, s 38C.

[185]   Town and Country Planning Act 1990, Sch 4B, para 12(4) as applied to neighbourhood plans by the Planning and Compulsory Purchase Act 2004, s 38C.

[186]   Town and Country Planning Act 1990, Sch 4B, para 12(5) as applied to neighbourhood plans by the Planning and Compulsory Purchase Act 2004, s 38C.

[187]   Town and Country Planning Act 1990, Sch 4B, para 12(6) as applied to neighbourhood plans by the Planning and Compulsory Purchase Act 2004, s 38C.

[188]   Town and Country Planning Act 1990, Sch 4B, para 12(10) as applied to neighbourhood plans by the Planning and Compulsory Purchase Act 2004, s 38C.

[189]   Town and Country Planning Act 1990, Sch 4B, para 10(7) and (8) as applied to neighbourhood plans by the Planning and Compulsory Purchase Act 2004, s 38C.

[190]   Neighbourhood Planning (General) Regulations 2012, reg 18. These documents must be published on the local planning authority's website and in any other ways to bring them to locals' attention and notice given of where they can be inspected: reg 18(2).

is being considered by the Council's cabinet then it will need to be published as part of the agenda in advance of the meeting in any event.

10.118 Following the examination, the local planning authority must publish on its website and to the locality its decision either to refuse the draft neighbourhood plan proposal or to submit it to referendum (or referendums) together with the reasons for making any decision (together called a decision statement), when and where the statement can be examined and the examiner's report.[191] The local planning authority must send a copy of those matters to be published to the qualifying body.[192]

10.119 Where the local planning authority proposes to make a decision which is different from that recommended by the examiner (apart from in relation to the area in which a referendum is to take place[193]), and the reason for the differences in the decision 'is (wholly or partly) as a result of new evidence or a new fact or a different view taken by the authority as to a particular fact', it must give notice of its proposed decision (and reasons for it) and invite representations.[194] Notice is given to the parish council or neighbourhood forum, any person who made representations in the statutory consultation by the local planning authority and which were then sent to the examiner, and any consultation body referred to in the qualifying body's consultation statement.[195] Any representations on the modifications must be made within six weeks from the notice being given.[196] Where the local planning authority considers it appropriate it may refer the issue to independent examination.[197]

10.120 The local planning authority has discretion to make modifications which have not been recommended by the examiner or to reject or approve the plan contrary to the examiner's report, and if so, whether to hold a further examination give rise to issues of fairness and procedure. The discretion is similar to the position of pre-2004 development plans where Inspector's reports were not binding on local planning authorities. Those authorities had to invite representations and could hold a second inquiry if they rejected recommendations or proposed further modifications.[198] In *Warren v Uttlesford District Council* Schiemann LJ considered the role of fairness when deciding whether to hold second inquiries in such cases:[199]

> 'Clearly, if the Authority, in not arranging for a new inquiry, behaved in a manner which was outside the limits of the discretion given to it by the Act or failed to take into account

---

[191] Town and Country Planning Act 1990, Sch 4B, para 12(11) as applied to neighbourhood plans by the Planning and Compulsory Purchase Act 2004, s 38C; Neighbourhood Planning (General) Regulations 2012, reg 18(2).

[192] Town and Country Planning Act 1990, Sch 4B, para 12(12) as applied to neighbourhood plans by the Planning and Compulsory Purchase Act 2004, s 38C. The notification of other persons can be, but has not been, required by regulations. A person who asks to be notified of the decision whilst making representations is entitled to be told of the decision whether to make the plan following a referendum rather than the decision following the examination: see Neighbourhood Planning (General) Regulations 2012, reg 16(a)(iv).

[193] Town and Country Planning Act 1990, Sch 4B, para 13(14) as applied to neighbourhood plans by the Planning and Compulsory Purchase Act 2004, s 38C.

[194] Town and Country Planning Act 1990, Sch 4B, para 13(1) as applied to neighbourhood plans by the Planning and Compulsory Purchase Act 2004, s 38C.

[195] Neighbourhood Planning (General) Regulations 2012, reg 17A(2).

[196] Neighbourhood Planning (General) Regulations 2012, reg 17A(3).

[197] Town and Country Planning Act 1990, Sch 4B, para 13(2) as applied to neighbourhood plans by the Planning and Compulsory Purchase Act 2004, s 38C.

[198] Town and Country Planning (Development Plans) (England) Regulations 1999, SI 1999/3280, regs 27–29.

[199] [1997] JPL 1130, at 1134 and 1135.

a relevant matter such as any unfairness to the applicants then the Plan would be liable to be struck down. … the correct approach by this court is to ask itself whether, on normal judicial review principles as applied to local authorities, the decision not to open a new inquiry was an illegal one.

Some things are clear and I think common ground.

1.   One of the matters which an LPA has to consider when deciding whether or not to open an inquiry to consider objections to proposed modifications is whether a decision not to do so will be unfair to the counter-objectors. If it fails to consider the point or comes to a perverse conclusion then its decision is liable to be struck down.

2.   For its part, the court in deciding whether or not the decision not to open a new inquiry was procedurally fair, needs to bear in mind the position not merely of the parties before the court but also all others who might be affected by an order of the court quashing the adoption of the plan.

3.   The court in coming to a conclusion as to whether a decision not to open a new inquiry was procedurally unfair must give weight to the LPA's "view of the general situation" …'

10.121   In *Drexfine Holdings Ltd v Cherwell District Council* various relevant considerations for deciding upon pre-2004 second inquiries were identified:[200]

'(1)   Whether or not the issue raised had been previously subject to independent scrutiny by an inspector so as to provide independent evaluation of the opposing contentions;

(2)   The current advice in paragraph 69 of annex A to PPG12;

(3)   The practical implications of a second inquiry and, in particular, whether it would potentially be of material benefit to the decision making process;

(4)   Delay and the desirability of securing an up to date adopted development plan; and

(5)   Fairness to the objector and to other parties; as with all decisions of this kind, the determination whether or not to hold a further inquiry should seek to achieve fairness, balancing the interests of all relevant parties; however, in the light of the Court of Appeal decision in Warren it is not appropriate in the context of a challenge to a decision whether or not to hold a new inquiry to elevate the consideration of fairness to an administrative law obligation that goes beyond usual Wednesbury principles.'

10.122   Due to government concern about delays in making neighbourhood plans, the Housing and Planning Act 2016 allowed deadlines to be set for local authorities' decisions following examinations.[201] Unless a different date is agreed by the qualifying body and the local planning authority, the date is five weeks from the date of receipt of the original examiner's report or, if the authority recommends and consults upon its own modifications, five weeks from the receipt of the second examiner's report or the close of consultations (if there is no further examination).[202] This date ought to be the final date for a decision, particularly as the regulation-making power is for requiring action 'to be taken by a prescribed date'.[203] However, the Regulations say that the authority must decide what action to take 'on or after the date prescribed in

---

[200]   [1998] JPL 361, at 372 and 373 per Robin Purchas QC. Followed in *Bersted Parish Council v Arun District Council* [2003] EWHC 3149 (Admin), [2004] JPL 1235, at para 39 per Richards J.

[201]   Town and Country Planning Act 1990, Sch 4B, para 13A(a), inserted by the Housing and Planning Act 2016, s 140(1).

[202]   Neighbourhood Planning (General) Regulations 2012, reg 17A(5).

[203]   Town and Country Planning Act 1990, Sch 4B, para 13A(a).

paragraph (5)'[204] which would have the effect of delaying decisions for no reason and not providing a deadline. This seems to be an obvious error in the Regulations and should be read as 'on or before', consistently with the Town and Country Planning Act 1990.

Secretary of State's power to intervene

10.123 The parish council or neighbourhood forum may ask the Secretary of State to intervene if the local planning authority:[205]

(a)   has not made a decision whether to hold a referendum within the five week or otherwise agreed period;

(b)   has not followed a recommendation of the examiner;

(c)   has made a modification which was not recommended by the examiner, was not considered by the authority to be necessary to ensure compatibility with European obligations or Convention rights, nor was for the purpose of correcting an error.

10.124 The reasoned request must be made in writing[206] within six weeks of the local planning authority's decision not to follow the examiner's recommendation or to make a modification in the circumstances in (c) above.[207] A non-determination request can be made as long as the decision is late and has not yet been taken.

10.125 As a first step, the Secretary of State may appoint an Inspector to exercise his intervention powers.[208] In this section, references to the Minister include an Inspector. The Minister may then make a holding direction preventing the authority from making a decision on the report or following the authority's additional consultation.[209]

10.126 Once the parish council or neighbourhood forum has requested an intervention, the local planning authority shall send to the Minister (or the appointed Inspector) the examiner's report, any decision by the authority on the report, the documents which the authority had sent to the examiner on appointment,[210] any representations received on a post-examination consultation and any other document the authority consider to be relevant to the request.[211] If requested by the Minister or the Inspector, they must produce any other document which they hold.[212]

10.127 The Minister may then exercise the local planning authority's powers to consider the examiner's report and any other matters.[213] If the Minister is satisfied

---

[204]   Neighbourhood Planning (General) Regulations 2012, reg 17A(4).
[205]   Town and Country Planning Act 1990, Sch 4B, para 13B(1), as inserted by the Housing and Planning Act 2016, s 141(1) and as applied to neighbourhood plans by the Planning and Compulsory Purchase Act 2004, s 38C.
[206]   Neighbourhood Planning (General) Regulations 2012, reg 31A(2).
[207]   Neighbourhood Planning (General) Regulations 2012, reg 31A(3), (4).
[208]   Neighbourhood Planning (General) Regulations 2012, reg 31A(5).
[209]   Neighbourhood Planning (General) Regulations 2012, reg 31A(6).
[210]   Under the Neighbourhood Planning (General) Regulations 2012, reg 17.
[211]   Neighbourhood Planning (General) Regulations 2012, reg 31B(a)–(c), (e), (f).
[212]   Neighbourhood Planning (General) Regulations 2012, reg 31B(g).
[213]   Town and Country Planning Act 1990, Sch 4B, para 13B(2).

that the plan meets the basic conditions, is compatible with Convention rights and meets the formal requirements, with or without amendment, then he may direct the authority to take the plan to referendum. If not so satisfied, he may direct refusal.[214] The Minister may also direct the authority to extend the referendum area and publicise the enlargement.[215] Any direction to hold the referendum, to refuse the plan proposal or to extend the voting area must be accompanied by a statement of reasons.[216] The direction and reasons, along with the examiner's report if that has not been published, should be published by the local planning authority on its website and brought to the attention of local people.[217] The authority will also send a copy of the direction and reasons to the qualifying body.[218]

10.128   If the Secretary of State directs the authority to take the plan to referendum (with or without modifications), the authority is still able to modify the plan to secure compliance with European law or Convention rights or to correct errors.[219] The Minister therefore just takes over the ability to decide whether the basic conditions are met. If the Minister proposes to direct the authority to act other than in accordance with the examiner's recommendations because of new evidence, a new fact or a different view taken as to a particular fact then the Minister may direct the authority to carry out a notification and invite representations.[220] Whilst the criteria are unchanged, the Minister is under a discretion to consult, unlike the duty on authorities to notify persons in similar cases.[221]

Referendums

10.129   The Neighbourhood Planning (Referendums) Regulations 2012[222] ('Referendums Regulations') provide for the conduct of neighbourhood plan referendums. They are extremely detailed and govern the minutiae of holding a referendum. Necessarily this book does not cover all that is therein and readers are advised to consult the Regulations as necessary. This section of the chapter seeks to give an overview of what is required from a local authority.

10.130   The Referendums Regulations set the question to be asked in any referendum in relation to a neighbourhood plan. The question states:

> 'Do you want [insert name of local planning authority] to use the neighbourhood plan for [insert name of neighbourhood area] to help it decide planning applications in the neighbourhood area?'[223]

---

[214] Town and Country Planning Act 1990, Sch 4B, para 13B(2).
[215] Town and Country Planning Act 1990, Sch 4B, para 13B(3).
[216] Neighbourhood Planning (General) Regulations 2012, reg 31D(2).
[217] Neighbourhood Planning (General) Regulations 2012, reg 31D(3)(a).
[218] Neighbourhood Planning (General) Regulations 2012, reg 31D(3)(b).
[219] Town and Country Planning Act 1990, Sch 4B, para 13B(5), (6).
[220] Town and Country Planning Act 1990, Sch 4B, para 13B(4). Any notice would be given to the parish council or neighbourhood forum, those who made representations on the proposals in the regulation 17 period and any consultation body referred to in the consultation statement: Neighbourhood Planning (General) Regulations 2012, reg 31C.
[221] Cf. Town and Country Planning Act 1990, Sch 4B, para 13.
[222] Made pursuant to Town and Country Planning Act 1990, Sch 4B, para 16 and the Planning and Compulsory Purchase Act 2004, s 38A.
[223] Referendums Regulations, Sch 1, para 1 read with reg 3.

10.131 Where a referendum is held the local planning authority must ensure that the information statement and the specified documents are published on the local authority's website,[224] made available for inspection during the referendum period at the local authority's principal offices and where the local authority controls any premises which is open to the public in the referendum area, at such of those premises as the local authority considers appropriate having regard to the desirability of ensuring a geographical distribution of premises where the statement and documents are made available (provided that in all cases they are available in one such premises).[225] Additionally, where a 'business referendum' is required to be held the documents should be made available during the referendum period in such other manner as the proper officer[226] considers necessary to bring them to the attention of those likely to vote.[227]

10.132 An 'information statement' is a statement which specifies that a referendum will be held (or two will be held if one is a business referendum), the date on which the referendum/s will be held, the question to be asked in the referendum/s, a map of the referendum area, a map of the neighbourhood area (if not identical to the referendum area), a description of those entitled to vote in the referendum/s, the referendum expenses limit[228] which will apply to the referendum/s and the number of persons by reference to which that limit has been calculated, that the referendum/s will be conducted in accordance with procedures similar to those used in local government elections and the address and times at which a copy of the specified documents can be inspected.[229]

10.133 The specified documents which are to be published and available for inspection are: the draft neighbourhood plan; the independent examiner's report; a summary of any representations submitted to the independent examiner; a statement that the local planning authority is satisfied the draft plan meets the basic conditions and complies with provisions made by or under ss 38A and 38B of the Planning and Compulsory Purchase Act 2004; and a statement that sets out general information as to town and country planning (including neighbourhood planning) and the referendum and has regard to any guidance issued by the Secretary of State.[230]

10.134 It is clear that during a referendum, a local planning authority is to take a neutral role.[231] The conduct of a referendum is regulated by the 'Neighbourhood Planning Referendums Rules' which are set out in Sch 3 to the Referendums Regulations.[232] The conduct of business referendums is governed by the 'Neighbourhood Planning Business Referendums Rules' at Sch 7 to the Referendums Regulations.[233]

---

[224] The information statement and specified documents must be published either in the case of a business referendum, 56 days before the date on which the referendums will be held, or in any other case 28 days before the date on which the referendum will be held (reg 4(1A)). This excludes Saturdays, Sunday's, Christmas Eve, Christmas Day, Good Friday, Bank Holidays and any day appointed as a day of public thanksgiving or mourning in England (see Referendums Regulations, reg 4(5)).

[225] Referendums Regulations, reg 4(1)(a) and (b).

[226] The officer appointed for that purpose by the local authority (see the Local Government Act 1972, s 270(3) and the Referendums Regulations, reg 2).

[227] Referendums Regulations, reg 4(1)(c).

[228] As defined and limited in the Referendums Regulations, regs 6 and 7.

[229] Referendums Regulations, reg 4(3)(a).

[230] Referendums Regulations, reg 4(3)(b).

[231] Referendums Regulations, reg 5.

[232] See also, in particular, the Referendums Regulations, regs 8–13 and Schs 4–6.

[233] See also the Referendums Regulations, reg 17 and Sch 6.

10.135 The minimum area in which the referendum (or referendums) must take place is the neighbourhood area to which the neighbourhood plan relates.[234] The local planning authority may extend the area of the referendum (or referendums) if they consider it appropriate to do so. Where it decides to extend the area the local planning authority must publish a map of that area.[235]

10.136 A 'paragraph 14' referendum is for local electors and is held in all cases when the local planning authority decides to take the plan to referendum or when the Secretary of State directs a referendum to be held.[236] A district council, London borough council, metropolitan district council or county council (where there is no district council) must make arrangements for the referendum to take place in so much of their area as falls within the area in which the referendum is to take place ('the referendum area').[237]

10.137 A person will be eligible to vote if on the day the referendum is held[238] they are entitled to vote in the election of any councillors of the district council, London borough council, metropolitan district council or county council (where there is no district council) and their 'qualifying address'[239] for the election is within the referendum area.[240]

10.138 An additional referendum ('paragraph 15 referendum') must be held to allow businesses to vote if the draft neighbourhood plan relates to a neighbourhood area which has been designated as a business area.[241] A person may vote if they are a non-domestic ratepayer in the area.[242]

10.139 The success rate of referendums has been overwhelming. At the present time, only one plan has been rejected at a referendum. In October 2016, residents rejected the Swanwick Neighbourhood Plan with 85% opposition after the parish council's plan steering group campaigned for a 'no' vote following a dispute with the local planning authority. In only three successful plans has the approval been less than 60%.[243]

---

[234] Town and Country Planning Act 1990, Sch 4B, para 12(7) as applied to neighbourhood plans by the Planning and Compulsory Purchase Act 2004, s 38C.

[235] Town and Country Planning Act 1990, Sch 4B, para 12(8) and (9) as applied to neighbourhood plans by the Planning and Compulsory Purchase Act 2004, s 38C.

[236] Town and Country Planning Act 1990, Sch 4B, para 12(4) as applied to neighbourhood plans by the Planning and Compulsory Purchase Act 2004, s 38C.

[237] Town and Country Planning Act 1990, Sch 4B, para 14(2) and (3) as applied to neighbourhood plans by the Planning and Compulsory Purchase Act 2004, s 38C. Usually the council will also be the local planning authority, but that will not always be the case, for example, if there is a development corporation. In such cases the two bodies must co-operate in holding the poll: Neighbourhood Planning (Referendums) Regulations 2012, reg 16.

[238] This is the date prescribed by the Neighbourhood Planning (Prescribed Dates) Regulations 2012, reg 2(1).

[239] 'Qualifying address' has the same meaning as in the Representation of the People Act 1983, s 9.

[240] Town and Country Planning Act 1990, Sch 4B, para 14(4) as applied to neighbourhood plans by the Planning and Compulsory Purchase Act 2004, s 38C. This does not apply to any part of a referendum area which falls within the City of London (including Inner Temple and Middle Temple) where a person will be entitled to vote in the referendum if on the day of the poll they are entitled to vote in an Mayor of London or Greater London Assembly election (see Town and Country Planning Act 1990, Sch 4B, para 14(5), (6) and the Representation of the People Act 1983, s 203(1)) and the person's qualifying address for the election is in the City of London.

[241] Town and Country Planning Act 1990, Sch 4B, para 15, (as applied to neighbourhood plans by Planning and Compulsory Purchase Act 2004, ss 38A(3), 38C) Business areas are identified under the Town and Country Planning Act 1990, s 61H.

[242] Town and Country Planning Act 1990, Sch 4B, para 15(3).

[243] *Planning*, 16 June 2017.

MAKING OF NEIGHBOURHOOD PLANS

10.140   Where a single referendum is held the local planning authority must make the plan if more than half of those voting in each referendum voted in favour,[244] unless it would contravene European Union law or the European Convention on Human Rights.[245] Where the duty arises the plan must be made as soon as reasonably practicable after the referendum has been held[246] and in any event within eight weeks beginning the day after the last applicable referendum has been held.[247]

10.141   If there is a split result, with a majority for it in one referendum but not in the other, the local planning authority has a discretion whether to make the plan.[248]

10.142   Once the authority has decided to make the plan or to decline to do so following the voting it must publish a decision statement setting out its decision, with reasons, and how that statement can be inspected.[249] A copy of the decision statement has to be sent to the qualifying body and any person who asked to be notified of the decision.[250]

10.143   There is, somehow, a distinction drawn in the Regulations between a decision to make the plan and its actual making as both actions have to be published. Since no formality is required to physically turn the document into a 'made' plan, the reason for this is not apparent.

10.144   As soon as possible after making a neighbourhood development plan the local planning authority must publish it on its website (together with details of where and when it may be inspected) and must notify any person who asked to be so notified that it has been made and where it may be inspected.[251]

Authorisation in local planning authorities

10.145   A local planning authority should ensure that it has a scheme of delegation in place for decision-making on neighbourhood plans and that it is adhered to. In the *Crownhall* litigation two decisions were rescinded because council officers had acted without authority. Firstly, a decision was taken that SEA was not required when officers had no authority to decide that question at all. Following the quashing of the first referendum result, the second referendum was cancelled after another judicial review was brought because officers only had authority to send a plan to referendum if the examiner had recommended it to proceed as submitted and instead modifications were proposed.[252]

---

[244]   Planning and Compulsory Purchase Act 2004, s 38A(4)(a).

[245]   Planning and Compulsory Purchase Act 2004, s 38A(6).

[246]   Planning and Compulsory Purchase Act 2004, s 38A(4)(b).

[247]   Neighbourhood Planning (General) Regulations 2012, reg 18A(1). The eight-week period does not apply if a High Court challenge has already been brought: reg 18A(2), although the duty to make the plan as soon as reasonably practicable will still apply.

[248]   Planning and Compulsory Purchase Act 2004, s 38A(5).

[249]   Planning and Compulsory Purchase Act 2004, s 38(9); Neighbourhood Planning (General) Regulations 2012, reg 19(a).

[250]   Planning and Compulsory Purchase Act 2004, s 38(10); Neighbourhood Planning (General) Regulations 2012, reg 19(b).

[251]   Neighbourhood Planning (General) Regulations 2012, reg 20.

[252]   See *R (on the application of Crownhall Estates Ltd) v Chichester District Council* [2016] EWHC 73 (Admin), at paras 4 and 7 per Holgate J.

REVOCATION AND MODIFICATION OF NEIGHBOURHOOD PLANS

10.146 Tensions exist in how to change or discard a neighbourhood plan. It has not simply been prepared by the parish council or neighbourhood forum and approved by the local planning authority but will have passed through examination and been approved by referendum. It is not simply the bodies' plan to change. Whilst it will have made the plan, the authority might not like it. The popular vote is important, but holding a fresh referendum could be seen as excessively expensive (and in the public view, pointless) for modest changes of no great interest. Conversely, some changes might require a public vote, or at least be seen in some quarters as undermining the will of the people. Parliament has sought to grapple with these issues, most recently in the Neighbourhood Planning Act 2017.

10.147 Several powers exist or are being introduced to modify or revoke a neighbourhood plan:

(i) the local planning authority may modify the plan for the purpose of correcting errors;

(ii) a plan may be revised by going through the conventional plan-making process;

(iii) a non-substantial modification process can avoid the need for a referendum;

(iv) non-material modifications may be made by the local planning authority;

(v) the Secretary of State may revoke the plan;

(vi) the local planning authority may revoke the plan with the Secretary of State's consent.

Correction of errors

10.148 A local planning authority may, at any time, modify a neighbourhood development plan for the purpose of correcting errors.[253] However, where the qualifying body which initiated the neighbourhood plan process is still authorised to act for the purpose of that plan the local planning authority must gain their consent to correct any errors.[254] Any such modification is done by replacing the development plan with a new one containing the modification.[255] A modification document setting out the details of the modification is to be published by the local planning authority on its website and by the other usual means. Unlike other provisions in the Regulations, there is no requirement for the document to contain the reasons for the modification. However, it may be useful to explain what the reasons are if they are not obvious. Copies of the document must also be sent to the qualifying body and anyone who was notified of the making of the plan.[256]

---

[253] Town and Country Planning Act 1990, s 61M(4) as applied to neighbourhood plans by the Planning and Compulsory Purchase Act 2004, s 38C.

[254] Town and Country Planning Act 1990, s 61M(5) as applied to neighbourhood plans by the Planning and Compulsory Purchase Act 2004, s 38C.

[255] Town and Country Planning Act 1990, s 61M(6) as applied to neighbourhood plans by the Planning and Compulsory Purchase Act 2004, s 38C.

[256] Neighbourhood Planning (General) Regulations 2012, reg 30.

Revision by the conventional plan-making process

10.149 A neighbourhood plan can be revised by going through the plan-making process again. This route has historically been used for development plan revisions and can accommodate either a partial review (of a particular policy) or a full review, with the plan period extended. It does involve going through all plan preparation stages, including an examination and referendum. The cost and effort involved may therefore be sizeable and it may be seen to be disproportionate to put modest changes to a referendum.

The non-substantial modification process

10.150 The Neighbourhood Planning Act 2017 introduces a simplified modification process for changes which do not alter the nature of the plan. These are still subject to an independent examination but no referendum. The 2017 Act inserts a new Sch A2 into the Planning and Compulsory Purchase Act 2004.[257]

10.151 The qualifying body will be able to apply, in a prescribed form, to the local planning authority for a modification.[258] Regulations may require the body to consult on the proposals prior to submission. The modifications will then be considered by the authority. If the authority thinks that 'the modifications contained in the draft plan to which it relates are so significant or substantial as to change the nature of the neighbourhood development plan' then they will be subjected to the conventional plan-making process.[259] If it does not, then the authority must consider the formal compliance of the modifications and then send them to an independent examination. The first responsibility of the examiner is to consider whether the modifications are so significant or substantial as to change the nature of the plan. Reasons have to be given for any decision that the changes are so significant. In such a case the changes will go through the conventional process unless they are withdrawn by the qualifying body.[260]

10.152 If the alterations are not that substantial then the examiner will continue with the examination. There are some differences from a new plan examination. The general rule remains that the examination will be conducted in writing, but a hearing must be held if there are exceptional reasons for doing so or in other prescribed circumstances.[261] The same basic conditions are applied,[262] but the referendum issues do not arise.

10.153 The examiner's recommendations are binding on the local planning authority who must make the modification within five weeks of receiving the report unless it considers that they would cause a breach of European law or Convention rights.[263]

---

[257] Inserted by the Neighbourhood Planning Act 2017, s 4(5) and Sch 1. Consequential amendments are made to the 2012 Regulations by the Neighbourhoood Planning (General) and Development Management Procedure (Amendment) Regulations 2017, SI 2017/1243. This mechanism only applies to neighbourhood development plans, not neighbourhood development orders.

[258] Proposed Planning and Compulsory Purchase Act 2004, Sch A2, para 1.

[259] Proposed Planning and Compulsory Purchase Act 2004, Sch A2, para 7(1)(c), (2).

[260] Proposed Planning and Compulsory Purchase Act 2004, Sch A2, para 10.

[261] Proposed Planning and Compulsory Purchase Act 2004, Sch A2, para 12.

[262] Set out in proposed Planning and Compulsory Purchase Act 2004, Sch A2, para 11(2).

[263] Proposed Planning and Compulsory Purchase Act 2004, Sch A2, para 14, Neighbourhood Planning (General) Regulations 2012, reg 18A(3).

Non-material modifications

10.154 The Neighbourhood Planning Act 2017 will also introduce a power for the local planning authority to modify a neighbourhood plan at any time, if it considers that the modification does not materially affect the policies in the plan.[264]

Revocation by the Secretary of State

10.155 The Secretary of State may revoke a neighbourhood plan.[265] A local planning authority may also revoke a neighbourhood plan which it has made, however, the consent of the Secretary of State is required for such revocation.[266] Reasons must be given for any revocation.[267] Revocations are publicised by the local planning authority preparing a revocation document setting out the revocation and the reasons for it.[268] This will be published on the authority's website and in other ways to bring it to local people's attention and to say where physical copies can be inspected. Notice of the revocation must also be given to the qualifying body, anybody notified of the original making of the plan and any other person the local planning authority consider necessary in order to bring the revocation to the attention of people who live, work or carry on business in the area.[269]

10.156 The local planning authority is also required to cease making the revoked neighbourhood plan available on its website or any other place where it made it available for inspection.[270]

LEGAL CHALLENGES TO NEIGHBOURHOOD DEVELOPMENT PLANS

10.157 Neighbourhood plan decisions may be challenged in the High Court by judicial review. Judicial review of decisions whether to proceed to referendum or whether to make the plan following referendum(s) or the conduct of a referendum may only be brought under the Town and Country Planning Act 1990, s 61N. In these cases, proceedings have to be brought within six weeks form the particular act and that period cannot be extended.

10.158 Legal challenges to neighbourhood plans along with other development plan documents are dealt with in Chapter 22 of this book.

---

[264] Proposed Town and Country Planning Act 1990, s 61M(4A), as applied and modified by the Planning and Compulsory Purchase Act 2004, s 38C(2), (3), to be inserted by the Neighbourhood Planning Act 2017, s 4(2), (8).
[265] Town and Country Planning Act 1990, s 61M(1) as applied to neighbourhood plans by the Planning and Compulsory Purchase Act 2004, s 38C.
[266] Town and Country Planning Act 1990, s 61M(2) as applied to neighbourhood plans by the Planning and Compulsory Purchase Act 2004, s 38C.
[267] Town and Country Planning Act 1990, s 61M(3) as applied to neighbourhood plans by the Planning and Compulsory Purchase Act 2004, s 38C.
[268] Neighbourhood Planning (General) Regulations 2012, reg 31(a).
[269] Neighbourhood Planning (General) Regulations 2012, reg 31(b).
[270] Neighbourhood Planning (General) Regulations 2012, reg 31(c).

Chapter 11

Supplementary Planning Documents and other Non-development Plan Policy

11.1 Various tiers of planning policy which sit below the development plan are produced by local planning authorities. These consist of:

- supplementary planning documents ('SPDs') which are subject to a statutory consultation process;

- a residual category of local development documents which may contain policy but which are not subject to the SPD statutory formalities.

SPDs and the residual documents are formally subservient to the development plan and usually in practice provide detail to support development plan policies. However, that is not always the case and one contentious area has been the use of informal documents to supersede development plan policies. These documents are governed by Pt 2 of the Planning and Compulsory Purchase Act 2004 and the Town and Country Planning (Local Planning) (England) Regulations 2012[1] ('Local Planning Regulations'). The residual category was created by those 2012 Regulations, probably by a drafting accident, SPDs having previously been the exclusive means for a local planning authority to set out sub-development plan policy.

THE EVOLUTION OF NON-DEVELOPMENT PLAN POLICY

11.2 As a planning decision-maker, it has always been possible for local planning authorities to prepare policies which relate to the exercise of their powers. Policies prepared without statutory formalities included Supplementary Planning Guidance ('SPG') and a miscellany of other documents with titles such as interim policy statements.

These processes were wrapped up in the comprehensive definition of local development documents in the Planning and Compulsory Purchase Act 2004 as documents which:[2]

'... must (taken as a whole) set out the authority's policies (however expressed) relating to the development and use of land in their area.'

---

[1]   SI 2012/767.
[2]   Planning and Compulsory Purchase Act 2004, s 17(3).

The Town and Country Planning (Local Development) (England) Regulations 2004[3] ('Local Development Regulations') defined various documents which had to be development plan documents[4] and then said that a SPD means:[5]

> 'an LDD which is not a DPD, but does not include the local planning authority's statement of community involvement'

SPDs were therefore a residual category which caught every non-development plan statement of the authority's policies on the development and use of land in their area. The SPD procedure in the Local Development Regulations was therefore obligatory.

In 2012, the Local Planning Regulations defined a SPD as:[6]

> 'any document of a description referred to in regulation 5 (except an adopted policies map or a statement of community involvement) which is not a local plan'

Regulation 5 lists a variety of matters which could be covered by documents and reg 6 provides that in all, but two cases, those matters have to be contained in local plans. The adopted policies map is one of those exclusions.[7] An SPD is therefore any non-local plan document containing statements regarding:[8]

> 'any environmental, social, design and economic objectives which are relevant to the attainment of the development and use of land [which the local planning authority wish to encourage during any specified period]'

Under the Local Development Regulations these objectives had to be contained in a core strategy as part of the development plan.[9] The consequences of the 2012 changes are that matters which previously had to be included in development plan documents were now left to SPDs and any matter which was previously in an SPD would not be an SPD in future. A residual category of non-SPD local development documents was therefore created which was not subject to the SPD adoption procedure. This change appears to have been entirely inadvertent. The consultation draft of the Local Planning Regulations defined an SPD as 'an LDD which is not a DPD or a statement of community involvement' whilst objectives had to be contained in a development plan document.[10] The final text of the Regulations was heavily revised, in particular to introduce the expression local plan. Whilst the changes included transferring objectives from development plans to SPDs, there is no hint in the government response to the consultation that it was intended to create the residual category of local development documents.[11]

Having arrived by accident, the residual category means that matters that would conventionally have been thought to be suitable for supplementary policies are not capable of being in the SPDs which are meant to cover them. Whilst no SPD has been challenged on the unmeritorious ground that it should be a residual local development

---

[3]   SI 2004/2204.
[4]   Local Development Regulations, regs 6, 7.
[5]   Local Development Regulations, reg 2(1).
[6]   Local Planning Regulations, reg 2(1).
[7]   Local Planning Regulations, regs 5(1)(b), 6.
[8]   Local Planning Regulations, reg 5(1)(a)(iii) referencing sub-paragraph (i).
[9]   Local Development Regulations, regs 6(1)(a)(iii),(3), 7.
[10] 'Local Planning Regulations consultation' (July 2011) proposed regs 2, 6.
[11] 'Local planning regulations: Consultation Summary of responses' (March 2012).

document, an informal set of planning policy is now permitted. That risks ad-hoc, but sometimes important, changes being made without consultation.

The sometimes contentious issue of the division between development plan and non-development plan matters is considered in Chapter 7.

THE CONTENT OF A SUPPLEMENTARY PLANNING DOCUMENT

11.3   SPDs and the residual category of local development documents may contain policy as the Planning and Compulsory Purchase Act 2004 says that the local development documents, taken as a whole, shall set out the authority's policies.[12] The inclusion of policies within an SPD is confirmed by the Regulations which require an SPD to 'contain a reasoned justification of the policies contained in it'.[13] They are confined to objectives relevant to the development and use of land which the local planning authority wish to encourage. In practice, this means more detail of how such development could be carried out, usually building on policy in the development plan.

An adopted SPD must contain the date of adoption and say that it is a supplementary planning document.[14]

THE PREPARATION OF A SUPPLEMENTARY PLANNING DOCUMENT

11.4   SPDs are adopted following Pt 2 of the Planning and Compulsory Purchase Act 2004, under the procedure in Pt 5 of the Local Planning Regulations and must also comply with the authority's statement of community involvement ('SCI').[15] The SCI must include a statement of the authority's policy on the exercise of its functions under s 19 of the Planning and Compulsory Purchase Act 2004 which include the preparation of all local development documents.[16]

In preparing an SPD the local planning authority must have regard to national, regional, strategic policy, the authority's other local development documents, local transport plans, major accident hazards and the resources available for implementing the SPD as it does when preparing local plans.[17] They must also exercise the powers with the objective of promoting sustainable development.[18]

An SPD would be subject to the duty to co-operate if it relates to a strategic matter.[19] An SPD might have a significant impact on two or more planning areas if it imposes a moratorium on development or is the design brief for a strategic site. Minerals and

---

[12] Planning and Compulsory Purchase Act 2004, s 17(3).
[13] Local Planning Regulations, reg 8(2). See also reg 8(3) which prohibits policies in SPDs from conflicting with the development plan.
[14] Local Planning Regulations, reg 8(1).
[15] Planning and Compulsory Purchase Act 2004, s 19(3).
[16] Planning and Compulsory Purchase Act 2004, s 18(2). SCIs are discussed further in Chapter 7 at 7.17.
[17] Planning and Compulsory Purchase Act 2004, ss 19(2), 34; Local Planning Regulations, reg 10: see Chapter 7 at 7.31.
[18] Planning and Compulsory Purchase Act 2004, s 39.
[19] Planning and Compulsory Purchase Act 2004, s 33A(3). See Chapter 7 at 7.34–7.36.

waste SPDs are subject to the duty to co-operate as they relate to county matters in two tier areas.[20]

The local planning authority must publish the SPD in draft with a statement setting out the persons consulted in preparing the SPD, a summary of the main issues they raised and how those have been addressed.[21] It is therefore assumed in the legislation that consultation will take place in advance of producing the draft, although that is not required. The SCI should indicate what consultation is likely to take place, although the persons to be specifically consulted at this early stage may vary depending upon the subject of the proposed SPD. If strategic environmental assessment is being carried out then the environmental report should be published with the draft SPD.[22] Otherwise the production of supporting material is a matter for the authority, although some explanation of the proposals is likely to be required, with at least links to relevant published documents.

The draft SPD and the consultation statement must be published by being made available for inspection at the authority's principal office (and any other places they consider appropriate) during normal office hours and published on the authority's website. The address for sending comments and the deadline for these must also be published in the same way.[23] Previous requirements to send the documents to public bodies and to publish a local newspaper advertisement[24] have been removed. Authorities should though consider how to best inform those who might be interested in the SPD, including statutory bodies, developers and residents' associations.

A minimum consultation period of four weeks from the start of the statutory publicity is provided for representations.[25] Representations should be made in writing. No soundness tests apply, so comments should be based on the planning merits of the SPD, particularly drawing on development plan and national policy. Issues might also arise as to whether parts of the SPD should be in a local plan and whether there is conflict with the development plan.

Sustainability appraisal and strategic environmental assessment

11.5   There is no requirement for a draft SPD (or other non-development plan local development document) to be accompanied by a sustainability appraisal. The original 2004 duty to have sustainability appraisal of all local development documents was repealed in 2009.[26]

An SPD may require strategic environmental assessment ('SEA'). As with other plans, the issue is whether it sets the framework for development consent for projects in the annexes in the Environmental Impact Assessment Directive 2011/92/EU, as amended.[27] With a lower tier document such as an SPD it is necessary to consider what

---

[20]   Planning and Compulsory Purchase Act 2004, s 33A(4).
[21]   Local Planning Regulations, reg 12(a).
[22]   See 11.5 below and Chapter 3.
[23]   Local Planning Regulations, reg 12(b), 35(1).
[24]   Local Development Regulations, reg 17.
[25]   Local Planning Regulations, reg 12(b)(i).
[26]   See Planning and Compulsory Purchase Act 2004, s 19(5), amended by the Planning Act 2008, s 180(5).
[27]   Environmental Assessment of Plans and Programmes Regulations 2004, SI 2004/1633 ('SEA Regulations'), reg 5. See Chapter 3 above.

it adds to the existing policy framework and what the environmental consequences of that addition may be. Often an SPD will simply be supplying detail which would not alter environmental effects beyond those proposed by development plan policies. In such cases either it will not set the framework for development consent and so will be outside the SEA regime entirely, or the authority could screen away the requirement for SEA by considering that it determines the use of a small area at local level or was in substance no more than a minor modification to an existing plan and in either case was not likely to have significant environmental effects.[28] In *R (on the application of Wakil) v Hammersmith and Fulham London Borough Council* an SPD promoting town centre regeneration was quashed in the absence of SEA or a negative screening decision.[29] The Court also held that the SPD should have been a development plan document, underlining the scale of its potential impact.

Ministerial powers

11.6   The Secretary of State can direct modifications to a SPD prior to its adoption[30] but the Minister does not have a power to call in the document. So that the Minister has an opportunity to consider whether to require modifications, he may direct the authority not to adopt the SPD.[31] Such a direction will remain in force until the Minister makes a direction requiring modifications, says that no such direction will be made or withdraws the direction.[32]

Modifying and adopting a draft supplementary planning document

11.7   When deciding whether to adopt the SPD, with or without modifications, the authority must consider the representations along with the material they have published. A local development document may be modified prior to adoption to take into account any representations received and any other matter which the authority think is relevant.[33] In practice the representations received will have to be summarised in a report to the political decision-maker (whether an elected mayor, cabinet or cabinet member) along with a proposed response.

Post-adoption publicity

11.8   As soon as reasonably practicable after its adoption, the local planning authority must make the SPD and an adoption statement available on its website and for inspection at the authority's principal offices and any other locations it chooses.[34] The adoption statement will also be sent to any person who asked to be notified of the adoption.[35]

---

[28]   SEA Regulations, reg 5(6).
[29]   [2012] EWHC 1411 (QB), [2013] Env LR 3, at paras 91–99 per Wilkie J.
[30]   Planning and Compulsory Purchase Act 2004, s 21(1). Procedural requirements are at regs 22 and 23 of the Local Planning Regulations.
[31]   Local Planning Regulations, reg 16(1). The direction can also require a copy of the SPD to be provided but the Minister would undoubtedly already have seen it.
[32]   For the first two situations, see Local Planning Regulations, reg 16(2). It must be implicit that the holding direction can be withdrawn, even if the Minister is silent on whether to a modification will be required.
[33]   Planning and Compulsory Purchase Act 2004, s 23(1).
[34]   Local Planning Regulations, regs 14, 35.
[35]   Local Planning Regulations, reg 14((b).

An adoption statement will contain the date of adoption, any modifications made to the draft SPD and say to this effect:[36]

> 'a person with sufficient interest in the decision to adopt the supplementary planning document may apply to the High Court for permission to apply for judicial review of the decision and any such application must be made promptly and in any event not later than three months after the date on which the supplementary planning document was adopted.'

Lack of conflict by supplementary planning documents

11.9   Any policies in a SPD 'must not conflict with the adopted development plan'.[37] This is an important change introduced by the 2004 regime. Previously non-statutory supplementary planning guidance or planning briefs could be adopted which were inconsistent with the development plan.[38] For example, this might arise where a major development proposal came forward outside the plan or changes to housing policy in PPG3 were reflected in supplementary policy before the development plan was changed. Whilst PPG12 discouraged such policies,[39] they were lawful.

The Local Development Regulations required the policies in an SPD to be in conformity with development plan documents and any old local parts of the development plan.[40] Policy changes were now to be made by amendments to local plans where they are inconsistent with the new policy, rather than authorities being able to rely on an informal policy.

Since the adopted development plan now includes any neighbourhood plans in addition to the local plan and, where relevant, the London Plan or a spatial development strategy, care needs to be taken by local planning authorities to ensure that their SPDs respect neighbourhood planning. It might be possible, although not particularly useful, to say that the SPD is subject to any neighbourhood plan policies. However, the reader would want to be able to understand the policies as a whole and having two documents in conflict is not helpful if it is not apparent that there is a conflict and how it should be resolved. An SPD ought to cross-reference to any relevant neighbourhood plans and identify any parts of the document which do not apply in identified areas with neighbourhood plans. In some circumstances a neighbourhood plan might entirely supplant a need for a SPD in its area.

Whether SPD policies conflict with the development plan is a matter to be determined by the local planning authority subject to review on public law grounds by the Court.[41] Whether there is a conflict may be a matter of logical or literal inconsistency, but those problems might rarely if ever arise. Conversely, the application of the SPD in practice might conflict with the development plan if it points in the opposite direction. In *R (on the application of RWE Npower Renewables Ltd) v Milton Keynes Council* it was found that the only rational conclusion was that a conflict arose where the development plan required wind turbines to be sited 'at least 350m from

---

[36]   Local Planning Regulations, reg 11(2). The promptly and within three-month time limit continues to apply as the document is adopted under the Planning and Compulsory Purchase Act 2004 rather than the Town and Country Planning Act 1990.

[37]   Local Planning Regulations, reg 8(3).

[38]   *R (on the application of Bedford) v London Borough of Islington and Arsenal Football Club* [2002] EWHC 2044 Admin, at paras 51–64 per Ouseley J.

[39]   PPG12, para 3.15. See 11.13 below.

[40]   Local Development Regulations, reg 13(8).

[41]   *R (on the application of RWE Npower Renewables Ltd) v Milton Keynes Council* [2013] EWHC 751 (Admin), at paras 102–106 per John Howell QC.

any dwellings' and an SPD required turbines higher than 25 metres to be at greater distances away.[42]

In considering the earlier conformity requirement in *Wakil*, Wilkie J considered that an SPD was in conformity with the development plan policy to retain and improve an existing market where it proposed to regenerate the market and the adjoining area.[43]

Relationship with the London Plan and spatial development strategies

11.10   Local development documents, including SPDs, must be in general conformity with the London Plan where they apply to land within Greater London.[44] In addition, the duty for the policies not to conflict with the adopted development plan[45] applies in respect of the London Plan as well as spatial development strategies adopted by combined authorities.

WITHDRAWAL OF A SUPPLEMENTARY PLANNING DOCUMENT

11.11   The local planning authority may withdraw an SPD prior to adoption.[46] If that is done then the authority must as soon as reasonably practicable, have a statement published on its website and made available for inspection.[47] Any person who made representations on the SPD must be notified of its withdrawal.[48] It is also required to cease to make the SPD and other published documents available for inspection or on its website.[49] Whilst there is a case for decluttering the planning office reception, it is useful for the documents to stay on the website as long as it is stated that the SPD has been withdrawn.

REVOCATION OF A SUPPLEMENTARY PLANNING DOCUMENT

11.12   An SPD may be revoked by the local planning authority.[50] Following revocation, the authority must seek to make the SPD available for inspection or on its website and take such other steps it considers necessary to draw the revocation to the attention of persons living or working in their area.[51]

PREPARATION OF NON-SPD LOCAL DEVELOPMENT DOCUMENTS

11.13   There are no statutory procedures for the making of local development documents which are not SPDs. The Local Planning Regulations do not address them

---

42   [2013] EWHC 751 (Admin), at para 107–135 per John Howell QC.
43   *R (on the application of Wakil)* v *Hammersmith and Fulham London Borough Council* [2012] EWHC 1411 (QB), [2013] Env LR 3, at paras 74, 75. The SPD was quashed on other grounds.
44   Planning and Compulsory Purchase Act 2004, s 24(1).
45   Local Planning Regulations, reg 8(3).
46   Planning and Compulsory Purchase Act 2004, s 22.
47   Local Planning Regulations, reg 15(1)(a) applying reg 35.
48   Local Planning Regulations, reg 15(1)(b).
49   Local Planning Regulations, reg 15(1)(c).
50   Local Planning Regulations, reg 15(2), made under the Planning and Compulsory Purchase Act 2004, s 25.
51   Local Planning Regulations, reg 15(3).

at all, possibly because it was not intended to create this residual category. These documents must though be prepared in accordance with authority's SCI[52] and the statement must have explained how they are prepared.[53] That may be problematic if the SCI has not anticipated the existence of these documents.

A residual local development document can be subject to the duty to co-operate although that is most likely to arise on county matters in two tier areas.[54]

These residual documents are subject to the same duties to have regard to various matters as SPDs.[55] If within Greater London, they must be in general conformity with the London Plan. However, there is no obligation to avoid conflict with the development plan.

A residual local development document may be withdrawn prior to adoption[56] or modified prior to adoption.[57]

An unintentional side effect of the creation of residual local development documents in 2012 is that the local planning authority has no power to revoke them. By s 25 of the Planning and Compulsory Purchase Act 2004 the minister may prescribe categories of local development documents which a local planning authority may revoke themselves. Whilst they may revoke SPDs,[58] no provision has been made for other local development documents. The authority would have to ask the Secretary of State to revoke the document.[59]

Supplementary Planning Guidance before the 2004 Act

11.14   Prior to the Planning and Compulsory Purchase Act 2004, the adoption of non-development plan policy was entirely non-statutory, although it could not trespass on matters that had to be in a development plan.[60] This was usually styled as Supplementary Planning Guidance ('SPG'), although proposals for individual sites would be development briefs. More informal policies had a habitat of appearing, sometimes as interim policies. National policy encouraged the use of SPG, in particular for design guides and development briefs. It did though emphasise that SPG should be consistent with national, regional and local policy and prepared following a thorough consultation process.

Some pre-2004 SPG still remains in operation although any new documents had to be prepared under the 2004 Act.[61]

Guidance on the use of SPG was provided in PPG12: *Development Plans*:

---

[52]   Planning and Compulsory Purchase Act 2004, s 19(3).
[53]   Planning and Compulsory Purchase Act 2004, s 18(2).
[54]   Planning and Compulsory Purchase Act 2004, s 33A(3), (4). See Chapter 7 at 7.34–7.36 above.
[55]   See 7.31 and 11.4.
[56]   Planning and Compulsory Purchase Act 2004, s 22.
[57]   Planning and Compulsory Purchase Act 2004, s 23(1).
[58]   Local Planning Regulations, reg 15(2).
[59]   Planning and Compulsory Purchase Act 2004, s 25(a).
[60]   See *Westminster City Council v Great Portland Estates Plc* [1985] AC 661 and the discussion in Chapter 2 at 2.34 above.
[61]   Planning Policy Statement 12 (2004), paras 5.22–5.24.

'3.14 As indicated above, policies in development plans should concentrate on those matters which are likely to provide the basis for considering planning applications or for determining conditions to be attached to planning permissions. Excessive detail should be avoided. Local authorities should therefore consider the use of supplementary planning guidance as a means of setting out more detailed guidance on the way in which the policies in the plan will be applied in particular circumstances or areas.

Supplementary Planning Guidance

3.15 Supplementary planning guidance (SPG) does not form a part of the plan. It can take the form of design guides or area development briefs, or supplement other specific policies in a plan. SPG must itself be consistent with national and regional planning guidance, as well as the policies set out in the adopted development plan. It should be clearly cross-referenced to the relevant plan policy or proposal which it supplements. It should be issued separately from the plan and made publicly available; consultation should be undertaken, and the status of the SPG should be made clear. SPG should be reviewed on a regular basis alongside reviews of the development plan policies or proposals to which it relates.

3.16 While only the policies in the development plan can have the status that Section 54A of the 1990 Act provides in deciding planning applications, SPG may be taken into account as a material consideration. The Secretary of State will give substantial weight in making decisions on matters that come before him to SPG which derives out of and is consistent with the development plan, and has been prepared in the proper manner. SPG should be prepared in consultation with the general public, businesses, and other interested parties and their views should be taken into account before it is finalised. It should then be the subject of a council resolution to adopt it as supplementary guidance. On adoption, a statement of the consultation undertaken, the representations received and the local authority's response to those representations should be made available with each copy of the SPG (either in an annex or in a separate document).

3.17 SPG can play a valuable role in supplementing plan policies and proposals. However, it is emphasised that SPG must not be used to avoid subjecting to public scrutiny, in accordance with the statutory procedures, policies and proposals which should be included in the plan. Plan policies should not attempt to delegate the criteria for decisions on planning applications to SPG or to development briefs.

3.18 Before preparing SPG, local authorities may find it useful to discuss its proposed scope and content with the appropriate Government Office for the Region. Further guidance on good practice, particularly in respect of site specific SPG is contained in Planning and Development Briefs: A Guide to Better Practice (DETR, 1998)'

Chapter 12

National Planning Policy – Wales

12.1 Planning policy at the Welsh national level is principally contained in non-statutory national policy adopted by the Welsh Ministers in the form of Planning Policy (Wales) and Technical Advice Notes ('TANs') along with older circulars and the Wales Spatial Plan adopted under the Planning and Compulsory Purchase Act 2004. National Policy Statements also apply in Wales. A National Development Framework for Wales will be introduced by the Planning (Wales) Act 2015 as a replacement for the Wales Spatial Plan.

The relationship between the documents is set out in *Planning Policy Wales*:[1]

> '*Planning Policy Wales* (PPW) sets out the land use planning policies of the Welsh Government. It is supplemented by a series of Technical Advice Notes (TANs, listed in Annex 1). Procedural advice is given in circulars and policy clarification letters.'

The role of the Wales Spatial Plan is described as:[2]

> 'The Wales Spatial Plan *People, Places, Futures* sets a strategic framework to guide future development and policy interventions. It integrates the spatial aspects of national strategies for social inclusion and economic development, health, transport and environment, translating the Welsh Government's sustainable development duty into practice.'

Welsh planning policy has not received the drastic pruning (or more accurately, pollarding) given to English guidance. There are therefore a significant number of circulars, practice guidance documents (of various descriptions), circular letters, policy clarification letters, dear chief planning officer letters, Minerals Planning Guidance notes ('MPG') and even parts of a Planning Policy Guidance note ('PPG') which are still in force in Wales. A letter to an Assembly Member and a Ministerial speech are listed by the Welsh Government as relevant to planning policy.[3]

The majority of this policy is non-statutory, in that it relies upon the Welsh Government's general role in the planning process.[4]

The statutory planning policies produced by the Welsh Government are the Wales Spatial Plan and the forthcoming National Development Framework for Wales.

---

1   *Planning Policy Wales*, 9th edn (November 2016), para 1.1.1.
2   *Planning Policy Wales*, 9th edn (November 2016), para 1.1.3.
3   Letter from the Cabinet Secretary for Environment and Rural Affairs to Janet Finch-Saunders AM re: Technical Advice Note 1 Joint Housing Land Availability Studies and Speech by Carl Sargeant, Minister for Housing and Regeneration, to the Royal Town Planning Institute Cymru Annual Conference 2014.
4   In the same way as the English position considered in *Hopkins Homes Ltd v Secretary of State for Communities and Local Government* [2017] UKSC 37, [2017] 1 WLR 1865, at para 19, 20 per Lord Carnwath JSC. See Chapter 2.

National Policy Statements published by UK Ministers also apply, but only in respect of nationally significant infrastructure projects which are subject to the development consent order procedure.[5] Waste management plans are also adopted as part of the implementation of the Waste Framework Directive.[6]

An *Index of Planning Policy Guidance for Wales* is published occasionally, although the current version was published in December 2015, and so is out of date in various respects.

PLANNING POLICY WALES

12.2   The *Planning Policy Wales* ('PPW') has functioned as the principal policy tool for the Welsh Ministers. It has set out criteria for development plan preparation and development management as well as explanations of how the planning system operates. The PPW therefore goes beyond the pure policy role of the English National Planning Policy Framework to include explanatory material of a nature found in England's Planning Practice Guidance.

The PPW has been re-issued in virtually annual editions. The present version is the 9th edition published in November 2016. The Welsh Government's practice is to consult on amendments and then the final changes are published in a new and complete edition. The PPW is only available electronically.

Technical Advice Notes

12.3   Technical Advice Notes ('TANs') are published by the Welsh Ministers on a non-statutory basis and are a combination of policy and guidance on the operation of the planning system. They began to be published in the 1990s as the style of Welsh and English national policy began to separate. Previously, the Secretaries of State for Environment and for Wales had tended to issue joint circulars, or separate circulars which were virtually identical. Whilst English ministers produced Planning Policy Guidance Notes ('PPGs'), the Welsh Office prepared TANs. These still shared many similarities, both in overall form and in detail but there has been a progressive evolution in the substance of the policies.

The TANs are:

- TAN 1 Joint Housing Land Availability Studies (2015);

- TAN 2 Planning and Affordable Housing (2006);

- TAN 3 Simplified Planning Zones (1996);

- TAN 4 Retail and Commercial Development (2016);

- TAN 5 Nature Conservation and Planning (2009);

- TAN 6 Planning for Sustainable Rural Communities (2010);

- TAN 7 Outdoor Advertisement Control (1996);

---

[5]   See Chapter 5.
[6]   See Chapter 6.

- TAN 8 Renewable Energy (2005);
- TAN 9 Enforcement of Planning Control (1997);
- TAN 10 Tree Preservation Orders (1997);
- TAN 11 Noise (1997);
- TAN 12 Design (2016);
- TAN 13 Tourism (1997);
- TAN 14 Coastal Planning (1998);
- TAN 15 Development and Flood Risk (2004);
- TAN 16 Sport, Recreation and Open Space (2009);
- TAN 18 Transport (2007);
- TAN 19 Telecommunications (2002);
- TAN 20 Planning and the Welsh Language (2013);
- TAN 21 Waste (2014); and
- TAN 23 Economic Development (2014).

In addition, there are two Minerals Technical Advice Notes:

- MTAN 1 Aggregates (2004); and
- MTAN 2 Coal (2009).

Minerals Planning Policy Guidance

12.4   For many years land use planning policies for minerals were set out in *Minerals Planning Policy Wales* (2000). This guidance was cancelled and replaced by a new chapter 14 in *Planning Policy Wales* in January 2016.[7]

Ten of the Minerals Planning Guidance notes which had been jointly produced in England and Wales remain wholly or partly in force in Wales. These are:

- Mineral Planning Guidance 2: Applications, Permissions and Conditions (July 1998);[8]
- Mineral Planning Guidance 4: The Review of Mineral Working Sites (September 1988);
- Mineral Planning Guidance 5: Minerals Planning and the General Development Order (December 1988);
- Mineral Planning Guidance 7: The Reclamation of Mineral Workings (August 1989);[9]

---

[7]   *Planning Policy Wales*, 8th edn (January 2016), para 1.1.6.
[8]   Paragraphs 7 to 10 are cancelled.
[9]   Paragraphs 3 and 4 have been cancelled generally. This note has also been cancelled for aggregates-related development by MTAN (Mineral Technical Advice Note) 1: Aggregates and for coal-related development by MTAN 2: Coal.

- Mineral Planning Guidance 8: Planning and Compensation Act 1991: Interim Development Order Permissions (IDOs) – Statutory Provisions and Procedures (September 1991);

- Mineral Planning Guidance 9: Planning and Compensation Act 1991: Interim Development Order Permissions (IDOs) – Conditions (March 1992);

- Mineral Planning Guidance 10: Provision of Raw Material for the Cement Industry (1991);[10]

- Mineral Planning Guidance 11: The Control of Noise at Surface Mineral Workings (April 1993);[11]

- Mineral Planning Guidance 12: Treatment of Disused Mine Openings and Availability of Information on Mined Ground (April 1994); and

- Mineral Planning Guidance 14: Environment Act 1995: Review of mineral planning permissions (September 1995).

These documents are incredibly dated and should only be used with care.

PLANNING POLICY GUIDANCE NOTE 14

12.5 Unusually persistent material is contained in Appendices A (Causes of Instability) and B (Sources of information) of the 1990 Planning Policy Guidance Note 14: Development on Unstable Land.[12] Appendix B on sources of information is particularly dated.

CIRCULARS

12.6 Circulars were published by the Welsh Office ('WO' prefix), the National Assembly for Wales ('NAW'), the Welsh Assembly Government ('WAGC') and now by the Welsh Government ('WGC').

Some of these are still important, in particular WO Circular 23/93 on the Award of Costs in Planning and other proceedings. WO Circular 13/97 on Planning Obligations, National Assembly for Wales circulars on hazardous substances (NAW 20/01), safeguarding aerodromes (NAW 01/03) and compulsory purchase orders (NAW 14/04). The referral of planning applications to Welsh Ministers is governed by a WGC 07/2012 The Town and Country Planning (Notification) (Wales) Direction 2012, and important advice is contained in WGC 016/2014 The Use of Planning Conditions for Development Management.

LETTERS AND PRACTICE GUIDANCE

12.7 The final categories of policy and guidance are circular letters or policy clarification letters (such as CL-03-10 Design and Access Statements), Dear Chief Planning Officer letters (which are unnumbered) and various practice guidance.

---

[10] Paragraphs 22–31 and 38–63 have been cancelled.

[11] Paragraphs 31–42 have been cancelled in relation to aggregates-related development by MTAN (Mineral Technical Advice Note) 1: Aggregates and for coal-related development by MTAN 2: Coal.

[12] The PPG was cancelled in England by the National Planning Policy Framework.

WALES SPATIAL PLAN

12.8   The Planning and Compulsory Purchase Act 2004, s 60 introduced a requirement for the National Assembly for Wales to approve a Wales Spatial Plan containing such of its policies as it thinks appropriate in relation to the development and use of land in Wales. The power to approve is exercised by the Assembly itself and cannot be delegated or transferred to the Welsh Ministers.[13]

However, there is no requirement for all of the Welsh Ministers' policies to be included in the Spatial Plan. Ministers have been able to put policies in other documents and have done so – in particular, *Planning Policy Wales*.

The Assembly is obliged to consult as it considers appropriate in preparing or reviewing the Wales Spatial Plan but there are otherwise no procedures imposed by the Act.

A consultation draft of the *Wales Spatial Plan – People, Places, Futures* was published in September 2003. Section 60 was brought into force on 14 July 2004.[14] By order, any step taken by the Assembly before that date on the Plan was treated as having been taken under s 60.[15] Section 60 came into force one week before the Environmental Assessment of Plans and Programmes Regulations 2004[16] came into force – so the Strategic Environmental Assessment Directive 2001/42/EC did not apply to the first Plan. Any review or revision would have been subject to strategic environmental assessment ('SEA').

The approved plan was published in November 2004. The Wales Spatial Plan Update 2008 was approved by the Assembly on 8 July 2008. Whilst the PPW has been reviewed on an annual basis, the Spatial Plan has not been changed more recently.[17]

These provisions are being replaced by the National Development Framework for Wales.

THE NATIONAL DEVELOPMENT FRAMEWORK FOR WALES

12.9   The National Development Framework is intended to replace the Wales Spatial Plan. In legislative terms the Planning (Wales) Act 2015 inserts a new s 60 into the Planning and Compulsory Purchase Act 2004.

The change is not simply one of name. The National Development Framework will have additional force in that it would become part of the development plan.[18] The Framework 'must set out such of the policies of the Welsh Ministers in relation to the

---

[13] Planning and Compulsory Purchase Act 2004, s 60(5), (6) (as in force prior to the Planning (Wales) Act 2015 amendments).

[14] Planning and Compulsory Purchase Act 2004 (Commencement No 1 and Transitional Provision) (Wales) Order 2004, WSI 2004/1814, art 2.

[15] Planning and Compulsory Purchase Act 2004 (Commencement No 1 and Transitional Provision) (Wales) Order 2004, art 3.

[16] SI 2004/1633.

[17] An SEA statement was published to monitor the effects of the Plan in 2011.

[18] Planning and Compulsory Purchase Act 2004, s 38(4), as amended by the Planning (Wales) Act 2015, s 9.

development and use of land in Wales as the Welsh Ministers consider appropriate'.[19] It is able to specify 'development of a particular description, in a particular area or location' as development of national significance for which planning permission must be sought from the Welsh Ministers.[20] The Framework's role is to identify particular projects, or at least particular types of projects in particular areas or locations which have to be treated as nationally significant development. Nationally significant developments can also be identified by applying criteria to be set out in regulations leaving the Framework to be concerned with types of projects in particular places rather than across the nation. Sometimes that might amount to identifying a particular scheme.

In addition to any policies and identified nationally significant development, the Framework must contain:

(a)   reasons for its policies and identified development;[21]

(b)   an explanation as to how any Welsh marine plan and the Wales Transport Strategy have been considered.[22]

The Framework will also specify the period for which it will have effect.[23] A sunset provision means that it will cease to be the National Development Framework at the end of that period.[24]

Preparation of the Framework involves public consultation on a draft Framework and then a subsequent consultation of the National Assembly on the draft with any revisions.

A preliminary step is for the Welsh Ministers to 'prepare and publish a statement of public participation setting out their policies relating to the consultation to be carried out in preparing' the Framework.[25] The statement must include the form that the consultation will take, when the consultation will take place, and the steps that will be taken to involve members of the public in the preparation of the Framework.[26] The

---

[19]   Planning and Compulsory Purchase Act 2004, s 60(2), as replaced by the Planning (Wales) Act 2015, s 3.
[20]   Planning and Compulsory Purchase Act 2004, s 60(3). The application process is under the Town and Country Planning Act 1990, s 62D, inserted by the Planning (Wales) Act 2015, s 19.
[21]   Planning and Compulsory Purchase Act 2004, s 60(4), as replaced by the Planning (Wales) Act 2015, s 3.
[22]   Planning and Compulsory Purchase Act 2004, s 60(5), as replaced by the Planning (Wales) Act 2015, s 3. A marine plan is adopted under Pt 3 of the Marine and Coastal Access Act 2009 and the Transport Strategy is published under s 2 of the Transport (Wales) Act 2006.
[23]   Planning and Compulsory Purchase Act 2004, s 60(6), as replaced by the Planning (Wales) Act 2015, s 3.
[24]   Planning and Compulsory Purchase Act 2004, s 60(7), as replaced by the Planning (Wales) Act 2015, s 3.
[25]   Planning and Compulsory Purchase Act 2004, s 60A(1), as inserted by the Planning (Wales) Act 2015, s 3. Whilst the associated consultation paper 'Positive Planning: Proposals to reform the planning system in Wales' envisaged statutory public consultation (para 4.18), this was not on the face of the draft Bill. Proposed s 60A(1)(c) had provided for the Welsh Ministers to 'consult such persons as they consider appropriate about the draft' before it was laid before the National Assembly for Wales. There was no obligation in the draft Bill for consultation with the public at large. This was changed to the wider public participation, which is now required.
[26]   Planning and Compulsory Purchase Act 2004, s 60A(2), as inserted by the Planning (Wales) Act 2015, s 3. The public participation statement may be subsequently revised and republished by Ministers: s 60A(4).

statement was published in November 2016 and revised in June 2017. It sets out a proposed timetable.

A non-statutory Call for Evidence and Projects was conducted between December 2016 and March 2017. The Welsh Ministers intend to consult on issues and options in April 2018. This will precede the statutory consultation on the draft plan.

A draft of the Framework must be published for a 12-week public consultation.[27] An appraisal of the sustainability of the Framework's policies has to be carried out at the same time.[28] Whilst not explicit in the legislation, the implication is that the sustainability appraisal will be published with the consultation draft. The consultation exercise must be carried out in accordance with the statement of public participation.[29]

The National Development Framework will be subject to the requirements of SEA and the Habitats and Birds Directives.[30]

Following the public consultation, the next step is for the draft Framework to be laid, with or without changes, before the National Assembly along with a report summarising the representations received and explaining how they have been taken into account.[31] The Assembly then has 60 days to consider the draft, beginning with the day it is put before it.[32] Welsh Ministers are required to have regard to any resolution of the National Assembly passed or any recommendation made by one of its committee about the draft in that period.[33] On or before the publication of the Framework, the Welsh Ministers must lay a statement before the Assembly explaining how they had regard to such resolutions or recommendations.[34] They are not obliged to accept the Assembly's view although it would be very difficult politically not to follow an Assembly resolution.

The public and other interested persons would have an opportunity to lobby the National Assembly and Welsh Ministers on this second draft of the Framework.

Welsh Ministers are required to keep the Framework under review and may revise it.[35] Regular reviews are anticipated and Ministers must either start a review or formally explain why they are not doing so at least once every five years. A five-year review

---

[27] Planning and Compulsory Purchase Act 2004, s 60A(3), as inserted by the Planning (Wales) Act 2015, s 3.

[28] Planning and Compulsory Purchase Act 2004, s 60B(1)(b), as inserted by the Planning (Wales) Act 2015, s 3. The sustainability appraisal will include the likely effects of the policies on the use of the Welsh language: s 60B(2).

[29] Planning and Compulsory Purchase Act 2004, s 60B(1)(c), as inserted by the Planning (Wales) Act 2015, s 3.

[30] The National Development Framework amongst the land use plans in the Conservation of Species and Habitats Regulations 2017, SI 2010/1012, reg 111(1).

[31] Planning and Compulsory Purchase Act 2004, s 60B(3), as inserted by the Planning (Wales) Act 2015, s 3.

[32] Disregarding any time when the National Assembly is dissolved or is in recess for more than four days: Planning and Compulsory Purchase Act 2004, s 60B(7), as inserted by the Planning (Wales) Act 2015, s 3.

[33] Planning and Compulsory Purchase Act 2004, s 60B(4), as inserted by the Planning (Wales) Act 2015, s 3.

[34] Planning and Compulsory Purchase Act 2004, s 60B(6), as inserted by the Planning (Wales) Act 2015, s 3.

[35] Planning and Compulsory Purchase Act 2004, s 60C(1),(2), as inserted by the Planning (Wales) Act 2015, s 3.

period will start with the first publication of the Framework and further five-year review periods will continue in sequence from that time. If the Welsh Ministers have not published a revised Framework or laid a draft of the revision before the National Assembly in that review period then they must publish and lay before the Assembly a statement with a reasoned assessment of whether the Framework should be reviewed and if they consider that it should be revised, setting out a timetable for doing so.[36]

The revision procedure is the same as for the adoption of the Framework.[37]

THE NATIONAL DEVELOPMENT FRAMEWORK AND STRATEGIC DEVELOPMENT PLANS AS PART OF THE DEVELOPMENT PLAN

12.10   Following the making of the National Development Framework the development plan for an area in Wales comprises:[38]

'(a) the National Development Framework for Wales,

(b) the strategic development plan for any strategic planning area that includes all or part of that area, and

(c) the local development plan for that area.'

Prior to the Planning (Wales) Act 2015, the development plan was the local development plan for the area which replaced the local planning authority's unitary development plan. The change is a profoundly important shift in the formality of control. In the event of a conflict between plans, the latest document will prevail.[39] The National Development Framework will therefore set aside all conflicting parts of local development plan documents on its making. The practical reality is less dramatic, since Ministers and Inspectors have tended to prefer national policy to development plan policy in any event, and local authorities know this well enough. The ability of a local development plan policy to prevail in the event of a clash is limited. A newer Framework would resolve the clash in favour of the Ministers' approach. The reverse might though apply for local development plans which post-date the Framework, although a review of the local document should ensure general conformity with the national policy.

Conformity between plans

12.11   Once the new regime is fully in force a strategic development plan must be in general conformity with the National Development Framework for Wales.[40]

On the next step down the hierarchy, a local development plan will be required to be:[41]

---

[36] Planning and Compulsory Purchase Act 2004, s 60C(6)–(8)), as inserted by the Planning (Wales) Act 2015, s 3.

[37] Planning and Compulsory Purchase Act 2004, s 60C(3), as replaced by the Planning (Wales) Act 2015, s 3.

[38] Planning and Compulsory Purchase Act 2004, s 38(4), as amended by the Planning (Wales) Act 2015, s 9.

[39] Planning and Compulsory Purchase Act 2004, s 38(5).

[40] Planning and Compulsory Purchase Act 2004, s 60I(3), as inserted by the Planning (Wales) Act 2015, s 6.

[41] Planning and Compulsory Purchase Act 2004, s 62(3A), as inserted by the Planning (Wales) Act 2015, s 7.

'in general conformity with—

(a) the National Development Framework for Wales, and

(b) the strategic development plan for any strategic planning area that includes all or part of the area of the authority.'

Since Supplementary Planning Guidance ('SPG') is non-statutory, there is no statutory requirement for SPG to be in conformity or consistency with any other document, although policy is more restrictive.[42]

The general conformity requirement upon local development plans introduces a degree of ministerial control which is unprecedented in England and Wales. The nearest comparison is the existence of regional strategies (formerly regional spatial strategies) but regional strategies were still largely drawn up in their region and have been almost entirely revoked. The Planning and Compulsory Purchase Act 2004 provided for regional spatial strategies to be part of the development plan and to require other development plan documents to be in general conformity with them.

---

[42] See *Planning Policy Wales* 9th edn (November 2016), para 2.3.1, discussed in Chapter 15 below.

Chapter 13

Strategic Plans – Wales

INTRODUCTION

13.1   From evidence gathered from the preparation of local development plans in Wales, the Welsh Government formed the view that some local planning authorities had found it difficult to address strategic planning issues (such as housing, strategic employment sites and transport infrastructure) in isolation whilst preparing their plans.[1] As such, the Welsh Government decided to introduce the ability for local planning authorities to co-operate and prepare strategic development plans which cross local authority borders. The Welsh Government has expressed the view that large urban areas such as Cardiff and Swansea are most likely to benefit from the preparation of strategic plans.[2] The Welsh Government says it is not necessary for strategic development plans to cover the whole of Wales.

Strategic development plans will form part of the development plan for the areas falling within them.[3]

THE PLANNING (WALES) ACT 2015

13.2   The mechanisms for the introduction of strategic development plans are contained within the Planning (Wales) Act 2015 which has introduced a number of provisions into the Planning and Compulsory Purchase Act 2004. The provisions enable the Welsh Ministers (by regulations) to designate areas within Wales as 'strategic planning areas' and to establish 'strategic planning panels' for those areas.[4] As yet, no strategic planning areas and/or panels have been established by the Welsh Ministers.

STRATEGIC PLANNING AREAS

13.3   The legislation provides that a strategic planning area must comprise all of the area of one local planning authority and all or part of the area of at least one other local planning authority.[5] Prior to the regulations being made for the particular strategic planning area and panel, the Welsh Ministers are required to:

---

[1]   Welsh Government Development Planning website at: http://gov.wales/topics/planning/legislation/planning-wales-act-2015/development-planning/?lang=en (last checked on 25 September 2017).
[2]   See: http://gov.wales/topics/planning/legislation/planning-wales-act-2015/development-planning/?lang=en.
[3]   Planning and Compulsory Purchase Act 2004, s 38(4) to be inserted by the Planning (Wales) Act 2015, s 9.
[4]   Planning and Compulsory Purchase Act 2004, s 60D, inserted by the Planning (Wales) Act 2015, s 4.
[5]   Planning and Compulsory Purchase Act 2004, s 60D(2), inserted by the Planning (Wales) Act 2015, s 4.

(a)   give a direction to one or more local planning authorities the part or whole of whose area is included in the proposed strategic planning area. The direction does not have to be given to all authorities whose areas are proposed to be included in the strategic plan area;

(b)   either:

    (i)   a proposal for an area to be designated has been submitted by that authority or authorities; or

    (ii)   the period for complying the proposal requirement has ended without a proposal being made (the period is either as specified in the direction or, if no period is specified, then before the end of six months[6]. The time period may be extended by the Welsh Ministers[7]); and

    (iii)   carry out any consultation required by s 60F(1) (see below).

Section 60E of the Planning and Compulsory Purchase Act 2004 enables the Welsh Ministers to direct one or more local planning authorities to submit a proposal for an area to be designated as a strategic planning area. That authority or those authorities are then required to prepare the proposal.[8] Before submitting that proposal, they are required to consult each local planning authority who was not one of the directed authorities but part or all of whose area is proposed to be included in the strategic planning area and any other persons who are specified in the direction.

The submitted proposal is required to contain:

(a)   the proposal, including:

    (i)   a map showing the boundaries of the proposed strategic planning area;

    (ii)   a statement of reasons for proposing that area; and

    (iii)   any other information specified in the Welsh Ministers' direction; and

(b)   a report about the consultation carried out.[9]

Having made a direction to prepare a proposal, the Welsh Minsters are entitled to decide not to designate the proposed strategic planning area. If this is the case they must give notice of their decision and their reasons for it to the local authority or authorities who prepared the proposal and to each local authority part or all of whose area falls within the proposed strategic planning area.[10]

The Welsh Ministers themselves are required to carry out consultation under s 60F if they propose to make regulations designating a strategic planning area and:

(a)   its boundaries differ from the boundaries put forward by the local authority or authorities in their proposal following a direction;

(b)   no proposal has been submitted in the time period set for the direction; or

---

[6]   Planning and Compulsory Purchase Act 2004, s 60E(8)(d).
[7]   Planning and Compulsory Purchase Act 2004, s 60E(9).
[8]   Planning and Compulsory Purchase Act 2004, s 60E(4). A research report commissioned by the Welsh Government suggests a framework for developing the proposal: *Exploring methods for the identification of Strategic Planning Areas* (October 2015).
[9]   Planning and Compulsory Purchase Act 2004, s 60E(7).
[10]   Planning and Compulsory Purchase Act 2004, s 60E(12).

(c)   their regulations will revoke or amend previous designating regulations.

Section 60F requires that the Welsh Ministers consult the relevant local planning authorities and any other persons they consider appropriate.[11] Where a new or enlarged strategic plan area is proposed, the Minister must consult all local planning authorities whose area, in whole or part, is included with the proposed land. If the Minister proposes to amend or revoke a strategic plan area then consultation is also required with all authorities whose area includes part the existing strategic area.[12]

STRATEGIC PLANNING PANELS

13.4   The status and membership of strategic planning panels is set out in Sch 2A to the Planning and Compulsory Purchase Act 2004. They are corporate bodies whose names are determined by the regulations establishing them.[13]

The membership of a strategic planning panel is comprised of both local planning authority members and nominated members.[14] The number of members and their composition (planning authority versus nominated members) must be specified in the regulations establishing them.[15] However, the number of local planning authorities must be at least that of the number of constituent local planning authorities and must be two-thirds of the total membership of the panel (rounded to the nearest whole number).[16] The number of nominated members must be one-third of the total membership, rounded to the nearest whole number.[17]

A person may not be a member of the strategic planning panel if the person is a member of the panel's staff.[18]

STRATEGIC DEVELOPMENT PLANS

13.5   Once established, a strategic planning panel is required to prepare a strategic development plan for its area.[19] The plan must set out: (a) the panel's objectives in relation to the development and use of land in its area, and (b) the panel's policies for the implementation of those objectives.[20] The plan must be in 'general conformity' with the National Development Framework for Wales and must specify the period for which it is to have effect.[21]

In preparing a strategic development plan, the strategic planning panel is required to have regard to certain matters:

(a)   current national policies;

---

[11] Planning and Compulsory Purchase Act 2004, s 60F(1).
[12] Planning and Compulsory Purchase Act 2004, s 60F(4).
[13] Planning and Compulsory Purchase Act 2004, Sch 2A, para 1.
[14] Planning and Compulsory Purchase Act 2004, Sch 2A, para 2(1).
[15] Planning and Compulsory Purchase Act 2004, Sch 2A, para 2.
[16] Planning and Compulsory Purchase Act 2004, Sch 2A, para 2(3).
[17] Planning and Compulsory Purchase Act 2004, Sch 2A, para 2(4).
[18] Planning and Compulsory Purchase Act 2004, Sch 2A, para 2(5).
[19] Planning and Compulsory Purchase Act 2004, s 60I(1).
[20] Planning and Compulsory Purchase Act 2004, s 60I(2).
[21] Planning and Compulsory Purchase Act 2004, s 60I(3)–(4).

(b)   the National Development Framework for Wales;

(c)   the strategic development plan for any strategic planning area that adjoins the panel's area;

(d)   the local development plan for each area all or part of which is included in the panel's area;

(e)   the resources likely to be available for implementing the strategic development plan; and

(f)   any other matters prescribed by the Welsh Ministers in regulations.[22]

The panel is further required to carry out a sustainability appraisal of the plan and prepare a report of the findings of the appraisal.[23] This appraisal must include an assessment of the likely effects of the plan on the use of the Welsh language in the strategic planning area.[24]

There is no provision for a joint strategic plan, covering more than one strategic planning panel's area.[25]

Otherwise the Planning and Compulsory Purchase Act 2004 provisions on adopting a local development plan apply to the making of strategic plans.[26] As for local development plans, these will be subject to regulations

In order for a strategic development plan to come into being it must either be adopted by resolution of the strategic planning panel or approved by Welsh Ministers under ss 65 or 71 of the Planning and Compulsory Purchase Act 2004.[27] Strategic development plans automatically expire at the end of the period during which they are stated to have effect.[28]

The Planning (Wales) Act 2015 contains a provision, not yet in force, which will require strategic planning panels to keep under review the matters which may be expected to affect the development of its strategic planning area or the planning of the development of that area.[29] It will also require each strategic planning panel to survey its area and to keep events in neighbouring strategic planning areas under review.[30] The duty on local planning authorities to make an annual report to the Assembly does not apply to strategic planning panels.[31]

---

[22]   Planning and Compulsory Purchase Act 2004, s 60I(6).
[23]   Planning and Compulsory Purchase Act 2004, s 60I(7).
[24]   Planning and Compulsory Purchase Act 2004, s 60I(8).
[25]   The joint local development plan provisions in the Planning and Compulsory Purchase Act 2004, s 72 are not applied to strategic plans.
[26]   Planning and Compulsory Purchase Act 2004, s 60J.
[27]   Planning and Compulsory Purchase Act 2004, s 60I(9).
[28]   Planning and Compulsory Purchase Act 2004, s 60I(10).
[29]   Planning and Compulsory Purchase Act 2004, s 60H which is prospectively inserted by the Planning (Wales) Act 2015, s 5.
[30]   Planning and Compulsory Purchase Act 2004, s 61(2)–(5) as proposed to be applied by the Planning and Compulsory Purchase Act 2004, s 60H(2), (3) which is prospectively inserted by the Planning (Wales) Act 2015, s 5.
[31]   Planning and Compulsory Purchase Act 2004, s 76.

INTERACTION WITH LOCAL DEVELOPMENT PLANS

13.6   Local development plans are required to be in 'general conformity' with any strategic development plan for an area which includes all or part of the area of the authority.[32] Further, following the adoption or approval of a strategic development plan (or refused strategic development plan) a local authority all or part of whose area is included within that strategic planning area must consider whether to carry out a review of their development plan.[33]

---

[32]   Planning and Compulsory Purchase Act 2004, s 62(3A).
[33]   Planning and Compulsory Purchase Act 2004, s 68A(2).

Chapter 14

Welsh Local Development Plans

14.1   Individual local planning authorities are required to adopt local development plans for their areas. These plans were introduced by the Planning and Compulsory Purchase Act 2004 to replace unitary development plans.

Welsh planning policy had benefited from the introduction of unitary authorities in 1996. The only tier of principal councils is county councils or county borough councils. Below them sit community councils (the equivalent of parish or town councils in England) which are not plan-making authorities. Welsh devolution managed to stave off the bewildering series of plan documents (and their acronyms) introduced in England by the 2004 Act. The Welsh provisions, by contrast, had an easy ride through Parliament.

However, putting in place the new plans was no easier, and the experience of the Welsh plans was often even more painful than in England.

Local development plans are provided for by Pt 6 of the Planning and Compulsory Purchase Act 2004 (with the only significant amendments made by the Planning (Wales) Act 2015) and the Town and Country Planning (Local Development Plan) (Wales) Regulations 2005[1] ('Welsh Local Development Regulations'). Few changes have been made to those Regulations, which does leave them somewhat behind the attempts in England to speed up plan-making.

In the exercise of these plan-making functions the local planning authority 'must have regard to any guidance issued by the Assembly'.[2] Policy on the content of local development plans is given in *Planning Policy Wales*, in particular Chapter 2. Welsh Ministers have also produced a *Local Development Plan Manual* which is now in its second edition (August 2015) but is explicitly not policy[3] (and so not guidance). Other useful documents are produced by the Planning Inspectorate, *LDPs: Preparing for submission – Guidance for Local Planning Authorities* and *Local Development Plan Examinations: Procedure Guidance*, but these again would not be policy.[4]

---

[1]   WSI 2005/2839.
[2]   Planning and Compulsory Purchase Act 2004, s 75.
[3]   *Local Development Plan Manual*, Edition 2 (August 2015), para 1.2.1.
[4]   Both of these documents are currently in 2015 versions.

LOCAL DEVELOPMENT POLICIES

14.2   Welsh local planning authorities are required to keep under review matters which may affect the development of their area or its planning.[5] The local planning authorities are the county or county borough councils and national park authorities.[6]

These authorities must also produce a local development plan for their area.[7]

FORM AND CONTENT OF LOCAL DEVELOPMENT PLANS

14.3   A local development plan will set out the authority's objectives for the development and use of land in their area, general policies for the implementation of those objectives and may include specific policies for parts of their area.[8]

The form of the plan is set out in the Regulations. It must contain a title which gives the name of the local planning authority area and say that it is a local development plan.[9] A sub-title must state the expiry date of the plan.[10] If the plan has been adopted, the sub-title will also contain the date of adoption and if not, the stage at which the plan has reached and the publication date for that stage.[11]

Local development plans must contain reasoned justifications of the policies contained within them,[12] which must be 'readily distinguishable' from the policies.[13] This final requirement is not present in the English provisions.[14] Whilst an adopted plan which does intermingle policy within the reasoned justification would have to be treated as lawful if not challenged in the High Court in time, the requirement for a distinction between the two types of text is an indicator against finding new or altered policy in the reasoned justification. The explanatory text is still an aid to the interpretation of the policy and can lead to a nuanced interpretation of that policy.[15]

A proposals map will be part of the local development plan.[16] It will show the proposals, that is, site specific policies, for the development and use of land in its area.[17] The map will be based on an Ordnance Survey map, using National Grid lines and reference numbers.[18] It does not operate as a 'key diagram' but shows defined

---

[5]   Planning and Compulsory Purchase Act 2004, s 61.
[6]   Planning and Compulsory Purchase Act 2004, s 78(2), (3). National parks are of course within council areas and it is the national park authority which has jurisdiction in such areas.
[7]   Planning and Compulsory Purchase Act 2004, s 62(1).
[8]   Planning and Compulsory Purchase Act 2004, s 62(2), (3).
[9]   Welsh Local Development Regulations, reg 11(1)(a).
[10]   Welsh Local Development Regulations, reg 11(1)(b)(ii).
[11]   Welsh Local Development Regulations, reg 11(1)(b)(i), (iii).
[12]   Welsh Local Development Regulations, reg 11(2).
[13]   Welsh Local Development Regulations, reg 11(3).
[14]   See the Town and Country Planning (Local Planning) (England) Regulations 2012, SI 2012/767, reg 8.
[15]   For an explanation of the correct relationship between explanatory text and policy, see *R (on the application of Cherkley Campaign Ltd) v Mole Valley DC* [2014] EWCA Civ 567, [2014] 2 EGLR 98.
[16]   Welsh Local Development Regulations, reg 12(1). This is unlike the separate status of the adopted proposals map in the Town and Country Planning (Local Planning) (England) Regulations 2012, regs 2, 9.
[17]   Welsh Local Development Regulations, reg 12(1), (2).
[18]   Welsh Local Development Regulations, reg 12(1)(b), (c).

areas and boundaries. Inset maps may be used at a larger scale and policies for those parts will be solely on the inset maps.[19] The proposals map and any inset maps must contain the local development plan's title, the map's scale and explain any symbol or notation used (implicitly by the local planning authority) on the map.[20]

Community involvement schemes and local development plan timetables

14.4   Local planning authorities must prepare a community involvement scheme stating their policy on involving people in the preparation or review of their local development plan.[21] Unlike statements of community involvement in England, the schemes do not address consultation in development control.[22] The scheme must deal with the involvement of persons prescribed by the Welsh Assembly and may include other persons with an interest in development in the authority's area.[23] It is therefore not required to be comprehensive as to all who may be involved, but any category of person included will have the benefit of the scheme as it relates to them.

A Welsh scheme must include:[24]

'(a) a list of all those general and specific consultation bodies to be involved in the LDP procedure;

(b) the principles of the LDP participation strategy to be adopted by the LPA;

(c) the timing of, and the method by which—

   (i) participation will occur at each stage of the LDP procedure, and

   (ii) the LPA will respond to the participation process referred to in sub-paragraph (i);

(d) details of how the LPA will use those responses at each stage in developing the content of its LDP.'

The general consultation bodies are 'voluntary bodies, some or all of whose activities benefit any part of the authority's area' and bodies representing the interests of different racial, ethnic, national or religious groups, disabled persons, persons carrying on business or the interests of Welsh culture, all within the local planning authority's area.[25] Specific consultation bodies are identified in the regulations[26]:

'(a) the Natural Resources Body for Wales,

(b) Network Rail Infrastructure Limited;

(c) insofar as the Secretary of State exercises functions previously exercisable by the Strategic Rail Authority, the Secretary of State,

(d) the National Assembly,

(e) a relevant authority [defined as a local planning authority or a community council[27]] any part of whose area is in or adjoins the area of the LPA,

---

[19]   Welsh Local Development Regulations, reg 12(3), (4).
[20]   Welsh Local Development Regulations, reg 12(5).
[21]   Planning and Compulsory Purchase Act 2004, s 63(2).
[22]   See Planning and Compulsory Purchase Act 2004, s 18.
[23]   Planning and Compulsory Purchase Act 2004, s 63(3).
[24]   Welsh Local Development Regulations, reg 6.
[25]   Welsh Local Development Regulations, reg 2(1).
[26]   Welsh Local Development Regulations, reg 2(1).
[27]   Welsh Local Development Regulations, reg 2(1).

   (f) any person—

      (i) to whom the electronic communications code applies by virtue of a direction given under section 106(3)(a) of the Communications Act 2003, and

      (ii) who owns or controls electronic communications apparatus situated in any part of the area of the LPA (where known),

   (g) if it exercises functions in any part of the LPA's area—

      (i) a Local Health Board,

      (ii) a person to whom a licence has been granted under section 6(1)(b) or (c) of the Electricity Act 1989,

      (iii) a person to whom a licence has been granted under section 7(2) of the Gas Act 1986,

      (iv) a sewerage undertaker,

      (v) a water undertaker;'

The scheme should therefore identify and list the bodies which the authority considers fall within either category in respect of their area. Consultation with the following UK government departments is also encouraged by the *Local Development Plan Manual*:[28]

Department	Issues
Department for Transport	Rail, airport and maritime/port policy
Department of Energy and Climate Change (now Department of Business, Energy and Industrial Strategy)	UK energy policy
Home Office	Civil defence matters; policies for prisons etc[29]
Ministry of Defence ('MoD')	Matters likely to affect its land holdings and installations or where large scale disposals of MoD land may be being considered.

A list of other potential consultees is also included in the manual, covering various other government agencies, such as the Civil Aviation Authority, and business associations and interest groups.[30] The principles of the participation strategy and the details and timing of the preparation process must as a minimum meet the statutory requirements in the Act and the Regulations. As the authority's policy, it can go beyond those obligations and tailor consultation and publicity to what the authority considers appropriate in its area.

---

[28] *Local Development Plan Manual*, Edition 2 (August 2015), Annex B.
[29] Since prisons are no longer the responsibility of the Home Office, the manual is in error and the Ministry of Justice should be consulted instead.
[30] *Local Development Plan Manual*, Edition 2 (August 2015), Annex C.

Timetables are also prepared by local planning authorities for the preparation and adoption of the local development plan. Under the Local Plans Regulations:[31]

> 'The timetable must include all key dates—
>
> (a) specified in guidance made under section 75, which must include—
>
>   (i)   a definitive date for each stage of the LDP procedure up to deposit stage, and
>
>   (ii) indicative dates up to adoption of the LDP,
>
> (b) for the preparation and publication of—
>
>   (i)   the sustainability appraisal report, and
>
>   (ii) the annual monitoring report.'

Welsh Ministers have declined to specify a standard prescribed timetable, but expect a replacement local development plan to be prepared within considerably less than four years from the decision to start the process.[32]

The procedure for preparing these documents is prescribed by the Assembly.[33] In preparing the community involvement scheme the local planning authority must involve those general consultation bodies which appear to have an interest to the development in the area.[34] Conversely, the specific consultation bodies must be consulted in the preparation of the timetable.[35]

The community involvement scheme and timetable are packaged together as a delivery agreement and approved by resolution of the local planning authority before being submitted for the approval of the Welsh Ministers.[36] The Welsh Ministers must respond to the submission within four weeks of receipt of the documents unless they have notified the local planning authority within that period that more time is required: reg 9(2). By reg 9(3), if the period expires without a response then the delivery agreement is deemed to be approved. This throws up a number of points. Firstly, and most obviously, the Ministers cannot extend the period after it has expired. The next issue is whether any extension must be for a defined period. Paragraph (3) deems approval at the end of 'the period' mentioned in para (2). The period must be the four-week period or any extended period. An indefinite extension would remove the effect of the deeming provision and risk delay to the plan preparation process. The implication is that any extension must be for a specified period. The final question is whether a further extension of time can be made, after the original four-week period. As the period in para (2) would seem to include any extended period, notice of more time can be given if done within the added period. This avoids a need for an excessive extension being made to cover the possibility of unexpected delays. In the absence of agreement to the community involvement scheme and timetable the Assembly can direct their terms.[37]

---

[31] Welsh Local Development Regulations, reg 8.
[32] *Planning Policy Wales*, 9th edn (November 2016), para 2.1.13.
[33] Planning and Compulsory Purchase Act 2004, s 63(7) and contained in the Welsh Local Development Regulations, regs 5–8.
[34] Welsh Local Development Regulations, reg 5.
[35] Welsh Local Development Regulations, reg 7.
[36] Welsh Local Development Regulations, reg 9(1).
[37] Planning and Compulsory Purchase Act 2004, s 63(4)–(6).

MATTERS TO CONSIDER WHEN PREPARING THE LOCAL DEVELOPMENT PLAN

14.5   Legislation sets out various matters that the local planning authority should consider when plan-making. Other matters may then be identified by policy and some will be readily apparent.

In preparing the local development plan, s 63(5) of the Planning and Compulsory Purchase Act 2004 requires the local planning authority to have regard to:[38]

'(a) current national policies;

(b) the National Development Framework for Wales;

(ba) the strategic development plan for any strategic planning area that—

(i)   includes all or part of the area of the authority, or

(ii) adjoins that area;

(bb) an area statement [published by Natural Resources Wales][39] which includes all or part of the area;

…

(d) any relevant local well-being plan;

…

(f)   the resources likely to be available for implementing the plan'

A local well-being plan is published by a public services board, setting out its local objectives and the steps it proposes to take to meet them.[40] A public services board is established for each local authority area, comprising the local authority, local health board, fire and rescue authority and the Natural Resources Body for Wales.[41]

A duty to exercise plan-making functions 'with the objective of contributing to the achievement of sustainable development' was introduced by the Planning and Compulsory Purchase Act 2004, s 39. This was replaced by the new sustainable development duty in the Planning (Wales) Act 2015, s 2 from 1 April 2016.[42] The new duty, which applies to all Welsh statutory planning policy-making, is discussed in Chapter 2 above.

In addition the Welsh Local Development Regulations require consideration of:[43]

'(a) any local transport plan, the policies of which affect any part of the LPA's area;

---

[38] Section 63(5)(c) requires regard to any English regional strategies whose area adjoins the authority's, but since none of those strategies adjacent to Wales remain, we have omitted it from the list.

[39] Environment (Wales) Act 2016, s 11.

[40] Well-being of Future Generations (Wales) Act 2015, s 39(1). A review of the plan may be carried out under s 44 of that Act.

[41] Well-being of Future Generations (Wales) Act 2015, s 29.

[42] If the local development plan had been submitted for examination prior to that date then the 2004 Act duty would apply up to its approval or adoption. Any review of the plan would be conducted under the new sustainable development duty: Planning (Wales) Act 2015 (Commencement No 2 and Transitional and Saving Provisions) Order 2015, SI 2015/1987, art 6.

[43] Welsh Local Development Regulations, reg 13(1). In para (a), the local transport plan is as defined in the Transport Act 2000, s 108(3), see Welsh Local Development Regulations, reg 13(3).

(b) any other policies prepared under section 108(1) and (2) of the Transport Act 2000 which affect any part of the LPA's area;

(c) the objectives of preventing major accidents and limiting the consequences of such accidents for human health and the environment by pursuing those objectives through the controls described in Article 13 of Directive 2012/18/EU;

(d) the need, in the long term—

  (i) to maintain appropriate safety distances between establishments and residential areas, buildings and areas of public use, recreational areas, and, as far as possible, major transport routes;

  (ii) to protect areas of particular natural sensitivity or interest in the vicinity of establishments, where appropriate through appropriate safety distances or other relevant measures;

  (iii) in the case of existing establishments, to take additional technical measures in accordance with Article 5 of Directive 2012/18/EU so as not to increase the risks to human health and the environment;

(e) the Waste Strategy for Wales;

(f) any marine plan adopted and published by the Welsh Ministers under Part 3 of the Marine and Coastal Access Act 2009 which affects any part of the LPA's area; and

(g) any local housing strategy, the policies of which affect any part of the LPA's area.'

Sub-paragraphs (c) and (d) are the Control of Major Accident Hazards ('COMAH') regime.

Local planning authorities are also required to keep various matters under review. Whilst entitled 'survey' in the Planning and Compulsory Purchase Act 2004, there is no methodology or reporting obligation. These are best seen as information relevant to policy formation and so should be considered when plan-making. The authority 'must keep under review the matters which may be expected to affect the development of their area or the planning of its development'.[44] These include:[45]

'(a) the principal physical, economic, social and environmental characteristics of the area of the authority (including the extent to which the Welsh language is used in the area);

(b) the principal purposes for which land is used in the area;

(c) the size, composition and distribution of the population of the area;

(d) the communications, transport system and traffic of the area;

(e) any other considerations which may be expected to affect those matters'

The authority has also to consider any changes which they think may occur and the effect such changes are likely to have on the development of the authority's area or on the planning of such development.[46] An authority may also keep under review and examine these matters in neighbouring areas insofar as they may affect the authority's area, provided it consults the neighbouring authority.[47] In practice though authorities are likely to commission joint work, share information or simply examine publically

---

[44] Planning and Compulsory Purchase Act 2004, s 61(1).
[45] Planning and Compulsory Purchase Act 2004, s 61(2).
[46] Planning and Compulsory Purchase Act 2004, s 61(3).
[47] Planning and Compulsory Purchase Act 2004, s 61(4), (5).

available data. It would be unlikely, potentially confusing and unproductive for a council to conduct a survey of businesses in the adjacent area.

The Welsh Assembly may prescribe further matters to be considered, or direct that they be considered in a particular case[48] but that has not been done.

Planning Policy Wales identifies the following key aspects of a local development plan:[49]

- '• it should be succinct, expressed in plain language avoiding jargon;

- it should not be long, complex, vague or over-detailed nor a compendium of policies to cover every eventuality;

- it should avoid repeating national planning policy;

- it should incorporate a concise, long-term vision and strategy;

- it should indicate clearly the plan's main objectives, along with the broad direction of change;

- it should indicate key spatial locations for development and the infrastructure required to achieve them;

- a clear focus should be on planning for places;

- a '**proposals map**' on a geographical Ordnance Survey base must delineate those policies and proposals with a spatial component;

- **deliverability and financial viability** are key considerations and costs such as infrastructure and affordable housing must be considered during preparation of the plan ...

- an appreciation of the **phasing and implementation** of proposals is essential to demonstrate delivery of the plan. Where phasing is included in an LDP it should take the form of a broad indication of the timescale envisaged for the release of development rather than an arbitrary numerical limit on permissions or a precise order of release of sites in particular periods;

- a reasonable degree of flexibility, both in terms of sites and numerical provision, should be embedded within the plan to enable it to respond to unforeseen circumstances that may arise over the plan period;

- the plan should include **policies** to achieve outcomes, support and identify site allocations/ development areas, define where constraints apply and set out the general criteria against which planning applications for the development and use of land and buildings will be considered, preferably by the use of generic policies rather than repetition;

- policies should be distinct from, but supported by, concise reasoned justification;

- an effective **monitoring framework** to deliver the plan.'

THE LOCAL DEVELOPMENT PLAN PROCESS

14.6   The local development plan-making process contains three rounds of statutory consultation followed by examination by an Inspector. The stages, as set out in the Welsh Local Development Regulations, are:

---

48 Planning and Compulsory Purchase Act 2004, s 61(2)(f).
49 *Planning Policy Wales*, 9 edn (November 2016), para 2.2.1.

- pre-deposit participation (reg 14);

- pre-deposit public consultation (reg 15);

- deposit of the proposed local development plan for consultation (regs 17, 18);

- submission of the plan to the Welsh Assembly Government (reg 22);

- independent examination (reg 23); and

- publication of the Inspector's report and adoption (reg 24, 25).

Compliance with the community involvement scheme

14.7   The local development plan must be prepared in accordance with the community involvement scheme and the approved timetable.[50]

The Regulations do provide a let out, that the authority 'does not need to comply with a particular requirement of its community involvement scheme if it has reasonable grounds to believe that it is not likely to prejudice any person's opportunity to be involved in the exercise of the LPA's functions under Part 6 of the Act if it does not comply with that requirement'.[51]

SUSTAINABILITY APPRAISAL

14.8   A sustainability appraisal is required, consisting of an appraisal of the sustainability of the plan and a report of the findings of the appraisal.[52] The report on the sustainability appraisal is required to include any necessary environmental report carried out under strategic environmental assessment.[53] This is a bringing together of the two regimes which formally is not required in England and which the Local Plans Expert Group had recommended that English practice treat separately. In another departure from the English approach, the appraisal must include an assessment of the likely effects of the plan on the use of the Welsh language in the area of the authority.[54]

The sustainability appraisal report is published with the deposit draft of the local development plan.[55]

PRE-DEPOSIT PARTICIPATION (REG 14)

14.9   The first formal stage of the plan-making process is pre-deposit participation under the Welsh Local Development Regulations, reg 14. This precedes the production of a draft plan and instead is for:

---

[50] Planning and Compulsory Purchase Act 2004, s 63(1). There would in any event be a legitimate expectation that the scheme would be complied with: *R (Majed) v London Borough of Camden* [2009] EWCA Civ 1029, [2010] JPL 621.
[51] Welsh Local Development Regulations, reg 9(6). This slightly surprising provision is sanctioned by the Planning and Compulsory Purchase Act 2004, s 63(7)(f) which allows the Assembly to prescribe 'circumstances in which the requirements of the documents need not be complied with'.
[52] Planning and Compulsory Purchase Act 2004, s 62(6).
[53] Welsh Local Development Regulations, reg 2(1).
[54] Planning and Compulsory Purchase Act 2004, s 62(6A).
[55] Welsh Local Development Regulations, reg 17(c)(ii).

- generating alternative strategies and options; and

- requesting nominations for sites to include in the plan.

To generate alternative strategies and options the authority is required to 'engage' those specific consultation bodies that it thinks are affected by the proposed plan and those general consultation bodies that the authority considers appropriate.[56] There is no restriction upon the authority engaging in a wider consultation exercise, both in terms of consulting more parties or the public at large, and in what is covered.

The site nomination process is thrown open widely. The request for nominations must be published on the local planning authority's website and 'by such other means as it considers appropriate'[57]. These might include local advertisement, a general mailing to persons it believes to be interested in planning and development matters or approaches to landowners about particular potential sites. All sites nominated by the published closing date must be put into a list by the authority,[58] known as the candidate sites register.[59] These are to be considered before the deposit draft plan (reg 17) is published[60] but do not have to be addressed before the regulation 15 pre-deposit draft is produced for consultation. A nomination may be made by any person: they do not need to be the owner or a prospective developer of the site.

PRE-DEPOSIT PUBLIC CONSULTATION (REG 15)

14.10   The next stage is pre-deposit consultation on the authority's proposals. This does not have to be a draft of the plan, but sets out the preferred strategy, options and proposals along with alternatives and implications. One form may be to show a preferred, proposed policy followed by rejected alternatives.

Pre-deposit proposals documents are:[61]

> '[the local planning authority's] preferred strategy, options and proposals for the LDP and the implications of these, with earlier alternatives and implications made explicit, the candidate sites register and any review report, together with such supporting documents as in the opinion of the [local planning authority] are relevant to those documents'

A review report is prepared before the preparation of a full or selective review of a local development document.[62]

Pre-deposit matters are:[63]

> '(a) the title of the LDP;
>
> (b) the period within which representations on the proposals may be made …;

---

[56] Welsh Local Development Regulations, reg 14(1).
[57] Welsh Local Development Regulations, reg 14(3).
[58] Welsh Local Development Regulations, reg 14(4).
[59] Welsh Local Development Regulations, reg 2(1).
[60] Welsh Local Development Regulations, reg 14(5).
[61] Welsh Local Development Regulations, reg 2(1).
[62] Defined in the Welsh Local Development Regulations, reg 2(1). A report is required under the Planning and Compulsory Purchase Act 2004, s 69(2) (for a full review) and the Welsh Local Development Regulations, reg 41(4) (for a selective review).
[63] Welsh Local Development Regulations, reg 2(1).

(c) the address to which and, where appropriate, the person to whom representations (whether made by way of electronic communications or otherwise) must be sent …;

(d) a statement that any representations may be accompanied by a request to be notified at a specified address that the LDP has been submitted to the National Assembly for independent examination under section 64 and of the adoption of the LDP'

The pre-deposit proposals documents and a statement of the pre-deposit matters will be published on the authority's website and made available for inspection during normal office hours at the authority's principal office and any other places within its area that it chooses. Copies will also be sent to those specific and general consultation bodies who were engaged at the regulation 14 stage. A notice of where the documents can be physically inspected will be posted on the website and circulated to the consultees.[64] However, a requirement to place a local advertisement was revoked in 2015.[65]

A six-week representation period is provided, starting on the day that the documents are made available for physical inspection and sent to consultees.[66,67] Any person may make representations at this stage.[68] Representations made in time and sent to the address (and, if identified, person at the authority) given for comments must then be considered by the local planning authority before it decides the deposit plan.[69]

Following the regulations 14 and 15 rounds of consultation the authority must prepare an initial consultation report which sets out:[70]

'(a) which bodies it has engaged, notified or consulted pursuant to regulations 14 and 15;

(b) a summary of the main issues raised in, and responses from, those engagements, notifications and consultations;

(c) in relation to the LDP to be deposited in accordance with regulation 17—

(i) how those main issues have been addressed; and

(ii) the extent to which those responses have been addressed;

(d) the total number of representations received pursuant to regulation 16; and

(e) any deviation from the community involvement scheme.'

DEPOSIT OF THE PROPOSED LOCAL DEVELOPMENT PLAN FOR CONSULTATION (REGS 17, 18)

14.11 The deposit stage is the production of the complete draft of the local development plan for representations to be made and for examination. Published

---

[64] Welsh Local Development Regulations, reg 15. Curiously, the consultees are only entitled to receive notice of the pre-deposit matters rather than the matters themselves, even though they can be set out in a few lines.

[65] Welsh Local Development Regulations, reg 15(d), revoked by the Town and Country Planning (Local Development Plan) (Wales) (Amendment) Regulations 2015, WSI 2015/1598, reg 2(11)(a).

[66] There is an error in the Regulations. Regulation 16(2)(a) starts the period running from compliance with reg 15(a), (c) and (d). However, sub-paragraph (d) was the requirement for a local advertisement, revoked in 2015.

[67] Since the six-week period is starting on the day that the material is made available, that is the first day of the period. So a consultation starting on a Tuesday will end on a Monday: *Barker v Hambleton District Council* [2012] EWCA Civ 610, [2013] PTSR 41, at paras 14, 15 per Maurice Kay LJ.

[68] Welsh Local Development Regulations, reg 16(1).

[69] Welsh Local Development Regulations, reg 16(3).

[70] Welsh Local Development Regulations, reg 16A.

at that stage are the 'LDP documents' which are the deposit local development plan, the sustainability appraisal report, the initial consultation report, any relevant review report, any candidate sites register and such supporting documents as in the opinion of the local planning authority are relevant to the preparation of the local development plan.[71] The 'deposit matters' are an updated version of the pre-deposit matters, comprising the title of the local development plan; how and by when to make representations and a statement that representations may be accompanied by a request to be notified at a specified address of the publication of the inspector's recommendations or the plan's adoption or both.[72]

'The LPA must—

(a)   make copies of the LDP documents, and a statement of the deposit matters , available for inspection during normal office hours at the places at which the pre- deposit proposals documents were made available under regulation 15(a);

(b)   publish on its website—

(i)   the LDP documents,

(ii)   the deposit matters, and

(iii)   a statement of the fact that the LDP documents are available for inspection and of the places and times at which they can be inspected;'

The general and specific consultation bodies who were engaged at the first stage will be sent copies of:[73]

'(i)   the deposit LDP,

(ii)   the sustainability appraisal report,

(iii)   the initial consultation report,

(iv)   a list of such of the supporting documents as in the opinion of the LPA are relevant to the preparation of the LDP,

(v)   notice of the deposit matters, and

(vi)   the statement [that the LDP documents are available for inspection and of the places and times at which they can be inspected]'

The Regulations refer to 'such of the supporting documents' in reg 17, whereas in the definition of LDP documents and at the earlier stages they consider 'such supporting documents' as are relevant to the plan or particular consultees. The implication is that the obligation is to filter documents from the previous list of supporting documents rather that to provide new supporting documents. Such a restriction may be undesirable and not the intended consequence of the provision.

One copy of these documents has to be sent to the Welsh Government as a specific consultation body, but guidance asks for four copies of the deposit plan, two copies of any other documents and an electronic copy where practicable.[74]

---

[71]   See definition in Welsh Local Development Regulations, reg 2(1).

[72]   Welsh Local Development Regulations, reg 2(1).

[73]   Welsh Local Development Regulations, reg 17(c).

[74]   *Local Development Plan Manual*, Edition 2 (August 2015), para 7.4.1.2.

Representations can be made by any person in the six weeks starting with the documents being made available for inspection and sent to the consultees.[75] Model representation forms for submission plans and focused changes are published by the Welsh Government.

Copies of the representations should be made available for inspection where the pre-deposit documents were available as soon as possible after their receipt.[76] Where practical, these are also to be put on the authority's website with a statement as to how they can be inspected.[77] Practicality depends upon the size of the documents and whether they were received electronically.

The local planning authority has a discretion to accept late representations. The Regulations do not require representations to be made within the period and it is said that the authority 'need not' comply with the duty to make representations available for inspection if they were made late.[78] That discretion to accept late submissions must be exercised reasonably and fairly between potential participants and in accordance with any provision in the community involvement scheme. Whilst the *Local Development Plan Manual* advises that late representations should only be considered in exceptional circumstances[79], it is explicitly not national policy.

The *Local Development Plan Manual* says that there should be an allowance for public holidays in the representation period.[80] There is no automatic provision, but an authority could use its discretion to announce an extended deadline.

Consideration of regulation 18 representations and the decision to submit

14.12   The next stage is for the local planning authority to send the local development plan to the Welsh Assembly Government for independent examination.[81] It may only be submitted after the authority has considered the representations made at the regulation 18 stage.

If representations at any stage of the process are in respect of anything which is done or is proposed to be done in pursuance of certain Highways Act orders or schemes or the creation of a New Town, then they may be disregarded by the local planning authority or the Welsh Assembly.[82] There is of course no value in objecting to an order or scheme that has been made, and comments on one which is being progressed should be made in that exercise. More difficult is a policy advocating a new road, bridge or new town which would be progressed under those powers. Such schemes would need planning permission and representations can relate to land allocations which would be built out under this legislation or designations or policies which may hinder or assist such schemes.

---

[75] Welsh Local Development Regulations, reg 18. The first day of the six-week period is the date on which the requirements are met.
[76] Welsh Local Development Regulations, reg 19(2)(a).
[77] Welsh Local Development Regulations, reg 19(2)(b).
[78] Welsh Local Development Regulations, reg 19(3).
[79] *Local Development Plan Manual*, Edition 2 (August 2015), para 7.4.4.2.
[80] *Local Development Plan Manual*, Edition 2 (August 2015), para 7.4.1.1.
[81] Planning and Compulsory Purchase Act 2004, s 64(1).
[82] Planning and Compulsory Purchase Act 2004, s 73. The highways schemes are at ss 10 (trunk roads), 14 (side roads), 16 and 18 (motorways), 106(1) or (3) (bridges and tunnel orders and schemes) or 108(1) (diverting navigable watercourses) of the Highways Act 1980 and their predecessor provisions.

SUBMISSION OF THE PLAN TO THE WELSH ASSEMBLY GOVERNMENT (REG 22)

14.13   To be able to submit, the authority must have complied with the relevant requirements in the Welsh Local Development Regulations and 'think the plan is ready for independent examination'.[83] In practical terms the latter requirement means that they believe the plan can be adopted as being sound whether as proposed or with modifications which may be recommended by the Inspector. They must also have considered the representations made on the deposit plan prior to submitting it.[84]

There is no statutory power for the local planning authority to change the plan in the light of the representations. Local planning authorities are, however, encouraged to prepare 'focussed changes' if they consider that soundness problems have been identified. Authorities are asked to advertise them for a six-week period for representations immediately before the submission of plan to the Welsh Ministers.[85]

The local development plan (or revision) is submitted[86] along with:[87]

'(a) the sustainability appraisal report;

(b) the community involvement scheme;

(c) a consultation report setting out—

   (i) which of the bodies they have engaged or consulted pursuant to regulations 14, 15 and 17,

   (ii) a summary of the main issues raised in those engagements, consultations and representations,

   (iii) in respect of the main issues raised under regulation 16, how those main issues have been addressed in the LDP,

   (iv) the total number of representations received pursuant to each of regulations 16 and 18,

   (v) its recommendations as to how it considers the main issues raised in the representations received pursuant to regulation 18 should be addressed in the LDP,

   (vi) its recommendations as to how it considers each of the representations received pursuant to regulation 18 should be addressed in the LDP, and

   (vii) any deviation from the community involvement scheme;

(ca) any relevant review report;

(cb) any candidate sites register;

(d) a copy of the representations received pursuant to regulation 18; and

(e) such supporting documents as the LPA considers relevant to the preparation of the LDP.'

---

[83] Planning and Compulsory Purchase Act 2004, s 64(2).
[84] Welsh Local Development Regulations, reg 22(1).
[85] *Local Development Plan Manual*, Edition 2 (August 2015), para 7.6.4.
[86] Planning and Compulsory Purchase Act 2004, s 64(1).
[87] Welsh Local Development Regulations, reg 22(2) required under the Planning and Compulsory Purchase Act 2004, s 64(3).

Four paper copies and an electronic copy of the documents are to be sent to the Welsh Ministers except that only a single paper copy of the representations is required.[88]

The local planning authority will publish on its website that the plan has been submitted. The submitted documents will all be made available for public inspection and published on the authority's website.[89]

Notice of the submission has to be sent to those who had asked to be informed.[90]

Focused changes

14.14 There is no mechanism for the authority to amend the local development plan following publication of the deposit draft, but it may propose changes for the Inspector to adopt in order to address any failure to achieve soundness. Those proposed changes can be published as 'focused changes'. In the Inspectorate's view, 'these should be exceptional and should clearly relate to potential soundness issues'.[91] Consultation on the proposed changes and their support by any necessary amendments to a sustainability appraisal, SEA environmental report or habitats assessment is encouraged.[92]

However, the *Planning Policy Wales* view that focussed changes can be treated as part of the submitted local development plan or plan revisions is not correct.[93] The submitted plan remains that which was deposited and further changes proposed by the authority are only suggested modifications which the Inspector might recommend to make the plan sound. The question is not whether the plan with its focused changes is sound, but whether the plan without those changes is unsound and the change would, perhaps with others, make it sound.

If the authority wishes to make changes because of a different view of the merits of the plan, or which are not corrections for soundness, then it can withdraw the current deposit plan and re-deposit (and re-consult on) a revised version.

INDEPENDENT EXAMINATION (REG 23)

14.15 The plan will then be examined by a person appointed by the Welsh Ministers[94], invariably a Planning Inspector. The Inspector's task is to decide:[95]

---

[88] Welsh Local Development Regulations, reg 22(3), (4). The supporting documents (para (e)) do not have to be sent electronically if it would not be practicable to do so, although these days it is hard to see how that would be the case.

[89] The new documents (para (c) and (e)) have to be made available and published under reg 22(5). Other documents are already published under regs 17, 19. Supporting documents are only published electronically if it is practicable to do so: reg 22(5)(d).

[90] Welsh Local Development Regulations, reg 22(5).

[91] *Local Development Plan Examinations Procedure Guidance* (August 2015), para 2.5.

[92] *Planning Policy Wales*, 9th edn (November 2016), para 2.7.1; *Local Development Plan Examinations Procedure Guidance* (August 2015), para 2.6.

[93] *Planning Policy Wales*, 9th edn (November 2016), para 2.7.1, and also see the *Local Development Plan Examinations Procedure Guidance* (August 2015), para 2.6.

[94] Planning and Compulsory Purchase Act 2004, s 64(4).

[95] Planning and Compulsory Purchase Act 2004, s 64(5). The section 62 and 63 requirements set out the authority's policies (as far as necessary), with regard to identified matters, sustainability appraisal and compliance with the community involvement scheme and timetable, The Regulations are the Welsh Local Development Regulations.

'(a) whether it satisfies the requirements of sections 62 and 63 and of regulations under section 77;

(b) whether it is sound.'

There is no statutory definition of 'sound' nor is the legal meaning altered by policy. *Planning Policy Wales* specifies soundness as:[96]

'1. **Does the plan fit?** (i.e. is it clear that the LDP is consistent with other plans?);

2. **Is the plan appropriate?** (i.e. is the plan appropriate for the area in the light of the evidence?);

3. **Will the plan deliver?** (i.e. is it likely to be effective?).'

As a preliminary step following receipt of the submitted plan, the Inspectorate will carry out a screening exercise to check that the procedural requirements have been met.[97]

There are very few statutory rules for the conduct of the examination. Any person who made representations seeking to change the plan must (if he so requests) be given the opportunity to appear before Inspector.[98] The Inspector is obliged to consider all of the regulation 18 representations,[99] whether pursued orally or not.

Otherwise the only statutory requirement is for the local planning authority to publish on its website and notify those who had made (and not withdrawn) representations under reg 18 of the time and place of the examination hearing (in practice the first day) and the name of the Inspector.[100]

PUBLICATION OF THE INSPECTOR'S REPORT AND ADOPTION (REGS 24, 25)

14.16   The Inspector will prepare a report, making recommendations and giving reasons for those recommendations.[101] The local planning authority must publish the Inspector's report,[102] at the latest when the plan is adopted.[103] In reality the report will have to be published before the Council decides whether to adopt the plan and it ought to be released shortly after receipt. Publication is actioned by putting the report on the authority's website, making it available for physical inspection in the same way as other documents and informing those who asked to be notified of the publication of the report.[104]

---

[96]   *Planning Policy Wales*, 9th edn (November 2016), para 2.7.2.
[97]   *LDPs Preparing for submission Guidance for local planning authorities* (August 2015), para 6. The exercise uses a checklist in Appendix 2.
[98]   Planning and Compulsory Purchase Act 2004, s 64(6).
[99]   Welsh Local Development Regulations, reg 23(3).
[100] Welsh Local Development Regulations, reg 23(1).
[101] Planning and Compulsory Purchase Act 2004, s 64(7).
[102] Planning and Compulsory Purchase Act 2004, s 64(8).
[103] Welsh Local Development Regulations, reg 24(1). If the Welsh Ministers have directed a modification or that the plan is referred to them following the Inspector's report (Planning and Compulsory Purchase Act 2004, s 65(1), (4)), then the report must be published as soon as reasonably practicable after the direction: reg 24(1).
[104] Welsh Local Development Regulations, reg 24(2).

There are three potential steps which the authority may take following receipt of the Inspector's report, all of which are dictated by either the Inspector's recommendations or the actions of the Welsh Ministers:

(i)   adopt the local development plan as originally prepared if that is the Inspector's recommendation;[105]

(ii)   adopt the local development plan with modifications if the Inspector recommends those modifications;[106]

(iii)   withdraw the development plan if the Inspector recommends that course of action.

The authority has to adopt the local development plan (or, in practice, withdraw it in accordance with the Inspector's recommendation) within eight weeks of receipt of the recommendations and reason.[107]

POWERS OF THE WELSH ASSEMBLY GOVERNMENT

14.17   The Welsh Assembly Government may direct modifications to a local development plan which is going through the adoption process or call it in for approval.[108] These intervention powers are relatively basic and have not been subject to the refinements made to the English provisions in the Housing and Planning Act 2016.

Directing modifications to a plan

14.18   Modifications may be directed if the Ministers consider that the plan is 'unsatisfactory'.[109] Unsatisfactory is not further defined but is not to be equated with unsound. An unsound plan will be dealt with by the Inspector. A plan may be sound but in Minsters' eyes, unsatisfactory. A direction may be given, with reasons, at any time prior to the adoption of the plan.[110] For a direction to be made, a plan must exist so the power can only arise once the deposit local development plan has been made available for representations. Earlier problems can be addressed under the Ministers' intervention powers. In practice, a direction is more likely to be made if the plan has emerged from the examination in a form unacceptable to the Welsh Assembly Government.

The plan-making authority must comply with any direction.[111] They would have to modify the plan and inform the Ministers of the modification as they may only adopt the plan if the Minister gives notice that the direction has been complied with.[112] A direction may be withdrawn by the Minister.[113]

---

[105]   Planning and Compulsory Purchase Act 2004, s 67(1).
[106]   Planning and Compulsory Purchase Act 2004, s 67(2).
[107]   Welsh Local Development Regulations, reg 25(1). The duty is to adopt within that period.
[108]   Planning and Compulsory Purchase Act 2004, s 65.
[109]   Planning and Compulsory Purchase Act 2004, s 65(1).
[110]   Planning and Compulsory Purchase Act 2004, s 65(1).
[111]   Planning and Compulsory Purchase Act 2004, s 65(2)(a). Beyond political persuasion, its only remedy would be judicial review.
[112]   Planning and Compulsory Purchase Act 2004, s 65(2)(b).
[113]   Planning and Compulsory Purchase Act 2004, s 65(3).

Taking over the plan

14.19   Alternatively, the Minister may direct that the plan is submitted to him for approval.[114] There is no statutory criterion for deciding to take over the plan: unlike a direction, the Minister does not have to consider that it is unsatisfactory. The reason may be to allow the Minister to control a plan which is sufficiently important that he considers he ought to deal with it but where he does not have a settled view on what should happen. Conversely, a modification direction requires the Minister to have decided that the plan should be changed. In addition, a takeover might also be executed where the plan has stalled.

As with requiring a modification, such a direction may be made at any time before the plan is adopted, but the power presupposes that there is a draft plan in existence. If the direction is given before the plan has been submitted to the Minister then the Minister must hold an independent examination, if the takeover occurs following submission but before the Inspector has reported, then the report is made to the Minister.[115] The Minister would then publish the report.[116]

Default powers to prepare, revise and adopt a plan

14.20   The Welsh Ministers have default powers if they think 'that a local planning authority are failing or omitting to do anything it is necessary for them to do in connection with the preparation, revision or adoption of a local development plan'.[117] These powers are poorly set out, leading to the replacement of similar provisions in England by the Housing and Planning Act 2016. The Ministers may prepare or revise the local development plan and adopt it. These will allow the Minister to start and then complete plan preparation or revision. Default powers might also be available when a plan or revision is part of the way through preparation: the failure could relate to adoption. However, takeover powers may be more appropriate in such cases.

Where the default power is exercised, the Ministers must hold an independent examination and publish the examiners' recommendations and reasons.[118] They are not however bound by the recommendations made by the examiner.[119]

Joint local development plans

14.21   The Welsh Ministers may direct two or more local planning authorities (not including a national park authority) to prepare a joint local development plan.[120] Alternatively, two or more local authorities may just agree to prepare joint local development plans.[121]

---

[114]   Planning and Compulsory Purchase Act 2004, s 65(4).
[115]   Planning and Compulsory Purchase Act 2004, s 65(5)(b), (c).
[116]   Planning and Compulsory Purchase Act 2004, s 65(6).
[117]   Planning and Compulsory Purchase Act 2004, s 71(1).
[118]   Planning and Compulsory Purchase Act 2004, s 71(2), (3).
[119]   The power to adopt under the default provisions is in s 71, rather than the constrained powers of local planning authorities to adopt under s 67.
[120]   Planning and Compulsory Purchase Act 2004, s 72(A1), (A2). Reasons have to be given for a direction: s 72(1A).
[121]   Planning and Compulsory Purchase Act 2004, s 72(1).

General

14.22   The Assembly may direct that the local development plan does not extend to the area of an urban development corporation.[122] Matching the English provisions, local planning authorities must have regard to any guidance issued by the Assembly in exercising Part 6 powers[123].

REVIEWS OF LOCAL DEVELOPMENT PLANS AND REVISIONS TO THEM

14.23   Reviews and revisions are two distinct processes in Welsh policy-making:[124]

- a local planning authority carries out a *review* of a local development plan to decide whether it ought to institute the process of changing the plan – it does not itself change the plan;

- a *revision* is the whole process of changing the local development plan.

A review of a local development plan must be commenced not later than four years following its adoption (or the adoption of the last review).[125] Additionally, following the publication of the National Development Framework for Wales or a revised Framework or the adoption or approval of a strategic development plan or revised strategic development plan for land that includes part of the local development plan area, the local planning authority must consider whether to carry out a review.[126]

If a statutory review is carried out then the authority must prepare a review report and send it to the Welsh Ministers.[127] An authority can informally consider whether the plan should be revised but if it decides on a revision then it must carry out a formal review first.

An authority may prepare a revision of a local development plan at any time,[128] but must first carry out a review.[129] It must revise the plan if following a review it decides that the plan should be revised or the Welsh Assembly Government direct that it be revised.[130]

Full or partial revisions of development plans have traditionally been carried out under the same procedure as for adopting a new plan. This route is available and sometimes necessary to make revisions of local development plans. However, whilst the provisions of the Planning and Compulsory Purchase Act 2004 apply to revisions as well as the initial adoption of the plan,[131] an altered procedure is made available by

---

[122] Planning and Compulsory Purchase Act 2004, s 74.
[123] Planning and Compulsory Purchase Act 2004, s 75.
[124] The point is worth emphasising as a plan review has generally (and in England still is) used to describe the making of a change to an adopted development plan or the adopted plan as changed.
[125] Welsh Local Development Regulations, reg 41(1).
[126] Planning and Compulsory Purchase Act 2004, ss 68A, 69(1).
[127] Defined in Welsh Local Development Regulations, reg 2(1). A report is required under the Planning and Compulsory Purchase Act 2004, s 69(2) (for a full review) and the Welsh Local Development Regulations, reg 41(4) (for a selective review).
[128] Planning and Compulsory Purchase Act 2004, s 70(1).
[129] Welsh Local Development Regulations, reg 41(2).
[130] Planning and Compulsory Purchase Act 2004, s 70(2).
[131] Planning and Compulsory Purchase Act 2004, s 70(3).

regulations. If it appears to the local planning authority that 'the issues involved are not of sufficient significance to justify undertaking the full procedure for' pre-deposit participation and pre-deposit public participation,[132] then a simplified approach to the early stages can be adopted.[133] The 'short-form' process is in Pt 4A of the Welsh Local Development Regulations.

Short-form procedure for revisions

14.24   The short-form procedure contains two pre-examination stages:

(i)   consultation with particular bodies and, if the revision includes identifying land for development, a call for sites;

(ii)   deposit of the proposed revision for representations.

This process therefore abandons the consultation on the pre-deposit draft plan.

Pre-deposit requirements on revisions

14.25   The local planning authority must ask the specific consultation bodies which it considers may have an interest in the subject of the proposed revision and those general consultation bodies which it considers appropriate to make representations on what the revision should include.[134] The selection of bodies to consult is therefore related to the scope of the intended revisions. A narrowly based revision, for example, updating nature conservation policies, could justify informing only a small number of consultees.

However, a wider exercise is required if 'the proposed revision includes land identified for development' where a request for site nominations must be published on the authority's website and in any other way it considers appropriate.[135] A revision which proposes to add allocations will have to be subject to the site search. An alteration to an existing allocation might also trigger the duty. A clear example would be changing an employment site to a housing-led, mixed use site. 'Includes' is not on its face confined to adding sites for development (or since much land is developed, allocating it for different development) but the meaning and scope of the term is not clear. In practice a change to the quantum of development on a site might prompt other sites to come forward but an alteration to the design detail of an allocation might not do so.

Planning authorities can choose to consult more widely at this pre-deposit stage and would be acting sensibly to do so. Since any changes to the deposit draft can only be made on soundness grounds, this is the only statutory stage at which the authority can be persuaded to include, alter or exclude particular policies.

Duly made representations made by consultation bodies and site nominations put forward must be considered by the authority before deciding on the deposit draft of the revisions.[136]

---

[132] That is, in the Welsh Local Development Regulations, regs 14–16.
[133] Welsh Local Development Regulations, reg 13A.
[134] Welsh Local Development Regulations, reg 26A(1), (2).
[135] Welsh Local Development Regulations, reg 26A(6), (7).
[136] Welsh Local Development Regulations, reg 26A(3), (9).

A report on the consultation process[137] and list of nominated sites will be produced by the authority.[138]

Deposit of the review

14.26   The review with the accompanying local development plan documents and statement of deposit matters will be made available for inspection, published on the authority's website and sent to those specific or general consultation bodies who were previously notified, in a similar manner to the publication of the documents with a new plan or conventional review.[139] In the same way a six-week period is allowed for representations[140] and representations which are made in time are to be available for inspection and where possible put on the authority's website.[141]

Submission, independent examination, publication of recommendations, adoption and withdrawal provisions for a plan apply in the same way to the short form review procedure.[142]

Revisions of plans generally

14.27   Whether the short-form revision process or the conventional process is used for a revision, several points are worthy of note.

The scope of the representations and the examination process will usually be defined by the review report.[143] Other issues ought not to be considered, although review topics might have implications for parts of the plan which the authority does not propose to revise. That might raise soundness issues, which will have to be considered.

The Inspectorate's guidance is for authorities to submit marked-up versions of the revised plan (with text underlined or struck through) if only certain sections of the plan are being revised, whilst a clean version of the plan should be submitted if there are substantial revisions or a replacement plan is being produced.[144] However, since the remit of the Inspector is to make recommendations on the revisions which are being proposed, they need to be clearly identified. So if a clean version of the proposed revised plan is being submitted then a separate list of the actual revisions is necessary. A replacement plan can simply be submitted as such.

Sustainability appraisal must be carried out for all revisions[145] but strategic environmental assessment is not required if 'minor modifications' are proposed which would not be likely to have significant environmental effects.[146] Habitats Regulations assessment may also be necessary.

---

[137] The report will meet the requirements of an initial consultation report under reg 16A (discussed in 14.10 above): Welsh Local Development Regulations, reg 26A(5).
[138] Welsh Local Development Regulations, reg 26A(4), (8).
[139] Welsh Local Development Regulations, reg 26B, see reg 17 discussed in 14.11 above.
[140] Welsh Local Development Regulations, reg 26C.
[141] Welsh Local Development Regulations, reg 26D.
[142] Welsh Local Development Regulations, reg 26E.
[143] *LDPs: Preparing for submission, guidance for local planning authorities* (August 2015), para 12.
[144] *LDPs: Preparing for submission, guidance for local planning authorities* (August 2015), paras 13, 14.
[145] Planning and Compulsory Purchase Act 2004, s 62(6).
[146] Environmental Assessment of Plans and Programmes Regulations 2004, SI 2004/1633, reg 5(6)(b). See 3.10 above.

ANNUAL MONITORING REPORT

14.28   Each local planning authority must make an annual monitoring report to the Welsh Government.[147] The report is to be submitted and published on the authority's website by 31 October for the preceding period 1 April to 31 March.[148]

A report will specify the housing land supply taken from the current Housing Land Availability Study and the number of net additional affordable and general market dwellings built in the authority's area in the report year and since the local development plan was adopted.[149] It will also identify local development plan policies which are not being 'implemented'.[150]

---

[147]   Planning and Compulsory Purchase Act 2004, s 76.
[148]   As specified in *Planning Policy Wales*, 9th edn (November 2016), para 2.11.1, compliance with which is required by the Welsh Local Development Regulations, reg 37(1).
[149]   Welsh Local Development Regulations, reg 37(4).
[150]   Welsh Local Development Regulations, reg 37(2).

Chapter 15

Welsh Supplementary Planning Guidance

15.1   Supplementary Planning Guidance is a tier of planning 'advice' prepared by local planning authorities which sits below the local development plan in the hierarchy. It does not have development plan status for the purpose of the section 38(6) presumption in favour of the plan.[1] Welsh Supplementary Planning Guidance is entirely non-statutory.[2] The ability to issue such guidance therefore arises out of the authorities' general planning responsibilities.[3]

Advice on Supplementary Planning Guidance is given in *Planning Policy Wales*[4] ('PPW') and the *Local Development Plan Manual*.[5]

THE ROLE AND CONTENT OF SUPPLEMENTARY PLANNING GUIDANCE

15.2   The content of Supplementary Planning Guidance ('SPG') is limited by the requirement that the local development plan contains the authority's objectives in respect of the development and use of land and their general policies for the implementation of those objectives.[6] A local development plan may contain specific policies for any part of the area.[7] SPG cannot contain anything which ought to be contained in a development plan.[8]

Planning Policy Wales seeks to constrain the scope of SPG much further. Whilst the PPW does not have to be followed, it should be considered and the Welsh Ministers and Inspectors are likely to give much less weight to SPG which does not accord with it. It advises that SPG is a 'means of setting out more detailed thematic or site specific guidance on the way in which the policies of an LDP are to be interpreted and applied in particular circumstances or areas'.[9] The distinction between policy not included within the development plan and guidance is seen by government as being real but is not in reality recognised by the courts. Problematically, the PPW says that SPG can be used to interpret policies in the development plan.[10] That is questionable: the meaning of the development plan ought to be capable of being understood from

---

[1]   Planning and Compulsory Purchase Act 2004, s 38(6).
[2]   Unlike supplementary planning documents in England, see Chapter 11.
[3]   See Chapter 2 above.
[4]   *Planning Policy Wales*, 9th edn (November 2016), section 2.3.
[5]   *Local Development Plan Manual*, Edition 2 (August 2015), section 7.3.
[6]   Planning and Compulsory Purchase Act 2004, s 62(2).
[7]   Planning and Compulsory Purchase Act 2004, s 62(3).
[8]   See *Westminster City Council v Great Portland Estates plc* [1985] AC 661 and the other cases discussed in 2.34.
[9]   *Planning Policy Wales*, 9th edn (November 2016), para 2.3.1.
[10] *Planning Policy Wales*, 9th edn (November 2016), para 2.3.1.

an objective reading of the document itself and not be susceptible to change by a document prepared later, less formally and without the safeguards attaching to the development plan process.[11] The local development plan can though defer the detail on some matters to SPG and it is best to do so explicitly. For SPG to give guidance on how development plan policies are to be applied is perfectly legitimate.

The *Local Development Plan Manual* says: 'LDP contains policy; SPG contains guidance and advice only. All SPG should derive from a generic policy or – in the case of a brief – from a site allocation. SPG should not be used to determine the appropriate type, scale and level of development for particular sites.'[12]

It is best if SPG is prepared or revised in accordance with an approach outlined in a local development plan. Plans can be strengthened by explaining what topics will be developed in SPG and so there is a coherent body of council planning advice. In structuring an authority's planning guidance it is useful to have a view of what will be in the development plan and what in supplementary guidance.[13] Signalling the use of SPG may help keep plans shorter and smooth the examination process as an answer to concerns that policies or site details are unduly brief.

The PPW advises that the Welsh Government and the Planning Inspectorate will give 'substantial weight to approved SPG which derives from and is consistent with the development plan, and has been the subject of consultation'.[14] There is, however, no legal bar on SPG which is not based on a development plan policy.

Joint SPG might be adopted[15] although it is difficult to see the value in this unless there is a genuinely common issue crossing authority boundaries. Common templates or text might be useful as a starting point, but there is no value in local policy unless it is genuinely local, reflecting local circumstances and local views as to the outcomes of planning decisions.

Several practical matters arise. SPG should focus on what it adds to the planning process but it fits into a context of local, strategic and national policy as well as some legislation. In light of that other material, SPG should not be longer than it needs to be and there is no benefit in simply summarising other policy but it needs to explain how it fits into the development plan material. It may also usefully provide illustrative material or examples but should be clear on its status.

The non-statutory nature of SPG makes it important to identify whether a document is a planning document or not. For example, in *R (on the application of Long) v Monmouthshire County Council*[16] an Urban Design Framework was not SPG or any other planning policy document, being commissioned by the Council as landowner.

---

11   See *Tesco Stores Ltd v Dundee City Council* [2012] UKSC 13.
12   *Local Development Plan Manual*, Edition 2 (August 2015), para 7.3.1, also para 7.3.4.
13   It is also important in structuring the planning policy team's workload.
14   *Planning Policy Wales*, 9th edn (November 2016), para 2.3.4. In *R (on the application of Jones) v City and County of Swansea* [2007] EWHC 213 (Admin), at paras 11, 12, 14, 15 per Wyn Williams J, a failure to consider window separation distances in a Household Extension Design Guide (which was itself referred to in a local plan) was unlawful although planning permission was not quashed. It was also common ground in *Rhoscrowther Wind Farm Ltd v Welsh Ministers* [2016] EWHC 1388 (Admin), at para 2 per Hickinbottom J, that SPG was a material consideration.
15   *Local Development Plan Manual*, Edition 2 (August 2015), para 7.3.4.
16   [2012] EWHC 3130 (Admin), at para 59, 92 per Nicola Davies J.

The preparation of Supplementary Planning Guidance

15.3   Since SPG is not mentioned in legislation at all there are few legal requirements for how to make it. Strategic environmental assessment ('SEA') may be required and the Habitats Regulations may apply, otherwise control is left to public law principles having regard to national policy on preparing SPG.

The *Local Development Plan Manual* says that the LDP delivery agreement with the Welsh Assembly Government should set out the procedures to be applied to SPG-making and could indicate the SPG proposed for consultation.[17] However, the Town and Country Planning (Local Development Plan) (Wales) Regulations 2005[18] refer to the delivery agreement and the community involvement strategy solely in development plan-making.

The process adopted should seek to ensure that the SPG is right, will carry weight with decision-makers and those affected and is lawful. Authorities may wish to have guidance on the procedure they might follow. This will avoid inventing a new process on every occasion and promotes consistency in the process. However, any such process needs to be followed, or only departed from for good reason, as failures to follow it may give rise to a breach of legitimate expectation[19] or political criticism.

In practice, there are two critical points on the process. Whilst there is no legal need to do so (unless SEA takes place) consultation ought to be carried out on a draft SPG. It will tend to produce a better document and one which is more likely to be accepted by those involved in the planning process. Guidance emphasises that Inspectors and the Welsh Ministers are more likely to attach weight to SPG which has been the subject of consultation.

Secondly, there should be formal adoption by councillors. SPG represents the authority's guidance on particular issues and so has a political context. A formal member decision also makes the status of the document clear and improves the public accountability of the decision-making. SPG would be adopted by a council's executive or an individual executive member unless the full council decides to take it over.[20]

---

[17] *Local Development Plan Manual*, Edition 2 (August 2015), para 7.3.3.
[18] WSI 2005/2839.
[19] See *R (Majed) v London Borough of Camden* [2009] EWCA Civ 1029, [2009] JPL 621 on English statements of community involvement.
[20] Local Authorities (Executive Arrangements) (Functions and Responsibilities) (Wales) Regulations 2007, SI 2007/399, reg 6(1), Sch 4.

Chapter 16

Northern Ireland: Plans and Policies Adopted by Ministers

16.1   Until 2015 the planning system in Northern Ireland was entirely centralised. All planning policy emanated from the province's administration, whether under direct rule or from the Northern Ireland Executive. Planning applications were made to, and decided by, the Department of the Environment. Local authorities were consulted on applications, but had no powers to make planning decisions.

Consequently, Northern Irish Ministers were responsible for adopting what in other jurisdictions would be seen as national policy (planning principles to be applied), strategic policy at the regional level and development plans at the local level. In April 2015, councils obtained powers over planning applications and local policy. Ultimately the area plans made by the Department will be replaced by local development plans made by the local planning authorities and considered in the next chapter. In the meantime, Northern Irish planning policy is in a state of transition.

In the Northern Ireland administration planning functions were exercised by the Department for the Environment. Those powers are now carried out by the Department for Infrastructure.[1]

The Department for Infrastructure is required to 'formulate and co-ordinate policy for securing the orderly and consistent development of land and the planning of that development'.[2] These policies must be formulated with 'the objective of furthering sustainable development and promoting or improving well-being'.[3] Sustainable development and well-being are to be considered having regard to Northern Ireland Executive policy and guidance and any other relevant matters.[4]

As part of its planning responsibilities, the Department is able to carry out or commission surveys and studies including on physical, economic, social and environmental characteristics of areas, population and transport.[5]

---

[1]   Legislation ascribes powers to particular departments, unlike the English approach of giving power to the Secretary of State with it being an administrative decision as to which Minister exercises the power. In *Re Omagh District Council's Application* [2007] NIQB 61 Gillen J held that the Department of Regional Development had no statutory authority to make substantive planning policy, that being a matter which fell exclusively within the remit of the then Department of the Environment. The judgment was affirmed in *Central Craigavon Ltd v Department of the Environment for Northern Ireland* [2011] NICA 17, at para 11 per Girvan LJ. Power sharing arrangements make the identity of the decision-maker even more fraught.

[2]   Planning Act (Northern Ireland) 2011, s 1(1). The same duty existed under the Planning (Northern Ireland) Order 1991, SR 1991/1220, art 3(1).

[3]   Planning Act (Northern Ireland) 2011, s 1(2)(b).

[4]   Planning Act (Northern Ireland) 2011, s 1(3).

[5]   Planning Act (Northern Ireland) 2011, s 1(4).

STATEMENT OF COMMUNITY INVOLVEMENT

16.2   The Department has to publish a statement of community involvement which sets out its policy on the involvement of persons who appear to be interested in development in the exercise of the Department's development management functions.[6] These include planning applications, appeals, call-ins and simplified planning zones.[7] There would be a legitimate expectation that the Department would comply with any promises in the statement.[8]

CONSULTATION ON THE PREPARATION OF POLICY

16.3   Ministerial practice and policy has to been to consult on changes to planning policy. In *Central Craigavon Ltd*[9] Ministerial statements to the Assembly on the weight to be given to economic benefits in planning decisions and restricting the use of prematurity to refuse planning permission were quashed. Having incorrectly said that these statements were not changes to planning policy, consultation should have been undertaken because of a legitimate expectation arising 'from the clear and unambiguous representation by the respondent's department to the Northern Ireland public at large that it would consult on new planning policy as per para.9 of PPS1'.[10] Planning Policy Statement 1 has since been cancelled and a similar promise is not contained in the replacement Strategic Planning Policy Statement. Whilst the government 'acknowledged that consultation is a requirement of fairness in the context of establishing the policy framework'[11] the High Court relied upon a representation to consult on planning policy.[12]

REGIONAL DEVELOPMENT STRATEGY

16.4   The Regional Development Strategy ('RDS') is 'a strategy for the long-term development of Northern Ireland'[13] which was prepared initially by the Department for Regional Development, with the responsibility now lying with the Department for Infrastructure. The only procedural requirement in the relevant order is for the Department to consult with the other departments.[14]

The Department is required to provide policy guidance and advice in relation to its RDS and the implementation thereof and co-ordinate the implementation of that strategy.[15]

Considerable importance is attached to the RDS. The Department's own policies for the development of land and its planning are required to be in general conformity

---

[6]   Planning Act (Northern Ireland) 2011, s 2.
[7]   The statement covers the functions in the Planning Act (Northern Ireland) 2011, Pt 3.
[8]   See *R (on the application of Majed) v London Borough of Camden* [2009] EWCA Civ 1029, [2010] JPL 621.
[9]   [2010] NIQB 102.
[10]   At para 37 per Treacy J.
[11]   At para 29 per Treacy J.
[12]   See paras 31, 39.
[13]   Strategic Planning (Northern Ireland) Order 1999, SR 1999/660, art 3(1).
[14]   Strategic Planning (Northern Ireland) Order 1999, art 3(1).
[15]   Strategic Planning (Northern Ireland) Order 1999, art 4.

with the strategy.[16] Old style development plans made by the Department also had to be in general conformity with the RDS.[17] As an important contrast, when councils prepare the new local development plans they are simply required to have regard to the RDS.[18] Any Northern Ireland department or UK government department is required to have regard to the regional development strategy when exercising functions in relation to development in Northern Ireland.[19]

The current Regional Development Strategy 2035 was published in 2010. It contains strategic guidance which applies across Northern Ireland as well as specific chapters on the Belfast Metropolitan Urban Area and the North West region centred on Londonderry. Housing growth forecasts are projected for 2008 to 2025, although these have been superseded by new forecasts for 2012 to 2025 which are mentioned below.

HOUSING GROWTH INDICATORS ('HGIS')

16.5   The Department for Infrastructure publishes an estimate of future housing need as housing growth indicators ('HGIs'). The current indicators are for the period 2012 to 2025.

STRATEGIC PLANNING POLICY STATEMENT FOR NORTHERN IRELAND 'PLANNING FOR SUSTAINABLE DEVELOPMENT'

16.6   The Strategic Planning Policy Statement for Northern Ireland ('SPPS'), 'Planning for Sustainable Development' sets out policy to be taken into account in plan-making and development management decisions.[20] It was adopted by the Department of the Environment (now the Department for Infrastructure) in September 2015 as part of its duty to formulate policy under the Planning Act (Northern Ireland) 2011.[21]

The SPPS contains a mix of planning policy and guidance on the operation of the planning process. It does not generally supersede existing Departmental policy[22], but conflicts between the SPPS and older Departmental policies (except for the RDS) are resolved in favour of the SPPS.[23]

---

[16]   Planning Act (Northern Ireland) 2011, s 1(2)(a).
[17]   Planning (Northern Ireland) Order 1991, art 4(1A).
[18]   Planning (Northern Ireland) Act 2011, ss 8(5), 9(6). Taking account of the RDS is also one of the soundness tests: test C1, in Development Plan Practice Note 5: *Soundness*.
[19]   Planning (Northern Ireland) Order 1991, art 5.
[20]   SPPS, para 1.5.
[21]   Planning Act (Northern Ireland) 2011, s 1(1). See SPPS, para 1.4. The document was subject to strategic environmental assessment ('SEA') under the Environmental Assessment of Plans and Programmes Regulations (Northern Ireland) 2004, SR 2004/280: SPPS, para 1.4.
[22]   The SPPS did cancel Planning Policy Statement PPS 1: General Principles, PPS 5: Retailing and Town Centres and PPS 9: The Enforcement of Planning Control: SPPS, para 1.16.
[23]   SPPS, para 1.12. However, 'where the SPPS is silent or less prescriptive on a particular planning policy matter than retained policies this should not be judged to lessen the weight to be afforded to the retained policy': SPPS, para 1.12.

PLANNING POLICY STATEMENTS

16.7   Planning Policy Statements were made by the Department for the Environment under their general duty to formulate policy in the Planning (Northern Ireland) Order 1991, art 3(1).[24] In *Central Craigavon Ltd* the Court of Appeal held that Planning Policy Statement 5: Retailing, Town Centres and Commercial Leisure Developments was a policy rather than a plan and so did not need to be subject to strategic environmental assessment.[25]

DEPARTMENTAL POLICIES AND TRANSITIONAL ARRANGEMENTS

16.8   The local development plan process is intended to enable local authorities to set their own planning policies within a much simplified regional policy context. In the meantime there is a great deal of Departmental policy. Until the council's first development plan document, the Plan Strategy, is adopted, the SPPS expects authorities to apply retained Departmental policy, relevant supplementary and best practice guidance and the SPPS.

By paragraph 1.11 of the SPPS:

> 'Where a council adopts its Plan Strategy, existing policy retained under the transitional arrangements shall cease to have effect in the district of that council and shall not be material from that date, whether the planning application has been received before or after that date.'

The old policy will therefore be displaced on an area-by-area basis. Councils will need to be careful to avoid leaving a vacuum, as many of the detailed development management policies will be in their Local Policies Plan which will be adopted some time after the Plan Strategy. A Plan Strategy could extend the transition until the later plan is adopted, subject to the Plan Strategy prevailing over the Departmental Policies in the event of conflict.

The 'policy provisions' of the Planning Policy Statements ('PPSs') below are retained by the SPPS in the transitional period:[26]

- PPS 2: Natural Heritage;

- PPS 3: Access, Movement and Parking;

- PPS 3 (Clarification): Access, Movement and Parking;

- PPS 4: Planning and Economic Development;

- PPS 4: Clarification of PED 7;

- PPS 6: Planning, Archaeology and The Built Heritage;

---

[24]   Planning Policy Statements could not be made by other departments: *Re Omagh District Council's Application* [2007] NIQB 61.
[25]   [2011] NICA 17, at para 43 per Girvan LJ, affirming [2010] NIQB 73 at para 19 per Morgan LCJ. Permission to appeal to the Supreme Court was granted but the appeal was withdrawn. The decision is criticised in Gregory Jones QC, Ned Westaway and Roger Watts, 'Why Central Craigavon was wrongly decided (and other problems with the incorporation of the Strategic Environmental Assessment Directive into domestic law)' [2013] JPL 1074.
[26]   SPPS, para 1.13.

16.8 *Northern Ireland: Plans and Policies Adopted by Ministers*

- PPS 6 (Addendum): Areas of Townscape Character;

- PPS 7: Quality Residential Environments;

- PPS 7: (Addendum): Residential Extensions and Alterations ;

- PPS 7: (Addendum): Safeguarding the Character of Established Residential Areas;

- PPS 8: Open Space, Sport and Outdoor Recreation;

- PPS 10: Telecommunications;[27]

- PPS 11: Planning and Waste Management;

- PPS 12: Housing in Settlements;

- PPS 12: Policy HS 3 (Amended) 'Travellers Accommodation';

- PPS 13: Transportation and Land Use;

- PPS 15 Revised: Planning and Flood Risk;

- PPS 16: Tourism;

- PPS 17: Control of Outdoor Advertisements;

- PPS 18: Renewable Energy;

- PPS 21: Sustainable Development in the Countryside; and

- PPS 23: Enabling Development.

The relevant provisions of 'A Planning Strategy for Rural Northern Ireland'[28] are also retained. Other Departmental planning documents which are treated as material considerations in the transitional period are listed on the Department's website and include:[29]

- Airport Public Safety Zones (2007);

- 'Living Places' – An Urban Stewardship and Design Guide for Northern Ireland;

- 'Building on Tradition' – A Sustainable Design Guide for the Northern Ireland Countryside;

- 'Creating Places' – Achieving quality in residential developments';

- Best Practice Guidance to PPS 18 'Renewable Energy';

- Wind Energy Development in Northern Ireland Landscapes (August 2010);

- Development Control Advice Notes; and

- Supplementary Planning Guidance to Policy PED 8 'Development Incompatible with Economic Development Uses'.

---

[27] Except Policy TEL2 which was cancelled by the SPPS.
[28] Department of the Environment, 1993.
[29] As listed in SPPS, para 1.14.

DEPARTMENTAL DEVELOPMENT PLANS

16.9   Prior to the granting of planning powers to local authorities in 2015, local planning policy was a matter for the Northern Ireland Executive. The Planning (Northern Ireland) Order 1991 empowered the Department to make, alter, repeal or replace a development plan for any area.[30] The development plan would consist of map and a written statement formulating proposals for the development or other use of land in the area and any further descriptive material.[31]

The plan was required to be in general conformity with the regional development strategy.[32]

Two alternative procedures were laid out. The full procedure applied where the Department proposed to make a development plan or to alter, repeal or replace a plan, unless in the latter cases the issues did not warrant this procedure. Two rounds of consultation would take place under the full procedure:

(i)   consultation with the district council for the area and the public at large on the Department's proposals or the issues involved. A period for representations would be provided;[33]

(ii)   after considering the representations made, the Department would prepare the plan, alterations, instrument of repeal or replacement plan and publicise them for statutory consultation to invite objections.[34]

If the proposal was to alter, repeal or replace a development plan for an area and it appeared to the Department that the issues involved were not of sufficient importance to warrant the full procedure set out in art 5 then the first stage could be omitted. Consultation would just take place on the draft documents.[35]

Whichever procedure had been adopted, the Department had a discretion to have an independent examination to be carried out by the Planning Appeals Commission to consider objections which had been made.[36] Whilst there was no right to have an examination, if one was held then any person who objected to the proposal would have an opportunity to appear at the examination.[37] The Department would then be able to make an order adopting the plan, or providing for its alteration, repeal or replacement after considering any representations made and any examiner's report.[38]

---

[30]   Planning (Northern Ireland) Order 1991, art 4(1).
[31]   Planning (Northern Ireland) Order 1991, art 4(2).
[32]   Planning (Northern Ireland) Order 1991, art 4(1A).
[33]   Planning (Northern Ireland) Order 1991, art 5(2), (3).
[34]   Planning (Northern Ireland) Order 1991, art 5(4)–(6). Whilst the initial consultation sought 'representations', the second round was to allow persons to make objections.
[35]   Planning (Northern Ireland) Order 1991, art 6.
[36]   Planning (Northern Ireland) Order 1991, art 7(1). The examination provisions had replaced an inquiry process in 2006: Planning Reform (Northern Ireland) Order 2006, SR 2006/1252, arts 1, 5. Reflecting previous legislation rather than post-2006 approaches this was an examination into objections rather than an examination of the plan.
[37]   Planning (Northern Ireland) Order 1991, art 7(2).
[38]   Planning (Northern Ireland) Order 1991, art 8(1). Article 8 requires objections to be considered before the proposal is adopted, but any representations made in the short consultation had to be taken into account: art 6(5).

Up to the turn of the century, the adoption of department development plans went relatively smoothly. Since then, two court cases have caused severe delays to the last round of plans.

The draft Northern Area Plan and draft Magherafelt Area Plan were subject to the first UK judicial reviews on strategic environmental assessment grounds in Seaport Investments Ltd. On 9 September 2007, Weatherup J found four errors.[39] First, the designation of the Department of the Environment as the consultation body contravened Directive 2001/42/EC ('SEA Directive') because it was not independent of itself. Secondly, the failure to set timeframes for consultation in the Environmental Assessment of Plans and Programmes Regulations (Northern Ireland) 2004 ('SEA Regulations') was also a transposition error. The environmental reports prepared for the plans were not in substantial compliance with the contents required by the SEA Regulations and the SEA Directive. Finally, the draft plans had preceded the environmental reports. Declarations were made about those transposition errors and the plans.[40]

The first attempt by the courts to refer the case to the European Court of Justice ('ECJ') was ruled inadmissible because it was inadequately drafted.[41] Consequently, the first two findings were not overturned by the ECJ until 20 October 2011.[42]

One of the other area plans which was progressing was the Belfast Metropolitan Area Plan ('BMAP').[43] Whether BMAP should restrict the expansion of the Sprucefield Regional Shopping Centre to bulky goods only was a major controversial issue amongst Northern Ireland Executive ministers. After the dispute had raged for over a year and a half, the Minister for the Environment made the plan on 3 September 2014. Judicial review proceedings were brought against the plan by the Minister for Enterprise, Trade & Investment. Treacy J held that the Minister needed the approval of the ministerial Executive Committee as it cut across the responsibilities of other ministers and was a 'significant or controversial matter'.[44]

In consequence, the High Court declared that BMAP had been unlawfully made, but at the Ministers' request made declarations which gave effect to a purported retrospective approval of BMAP by the Northern Ireland Executive, except for the contentious bulky goods restriction at Sprucefield. The Court of Appeal found this to be impermissible.[45] The making of BMAP had been unlawful and the remaining parts of the declaration were 'included with the intention of giving effect to political policy decisions about the content of BMAP that had played no part in the matters argued before or decided by the judge who was not at all concerned with the contents of the draft BMAP but only with what he held to be the invalidity of its purported adoption'.[46]

---

[39] *Re* Seaport Investments Ltd's Application [2007] NIQB 62, [2008] Env LR 23.
[40] [2007] NIQB 103.
[41] Case C-454/08, *Seaport Investments Ltd v Department of the Environment for Northern Ireland* [2009] ECR I-92.
[42] Case C-474/10, *Department of the Environment for Northern Ireland v Seaport Ltd (NI)*, [2011] ECR I-10227, [2012] Env LR 21.
[43] Pronounced 'B Map'.
[44] Northern Ireland Act 1998, s 20(3), (4).
[45] *Belfast City Council v Minister of Enterprise, Trade & Investment* [2017] NICA 28.
[46] At para 17 per Weir LJ.

Whilst the Court made a declaration rather than a quashing order, the adoption is being treated as not having legal effect. In practice weight continues to be given to the 2004 draft BMAP but the future of the plan remains to be decided. It may be that with the suspension (at the time of writing) of the Northern Ireland Executive and progress on local development plans that BMAP never finally and lawfully comes into effect.

Transition of the area plans

16.10   Other than BMAP, the area plans remain in force, although most are quite dated. They will be progressively replaced by local development plans.

Once a plan strategy is adopted by a council or approved by the Department for the council area, then the local development plan will be the plan strategy and the departmental development plan.[47] As would be expected, any conflict between the two documents is resolved in favour of the plan strategy.[48] When the local policies plan comes into force, the departmental development plan will cease to have any effect.[49]

---

[47]   Planning (Local Development Plan) Regulations (Northern Ireland) 2015, SR 2015/62, Sch 1, para 3(a).

[48]   Planning (Local Development Plan) Regulations (Northern Ireland) 2015, Sch 1, para 3(b).

[49]   Planning (Local Development Plan) Regulations (Northern Ireland) 2015, Sch 1, para 4.

Chapter 17

Local Development Plans in Northern Ireland

17.1 An essential part of the devolution of power within Northern Ireland is handing control of most planning matters to the local councils. They are now responsible for preparing local development plans, replacing the departmental development plans. The role of the Northern Ireland Executive in the process remains considerable, principally carried out by the Department for Infrastructure ('the Department').

The relevant legislation is Pt 2 of the Planning Act (Northern Ireland) 2011, the Planning (Local Development Plan) Regulations (Northern Ireland) 2015[1] and the Planning (Statement of Community Involvement) Regulations (Northern Ireland) 2015.[2] Policy and guidance on how to make the plans is in the Strategic Planning Policy Statement for Northern Ireland ('SPPS') and nine Development Plan Practice Notes ('DPPNs').[3] The DPPNs are:

- Development Plan Practice Note 01 Introduction: *Context for Local Development Plans* (April 2015);

- Development Plan Practice Note 02: *Statement of Community Involvement (SCI)* (Version 2/August 2015);

- Development Plan Practice Note 03: *Timetable* (April 2015);

- Development Plan Practice Note 04: *Sustainability Appraisal incorporating Strategic Environmental Assessment* (April 2015);

- Development Plan Practice Note 05: *Preferred Options Paper* (April 2015);

- Development Plan Practice Note 06: *Soundness* (Version 2/May 2017);

- Development Plan Practice Note 07: *The Plan Strategy* (April 2015);

- Development Plan Practice Note 08: *The Local Policies Plan* (April 2015); and

- Development Plan Practice Note 09: *Submission and Handling of Representations* (Version 2/December 2016).

---

[1] SR 2015/62.
[2] SR 2015/63. The Regulations contain a variety of drafting quirks which could be usefully ironed out and are discussed as they arise in this chapter.
[3] Councils are required to have regard to any guidance issued by the Department for Infrastructure, the Department for Regional Development and the Office of the First Minister and deputy First Minister when exercising their functions under Pt 2 of the Act: Planning (Northern Ireland) Act 2011, s 20. There is also a duty to have regard to policies and guidance issued in respect of sustainable development: Planning (Northern Ireland) Act 2011, s 5(2).

Examination practice is explained in the Planning Appeals Commission's *Procedures for Independent Examination of Local Development Plans.*[4]

Plans will invariably be subject to strategic environmental assessment under the Environmental Assessment of Plans and Programmes Regulations (Northern Ireland) 2004.[5]

THE LOCAL DEVELOPMENT PLAN

17.2   A local development plan will comprise two development plan documents:

- a plan strategy detailing the council's objectives in relation to the development and use of land in its district and its strategic policies;[6] and

- a local policies plan setting out the council's policies in relation to the development and use of land in its district.[7]

Government guidance is that strategic site allocations should be in the plan strategy, with other sites in the local policies plan.[8] As with all development plan-making, the councils should consider what the documents will add. There is no value in repeating matters in the SPPS or the Regional Development Strategy 2035 ('RDS') and some of their policies could be incorporated by reference. Authorities need to consider whether some details can be left to non-statutory Supplementary Planning Guidance. Each plan will contain its own proposals map (which might be several maps) to illustrate the document's policies and proposals spatially as far as possible.[9]

The two documents are prepared as part of a single process, carried out, it is hoped, in accordance with a timetable agreed with the Northern Ireland Executive.[10] The plans will be prepared in accordance with the requirements of the Planning Act (Northern Ireland) 2011 and Regulations and the statement of community involvement prepared by each council and agreed with the Department.[11]

Matters to be considered

17.3   The development plan preparation functions are to be exercised 'with the objective of furthering sustainable development'.[12] This duty extends to councils, examiners and the Department. For these purposes regard is to be had to policies and guidance issued by the Office of the First Minister and deputy First Minister or by the Department for Regional Development along with any other matters that appear to be relevant.[13]

---

[4]   April 2017.
[5]   SR 2004/280.
[6]   Planning (Northern Ireland) Act 2011, s 8(2).
[7]   Planning (Northern Ireland) Act 2011, s 9(2).
[8]   See DPPN 7: *The Plan Strategy*, para 5.8.
[9]   Planning (Local Development Plan) Regulations (Northern Ireland) 2015, reg 13(1).
[10] Planning (Northern Ireland) Act 2011, s 7.
[11] Planning (Northern Ireland) Act 2011, s 4.
[12] Planning (Northern Ireland) Act 2011, s 5(1).
[13] Planning (Northern Ireland) Act 2011, s 5(2).

In preparing each development plan document, the council is required to have regard to the RDS, the council's current community strategy, any policy or advice contained in guidance published by the Department and any matters prescribed, or in a particular case, directed by the Department.[14] The only prescribed matters are the Control of Major Accident Hazards duties.[15]

A vital part is the preparation of the evidence base: this has been the main source of failure elsewhere in the UK. Critical topics including housing and employment market analysis and availability, environmental impacts, viability and infrastructure requirements.[16] The SPPS says that housing allocations in local development plans should be informed by RDS housing growth indicators ('HGIs') of dwelling numbers and distributions, the RDS housing evaluation framework, urban capacity studies, a locally calculated windfall allowance, a sequential approach to large settlements (usually over 5,000 population), a housing needs assessment/housing market analysis carried out by the Northern Ireland Housing Executive and transport assessments.[17]

Some advice on how to carry out these assessments is given in regional policy, in particular the RDS.[18]

Sustainability appraisal is required by the Planning Act (Northern Ireland) 2011[19] and this is viewed by DPPN4 as an ongoing process. Care does need to be taken to ensure that it produces useful documents which address the real sustainability and environmental issues arising on the plan.

Equality impact assessments ('EQIAs') are expected for policies which have a major potential to impact on equality of opportunity and good relations.[20]

As well as the danger of having an inadequate evidence base, there is a risk of too much material being produced. Particularly when plans are submitted to the Department, councils should ask themselves whether supporting material is likely to be referred to in the examination.

Statement of community involvement

17.4   Each council must prepare a statement of community involvement[21] which is:[22]

> 'a statement of the council's policy as to the involvement in the exercise of the council's functions under this Part and Part 3 of persons who appear to the council to have an interest in matters relating to development in its district.'

---

[14] Planning (Northern Ireland) Act 2011, ss 8(5), 9(6).
[15] Planning (Local Development Plan) Regulations (Northern Ireland) 2015, reg 14.
[16] An extensive list of topics for information gathering is in DPPN 4: *Preferred Options Paper*, para 5.4.
[17] SPPS, para 6.139.
[18] Guidance and advice from the mainland is also helpful. The Local Plans Expert Group considered what was required for the evidence base: www.lpeg.org
[19] Planning Act (Northern Ireland) 2011, ss 8(6), 9(7).
[20] *Section 75 of the Northern Ireland Act 1998, A Guide for Public Authorities* (April 2010), chapter 7. This statutory guidance should be reflected in authorities' equality schemes: Northern Ireland Act 1998, Sch 9, para 4(3).
[21] Planning (Northern Ireland) Act 2011, s 4(1). This is closely based on the English provisions in the Planning and Compulsory Purchase Act 2004, s 18.
[22] Planning (Northern Ireland) Act 2011, s 4(2).

It therefore covers plan-making under Pt 2 and planning applications under Pt 3. The statement must set out 'the principles of how the council will involve the community' in these matters[23] and in particular:[24]

> '(b) the timing of, and the method by which—
>
>> (i) participation will occur at each stage of the local development plan procedure, and
>>
>> (ii) the council will respond to the participation process referred to in sub-paragraph (i);
>
> (c) details of how the council will use those responses at each stage in developing the content of its local development plan;'

This will have to accord with the legislative requirements but may go further.

The procedural requirements for making the statement are themselves short. Before preparing the statement the council has to consider whether to consult persons interested in development in its area.[25] If it does consult, then it will need to take into account the responses received.[26] The council and the Department must attempt to agree the terms of the statement of community involvement.[27] Following approval by resolution of the council, the draft is to be submitted to the Department.[28] The Department then has four weeks to consider the draft.[29] Within that period it may agree the draft, make a direction specifying the terms of the statement[30] or require extra time.[31] If it has not taken any step within the four-week period then it is deemed to have approved the statement.[32]

Once actual or deemed approval has been given, with any modifications, the council will then make the agreed statement available for public inspection at its principal office and publish it on its website.[33] Local advertisements must say that the statement is available for inspection and where and when it can be inspected.[34]

DPPN2 gives advice on statements of community involvement, emphasising a desire for 'front loading' public involvement in the plan-making process.[35] The types of persons likely to be interested are listed as people living within the area/neighbourhood, elected representatives, voluntary groups, community forums/groups/umbrella organisations, environmental groups, residents groups, business

---

[23] Planning (Statement of Community Involvement) Regulations (Northern Ireland) 2015, reg 4(a), (d).

[24] Planning (Statement of Community Involvement) Regulations (Northern Ireland) 2015, reg 4(b), (c).

[25] Planning (Statement of Community Involvement) Regulations (Northern Ireland) 2015, reg 5(1).

[26] Planning (Statement of Community Involvement) Regulations (Northern Ireland) 2015, reg 5(3).

[27] Planning (Northern Ireland) Act 2011, s 4(3).

[28] Planning (Statement of Community Involvement) Regulations (Northern Ireland) 2015, reg 6(1).

[29] Planning (Statement of Community Involvement) Regulations (Northern Ireland) 2015, reg 6(2).

[30] Planning (Northern Ireland) Act 2011, s 4(4), (5).

[31] Planning (Statement of Community Involvement) Regulations (Northern Ireland) 2015, reg 6(2).

[32] Planning (Statement of Community Involvement) Regulations (Northern Ireland) 2015, reg 6(3).

[33] Planning (Statement of Community Involvement) Regulations (Northern Ireland) 2015, reg 7(1)(a), (c). Unlike other development plan provisions, there is no need to consider making copies of the statement available for inspection elsewhere.

[34] Planning (Statement of Community Involvement) Regulations (Northern Ireland) 2015, reg 7(1)(b). Local advertisement means an advertisement for two successive weeks in at least one newspaper circulating in the district: Planning (Statement of Community Involvement) Regulations (Northern Ireland) 2015, reg 2(1).

[35] DPPN 2, para 3.6.

interests, developers/landowners.[36] An 'example' statement of community involvement is set out as Annex 1 of the DPPN. This promises consultation and publicity well beyond the requirements of the Local Development Plan Regulations, including press releases, public exhibitions and writing to various persons. Councils therefore need to be careful in deciding that they wish to take these further steps and ensure that they do comply with them.

When plan-making, compliance with the statement is required in preparing each type of plan.[37] A statement may create a legitimate expectation that it will be complied with in development management matters.[38]

The council must keep the statement of community involvement under regular review with any revision complying with the same procedure.[39] Additionally, the statement might set out the procedure for its own revision, and so create a legitimate expectation that should be followed.

Timetable

17.5   A statutory timetable for local development plan preparation will be prepared by the council.[40] Following approval by a resolution of the authority, it will be submitted to the Department. The Department and the council must try to agree the timetable, but in the event of dispute the Department may direct the terms of the timetable.[41]

Initial consultation

17.6   The first stage is for the council to engage with Northern Ireland government departments, adjoining councils, the Housing Executive, Civil Aviation Authority, water, sewerage, electronic communications, electricity and gas undertakers[42] 'for the purpose of generating alternative strategies and options': see reg 9. Whilst in England, similar provisions have been broadened in practice to involve public consultation on an issues and options paper, the Northern Irish practice has been more confined. Sometimes topic papers have been published, but it has not tended to be a public process.

Liaison with neighbouring councils is important. Authorities will need to show that they have considered joint issues, for example, market areas which cross boundaries, such as housing and waste, and the effects of development in one area on infrastructure

---

[36]   DPPN 2, para 3.1.
[37]   Planning (Northern Ireland) Act 2011, ss 8(4)(b), 9(4)(b), respectively.
[38]   *R (on the application of Majed) v London Borough of Camden* [2009] EWCA Civ 1029, [2010] JPL 621. For statements of community involvement and development management, see Richard Harwood, *Planning Permission* (Bloomsbury, 2016), paras 6.111–to 6.116.
[39]   Planning (Statement of Community Involvement) Regulations (Northern Ireland) 2015, reg 6(5).
[40]   Planning Act (Northern Ireland) 2011, s 7.
[41]   Planning Act (Northern Ireland) 2011, s 7(2), (3). The Department must respond within four weeks of the submission of the timetable, if only by extending time for consideration: Planning (Local Development Plan) Regulations (Northern Ireland) 2015, reg 7(2). If it does not then the timetable is deemed to be agreed: reg 7(3).
[42]   Defined as the 'consultation bodies': Planning (Local Development Plan) Regulations (Northern Ireland) 2015, reg 2(1).

in another. It would not be sufficient to have simply invited comments or to have considered adjoining authorities' policies.

Preferred Options Paper

17.7   The next step is the publication of a Preferred Options Paper for public consultation: reg 10. An uninspiring, and uninformative definition is given to this as 'a consultation document prepared by the council for the purpose of consulting the public before a local development plan is prepared'.[43] Preferred Options is a critical stage as it is the only consultation which will enable a council to change the plan on its merits, since later submission documents can only be modified by the Department and their examination considers whether they are sound. A single Preferred Options Paper will cover both the plan strategy and local policies plan.

DPPN 5: *Preferred Options Paper* advises 'as the preparation of the POP involves formulating options for growth and deciding on a preferred option, it is not necessary at this stage to request or gather detailed information on smaller individual sites'.[44] That understates the extent of the task. The Preferred Options Paper will influence the plan strategy and local policies plan,[45] and since the council cannot change the submitted documents, the opportunity for local influence is at the Preferred Options stage. Developers will want to have their sites considered at that point. Additionally, the requirements identified in the plan strategy, and the spatial policy to meet them, have to be realistic. It must be possible to have confidence that if (say) new housing is to be concentrated in existing built up areas that enough homes can be built out on that land. Testing the soundness of a target or strategy does involve consideration of non-strategic sites.

The evidence base will need to be in good shape for the preparation of the Preferred Options Paper. Councils will have to know what is happening, and might happen, in their area to be able to decide what ought to happen. The paper should explain what the council's preference is and offer reasonable alternatives to it. Those options 'should be realistic and deliverable'.[46] There is no value in alternatives which are simply implausible, perhaps because of fundamental incompatibilities with regional policy, the proposed plan's objectives or finance. Conversely, an argument that there is no alternative will rarely be plausible. The key is to cover the main alternatives and these may be easier to identify if there has been earlier consultation or discussion.

Consultation on the Preferred Options Paper

17.8   A public consultation is carried out on the Preferred Options Paper. It is to be made available for inspection during normal office hours at the council's principal offices and any other locations in the council's area which it considers appropriate.[47] The paper will be deposited with 'such supporting documents as in the opinion of the

---

[43]   Planning (Local Development Plan) Regulations (Northern Ireland) 2015, reg 2(1).

[44]   Para 6.6. The DPPN also warns 'too much detail may lead to increased focus on site specific issues which should be dealt with at the later stages of plan preparation': para 8.7.

[45]   As DPPN 5 says at para 7.3.

[46]   DPPN 5, para 7.4.

[47]   Planning (Local Development Plan) Regulations (Northern Ireland) 2015, reg 10(a), (b).

council are relevant to that paper' along with a statement on the consultation period and where representations should be sent.[48]

The consultation bodies are to be sent 'the information set out at paragraph (a)'.[49] It is unclear whether the information is the notice of the consultation period and address for response or includes the Paper and supporting documents (as all of the documents in paragraph (a)).[50] The practical, and cautious, approach may be to provide all documents electronically.

The statement of community involvement should set out the locations or types of locations which will be used. Examples of other places for depositing documents would be local offices of the authority or public libraries. Physical inspection of documents is less important given internet access, but local authorities should consider where there is likely to be interest in physical copies. Over the course of the development plan process a large number of documents will have to be made available, including all representations made. Whilst they do not strictly have to be deposited at the same locations, it is better to be consistent. Councils therefore should be careful not to impose too great a burden on themselves by promising to have too many inspection points.

Notice is given by local advertisement[51] of:[52]

'(i)   the title of the local development plan,

(ii)   a statement of the fact that the preferred options paper is available for inspection and the places and times at which it can be inspected,

(iii)   a brief description of the content and purpose of the preferred options paper, and

(iv)   details of how further information on the preferred options paper may be obtained;'

Finally, the council will publish on its website the Preferred Options Paper, the relevant supporting documents, the statement of the consultation period and where representations can be made.[53]

The consultation period is not less than eight weeks and not more than 12 weeks starting on the day on which the council deposits the documents for inspection at its principal offices and the other physical locations.[54]

---

[48]   Planning (Local Development Plan) Regulations (Northern Ireland) 2015, reg 10(a).

[49]   Planning (Local Development Plan) Regulations (Northern Ireland) 2015, reg 10(c).

[50]   Contrast the submission stage which requires 'a copy of the documents' to be sent (Planning (Local Development Plan) Regulations (Northern Ireland) 2015, reg 15(c)) and the explicit requirements for the pre-submission and other relevant documents to be sent in Wales (Town and Country Planning (Local Development Plan) (Wales) Regulations 2005, WSI 2005/2839, reg 15(c)) and simply notice of the process in England (Town and Country Planning (Local Planning) (England) Regulations 2012, SI 2012/767, reg 19).

[51]   'Local advertisement' means 'an advertisement for two successive weeks in at least one newspaper circulating in the district of the council': Planning (Local Development Plan) Regulations (Northern Ireland) 2015, reg 2(1).

[52]   Planning (Local Development Plan) Regulations (Northern Ireland) 2015, reg 10(d).

[53]   Planning (Local Development Plan) Regulations (Northern Ireland) 2015, reg 10(e).

[54]   Planning (Local Development Plan) Regulations (Northern Ireland) 2015, reg 11(2). As the period starts on the day of deposit, that is the first day of the period. So if the papers are first available for inspection on a Wednesday the latest possible day for statutory representations is the Tuesday 12 weeks later.

SUSTAINABILITY APPRAISAL AND STRATEGIC ENVIRONMENTAL ASSESSMENT

17.9   Sustainability appraisal and strategic environmental assessment have to be carried out on the plan strategy and the local policies plan. Sustainability appraisal is required by the Planning Act (Northern Ireland) 2011, by which the council must:[55]

(a)   carry out an appraisal of the sustainability of the plan strategy/local policies plan; and

(b)   prepare a report of the findings of the appraisal.

Strategic environmental assessment ('SEA') is carried out under the Environmental Assessment of Plans and Programmes Regulations (Northern Ireland) 2004.[56] A new district wide plan (of either type) will require SEA. A subsequent revision of an adopted plan might not have a likely significant effect on the environment and so the relevant council could decide that SEA is not required. Sustainability appraisal must though be carried out for any revisions.[57]

Advice is given in DPPN 4: *Sustainability Appraisal incorporating Strategic Environmental Assessment*. The Department sees the purpose of sustainability appraisal as promoting sustainable development through the integration of social, environmental and economic considerations into local development plan preparation.[58]

The DPPN envisages the production of a scoping report and then an interim sustainability appraisal at the preferred options paper stage, followed by sustainability appraisal reports (incorporating the SEA environmental report) for each plan strategy and local policies plan.[59]

THE FORM AND CONTENT OF A DEVELOPMENT PLAN DOCUMENT

17.10   Every development plan document must contain policies and a reasoned justification of those policies.[60] The policies and their reasoned justification must be readily distinguishable,[61] for example, by numbering or format. Each document will contain a proposals map 'describing the policies and proposals set out in the development plan document so far as practicable to illustrate such policies or proposals spatially.'[62] The proposals map will be at a sufficient scale to show the boundaries of any allocations.[63] Several maps may comprise the proposals map,[64] although since maps are generally viewed online it may be easier to have a single electronic map which viewers can zoom in on. If a number of maps are used then they ought not to overlap to reduce the risk of inconsistency. Larger scale maps could

---

[55]   Planning Act (Northern Ireland) 2011, ss 8(6), 9(7).
[56]   SR 2004/280.
[57]   See the Planning Act (Northern Ireland) 2011, s 14(3) which applies the remainder of the Part to revisions.
[58]   See DPPN 4, para 3.1.
[59]   DPPN 4, section 6.
[60]   See Planning (Local Development Plan) Regulations (Northern Ireland) 2015, reg 12(2).
[61]   Planning (Local Development Plan) Regulations (Northern Ireland) 2015, reg 12(3).
[62]   Planning (Local Development Plan) Regulations (Northern Ireland) 2015, reg 13(1).
[63]   Planning (Local Development Plan) Regulations (Northern Ireland) 2015, reg 13(2).
[64]   Planning (Local Development Plan) Regulations (Northern Ireland) 2015, reg 13(1).

be inset (for example, for a town centre), leaving a blank in the main, small scale map. The written text of the document will prevail in the event of any conflict with the proposals map.[65]

In formal matters, any development plan document must include in its title the name of the district and whether it is the plan strategy or local policies plan. Its date of adoption will be shown, as a sub-title.[66]

THE PLAN STRATEGY

17.11   Following the consultation on the Preferred Options Paper the council will prepare the plan strategy. The plan strategy must contain the council's objectives in relation to the development and use of land in its district and its strategic policies for the implementation of those objectives.[67] DPPN 7: *The Plan Strategy* neatly sets out the role of this plan:[68]

> 'The PS should set out an ambitious but realistic vision for the council area as well as the objectives and strategic policies required to deliver that vision. The PS should be strategic, concise and distinctive to the council area and aim to address the challenges that it faces. It should also ensure that its objectives are integrated with, add value to and assist in the delivery of national, regional and local policies and strategies within Northern Ireland, the council area and other district councils.'

The plan strategy should have a clear and understandable vision. It is the opportunity for the council to say how its area should develop. That vision might or might not be one of dramatic change. 'Steady as she goes' can still be an objective, but that would need to be a deliberate choice rather than inertia. The plan needs to be realistic: there needs to be a sufficient basis for believing that its aims can be achieved in the light of demand, viability, the objectives of other public bodies and the tools at the council's disposal.

The DPPN says the objectives should aim, whilst having regard to the Department's policies:[69]

- '• reflect longer term local aspirations, based on a vision, objectives and strategic policies agreed to by the community and stakeholders;

- • provide a plan-led strategy specific to the area covered, to act as a basis for rational and consistent decisions about the use and development of land and identify interdependencies and relationships between places both within and across administrative boundaries;

- • provide a settlement hierarchy which identifies settlements and their role within the hierarchy …;

- • allocate land for housing … ;

- • facilitate economic development and the creation of employment …;

---

[65]   Planning (Local Development Plan) Regulations (Northern Ireland) 2015, reg 13(3).
[66]   Planning (Local Development Plan) Regulations (Northern Ireland) 2015, reg 12(1).
[67]   Planning Act (Northern Ireland) 2011, s 8(2). Further content could be prescribed but this has not been done.
[68]   DPPN 7, para 1.3.
[69]   DPPN 7, para 5.4.

- facilitate sustainable patterns of growth and regeneration whilst promoting compact urban forms and protecting and maintaining distinctive local character and viability. This may include strategic zonings and/or policy areas where considered necessary;

- identify and define, as appropriate, transportation related proposals, …;

- conserve, sustain and enhance the area's environmental qualities, local distinctiveness and sites of environmental importance in terms of landscape character and diversity, wildlife and habitats, townscape and archaeology;

- promote the development of sustainable tourism, recreational and other community facilities that will positively contribute to the amenity and well being of the population; and

- facilitate the promotion of equality of opportunity and good relations between persons of different religious belief, political opinion or racial group.'

A suggested structure for the plan strategy is provided by the DPPN 7: vision; objectives; regional policy; settlement hierarchy, growth strategy and strategic sites; strategic topic based policies; the proposals map; and finally implementation, monitoring and review provisions.[70] Ultimately, the structure will follow out of the council's policy approach. It may be difficult to separate out vision and objectives, without one of them becoming banal and regional policy might be best referenced in the reasoned justification to individual policies rather than summarised at length.

Guidance on various topic policies is contained in DPPN 7, drawing on regional policy, but with useful assistance on the assessments required. The plan strategy can include strategic allocations. These are not defined and will vary between council areas and objectives. Broadly speaking, these are large sites (at least several hundred homes or equivalent as a minimum) whose failure to deliver would be a singular misfortune.

THE LOCAL POLICIES PLAN

17.12   The council must prepare the local policies plan after the plan strategy has been adopted or approved.[71] This will contain the council's policies in relation to the development and use of land in its district,[72] leaving aside the strategic policies which are in the plan strategy. Whilst the formal local policies plan steps will have to await the coming into force of the strategic plan, they cannot in practice be seen as separate processes. The Preferred Options Paper precedes the draft plan strategy and will have to cover both documents. Additionally, much of a plan strategy will depend upon what can be delivered in a local policies plan. The amount of housing and employment land, its spatial distribution and site selection criteria relies upon what can be delivered and where. It would be difficult to find a plan strategy sound unless there is a good understanding of the type of sites which are likely to go into the local policies plan.

The local policies plan will contain allocations, land designations and development management policies insofar as they are not included in the strategic policies in the

---

[70]   DPPN 7, para 5.8.
[71]   Planning Act (Northern Ireland) 2011, s 9(1).
[72]   Planning Act (Northern Ireland) 2011, s 9(1).

plan strategy.[73] For example, DPPN8 proposes that the local policies plan proposals map set out the development limits for the settlement hierarchy which has been identified in the plan strategy.[74]

The local policies plan must be consistent with the plan strategy.[75] This involves comparing the content of each document and whether there is consistency when the two are applied in practice.[76] That is a matter of planning judgment[77] rather than strict literal interpretation.[78] Consistency is expressed to be required between the plan and the strategy as a whole, not between individual policies,[79] but some individual departures will be more important than others. A difference which is liable to frustrate the ability to achieve the numbers required by the plan strategy or undermine its spatial approach may well result in a lack of consistency.

THE DEVELOPMENT PLAN DOCUMENT-MAKING PROCESS

17.13   The statutory process of taking a development plan document from draft to final adoption or approval is the same for plan strategies and local policies plans.

The draft development plan document[80] is made available for public inspection along with the sustainability appraisal report and 'such supporting documents as in the opinion of the council are relevant to the preparation of the local development plan'.[81] Supporting documents are therefore those relevant to the plan as a whole rather than necessarily the particular development plan document.

All of these documents will be deposited with a statement indicating the period for representations to be made and notice of the address to which they should be sent.[82] They will be made available at the council's principal offices and such other places within the council's district as the council considers appropriate.[83]

---

73 See DPPN 8: *the Local Policies Plan*, paras 5.3–5.6. As with plan strategies, a broad structure is proposed at para 5.9.

74 DPPN 8, para 5.6.

75 Planning Act (Northern Ireland) 2011, s 9(5). A comparison can be drawn with the requirements of general conformity neighbourhood development plans with strategic policies in the development plan in England (Town and Country Planning Act 1990, Sch 4B, para 8(2)), any policies in a supplementary planning document not conflicting with the development plan (Town and Country Planning (Local Planning) (England) Regulations 2012, reg 8(3) and a local development plan in Wales being in general conformity with the higher level development plans: Planning and Compulsory Purchase Act 2004, s 62A(3A).

76 See on 'conflict' by English supplementary planning documents: *RWE Npower Ltd v Milton Keynes Borough Council* [2013] EWHC 751 (Admin), at paras 99–104 per John Howell QC.

77 *Persimmon Homes v Stevenage Borough Council* [2006] 1 WLR 334, at 334–345, 347–348 per Laws LJ (structure plans) and *R (DLA Delivery Ltd) v Lewes District Council* [2017] EWCA Civ 58, at para 23 per Lindblom LJ.

78 *RWE Npower*, at paras 99–104 per John Howell QC.

79 See on English neighbourhood plans, *BDW Trading Ltd v Cheshire West and Chester Borough Council* [2014] EWHC 1470 (Admin), at para 82 per Supperstone J.

80 The legislation refers to the document at this stage as 'a development plan document' rather than 'a draft development plan document' but for clarity the unadopted document will be referred to here as a draft.

81 Planning (Local Development Plan) Regulations (Northern Ireland) 2015, reg 15(a)(i)–(iii).

82 Planning (Local Development Plan) Regulations (Northern Ireland) 2015, reg 15(a).

83 Planning (Local Development Plan) Regulations (Northern Ireland) 2015, reg 15(b).

A copy of the development plan document, sustainability appraisal report, supporting documents and the details of when and how to make representations are to be sent to each of the consultation bodies.[84] Notice is to be given in the Belfast Gazette and by local advertisement of the document's title and where and when it can be inspected.[85] Whilst the local advertisement in at least one newspaper circulating in the district must be given for two successive weeks[86], the Belfast Gazette notice only needs to be posted once. The advertisement does not have to set out the consultation period but it makes sense to do so.

On the council's website should be published the draft development plan document, supporting documents and the consultation period.[87] The website provision is oddly drafted. It omits mention of the sustainability appraisal report although it is obvious that should be published with the other supporting documents. It describes supporting documents as 'such of the supporting documents as in the opinion of the council are relevant' when the physically deposited documents are 'such supporting documents as in the opinion of the council are relevant to the preparation of the local development plan'. It is not apparent whether or why there is a difference but it is sensible for the same documents to be on the website and available for physical inspection. Finally, the statement of the representation period has to be on the website but not the notice of the address to send the responses to.[88] Again, it is sensible for that address to be provided along with the ability to submit representations online.

Representations may be made by any person[89] within an eight-week period starting on the day the council 'complies with regulation 15(d)'[90] which is the requirement for notice in the Belfast Gazette and local newspapers. Since the local newspaper advertisement has to be carried for two successive weeks, the representation period starts on the day of the final advertisement (assuming that the Belfast Gazette notice is given by that time). This is different to Preferred Options Paper consultation period which starts on the day of physical deposit of the papers and is not tied to press advertisement.[91]

Under the Regulations any representation must be made within that eight-week period and sent to the address specified in the notice.[92] Councils do though have a discretion to accept representations made outside that period: they are told that they need not publish representations made after the period[93] so there will be a discretion to do so. The Regulations do not refer to representations made after the submission plan has been published but before the second advertisement and the start of the eight-week period, but a discretion must also exist to accept those earlier representations. Those

---

[84]   Planning (Local Development Plan) Regulations (Northern Ireland) 2015, reg 15(c).
[85]   Planning (Local Development Plan) Regulations (Northern Ireland) 2015, reg 15(d).
[86]   Planning (Local Development Plan) Regulations (Northern Ireland) 2015, reg 2(1).
[87]   Planning (Local Development Plan) Regulations (Northern Ireland) 2015, reg 15(e).
[88]   Unlike publicity for the Preferred Options Paper: Planning (Local Development Plan) Regulations (Northern Ireland) 2015, reg 10(e)(iii).
[89]   Planning (Local Development Plan) Regulations (Northern Ireland) 2015, reg 16(1).
[90]   Planning (Local Development Plan) Regulations (Northern Ireland) 2015, reg 16(2)(a).
[91]   Planning (Local Development Plan) Regulations (Northern Ireland) 2015, reg 11(3).
[92]   Planning (Local Development Plan) Regulations (Northern Ireland) 2015, reg 16(2).
[93]   Planning (Local Development Plan) Regulations (Northern Ireland) 2015, reg 17(2).

discretions must be exercised reasonably[94] and it is hard to see how post-publication but premature representations could be lawfully disregarded.[95]

Once the period for representations has ended, the council must make copies of the representations available at the council's principal offices, any other places which it considers appropriate in its district and publish them on its website.[96] Notice of the availability of the representations and the times and places for inspection is to be given in the Belfast Gazette and by local advertisement and also notified to the consultation bodies.[97] Those who made representations are also to be informed of 'those matters' unless they have withdrawn their representation.[98] Again, the publicity requirements are incomplete as the opportunity for counter-representations needs only be set out in the physical inspection and it is unclear whether 'those matters' include notice of that further consultation period. Councils should, as a matter of practice, provide the counter-representations period and address with all of their publicity of the ability to inspect.

The council's equality scheme will include the authority's arrangements for consulting on matters to which their section 75 equalities duty is likely to be relevant (including details of the persons to be consulted).[99] Specifically, the scheme will explain 'assessing and consulting on the likely impact of policies adopted or proposed to be adopted by the authority on the promotion of equality of opportunity'.[100] These schemes must conform to the guidance issued by the Equality Commission Northern Ireland.[101] This recommends that the list of consultees includes the Equality Commission and a range of voluntary, community and trades unions, business organisations and organisations representing the various categories included in s 75. It recommends a consultation period of a minimum of 12 weeks to allow groups to consult amongst themselves. However, the periods for local development plans are fixed by the legislation.

Site specific policy representations

17.14   A further round of consultation is provided on representations made about sites on the basis that these may raise issues which other persons might not have been able to anticipate in the submission consultation period. A site specific policy is 'a policy in a development plan document which identifies a site for a particular use or development',[102] that is, one which proposes that particular development is carried

---

[94]   In *R v Hinckley and Bosworth BC ex p FL Fitchett & JS Bloor (Services) Ltd* (1997) 74 P & CR 52 it was irrational to refuse to accept a representation which was physically received four minutes late. That case also suggested, obiter, that the authority was estopped from refusing to consider representations made within a published, but erroneous, time period.
[95]   Representations made prior to the plan being made available under reg 15 might be disregarded. These could arise if representations are made when the draft document is published for consideration by councillors.
[96]   Planning (Local Development Plan) Regulations (Northern Ireland) 2015, reg 17(1)(a), (b), (c). These are not necessarily the same 'other places' as for the earlier deposits of documents, although consistency is preferable.
[97]   Planning (Local Development Plan) Regulations (Northern Ireland) 2015, reg 17(1)(d), (e).
[98]   Planning (Local Development Plan) Regulations (Northern Ireland) 2015, reg 17(1)(f).
[99]   Northern Ireland Act 1998, Sch 9, para 4(2)(a).
[100] Northern Ireland Act 1998, Sch 9, para 4(2)(b).
[101] Northern Ireland Act 1998, Sch 9, para 4(3)(a). The guidance is in chapters 5, 6 and 7 of *Section 75 of the Northern Ireland Act 1998, A Guide for Public Authorities* (April 2010).
[102] Planning (Local Development Plan) Regulations (Northern Ireland) 2015, reg 2(1).

out there. It will not include a policy which restrains development on the site. A 'site specific policy representation' is:[103]

> 'any representation which seeks to change a development plan document by—
>
> (a)   adding a site specific policy to the development plan document; or
>
> (b)   altering or deleting any site specific policy in the development plan document'

If a site specific policy representation is made then there is an eight-week period for 'counter-representations' to be made, starting on the day that the council makes the representations and notice of counter-representation arrangements available for inspection.[104] If counter-representations may be made in respect of site specific policy representations then the time for such comments and the address to send them to must be available for physical inspection.[105]

Counter-representations may not propose any changes to the development plan document,[106] which seems to prohibit representations from being made at this stage in support of the site representations. Whilst no doubt seeking to avoid further issues being raised, the counter-representations stage is not suited to ascertaining support for proposed sites or developing compromises.

Counter-representations must be made available by the council at its principal offices, any other location it chooses and on its website as soon as reasonably practicable following the consultation period.[107] Again, there is a discretion not to publish late counter-representations,[108] which implies that there is a discretion to accept and take them into account.

Consideration of representations on the development plan document

17.15   Representations and counter-representations[109] have to be considered by the council before submitting the development plan document to the Department for examination.[110] There is no formal opportunity for the council to modify the plan in the light of those representations. It could withdraw the plan prior to its submission to the Department[111] and publish a modified plan for further consultation. Alternatively, the plan could be submitted along with proposed modifications, but those changes could only be made with the Department's approval following the examination and the examiner would need to consider that the plan would be unsound without them.

The examination guidance does ask the council to 'set out its views on the main issues identified, perhaps in a series of topic papers, as well as its comments on all the representations' when submitting the plan.[112]

---

[103]   Planning (Local Development Plan) Regulations (Northern Ireland) 2015, reg 2(1).
[104]   Planning (Local Development Plan) Regulations (Northern Ireland) 2015, reg 18(2).
[105]   Planning (Local Development Plan) Regulations (Northern Ireland) 2015, reg 17(1)(a)(ii), (iii).
[106]   Planning (Local Development Plan) Regulations (Northern Ireland) 2015, reg 18(3).
[107]   Planning (Local Development Plan) Regulations (Northern Ireland) 2015, reg 19(1).
[108]   Planning (Local Development Plan) Regulations (Northern Ireland) 2015, reg 19(2).
[109]   Made under Planning (Local Development Plan) Regulations (Northern Ireland) 2015, regs 16 and 18.
[110]   Planning (Local Development Plan) Regulations (Northern Ireland) 2015, reg 20(1).
[111]   Planning Act (Northern Ireland) 2011, s 11(1).
[112]   *Procedures for Independent Examination of Local Development Plans* (April 2017), para 21.

Before submitting the plan, the council must think 'the document is ready for independent examination'[113] which simply means that the council consider it to be sound.

The submission of the plan to the Department

17.16 Along with the plan,[114] the council will send to the Department:[115]

(a)   the sustainability appraisal report;

(b)   the statement of community involvement;

(c)   evidence that the council has complied with its statement of community involvement;

(d)   copies of the notices of the consultations on the Preferred Options Paper, submission draft and site specific representations;[116]

(e)   the timetable;

(f)   a statement setting out:

    (i)   a summary of the main issues raised in representations made in time on the preferred options paper; and

    (ii)   how those main issues have been taken into account in the preparation of the development plan document;

(g)   a statement setting out:

    (i)   if representations were made in time on the submission and site specific stages, the number of representations made and a summary of the main issues raised in those representations; or

    (ii)   that no such representations were made;

(h)   copies of any timely representations made on submission and site specific stages; and

(i)   such supporting documents as in the opinion of the council are relevant to the preparation of the development plan document.

Additionally, when the local policies plan is submitted, it should be accompanied by a copy of the adopted plan strategy.[117]

Availability of the submission documents

17.17 As soon as reasonably practicable after the submission of the development plan document, the council shall make available for inspection the submitted

---

[113] Planning Act (Northern Ireland) 2011, s 10(2)(b).

[114] Planning (Local Development Plan) Regulations (Northern Ireland) 2015, reg 20(3)(a), (b)(i).

[115] Planning (Local Development Plan) Regulations (Northern Ireland) 2015, reg 20(2), prescribed pursuant to the Planning Act (Northern Ireland) 2011, s 10(3).

[116] Curiously, the Regulations refer to providing the notices of the address to which representations should be sent on preferred options and sites under regs 10(a)(iv), and 17(1)(a)(iii) but not the time for making those comments (in regs 10(a)(iii) and 17(a)(ii)), and conversely ask for the document giving the time period for comments on the submission draft under reg 15(a)(iv) but not the notice of where they should be sent (reg 15(a)(v)).

[117] Planning (Local Development Plan) Regulations (Northern Ireland) 2015, reg 20(3)(b).

documents and 'such other documents as in the opinion of the council are relevant to the preparation of the development plan document'.[118] This final category is strange, as the council was required to submit those same documents to the Department so it is not apparent why there should be further documents available for inspection but not sent in with the plan.

As before, the documents are to be available for inspection at the council's principal offices and such other places in the district which it considers appropriate.[119] The consultation bodies and those who made representations on the submission draft and any later site specific representations are to be notified of where and when the documents can be inspected.[120] A notice of the submission is to be published in the Belfast Gazette and by local advertisement (on two consecutive weeks) and put on the council's website.[121] There is no requirement under these provisions to publish the documents on the website, although the plan, sustainability appraisal report and supporting material should already have gone online.[122]

The examination

17.18   Following the submission of a plan, the Department will hold an independent examination unless it intends to direct that the document is withdrawn or modified.[123] The latter exception is problematic. Whilst there is limited value in examining a plan that the Department says should be withdrawn (although that would deprive the council of the ability to make oral representations to an examiner), adopting a plan in a modified form will affect numerous interests. It is difficult to see how an examination can be avoided in such cases.

Examinations are conducted by the Planning Appeals Commission unless the Department considers it expedient to appoint someone else having regard to the statutory timetable.[124] This would allow examiners who are not commissioners to be used, such as current or former inspectors or reporters from the mainland, if the Commission is unable to deal with plans given its other responsibilities.

By s 10(6):[125]

> 'The purpose of an independent examination is to determine in respect of the development plan document–
>
> (a)   whether it satisfies the requirements of sections 7 and 8 or, as the case may be, sections 7 and 9, and any regulations under section 22 relating to the preparation of development plan documents;
>
> (b)   whether it is sound.'

---

[118] Planning (Local Development Plan) Regulations (Northern Ireland) 2015, reg 21(a).

[119] Planning (Local Development Plan) Regulations (Northern Ireland) 2015, reg 21(b).

[120] Planning (Local Development Plan) Regulations (Northern Ireland) 2015, reg 21(c), (d).

[121] Planning (Local Development Plan) Regulations (Northern Ireland) 2015, reg 21(e), (f).

[122] Mainly when published for consultation (Planning (Local Development Plan) Regulations (Northern Ireland) 2015, reg 15(e)) but the timetable will be online under reg 8(c).

[123] Planning Act (Northern Ireland) 2011, s 10(4) referring to the powers to direct withdrawal under s 11(2) and modification under s 15(1).

[124] Planning Act (Northern Ireland) 2011, s 10(4), (5).

[125] Planning Act (Northern Ireland) 2011, s 10(6).

Section 7 is the timetable, and ss 8 and 9 concern the content and making of the plan strategy and local policies plan respectively. The Regulations referred to are the Planning (Local Development Plan) Regulations (Northern Ireland) 2015.

As in other jurisdictions, 'sound' is not defined in the Planning Act (Northern Ireland) 2011 nor in secondary legislation. Whilst policy does say what the Department considers it to be, this does not define or alter its meaning in law.[126] There is therefore a generally expressed legal test but in practice a policy-based test is applied. That the policy does not simply explain what the legislation means is illustrated by there being differences in policy between England, Wales and Northern Ireland and the periodic changes to those policies.

All that the SPPS says on soundness is 'The tests of soundness include procedural, consistency, and coherence and effectiveness tests'.[127] The DPPN 6: *Soundness* sets out the various tests which it summarises as:[128]

'Procedural tests

P1 Has the DPD been prepared in accordance with the council's timetable and the Statement of Community Involvement?

P2 Has the council prepared its Preferred Options Paper and taken into account any representations made?

P3 Has the DPD been subject to sustainability appraisal including Strategic Environmental Assessment?

P4 Did the council comply with the regulations on the form and content of its DPD and procedure for preparing the DPD?

Consistency tests

C1 Did the council take account of the Regional Development Strategy?

C2 Did the council take account of its Community Plan?

C3 Did the council take account of policy and guidance issued by the Department?

C4 Has the plan had regard to other relevant plans, policies and strategies relating to the council's district or to any adjoining council's district?

Coherence and effectiveness tests

CE1 The DPD sets out a coherent strategy from which its policies and allocations logically flow and where cross boundary issues are relevant it is not in conflict with the DPDs of neighbouring councils;

CE2 The strategy, policies and allocations are realistic and appropriate having considered the relevant alternatives and are founded on a robust evidence base;

---

[126] *Grand Union Investments Ltd v Dacorum Borough Council* [2014] EWHC 1894 (Admin), at para 59 per Lindblom J.
[127] SPPS, para 5.31.
[128] DPPN 6, version 2, May 2017, para 3.1.

CE3 There are clear mechanisms for implementation and monitoring; and

CE4 It is reasonably flexible to enable it to deal with changing circumstances.'

The DPPN describes all of these as tests of soundness but the procedural and consistency tests are principally legal matters falling within s 10(6)(a). Apart from the carrying out of strategic environmental assessment (under regulations which are not made under the Planning Act (Northern Ireland) 2011), they are tests of compliance with the Act or the Planning (Local Development Plan) Regulations (Northern Ireland). Failure to comply with the timetable can be excused provided that it is revised and the Department seeks an explanation for the delay.[129] The DPPN does though look for more justification under some of these heads, in particular why the preferred options were chosen in the preferred options paper.[130] Compliance with all of the legal tests will need to be documented.

Whilst headed as 'Consistency tests' the second set of tests concern taking account of or having regard to various policies rather than requiring the plan to be consistent with them.[131] The DPPN expects councils to explain how they have taken into account the various policies and, at least with regard to the RDS, provide 'robust evidence of a local justification for departure'.[132] It says that the plan ought to show how the policies and proposals of the plan 'implement the core principles, aims and objectives' of the SPPS and any relevant Planning Policy Statement[133] but even that expectation is far short of an obligation to accord with the detailed policies in them. For the community plan, however, advice is given that:[134]

'A council should ensure that the vision and objectives of the DPD reflect the spatial aspirations of the Community Plan.'

Since both plans are prepared by the same authority they ought to be consistent. The statutory requirement for the local policies plan to be consistent with the plan strategy arises separately.

The coherence and effectiveness tests are more demanding. The need in test CE1 is for a coherent strategy to deliver the vision, aims and objectives for the council's area which are in the plan.[135] Emphasis is placed on the need for the plan to 'add value to' and assist the delivery of other policies.[136] It is also expected that the plan will not conflict with the plans of neighbouring authorities.[137] That may give rise to issues of timing if councils are at different stages of plan adoption or review and whilst an agreed approach to cross-authority issues (for example numbers in the same market area or spatial strategy) is desirable, councils will need to proceed in the best way they can without undue delay. If councils cannot agree then the need to avoid conflict amounts to taking account of how other authorities intend to proceed rather than have policies which assume that they will take a right, but different, approach.

---

[129] See DPPN 6, para 5.3.2.
[130] DPPN 6, para 5.3.8.
[131] Unlike, for example, the National Planning Policy Framework's test of soundness: para 182.
[132] DPPN 4, para 5.4.3.
[133] DPPN 6, para 5.4.3.
[134] DPPN 6, para 5.4.6.
[135] DPPN 6, para 5.5.2, 5.5.5.
[136] DPPN 6, para 5.5.4.
[137] DPPN 6, para 5.5.4.

Test CE2 is the principal soundness ground: the need for the strategy, policies and allocations to be realistic and appropriate, having regard to relevant alternatives and on a robust evidence base. The emphasis is on the justification for the plan proposed, why one of several potential reasonable alternatives have been chosen and the evidence which underpins the plan.[138]

These tests are closely based on the original tests of soundness in the 2004 version of the English Planning Policy Statement 12.[139] The original 2016 version of the DPPN repeated a mistake made by PPS 12. It said 'the presumption will be that the DPD is sound unless it is shown to be otherwise as a result of evidence considered at [the Independent Examination]'.[140] However, the statute does not allow a presumption that the plan is sound and an examiner who took that approach would be in error.[141] This was corrected by version 2 of DPPN 6 which says 'There is no presumption of soundness in legislation for a DPPN'.[142]

The conduct of the examination

17.19   The examination process is considered in Chapter 21. The Northern Irish procedural guidance is in the Planning Appeals Commission's *Procedures for Independent Examination of Local Development Plans*[143] which draws on the English and Welsh experiences.

There are a few matters set out in legislation. A person who makes representations seeking to change the document has a right to be heard (if requested) at the examination.[144] Implicitly the right is only given to someone who made representations in time in accordance with the Regulations. All representations made in accordance with the Regulations on the submission draft and as counter-representations to any site specific representations must be considered by the examiner.[145] Implicitly withdrawn representations do not need to be considered as their makers are saying they have been superseded or no longer represent their position.

At least four weeks' notice of 'the opening of an independent examination' has to be given to the consultation bodies and any person who made representations in time on the submission or site specific consultations (which have not been withdrawn) along with notice in the Belfast Gazette, by local advertisement and on the council's website.[146] The notice must set out 'the time and place at which the examination is to be held' and whether the examination is to be carried out by the Planning Appeals Commission or a named person.[147] In these provisions the Regulations treat the examination as consisting of hearings. However, the examination is the whole

---

[138] See DPPN 6, paras 5.5.8–5.5.13.
[139] PPS 12, para 4.24 (2004). They do though omit the question whether the plan is consistent with national policy.
[140] DPPN 6, version 1, 2016, para 4.1.
[141] *Persimmon Homes (North East) Ltd v Blyth Valley Borough Council* [2008] EWCA Civ 861, [2009] JPL 335, at para 40 per Keene LJ, followed in *Capel Parish Council v Surrey County Council* [2009] EWHC 350 (Admin); [2009] JPL 1302, at para 16 per Collins J.
[142] DPPN 6, version 2, 2017, para 4.1.
[143] April 2017.
[144] Planning Act (Northern Ireland) 2011, s 10(7).
[145] Planning (Local Development Plan) Regulations (Northern Ireland) 2015, reg 22(3).
[146] Planning (Local Development Plan) Regulations (Northern Ireland) 2015, reg 22(1).
[147] Planning (Local Development Plan) Regulations (Northern Ireland) 2015, reg 22(2).

process from the receipt of the papers by the examiner to the submission of the report. Publicity is therefore strictly required for the first day of hearings and the date ought of course to be included with the time of the examination. Examination timetables may change and the notice does not have to contain further programmed dates. Since a local advertisement must be published on two consecutive weeks, it is prudent for the second notice to be out more than four weeks before the first hearing.

At the end of the process the examiner must make recommendations to the Department,[148] giving reasons for those recommendations.[149]

The final decision on the plan: adoption, modification or withdrawal

17.20   Adoption of the document is carried out by the council but the decision whether to adopt is taken by the Department of Infrastructure. This gives rise to three significant differences to England and Wales. Firstly, the decision on how to respond to the examiner's report is taken by a body who did not draft the plan and so comes to it afresh. Secondly, the Department is not bound by the examiner's recommendations. Thirdly, the Department's consideration is not confined to the issues of procedural compliance and soundness which the examiner has considered. Its role is to consider both the response to the report and whether to exercise ministerial powers of intervention. In England and Wales, those intervention powers are rarely exercised. In Northern Ireland, Ministers will have to routinely ask themselves what the appropriate plan policies should be.

The ability though to rewrite the plan at the last stage is limited. Changes might not be examined or supported by a significant evidence base, unless they are approaches which have already been raised and discussed. Productive departmental input into the early stages of a plan will be necessary to enable the Minister to depart from the examiner's report.

Three overlapping powers are given to the Department to intervene on plan documents: directing, adoption, modification or withdrawal on consideration of the examiner's report under s 12; and general powers to direct changes to a development plan document under s 15 or its withdrawal under s 11.

Consideration of the examiner's report

The Department will consider the examiner's report and:[150]

> 'direct the council to—
>
> (a) adopt the development plan document as originally prepared;
>
> (b) adopt the development plan document with such modifications as may be specified in the direction; or
>
> (c) withdraw the development plan document.'

---

[148] Planning Act (Northern Ireland) 2011, s 12(1) and Planning (Local Development Plan) Regulations (Northern Ireland) 2015, reg 24(1).
[149] Planning Act (Northern Ireland) 2011, s 10(8).
[150] Planning Act (Northern Ireland) 2011, s 12(1).

The direction must be accompanied by reasons.[151]

Intervention by the Department

17.21 If the Department thinks that a development plan document is unsatisfactory it may, at any time before the document is adopted direct the council to modify the document in accordance with the direction.[152] This power arises at any point once the document has come into existence.

As usual, reasons must be given for any direction[153] and the council must comply with it.[154]

Withdrawal of drafts of development plan documents

17.22 A council may withdraw a submission draft development plan document at any time before it is submitted to the Department.[155] Once the plan has been submitted it can only be withdrawn on a direction by the Department.[156] The power to direct withdrawal arises from submission and can be exercised before an examination is held. A council might though suggest that as a matter of politics, or in law, reasonableness and fairness, it ought to be able to present its plan to an examiner for a detailed view before it is terminated by the Minister.

As soon as reasonably practicable, the council must publicise the withdrawal of a development plan document and the reason for it by notice in the Belfast Gazette, local advertisement, on its website, and by notice to the consultation bodies and those with duly made representations on the document.[157] It is also required to 'remove any material or documents made available or published' under the Regulations for the timetable, preferred options paper, consultation on development plan document, submission and site specific representations and the formal submission of the document.[158] However, the preferred options paper might provide the base for an adopted plan strategy (if the local policies plan has failed) or a new development plan document so should not necessarily be discarded. The timetable will need revision for a new document to be worked up. With the withdrawal of a document, its drafts and supporting material will have no formal status, but they may provide some of the evidence for a new development plan document and assist with planning application. There is no need to have this latter material immediately available for physical inspection, but retaining the draft document and the supporting material published with it on the council's website would be useful. This provision does seem to go further than it needs to in wiping the slate clean.

---

[151] Planning Act (Northern Ireland) 2011, s 12(2).
[152] Planning Act (Northern Ireland) 2011, s 15(1).
[153] Planning Act (Northern Ireland) 2011, s 15(2).
[154] Planning Act (Northern Ireland) 2011, s 15(3).
[155] Planning Act (Northern Ireland) 2011, s 11(1).
[156] Planning Act (Northern Ireland) 2011, ss 11(2) (at any time) and 12(1)(c) (following the examiner's report).
[157] Planning (Local Development Plan) Regulations (Northern Ireland) 2015, reg 23(a)–(d). There is no mention of notice only being given to those who have not withdrawn their representations so it appears that they should also be informed. It is quite likely that even the makers of withdrawn representations would be interested in what had happened to the plan.
[158] Planning (Local Development Plan) Regulations (Northern Ireland) 2015, reg 23(e).

Adoption

17.23   A council is required to comply with a direction to adopt (with or without modifications) 'as soon as reasonably practicable'.[159] Curiously, a similar timescale is not applied for the withdrawal of a plan but only for its advertisement following a withdrawal.[160] In practice authorities would be expected to take any of these steps quickly. If they wish to bring judicial review proceedings then they should do so against the direction and hold off from complying with it. The effective decision on adoption is the direction of the Department rather than the council acting on it, and so directions could also be challenged by other persons unhappy at the proposed decision.

JOINT PLANS

17.24   There will be issues which cross local authority boundaries and benefit from a co-ordinated response, for example, housing or employment requirements or strategic growth. Councils could agree a common approach and then seek to progress that resolution through their own individual local plans. As an alternative, they can prepare joint plans, either for strategic matters or generally. The options therefore are to agree to prepare:[161]

   '(a)   a joint plan strategy; or

   (b)   a joint plan strategy and joint local policies plan.'

The former may be more likely, with the spatial strategy and the requirements produced jointly, whilst detailed policies and non-strategic sites are left to each council. The plan-making steps laid down in the legislation are then to be carried out by each council.[162]

If a council withdraws from the agreement to prepare a joint plan then what has been done so far can be treated by the other councils has having been done by them for any replacement plan which is substantially the same effect as the original joint plan.[163] The council which has withdrawn from the agreement cannot rely on those steps,[164] but having decided to drop the joint plan, it is unlikely to want to do so. However, the plan would have been drafted to cover common issues across several authorities and so is unlikely to work for one council. More significant than matters of wording, a council is only likely to withdraw from preparing a joint plan if it has a serious disagreement meaning that a large part of the joint strategy would have been disowned. The spatial approach in the other council area or areas is unlikely to survive that breakup.

---

[159] Planning (Local Development Plan) Regulations (Northern Ireland) 2015, reg 24(2) made under the Planning Act (Northern Ireland) 2011, s 12(3).

[160] Compare the Planning (Local Development Plan) Regulations (Northern Ireland) 2015, regs 23 and 24(2).

[161] Planning Act (Northern Ireland) 2011, s 17(1).

[162] Planning Act (Northern Ireland) 2011, s 17(3).

[163] Planning Act (Northern Ireland) 2011, s 17(5) and Planning (Local Development Plan) Regulations (Northern Ireland) 2015, reg 30(2)(b). The replacement may be a joint or single authority plan and is referred to as a corresponding plan.

[164] Planning (Local Development Plan) Regulations (Northern Ireland) 2015, reg 30(2)(a).

ANNUAL MONITORING REPORT

17.25   Each council is required to send an annual monitoring report to the Department.[165] A report will cover the 12-month period ending on 31 March and must be published by the end of September following that period, unless another time is agreed by the Department.[166]

Much of the detail of the report is prescribed.[167] It will set out:[168]

(a)   the housing land supply at the beginning and end of the period;

(b)   the number of net additional housing units built in the council's district in that year and since the local policies plan was first adopted or approved;

(c)   the land supply for economic development purposes in the council's district; and

(d)   such other issues as appear to the council to be relevant to the implementation of the local development plan.

The SPPS expects that a 'plan, monitor and manage' approach is taken to ensure that there is a minimum of a five-year housing land supply.[169] Annual monitoring reports should contain information on building rates, densities and the accuracy of windfall predictions.[170]

If a local development plan policy is not being implemented then the report must explain why, what steps (if any) the council intend to take to secure its implementation and whether it is intended to revise the plan to replace or amend the policy.[171] 'Implemented' is not defined, but since the policies must all be relevant to development management decisions, they cannot be overlooked. A failure to implement must mean that the policy is either not being followed in practice and exceptions are being made to it, or it is not being achieved, for example, where employment land targets are not being met.

The annual monitoring report is to be made available for inspection at the council's principal offices and at any other places in the district it considers appropriate as well as being published on the council's website.[172] Local advertisements should be published explaining where and when the report can be inspected.[173]

LOCAL DEVELOPMENT PLAN REVIEW

17.26   Authorities are required to carry out periodic reviews to consider whether their local development plan ought to be revised.[174] They might of course conclude

---

[165]   Planning Act (Northern Ireland) 2011, s 21(1).
[166]   Planning (Local Development Plan) Regulations (Northern Ireland) 2015, reg 25(1).
[167]   Planning (Local Development Plan) Regulations (Northern Ireland) 2015, reg 25.
[168]   Planning (Local Development Plan) Regulations (Northern Ireland) 2015, reg 25(2).
[169]   SPPS, para 6.140.
[170]   SPPS, para 6.140.
[171]   Planning (Local Development Plan) Regulations (Northern Ireland) 2015, reg 25(3).
[172]   Planning (Local Development Plan) Regulations (Northern Ireland) 2015, reg 27(a), (c).
[173]   Planning (Local Development Plan) Regulations (Northern Ireland) 2015, reg 27(b).
[174]   Planning Act (Northern Ireland) 2011, s 13.

that no revision is required at that time. A review of the local development plan must be carried out every five years and no later than five years from the date that the local policies plan was first adopted or approved.[175] This appears to mean that the first review is required within five years of the second part of the local development plan coming into force.[176]

The findings of the review must be reported to the Department for Infrastructure.[177] In the same way as for the annual monitoring report, the report of the review must be published on the council's website, made available for inspection and published by local advertisement.[178]

DEPARTMENTAL DEVELOPMENT PLANS

17.27 The previous departmental development plans[179] will remain in force until the local policies plan for the area comes into force.[180] Prior to that stage, the plan strategy and the departmental development plan will collectively be the local development plan, once the strategy has been adopted or approved.[181] Any conflict between those two documents has to be resolved in favour of the later plan strategy.[182]

---

[175] Planning (Local Development Plan) Regulations (Northern Ireland) 2015, reg 26(1).

[176] Or put another way, from when the local development plan is complete.

[177] Planning Act (Northern Ireland) 2011, s 13(2); Planning (Local Development Plan) Regulations (Northern Ireland) 2015, reg 26(2).

[178] Planning (Local Development Plan) Regulations (Northern Ireland) 2015, reg 27.

[179] Adopted under the Planning (Northern Ireland) Order 1972, SI 1972/1634 or the Planning (Northern Ireland) Order 1991, SI 1991/1220. See Chapter 16 above.

[180] Planning (Local Development Plan) Regulations (Northern Ireland) 2015, Sch, para 1, 2, 4.

[181] Planning (Local Development Plan) Regulations (Northern Ireland) 2015, Sch, para 3(a).

[182] Planning (Local Development Plan) Regulations (Northern Ireland) 2015, Sch, para 3(b).

Chapter 18

Marine Planning

INTRODUCTION AND THE DEVELOPMENT OF MARINE PLANNING

18.1   Marine planning is a relatively new area of spatial planning. It was introduced in 2009 by the Marine and Coastal Access Act 2009 ('MCAA 2009'). Its emergence is perhaps the inevitable result of the seas around the country getting steadily busier; playing host to such development and activity as: offshore energy projects, undersea cables, shipping, aggregates and fishing. Equally, the seas play host to species and habitats which planning can play a role in protecting. Given the increasing activities on and under the seas in the UK, it can safely be assumed that marine plans are likely to increase in their significance for planning practitioners over the next few decades.

In April 2009, the government and the devolved administrations jointly published the 'high level marine objectives' which were to underpin national marine policy. The objectives usefully highlight the competing and complementary interests active in the seas around the UK. The objectives are:

'**Achieving a sustainable marine economy**

- Infrastructure is in place to support and promote safe, profitable and efficient marine businesses.

- The marine environment and its resources are used to maximise sustainable activity, prosperity and opportunities for all, now and in the future.

- Marine businesses are taking long-term strategic decisions and managing risks effectively. They are competitive and operating efficiently.

- Marine businesses are acting in a way which respects environmental limits and is socially responsible. This is rewarded in the marketplace.

Ensuring a strong, healthy and just society

- People appreciate the diversity of the marine environment, its seascapes, its natural and cultural heritage and its resources and act responsibly.

- The use of the marine environment is benefiting society as a whole, contributing to resilient and cohesive communities that can adapt to coastal erosion and flood risk, as well as contributing to physical and mental wellbeing.

- The coast, seas, oceans and their resources are safe to use.

- The marine environment plays an important role in mitigating climate change.

- There is equitable access for those who want to use and enjoy the coast, seas and their wide range of resources and assets and recognition that for some island and peripheral communities the sea plays a significant role in their community.

- Use of the marine environment will recognise, integrate with, defence priorities, including the strengthening of international peace and stability and the defence of the United Kingdom and its interests.

Living within environmental limits

- Biodiversity is protected, conserved and, where appropriate, recovered, and loss has been halted.

- Healthy marine and coastal habitats occur across their natural range and are able to support strong, biodiverse biological communities and the functioning of healthy, resilient and adaptable marine ecosystems.

- Our oceans support viable populations of representative, rare, vulnerable, and valued species.

Promoting good governance

- All those who have a stake in the marine environment have an input into associated decision-making.

- Marine, land and water management mechanisms are responsive and work effectively together for example through integrated coastal zone management and river basin management plans.

- Marine management in the UK takes account of different management systems that are in place because of administrative, political or international boundaries.

- Marine businesses are subject to clear, timely, proportionate and, where appropriate, plan-led regulation.

- The use of the marine environment is spatially planned where appropriate and based on an ecosystems approach which takes account of climate change and recognises the protection and management needs of marine cultural heritage according to its significance.

Using sound science responsibly

- Our understanding of the marine environment continues to develop through new scientific and socio-economic research and data collection.

- Sound evidence and monitoring underpins effective marine management and policy development.

- The precautionary principle is applied consistently in accordance with the UK Government and Devolved Administrations' sustainable development policy.'[1]

As stated above, the high level objectives were used to underpin the UK's first Marine Policy Statement. This in turn has set the framework for individual marine plans which must be consistent with it. The statutory basis for the preparation and publication of MPS' and marine plans is set out below.

MARINE POLICY STATEMENT

18.2   The Marine Policy Statement ('MPS') is a national policy document which sets out general policies 'for contributing to the achievement of sustainable development in the UK marine area'.[2] It is a high level document which is prepared

---

[1]   DEFRA, 'Our seas – a shared resource. High level marine objectives' (2009).
[2]   MCCA 2009, s 44(1)(a).

by all of the policy authorities (the Secretary of State, the Scottish Ministers, the Welsh Ministers and the Department of the Environment in Northern Ireland[3]) acting jointly.[4] Or, it may be prepared by the Secretary of State acting with one or more of the other policy authorities. The Secretary of State is able to prepare an MPS alone but only where he has invited each of the other policy authorities to participate in preparing the MPS.[5] As intended, the first MPS has been prepared by the four authorities.

Statement of public participation

18.3   In preparing an MPS, the policy authorities must comply with Sch 5 of the MCAA 2009. It requires the policy authorities preparing the plan to prepare and publish a statement of public participation ('SPP'). This is a statement of the policies settled by the relevant policy authorities for or in connection with the involvement of interested persons in the preparation of the MPS.[6] Interested persons are defined as both the general public and those 'appearing to the relevant authorities to be likely to be interested in, or affected by, policies proposed to be included in the relevant document'.[7]

The SPP must include a proposed timetable which includes provision for the preparation and publication of the consultation draft, the making of representations on the consultation draft, the consideration of those representations and the adoption and publication of the MPS.[8] It must also state the period which it proposes to allocate for the legislative scrutiny of the consultation draft (see below).[9]

The relevant policy authorities are required to keep the SPP under review and if at any time consider that it is necessary or expedient to revise it then they must do so and publish the revised version.[10]

Consultation

18.4   The relevant policy authorities are required to prepare and publish a consultation draft of an MPS and bring it to the attention of the general public and any persons the relevant authorities consider are likely to be interested in or affected by the proposed policies.[11] Any representations on the consultation draft must be made in line with the SPP and must be taken into account by the relevant policy authorities when drafting the final text of the policies.[12]

The consultation draft must also undergo legislative scrutiny. It must be laid before the appropriate legislature: Parliament for the Secretary of State, the Scottish Parliament for the Scottish Ministers, the National Assembly for Wales for the Welsh

---

3   The policy authorities are defined by s 44(4) of MCCA 2009.
4   MCCA 2009, s 44(1)(a).
5   MCCA 2009, s 45(2).
6   MCCA 2009, Sch 5, para 4(2).
7   MCCA 2009, Sch 5, para 4(4).
8   MCCA 2009, Sch 5, para 2.
9   MCCA 2009, Sch 5, para 5(5).
10 MCCA 2009, Sch 5, para 6.
11 MCCA 2009, Sch 5, para 8.
12 MCCA 2009, Sch 5, para 9.

Ministers and the Northern Ireland Assembly for the Department of the Environment in Northern Ireland. If during the period it is laid[13] before a legislature the legislative body or one of its committees makes a resolution or recommendations in relation to it, the policy authority must respond.[14]

Sustainability appraisal

18.5   The MCAA 2009 requires that a sustainability appraisal ('SA') of an MPS be carried out and be included within it.[15] A report of the results of the SA must be published with the consultation draft. The relevant policy authorities are required to take the SA into account and the MCAA 2009 states that they may only proceed with proposals in an MPS if the SA indicates that it is appropriate to proceed.[16] Strategic environmental assessment may also be required under the Environmental Assessment of Plans and Programmes Regulations 2004.[17]

Adoption, monitoring and review

18.6   The final text is adopted by each policy authority by decision. Notice of that decision must be given to each of the other policy authorities. It must then be published by all of the relevant authorities acting jointly as soon as possible after it has been adopted by each of them.[18] Where there are any differences between the consultation draft and the final text of the MPS the relevant authorities must publish a summary of the differences and a statement of the reasons for them.[19]

The policy authorities who prepared the MPS must review that MPS when they consider it appropriate to do so.[20] It may be amended by the policy authorities who prepared and adopted it in accordance with Sch 5.[21]

The MCAA 2009 also contains provisions for the withdrawal of an MPS or the withdrawal of a policy authority from being treated as one who adopted and published the MPS.[22]

The current MPS

18.7   The current MPS (and the first one ever prepared) was adopted and published by all of the policy authorities in March 2011 and can be found on the MMO's website. Its introduction states that it is a key step to achieving the vision of having 'clean, healthy, safe, productive and biologically diverse oceans and seas'.[23] The introduction further states:

---

[13]   The period is that which is specified by the policy authority: MCCA 2009, Sch 5, para 10(6) and (7).
[14]   MCCA 2009, Sch 5, para 10.
[15]   MCCA 2009, Sch 5, para 7.
[16]   MCCA 2009, Sch 5, 7(2).
[17]   SI 2004/1633. See Chapter 3 above.
[18]   MCCA 2009, Sch 5, para 12.
[19]   MCCA 2009, Sch 5, para 11.
[20]   MCCA 2009, s 46.
[21]   MCCA 2009, s 47.
[22]   MCCA 2009, s 48.
[23]   The objectives come from DEFRA, 'Safeguarding our seas report' (2002).

'The MPS will facilitate and support the formulation of Marine Plans, ensuring that marine resources are used in a sustainable way in line with the high level marine objectives and thereby:

- Promote sustainable economic development;

- Enable the UK's move towards a low-carbon economy, in order to mitigate the causes of climate change and ocean acidification and adapt to their effects;

- Ensure a sustainable marine environment which promotes healthy, functioning marine ecosystems and protects marine habitats, species and our heritage assets; and

- Contribute to the societal benefits of the marine area, including the sustainable use of marine resources to address local social and economic issues.'[24]

It is this MPS which sets the direction for marine plans which sit on the next rung down the marine planning ladder.

MARINE PLANS

The marine planning regions

18.8   The UK marine area is divided into eight marine planning regions: the English inshore region, the English offshore region, the Scottish inshore region, the Scottish offshore region, the Welsh inshore region, the Welsh offshore region, the Northern Ireland inshore region, and the Northern Ireland offshore region.[25] Each of the marine planning regions has a marine plan authority ('MPA') (apart from the Scottish inshore region and the Northern Ireland inshore region).[26]

The Secretary of State for Environment Food and Rural Affairs is the MPA for the English inshore region and the English offshore region. The Welsh Ministers are the MPA for the Welsh inshore region and the Welsh offshore region. The Scottish Ministers are the MPA for the Scottish offshore region and the Department of the Environment in Northern Ireland is the MPA for the Northern Ireland offshore region.[27]

The MPAs are able to direct that any of their delegable marine plan functions are to be exercisable by another public body (with that public body's consent).[28] The delegable marine plan functions are those contained under Chapter 2 of Pt 3 of the MCAA 2009 (marine plans) and also the monitoring and implementation functions under s 61 of that Act. However, these exclude the power to decide whether to publish a marine plan or any amendment to it (under para 15 of Sch 6) and deciding whether to withdraw a marine plan under s 53.[29] Certain other functions are specifically excluded from the power to delegate (s 55(7)).

---

[24]   At p 3.
[25]   MCCA 2009, s 49, each is defined in s 322.
[26]   MCCA 2009, s 50(1).
[27]   MCCA 2009, s 50(2).
[28]   MCCA 2009, s 55.
[29]   MCCA 2009, s 55(6).

The Marine Maritime Organisation

18.9   Since 18 March 2010, marine planning in England has been largely the responsibility of the Marine Maritime Organisation ('MMO'), the relevant functions having been delegated by direction by the Secretary of State for Environment, Food and Rural Affairs.[30] The specific functions delegated to the MMO are set out in the schedule which accompanies the delegation direction. They are:

Function	Provision in the Act	Conditions
To prepare marine plans (and amendments to marine plans) for the English inshore region and the English offshore region, having regard to the matters set out in Sch 6, para 9	ss 51 and 52 and Sch 6, para 9	The MMO must comply with the relevant provisions of Sch 6 (see below). The MMO only to prepare amendments to a marine plan if the Secretary of State agrees
To notify related planning authorities	Sch 6, para 1	
To prepare, publish and keep under review statements of public participation ('SPPs') and to take all reasonable steps to comply with them	Sch 6, para 3	
To prepare publish and keep under review SPPs and to take all reasonable steps to comply with them	Sch 6, paras 5–7	The MMO must submit draft SPPs to the Secretary of State for approval before publication
To seek expert advice and assistance (to include the convening of consultative groups)	Sch 6, para 8	
To carry out a sustainability appraisal of its proposals for inclusion in a marine plan and to publish a report of the results of the appraisal	Sch 6, para 10	
To prepare and publish consultation drafts of marine plans	Sch 6, para 11	The MMO must submit the consultation draft to the Secretary of State for approval before publication
To consider representations made about a consultation draft when settling the text of a marine plan	Sch 6, para 12	

---

[30]   Delegation made under s 55 of MCCA 2009. The direction can be found at: https://www.gov.uk/government/uploads/system/uploads/attachment_data/file/312292/delegation.pdf.

Function	Provision in the Act	Conditions
To settle the text of a marine plan for adoption and publication	Sch 6, para 14	(1) The MMO must have regard to any recommendations by an independent investigator and to any reasons given for such recommendations (2) The MMO must liaise very closely with the Secretary of State and must not settle the final text without the approval of the Secretary of State
To prepare and arrange for the publication of the changes made to a marine plan between consultation and adoption, reasons for the changes and reasons for not implementing any recommendations by an independent investigator	Sch 6, para 15	
To arrange for the publication of a marine plan	Sch 6, para 15	The decision to publish must be taken by the Secretary of State (section 55(6)(a))
To keep matters relevant to marine planning under review	s 54	
To monitor and report on the effects and effectiveness of marine plans	s 61	The decision to lay and what to lay under s 61(1)(b) and (c) must be taken by the Secretary of State

The MMO was itself founded in 2010 pursuant to s 1 of MCCA 2009. The MMO is required by that statute to ensure that its functions are carried out with 'the objective of making a contribution to the achievement of sustainable development'.[31]

MARINE PLANS – PREPARATION, PUBLICATION AND ADOPTION

18.10   The first set of marine plans to be adopted were the 'East Marine Plans' which were published on 2 April 2014. They relate to the East Marine Inshore and East Marine Offshore regions. Between them they cover about 55,000 square

---

[31]   MCCA 2009, s 2(1)(a).

kilometres of sea. As the executive summary to the pans states this is the equivalent of developing a land-use plan for around 40% of England's land area.[32]

The statutory basis for marine planning is contained within Pt 3 of MCCA 2009. It defines marine plans as documents which:

'(a) have been prepared and adopted for a marine plan area by the appropriate marine plan authority in accordance with Schedule 6,

(b) states the authority's policies (however expressed) for and in connection with the sustainable development of the area, and

(c) states that it is a marine plan prepared and adopted for the purposes of [s 51 of MCCA 2009].'

By virtue of s 51 of that Act an MPA may prepare a marine plan for an area making up the whole or part of its marine planning region.[33] Schedule 6 to the MCAA 2009 governs the preparation and adoption of marine plans. An MPA must seek to ensure that every part of its marine planning region is covered by a marine plan.[34]

A marine plan must be in conformity with any MPS which applies to the marine plan area unless 'relevant considerations indicate otherwise'.[35] The MPAs for the English inshore region and the Welsh inshore region are required to 'take all reasonable steps to ensure that any marine plan for a marine plan area in its marine planning region is compatible with the relevant Planning Act plan for any area in England, Wales or Scotland which is related to the marine plan area.'[36] An area is related to another if it adjoins it, lies wholly or partly within it, or its whole or part of it is affected by the whole or part of the other.[37] In England the relevant Planning Act plan is the development plan. In Wales it is the development plan and/or the Wales Spatial Plan.[38]

Before beginning to prepare a marine plan, an MPA must give notice of its intention to prepare such a plan to the 'related planning authorities'.[39] These are:

(a)   the Secretary of State (unless he is the MPA);[40]

(b)   any MPA whose marine planning region adjoins or is adjacent to the marine plan area;

(c)   if the MPA adjoins or is adjacent to the Scottish inshore region, the Scottish Ministers;

(d)   any local planning authority whose area adjoins or is adjacent to the MPA; and

---

[32]   HM Government DEFRA, East Inshore and East Offshore Marine Plans, Executive Summary (April 2014), para.1, at: https://www.gov.uk/government/uploads/system/uploads/attachment_data/file/312493/east-plan-executivesummary.pdf.
[33]   Subsection 1.
[34]   MCCA 2009, s 51(2).
[35]   MCCA 2009, s 51(6).
[36]   MCCA 2009, Sch 6, para 3(2).
[37]   MCCA 2009, Sch 6, para 3(3).
[38]   MCCA 2009, Sch 6, para 3(4).
[39]   MCCA 2009, Sch 6, para 1(1).
[40]   Where notice is required to be given to the Secretary of State it must state whether the MPA proposes to include provisions relating to retained functions in the marine plan and whether the MPA proposes to prepare the marine plan in a way which will not be in conformity with any MPS which governs the marine plan area (MCCA 2009, Sch 6, para 2).

(e)   any responsible regional authorities whose region adjoins or is adjacent to the MPA.[41]

The MPA must also, before preparing a marine plan, prepare and publish an SPP.[42] Like with the MPS, the SPP is a statement of policies which relate to the involvement of interested persons in the preparation of the marine plan.[43] It must:

(a)   identify the area for which the marine plan is being prepared;[44]

(b)   state whether the MPA intends to include provision relating to the retained functions (if it does then it may only publish the SPP with the agreement of the Secretary of State);[45]

(c)   invite the making of representations as to matters to be included in the marine plan (made in accordance with the SPP);[46]

(d)   include a proposed timetable for the preparation and publication of a consultation draft, the making of representations on that draft, the consideration of those representations, the settling of the text and the marine plan's adoption;[47] and

(e)   include provision about making representations in response to the invitation regarding matters to be included in the proposed plan and also about the consultation draft (including how those representations may be made and the time when they must be made.[48]

The SPP must be kept under review by the MPA and if at any time the MPA considers it necessary or expedient to amend it, then it must do so and publish the revised version.[49]

The statute includes specific provision for the MPA to seek advice from any expert body or person in connection with the preparation of a marine plan.[50]

The MPA is required by statute to have regard to certain matters in preparing a marine plan. These are:

(a)   the requirement for the marine plan to be in conformity with any MPS which governs marine planning for the marine plan area, unless relevant considerations indicate otherwise (under s 51(6));

(b)   the duties with respect of securing compatibility of marine plans or land use plans for areas related to the marine plan area (under Sch 6, para 3(1) and (2));

(c)   the effect which any proposal for inclusion in the plan is likely to have on any area which is related to the marine plan area;

---

41   MCCA 2009, Sch 6, para 1(2).
42   MCCA 2009, Sch 6, para 5(1).
43   MCCA 2009, Sch 6, para 5(2).
44   MCCA 2009, Sch 6, para 5(3).
45   MCCA 2009, Sch 6, para 5(4).
46   MCCA 2009, Sch 6, para 5(5).
47   MCCA 2009, Sch 6, para 6(2).
48   MCCA 2009, Sch 6, para 6(4).
49   MCCA 2009, Sch 6, para 7(1), (2) and (4).
50   MCCA 2009, Sch 6, para 8(1).

(d)   the results of the requirement under s 54 to keep the identification of areas which are to be marine plan areas and the preparation, adoption, review, amendment or withdrawal of marine plans for those areas under review;

(e)   the SPP;

(f)   any representations made in response to the invitation for representations on the content of a marine plan under Sch 6, para 5(5);

(g)   any expert advice received under Sch 6, para 8(1);

(h)   any plan (not falling within Sch 6, para 3(1) or (2)) prepared by a public or local authority in connection with the management or use of the sea or the coast, or of marine or coastal resources, in the marine plan area or in any adjoining or adjacent area in England or Wales, Scotland or Northern Ireland; and

(i)   the powers and duties of the Crown Estate Commissioners under the Crown Estate Act 1961.

Sustainability appraisal

18.11   The MPA must carry out a sustainability appraisal of its proposals for inclusion within a marine plan and the MPA may only continue with those proposals if 'it considers that the results of the appraisal indicate that it is appropriate to do so.'[51] The sustainability appraisal must be published alongside the consultation draft of the marine plan.[52]

Consultation and examination

18.12   A consultation draft is required to be published pursuant to Sch 6, para 11 and any person may make representations on it in line with the SPP.[53] Such representations must be considered by the MPA in the course of settling the text of the marine plan.[54]

Having published the consultation draft, the MPA must consider appointing an independent person to investigate the proposals and report upon them.[55] In deciding whether to make such an appointment the MPA must have regard to: (a) any representations received as to the matters to be included in the marine plan pursuant to the invitation made under Sch 6, para5(5); (b) any representations received on the consultation draft; and (c) the extent to which any representations have not been resolved. If appointed the independent person must make recommendations supported by reasons.[56] These recommendations and their reasons are to be published by the MPA.[57] The MPA is required to have regard to any recommendations when settling the text for the marine plan. It may also have regard to any other matters it considers relevant.[58]

---

[51]   MCCA 2009, Sch 6, para 10(2).
[52]   MCCA 2009, Sch 6, para 10(4).
[53]   MCCA 2009, Sch 6, para 12(1) and (2).
[54]   MCCA 2009, Sch 6, para 12(3).
[55]   MCCA 2009, Sch 6, para 13(1).
[56]   MCCA 2009, Sch 6, para 13(3).
[57]   MCCA 2009, Sch 6, para 13(4).
[58]   MCCA 2009, Sch 6, para 14.

Publication and adoption

18.13   A marine plan is adopted when the MPA decides to publish the plan.[59] It may only be adopted by, or with the agreement of, the Secretary of State unless it only applies to the Welsh inshore region and does not contain provision relating to retained functions.[60] The MPA is required to publish the plan as soon as reasonably practicable after its adoption. The plan must be accompanied by statements of: (a) modifications that have been made to the proposals published in the consultation draft; (b) reasons for those modifications; (c) where any recommendations made by an independent person appointed under Sch 6, para 13 have not been implemented, the reasons why.[61]

Continuing review

18.14   Where an MPA has prepared and adopted a marine plan, there is a statutory duty on that MPA to keep that plan under review. This includes reviewing the effects of the policies in the marine plan, the effectiveness in securing the objectives for which the plan was prepared and adopted are met, the progress being made towards securing those objectives and where an MPS governs marine planning for the MPA's region, the progress being made towards securing that the objectives for which the MPS was prepared and adopted are met in that region. The MPA must report on those matters at least every three years and lay it before the Secretary of State, the Scottish Ministers, the Welsh Ministers or the Department of the Environment in Northern Ireland (whichever body is appropriate).[62] It must also, at least every six years, prepare and lay a report on any marine plans it has prepared and adopted, its intentions for their amendment, and its intentions for the preparation and adoption of any further marine plans.[63] A marine plan may be amended from time to time by the MPA.[64] It may also be withdrawn in accordance with the provisions of s 53 of the MCAA 2009.

THE INTERRELATIONSHIP WITH LAND-USE AND OTHER PLANS

18.15   Many of the types of development typically located in the sea also have an impact on the land. For example, offshore wind turbines require cabling to transport the electricity to the shore. There may be substantial onshore facilities such as electricity converter stations on the land. It is therefore necessary for there to be joined-up thinking between marine plans and land-use plans.

The MMO is listed as one of the prescribed bodies which are subject to the duty to co-operate under s 33A of the Planning and Compulsory Purchase Act 2004[65]. It is therefore required to co-operate with local planning authorities, county councils (who are not local planning authorities) and other prescribed bodies. Further, the prescribed activities which are caught by the duty include the preparation of marine

---

[59]   MCCA 2009, Sch 6, para 15(1).
[60]   MCCA 2009, Sch 6, para 15(1) and (3).
[61]   MCCA 2009, Sch 6, para 7.
[62]   MCCA 2009, s 61(1)(b) and (14).
[63]   MCCA 2009, s 61(1)(c).
[64]   MCCA 2009, s 52(1).
[65]   See Chapter 7 for more on the duty to co-operate.

plans under the MCAA 2009 for the English inshore region, the English offshore region or part thereof.[66] The government's intention for the working of the duty to co-operate is clear from the Planning Policy Guidance ('PPG') which states:

> 'The Marine Management Organisation's inclusion in the duty to cooperate will contribute to strengthening the integration between marine and terrestrial planning, which is also facilitated by requirements within the Marine and Coastal Access Act 2009 and the National Planning Policy Framework'[67]

MPAs extend up to the level of the mean high water spring tides. Local plans in coastal areas generally extend to the mean low water spring tides. Therefore the MPA will physically overlap with that of terrestrial plans.[68] The MPS states that '... the coast and estuaries are highly valued environments, as well as social and economic assets. The UK Administrations are committed to ensuring the coastal areas, and the activities taking place within them, are managed in an integrated and holistic way in line with the principles of Integrated Coastal Zone Management (ICZM)'[69,70]

MARINE PLANS AND DECISION-TAKING

18.16   Although this book is focussed upon the preparation and adoption of planning policy, it is worth briefly considering the impact of marine plans on decision-taking. Public authorities are required to take any authorisation or enforcement decision[71] in accordance with the appropriate marine policy documents, unless relevant considerations indicate otherwise.[72] This presumption, in favour of marine policy documents, mirrors that contained in s 38(6) of the Planning Compulsory Purchase Act 2004 which states that planning decisions must be taken in accordance with the development plan unless material considerations indicate otherwise. Where such a decision is taken otherwise than in accordance with appropriate marine policy documents, the public authority must give reasons for that decision.[73]

When making a decision as to whether to confirm a Nationally Significant Infrastructure Project the Secretary of State is required, amongst other considerations, to have regard to the appropriate marine policy documents determined in accordance with s 59 of the MCAA 2009.[74]

There is also a statutory requirement for public authorities to have regard to the appropriate marine policy documents in taking any decision which relates to the

---

[66]   Planning and Compulsory Purchase Act 2004, s 33A(3)(c).
[67]   PPG Ref ID: 9-023-20140306.
[68]   MPS, para.1.3.3
[69]   MPS, para.1.3.5
[70]   Integrated Coastal Zone Management is currently the subject of a draft EU directive establishing a framework for maritime spatial planning and integrated coastal management. It follows the EU Council's recommendation on Integrated Coastal Zone Management of 2002 and the Protocol to the Barcelona Convention on Integrated Coastal Zone Management (ratified by the EU in 2010) (see: http://ec.europa.eu/environment/iczm/prop_iczm.htm).
[71]   As defined in s 58(4) of MCCA 2009
[72]   MCCA 2009, s 58(1).
[73]   MCCA 2009, s 58(2).
[74]   Planning Act 2008, s 104(2)(aa).

exercise of any function capable of affecting the whole or any part of the UK marine area, but which is not an authorisation or enforcement decision.[75]

'Appropriate marine policy documents' are defined in s 59 of the MCAA 2009. They include:

(a)   where a decision relates to an MPA, the marine plan which is in effect for that area;

(b)   where the authorisation or enforcement decision involves retained functions[76] the marine plan will only be an appropriate marine policy document where:

   (i)   it contains a statement under s 51(8) that it includes provision relating to retained functions;

   (ii)   it was adopted with the agreement of the Secretary of State under para 15(2) of Sch 6; and

   (iii)   it was prepared and adopted at a time when an MPS was in effect and governed marine planning for the marine planning region;[77]

(c)   any marine policy statement which is in effect as an appropriate marine policy document for any:

   (i)   minister of the crown;

   (ii)   government department;

   (iii)   devolved policy authority;[78]

   (iv)   non-departmental public authority so far as it is carrying out functions in relation to the English inshore region or the English offshore region;

   (v)   non-departmental public authority in so far as it is carrying out retained functions in relation to a devolved marine planning region; and

   (vi)   non-departmental public authority so far as it is carrying out secondary devolved functions in relation to a marine planning region whose marine plan authority is a policy authority which adopted the MPS.[79]

---

[75]   MCCA 2009, s 58(3).
[76]   As defined in s 60 of MCCA 2009.
[77]   MCCA 2009, s 59(4).
[78]   I.e. the Scottish Ministers, the Welsh Ministers and the Department of the Environment in Northern Ireland (see s 59(7) of MCCA 2009).
[79]   MCCA 2009, s 59(5).

Chapter 19

National Agencies' Policies

INTRODUCTION

19.1   The UK government website lists 376 Government 'agencies and other public bodies' and 10 public corporations. The policies of a number of these agencies, public bodies and corporations are material to planning. Those agencies, public bodies and corporations include:

Agencies and public bodies

- Historic England;
- Natural England;
- Environment Agency;
- Forestry Commission (non-Ministerial department);
- Advisory Committee on Releases to the Environment, Agriculture and Horticulture Development Board;
- Building Regulations Advisory Committee;
- Centre for the Protection of National Infrastructure;
- Coal Authority;
- Committee on Climate Change;
- the Crown Estate;
- Ebbsfleet Development Corporation;
- Health and Safety Executive;
- High Speed Two Limited;
- Highways England;
- Homes and Communities Agency;
- Marine Management Organisation;
- National Infrastructure Commission;
- Natural Resources Wales;
- Planning Inspectorate;
- Public Health England;
- Public Health Wales;

- Royal Parks;

- Sport England; and

- Sports Council for Wales.

Public corporations

- Civil Aviation Authority;

- Historic Royal Palaces;

- Office for Nuclear Regulation; and

- the Oil and Pipelines Agency.

This chapter does not seek to address all of the plans, policies and guidance published by the above bodies. Rather, it makes some general comments on the status of the policies and guidance of national agencies and corporations and then discusses some of the policies and guidance issued by the more significant national agencies, these are: the Environment Agency, Natural England and Historic England.

THE STATUS OF NATIONAL AGENCIES'/CORPORATIONS' POLICIES AND GUIDANCE

19.2   As will be seen from the examples below, a number of the national agencies, public bodies and corporations have adopted policies and guidance dealing with matters within their remit. The status of the particular plan, policy or guidance in question will depend on whether it has been given statutory status. Where the plan/policy/guidance has no statutory status then it is capable of being a material consideration An example of this can be found in *R (on the application of Young) v Oxford City Council* which explored advice from Historic England with regards to how to deal with the effect of development upon heritage and the planning system.[1]

The following sections address the plans and policies of: the Environment Agency, Natural England, and Historic England.

THE ENVIRONMENT AGENCY

Introduction

19.3   The Environment Agency ('EA') was established by s 1 of the Environment Act 1995. The Environment Act 1995 sets out the statutory 'aim' of the EA which is, in discharging its functions, 'to protect or enhance the environment, taken as a whole, as to make the contribution towards attaining the objective of achieving sustainable development ...'.[2] In exercising its functions it must have regard to guidance given to it by the Secretary of State and issued in accordance with s 4 of the Environment Act 1995.

---

[1]   [2002] EWCA Civ 990, [2003] JPL 232.
[2]   Environment Act 1995, s 4.

Chapter 1A of the Environment Act 1995 sets out the general functions of the EA within a number of its different competencies, these are: pollution control, water, environmental and recreational duties, environmental duties with respects to sites of special scientific interest, codes of practice with respect to environmental and recreational duties and a duty to co-operate with the Natural Resources Body for Wales.

The Environment Act 1995 enables the EA to 'do anything which, in its opinion, is calculated to facilitate, or is conducive or incidental to, the carrying out of its functions'.[3] This broad power enables the EA to develop plans and policies which are material considerations in planning decisions.

The EA is also tasked by statute with the development of the flood and coastal erosion management strategy for England, discussion of which follows below.

National Flood and Coastal Erosion Risk Management Strategy

19.4   Pursuant to s 7 of the Flood and Water Management Act 2010 the EA is required to develop, maintain, apply and monitor a strategy for flood and coastal erosion risk management in England. The strategy is required to specify:

(a)   the English risk management authorities;

(b)   the flood and coastal erosion risk management functions that may be exercised by those authorities in relation to England;

(c)   the objectives for managing flood and coastal erosion risk;

(d)   the measures proposed to achieve those objectives;

(e)   how and when the measures are to be implemented;

(f)   the costs and benefits of those measures, and how they are to be paid for;

(g)   the assessment of flood and coastal erosion risk for the purpose of the strategy;

(h)   how and when the strategy is to be reviewed;

(i)   the current and predicted impact of climate change on flood and coastal erosion risk management; and

(j)   how the strategy contributes towards the achievement of wider environmental objectives.[4]

The Flood and Water Management Act 2010 sets out a wide definition for 'flood'. It is defined as including any case where land not normally covered by water becomes covered by water. It does not matter whether such a flood is caused by heavy rainfall, a river overflowing its banks, a dam being breached, tidal waters, groundwater or anything else.[5] However, it does not include a flood from any part of a sewerage system unless that flood is wholly or partly caused by an increase in the volume of rainwater entering or otherwise effecting the system. Neither does it cover a flood caused by a burst water main.[6]

---

[3]   Environment Act 1995, s 37(1)(a).
[4]   Flood and Water Management Act 2010, s 7(2).
[5]   Flood and Water Management Act 2010, s 1(1) and (2).
[6]   Flood and Water Management Act 2010, s 1(3).

19.5 *National Agencies' Policies*

The EA is required to consult certain bodies and the public about the National Flood and Coastal Erosion Risk Management Strategy ('NFCERMS').[7] These are: the English risk management authorities,[8] the public, and so far as the strategy may affect flood and coastal erosion risk management in either Wales or Scotland, the Welsh Ministers and Scottish Ministers respectively.

The EA is empowered to issue guidance as to the application of the strategy.[9] That guidance, and the strategy must be submitted to the Secretary of State for his/her approval. The Secretary of State may approve the draft strategy or guidance with or without modification. Where the Secretary of State approves a strategy or guidance, the Minister is required to lay it before Parliament and it may not be issued if, within 40 days of it being so laid, either House of Parliament resolves that it should not be issued.[10]

The corresponding duties, in terms of the preparation of a NFCERMS and guidance in Wales, is contained within s 8 of the Flood and Water Management Act 2010.

The current NFCERMS for England is entitled 'Understanding the risks, empowering communities, building resilience' (2011).

Flood risk management plans

19.5   Flood risk management plans are defined as plans for the 'management of significant flood risk'.[11] The duty to provide them stems from the EU Floods Directive 2007/60/EC which came into force in November 2007. The Directive is implemented in England and Wales by the Flood Risk Regulations 2009.

The EA has a duty to prepare a flood risk management plan in relation to each relevant flood risk area.[12] Flood risk areas are those areas identified by the EA under reg 13 of the Flood Risk Regulations 2009 (those areas determined by the EA in relation to each river basin district to be at significant flood risk from the sea, main rivers and reservoirs) and those areas in an English cross border area[13] in which the Secretary of State and Scottish Ministers have identified (under reg 14A) that there is a significant flood risk from the sea, main rivers or reservoirs.[14]

Flood risk management plans are required to include details of:

'(a) objectives set by the EA for the purpose of managing the flood risk, and

(b) the proposed measures for achieving those objectives ...'[15]

---

7   Flood and Water Management Act 2010, s 7(3).

8   These are defined in s 6(13) of the Flood and Water Management Act 2010 as: the Environment Agency, the Natural Resources Body for Wales, a lead local flood authority, a district council for an area where there is no unitary authority, an internal drainage board, a water company and a highway authority.

9   Flood and Water Management Act 2010, s 7(5).

10   Flood and Water Management Act 2010, s 7(9).

11   Flood Risk Regulations 2009, SI 2009/3042, reg 27(1).

12   Flood Risk Regulations 2009, reg 25(1).

13   Defined in reg 5A of the Flood Risk Regulations 2009 as an area identified on the Cross Border Map consisting, in relation to a river basin which is partly in England and partly in Scotland, of the part of the basin that is in England.

14   Flood Risk Regulations 2009, reg 25(2).

15   Flood Risk Regulations 2009, reg 27(2).

In setting objectives, the EA must have regard to the desirability of:

'(a) reducing the adverse consequences of flooding for—

  (i) human health,

  (ii) economic activity, or

  (iii) the environment (including cultural heritage), and

(b) reducing the likelihood of flooding, whether by exercising powers to carry out structural work or otherwise.'[16]

The measures included within the plan must include measures relating to the prevention of flooding, the protection of individuals, communities and the environment against the consequences of flooding, and arrangements for forecasting and warning.[17] In determining the proposed measures the EA is required to have regard to:

'(a) the costs and benefits of different methods of managing the flood risk,

(b) the information included in the flood hazard map and the flood risk map,

(c) the river basin management plan for the area,

(d) the effect of floodplains that retain flood water,

(e) the environmental objectives, within the meaning of regulation 2 of the Water Environment Regulations, and

(f) the likely effect of a flood, and of different methods of managing a flood, on the local area and the environment.'[18]

Each flood risk management plan must include:

'(a) a map showing the boundaries of the flood risk area,

(b) a summary of the conclusions drawn from the flood hazard maps and flood risk maps for the area,

(c) a description of the proposed timing and manner of implementing the measures mentioned in paragraph (2)(b), including details of the bodies responsible for implementation,

(d) a description of the way in which implementation of those measures will be monitored,

(e) a report of the consultation under paragraph (7), and

(f) where the EA thinks it appropriate, information about how the implementation of measures under the flood risk management plan and the river basin management plan for the area will be co-ordinated.'[19]

The EA is required to consult the public together with the authorities listed in reg 36(3) as to the proposed content of a flood risk management plan.[20]

The current gamut of flood risk management plans were published in March 2016. Each of the English management plans has been published as six documents:

---

[16] Flood Risk Regulations 2009, reg 27(3).
[17] Flood Risk Regulations 2009, reg 27(4).
[18] Flood Risk Regulations 2009, reg 27(5).
[19] Flood Risk Regulations 2009, reg 27(6).
[20] Flood Risk Regulations 2009, reg 27(7).

- a summary giving an overview of the flood risk management plan;

- part A which includes the legislative background and information for the whole river basin district;

- part B which includes detail about each catchment, flood risk areas and other strategic areas;

- part C which includes measures identified to manage flood risk across the river basin district;

- a strategic environmental assessment; and

- a habitats regulation assessment.

Catchment flood management plans

19.6 The EA has produced 77 catchment flood management plans ('CFMPs').[21] These assess inland flood risk across England and Wales. This is flooding from rivers, ground water, surface water and tidal flooding. They do not consider coastal flooding which is the subject of shoreline management plans.[22] Each CFMP considers the risks of flooding across a catchment and also the potential effect of climate change upon these risks. The EA's commitment to produce and monitor CFMPs can be found in the CEFRMS.[23]

Draft guidelines for the preparation of CFMPs were consulted upon in March 2004. The draft was prepared by the EA, the Department for Environment, Food and Rural Affairs and the Welsh Assembly. The guidelines were published in two volumes. Volume I provides policy guidance on the vision, purpose and stages of producing a CFMP. Volume II sets out procedures for each step of the process and sets out practical guidance on appropriate methodologies for developing a CFMP. The guidelines do not appear to have been finalised/confirmed and remain in draft.

The CEFRMS includes some guidance relevant to the preparation of catchment flood management plans. For example, the boundaries for the various CFMPs are shown in Annex 1 of that document.

Shoreline management plans

19.7 The EA plays a significant role in the preparation of shoreline management plans, which are covered in Chapter 20. The CEFRMS includes a commitment by the EA to ensure that shoreline management plans are prepared and monitored.[24]

NATURAL ENGLAND

19.8 Natural England was established by the Natural Environment and Rural Communities Act 2006 (its predecessors English Nature and the Countryside Agency

---

[21] These can be found at: https://www.gov.uk/government/collections/catchment-flood-management-plans where they are grouped by river basin district.
[22] Chapter 7.
[23] At p 9.
[24] At p 19.

were dissolved under that Act). Its general purpose is set out in s 2(1) as 'to ensure that the natural environment is conserved, enhanced and managed for the benefit of present and future generations, thereby contributing to sustainable development'.

Management schemes for SSSI

19.9   Under s 28J of the Wildlife and Countryside Act 1981 Natural England is empowered to formulate management schemes for all or part of any site of special scientific interest ('SSSI'). A management scheme is for: (a) conserving the flora, fauna, or geological or physiographical features by reason of which the land (or the part of it to which the scheme relates) is of special interest; or (b) restoring them, or (c) both.[25]

Natural England is required to serve notice of a proposed management scheme on every owner and occupier of the land to which it relates but only after they have been consulted on the proposed management scheme.[26] The owners and occupiers must be given at least three months to make representations and Natural England is required to take any representation (duly made) into account.[27]

Within nine months of giving notice to the owners and occupiers Natural England may give notice to the owners and occupiers withdrawing the notice or may give notice to them confirming the management scheme (with or without modifications which must not be more onerous).[28]

Natural England may cancel or propose a modification to a management scheme at any time.[29]

Natural England has the power to serve management notices on any owner or occupier who is not giving effect to a provision of the management scheme and as a result any flora, fauna or geological or physiographical features by reason of which the land is of special interest are being inadequately conserved or restored.[30] The management notice may require the owner to carry out certain works on the land within a specified period. Appeals to the Secretary of State against such notices are governed by s 28L of the Wildlife and Countryside Act 1981.

HISTORIC ENGLAND

19.10   Officially known as the Historic Buildings and Monuments Commission for England, Historic England was set up by the National Heritage Act 1983. Its general functions are set out in s 33 of that Act. Historic England has the following duties:

(a)   to secure the preservation of ancient monuments and historic buildings situated in England;

---

[25]   Wildlife and Countryside Act 1981, s 28J(2).
[26]   Wildlife and Countryside Act 1981, s 28J(2) and (3).
[27]   Wildlife and Countryside Act 1981, s 28J(2) and (7).
[28]   Wildlife and Countryside Act 1981, s 28J(2) and (8).
[29]   Wildlife and Countryside Act 1981, s 28J(2) and (11).
[30]   Wildlife and Countryside Act 1981, ss 28K and 28J(2).

(b) to promote the preservation and enhancement of the character and appearance of conservation areas situated in England; and

(c) to promote the public's enjoyment of, and advance their knowledge of, ancient monuments and historic buildings situated in England and their preservation.[31]

Historic England does not have statutory responsibility for drawing up any particular plans or policies. However, it has developed planning advice which is capable of being material considerations in planning decisions. Its own approach is contained in 'Conservation Principles, Policies and Guidance'. Historic England advice comes in two forms: Good Practice Advice and Historic England Advice Notes.

Historic England's Good Practice Advice sets out information on 'good practice' in plan-making and the taking of planning decisions in relation to those plans and decisions which affect heritage assets. At present, the following pieces of Good Practice Advice ('GPA') have been promulgated by Historic England:

- GPA1 – Local Plan Making;

- GPA2 – Managing Significance in Decision-Taking in the Historic Environment; and

- GPA3 – Setting and Views.

Historic England is in the process of drawing up GPA4 on Enabling Development to replace 'Enabling development and the conservation of significant places'.

Each of the GPAs was prepared following public consultation.

Historic England's Advice Notes contain practical advice on how to implement national planning policy and guidance. Like with GPAs, they have been prepared following public consultation. At present, the Historic England Advice Notes are:

- Historic England Advice Note 1 – Conservation Areas

- Historic England Advice Note 2 – Making Changes to Heritage Assets

- Historic England Advice Note 3 – The Historic Environment and Site Allocations in Local Plans

- Historic England Advice Note 4 – Tall Buildings

- Historic England Advice Note 5 – Setting up a Listed Building Heritage Partnership Agreement

- Historic England Advice Note 6 – Drawing up a Local Listed Building Consent Order

- Historic England Advice Note 7 – Local Heritage Listing

- Historic England Advice Note 8 – Sustainability Appraisal and Strategic Environmental Assessment

- Historic England Advice Note 9 – The Adaptive Reuse of Traditional Farm Buildings.

---

[31] National Heritage Act 1983, s 33(1).

Chapter 20

Local Policies

INTRODUCTION

20.1   There exist a number of other types of plans/policies which are created at a local level. Their production is governed either by statute or guidance. This chapter discusses the following:

- river basin management plans;

- local flood risk management strategies;

- shoreline management plans;

- National Park plans;

- area of outstanding natural beauty ('AONB') management plans;

- conservation area management plans;

- local transport plans;

- the Lee Valley Park Plan; and

- air quality management area action plans.

RIVER BASIN MANAGEMENT PLANS AND RIVER BASIN PROGRAMMES OF MEASURES

Introduction

20.2   River basin management plans ('RBMPs') are creatures of European law. They are plans which seek to protect and improve the water environment in a river basin district. Each plan sets out the baseline from which improvements are sought and against which the EU Water Framework Directive's (2000/60/EC) 'no deterioration in status' objective is measured. The plans also set out actions expected to improve water quality through contributions from various organisations and agencies working in partnership with the Environment Agency.

The first RBMPs were published in 2009. They were updated in 2015/6. Each RBMP consists of a number of documents and is presented in two parts. Part 1 is the RMBP, part 2 includes a planning overview and additional information. Each RBMP is accompanied by an impact assessment, a strategic environmental assessment and a habitat regulation assessment.

There are eight RBMPs in England (each published in 2015). These are: Anglian river basin district RBMP, Humber river basin district RBMP, Northumbria river basin district RBMP, North West river basin district RBMP, Severn river basin district RBMP[1], South East river basin district RBMP, South West river basin district RBMP and Thames river basin district RBMP.

The requirement for RBMPs originates from the Water Framework Directive which sets out its purpose in Article 1. It aims to establish a framework for the protection of inland surface waters, transitional waters, coastal waters and groundwater which:

(a)   prevents further deterioration and protects and enhances the status of aquatic ecosystems;

(b)   promotes sustainable water use based on a long-term protection of available water resources;

(c)   aims at enhanced protection and improvement of the aquatic environment;

(d)   ensures the progressive reduction of pollution of groundwater and prevents its further pollution; and

(e)   contributes to mitigating the effects of floods and droughts.

The Water Framework Directive has been transposed into English and Welsh law by the Water Environment (Water Framework Directive) (England and Wales) Regulations 2017[2] ('Water Environment Regulations 2017'). These Regulations relate to those river basin districts wholly within England and/or Wales. Where a river basin district straddles England and Scotland separate regulations adapt the provisions of the 2017 Regulations and the relevant Scottish legislation (the Water Environment and Water Services (Scotland) Act 2003) to ensure that the requirements of the Directive are met. The relevant Regulations are:

•   Water Environment (Water Framework Directive) (Northumbria River Basin District) Regulations 2003;[3] and

•   Water Environment (Water Framework Directive) (Solway Tweed River Basin District) Regulations 2004.[4]

River basin Planning Guidance (July 2014)[5] published by the Department for Environment, Food and Rural Affairs ('DEFRA') and Welsh Ministers contains guidance on the practical implementation of the Water Framework Directive (and therefore the preparation of RBMPs) and is addressed to the Environment Agency ('EA') and the Natural Resources Body for Wales ('NRBW').

River basin districts, appropriate agencies and appropriate authorities

20.3   Under Article 3 of the Water Framework Directive, Member States are required to identify the individual river basins within their territory and assign them to individual river basin districts. Member States must put in place administrative

---

[1]   This also covers part of Wales.
[2]   SI 2017/407. They replace the Water Environment (Water Framework Directive) (England and Wales) Regulations 2003, SI 2003/3242, for consolidation purposes and to address transposition issues raised by the European Commission.
[3]   SI 2003/3245.
[4]   SI 2004/99.
[5]   Issued under reg 20(3) of the Water Environment Regulations 2003.

arrangements including identifying an appropriate competent authority to oversee the application of the Directive within each river basin district.

The river basin districts in England and Wales are set out on the 'official maps' produced by the EA and NRBW and displayed on their websites.[6]

Statutory functions in relation to river basin districts are carried out by 'appropriate agencies' and 'appropriate authorities'.

In relation to river basin districts wholly in England the appropriate agency is the EA. In relation to those wholly in Wales the appropriate agency is the NRBW. Where the river basin district which is partly in both, the EA and NRBW are both the appropriate authority (acting jointly).[7]

The appropriate authority in relation to a river basin district wholly in England is the Secretary of State. Where the river basin district is wholly in Wales, the appropriate authority is the Welsh Ministers. Where a river basin district is partly within both England and Wales, the Secretary of State and the Welsh Ministers act jointly as appropriate authority.[8]

Regulation 3 of the Water Environment Regulations 2017 sets out general duties of the appropriate authorities and the appropriate agencies. They are required to exercise their functions under the Regulations and statutes listed in Pts 1 and 2 of Sch 2 ('relevant functions') so as to secure compliance with the requirements of the Water Framework Directive, the Environmental Quality Standards Directive 2008/105/EC ('EQS Directive') and the Groundwater Directive 2006/118/EEC. They must further exercise their relevant functions so as to best secure that the requirements under the Directives are co-ordinated.

River basin management plans

20.4   Article 13 of the Water Framework Directive requires Member States to ensure that a river basin management plan is prepared for each river basin district lying within its territory. It is required to contain all of the information detailed in Annex VII. This includes information in relation to:

(1)   a general description of the characteristics of the river basin district required under Article 5 and Annex II;

(2)   a summary of significant pressures and impact of human activity on the status of surface water and groundwater;

(3)   identification and mapping of protected areas as required by Article 6 and Annex IV;

(4)   a map of the monitoring networks established for the purposes of Article 8 and Annex V, and a presentation in map form of the results of the monitoring programmes carried out under these provisions for the status of surface water, groundwater and protected areas;

---

[6]   Water Environment Regulations 2017, reg 4.
[7]   Water Environment Regulations 2017, reg 2(1).
[8]   Water Environment Regulations 2017, reg 2(1).

(5)   a list of environmental objectives established under Article 4 for surface waters, groundwaters and protected areas;

(6)   a summary of the economic analysis of water use as required by Article 5 and Annex III;

(7)   a summary of the programme or programmes of measures adopted under Article II;

(8)   a register of any more detailed programmes and management plans for the river basin district dealing with particular sub-basins, sectors, issues or water types;

(9)   a summary of the public information and consultation measures taken, their results and the changes to the plan made as a consequence;

(10)   a summary of the public information and consultation measures taken, their results and the a list of competent authorities; and

(11)   a summary of the public information and consultation measures taken, their results and the the contact points and procedures for obtaining the background information referred to in Article 14(1).

Regulation 11 of the Water Environment Regulations 2003 governs the preparation of river basin management plans in England and Wales. It requires the appropriate agencies to (by such date as the appropriate agency may direct) prepare and submit a river basin management plan for each river basin district. The Regulation requires that it must include the relevant information as specified in the Water Directive and the EQS Directive. It required that the initial management plans were published by 22 December 2009 and that they will be periodically reviewed and where appropriate updated every six years.

Public participation in river basin management plans

20.5   The Water Framework Directive provides for public involvement and consultation in the preparation of river basin management plans (and updates thereto). The requirements are that Member States publish and make available for comment:

(a)   a timetable and work programme for the production of the plan, including a statement of the consultation measures to be taken, at least three years before the beginning of the period to which the plan refers;

(b)   an interim overview of the significant water management issues identified in the river basin, at least two years before the beginning of the period to which the plan refers; and

(c)   draft copies of the river basin management plan, at least one year before the beginning of the period to which the plan refers (Article 14(1)).

Member States are required to allow at least six months for the public to comment in writing on each of those documents (Article 14(2)).

Regulation 12 of the Water Environment Regulations 2003 governs public participation in the production of river basin management plans. It mirrors Article 14 of the Water Framework Directive. It requires the appropriate agency to publish a statement of the steps and consultation measures which it intends to take in connection with the preparation of the plan and the dates by which those steps are to be taken at least three years before the beginning of the plan period. The appropriate agency must also publish a summary of the significant water management matters which it considers arise for consideration in relation to the river basin district, not less than two years before the beginning of the plan period. Finally, the appropriate agency must publish the draft plan at least a year before the beginning of the plan period.[9]

As well as the general public, reg 12 also lists specific persons to be consulted on the plan at subsection 4.

Regulation 12(6) requires the appropriate agency to take into account any representations received within six months following the date of publication, or such longer period as the appropriate authority directs.[10]

Publication

20.6   On submission of the RBMP, the appropriate agency must make the plan accessible to the public and publish a notice stating it has been submitted and specifying the arrangements for making the plan accessible to the public.[11] The submitted plan must be accompanied by a statement of steps taken in order to comply with the publicity and consultation requirements under reg 12(1)–(4)[12] and a summary of any representations considered in line with reg 12(6) and of any changes made to the plan in light of those representations.[13]

Where the appropriate authority considers that the appropriate agency should take further action in relation to the publicity and consultation requirements set out in reg 12 (2)–(4) it may direct that the appropriate authority takes further steps and resubmits the plan within such a period as the authority specifies.[14] Reasons must be given for such a direction.[15]

Having considered the submitted RBMP the appropriate authority may approve it in whole or in part as submitted, approve it in whole or in part either with modifications or subject to modifications which it directs the appropriate agency to make, or reject it.[16] Where its approval is subject to modifications, or where the authority rejects a plan, reasons must be given for that decision.[17] Where the appropriate authority rejects a plan it must direct the appropriate agency to resubmit the plan within a certain time frame with modifications as contained within

---

9   Water Environment Regulations 2003, reg 12(1). See also reg 12(2), (3) for the required format and method for the publicity of the statements/draft plan.
10   Water Environment Regulations 2003, reg 12(6).
11   Water Environment Regulations 2003, reg 13(1).
12   This includes the publication (three years before the beginning of the plan period) of the steps and consultation measures the appropriate agency will take, the publication (not less than two years before the beginning of the plan period) of a summary of the significant water management matters which the appropriate agency considers arise for consideration in relation to the river basin district, the publication of the draft plan not less than one year before the beginning of the plan period and consultation of certain persons and organisations.
13   Water Environment Regulations 2003, reg 13(2).
14   Water Environment Regulations 2003, reg 13(3).
15   Water Environment Regulations 2003, reg 13(4).
16   Water Environment Regulations 2003, reg 14(1).
17   Water Environment Regulations 2003, reg 14(1).

the direction or as the authority considers appropriate.[18] Where the appropriate authority approves a RBMP the appropriate agency must publish that plan in accordance with reg 14(3).

Review

20.7   The Water Framework Directive requires that RBMPs are reviewed and, if necessary, updated 15 years from the date of the Directive's entry into force and every six years thereafter (Article 13(7)). This requirement is contained in domestic legislation in reg 15 of the Water Environment Regulations 2003.

Supplementary plans

20.8   Pursuant to reg 16 of the Water Environment Regulations 2003 the appropriate agency may prepare supplementary plans in order to supplement RBMPs. These may relate to a particular body of water, a particular catchment or geographical area, a particular matter relating to or aspect of the water environment; or a particular description of user of water resources.[19] The appropriate agency must consult the persons specified in reg 12(4) and such other persons likely to be interested in or affected by that plan as the appropriate agency thinks fit. The appropriate agency must take into account the views of those consulted.[20]

The status of RBMPs and supplementary plans

20.9   The Secretary of State, the Welsh Ministers, the EA and NRBW and each public body must in exercising their functions so far as affecting a river basin district have regard to the RBMP as approved under reg 14 and any supplementary plan prepared under reg 16 of the of the Water Environment Regulations 2003.[21]

Environmental objectives and programmes of measures

20.10   Pursuant to reg 10(1) of the Water Environment Regulations 2003 for the purposes of each RBMP the appropriate agency must prepare (by such date as the appropriate authority may direct) and submit to the authority proposals for:

(a)   the environmental objectives for the river basin district; and

(b)   a programme of measures to be applied in order to achieve those objectives.[22]

The requirement for a programme of measures comes from Article 11 of the Water Framework Directive and the objectives for programmes of measures are found at Article 4. Under Article 11 Each programme of measures must contain the 'basic measures' in Article 11(3) and where necessary 'supplementary measures' which are defined as 'those measures designed and implemented in addition to the basic measures with the aim of achieving the objectives established pursuant to Article 4'.[23]

---

[18]   Water Environment Regulations 2003, reg 14(2).
[19]   Water Environment Regulations 2003, reg 16(2).
[20]   Water Environment Regulations 2003, reg 16(3).
[21]   Water Environment Regulations 2003, reg 17.
[22]   Water Environment Regulations 2003, reg 10(1).
[23]   Water Framework Directive, Art 11(4).

A non-exhaustive list of supplementary measures can be found in Part B of Annex VI of the Directive.

The basic measures which must be included in a programme of measures are:[24]

'(a) those measures required to implement Community legislation for the protection of water, including measures required under the legislation specified in Article 10 and in part A of Annex VI;

(b) measures deemed appropriate for the purposes of Article 9;

(c) measures to promote an efficient and sustainable water use in order to avoid compromising the achievement of the objectives specified in Article 4;

(d) measures to meet the requirements of Article 7, including measures to safeguard water quality in order to reduce the level of purification treatment required for the production of drinking water;

(e) controls over the abstraction of fresh surface water and groundwater, and impoundment of fresh surface water, including a register or registers of water abstractions and a requirement of prior authorisation for abstraction and impoundment. These controls shall be periodically reviewed and, where necessary, updated. Member States can exempt from these controls, abstractions or impoundments which have no significant impact on water status;

(f) controls, including a requirement for prior authorisation of artificial recharge or augmentation of groundwater bodies. The water used may be derived from any surface water or groundwater, provided that the use of the source does not compromise the achievement of the environmental objectives established for the source or the recharged or augmented body of groundwater. These controls shall be periodically reviewed and, where necessary, updated;

(g) for point source discharges liable to cause pollution, a requirement for prior regulation, such as a prohibition on the entry of pollutants into water, or for prior authorisation, or registration based on general binding rules, laying down emission controls for the pollutants concerned, including controls in accordance with Articles 10 and 16. These controls shall be periodically reviewed and, where necessary, updated;

(h) for diffuse sources liable to cause pollution, measures to prevent or control the input of pollutants. Controls may take the form of a requirement for prior regulation, such as a prohibition on the entry of pollutants into water, prior authorisation or registration based on general binding rules where such a requirement is not otherwise provided for under Community legislation. These controls shall be periodically reviewed and, where necessary, updated;

(i) for any other significant adverse impacts on the status of water identified under Article 5 and Annex II, in particular measures to ensure that the hydromorphological conditions of the bodies of water are consistent with the achievement of the required ecological status or good ecological potential for bodies of water designated as artificial or heavily modified. Controls for this purpose may take the form of a requirement for prior authorisation or registration based on general binding rules where such a requirement is not otherwise provided for under Community legislation. Such controls shall be periodically reviewed and, where necessary, updated;

(j) a prohibition of direct discharges of pollutants into groundwater subject to the following provisions:

Member States may authorise reinjection into the same aquifer of water used for geothermal purposes;

---

[24] Water Framework Directive, Art 11(3).

They may also authorise, specifying the conditions for:

- injection of water containing substances resulting from the operations for exploration and extraction of hydrocarbons or mining activities, and injection of water for technical reasons, into geological formations from which hydrocarbons or other substances have been extracted or into geological formations which for natural reasons are permanently unsuitable for other purposes. Such injections shall not contain substances other than those resulting from the above operations,

- reinjection of pumped groundwater from mines and quarries or associated with the construction or maintenance of civil engineering works,

- injection of natural gas or liquefied petroleum gas (LPG) for storage purposes into geological formations which for natural reasons are permanently unsuitable for other purposes,

- injection of natural gas or liquefied petroleum gas (LPG) for storage purposes into other geological formations where there is an overriding need for security of gas supply, and where the injection is such as to prevent any present or future danger of deterioration in the quality of any receiving groundwater,

- construction, civil engineering and building works and similar activities on, or in the ground which come into contact with groundwater. For these purposes, Member States may determine that such activities are to be treated as having been authorised provided that they are conducted in accordance with general binding rules developed by the Member State in respect of such activities,

- discharges of small quantities of substances for scientific purposes for characterisation, protection or remediation of water bodies limited to the amount strictly necessary for the purposes concerned provided such discharges do not compromise the achievement of the environmental objectives established for that body of groundwater;

(k) in accordance with action taken pursuant to Article 16, measures to eliminate pollution of surface waters by those substances specified in the list of priority substances agreed pursuant to Article 16(2) and to progressively reduce pollution by other substances which would otherwise prevent Member States from achieving the objectives for the bodies of surface waters as set out in Article 4;

(l) any measures required to prevent significant losses of pollutants from technical installations, and to prevent and/or to reduce the impact of accidental pollution incidents for example as a result of floods, including through systems to detect or give warning of such events including, in the case of accidents which could not reasonably have been foreseen, all appropriate measures to reduce the risk to aquatic ecosystems.'

In 2015, the 2003 Regulations were amended in order to take account of amendments to the Water Framework Directive and the EQS Directive made by virtue of Directive 2013/39/EU. This included the insertion of reg 10A which requires that the appropriate agency must also, by 22 December 2018, establish a preliminary programme of measures for each river basin district in relation to certain priority substances by 22 December 2018. Thereafter the appropriate authority is required to prepare and submit a final version of this programme of measures (by such date as the appropriate authority directs) in relation to the next round of updated programmes of measures (22 December 2021) 'for the purposes of aiming to achieve good surface water chemical status in relation to certain priority substances by 22 December 2027 and preventing deterioration in the chemical status of each body of surface water in relation to those substances'.[25]

The environmental objectives in Article 4 are divided into objectives for: surface waters, groundwater and protected areas. They are:

'(a) for surface waters

(i) Member States shall implement the necessary measures to prevent deterioration of the status of all bodies of surface water, subject to the application of paragraphs 6 and 7 and without prejudice to paragraph 8;

(ii) Member States shall protect, enhance and restore all bodies of surface water, subject to the application of subparagraph (iii) for artificial and heavily modified bodies of water, with the aim of achieving good surface water status at the latest 15 years after the date of entry into force of this Directive, in accordance with the provisions laid down in Annex V, subject to the application of extensions determined in accordance with paragraph 4 and to the application of paragraphs 5, 6 and 7 without prejudice to paragraph 8;

(iii) Member States shall protect and enhance all artificial and heavily modified bodies of water, with the aim of achieving good ecological potential and good surface water chemical status at the latest 15 years from the date of entry into force of this Directive, in accordance with the provisions laid down in Annex V, subject to the application of extensions determined in accordance with paragraph 4 and to the application of paragraphs 5, 6 and 7 without prejudice to paragraph 8;

(iv) Member States shall implement the necessary measures in accordance with Article 16(1) and (8), with the aim of progressively reducing pollution from priority substances and ceasing or phasing out emissions, discharges and losses of priority hazardous substances without prejudice to the relevant international agreements referred to in Article 1 for the parties concerned;

(b) for groundwater

(i) Member States shall implement the measures necessary to prevent or limit the input of pollutants into groundwater and to prevent the deterioration of the status of all bodies of groundwater, subject to the application of paragraphs 6 and 7 and without prejudice to paragraph 8 of this Article and subject to the application of Article 11(3)(j);

(ii) Member States shall protect, enhance and restore all bodies of groundwater, ensure a balance between abstraction and recharge of groundwater, with the aim of achieving good groundwater status at the latest 15 years after the date of entry into force of this Directive, in accordance with the provisions laid down in Annex V, subject to the application of extensions determined in accordance with paragraph 4 and to the application of paragraphs 5, 6 and 7 without prejudice to paragraph 8 of this Article and subject to the application of Article 11(3)(j);

(iii) Member States shall implement the measures necessary to reverse any significant and sustained upward trend in the concentration of any pollutant resulting from the impact of human activity in order progressively to reduce pollution of groundwater. Measures to achieve trend reversal shall be implemented in accordance with paragraphs 2, 4 and 5 of Article 17, taking into account the applicable standards set out in relevant Community legislation, subject to the application of paragraphs 6 and 7 and without prejudice to paragraph 8;

---

[25] Water Environment Regulations 2003, reg 10A inserted by the Water Environment (Water Framework Directive) (England and Wales) (Amendment) Regulations 2015, SI 2015/1623, reg 7.

(c)   for protected areas

> Member States shall achieve compliance with any standards and objectives at the latest 15 years after the date of entry into force of this Directive, unless otherwise specified in the Community legislation under which the individual protected areas have been established.'

Where more than one of the objectives above applies to a given body of water then the most stringent objective applies.[26] Article 11 contains further provisions with regards to extending deadlines for achieving the objectives[27] and applying less stringent objectives for certain bodies of water.[28]

In preparing the environmental objectives and a programme of measures the appropriate agencies must take into account the characterisation of, and economic analysis of water use in the relevant river basin district (and any review of this) as required to be carried out under regs 5 and 6.[29] The appropriate agency must also take such steps as it thinks fit (or as the appropriate authority may direct) to:

(i)   provide opportunities for the general public and those persons likely to be interested in or affected by the proposals to participate in discussion and the exchange of information or views in relation to the preparation of those proposals;

(ii)   publicise the draft proposals to those persons; and

(iii) consult those persons in relation to those proposals.[30]

Where proposals for environmental objectives or for a programme of measures has been submitted to it, the appropriate authority may, having considered it and any representations received on it, approve them in the form submitted, approve them with modifications or such modifications as the authority may direct the appropriate agency to make; or reject them. Where the authority proposes to approve the objectives or the programme with modifications or to reject them then it must give its reasons for so doing.[31] Where the authority rejects any proposals then it must direct that the appropriate agency resubmits the proposals with modifications.[32]

In line with the requirements of the Water Framework Directive, the Water Environment Regulations 2003 provided that the appropriate authorities must ensure that a programme of measures was in place for each river basin district by 22 December 2009, made operational by 22 December 2012 and periodically reviewed and where appropriate updated, initially by 22 December 2015 and every six years thereafter.[33]

In England and Wales each of the original RBMPs has as an annex entitled 'Water body status objectives' which are the environmental objectives mandated under Article 4 of the Water Framework Directive and an annex entitled 'Actions to deliver

---

[26]   Water Framework Directive, Art 11(2).
[27]   Water Framework Directive, Art 11(4).
[28]   Water Framework Directive, Art 11(5).
[29]   Water Environment Regulations 2003, reg 10(2)(a).
[30]   Water Environment Regulations 2003, reg 10(2)(b).
[31]   Water Environment Regulations 2003, reg 10(3).
[32]   Water Environment Regulations 2003, reg 10(4).
[33]   Water Environment Regulations 2003, reg 10(5).

objectives' which are the programmes of measures required under Article 11. The latest round of RMBPs (2015) now includes links to the environmental objectives and programmes of measures within Part 2 of each RMBP.

LOCAL FLOOD RISK MANAGEMENT STRATEGIES

20.11   Lead local flood authorities in England and Wales are required by statute to develop, maintain, apply and monitor a strategy for local flood risk management in its area.[34] Lead local flood authorities are defined in England as the unitary authority for the area or if there is no unitary authority, the county council.[35] In Wales lead local flood authorities are the county council for the area and the country borough council for the area.[36] Local flood risk is defined as flood risk from surface runoff, groundwater and ordinary watercourses.

Local flood risk management strategies must be consistent with the national flood and coastal erosion risk management strategy for England or Wales (as relevant).[37] This is discussed in Chapter 19 of this book.

Local flood risk management strategies are required to specify the following:

(a)   the risk management authorities in the authority's area;

(b)   the flood and coastal erosion risk management functions that may be exercised by those authorities in relation to the area;

(c)   the objectives for managing local flood risk (including any objectives included in the authority's flood risk management plan prepared in accordance with the Flood Risk Regulations 2009);

(d)   the measures proposed to achieve those objectives;

(e)   how and when the measures are expected to be implemented;

(f)   the costs and benefits of those measures, and how they are to be paid for;

(g)   the assessment of local flood risk for the purpose of the strategy;

(h)   how and when the strategy is to be reviewed; and

(i)   how the strategy contributes to the achievement of wider environmental objectives.[38]

Lead local flood authorities may issue guidance about the application of the local flood risk management strategy in its area.[39] In Wales a lead local flood authority must submit a draft of any strategy and guidance prepared under s 10 of the Flood and Water Management Act 2010 for their approval. The Welsh Ministers may approve the strategy and/or guidance with or without modification or reject it.[40]

---

[34]   Flood and Water Management Act 2010, ss 9, 10.
[35]   Flood and Water Management Act 2010, s 6(7).
[36]   Flood and Water Management Act 2010, s 6(9).
[37]   Flood and Water Management Act 2010, ss 9(5) and 10(5).
[38]   Flood and Water Management Act 2010, ss 9(4) and 10(4).
[39]   Flood and Water Management Act 2010, s 9(7) and (8).
[40]   Flood and Water Management Act 2010, s 10(10).

20.12 *Local Policies*

Lead local flood authorities are required to consult any risk management authorities[41] which may be affected by the strategy and the public on its local flood risk management strategy.[42] They must also publish a summary of its local flood risk management strategy together with guidance as to the availability of relevant information.[43]

Status of local flood risk management strategies

20.12　When exercising flood and coastal risk management functions, English and Welsh risk management authorities are required to:

(a)　act in a manner which is consistent with the national strategy and guidance; and

(b)　except in the case of a water company, act in a manner which is consistent with the local strategies and guidance.[44]

However, that requirement does not apply to the function of the Environment Agency in developing, maintaining, applying and monitoring the National Flood and Coastal Erosion Risk Management Strategy ('NFCERMS') under s 7 of the Flood and Water Management Act 2010. In exercising that function it must instead 'have regard to the national and local strategies and guidance'.[45]

Where an English or Welsh risk management authority is exercising a function which is not a flood and coastal risk management function but which may affect a flood risk or coastal erosion risk, it is required to have regard to the national and local strategies and guidance.[46]

SHORELINE MANAGEMENT PLANS

Introduction

20.13　Shoreline management plans ('SMPs') are non-statutory plans. They are described in the current guidance as:

> '... a large scale assessment of the risks associated with coastal processes...and helps to reduce these risks to people and the developed historic and natural environment. In doing so, it is an important part of our and the Welsh Assembly Government's strategy for managing flooding and coastal erosion. The strategy aims to manage risks ... by using a range of methods which reflect both national and local priorities, to:
>
> • reduce the threat of flooding and erosion to people and their property; and
>
> • benefit the environment, society and the economy as far as possible, in line with the Government's 'sustainable development principles ...'[47]

---

[41]　Defined in s 6(13) of the Flood and Water Management Act 2010 as: the EA, NRBW, a lead local flood authority, a district council for where there is no unitary authority, an internal drainage board, a water company, and a highway authority.

[42]　Flood and Water Management Act 2010, s 9(6).

[43]　Flood and Water Management Act 2010, s 9(7).

[44]　Flood and Water Management Act 2010, ss 11(1) and 12(1).

[45]　Flood and Water Management Act 2010, s 11(2)(b).

[46]　Flood and Water Management Act 2010, s 11(4) and 12(3).

[47]　DEFRA, 'Shoreline management plan guidance, Volume 1 Aims and requirements' (March 2006), p 4.

Despite their preparation not being required by statute, SMPs cover the entirety of the English and Welsh coastline. Schedule IV of the Coast Protection Act 1949 defines the upstream limits of the 'coast' in rivers and estuaries. However, these do not necessarily dictate the limits of shoreline management plans. The fact of coastal processes means that plans are required to be flexible.[48]

The English and Welsh shoreline was originally divided into 11 'major sediment cells'. These have each been sub-divided into 'sediment sub-cells'. However, the current guidance states that the coast will be divided into 'policy units' which are defined as 'lengths of shoreline for which a separate shoreline management policy applies'.[49]

The guidance

20.14   The guidance for the preparation of SMPs was first introduced in 1995 by the Ministry of Agriculture Fisheries and Food ('MAFF') and the Welsh Office. The first round of plans were completed by 2000. The MAFF was disbanded in 2001 and its responsibilities transferred to DEFRA. The most recent guidance was issued by DEFRA in March 2006 in which it identified shortcomings in the existing SMPs. It identified that they required: more emphasis on improved links with the planning system, more consideration of effects on the environment, and longer term coastal policies.[50] It required the second round of SMPs to be a review of the first generation SMPs.[51]

The current guidance comprises two volumes and a number of appendices. Volume 1 is entitled 'Aims and requirements' and defines an SMP and what it should include. Volume 2 is entitled 'Procedures' and provides guidance on how to produce an SMP.

Operating authorities

20.15   The SMP process is overseen by a group of operating authorities which supervises the process by which the SMP is put into place, monitors progress, acts as the client steering group while reviewing and amending the SMP and works closely with the Regional Coastal Authority Group on costal issues.[52] The group of operating authorities will generally include: a chairperson and technical secretary (preferably from the lead authority), all authorities with operational responsibility in the plan area (including a representative from the Environment Agency), a representative from the relevant regional or local planning authorities, Natural England and the Countryside Council for Wales, important organisations who have an interest in the shoreline and Defra Flood Management Division and the Welsh Assembly Government.[53]

Individual SMPs and their reviews are overseen by maritime local authorities and the Environment Agency (the operating authorities). A lead authority from the relevant

---

[48]   DEFRA, 'Shoreline management plan guidance, Volume 1 Aims and requirements' (March 2006), p 33.
[49]   DEFRA, 'Shoreline management plan guidance, Volume 1 Aims and requirements' (March 2006), p 12.
[50]   DEFRA, 'Shoreline management plan guidance, Volume 1: Aims and requirements' (March 2006), Foreword.
[51]   DEFRA, 'Shoreline management plan guidance, Volume 2: Procedures' (March 2006), p 11.
[52]   DEFRA, 'Shoreline management plan guidance, Volume 2: Procedures' (March 2006), p 6.
[53]   DEFRA, 'Shoreline management plan guidance, Volume 2: Procedures' (March 2006), p 6.

20.16 *Local Policies*

operating authority takes responsibility. There are currently 22 SMPs in place in England and Wales.[54]

Content and policies

20.16 Each SMP is required to be in line with the government's strategy for managing risks from floods and coastal erosion.[55] SMPs should also:

- set out the risks from flooding and erosion to people and the developed, historic and natural environment within the SMP area;

- identify opportunities to maintain and improve the environment by managing the risks from floods and coastal erosion;

- identify the preferred policies for managing risks from floods and erosion over the next century;

- identify the consequences of putting the preferred policies into practice;

- set out procedures for monitoring how effective these policies are;

- inform others so that future land use, planning and development of the shoreline takes account of the risks and the preferred policies;

- discourage inappropriate development in areas where the flood and erosion risks are high; and

- meet international and national nature conservation legislation and aim to achieve the biodiversity objectives.[56]

Perhaps uniquely amongst strategic planning documents, SMPs are required to 'identify the best approach or approaches to managing risks over the next 100 years from flooding and coastal erosion'.[57] They are required to 'identify the combination of policies that are likely to be practical and acceptable over the next 100 years.'[58]

An SMP may adopt any of the following four policies:

- *Hold the existing defence line* by maintaining or chanting the standard of protection.

- *Advance the existing defence line* by building new defences on the seaward side of the original defences.

- *Managed realignment* by allowing the shoreline to move backwards or forwards, with management to control or limit movement (such as reducing erosion or building new defences on the landward side of the original defences).

- *No active intervention*, where there is no investment in coastal defences.[59]

---

54 See: https://www.gov.uk/government/publications/shoreline-management-plans-smps/shoreline-management-plans-smps for a full list and their lead authorities.
55 DEFRA, 'Shoreline management plan guidance, Volume 2: Procedures' (March 2006), p 11.
56 DEFRA, 'Shoreline management plan guidance, Volume 2: Procedures' (March 2006), p 11, see also the glossary.
57 DEFRA, 'Shoreline management plan guidance, Volume 2: Procedures' (March 2006), p 11.
58 DEFRA, 'Shoreline management plan guidance, Volume 2: Procedures' (March 2006), p 12.
59 DEFRA, 'Shoreline management plan guidance, Volume 2: Procedures' (March 2006), pp 13, 14.

The policies together with objectives and management requirements are chosen in relation to three time periods: the short term (0–20 years), the medium term (20–50 years) and the long term (50–100 years).[60]

Each policy should be assessed in relation to: coastal defences, how land is used, historic and archaeological features, landscape and the natural environment (including biodiversity).[61]

Public participation/consultation

20.17   The Guidance divides the plan preparation into six stages and requires consultation as follows:

'*Stage 1*

You should contact all stakeholders to:

- let them know that you are preparing an SMP and make them more aware of the SMP's aims and objectives;

- ask for relevant information so that they are involved in the project as far as possible; and

- identify the main stakeholders and other people you can consult.

Stages 2 and 3

You should involve stakeholders (including councillors and regional flood defence committees) to:

- make sure all the information you use is correct;

- make them more aware of coastal change and risks; and

- make sure that representatives of interested people have an opportunity to tell you their *ideas, opinions and concerns.*

Stage 4

You should consult your stakeholders and the general public to:

- let them know that you have prepared an SMP; and

- give them the opportunity to support or object to the proposals.

Stage 5

You should contact councillors, regional flood defence committees, planners and so on to:

- let them know about proposed changes to the final SMP (based on consultation responses);

  and

- request that they adopt the SMP.

---

[60] DEFRA, 'Shoreline management plan guidance, Volume 2: Procedures' (March 2006), p 12.
[61] DEFRA, 'Shoreline management plan guidance, Volume 2: Procedures' (March 2006), p 23.

20.18 *Local Policies*

Stage 6

You should make the general public and everyone you have consulted aware of:

- where they can see a copy of the adopted SMP; and
- how you are putting the agreed actions into practice.'[62]

Interaction with other plans

20.18   The National Planning Policy Framework ('NPPF') requires local planning authorities whose administrative area includes a coastline to identify 'Coastal Change Management Areas' which are areas likely to be affected by physical changes to the coast.[63] The Planning Policy Guidance ('PPG') further states that Coastal Change Management Areas should only be defined as such where rates of shoreline change are significant over the next 100 years.[64] However, they will not need to be so defined where the shoreline management policy is to hold or advance the line for the whole period covered by the plan.[65]

The PPG requires local planning authorities to demonstrate that they have considered shoreline management plans and that those plans should provide the primary source of evidence in defining any coastal change management area and inform land allocation within it.[66]

NATIONAL PARK AUTHORITIES

Introduction

20.19   There are nine National Parks in England and three in Wales. These are designated by Natural England or the Natural Resources Body for Wales before being confirmed by the Minister under the provisions of the National Parks and Access to the Countryside Act 1949 ('NPACA 1949').[67] Each of them is overseen by a National Park Authority.[68] National Park authorities are the local planning authorities for their parks.[69] Their role in adopting the development plan and supplementary planning policies is considered under the relevant chapters.

The National Park authorities therefore cover the Brecon Beacons, Dartmoor, Exmoor, the Lake District, the New Forest, the North York Moors, the Northumberland

---

[62]   DEFRA, 'Shoreline management plan guidance, Volume 2: Procedures' (March 2006), p 16.
[63]   NPPF, para 106.
[64]   Paragraph: 072 Reference ID: 7-072-20140306.
[65]   Paragraph: 072 Reference ID: 7-072-20140306.
[66]   Paragraph: 072 Reference ID: 7-072-20140306.
[67]   See ss 4a–7 in particular. There are two national parks in Scotland. There are currently no national parks in Northern Ireland, although they can be designated under the Nature Conservation and Amenity Lands (Northern Ireland) Order 1985, art 12.
[68]   Established under ss 63 and 64 of the Environment Act 1995 in England and Wales.
[69]   Town and Country Planning Act 1990, s 4A as inserted by the Environment Act 1995, s 67. For consideration of the designation criteria, see *Meyrick Estate Management Ltd v Secretary of State for the Environment, Food and Rural Affairs* [2007] EWCA Civ 53, [2007] Env LR 26 affirming [2005] EWHC 2618 (Admin), [2006] JPL 1049. On the handling of planning applications which fall partially outside of a national park, see *R v Northumberland National Park Authority ex p Secretary of State for Defence* (1999) 77 P&CR 120

National Park Authority, the Peak District National Park Authority, Pembrokeshire Coast, the South Downs, Snowdonia and the Yorkshire Dales. Whilst branding its area the Broads National Park, the Broads are not a national park and the Broads Authority is not a National Park Authority.[70] It is instead governed by the Norfolk and Suffolk Broads Act 1988.

Statutory purposes

20.20　The NPACA 1949 amended by the Environment Act 1995 sets out two statutory purposes for National Parks in England and Wales these are: (1) to conserve and enhance the natural beauty, wildlife and cultural heritage and (2) promote opportunities for the understanding and enjoyment of the special qualities of national parks by the public.[71] The NPACA 1949 further provides that in pursuing those purposes, a National Park Authority must 'seek to foster the economic and social well-being of local communities within the National Park and shall for that purpose co-operate with local authorities and public bodies whose functions include the promotion of economic or social development within the area of the National Park.'[72]

A 'relevant authority' must, in performing any of its functions in relation to land in a National Park, have regard to those purposes.[73] Relevant authorities include: any ministers of the Crown, any public body, any statutory undertaker and any person holding public office.[74] The statutory duty to have regard to the purposes of the national park therefore applies to the drawing up and application of planning policy by those bodies.

National Park management plans

20.21　A National Park Authority has a duty to 'prepare and publish a plan, to be known as a National Park management plan, which formulates its policy for the management of the relevant Park and for the carrying out of its functions in relation to that Park.'[75] It is required to review the plan at least every five years.[76]

Before a National Park Authority prepares a plan for the National Park (or alters or adds to it) they must consult with Natural England and take into account any observations made by them.[77] Further, when a National Park Authority is proposing to publish, adopt or review any plan it must give notice of the proposal (and send a copy of the plan and any proposed amendments) to every principal council whose

---

[70] For an unsuccessful challenge to that branding decision, see *R (on the application of Harris) v Broads Authority* [2016] EWHC 799 (Admin), [2017] 1 WLR 567.

[71] See s 5 of NPACA 1949 and s 61 of the Environment Act 1995. Where there is a conflict between these two purposes, s 11A(2) of NPACA 1949 provides that greater weight should be attached to the purpose of conserving and enhancing the natural beauty, wildlife and cultural heritage of the area comprised in the National Park.

[72] NPACA 1949, s 11A(1). Note that ss 37 and 38 of the Countryside Act 1968 (general duties as to the protection of interests of the countryside and the avoidance of pollution) also apply to National Park authorities by virtue of s 65 of the Environment Act 1995.

[73] NPACA 1949, s 11A(2).

[74] NPACA 1949, s 11A(3).

[75] Environment Act 1995, s 66(1).

[76] Environment Act 1995, s 66(4).

[77] NPACA 1949, s 9.

area is wholly or partly within the relevant Park and to Natural England or Natural Resources Wales (depending on whether the Park is in England or Wales) and to take into consideration any observations made by those bodies.[78]

When publishing, adopting or reviewing a plan, a national park authority for a park in Wales must also have regard to the 'state of natural resources report' which is published by Natural Resources Wales ('NRW') on the extent to which sustainable management of natural resources is taking place, biodiversity, trends and factors affecting the state of natural resources and any deficiencies in information.[79] It must also consider any area statement published by NRW on the state of an area that includes all or part of the park and NRW's proposals to address priorities, risks and opportunities.[80]

The National Park Authority must also send to the Secretary of State a copy of every plan, notice or report which it is required to publish under s 66 of the Environment Act 1995.[81]

The Broads Plan

20.22 The Broads is identified by the Norfolk and Suffolk Broads Act 1988.[82] The general duty of the Broads Authority is to manage the Broads for the purposes of conserving and enhancing the natural beauty, wildlife and cultural heritage of the Broads; promoting opportunities for the understanding and enjoyment of the special qualities of the Broads by the public; and protecting the interests of navigation.[83] It is the latter navigational responsibility which distinguishes the Broads regime from the National Park legislation.

In carrying out its functions, the Broads Authority must have regard to the national importance of the Broads as an area of natural beauty and one which affords opportunities for open-air recreation; the desirability of protecting its natural resources from damage; and the needs of agriculture and forestry and the economic and social interests of those who live or work in the Broads.[84]

The Broads Authority has prepared the Broads Plan which sets out its policy with respect to the exercise of its functions.[85] The plan must be reviewed at least once in every five years.[86]

As a result of any such review, if the Authority is of the opinion that it is appropriate to vary the Broads Plan, it shall do so in such manner as it thinks fit.[87] It must publish a draft of its proposals; and consult each of the appointing authorities (the local

---

[78] Environment Act 1995, s 66(7).
[79] Published under the Environment (Wales) Act 2016, s 8.
[80] Published under the Environment (Wales) Act 2016, s 11. The duty to consider these documents is under s 66(7A) of the Environment Act 1995.
[81] Environment Act 1995, s 66(8).
[82] On a deposited map subject to certain variations: Norfolk and Suffolk Broads Act 1988, s 2(3).
[83] Norfolk and Suffolk Broads Act 1988, s 2(1).
[84] Norfolk and Suffolk Broads Act 1988, s 2(4).
[85] Norfolk and Suffolk Broads Act 1988, s 3(1).
[86] Norfolk and Suffolk Broads Act 1988, s 3(2).
[87] Norfolk and Suffolk Broads Act 1988, s 3(3).

authorities who appoint members to it and the Secretary of State[88]), the internal drainage board for each internal drainage district which is wholly or partly within the Broads and such other bodies as appear to it to represent interests likely to be concerned.[89]

A new Broads Plan 2017 was adopted in March 2017. The draft plan had been accompanied by a sustainability appraisal, including an environmental report under the strategic environmental assessment regime, and a Habitats Regulations assessment.

The Authority is required to publish a report on the result of any review and any variations made.[90] A copy of any plan or variation has to be sent to the Secretary of State.[91]

AREA OF OUTSTANDING NATURAL BEAUTY MANAGEMENT PLANS

Introduction – AONBs

20.23   Originally, areas of outstanding natural beauty ('AONBs') were created under the National Parks and Access to the Countryside Act 1949, with the first AONB being designated in 1956 (the Gower Peninsula). However, they are now created under the Countryside and Rights of Way Act 2000. They are designated by Natural England (in England) and NRW (in Wales) where it appears to either of those bodies that the area in question is not a National Park but is 'of such outstanding natural beauty that it is desirable [that the legislative protections under Pt IV of the Countryside and Rights of Way Act 2000] should apply to it … for the purpose of conserving and enhancing the natural beauty of the area'.[92] The procedure for designation is contained within s 83 of the Countryside and Rights of Way Act 2000.

There are currently 33 AONBs in England, four in Wales and one (Wye Valley AONB) which straddles the two. There are eight AONBs in Northern Ireland, being designated under the Nature Conservation and Amenity Lands (Northern Ireland) Order 1985,[93] art 14.

In 'exercising or performing any functions in relation to, or so as to affect, land in an area of outstanding natural beauty' relevant authorities (Ministers of the Crown, public bodies, statutory undertakers and any person holding public office[94]) 'shall have regard to the purpose of conserving and enhancing the natural beauty of the area of outstanding natural beauty'.[95]

---

[88]   Norfolk and Suffolk Broads Act 1988, ss 1(3), 25(1).
[89]   Norfolk and Suffolk Broads Act 1988, s 3(5).
[90]   Norfolk and Suffolk Broads Act 1988, s 3(4).
[91]   Norfolk and Suffolk Broads Act 1988, s 3(6).
[92]   Countryside and Rights of Way Act 2000, s 82(1) in relation to Natural England and s 82(2) in relation to NRW.
[93]   NI 1985/170.
[94]   Countryside and Rights of Way Act 2000, s 85(2) and (3).
[95]   Countryside and Rights of Way Act 2000, s 85(1).

Conservation boards and the requirement to produce an AONB management plan

20.24   The Secretary of State (in England) and the Welsh Assembly Government have the power to establish 'conservation boards' to carry out functions in relation to AONBs (either already in existence or in conjunction with their designation).[96] They may also, by order, provide for the transfer of certain[97] local authority functions to the conservation boards or provide that such functions be carried out jointly so long as such an order has the purpose of conserving and enhancing the natural beauty of the AONB or of increasing the understanding and enjoyment by the public of the special qualities of the AONB.[98,99]

The statutory purposes and powers of conservation boards are set out in s 87 of the Countryside and Rights of Way Act 2000 which provides:

'(1) It is the duty of a conservation board, in the exercise of their functions, to have regard to—

(a) the purpose of conserving and enhancing the natural beauty of the area of outstanding natural beauty, and

(b) the purpose of increasing the understanding and enjoyment by the public of the special qualities of the area of outstanding natural beauty,

but if it appears to the board that there is a conflict between those purposes, they are to attach greater weight to the purpose mentioned in paragraph (a).'

Having regard to these purposes conservation boards should also seek to foster the economic and social well-being of local communities within the AONB. For these purposes they shall 'co-operate with local authorities and public bodies whose functions include the promotion of economic or social development' within the AONB.

The conservation board is required to have due regard to the needs of agriculture and forestry and to the economic and social interests of rural areas and to the protection against pollution of any water, whether on the surface or underground, which belongs to the EA, NRW or a water undertaker or which the Agency, the NRW or a water undertaker are authorised to take.[100]

A conservation board has powers to do anything which, in its opinion of the board, is calculated to facilitate, or is conducive or incidental to

'(a) the accomplishment of the purposes mentioned in subsection (1), or

(b) the carrying out any other function conferred on it ...'[101]

---

[96]   Countryside and Rights of Way Act 2000, s 86(1) and also s 88.

[97]   These exclude functions of local authorities under Pts III (development control), VII (enforcement) or XIII (Crown land) of the Town and Country Planning Act 1990 or the policy-making powers under Pt 2 or 6 (local development and Wales) of the Planning and Compulsory Purchase Act 2004 by virtue of s 86(3) of the Countryside and Rights of Way Act 2000.

[98]   Countryside and Rights of Way Act 2000, s 87(1).

[99]   The consultation provisions in s 86 of the Countryside and Rights of Way Act 2000 must be followed in making such an order.

[100]   Countryside Act 1968, ss 37, 38 respectively, applied by the Countryside and Rights of Way Act 2000, s 87(3).

[101]   Countryside and Rights of Way Act 2000, s 87(4 . Supplemental provisions on powers are in s 87(5)–(7) and Sch14.

Every conservation board is required by statute to prepare and publish an AONB management plan 'which formulates their policy for the management of their area of outstanding natural beauty and for the carrying out of their functions in relation to it' within two years from the date that they are established.[102]

Unless a conservation board has been established, each 'relevant local authority' in respect of an AONB is required to prepare and publish a management plan within three years either from 1 April 2001 or the date on which an area is designated as an AONB (whichever is the later).[103] They must review such plans ever five years.[104]

Where there was an AONB management plan in existence prior to 1 April 2001 the conservation board or local authority may, instead of preparing a new plan, review the existing plan, adopt it as reviewed and publish it.[105]

Where there was an AONB management plan prepared by a local authority and in existence prior to the establishment of a conservation board, that conservation board may adopt and publish that AONB management plan within six months of their establishment.[106] The first review of a plan adopted by this method must take place within three years from the date the plan was published.[107]

Publicity and consultation

20.25   Where the conservation board or relevant local authority is proposing to publish, adopt or review any AONB management plan it must give notice of the proposal and send a copy of the plan to Natural England (in England) and to NRW (in Wales).[108] Where a conservation board is proposing to publish, adopt or review an AONB management plan it must give notice (and send a copy of the plan) to every local authority whose area is wholly or partly comprised in the AONB. [109] The conservation body, or local authority (where relevant) must take into consideration the observations made by anybody who is required to be consulted in this way.[110]

If a plan is being reviewed, the conservation board or relevant local authority must decide whether it would be expedient to amend the plan, make any amendments that they consider appropriate, and publish a report on the review specifying any such amendments.[111]

In relation to an AONB in Wales where the conservation board or relevant local authority is proposing to publish, adopt or review a plan under s 89 of the Countryside and Rights of Way Act 2000 it must have regard to the state of natural resources

---

[102] Countryside and Rights of Way Act 2000, s 89(1). An AONB management plan can be material to the determination of a planning application, but its significance will depend upon the circumstances including what it adds: see *R (on the application of Higham) v Cornwall Council* [2015] EWHC 2191 (Admin), at para 58 to 75 per Supperstone J.
[103] Countryside and Rights of Way Act 2000, s 89(2).
[104] Countryside and Rights of Way Act 2000, s 89(7).
[105] Countryside and Rights of Way Act 2000, s 89(5).
[106] Countryside and Rights of Way Act 2000, s89(6).
[107] Countryside and Rights of Way Act 2000, s 89(8).
[108] Countryside and Rights of Way Act 2000, s 90(1)(a).
[109] Countryside and Rights of Way Act 2000, s 90(1)(a)(iii).
[110] Countryside and Rights of Way Act 2000, s 90(1)(c).
[111] Countryside and Rights of Way Act 2000, s 89(10).

report published under s 8 of the Environment (Wales) Act 2000 and also any area statement published under s 11 of the Environment (Wales) Act 2016 for an area that includes all or part of the AONB.

Conservation boards or relevant local authorities are required to send a copy of every plan, notice or report which they are required to publish under s 89 of the Countryside and Rights of Way Act 2000 to the Secretary of State (in England) or the Welsh Government.

CONSERVATION AREA MANAGEMENT PLANS

Management of conservation area

20.26   Local planning authorities have a duty under s 69(1) and (2) of the Planning (Listed Buildings and Conservation Areas) Act 1990 ('Listed Buildings Act 1990') to designate areas of special architectural or historic interest, the character or appearance of which it is desirable to preserve or enhance as conservation areas, and to review those designations:

'(1) Every local planning authority—

   (a)   shall from time to time determine which parts of their area are areas of special architectural or historic interest the character or appearance of which it is desirable to preserve or enhance, and

   (b)   shall designate those areas as conservation areas.'

After a conservation area has been designated the local planning authority is under a duty 'from time to time to formulate and publish proposals for the preservation and enhancement' of any conservation areas in their area.[112] The proposals shall be considered at 'a public meeting in the area to which they relate'.[113] The legislation is unclear whether 'the area' means one of the conservation areas, the local authority area or an area within the local authority area which contains the particular conservation area or areas. There might not be suitable rooms for public meetings in a particular conservation area but holding a meeting at the other end of the district might undermine the utility of the meeting. The duty to have regard to what is said at the meeting, which would arise in public law in any event, is written into the statute.[114]

The bare bones of s 71 of the Listed Buildings Act 1990 have been fleshed out by guidance, in particular, Historic England's *Conservation Area Designation, Appraisal and Management: Historic England Advice Note 1*.[115] Authorities are advised to produce a management plan, drawing on a character appraisal. The management plan may include the application of policy guidance, the council's proposals for the use of its statutory powers, and proposals for enhancement schemes, regeneration strategies, street and traffic management, tree, open space and infrastructure strategies, and an enforcement and remediation strategy.[116] The point is fairly made that:[117]

---

[112] Listed Buildings Act 1990, s 71(1).
[113] Listed Buildings Act 1990, s 71(2).
[114] Listed Buildings Act 1990, s 71(3).
[115] Part 2.
[116] See paras 33–37 in particular.
[117] At para 24. The involvement of utility companies, statutory undertakers and the highway authority is emphasised: para 26.

'There are major advantages, particularly in public support, in encouraging owners, residents' groups, amenity groups, businesses and community organisations to discuss the issues facing the area and how these might be addressed. Management plans, like appraisals, which are drawn up without effective consultation are likely to be misunderstood and ineffective.'

The proposals prepared under s 71 will not be part of the development plan nor be supplementary planning documents unless the local planning authority chooses to go through the adoption processes for those types of documents.[118] An authority is able to reconsider a conservation area plan made under s 71 at any time.[119]

LOCAL TRANSPORT PLANS

Introduction

20.27   This type of local plan falls under the competency of local transport authorities. In England these are county councils, unitary authorities and integrated transport authorities.[120] Responsibilities in Wales are taken by the county councils and county borough councils.[121]

By virtue of s 108 of the Transport Act 2000, local transport authorities are required to 'develop policies for the promotion and encouragement of safe, integrated, efficient and economic transport to, from and within their area'. They are also required to 'carry out their functions so as to implement those policies'.

In both England and Wales, transport authorities must develop local transport plans which contain these policies.[122] In Wales, local transport authorities are also required to develop policies which implement the Wales Transport Strategy in their area; these should also be included within the local transport plans.[123]

The definition of transport in this context includes that which is 'required to meet the needs of persons living or working in the authority's area, or visiting or travelling through that area' and 'the transport required for the transportation of freight'. It further includes 'facilities and services for pedestrians'.[124]

Content

20.28   In preparing their local transport plans, local transport authorities are required to have regard to guidance issued by the Secretary of State or, as the case may be, the National Assembly for Wales which concerns: the content of local

---

[118] Under Pt 2 of the Planning and Compulsory Purchase Act 2004. For discussion of the role of a particular management plan, see *R (TW Logistics Ltd) v Tendring District Council* [2013] EWCA Civ 9, [2013] 2 P & CR 9 affirming [2012] EWHC 1209 (Admin).
[119] *R (TW Logistics Ltd) v Tendring District Council* [2012] EWHC 1209 (Admin), at para 93 per Silber J.
[120] Established under s 77 of the Local Transport Act 2008 through the renaming of metropolitan county passenger transport authorities established under s 28(1) of the Local Government Act 1985.
[121] Transport Act 2000, s108(4).
[122] Transport Act 2000, s108(3) and (4).
[123] Transport Act 2000, s 108(3) and (3A).
[124] Transport Act 2000, s 108(2).

transport plans, the preparation of such plans, the alteration and replacement of such plans and the publication and making available of such plans.[125]

In preparing its transport policies, a local transport authority must also take into account government policy and have regard to any guidance issued by the Secretary of State under s 108(2ZB) with respect to the mitigation of or adaptation to climate change or otherwise with respect to the protection or improvement of the environment.[126]

Local transport authorities are also required under the Transport Act 2000 to have regard to the transport needs of disabled persons and of persons who are elderly or have mobility problems in developing and implementing their transport policies.[127]

Review and consultation – England

20.29   In England, local transport authorities are required to keep their local transport plans under review and alter them if they consider alterations appropriate.[128] In preparing their local transport plan, or keeping it under review, local transport authorities (other than integrated transport authorities or combined authorities) must consult the Secretary of State in relation to his/her functions as highway authority (by virtue of s 1 of the Highways Act 1980) or as traffic authority (by virtue of the Road Traffic Regulation Act 1984).[129] Further, if the local transport authority is a county council, it must consult the councils of the districts within that county.[130]

Where an integrated transport authority or combined authority is preparing its local transport plan or keeping it under review, it must consult:

(a)   each local traffic authority for any area within its area;

(b)   the Secretary of State in relation to its functions as highway authority and traffic authority; and

(c)   each county council and each district council within its area.[131]

Further, any transport authority must also consider such of the following as they consider appropriate:

(a)   operators of any network or station, or of any railway services, in their area;

(b)   operators or providers of other transport services in their area, or organisations appearing to the authority to be representative of the interests of such persons;

(c)   organisations appearing to the authority to be representative of the interests of users of transport services and facilities in their area;

(d)   other persons whom they consider appropriate.[132]

---

[125] Transport Act 2000, s 112(1).
[126] Transport Act 2000, s 108(2ZB).
[127] Transport Act 2000, s 112(2).
[128] Transport Act 2000, s 109(1).
[129] Transport Act 2000, s 109(2A)(a).
[130] Transport Act 2000, s 109(2A)(b).
[131] Transport Act 2000, s 109(2B).
[132] Transport Act 2000, s 109(2C).

Submission and approval

20.30   In Wales, local transport authorities must submit their local transport plans to the National Assembly for Wales for its approval.[133] The National Assembly for Wales may only approve a local transport plan if it considers that it is consistent with the Wales Transport Strategy and that the policies within the plan are adequate for the implementation of the Strategy in that area.[134] If the assembly refuses to approve the plan then it must give the local transport authority its reasons for refusal, and the authority must prepare another plan.[135]

Welsh transport authorities are further required to keep their local transport plans under review and alter them if they consider appropriate.[136] They are required to review the plan as soon as is practicable after the publication of the Wales Transport Strategy or any revision of it.[137] A local transport authority must replace their local transport plan every five years.[138]

LEE VALLEY PARK PLAN

Introduction

20.31   The Lee Valley Regional Park, running through parts of London, Essex and Hertfordshire, was established by the Lee Valley Regional Park Act 1966. The pre-amble described the Act as:

> 'An Act to establish the Lee Valley Regional Park Authority for the development, preservation and management for recreation, sport, entertainment and the enjoyment of leisure of an area adjoining the river Lee as a regional park …'

Section 12 of the Act sets out the general duty of the Park Authority which is:

> '… to develop, improve, preserve and manage or to procure or arrange for the development, improvement, preservation and management of the park as a place for the occupation of leisure, recreation, sport, games or amusements or any similar activity, for the provision of nature reserves and for the provision and enjoyment of entertainments of any kind.'

The plan

20.32   Section 14 of the Lee Valley Regional Park Act 1966 requires the Park Authority, after consultation with the local planning authorities[139] and appropriate statutory bodies, to prepare a plan 'showing proposals for the future use and development of the park, and shall from time to time review such proposals and shall

---

[133] Transport Act 2000, s 109A(1).
[134] Transport Act 2000, s 109A(4)(b).
[135] Transport Act 2000, s 109A(2).
[136] Transport Act 2000, s 109B(1).
[137] Transport Act 2000, s 109B(2).
[138] Transport Act 2000, s 109B(3).
[139] For the purposes of this section local planning authority is defined as those 'whose area or any part of whose area is situated within the park and includes any council to whom the functions of a local planning authority have been delegated' (Lee Valley Regional Park Act 1966, s14(11)).

consult with the appropriate statutory bodies and with the local planning authorities in relation to whose areas any amendment to such plan is proposed' (s 14 (1)).

The current regional park plan was adopted in April 2000. It is in two parts. Part one is entitled the Strategic Policy Framework and part two is the Statutory Plan of Proposals.

The status of the plan

20.33   The plan has a difficult relationship with the development plan. By s 14(2)(a):

> 'The local planning authorities shall from time to time include in their development plans or in any proposals for any alterations ... such part of the [Lee Valley Authority plan] or of any amendment to that plan as relates to their area.'

Copies of this plan and amendments must be sent by the authority to the local planning authorities and be kept available for public inspection. However, by s 14(2)(b), the inclusion of a part of the regional park plan in a local planning authority's development plan:

> 'shall not be treated as indicating the approval of the local planning authority to such plan ... nor shall such inclusion prejudice any representation to the Minister which the local planning authority may think fit to make thereon.'

At the time, development plans were prepared by local authorities but submitted to the Minister for approval.[140] The local planning authority therefore had to include the relevant parts in its draft plan but was able to ask the Minister to remove or alter them. How this relates to the current development plan system is a 'very difficult topic'.[141] The provision does not make the regional park plan automatically part of the development plan, nor is it entitled to be given the same weight.[142]

Under s 14(4) of the Lee Valley Regional Park Act 1966 a local planning authority is required to consult the Park Authority in relation to any application for planning permission for development where it appears that the development is likely to affect any part of the park. Once the local planning authority has considered the application it must give notice to the Authority of its determination. Similarly, local planning authorities shall notify the Park Authority of any proposal for development by the local planning authority which appears to it to affect any part of the Park.

Where the Park Authority is of the opinion that the determination of the local planning authority or the proposal for development by the local planning authority would materially conflict with the proposals in its plan then they may by notice (within 14 days or any longer period as agreed between the Park Authority and the local planning authority) to the local planning authority require it to refer the application or the proposal for development to the Minister for his consideration in order for him to decide whether to call in the application.[143]

---

[140] Town and Country Planning Act 1962, ss 4, 5.
[141] *R (on the application of Lee Valley Regional Park Authority) v Broxbourne Borough Council* [2015] EWHC 185 (Admin), at para 80 per Ouseley J.
[142] *Lee Valley*, at paras 81–84 per Ouseley J.
[143] Lee Valley Regional Park Act 1966, s.14(8).

AIR QUALITY MANAGEMENT AREAS ACTION PLANS

20.34 Local authorities are required to review 'from time to time' the current and projected air quality in their area. This review must include an assessment of whether air quality standards and objectives are being achieved or are likely to be achieved within the relevant period within their area.[144] Where objectives are not being achieved or are not likely to be achieved within the relevant period, the local authority is required to identify the parts of its area in which the standards are not likely to be achieved within the relevant period.[145] These are to be designated, by order, as 'air quality management areas' under s 83 of the Environment Act 1995 ('EA 1995').[146]

Where an order under s 83 of EA 1995 comes into an operation, the local authority who made that order must prepare a written action plan in pursuit of the achievement of air quality standards and objectives in the designated area.[147] The plan must include a statement of the time or times by or within which the local authority proposes to implement each of the proposed measures within the plan.[148] There is provision within EA 1995 for situations where county councils and district councils disagree over the content of an action plan.[149]

Where a local authority conducts an air quality review, an assessment under s 82 of EA 1995 or prepares an action plan or revision to an existing action plan, it must consult: the Secretary of State, the appropriate new Agency (defined as the EA or the Scottish Environment Protection Agency ('SEPA')[150]), the highway authority for any highway in the area to which the review, action plan or revision relates, every local authority whose area is contiguous to the authority's area, any county council in England whose area consists or includes the whole or any part of the authority's area, any National Park Authority for a National Park whose area consists of or includes the whole or any part of the authority's area, such public authorities exercising functions in, or in the vicinity of, the authority's area as the authority may consider appropriate, such bodies appearing to the authority to be representative of persons with business interests in the area to which the review or action plan relates as the authority may consider appropriate and such other bodies or persons as the authority considers appropriate.[151] Where a local authority's area falls within Greater London or is contiguous to it, it must also consult the Mayor of London.[152]

Where the local authority preparing an action plan is situated in Greater London, the Mayor is required (within the relevant period) to submit proposals to the authority for the exercise of Mayoral powers in pursuit of the achievement of air quality standards and objectives.[153] The Mayor must also submit a timetable for when he proposes to implement each of the proposals.[154] The eventual action plan must include a statement

---

[144] Environment Act 1995, s 82(2).
[145] Environment Act 1995, s 82(3).
[146] Environment Act 1995, s 83(1).
[147] Environment Act 1995, s 84(1).
[148] Environment Act 1995, s 84(3).
[149] Environment Act 1995, s 84(5), see also s 86 for the functions of county councils.
[150] Environment Act 1995, s 91.
[151] Environment Act 1995, Sch 11, para 1
[152] Environment Act 1995, Sch 11, para 1(2A), (2B).
[153] Environment Act 1995, s 86A(1).
[154] Environment Act 1995, s 86A(2).

of any Mayoral proposals and the time or times by which they are proposed to be implemented.[155]

Where a district council sits within the administrative area of a county council, the county council may make recommendations to a district council with respect to: an air quality review, any particular assessment under s 82 of EA 1995 or the preparation of any action plan or revision thereof.[156] A district council is required to take into account any such recommendations.[157] Where a district council is preparing an action plan, the county council is required to submit proposals to the district council of the exercise of county council powers in pursuit of the achievement of air quality standards and objectives.[158] It is also required to submit a statement of a timetable by which it proposes to implement each proposal.[159] The action plan should include a statement of the proposals and the timetable by which they are proposed to be implemented.[160]

If it appears to the Secretary of State that:

(a)   air quality standards or objectives are not being achieved or are not likely to be achieved within the relevant period within the area of a district council;

(b)   the county council has failed to discharge any duty imposed on it under or by virtue of Pt IV of EA 1995;

(c)   that the actions, or proposed actions, of the county council in purported compliance with the provisions of Pt IV of EA 1995 are inappropriate in all the circumstances of the case; or

(d)   that developments in science or technology, or material changes in circumstances have rendered inappropriate the actions or proposed actions of the county council in pursuance of Pt IV of EA 1995;

he may give directions to the county council.[161]

The Secretary of State may also give directions to county councils for areas where there are district councils requiring them to take such steps as he considers appropriate for the implementation of any UK obligations under the EU treaties or any international agreement to which the UK is a party so far as they relate to air quality.[162]

The EA reserves some further powers to the Secretary of State, Mayor of London and SEPA (in Scotland). It enables them to instigate:

(a)   a review of the current and the likely future air quality within the relevant period of air within the area of any local authority;

(b)   an assessment of whether air quality standards and objectives are being achieved or are likely to be achieved within the relevant period;

---

155   Environment Act 1995, s 86A(3).
156   Environment Act 1995, s 86(2).
157   Environment Act 1995, s 86(2).
158   Environment Act 1995, s 86(3).
159   Environment Act 1995, s 86(4).
160   Environment Act 1995, s 86(5).
161   Environment Act 1995, s 86(6).
162   Environment Act 1995, s 86(8).

(c)   an identification of any parts of the area of a local authority in which it appears that those standards or objectives are not likely to be achieved within the relevant period; and

(d)   an assessment of the respects in which it appears that air quality standards or objectives are not being achieved or are not likely to be achieved.[163] In certain circumstances the Secretary of State, the Mayor of London or SEPA may give directions to a local authority requiring it to take certain steps.[164] A local authority must comply with any such direction given to it.[165]

The Secretary of State may issue statutory guidance to local authorities pursuant to s 88 of EA 1995. In carrying out its functions under Pt IV of EA 1995, a local authority must have regard to any such guidance.[166]

DEFRA has issued statutory guidance entitled 'Local Air Quality Management, Policy Guidance (PG 16)' (April 2016). It relates to local authorities in England excluding those in London whose guidance is to be provided by the Mayor of London.[167] Guidance for London boroughs can be found in the London Local Air Quality Management ('LLAQM') Policy Guidance 2016 and the accompanying LLAQM Technical Guidance 2016.

A number of bodies have produced non-statutory guidance documents to assist local authorities in improving air quality. These include documents prepared by DEFRA, the Low Emissions Strategies Partnership[168], and Environmental Protection UK.[169]

---

[163] Environment Act 1995, s 85(1) and (2).
[164] Environment Act 1995, s 85(3)–(6).
[165] Environment Act 1995, s 85(7).
[166] Environment Act 1995, s 88(2).
[167] Para 1.5.
[168] A partnership of local authorities.
[169] These guidance documents can be found at: https://laqm.defra.gov.uk/action-planning/aqap-supporting-guidance.html.

Chapter 21

Representations and Examinations

21.1   There are many similarities in the ways in which representations are made and development plans examined across the different jurisdictions and types of plan. Whilst the relevant procedural rules for the type of plan will need to be considered there are some common matters of practice.[1] This chapter seeks to consider good practice from the perspective of plan making authorities, persons making representations and examiners. Procedural guidance has been published, the fullest advice being in the Planning Inspectorate's *Procedural Practice in the Examination of Local Plans*[2] for England.

The tests applied to determine the adequacy of plans do vary. As a matter of policy, 'sound' means different things in England, Wales and Northern Ireland. These tests are therefore addressed in the individual chapters.

THE EXAMINATION

21.2   Examinations contain a number of features which set the context for how they are conducted and the roles of the various participants:

- They consist of a review of the proposed plan by a person who is independent of the body who has prepared and (if different) will approve the plan.

- The review will apply various tests, laid down in statute or policy. Therefore the examiner will not be stating their own view of the appropriate planning approach but whether the plan maker's approach meets the tests.

- The first issue is whether the plan as submitted meets the tests. If so, modifications cannot be made simply because they would make the plan better.

- The examination will consider the plan on the basis of the issues which the examiner considers arise in it. These may include matters which have not been raised by representations. Unlike pre-2004 development plan inquiries, the statutory exercise is an examination into the plan not an inquiry to consider objections to it. Written questions from the examiner and hearings will be structured around the issues which the examiner identifies and not around the hearing of objections. The examiner is not confined to dealing with the issues raised in representations.

---

[1]   Local plan and local development plan examinations in England and Wales fall under the Tribunals and Inquiries Act 1992 (see Planning and Compulsory Purchase Act 2004, s 114) and instead dealt with by Ministers. The Law Commission has recommended abolishing this provision in Wales: *Planning law in Wales* (Law Com paper 233), para 6.41.
[2]   Planning Inspectorate, *Procedural Practice in the Examination of Local Plans* (June 2016), 4th edn, v.1.

- The examiner will though have to consider all the representations which have been made in accordance with the procedures and may be required to give objectors an oral hearing.

- The plan-making body and interested persons should have put in their evidence when the plan is submitted or consulted upon. In principle, further material should only be submitted at the examiner's request.

- The examination process is inherently flexible, but certain procedures are encouraged in guidance or have evolved in practice.

- The examination will culminate in a report making recommendations which might or might not be binding. In extremis, the recommendations may be for the withdrawal of the plan, but where possible they will be for modifications which enable the tests to be met. Usually the examination will be run as a collaborative process, with the examiner identifying problems and inviting suggested modifications as the examination goes on, rather than leaving their conclusions to the final report.

- The examination should be carried out in a way which should be, and be seen to be, open, transparent, fair and independent.

The plan-maker's evidence base

21.3   Most of the difficulties faced by plan-making authorities at examination arise from weaknesses in the evidence base. Since the examiner is concerned with whether the plan is justified according to the relevant tests, rather than whether it is right, much of the focus will be on whether there is evidence allowing the authority to write the plan it has done.

When an authority starts plan preparation it needs to consider what evidence it needs. In the first place this is derived from legal requirements and policy expectations, discussed elsewhere in this book. A checklist approach is useful.[3] The authority does also need to consider what arises on this particular plan. Some work might be particularly important, whilst other areas might not figure at all. The evidence needs to be sufficient and proportionate to the issues which arise on that document. For example, water supplies might be an important issue in some parts of the country, but not others. The depth of information will also vary. An examiner will want to know about the overall benefits and any harm of a particular proposal, along with whether there are any showstoppers which might prevent it coming forward at all. That does not require the depth of information required for a planning application: the interest will be in whether any problems can be overcome, not precisely how they will be dealt with.

Authorities will therefore have to consider what evidence to obtain. In particular they should take a view at an early stage whether consultants are required for particular matters, whether survey work is required and the budget and timescale for these exercises.

---

[3] There are rarely official lists of evidential requirements. The Local Plans Expert Group prepared a list for English local plans from the published sources.

21.4   *Representations and Examinations*

Representations made at earlier stages will add to the evidence base but may also identify deficiencies. Authorities should consider such points and decide whether more material is required. Authorities will also need to review their evidence themselves. This includes checking whether consultants' reports cover the necessary matters. It is useful for authorities to arrange an external check of their evidence base. Whilst an exhaustive review of the material will be disproportionate (and expensive), a short exercise should be able to identify any major issues which require correction before examination.

Dealing with problems in the evidence base which arise at examination is addressed below.

Representations on the submitted plan

21.4   Potential participants should involve themselves in the process at the earliest stage, seeking to influence the plan-makers from the outset. Since representations on the submission version are concerned with whether the plan meets the tests rather than the merits of its proposals, they should seek to persuade before the plan is written.

If those efforts are unsuccessful or the opportunity missed, then the focus will be on the representations at the submission stage. These should be directed to the tests which the examiner will be applying.

An objector will want to show:

- why the plan is unsound, fails to meet the basic conditions or is otherwise in breach of the examination tests; and then

- what the party's proposed modifications are and why they will cure the identified failing; or

- in an extreme case, why the failures cannot be cured and the plan should be withdrawn.

An objector who simply says, even persuasively, that their proposal is better will not succeed. They have to show that the plan as drafted would fail and that their proposals are the appropriate solution.

The examiner will be looking for a clear explanation of what parts of the plan are defective and why. This should be supported by references to the evidence base along with any further evidence which the party wishes to put in. That may include expert reports, legal opinions or submissions.

As with most planning appeals[4] there is no formal burden of proof on any particular party. The plan-maker is not required to prove that the plan meets the relevant tests, nor is an objector required to prove that it does not. That means there is no presumption that the submitted plan meets the tests[5] and the examiner is required to

---

[4]   The exception being 'legal' grounds of appeal under enforcement notices.

[5]   *Persimmon Homes (North East) Ltd v Blyth Valley Borough Council* [2008] EWCA Civ 861, [2009] JPL 335, at para 40 per Keene LJ.

reach a conclusion on the issues having considered the evidence provided. In practice of course, a person who advances a case should explain it and produce the evidence which is necessary and available to deal with it.

Preparation for the examination by the plan-making authority

21.5   A distinguishing feature of a development plan examination is that it involves one side who are permanently engaged in the process (the plan-making authority) and a large number of participants who are interested in individual topics and with different levels of activity. The plan-makers will have to deal with a very wide range of issues and a potentially huge number of critics. Those making representations need to be able to find the material relevant to their interests quickly and to organise their involvement in the examination.

Document handling

21.6   Documentation needs to be readily available and referenced. The examination has to be able to range over the material prepared by the plan-making authority, representations made and other relevant publications. Documents need to be available in hard copy and electronically.

The plan making authority[6] should have a dedicated webpage which then leads to all of the relevant material. It should be sufficiently well structured that a new visitor can quickly find documents and understand the stage to which they relate. New material must be posted promptly. This is particularly important during the examination itself when participants need to have immediate access to questions, agendas and letters from the examiner.

Paper copies of the documentation[7] will need to be prepared for the examiner, the authority's team and a library copy available for review, copying and judicious borrowing by participants and the public. Having physical copies of most of the documents available for inspection is a statutory requirement and they are often easier to work with.

The sheer volume of material means that a document-referencing system will have to be adopted and maintained. All participants should be encouraged to add the document references when citing material.

Programme officers

21.7   It has been common to employ a programme officer for examinations into local and strategic level plans. They will usually be an essential part of running an efficient examination into such plans. Programme officers are probably unnecessary for the smaller scale neighbourhood plan examinations or minor revisions to other development plans.

---

[6]   Or possibly for a neighbourhood development plan, the parish council or neighbourhood forum.
[7]   Except perhaps well-known national policy and guidance such as the National Planning Policy Framework or the Planning Practice Guidance.

21.8 *Representations and Examinations*

The programme officer will report to the examiner and will be independent of the plan-making authority even though in England and Wales they are appointed by that authority.[8] The appearance of independence is important: the officer should be seen as representing the examiner rather than the authority. Many programme officers are specialists, employed for individual examinations or provided by consultancies. Programme officers have sometimes been drawn from existing staff members of the authority, although this has tended to happen in planning appeals or call-in inquiries rather than development plan examinations. If so, the officers ought to be from outside the planning department.

A programme officer will provide administrative support to the examiner, organise the programme and be the main point of contact between the examiner and participants outside the hearings. They will be responsible for notifying participants of written questions and hearings in accordance with the examiner's decisions. In practice this makes them the conduit for debates on procedural and timetabling matters. Participants will normally try to sort these out with the programme officer before directly asking the examiner to rule. An examiner's decision on programming disputes, such as whether a party will be invited to a particular session, will often be relayed in a letter from the programme officer. Programme officers can also serve as an informal line of communication between the examiner and major participants. They will also maintain the hard copy of the library during the examination and ensure that documents are published on the website.

Consequently, the plan-making authority and major participants should establish and maintain good relations with the programme officer.

Venue for hearings

21.8 Any examination hearings should be held in a room which can conveniently seat the examiner and the hearing participants, along with the papers they need, and provide space for others to observe. A rectangular layout for the tables will often be best. To avoid excessive formality it is important that the examiner is sitting at the same level as the parties. The need will therefore be to provide adequate space for perhaps 10 parties at a single local development plan hearing. Ideally, there will be sufficient space for all the speakers for the parties to be sat at the table but there may be a need for the rest of their team to sit behind them. If there are several speakers for a party they may have to swap places during the hearing, but it is preferable for two speakers to be able to sit up front for each party.

The format therefore points to a large committee room in the council offices or a village hall sized space rather than a council chamber. If the examination is to run for a week or more there will need to be convenient rooms for the examiner, the programme officer and the examination library, the plan-making authority and for other parties. In practice wifi and copying facilities are important, given the range of materials which might be referred to. The plan-making authority and the examiner may need room to store papers overnight.[9]

---

[8] Programme officers for local development plans in Northern Ireland are appointed by the Planning Appeals Commission.

[9] Guidance on venues for examinations is given by the Planning Inspectorate in *Public Inquiries; Hearings and Examinations – Venue and Facility Requirements* (2013, updated 2017).

Preparation by the examiner

21.9   Key to the speedy and successful running of an examination is the examiner understanding the critical issues at an early stage. In such cases the written questions and any hearings can be focused on those matters and work can begin sooner on any further documentation or modifications. If a potential showstopper issue is identified early on then an exploratory meeting can be held to decide whether and how to proceed.

Such efficiency depends upon the examiner having, and taking, the opportunity to read into the examination once the papers are received. Sufficient time needs to be clear in the examiner's own diary for that reading and the subsequent drafting of written questions. The examiner's reading can be helped by the authority taking a proportionate approach to the evidence base which is submitted and using its documentation to draw out the important points. Major parties and any others who are professionally represented, should be as clear as possible in saying what are the major issues which arise on their points.

If the examiner is not able to identify early on what they consider to be the critical points then the risk is that the written questions will be generic and it only becomes apparent shortly before or at the hearing what the examination will turn on. An unnecessary number of hearings may be held and further work may have to follow those sessions.

Unless the examiner is already very familiar with the plan area,[10] it would be useful to do an unaccompanied drive around the area and briefly view some of the major sites from the highway before any hearings get underway.

Evidence

21.10   The parties' evidence ought to be complete when representations have been made on the draft document and any statutory response from the plan-preparing authority has been provided. It should not be assumed by the plan-maker that more material can be submitted. Explanatory reports from authorities, often called topic papers, should be provided at the consultation stage alongside the plan.[11] Even participants who are entitled to an oral hearing have no statutory right to submit further documents.

The examiner may, however, request documents or for further work to be done. It may also be that a legitimate answer to an examiner's question involves the provision of new or previously unproduced material.

Additionally, a party may ask the examiner for permission to put in more material. That may be a necessary plugging of gaps in the evidence. Whilst it is undesirable for the plan-maker to do so, since it can lead to further consultation being required or comments from other participants, there is no virtue in failing a plan because of a correctable error. Other parties can expect a little less sympathy: their case why the

---

[10]   The need for the examiner to independent would tend to preclude an examiner who lives in or close to the area or who has previously been employed by the local planning authority.

[11]   See Planning Inspectorate, *Procedural Practice in the Examination of Local Plans*, para 3.15.

plan fails the relevant tests should be deployed in the consultation period, and raising further points late harms rather than benefits the plan-making process.

More latitude does arise in respect of developments following the statutory consultation and submission to examination. Some changes in circumstances may need to be taken on board, for example, the grant of planning permission on an allocated site. Updating material can be useful.

Changes in planning circumstances during an examination

21.11   One issue which may arise is that underlying policy, figures or other circumstances change following the submission of the draft plan. Sometimes changes, for example, to household forecasts, may be significant. The response to changes should be pragmatic but supportive of proceeding with the plan without delay. New circumstances can be considered and, where both practical and necessary, accommodated in modifications. However, a plan should not be found to fail the relevant tests and be incapable of being modified to comply because of post-submission changes.[12] Any such modifications must be capable of being prepared (and if necessary, consulted upon) in the statutory examination timetable. This is reflective of the sensible approach which examiners will tend to take.

Constantly revising a submitted plan to catch up with the latest developments is likely to lead to delay and greater difficulty in keeping the submitted plan as a whole up to date. It is better to proceed with the submitted plan and any practical modifications and if necessary move to a swift partial review.

However, to keep a plan-making process manageable, and to ensure that it is able to reach a positive conclusion, there must be realism as to how far a submitted plan should try to keep up with a changing planning context.

EXAMINERS' WRITTEN QUESTIONS

21.12   The examination is the totality of the process from the receipt of the submitted plan to the delivery of the examiner's report.[13] Any hearings are only a part of the exercise. In a sense, this was always the case. Whilst the title has changed from an inquiry to an examination, local plan inquiries dealt with many objections by written representations.

Written questions are now an essential part of the examination procedure. Examiners should use them to probe the issues which arise on the particular plan and to seek any necessary further information. Questions should arise from the examiner's consideration of the plan, the supporting materials and the representations on it and be directed towards the examination tests. If the examiner is concerned by a matter which has not been raised, or not sufficiently explored, in the documents then this is best taken in the written questions. Generic questions,

---

[12]   This view was taken by the Local Plans Expert Group in *Report to the Communities Secretary and to the Minister of Housing and Planning* (March 2016), Appendix 10, para 66.

[13]   The expression 'examination in public' is still used for the hearing part of the scrutiny of a spatial development strategy.

which could be asked on any plan, should be avoided. Similarly, there may be live issues where the examiner considers that there is already sufficient information and no questions need to be put.

Responses and any additional material should be directed to answering the questions which have been put. This stage is not an opportunity to put in material more generally on the issues. That said, the questions will tend to go to the major areas of dispute and so participants will tend to be able to strengthen or re-emphasis their arguments and update the examiner in the course of legitimately responding to him or her.

Given the volume of material and the number of documents involved, representations ought to include the examination document references and page and paragraph numbers for any point they are referring to.

HEARINGS

21.13 Examination hearings are conducted by informal hearings. The original 2004 English scheme allowed for round table discussions, informal hearings and formal hearings. In practice though there was no difference between round tables and informal hearings as they would both be organised for particular issues with all of the interested parties who would be heard on that issue present.[14]

Hearings will take place on an issue by issue basis, rather than organised around particular participants.[15] The purpose of a hearing is two-fold: firstly to enable the examiner to properly understand and test the issues; and secondly to give a fair hearing to those entitled to one or who it is considered ought to be able to appear. Programming should be driven by the matters which the examiner wishes to hear more about. There is though only limited tension with the topics that objectors want to raise. Generally speaking, the major concerns raised in representations will tend to be the same topics that an examiner will have seen as important in any event. Whilst it is an examination of a plan rather than an inquiry into objections, the examiner will need to think whether there is something in apparently unpromising representations.

There is no standard structure to programming issues in hearings. Generally, it will make sense to deal with area-wide issues first, particularly where they raise substantial issues before moving onto individual sites or detailed development management policies. Legal compliance issues might fit towards the start, and monitoring and implementation of plans logically goes towards the end. However, it is important to only have hearings on issues which need an oral hearing. Similarly, an agenda which is set for a hearing ought to bring out the matters on which the examiner thinks that more needs to be said. Whilst there will be an element of ventilating opinion on the major points, it is more useful to focus on what the examiner sees as critical points and where more information is required. In an effort to reduce unnecessary hearings,

---

[14] Under the previous local plan inquiry system there would be a difference between the two formats. An informal hearing might be held into an objection with simply the particular objector and the local planning authority present, whilst a round table discussion (say on housing need) would involve a range of participants. Current informal hearings are therefore more like round table discussions.

[15] In contrast, local plan inquiries were into objections and so a session would be to hear a particular objector and then the same issues may be addressed with later objectors at other sessions.

the Local Plans Expert Group said that the use of standard issues and questions in examinations is not appropriate.[16]

The retention of the right of objectors to a hearing on local plans was supported by the Local Plans Expert Group:[17]

> 'The existence of the right to be heard in local planning does work well. Many of the important contributors will not be well-known or obvious candidates for an invitation, but oral representations by a small local developer, an ambitious landowner, a residents' group or simply the neighbours may turn out to be decisive. The Inspector still controls the agenda, so can decide who is able to speak at particular sessions and manages the hearings themselves. We do not consider that any difficulties have been caused by the right to be heard and it proves to be an important element in the acceptability of the process as a whole.'

Historically, any statutory right to require a hearing has been confined to objectors, who have made their representations in accordance with the rules. Legislation has not even given the right to the plan-making authority, although the bodies preparing neighbourhood plans will have a similar right.[18] In practice, of course, the plan-making authority will be the major participant in any hearing.

A person who supports the plan will not have a right to be heard,[19] the assumption being that their interests are promoted by the plan-making authority. Supporters have the following options to be heard:

(a)   Ask the examiner for permission to be heard. A request should draw attention to any matters that the plan making authority is not able to deal with, for example, requiring technical expertise or explaining the commitment to the project;

(b)   Appear as part of the plan-making authority's team. This does not require the examiner's agreement, but authorities are unlikely to agree except for strategic schemes;

(c)   Make representations seeking changes to details of the otherwise supportive policy. The person will then be an objector for the purpose of promoting those changes. However, examiners are wise to this old tactic and could seek to confine oral representations to the objection rather than the support. Protesting too much about the detail might undermine the merits of the main allocation.

Alternatively, they can just rely on their own written representations and offering any assistance to the plan making authority.

Objectors, who failed to make representations in sufficient time to have any entitlement to be heard, could ask to speak. However, the examination is meant to be the culmination of the process, and not an opportunity for new participants and

---

[16]   Local Plans Expert Group, *Report to the Communities Secretary and to the Minister of Housing and Planning*, para 9.35.

[17]   Local Plans Expert Group, *Report to the Communities Secretary and to the Minister of Housing and Planning*, Appendix 10, para 65.

[18]   Neighbourhood Planning Act 2017, s 7. See Chapter 10.

[19]   An examiner may have to hold a hearing in a neighbourhood plan examination to give someone 'a fair chance to put their case' (Town and Country Planning Act 1990, Sch 4B, para 9(1) and (2) as applied to neighbourhood plans by the Planning and Compulsory Purchase Act 2004, s 38C) but this is unlikely to be the case for a supporter.

new issues. Examiners will therefore tend to be wary of allowing late comers into the exercise.

The examiner may invite other persons to appear or to make written representations if they should have something important to contribute. Statutory consultees might be asked to attend, whether or not they had made representations on the particular topic.

In exercising any discretion whether to allow a person to appear, the examiner must act fairly. Fairness is not simply to the party who wishes to be heard, but to other actual and potential participants.

Practice at a hearing

21.14   The examiner should produce an agenda setting out the matters which he considers should be covered under the particular issue. This will include an 'any other matters' item at the end. The agenda should be circulated to the participants either shortly before or at the start of the hearing. Discussion should run through those matters in sequence as the number of speakers will mean that a less structured hearing will fail to follow through analysis of the issues.

The way to run the discussion of each matter will depend on the particular issues which arise. It may be useful for the parties to make their comments in sequence, or for the examiner to start with questions to one party. Varying which party starts off speaking on each matter will emphasise the even-handedness of the process. Whether or not they have started on a particular matter, the plan-making authority will need to be able to speak last, or almost last so that the examiner has their response to everything which has been said.

The ability of a planning officer or a consultant to express an expert view is important. The hearing format does benefit from lawyer involvement, as lawyers are trained to assemble material and to put an argument clearly and concisely. They are also able to deal with legal or procedural issues which may arise. Generally, parties (particularly authorities) benefit from a double act of a lawyer and a planning officer/expert. The Planning Inspectorate comments:[20]

> 'Lawyers have adapted well to the hearings procedure, sensing when best to contribute themselves and when to allow the specialist to comment.'

There is usually no formal presentation of evidence. Parties will either be asked to comment on particular issues or to answer questions put or relayed by the examiner. An advocate may manage the response, asking particular persons to comment, but usually a team can decide who is best to lead on a particular point without being formally called. Matters of professional opinion are best put by an expert, whilst legal, forensic or argumentative comments can be made by the advocate.

The hearing format can accommodate legal submissions, although ideally the nature of the arguments will have been indicated in advance by representations or skeletons. Such oral submissions would normally take the order taken in court, with one party

---

[20]   Planning Inspectorate, *Procedural Practice in the Examination of Local Plans*, para 5.11.

starting, others following and the initial party having a final say, rather than there being any more prolonged or unstructured debate.

Cross-examination

21.15   There may be circumstances in which the formal presentation of evidence followed by cross-examination and re-examination is required. The Inspectorate advises:[21]

> 'This will only happen in very exceptional instances where the Inspector is convinced that a formal approach is essential for adequate testing of the evidence. If any participant (including the LPA) wishes the Inspector to consider dealing with a particular subject using this formal approach, he/she must be prepared to make a strong case for this well in advance of the session. This is most likely to be appropriate where the Inspector considers that the issues raised are highly technical or complex. The final decision about whether a formal approach is appropriate rests with the Inspector. Participants will be informed in advance of the particular session that cross-examination is to be permitted on a particular subject and these are the only circumstances in which it will take place.'

The former formal hearings

21.16   The original Planning Policy Statement 12 ('PPS 12') in England included a mechanism for formal hearings, saying 'The existing traditional inquiry procedure has been adapted to form the formal hearing, where the inspector leads the process in an inquisitorial manner and advocates are permitted to be present to assist in the proper testing of evidence'.[22] As briefly expanded in Inspectorate guidance,[23] this was a mix of discussion and cross-examination.

As far as is known, the only formal hearing held under these procedures was into a proposed thermal treatment site at Clockhouse Brickworks, Capel, in the Surrey Waste Plan. The process ultimately adopted involved the production of statements in advance. Matters were considered on an issue by issue basis with some discussion, followed in rather ad-hoc fashion by cross-examination. Closing speeches were made at the end of the hearing. The session took three days, at least one day longer than would have been required in an informal hearing,[24] and failed to reach a lawful conclusion. Capel was the only site which was subsequently quashed in the High Court.[25]

Site visits

21.17   The examiner will need to see the various sites proposed and also have a good feel for the area. This can usually be done on an unaccompanied basis. Normally an examiner will be able to see sufficiently from a highway or other public land without the need to go on a proposed allocation or to view a potential scheme from

---

[21]   Planning Inspectorate, *Procedural Practice in the Examination of Local Plans*, para 5.12.

[22]   PPS 12, para D15 (2004).

[23]   Planning Inspectorate, *Development Plan Examinations – A Guide to Assessing the Soundness of Development Plan Documents* (2005), paras 2.3.5–2.3.7.

[24]   Just the view of Richard Harwood who appeared for the Council. Peter Village QC and James Strachan (now QC) appeared for the main objector, Capel Parish Council.

[25]   *Capel Parish Council v Surrey County Council* [2009] EWHC 350 (Admin), [2009] JPL 1302.

private land. The plan does not descend to the detail which is required to determine a planning application. Essentially therefore the examiner can decide when and how to carry out inspections. It may be thought useful to invite suggestions from participants on visits to undertake or particular views.

An examiner who goes onto private land ought to be accompanied by representatives of the particular sides involved in that particular issue. That will need prior arrangement. It is important that the examiner is not shown around simply by the plan-making authority.

The examiner's interim views

21.18   In legal form, an examination will be held, at the conclusion of which the examiner will report and the report then acted upon. That would leave any actions to address the examiner's conclusions to after the examination has concluded. Solutions would need to be identified by the examiner. It may take longer for problems to be resolved or for a fatally flawed plan to be put out of its misery.

The practice has therefore developed of an examiner indicating views as the examination proceeds. It is important that this is done on an informed basis and fairly. So unless an issue has been fully heard, any interim views should initially be provisional and invite representations from those interested. For example, on reading the plan documentation following submission the examiner might consider that the housing market evidence is fundamentally defective, rendering the plan unsound. Substantial time and resources may be wasted if he keeps this thought back until the formal report. Immediately writing to the authority failing the plan could though be based on an incomplete understanding and is likely to be seen to be unfair. The examiner should raise the issue promptly and invite representations before reaching a firm (if technically, interim) conclusion.

Such points should be raised in writing, in sufficient detail to be understood, and published on the examination website. Those who have made representations on the plan should be able to comment. The examiner may then decide to hold an early meeting, often called an exploratory meeting, to deal with the matter. This would be a formal session, in public, giving the plan making authority and other parties an opportunity to speak.

As the examination progresses the examiner may reach fairly definitive views having heard the full cases on a particular topic. There may be advantages in setting out those views as preliminary conclusions. If action ought to be taken in the plan process, such as the preparation of modifications, that can be put underway. A conclusion that an allocation is sound may allow the local planning authority to give sufficient weight to the policy to grant planning permission for the scheme. Whilst decision-makers may give indications in the course of hearings, any preliminary conclusions should be given or recorded in writing and published.

MODIFICATIONS DURING THE COURSE OF THE EXAMINATION

21.19   As the examination progresses the plan-making authority may decide that modifications should be made to the submitted plan. It may have changed its views or consider that the draft needs updating. Alternatively, the examiner may have suggested that the plan would fail without changes on particular points or the authority suspect that is the likely outcome of the examination. The examiner may propose modifications as the examination progresses or identify problems and invite the authority to bring forward changes. Objectors should set out any modifications which they seek.

The plan-making authority should have internal authorisations in place to enable proposed changes to be approved. Many could be dealt with at officer level, but others might require political consent.

Proposed modifications should be clearly referenced and set out in a schedule. Since the precise wording of the document may what be in issue, the text or map amendment proposed should be prepared. An indication of the nature of the change would not be enough.

There must be sufficient evidence to justify the modification, not merely to show the deficiencies in the submitted plan. For example, the implications of a change to the housing requirement must be understood before it is made: what effect does it have on the spatial strategy and what are its environmental consequences? Making a further allocation of land for development must be justified in the same way as any site included in the submitted plan. Hopefully there will be sufficient material in the authority's original evidence base, including any environmental report, and the material produced by the parties. There will though be situations when further evidence is required and potentially an addendum to an environmental report, to provide a proper basis for making the modification. If a plan requires modification to meet its tests but the work needed to decide what the modifications should be cannot be done in a reasonable time, then the examiner may need to recommend that the plan is withdrawn.

It is sensible to publish proposed modifications as they are proposed by the plan-making authority. Similarly, modifications which the examiner or a party suggest in writing should go on the examination website. A separate question arises as to whether there should be a non-statutory consultation on proposed modifications during the course of the examination. This will depend upon the significance of the changes, how far they have been ventilated in the course of the examination and the extent to which they might be of interest to persons who have not been actively engaged in the examination. As the Local Plans Expert Group said:[26]

> 'in general if a public body consults on proposals then it may make modifications in the light of that consultation without carrying out a further consultation exercise. The whole point of the original consultation is to see whether changes should be made. There will be situations where fairness or good decision making requires consultation on proposed modifications.'

An increase in the housing requirement is likely to require consultation since many people may wish to comment on the proposed housing figure and how it should be met. Conversely, a small amendment of a site specific policy might not need

---

[26] Local Plans Expert Group, *Report to the Communities Secretary and to the Minister of Housing and Planning,* Appendix 10, para 82.

consultation if it was discussed at a hearing involving anyone who in practice was interested. LPEG advised:[27]

> '… there should not be a presumption that all modifications will be consulted upon or that any consultation will be carried out in the same way, and for the same period, as the [statutory submission] consultation. Where consultation is appropriate, a much shorter period of two or three weeks may be sufficient, with the proposed change being publicised on the examination webpages and by email to participants. There will be occasions when the volume and complexity of the material requires a longer period or an entirely fresh issue is raised which may affect persons not already alert to the examination. In those circumstances a four week consultation and wider publicity may be needed. Any such consultation may take place during the course of the examination and will not necessarily be left until the close of the examination hearings.'

The report

21.20   The duties to give reasons are concerned with whether the plan complies with the requirements on it, such as soundness or the basic conditions, rather than with responding to the individual representations made.[28] A report will be read and understood in the context of the submitted plan and the evidence and representations which have been received. Consequently, there is no need to set out either the contents of the plan or of representations. However, the report does need to be readable and comprehensible to an interested reader. It ought to be possible to understand the thrust of the examiner's reasoning without having to cross-refer to other documents. The more detailed reasoning or its nuances might be more apparent by looking at what the examiner relies upon.

The structure of the report will tend to come out of the issues which the examiner identifies. Some may be based on the examination tests, for example, whether the duty to co-operate has been complied with. Other issues are likely to be topic based, for example, the retail strategy which is adopted or the acceptability of a major site.

---

[27]   Local Plans Expert Group, *Report to the Communities Secretary and to the Minister of Housing and Planning*, Appendix 10, para 83.

[28]   *Cooper Estates Strategic Land Ltd v Royal Tunbridge Wells Borough Council* [2017] EWHC 224 (Admin), at para 29 per Ouseley J.

Chapter 22

High Court Challenges

22.1 The exercise of public law powers is subject to the review of the courts. Since 6 April 2014, challenges to planning decisions in England and Wales have been heard in the Planning Court which is administered from the Administrative Court Office which is itself part of the Queen's Bench Division of the High Court.

This chapter concentrates on law and practice in England and Wales, before concluding with a short discussion of the less complicated procedures in Northern Ireland.

At common law public law challenges can be brought by judicial review unless statute provides for another form of proceedings or the point arises by way of a defence in other proceedings (a collateral challenge). Where statute provides another means of challenging the decision in the High Court, then claimants must take that route rather than judicial review.

Challenges to a number of planning policy documents discussed in this book are brought by way of particular statutory provisions. For example, challenges to the Wales Spatial Plan, a development plan document, a local development plan, the Mayor of London's spatial development strategy (or revisions or alterations thereto) must be brought pursuant to s 113 of the Planning and Compulsory Purchase Act 2004 ('PCPA 2004'). Challenges to a marine policy statement or marine plan my only be brought under s 62 of the Marine and Coastal Access Act 2009.

However, challenges to neighbourhood development plans may only be brought by way of judicial review under s 61N of the Town and Country Planning Act 1990. Similarly, s 13 of the Planning Act 2008 states that challenges to national policy statements may only be brought by judicial review and where there is no statutory provision for High Court proceedings then challenges must also be brought by way of judicial review, for example to planning practice guidance.[1]

This chapter deals with the legal grounds of challenge to planning policies, the Court's exercise of its powers, the rules for bringing a challenge and the practice of the Planning Court.

PUBLIC LAW GROUNDS OF REVIEW

22.2 The grounds on which decisions may be challenged before the High Court have essentially been derived from judicial decisions. The terminology therefore varies. It is

---

[1] See, for example, *R (on the application of West Berkshire DC and another) v Secretary of State for Communities and Local Government* [2016] EWCA Civ 441, [2016] 1 WLR 3923.

also possible for a single error of law to be characterised in numerous ways. However, there are three main categories of challenge: illegality, unreasonableness and natural justice. The grounds apply to judicial review claims as well as statutory challenges.

Illegality

22.3   This ground of challenge falls under two categories: error of law and error of fact.

If the decision maker makes an error of law in coming to the decision then it will be *ultra vires* as it will be outside of the decision-making power. Such errors may include misunderstanding legal powers and duties and a misinterpretation of policy. One example of this is the failure of a local planning authority to consider reasonable alternatives in an environmental report for a strategic environmental assessment ('SEA').[2] The misinterpretation of national policy when adopting a local development plan document may also lead to a successful legal challenge, as in *Gallagher Homes Ltd v Solihull MBC*.[3]

Traditionally errors of fact have been interpreted narrowly only allowing the Court to consider errors over a fact which is essential to the decision-maker's ability to exercise his power. However, more recently the Court has taken a broader approach to mistake of fact giving rise to unfairness. In *E v Secretary of State for the Home Department* the Court of Appeal held:[4]

> 'First, there must have been a mistake as to an existing fact, including a mistake as to the availability of evidence on a particular matter. Secondly, the fact or evidence must have been "established", in the sense that it was uncontentious and objectively verifiable. Thirdly, the appellant (or his advisers) must not been have been responsible for the mistake. Fourthly, the mistake must have played a material (not necessarily decisive) part in the tribunal's reasoning.'

Unreasonableness

22.4   This ground is also called irrationality. It is concerned with defects in which the way the decision was reached. Usually this is concerned with the exercise of discretion. Unreasonableness in its broad sense includes acting for an improper purpose; failing to take account of relevant considerations; taking account of immaterial considerations; opposing the policy of Parliament; and making a finding of fact on no evidence.

In its narrow sense, unreasonableness means making a decision which no reasonable decision maker could have come to. This is often known as '*Wednesbury* unreasonableness',[5] or sometimes as perversity. The premise of this narrow category

---

[2]   Environmental Assessment of Plans and Programmes Regulations 2004, SI 2004/1633, reg 12. See *Ashdown Forest Economic Development LLP v Secretary of State for Communities and Local Government* [2015] EWCA Civ 681, [2016] PTSR 78.

[3]   [2014] EWCA Civ 1610, [2015] JPL 713.

[4]   [2004] EWCA Civ 49, [2004] QB 1044, at para 66 per Carnwath LJ.

[5]   From Lord Greene MR's judgment in *Associated Provincial Picture Houses Ltd v Wednesbury Corpn* [1948] 1 KB 223 at 229. The categories of unlawfulness identified in *Wednesbury* do encompass the full range of legal error in the exercise of discretion and so *Wednesbury* unreasonableness also needs to be understood in a broad sense.

is that, having been unable to identify another specific error, the overall decision was not one that the decision-maker could have come to if they had been approaching their task properly. This narrow category is hard to demonstrate, particularly in planning cases where the courts are concerned not to be seen to be deciding the planning merits of a proposal.[6]

Natural justice

22.5   This ground is also known as procedural impropriety. It is concerned with errors in the way the decision was made and includes: failure to comply with procedural requirements, failure to give a fair hearing and appearance of bias.

With regards to the making of planning policy, certain procedural requirements are often set out in statute, rules or regulations. A failure to follow these procedures, or indeed a failure to give adequate or intelligible reasons may amount to a failure to comply with a procedural requirement. In *JJ Gallagher Ltd v Cherwell DC*[7] the High Court ruled that failing to give reasons for recommending the approval of a policy which included a restriction of built development in an area of Bicester was unlawful. The Court found in the alternative that the inspector was irrational in acting as he did without supplying reasons for so doing.[8]

Even where the procedural requirements of any statute, rules or regulations have been met, the decision-maker may have failed to give a party a fair opportunity to be heard, this may amount to a failure to give a fair hearing.

The test for the appearance of bias was set out by the House of Lords in *Porter v Magill*[9] it is whether a fair minded and informed observer would conclude that there was a real possibility of bias.

THE PLANNING COURT

22.6   From April 2014, the Planning Court became a specialist list within the Queen's Bench Division.[10] To what extent the running of the Planning Court is separate from the Administrative Court is a matter of opinion.[11] Planning Court claims are issued in the Administrative Court Office, either in the Royal Courts of Justice or one of its regional/national centres (Cardiff, Birmingham, Leeds or Manchester).[12] Such claims are stamped 'Planning Court' but as with cases in the Administrative Court cases are given a Crown Office number (CO/number/year) and an Administrative Court stamp. The Court is an evolution of the Planning Fast Track

---

[6]   See, for example, *IM Properties Development Ltd v Litchfield District Council* [2015] EWHC 2077 (Admin), [2015] PTSR 1536, at para 58 per Cranston J citing *Tesco Stores Ltd v Secretary of State for the Environment* [1995] 1 WLR 759, 780, per Lord Hoffmann.

[7]   [2016] EWHC 290 (Admin) (judgement upheld in Court of Appeal [2016] EWCA Civ 1007).

[8]   At para 69 per Patterson J.

[9]   [2001] UKHL 67, [2002] 2 AC 357.

[10]   CPR 54.22(1) inserted by the Civil Procedure (Amendment No 3) Rules 2014, SI 2014/610, r 3.

[11]   The Planning Court was at least to have its own letterhead (*Explanatory Memorandum to the Civil Procedure (Amendment No 3) Rules 2014* para 9.1) although the suggestion that its heraldic supporters should be a JCB digger and a Great Crested Newt was not taken up. The letterhead simply says 'Planning Court, Administrative Court Office'.

[12]   Practice Direction 54E, para 2.1.

which was introduced into the Administrative Court in July 2013. The aim of the Fast Track was to ensure that important planning cases were heard quickly before specialist judges.[13] A Liaison Judge is in charge of the Planning Court specialist list.[14] The first Planning Liaison Judge was Mr Justice Lindblom. He was followed by Mrs Justice Patterson. Following her tragically early death, the current Lead Judge is Mr Justice Holgate.

CPR 54.21(2) sets the jurisdiction of the Planning Court by defining a 'Planning Court claim' as:

'a judicial review or statutory challenge which:

(a)   involves any of the following matters:

   (i)   planning permission, other development consents, the enforcement of planning control and the enforcement of other statutory schemes;

   (ii)   applications under the Transport and Works Act 1992;

   (iii)   wayleaves;

   (iv)   highways and other rights of way;

   (v)   compulsory purchase orders;

   (vi)   village greens;

   (vii) European Union environmental legislation and domestic transpositions, including assessments for development consents, habitats, waste and pollution control;

   (viii)national, regional or other planning policy documents, statutory or otherwise; or

   (ix)   any other matter the judge appointed under rule 54.22(2) considers appropriate; and

(b)   has been issued or transferred to the Planning Court.'

The Planning Liaison Judge is able to categorise Planning Court claims as 'significant'.[15] This can be done by class as well as individually. According to the Practice Direction, significant Planning Court claims include claims which:[16]

'a)   relate to commercial, residential, or other developments which have significant economic impact either at a local level or beyond their immediate locality;

b)   raise important points of law;

c)   generate significant public interest; or

d)   by virtue of the volume or nature of technical material, are best dealt with by judges with significant experience of handling such matters.'

Parties may make representations as to whether a matter should be characterised as significant on issuing the claim or lodging an acknowledgment of service. To be

---

[13]   For a discussion of the evolution of the Planning Court proposals, see Richard Harwood QC, 'The High Court's New Planning Court' (February 2014).

[14]   CPR 54.22(2).

[15]   Practice Direction 54E, para 3.1. Categorisation involves a judicial decision, but whilst noted on the file, it is not contained in an order or routinely notified to the parties. It would be helpful if such notice was given.

[16]   Practice Direction 54E, para 3.2.

identified and dealt with promptly it is best if this is done in a separate document. One implication of being identified as significant is that the case should come before a specialist judge. The other consequence is that tight timescales apply to the handling of the case. By para 3.4 of the Practice Direction target timescales for hearing significant cases are:

'(a) applications for permission to apply for judicial review or planning statutory review are to be determined within three weeks of the expiry of the time limit for filing of the acknowledgment of service;

(b) oral renewals of applications for permission to apply for judicial review or planning statutory review are to be heard within one month of receipt of request for renewal;

(c) applications for permission under section 289 of the Town and Country Planning Act 1990 are to be determined within one month of issue;

(d) planning statutory reviews are to be heard within six months of issue; and

(e) judicial reviews are to be heard within ten weeks of the expiry of the period for the submission of detailed grounds by the defendant or any other party as provided in rule 54.14.'

This would mean that a judicial review substantive hearing should take place within six months of the claim being filed if permission to apply is granted by the Planning Court at a hearing.

The Planning Liaison Judge is able to direct the expedition of any Planning Court claim if it is necessary to deal with the case justly.[17]

The target timescales are subject to the overriding objective of the interests of justice but the parties should be prepared to meet them. In *London & Henley (Middle Brook Street) Ltd v Secretary of State for Communities and Local Government*[18] Mr Justice Lindblom agreed to the adjournment of a two-day substantive hearing of a compulsory purchase order challenge in 'truly exceptional circumstances' on the basis that it was effectively settled. He emphasised the loss of court time which had been caused by the late adjournment and took:[19]

'this opportunity to remind parties in proceedings such as these of the new targets for planning cases in the Administrative Court, which have been published on its website, and in particular the guidance given on listing. The guidance makes it clear that parties will be consulted before substantive hearings are listed, but – and this is important for parties to note – listing will respect the general timetable and targets. Dates may be imposed and counsel's availability will not be a reason for hearing a case significantly outside the target timetable.'

HIGH COURT CHALLENGES TO PLANNING POLICY DECISIONS

22.7 The lawfulness of decisions of public bodies is generally able to be challenged in the High Court. This will be by judicial review unless a statutory right of appeal or application to the Court is expressed to be exclusive or the Court considers that an alternative remedy is effective and convenient.[20]

---

17 Practice Direction 54E, para 3.6.
18 [2013] EWHC 4207 (Admin).
19 At para 17.
20 *R v Chief Constable of the Merseyside Police, ex p Calveley* [1986] 1 QB 424.

Challenges to planning policy decisions fall broadly into four categories:

(1) applications to the High Court under s 113 of PCPA 2004. These are:

    (a) challenges to a revision of a regional strategy;

    (b) challenges to the Wales Spatial Plan, National Development Framework for Wales (or revision thereof);

    (c) challenges to a development plan document (or revision thereof);

    (d) challenges to a local development plan (or revision thereof); and

    (e) challenges to a spatial development strategy (such as 'the London Plan') (or alteration or replacement thereof);

(2) applications to the High Court under s 62 of the Marine and Coastal Access Act 2009. These are:

    (a) challenges to a marine policy statement (or amendment thereof); and

    (b) challenges to a marine plan (or amendment thereof);

(3) judicial review applications where that procedure, in particular an exclusive time limit, is specified by statute:

    (a) under s 13 of the Planning Act 2008 – proceedings questioning a national policy statement or anything done or omitted to be done by the Secretary of State in the course of preparing such a statement;

    (b) under s 61N of the Town and Country Planning Act 1990 – challenges to neighbourhood development plans;

(4) other judicial review proceedings in the High Court.

Where a challenge falls within the remit of these statutory applications or judicial review under particular statutory provisions, the challenge may only be brought under that section and the validity of that policy document cannot be questioned in any other legal proceedings.[21]

Where the method of bringing proceedings is not prescribed by statute then proceedings should be brought by way of judicial review.

Amendments made in 2015 to legislation and the Civil Procedure Rules ('CPR') and Practice Directions have done much to standardise the different procedures. However, there are still important differences and it is crucial to identify which is the correct process to be used. This will also be important in ensuring that the correct court forms are used when issuing and defending a claim.

PROCEDURES FOR HIGH COURT CHALLENGES

22.8 Section 113 applications are made under the CPR 1998, Part 8. Judicial review proceedings are carried out under a highly modified form of Part 8 procedure under Part 54 CPR. The introduction of a permission stage in section 113 applications in October 2015 gave rise to new Part 8 proceedings for those challenges which are

---

[21] PCPA 2004, s113(2), Planning Act 2008, s 13 and Marine and Coastal Access Act 2009, s 62(3).

very similar to judicial review. Although the procedures for section 113 applications and judicial review applications are similar, there are important differences in the documentation required to commence proceedings, standing and time limits. These are therefore discussed first before the common processes for conducting the cases are dealt with.

There remains no permission stage in relation to challenges brought under s 62 of the Marine and Coastal Access Act 2009 challenges and therefore the procedures remain very different. As such, they are discussed entirely separately within this chapter.

APPLICATION TO THE HIGH COURT UNDER S 113

22.9   Challenges to the Wales Spatial Plan, the National Development Framework for Wales, a strategic development plan, a development plan document, a local development plan, the Mayor of London's spatial development strategy (or revisions or alterations thereto) must be brought pursuant to s 113 of PCPA 2004.

Grounds of challenge

22.10   A section 113 application is made on the grounds that:

(a)   the document is not within the appropriate power; and

(b)   a procedural requirement has not been complied with.[22]

The appropriate powers are listed within s113 as those under:

(a)   Pt 5 of the Local Democracy, Economic Development and Construction Act 2009 in the case of a revision of the regional strategy;

(b)   s 60 of the PCPA 2004 in the case of the Wales Spatial Plan, National Development Framework for Wales or any revision of it;

(c)   Pt 2 of PCPA 2004 in the case of a development plan document or any revision of it;

(d)   ss 62–78 of PCPA 2004 in the case of a local development plan or any revision of it;

(e)   ss 334–343 of the Greater London Authority Act 1999 in the case of the London Spatial Development Strategy or any alteration or replacement of it.[23]

Section 113 further states that a procedural requirement 'is a requirement under the appropriate power or contained within regulations or an order made under that power which relates to the adoption, publication or approval of a relevant document'.[24]

It is considered that the tests to be applied to a section 113 challenge are the same as those in judicial review. These include errors of law, unreasonableness in acting without evidence, taking into account irrelevant considerations or failing to take into account relevant considerations, failure to comply with the statutory procedures or failing to comply with the principles of natural justice.

---

[22]   PCPA 2004, s 113(3).
[23]   PCPA 2004, s 113(9).
[24]   PCPA 2004, s 113(10).

In the interim relief hearing of *Lisle-Mainwaring v Royal Borough of Kensington and Chelsea*[25] Cranston J appeared to be of the view, albeit expressed in *obiter* terms, that the ordinary grounds of judicial review did not apply to s 113.[26] However, the scope of 113 was dealt with in the ratio of Lang J's judgment in the substantive hearing of the section 113 challenge.[27] She held that the scope of section 113 challenges was the same as that which applied to ss 287 and 288 of the Town and Country Planning Act 1990, ie that 'the decision maker may be found to have acted outside his powers … not only by reference to the powers/duties and requirements expressly set out in the statute, but also because he has acted irrationally, or taken into account irrelevant, of failed to take into account relevant, considerations, applying conventional judicial review principles'.[28]

The exclusive nature of s 113 and exceptions

22.11   Section 113(2) of PCPA 2004 provides:

> 'A relevant document must not be questioned in any legal proceedings except in so far as is provided by the following provisions of this section.'

Challenges to those documents have to be brought by a section 113 application at the end of the plan-making process. In some cases it might be thought desirable, or even essential, that a challenge is brought to the plan making at an earlier stage.

In *Manydown Co Ltd v Basingstoke and Deane BC*[29] the High Court considered a challenge brought by way of judicial review to a pre-submission draft of a core strategy. As a preliminary issue the Court had to decide whether it had jurisdiction to hear the claim, or whether it should have been brought under s 113. Lindblom J concluded:

(a)   as with any statutory ouster of the Court's jurisdiction, s 113 should be interpreted strictly in accordance with the words chosen by Parliament;[30]

(b)   under the provisions of s 113(1)(c), (2), (3), (4) and (11)(c) it is a development plan document which may be questioned only upon its adoption (within six weeks of that date) not some prior step of the local planning authority and therefore it could not catch a decision taken earlier than the plan's adoption;[31]

(c)   in any event, the pre-submission draft of a core strategy does not qualify as a development plan document within s 113(1).[32]

The Court therefore concluded that the claim was not ousted by the operation of s 113 and could proceed by way of judicial review. Lindblom J went on to make the following observation:

> '87.   The conclusion that these proceedings are not ousted by s.113(2) seems both legally right and pragmatic. In a case such as this, an early and prompt claim for judicial

---

[25]   [2015] EWHC 1814 (Admin).
[26]   See paras 17–19.
[27]   [2015] EWHC 2105 (Admin).
[28]   At para 22
[29]   [2012] EWHC 977 (Admin), [2012] JPL 1188.
[30]   At para 81.
[31]   At paras 83 and 84.
[32]   At para 86.

review makes it possible to test the lawfulness of decisions taken in the run-up to a statutory process, saving much time and expense—including the expense of public money—that might otherwise be wasted. In principle, it cannot be wrong to tackle errors that are properly amenable to judicial review, when otherwise they would have to await the adoption of the plan before the court can put them right. Improper challenges—including those caught by the ouster provision in s.113(2) —can always be filtered out at the permission stage.'

The very early stage of plan preparation means that *Manydown* was correctly decided as there was no development plan document (in draft or adopted) to be protected by s 113(2). The wider comments about being able to challenge preparatory acts by judicial review are more difficult. Almost all legal defects in local plans will be traced back to an event which precedes the act of adoption, such as the Inspector's report or the SEA environmental report. Since authorities have to follow the recommendations made to them, adoption is rarely other than a formal act. If any preparatory act could be subject to judicial review then the statutory ouster would give no protection to an emerging plan.

In *R (on the application of IM Properties Development Ltd) v Lichfield District Council* judicial review of the decision of the local planning authority to endorse modifications during the course of the local plan examination was prohibited by the s 113(2) ouster.[33]

22.12   There are circumstances where a challenge might be contemplated to the Inspector's report in advance of adoption. One is when it is the local planning authority (or its supporters) who disagree with the report and wish to challenge its lawfulness. If an Inspector finds a plan unsound and recommends that it is not adopted or adopted subject to modifications which the authority opposes, then the local planning authority has few alternatives. Unless it persuades the Minister to intervene, it has to do what the Inspector says. Judicial review proceedings by the local planning authority in support of the submitted plan would not be questioning the validity of the plans and so would not fall foul of s 113(2).[34]

A further consequence of the s 113(2) ouster is that the lawfulness of an adopted document cannot be questioned at a later time. Once the challenge period has passed without s 113 proceedings being brought or any such claim finally fails, no further claim can be brought against it by judicial review or otherwise. It is also not possible to contend in a planning appeal or a later plan making process that the adopted document is unlawful.

Alternative remedies

22.13   The general rule is that a judicial review ought not to be brought where the potential claimant has an alternative remedy. The existence of an alternative remedy may thwart a challenge brought prematurely. In *R (on the application of IM Properties Development Ltd) v Litchfield DC*[35] the claimant brought an application for judicial

---

33   [2014] EWHC 2440 (Admin), [2014] PTSR 1484, at para 70 to 74 per Patterson J.

34   For example, the local planning authority could bring judicial review of the examining Inspector's interim finding that the duty to co-operate had not been complied with: *R (on the application of St Albans City and District Council) v Secretary of State for Communities and Local Government* [2017] EWHC 1751 (Admin).

35   [2014] EWHC 2440 (Admin), [2014] PTSR 1484.

review against the defendant's decision to endorse modifications to a draft local plan strategy. Mrs Justice Patterson found that the Court did not have jurisdiction to hear the claim under s 113 but also went on to state:

'114 The fact of the pending further examination is the answer to the claimant's complaints. The claimant will have ample opportunity at that hearing to raise all of these issues, if it thinks it is appropriate to do so, and to have the inspector's findings on them. I do not find that there has been any lack of fairness in the process thus far which seems to me to have been carried out in a thorough manner on the part of the local authority. However, the claimant is not deprived of any opportunity to make representations on the main modifications as the examination process is ongoing. In truth, the claimant has an alternative remedy for its complaints.'

Challenges to revisions of policy documents

22.14   When challenging revisions to a policy document, it will be necessary to consider whether the factor which is the subject of the challenge was in fact included in the original document and therefore whether a challenge should have been brought when the original document was published. This was indicated in *London Borough of Islington v The Mayor of London*[36] where, as part of the challenge, the claimants criticised the treatment of the entirety of London as a single housing market area in their challenge to the Mayor's publication of 'Revised Early Minor Alterations' ('REMA') to the London Plan. This was rejected by the Court which noted: 'It is apparent that London was identified as a single housing market in the London Plan published in 2011. Thus, if the Claimants had valid grounds for challenging this approach, they should have done so when the London Plan was published. They are now well outside the time limits prescribed by section 113 PCPA 2004 for bringing any such challenge'.[37]

Standing to bring section 113 applications

22.15   A challenge may only be brought by a 'person aggrieved'.[38] This is the same test for standing which applies to other statutory challenges under ss 287 and 288 of the Town and Country Planning Act 1990. It also applies to challenges brought under s 62 of the Marine and Coastal Access Act 2009. The test has been treated widely, though not as widely as the 'sufficient interest' test in judicial review. The reasons for the wide approach were set out by Lord Hope of Craighead DPSC in *Walton v Scottish Ministers*:[39]

'152 I think, with respect, that this is to take too narrow a view of the situations in which it is permissible for an individual to challenge a scheme or order on grounds relating to the protection of the environment. An individual may be personally affected in his private interests by the environmental issues to which an application for planning permission may give rise. Noise and disturbance to the visual amenity of his property are some obvious examples. But some environmental issues that can properly be raised by an individual are not of that character. Take, for example, the risk that a route used by an osprey as it moves to and from a favourite fishing loch will be impeded by the proposed erection across it of a cluster of wind turbines. Does the fact that this proposal cannot reasonably be said to affect any individual's

---

36   [2014] EWHC 751 (Admin)
37   At para 47 per Lang J.
38   PCPA 2004, s 113(3).
39   [2012] UKSC 44, [2013] PTSR 51.

property rights or interests mean that it is not open to an individual to challenge the proposed development on this ground? That would seem to be contrary to the purpose of environmental law, which proceeds on the basis that the quality of the natural environment is of legitimate concern to everyone. The osprey has no means of taking that step on its own behalf, any more than any other wild creature. If its interests are to be protected someone has to be allowed to speak up on its behalf.

153 Of course, this must not be seen as an invitation to the busybody to question the validity of a scheme or order under the statute just because he objects to the scheme of the development. Individuals who wish to do this on environmental grounds will have to demonstrate that they have a genuine interest in the aspects of the environment that they seek to protect, and that they have sufficient knowledge of the subject to qualify them to act in the public interest in what is, in essence, a representative capacity. …'

The majority of cases dealing with the 'person aggrieved' test have done so in the context of applications made under s 288 of the Town and Country Planning Act 1990. However, the issue did arise under s 113 in *Zurich Assurance Ltd v Winchester City Council*[40] where the Council argued that the claimant was not a 'person aggrieved' as it did not, itself, make representations at the examination of the impugned core strategy but instead instructed agents to do so. The agents did not make clear at the time that their representations were being made on behalf of the claimant. Sales J stated:

'82 The test to identify a "person aggrieved" (which is a concept with a lengthy history in planning legislation) is open-textured. Factors relevant to the assessment whether a person who objects to a planning decision qualifies as a "person aggrieved" by that decision include the nature of the decision and the directness of its impact on him, the grounds on which he claims to be aggrieved, whether he had a fair opportunity to participate in the relevant decision-making process to raise such grounds of objection and whether he did in fact make use of such opportunity to make those objections before the decision was taken. The approach to be adopted was *explained by the Court of Appeal in Ashton v Secretary of State for Communities and Local Government [2010] EWCA Civ 600*, at [53].

83 As the Lord President (Lord Rodger) explained in *Lardner v Renfrew DC*, 1997 SC 104 (Inner House), at 108:

"The particular circumstances of any case require to be considered and the question must always be whether the appellant can properly be said to be aggrieved by what has happened. In deciding that question it will usually be a relevant factor that, through no fault of the council, the appellant has failed to state his objection at the appropriate stage of the procedure laid down by Parliament since that procedure is designed to allow objections and problems to be aired and a decision then to be reached by the council. The nature of the grounds on which the appellant claims to be aggrieved may also be relevant. We express no view on the merits of those advanced by the appellant, but we observe that they all relate to matters which he could have put, or endeavoured to put, to the council or to the reporter at the inquiry. Had he done so, his objections could have been considered at the due time. Instead of that, the appellant now seeks to have these issues reopened after the decision has been taken in accordance with the prescribed procedure. In these circumstances, having regard both to the nature of his interest in the site and to his failure to take the necessary steps to state these objections at the due time, the appellant cannot properly be regarded as 'a person aggrieved' in terms of [the relevant statutory provision]."

---

[40]   [2014] EWHC 758 (Admin).

84   These observations have particular force in the present context. The Core Strategy is a plan document which operates at a high level of abstraction, with general impact across the whole of WCC's area. It is intended to provide a settled framework within which other, lower order development plan documents can be drawn up. An elaborate procedure of consultation and examination in public has been adopted to ensure that all relevant views on a core strategy document are brought into account and considered and weighed together, first by the plan-maker (here, WCC) and then by the Inspector: compare Ashton at [55]-[56]. The effectiveness and fairness of that system and the overall efficiency of the plan making process would be undermined if persons in the relevant area could come forward with new points raised only after a core strategy has been adopted, and seek to compel review of the core strategy on the basis of those new points. A person who has stood aside from the plan-making process but later seeks to challenge a core strategy by way of application under section 113 to raise objections which could have been raised in the course of that process will not usually be able to show that he is "a person aggrieved" for the purposes of that provision.'

Sales J concluded that there was sufficient participation by Zurich in the plan-making process, combined with their interests as a major landholder affected by the policies in the core strategy to justify the conclusion that Zurich was a person aggrieved under s 113.[41]

Cases in the context of s 288 of the Town and Country Planning Act 1990 have determined that persons aggrieved will include:

(i)   those who made representations against the decision which was finally taken;[42]

(ii)   those who would have made representations had they been aware of the process, usually being mislead or not being informed by error;[43]

(iii)   someone whose interests have been prejudicially affected by the decision, whether they had taken part in the process or not.[44]

However, where a person makes an objection to a scheme but later withdraws that objection they may fail to satisfy the person aggrieved test.[45]

Third party pressure groups have been allowed to challenge planning decisions.[46] Broadly speaking, a claimant must show that they took part in the appeal proceedings, were not told about the appeal and would have taken part if they had known, or are directly affected by the proposal.[47] A failure to take an opportunity to make representations may mean that a person does not have standing.[48] In *Ashton* a person who did not object but was a member of the local residents' company which

---

[41]   At para 90.
[42]   For example, *Turner v Secretary of State for the Environment* (1974) 28 P&CR 123; *Times Investments Ltd; and Walton v Scottish Ministers*, at paras 86–88 per Lord Reed JSC.
[43]   For example, *Wilson v Secretary of State for the Environment* [1973] 1 WLR 1083 where an inaccurate notice misled the public about which land was affected by a proposal.
[44]   *Ashton v Secretary of State for Communities and Local Government* [2010] EWCA Civ 600, [2010] JPL 1645.
[45]   *JB Trustees Ltd v Secretary of State for Communities and Local Government* [2013] EWHC 3555 (Admin), [2014] JPL 656.
[46]   Eg, *Save Britain's Heritage v Secretary of State for the Environment* [1991] 2 All ER 10.
[47]   See *Walton v Scottish Ministers* [2012] UKSC 44, [2013] PTSR 51; *Ashton v Secretary of State for Communities and Local Government* [2010] EWCA Civ 600, [2010] JPL 1645 and the Aarhus Convention on Access to Environmental Justice, Art 9.
[48]   *Lardner v Renfrewshire District Council* [1997] SCLR 454, at 457 per Lord Rodger (Lord President).

appeared at the inquiry (having asked them to make representations on his behalf) and who attended part of inquiry did not have standing.[49] Two claimants were found not to have standing in *Crawford-Brunt v Secretary of State for Communities and Local Government*.[50] Whilst living in separate properties adjoining the site, neither had made representations on the planning appeal. However one of the claimants had made representations on the planning application and the judgment overlooked that those representations would have been sent to the Inspectorate by the local planning authority with the appeal questionnaire and would have been considered and rejected by the inspector.[51] Representations on a planning application are also representations on any appeal which follows and in respect of that claimant, the decision is in error.

Person aggrieved status has also been refused in a number of cases where claimants become interested at the time of the decision and not before.[52] Care may need to be taken to identify the claimant. In *Eco-Energy (GB) Ltd v First Secretary of State* a consortium called Eco-Energy Group had applied for planning permission and appealed to the Minister but the High Court proceedings were brought by a company related to a party in the consortium. They were not a person aggrieved, although they might have been if an option in the land had been transferred to them. Whilst an interest in land can be transferred, enabling a person to apply to the High Court, an interest in a planning application or the right to bring proceedings as a person aggrieved cannot be transferred.[53] In another unusual case, an objector who withdrew their objections, believing that planning permission would give them a ransom strip, did not have standing when that turned out not to be the case.[54]

It is considered that these principles could equally apply to those bringing applications under s113. However, as was stated by Sales J in *Zurich Assurance* it will be necessary to consider all of the circumstances in order to conclude whether any particular person is a person aggrieved in the context of a particular challenge.

Standing to bring judicial review proceedings

22.16 A person may bring judicial review proceedings if they have 'sufficient interest' in the matter. A wide approach to standing was explained by Sedley J in *R v Somerset County Council ex p Dixon*:[55]

> 'Public law is not at base about rights, even though abuses of power may and often do invade private rights; it is about wrongs—that is to say misuses of public power; and the

---

[49] *Ashton*, at para 54 per Pill LJ.

[50] [2015] EWHC 3580 (Admin), [2016] JPL 573.

[51] See the Inspectorate's *Guide to taking part in planning, listed building and conservation area consent appeals proceeding by an inquiry – England* (April 2016), para 5.1 which promises that these will be 'fully considered by the Inspector who decides the appeal'. Third parties are only encouraged to send comments on the appeal if they have something to add: 'If you did not write at application stage, or you did write and now have something new to say, you can send us your representations about the appeal' (para 5.2).

[52] In *Morbaine Ltd v First Secretary of State* [2004] EHWC 1708 (Admin), [2005] JPL 377 one claimant was a rival developer who had taken no part in the appeal process and so did not have standing.

[53] *Eco-Energy* at 21 per Buxton LJ.

[54] *JB Trustees Ltd v Secretary of State for Communities and Local Government,* at paras 45, 46 per Lord Lindblom. An objector who withdrew on the basis that a particular condition would be included or obligation made might be a person aggrieved if that event does not happen.

[55] [1997] JPL 1030 at 1037.

courts have always been alive to the fact that a person or organisation with no particular stake in the issue or the outcome may, without in any sense being a mere meddler, wish and be well placed to call the attention of the court to an apparent misuse of public power. If an arguable case of such misuse can be made out on an application for leave, the court's only concern is to ensure that it is not being done for an ill motive. It is if, on a substantive hearing, the abuse of power is made out that everything relevant to the applicant's standing will be weighed up, whether with regard to the grant or simply to the form of relief.'

Once a person has standing to bring proceedings then they may challenge the decision on any grounds if they are issues which they do not have a personal interest in.[56] However a lack of interest in the particular issue might affect whether relief was refused because it was 'highly likely that the outcome for the applicant would not have been substantially different'[57] and in the exercise of the Court's discretion to quash.

The commencement of section 113 proceedings

22.17   The procedure is set out in CPR Part 8 and Practice Direction 8C. The Planning Court's Part 8 claim form[58] will identify the decision to be challenged and set out the grounds of challenge (or have those grounds appended to it). The claim form and grounds should be marked 'Planning Court'.[59]

With or on the claim form the claimant must give:[60]

'(a)   the name and address of any person that the claimant considers must be served in accordance with paragraph 4.1;

(b)   that the claimant is requesting permission to proceed with a claim for planning statutory review;

(c)   a detailed statement of the claimant's grounds for bringing the claim for planning statutory review;

(d)   a statement of the facts relied on;

(e)   any application for directions; and

(f)   the remedy being claimed (including any interim remedy).'

Usually the claim form will be accompanied by details of claim which set out the facts and grounds of the application. A claim which lacks any grounds capable of being within the statutory grounds of challenge and complying with the CPR will

---

[56]   *R (on the application of Kides) v South Cambridgeshire District Council* [2002] EWCA Civ 1370, [2003] 1 P&CR 19, applied to s 288 in *Ashton v Secretary of State for Communities and Local Government* [2010] EWCA Civ 600, [2010] JPL 1645, at para 37 per Pill LJ.

[57]   Senior Courts Act 1981, s 31(2A).

[58]   Form N208PC. If the application made using the wrong form, such as by a judicial review claim form or s 289 appeal, then the Court can allow an amendment to the correct form or for the erroneous document to stand as an application: *R v Secretary of State for the Environment, Transport and the Regions and the National Assembly for Wales* (CO/3109/99, 24 November 1999); *Thurrock Borough Council v Secretary of State for the Environment, Transport and the Regions and Holding* [2001] CP Rep 55.

[59]   Practice Direction 54E, para 2.2.

[60]   Practice Direction 8C, para 2.2.

not be valid[61] and is incapable of correction by amendment outside the time limit. Also, and more formally, the details should say that the application is brought under PCPA 2004, s113 and CPR Part 8.[62]

Details in section 113 cases have historically tended to be pleaded quite fully, explaining the facts and law, the headline of the grounds and reasoning why they are made out. In part this has been to seek to persuade the defendants to give in. With the introduction of a requirement for permission from the Court to bring the claim, the grounds need to be detailed as they must be persuasive to a judge reading the papers in an hour when faced with likely responses from the defendants.

Various other documents need to be filed with the claim and since these are identical to those required for judicial review, they are considered below.

Time for commencing proceedings

22.18   The time limit for challenging most planning policy decisions has been standardised as six weeks. However, even where the time limit is six weeks there remain some differences relating to the event which triggers the running of time and whether the Court is able to extend the time limit. Some judicial reviews will still enjoy a time limit of promptly and within three months. These are discussed below.

Section 113 applications

22.19   The time limit for bringing a section 113 challenge is six weeks from the day after the 'relevant date'.[63] That date will depend on the document being challenged. In relation to the Wales Spatial Plan it is the date of its approval by the Welsh Assembly Government. For a development plan document (or revision of it) it is the date it is adopted by the local planning authority or approved by the Secretary of State. For a local development plan (or revision thereto) it is the date when it is adopted by a local planning authority in Wales or approved by the Welsh Assembly Government, in relation to the spatial development strategy (or an alteration to or replacement of it) it is the date when it is published by the Mayor of London.[64]

The first day of the six-week period is the day after the relevant date, so if a local plan is adopted on a Tuesday then the last day for bringing a challenge is the Tuesday six weeks later.[65]

---

[61] See *R (on the application of A) v Secretary of State for Communities and Local* Government [2011] EWCA Civ 1253, [2012] JPL 579, at paras 64–66 per Sir Mark Potter. As discussed in that case, such failures have sometimes been characterised as concerning the statute authorising the application or of the Court's procedural rules. Whilst more detail is required under the Practice Direction, CPR 8.2(b)(ii) requires the claim to state 'the legal basis for the claim to that remedy'.

[62] CPR 8.2.

[63] PCPA 2004, s113(3B).

[64] PCPA 2004, s 113(11).

[65] This is the effect of amendments made by the Criminal Justice and Courts Act 2015. Previously, time had started to run on the day of the decision, so the period for challenging a plan adopted on a Tuesday expired on a Monday: *Hinde v Rugby Borough Council* [2011] EWHC 3684 (Admin), [2012] JPL 816; affirmed, *Barker v Hambleton District Council* [2012] EWCA Civ 610, [2013] PTSR 41. The 2015 changes equalised the starting point for time in planning challenges following amendments proposed by Bob Neill MP, see Richard Harwood QC, 'The Planning Court comes into being' [2014] JPL 699.

In Nottingham City Council v Calverton Parish Council[66] Mr Justice Lewis held that where the six-week period would otherwise expire on a non-working day (for example, a Bank Holiday) it would then be taken to expire on the following working day. He stated:

> 'In general terms however, where a statutory provision provides that proceedings must be brought no later than the end of a specified period, and the bringing of proceedings requires that the court office be functioning, and the last day of the prescribed period falls on a day when the court office is closed, then the statutory provision is to be interpreted as permitting the proceedings to be brought on the next day when the court office is open.'[67]

There is some debate as to what is a sufficient attempt to file the claim on a day that the Court office is open. In *Barker v Hambleton District Council*, a section 113 claim which was slipped under the front door of the Court building was considered not to be filed until the following day.[68] In *Croke v Secretary of State for Communities and Local Government*, the High Court held that a litigant was out of time when Court security prevented him from entering the building five minutes before the Court office was due to close.[69] Inconsistent High Court case law renders the challenge provisions unworkable.

Judicial review proceedings against neighbourhood plans

22.20   Judicial review proceedings on neighbourhood plans may only be brought within six weeks from various stages in the processes.[70] The stages are:

(i)   the decision by the local planning authority whether to take the draft plan or order to a referendum and whether to make modifications to it following the examiner's report, or a decision by the Secretary of State whether to intervene at that stage, under s 61N(2);

(ii)   the conduct of the referendum(s) (within six weeks of the declaration of the result) under s 61N(3);

(iii)   making or declining to make the plan following a referendum or referendums under s 61N(1).

These periods cannot be extended.

This overly complex provision raises important issues, none of which have been resolved by the courts.[71] Inconsistent High Court case law renders the challenge provisions unworkable.

The first is the extent to which errors earlier in the process can be challenged on the final making of the order. Provided the referendum(s) have supported the plan, the

---

[66]   [2015] EWHC 503 (Admin).
[67]   At para 38.
[68]   [2011] EWHC 1707 (Admin); the decision was upheld for different reasons: [2012] EWCA Civ 630, [2013] PTSR 41. The Court of Appeal left open the correctness of the out of hours ruling, Maurice Kay LJ describing it as not 'entirely straightforward' at para 15.
[69]   [2016] EWHC 2484 (Admin), [2017] PTSR 116. Permission to appeal has been granted and the appeal is pending: [2017] EWCA Civ 423.
[70]   Town and Country Planning Act 1990, s 61N as applied to neighbourhood plans by PCPA 2004, s 38C.
[71]   Unless pragmatically interpreted in decisions, the section should be recast.

local planning authority has to make it unless doing so would be contrary to European Union or human rights law.[72] Has therefore a challenge based on other grounds to the plan's preparation, the examiner's report or the authority's consideration of it to be brought when the authority consider the report or can it wait until the plan is made? In *R (on the application of Stonegate Homes Ltd) v Horsham District Council* the council unsuccessfully criticised a challenge to the making of the plan being based on errors at earlier stages. [73] However, in *R (on the application of Oyston Estates Ltd) v Fylde Borough Council* [74] Kerr J held that a legal error could only be raised at the step it occurred. In that case the Court held that an alleged unlawful failure to follow the examiner's recommendation and to carry out an appropriate assessment had to be challenged when the decision was made to hold a referendum rather than when the plan was made.

If proceedings are brought against an earlier stage, such as the decision to hold a referendum, the local planning authority may still continue past one or more further stage and then make the plan. In *R (on the application of Maynard) v Chiltern District Council*[75] a successful challenge to the decision of the local planning authority on the examiner's recommendations (brought under s 61N(2)) allowed a quashing of the subsequent referendum result. Similarly in *R (on the application of Crownhall Estates Limited) v Chichester District Council*[76] proceedings were brought against the decision to hold a referendum and then amended, with consent, to quash the later making of the plan. There is sense in that approach. On this basis a claim can be commenced at an early stage and continue without the need to start fresh proceedings just because the authority had continued with the process. However, in *R (on the application of Hoare) v Vale of White Horse District Council*[77] the High Court held that a challenge under s 61N(2) could not result in the quashing of the plan after the local planning authority had made it since s 61N(1) provides that only a claim brought within the post-making six-week period may do that. A further claim should have been brought under s 61N(1) to do that or an interim injunction obtained to prevent the plan being made.[78] The subsequent decision in *Oyston Estates* does not refer to *Hoare* and fails to recognise the contradiction: *Hoare* requires the making of a plan to be challenged by proceedings brought after the event but *Oyston Estates* limits the grounds to errors at that final stage. Unless the process is stopped by an interim order it would be impossible to challenge a plan because of an error by the examiner or in considering the examiner's report. The courts have rightly been very reluctant to hold plan-making processes with interim orders.[79]

As the Court recognised in *Hoare* it makes no sense to require a second claim to be brought to continue a challenge to the same point on the same plan. However, the uncertainty created by the statute and the decisions may result in just that practice being followed. It does though have the consequence that any error in the plan process can be challenged at the final stage when the plan is made. Otherwise if consideration

---

[72] Town and Country Planning Act 1990, s 61E(4), (8).
[73] [2016] EWHC 2512 (Admin), [2017] JPL 271, at paras 53, 106 per Patterson J.
[74] [2017] EWHC 3086 (Admin). The judge granted permission to appeal and the appeal is pending.
[75] [2015] EWHC 3817 (Admin), at para 7, 83 per Holgate J.
[76] See the subsequent substantive judgment at [2016] EWHC 73 (Admin), at para 10 per Holgate J.
[77] [2017] EWHC 1711 (Admin).
[78] At paras 181–186 per John Howell QC. He recognised at para 186 that 'this analysis of section 61N of the 1990 Act is one that may have unfortunate consequences for an unwary claimant that it is hard to imagine that Parliament intended'.
[79] See 22.34 below.

of the basic conditions is unlawful but the plan is made then judicial review under s 61N(2) would be unable to quash the plan but a later claim under s 61N(1) would be unable to consider that question.

Finally the exclusive provisions in s 61N are addressed to particular stages in the process and do not in terms prohibit judicial review of other stages. An issue may arise as to how far earlier claims are precluded in principle or seen to be premature in particular circumstances.

Judicial review proceedings on national policy statements

22.21   Challenges to national policy statements ('NPSs') are brought by judicial review under s 13 of the Planning Act 2008. It lists six scenarios in which challenges may be brought to an NPS by a judicial review application under s 13. They are:

(1)   questioning an NPS or anything done, or omitted to be done, by the Secretary of State in the course of preparing such a statement;

(2)   questioning a decision of the Secretary of State not to carry out a review of all or part of an NPS;

(3)   questioning a decision of the Secretary of State to carry out a review of all or part of an NPS;

(4)   questioning anything done, or omitted to be done, by the Secretary of State in the course of carrying out a review of all or part of an NPS;

(5)   questioning anything done by the Secretary of State under s 6(5) (amend, withdraw or leave the statement unchanged])after completing a review of all or part of an NPS;

(6)   questioning a decision of the Secretary of State as to whether or not to suspend the operation of all or part of an NPS under s11.

Section 13 provides that a challenge brought under that section may only be brought by judicial review and the claim form must be filed before the end of the period of six weeks beginning with the day after:[80]

(1)   in relation to a challenge questioning an NPS or anything done, or omitted to be done, by the Secretary of State in the course of preparing such a statement:

    (a)   the day on which the statement is designated as an NPS for the purposes of the 2008 Act;

    (b)   or, (if later) the day on which the statement is published;[81]

(2)   in relation to a challenge questioning a decision of the Secretary of State not to carry out a review of all or part of an NPS:

    (a)   the day of the decision not to carry out the review;[82]

---

[80]   The time limits in s 113 (and s 118 relating to challenges to development consent orders ('DCOs')) were amended.

[81]   s13(1) Planning Act 2008. Publishing is not defined in the Act and would be interpreted quite widely. Putting a DCO under the Act on the Inspectorate's website was sufficient to publish it: *R (on the application of Michael Williams) v Secretary of State for Energy and Climate Change* [2015] EWHC 1202 (Admin), at paras 44 and 45 per Lindblom J.

[82]   Planning Act 2008, s13(2)(b).

(3)   questioning a decision of the Secretary of State to carry out a review of all or part of an NPS:

   (a)   the day on which the Secretary of state complies with s 6(5) in relation to the review concerned;[83]

(4)   questioning anything done, or omitted to be done, by the Secretary of State in the course of carrying out a review of all or part of an NPS:

   (a)   the day on which the Secretary of State complies with s 6(5) in relation to the review concerned;[84]

(5)   questioning anything done by the Secretary of State under s 6(5) after completing a review of all or part of an NPS:

   (a)   the day on which the thing concerned is done;[85]

(6)   questioning a decision of the Secretary of State as to whether or not to suspend the operation of all or part of an NPS under s 11:

   (a)   the day of the decision.[86]

Section 13 therefore provides that certain challenges can only be brought by a judicial review under that section. The scope of those provisions needs to be determined, along with the time limits which apply.

In *R (on the application of Hillingdon London Borough Council) v Secretary of State for Transport*[87] the claimant local authorities challenged the Secretary of State's October 2016 announcement that the government's preferred option for delivering additional runway capacity in south east England is the north-west runway scheme and proposing to include this in a draft National Planning Statement which was to follow. The Secretary of State applied to strike out the proceedings arguing that the time limit in s 13(1) barred the claim being made. This raised two issues. First, whether the 'period of 6 weeks' prevented claims from being brought before the start of that period, and second, whether the challenge was to something the Secretary of State was doing in the 'course of preparing' a national policy statement, or whether it preceded that. In relation to the first issue the Court found, relying on the purpose behind the wording of the legislation, that the section did not allow for claims to commence before the start of the six weeks.[88] In relation to the second issue, it found a step in the course of preparing a national policy statement was not confined to statutory functions under the Act or required there to be a draft NPS. The announcement of the intention to prepare a draft NPS was sufficient to bring the challenge within the scope of s 13. The claim could not be brought until any NPS had been designated and was therefore struck out.[89]

Starting the six-week period running on the day after the event means that if the event was on Tuesday then the final day for bringing proceedings is Tuesday six weeks later. Prior to April 2015, the time had begun to run the day earlier but this

---

[83]   Planning Act 2008, s13(3)(b).
[84]   Planning Act 2008, s13(4)(b).
[85]   Planning Act 2008, s13(5)(b).
[86]   Planning Act 2008, s13(6)(b).
[87]   [2017] EWHC 121 (Admin), [2017] 1 WLR 2166, [2017] JPL 610, [2017] ACD 38.
[88]   At paras 57–64 per Cranston J.
[89]   At paras 71–73 per Cranston J.

was amended as part of the rationalisation of planning High Court time limits in the Criminal Justice and Courts Act 2015.[90]

Judicial reviews against other planning policy decisions

22.22   Unless statute provides that a public authority's decision is to be challenged by an application or appeal to the High Court (as in the Planning and Compulsory Purchase Act 2004, s 113) then it may be challenged by judicial review. In some circumstances the legislation says that judicial review is to be used and sets out a time limit (as with various national policy statements and neighbourhood development plan challenges). In the absence of legislative provision, judicial review proceedings are governed by the CPR, Part 54. There are though two potentially relevant time limits under CPR 54.

The conventional judicial review time limit is that:[91]

'The claim form must be filed:

(a)   promptly; and

(b)   in any event not later than 3 months after the grounds to make the claim first arose.'

The period for challenges under the 'Planning Acts' was changed to six weeks, with no promptness requirement, for decisions made from 1 July 2013.[92] Civil Procedure Rule 54.5(5) provides:

'Where the application for judicial review relates to a decision made by the Secretary of State or local planning authority under the Planning Acts, the claim form must be filed not later than six weeks after the grounds to make the claim first arose.'

The Planning Acts are as defined in the Town and Country Planning Act 1990: Town and Country Planning Act 1990, the Planning (Listed Buildings and Conservation Areas) Act 1990, the Planning (Hazardous Substances) Act 1990 and the Planning (Consequential Provisions) Act 1990.[93] They do not include PCPA 2004. The Secretary of State includes the Welsh Ministers and is likely to be taken to include the actions of planning inspectors or the Planning Inspectorate which are taken in the Minister's name. Many planning and related policies are made other than under the Planning Acts (as defined).

Since local planning policy is dealt within PCPA 2004, most judicial reviews will be subject to promptly and within the three-month time limit. These include challenges to:

•   supplementary planning documents and residual local development documents;

•   preparatory acts or steps involving local plans in England and local development plans in Wales which are not subject to s 113 of PCPA 2004, including any challenges to Inspector's reports;

•   the revocation of local plans.

---

[90]   Criminal Justice and Courts Act 2015, s 92 with effect from 13 April 2015.
[91]   CPR 54.5(1). The CPR time limit does not apply if statute provides for a shorter period: CPR 54.5(4), for example, the Planning Act 2008, s 13.
[92]   CPR 54.5(1) which contains the promptness requirement is disapplied entirely in Planning Acts cases: CPR 54.5(4).
[93]   Town and Country Planning Act 1990, s 336(1), applied by CPR 54.5(A1).

The various non-planning policies considered in this book will be subject to promptly and within three months, for example, National Park management plans and Historic England guidance.

Time limits for planning policies which do not have an explicit statutory base are more uncertain. National planning policy and the supplementary planning guidance of Welsh authorities and the Mayor of London are made pursuant to their planning responsibilities, some at least of which arise under the Planning Acts. It is debatable whether these policies are referable to the Planning Acts and, even so, being non-statutory whether they are made under them.

The one clear example of a plan which falls under the CPR six weeks is a conservation area management plan or proposals made under s 71 of the Planning ((Listed Buildings and Conservation Areas) Act 1990.

These issues can be avoided by filing proceedings within six weeks. The other time limit is promptly and within three months, so it is possible that a claim can be out of time as not prompt even if filed within three months.[94]

The final time for bringing a judicial review challenge runs from the issue of the decision notice.[95] The judicial review formulation 'after the grounds … arose' means that the six weeks start to be counted from the day after the decision. So if the decision was issued on a Tuesday then the period expires on the Tuesday six weeks later.[96]

Since bringing a planning statutory application or judicial review involves the filing of the claim form with the Court office, this can only be done on a day that the Court is open. Consequently, if the period would expire on a weekend or a public or Bank Holiday then filing may take place on the next working day.[97]

The six-week time limit has been held to be compatible with the right to a fair hearing under Article 6 of the European Convention on Human Rights and access to environmental justice under European law.[98]

The Court may grant an extension of time for bringing judicial review proceedings where the time limit is in the CPR rather than contained in an Act of Parliament, but extensions would only be granted in exceptional circumstances.[99] It should not be assumed that an extension would be granted. Long extensions of time have been granted in planning cases where there has been a failure to notify a neighbour of a

---

[94] See *R (on the application of Finn-Kelcey) v Milton Keynes Borough Council* [2008] EWCA Civ 1067, [2009] JPL 493.

[95] *R (on the application of Burkett) v London Borough of Hammersmith and Fulham* [2002] UKHL 23, [2002] 1 WLR 1593.

[96] *R (on the application of Berky) v Newport City Council* [2012] EWCA Civ 378, [2012] 2 CMLR 44.

[97] *Nottingham City Council v Calverton Parish Council* [2015] EWHC 503 (Admin), [2015] PTSR 1130 following *Kaur v S Russell & Sons Ltd* [1973] QB 336.

[98] See *Barker v Hambleton District Council* and *R (on the application of Blue Green London Plan) v Secretary of State for the Environment, Food and Rural Affairs* [2015] EWHC 495 (Admin) on analogous provisions and, for human rights, *Matthews v Secretary of State for the Environment* [2001] EWHC Admin 815, [2002] 2 P & CR 34, per Sullivan J at para 33 on section 288 applications.

[99] A lack of awareness of the matter until long after the decision, caused by an unlawful failure to be consulted, is the best justification for an extension of time. For the rejection of various reasons to extend time, see *R (on the application of Gerber) v Wiltshire Council* [2016] EWCA Civ 84, [2016] 1 WLR 2593.

planning application, for example, two years and eight months from the decision in *R (on the application of Gavin) v London Borough of Haringey*,[100] although the delay may mean that only declaratory relief is given.

PRE-ACTION PROCESSES

22.23   Judicial reviews in planning cases have been taken as being subject to the Judicial Review Pre-Action Protocol, although on its terms it does not apply if the decision-maker is unable to revisit its decision without the intervention of the Court. Where a plan has been adopted, the planning authority will not in practice be able to revoke it, so on that strict view the protocol would not apply in a number of planning policy cases. However, even prior to the protocol the courts had said that warning of planning judicial reviews should be given.[101] As a matter of practice it is useful to send a pre-action letter giving sufficient time (ideally two weeks) for a substantive response to be received. This will, at the least, allow any challenge to be better informed and focused. It might lead the local planning authority into agreeing to submit to judgment upon proceedings being brought.

The pre-action protocol sets out a list of matters to be included in pre-action letters and recommends a standard format. Most importantly the letter should identify the decision and the proposed grounds along with any information being requested. Formally, it should also identify the claimant and their legal team along with the proposed defendant and any interested parties. The defendant ought to reply substantively within the requested period. As a matter of practice, interested parties who wish to take part in any proceedings ought to do so as well, although the protocol does not require that.

The reduced period of six weeks for bringing almost all planning judicial reviews means that it is harder to comply with the pre-action procedures. The Pre-Action Protocol for Judicial Review now provides:[102]

> 'This protocol may not be appropriate in cases where one of the shorter time limits in Rules 54.5(5) or (6) applies. In those cases, the parties should still attempt to comply with this protocol but the court will not apply normal cost sanctions where the court is satisfied that it has not been possible to comply because of the shorter time limits.'

Section 113 applications are not subject to any pre-action protocol. Whilst formally the Practice Direction – Pre-Action Conduct and Protocols would apply and encourage a pre-action letter, such correspondence has not traditionally been sent. The view of central government has tended to be that a final decision will have been made and so any dispute could only be resolved in the courts.

SECTION 113 AND JUDICIAL REVIEW PROCEEDINGS FROM COMMENCEMENT

22.24   Once proceedings have been filed, the planning statutory review procedures are almost identical to the well-established judicial review processes. Reviews under

---

[100]   [2003] EWHC 2591 (Admin), [2004] 2 P & CR 13.
[101]   *R v Cotswold District Council ex p Barrington Parish Council* (1998) 75 P & CR 515, at 528 per Keene J.
[102]   Paragraph 6.

s 113 are dealt with by CPR Practice Direction 8C, which is based on CPR Part 54 and Practice Direction 54A which are used for judicial review.

Documentation filed with the proceedings

22.25   In addition to the claim form,[103] detailed grounds[104] and application fee, the claim must be accompanied by:[105]

'(a) any written evidence in support of the claim;

(b) a copy of any decision, order, relevant document or action that the claimant seeks to have quashed;

(c) copies of any documents on which the claimant proposes to rely;

(d) copies of any relevant statutory material; and

(e) a list of essential documents for advance reading by the court (with page references to the passages relied on).'

It is also helpful to include any judgments which the judge will need to refer to at the permission stage. The bundle must be paginated.[106]

The commencement of the proceedings

22.26   The proceedings should be filed with the relevant documents and fee in the Administrative Court Office at the Royal Courts of Justice or the relevant regional Administrative Court Office in the District Registry of the High Court at Cardiff, Birmingham, Leeds or Manchester.[107]

If the claimant considers that the case should be categorised as a significant planning case this should be indicated in a covering letter.[108]

Service of proceedings

22.27   Section 113 proceedings should be served within the six-week period[109] but judicial review proceedings are to be served within seven days of their commencement.[110] In either case the Court may extend time for service.[111]

---

[103] Form N208PC for s 113 and other statutory reviews; form N461PC for Planning Court judicial reviews.

[104] Usually called Details of Claim in planning statutory reviews and a Statement of Facts and Grounds in judicial review.

[105] Planning reviews: Practice Direction 8C, para 2.3. The judicial review requirements are to the same effect: Practice Direction 54A, para 5.7.

[106] It is useful to include a gap in the pagination between the grounds and the evidence to allow other pleadings and orders to be included in a trial bundle without upsetting the existing pagination.

[107] Practice Direction 54D. Filing the claim in the wrong office but in the right building can be excused: *Cala Homes (South) Ltd v Chichester District Council* (2000) 79 P & CR 430 (claim filed in Central office of the High Court rather than what was then the Crown Office), approved by in *San Vicente v Secretary of State for Communities and Local Government* [2013] EWCA Civ 817, [2014] 1 WLR 966, at para 52 per Beatson LJ.

[108] Practice Direction 54E, para 3.3.

[109] Practice Direction 8C, para 4.4. The certificate of service is form N215PC.

[110] CPR 54.7.

[111] For the principles on extending time for service in statutory applications such as s 113, see *Corus UK Ltd v Erewash Borough Council* [2006] EWCA Civ 1175, [2007] 1 P & CR 22.

Where a claim brought under s 113 relates to a decision/order made by on behalf of a Minister or government department then the claim form must be served on that Minister or government department. Where it relates to a document prepared by a local planning authority then it must be served on that local planning authority.[112] A challenge to the adoption of a local plan is brought against the local planning authority who adopted it, and not against the examining Inspector or the Secretary of State even if the grounds are concerned with an error by the Inspector. Usually there is no need to add other persons as interested parties. The Court has a discretion to allow other parties to appear if they might otherwise suffer injustice, but that discretion should be exercised very rarely or exceptionally. That the person has the benefit of an allocation which is under challenge will not necessarily be sufficient.[113]

In judicial review the claim form must be served on the defendant and any person whom the claimant considers to be an interested party.[114]

Acknowledgements of service and summary grounds

22.28   Since permission to proceed is required from the Court in judicial review and now in planning statutory reviews, a judge needs to form a view at an early stage whether there is an arguable case. The 2000 judicial review reforms had changed the application for permission (previously called leave) from a 'without notice' procedure (where the first the planning authority might know of the claim was on receipt of the permission decision) into a 'with notice' process where the relevant parties are expected to comment on merits from the beginning. This has been continued, almost in the same terms, in the new procedures for section 113 applications.

A person served with the claim who wishes to take part in the proceedings must file an acknowledgment of service and if intending to contest it, must provide summary grounds of resistance.[115] Summary grounds ought to be kept short, as Carnwath LJ explained 'The purpose of the "summary of grounds" is not to provide the basis for full argument of the substantive merits, but rather ... to assist the judge in deciding whether to grant permission, and if so on what terms'.[116] They might need to do little more than refer back to any pre-action correspondence and could make their points in a few pages. In some cases, of course, the claimant's explanation of the facts may be so unclear or incomplete from the defendant's perspective that a lengthier explanation is required. There is no provision for the production of evidence by

---

[112] Practice Direction 8C, para.4.1

[113] *IM Properties Development Ltd v Lichfield District Council (No 2)* [2015] EWHC 1982 (Admin), at para 62 per Holgate J, following *Capel Parish Council v Surrey County Council* [2008] EWHC 2364 (Admin), at para 11 per Sullivan J; *MA Holdings Ltd v George Wimpey UK Ltd* [2008] EWCA Civ 12, [2008] 1 WLR 1649, at para 28 per Dyson LJ; and *Warren v Uttlesford District Council* [1996] COD 262.

[114] CPR 54.7.

[115] Planning reviews: Practice Direction 8C, para 5.2, 5.5; judicial review: CPR 54.8(1), (4). The acknowledgment of service forms are N210PC and N462PC respectively.

[116] *R (on the application of Ewing) v Office of the Deputy Prime Minister* [2005] EWCA Civ 1583, [2006] 1 WLR 1260, at para 43. In *R (on the application of Davey) v Aylesbury Vale District Council* [2007] EWCA Civ 1166, [2008] 1 WLR 878 at 33, Sir Anthony Clarke MR said that the Court at the permission stage should 'decline to look at anything which goes beyond the "summary of grounds" described in *Ewing*'s case'.

defendants or interested parties at this stage, but it may be submitted.[117] This is best confined to critical issues going to whether permission should be granted.

Acknowledgments and summary grounds must be filed not more than 21 days after service of the claim form and then served on the claimant and the other parties as soon as practicable and, in any event, not later than seven days after filing.[118] No provision is made for any reply by the claimant, but that may be done. Any reply should be short and confined to making new and essential points arising from the summary grounds. On occasion, a reply may be ordered by the Court.

Consideration of permission

22.29   The permission application will then be considered by a judge on the papers.[119] In significant planning cases the target is for this to be done within three weeks of receipt of the expiry of the acknowledgment of service deadline.[120] A reasoned decision whether to grant or refuse permission will usually be given, and it is possible to grant permission only on certain grounds. Occasionally, the judge may decide that the application should be referred to a 'rolled-up' hearing to consider whether permission should be granted and, if so, whether the claim should succeed.

At the permission stage, the judge may mark the claim (or certain grounds) as 'totally without merit' under CPR 23.12, the effect of this is that the claimant may only appeal that decision to the Court of Appeal (ie they lose their right of an oral renewal hearing).[121]

Oral hearings will usually be listed for 30 minutes unless a longer listing has been requested.[122] There is no requirement to file skeleton submissions and the parties will need to consider what assists the Court given the submissions which will already be in.[123] A claimant may wish to respond to reasons for refusal given on the papers and it might be helpful to shortly guide the judge through the paperwork. Sometimes there is value in preparing a skeleton which is a revision of the grounds, picking up the issues as they have subsequently developed.[124]

On either the papers or following an oral hearing the judge may make directions. If the case is particularly urgent then expedition may be ordered, potentially with a hear-by date, and if it may need to be heard in August or September then it should be certified as fit for vacation business. If permission is refused then the Court will usually order the unsuccessful claimant to pay the costs of the decision maker's

---

[117] The requirement in CPR 8.5(3), (4) to serve evidence with an acknowledgement of service to a Part 8 claim is disapplied by Practice Direction 8C, para 12.3.

[118] Planning reviews: Practice Direction 8C, para 5.3; judicial review: CPR 54.8(2).

[119] Planning reviews: Practice Direction 8C, para 7.1; judicial review: CPR 54.8(2).

[120] Practice Direction 54E, para 3.4(a); judicial review; Practice Direction 54A, para 8.4.

[121] CPR 54.12(7); Practice Direction 8C, para 7.8.

[122] How long the hearing actually takes is down more to the judge and the number of cases in the list that day, followed by the extent of the issues and the nature of the parties' submissions.

[123] The Court does though informally request parties to file any skeletons one week before the hearing (or indicate that it is not proposed to file a skeleton). The production of skeletons may be directed by the judge. If further cases or legislation are to be cited then an authority's bundle (ideally agreed) ought to be filed.

[124] As with any written submissions, the objective is to find the most helpful and persuasive way of explaining the case to the judge given the material which is already before the Court.

acknowledgment of service and summary grounds but will not usually allow the decision maker to recover the costs of attending any renewal hearing.[125]

Where there has been undue delay in the proceedings, and so they are brought with an extension of time, then prejudice caused in the meantime to a developer who was unaware of a potential challenge may count against the grant of permission. This is relevant to discretion and also, in judicial review cases, to the application of the Senior Courts Act 1981, s 31(6) which provides:[126]

> 'Where the High Court considers that there has been undue delay in making an application for judicial review, the court may refuse to grant:
>
> (a)   leave for the making of the application; or
>
> (b)   any relief sought on the application,
>
> if it considers that the granting of the relief sought would be likely to cause substantial hardship to, or substantially prejudice the rights of, any person or would be detrimental to good administration.'

Further the Senior Courts Act 1981, s 31 also provides that the Court must refuse permission to apply for judicial review or relief if 'it appears to the court to be highly likely that the outcome for the applicant would not have been substantially different if the conduct complained of had not occurred'.[127] In those circumstances the Court must refuse permission or substantive relief unless there are reasons of exceptional public interest.[128] It remains to be seen how much practical difference this makes.

An issue may arise as to what extent new material needs to be produced showing that there might have been a different outcome so that, where appropriate, substantial prejudice had occurred and, in terms of discretion, that there was a real possibility of a different decision. A claimant who was unable to make representations because of a consultation error ought to indicate the nature of the comments which they would have made. In some circumstances expert evidence could be produced, although Collins J in *R v Bolsover District Council, ex p Paterson*[129] was of the view that this would be an excessive requirement upon claimants.

---

[125]   Costs for the acknowledgment of service and summary grounds should generally be awarded: *R (on the application of Mount Cook Ltd) v Westminster City Council* [2003] EWCA Civ 1346, [2004] JPL 470, at para 74, 76(1) per Auld LJ (but query whether more than one set of costs should be awarded unless justified under *Bolton Metropolitan Borough Council v Secretary of State for the Environment (Practice Note)* [1995] 1 WLR 1176). For the award of costs of permission hearings, see for planning reviews Practice Direction 8C, para 8.2 and for judicial review Practice Direction 54A, para 8.6: 'Where the defendant or any party does attend a hearing, the court will not generally make an order for costs against the claimant'. Defendant's costs of attending permission hearings should only be recovered in exceptional circumstances, some of which are identified in *Mount Cook*, at para 76(5).

[126]   The detrimental to good administration limb is less likely to help a defendant. As the Court of Appeal observed in *R (Burkett) v London Borough of Hammersmith and Fulham* [2001] Env LR 39 at para 29: 'Administration beyond law is bad administration. The courts exist to protect the former as jealously as to stop the latter, but they cannot know which they are dealing with unless they can hear out, and decide, viable challenges to the legality of administrative acts'.

[127]   Senior Courts Act 1981, s 31(3D) (at the permission stage) and s 31(2A) (at the substantive hearing). This applies only to proceedings brought from 13 April 2015: see Criminal Justice and Courts Act 2015 (Commencement No 1, Saving and Transitional Provisions) Order 2015, SI 2015/778, art 4, Sch 2, para 6.

[128]   Senior Courts Act 1981, s 31(3E) and s 31(2B) respectively.

[129]   [2001] JPL 211 at paras 15, 16.

The Court must have in mind that it is not qualified to determine planning merits which combine matters of professional judgment and political opinion.

Post-permission

22.30   The defendant and anyone else served with the claim form who wishes to defend the claim or support it on additional grounds must file and serve detailed grounds and any written evidence within 35 days after service of the order giving permission.[130] Any other evidence can only be submitted with the permission of the Court (or the agreement of the parties) and directions may provide time either in which the claimant is entitled to submit evidence in reply or to apply to be able to submit such evidence.

If permission is refused (without having been marked 'totally without merit') then the application may be renewed (with short grounds) to an oral hearing before a high court judge. Any request for reconsideration by the High Court or appeal to the Court of Appeal must be filed within seven days after service of the order and its reasons or the delivery of judgment.[131]

EVIDENCE IN STATUTORY APPLICATIONS AND JUDICIAL REVIEW

22.31   Evidential matters are dealt with in a similar manner in judicial review and the equivalent statutory applications and appeals, such as under s 113. First of all, the Court is concerned with the lawfulness of the decision or the decision-making process and so the evidence will usually just include what was in front of the decision-maker and what actually happened. That evidence must bear on the grounds which are raised. For example, if a challenge is confined to the lawfulness of the Inspector's handling of ecology then the ecological evidence in the application and appeal is likely to need to be before the Court, but the highways evidence is unlikely to be relevant.[132]

Material which was not in the decision-making process is rarely relevant, the exceptions generally being:

- if a complaint is that the claimant was not informed of a consultation/ examination or of some evidence then they may wish to indicate what would have been said about the matter;

- anything which as a matter of law had to be considered but was not, for example, parts of the development plan or national policy relevant to the grounds raised;

- subsequent developments but only if they materially assist in the exercise of the Court's discretion if the decision was unlawful. Discretion is primarily focused on the position at the date of the unlawful decision, so it would be rare for the court to conclude that on the circumstances of that time the policy should be quashed but later events mean that a quashing order should not now be made.

For the most part evidence can be dealt with by exhibiting documents. The course of events will be described in the grounds, with a statement of truth, and a witness

---

[130] Planning reviews: Practice Direction 8C, para 12.1; judicial review: CPR 54.14(1).
[131] Planning reviews: Practice Direction 8C, para 7.5 (reconsideration), CPR 52.15B(3) (appeal); judicial review: CPR 54.13(4) (reconsideration), CPR 52.15(2) (appeal).
[132] Whilst it might sometimes be useful to place the decision in an early and separate tab, evidential documents should otherwise be organised chronologically.

statement only needs to expand on matters if they are not in the contemporaneous documents. A claimant might need to explain their interest in the matter or that they were unaware of the policy document until it was too late to be involved.

Where a decision-maker is required to give reasons for their decision, their reasoning cannot be supplemented by witness evidence. In the context of a decision in relation to a planning permission the Court of Appeal endorsed Mr Justice Ouseley's first instance decision in *Ioannou v Secretary of State for Communities and Local Government*[133] where he stated:

> 'I would strongly discourage the use of witness statements from Inspectors in the way deployed here. The statutory obligation to give a decision with reasons must be fulfilled by the decision letter, which then becomes the basis for challenge. There is no provision for a second letter or for a challenge to it. A witness statement should not be a back door second decision letter. It may reveal further errors of law ...'[134]

Disclosure

22.32   There is no automatic disclosure in judicial review or statutory applications. In planning cases a great deal of the necessary evidence will already be available to the parties, published on websites or in files which are open to public inspection. There are circumstances where internal notes and emails are required. Occasionally an issue may arise on a claimant's involvement, knowledge or interest in a matter which requires documents.

Public law cases should be fought with all of the parties being in possession of the relevant material. All parties are under a duty of candour to make a full and frank disclosure of relevant facts to the Court.[135] Issues of the claimant's knowledge of the matter may be relevant to timing of the proceedings and standing and should be fully disclosed where they arise. The decision-making process may need to be honestly and fully explained by the defendant. As Sir John Donaldson MR pointed out in *R v Lancashire County Council, ex p Huddleston*[136] judicial review is:

> 'a process which falls to be conducted with all the cards face upwards on the table and the vast majority of the cards will start in the authority's hands.'

The obligation to make full and frank disclosure to the Court is particularly onerous where an application is made without notice to the other side, although in judicial reviews and statutory challenges this will only in practice arise in urgent injunction applications. Where all parties are aware of published documents a party need only put before the Court the documents which it considers to be relevant to the claim as put. The other parties can put other documents in if they wish, although it is prudent for any party to ensure that the unhelpful documents are produced and addressed.

---

[133] [2014] EWCA Civ 1432, [2015] 1 P& CR 10.

[134] At para 41 of the Court of Appeal judgement citing para 51 of Mr Justice Ouseley's first instance decision. For other examples of this principle, see *Rumsey v Secretary of State for the Environment, Transport and the Regions* (2000) 81 P & CR 32 and *R (on the application of Shasha) v Westminster City Council* [2016] EWHC 3283 (Admin), [2017] PTSR 306, [2017] JPL 539.

[135] See for application to the claimant: *Cocks v Thanet District Council* [1983] 2 AC 286, at 294G per Lord Bridge, and for defendants and interested parties: *Belize Alliance of Conservation Non-Governmental Organisations v Department of the Environment* [2004] UKPC 6, [2004] Env LR 761, at paras 86, 87 per Lord Walker of Gestingthorpe.

[136] [1986] 2 All ER 941.

A party seeking documents should request them in the context of the proceedings (to avoid potential delays if requests to public bodies are dealt with under the Freedom of Information Act/Environmental Information Regulations). An application for specific disclosure can be made. If documentation has been refused prior to the commencement of proceedings then a disclosure application can be included in the claim form, to be dealt with by the permission judge.

Cross-examination in statutory applications and judicial review

22.33   Cross-examination may be ordered in s 113 or judicial review proceedings.[137] In *Jones v Secretary of State for Wales*[138] the Court of Appeal ordered cross-examination of a Planning Inspector after a dispute about a conversation with a participant during an adjournment of the inquiry. Balcombe LJ said 'The principle is clear – that cross-examination will be allowed when the justice of the case requires and the decision whether justice so requires is a matter for the discretion of the judge'.[139]

Cross-examination in Administrative Court and Planning Court cases has been very rare although it is becoming less infrequent.[140] Lord Neuberger of Abbotsbury MR warned on judicial review in *Bubb v Wandsworth London Borough Council*:[141]

> 'for reasons of both principle and practice, such a course should only be taken in the most exceptional case. As its name suggests, judicial review involves a judge reviewing a decision, not making it; if the judge receives evidence so as to make fresh findings of fact for himself, he is likely to make his own decision rather than to review the original decision. Also, if judges regularly allow witnesses and cross-examination in judicial review cases, the court time and legal costs involved in such cases will spiral.'

There may be factual issues as to what was done or said which can only be resolved by live witnesses being heard and questioned. One example is if an explanation of the decision-maker's thinking is given in a witness statement and the issue is raised, in the absence of contemporaneous documents, as to whether that is accurate and whether it was in the authority's mind at the time of the decision or is an ex post facto rationalisation.[142]

Oral expert evidence is rarely of assistance in a statutory challenge or planning judicial review.[143]

---

[137] CPR 8.6(2), (3), in judicial review cases as applied by CPR 54.1.

[138] [1995] 2 PLR 26.

[139] *Jones*, at 30.

[140] One such example is cross-examination ordered of a council officer as to whether consideration was given to publishing an advertisement of an application due to potential effects on a listed building: *R (on the application of Embleton Parish Council) v Northumberland County Council* [2013] EWHC 3631 (Admin), [2014] Env LR 16, at paras 113–118 per judge Behrens.

[141] [2011] EWCA Civ 1285, [2012] PTSR 1011 at paras 24, 25.

[142] *R (Jedwell) v Denbighshire County Council* [2015] EWCA Civ 1232, [2016] PTSR 715, at paras 48–60 per Lewison LJ.

[143] See the comments of Dove J in *R (on the application of Groves) v Boston Borough Council* [2014] EWHC 3950 (Admin) at paras 22, 23 where the enforceability of a noise condition on a wind turbine planning permission was in issue. The judge did derive some benefit from a joint statement of experts which crystallised the issues.

Interim orders

22.34   The High Court is empowered under s113 to make an interim order suspending the operation of the relevant document wholly or in part, generally or as it affects the property of the applicant.[144] The tests for whether or not interim relief should be granted are found in the decision of *American Cyanamid v Ethicon Ltd*[145] (is there a serious issue to be tried and if so, what is the balance of convenience) but modified as appropriate to a public law challenge (see *Terry Adams Ltd v Bolton Metropolitan Borough Council*[146] and *R (on the application of Medical Justice) v Secretary of State for the Home Department*[147]). In *Medical Justice* the Court stated:

> '12. The more important issue in considering interim relief in this issue is where the balance of convenience lies. In judicial review, this consideration varies from its application in private law, because generally speaking damages will not be payable in the event of an unlawful administrative act, nor will a public authority suffer financial loss from being prevented from implementing its policy. The public interest is strong in permitting a public authority to continue to apply its policy when ex hypothesi it is acting in the public interest. That wider public interest cannot be measured simply in terms of the financial or individual consequences to the parties, a point made by Browne LJ in his judgment in *Smith v Inner London Education Authority* [1978] 1 All ER 411 , at 422 H.
>
> 13. The weight to be attached to that wider public interest turns in part on the juridical basis of the policy.'[148]

The particular issues associated with suspending the operation of a policy were identified by Cranston J in *Lisle-Mainwaring v Royal Borough of Kensington and Chelsea.*[149] That case considered an application for interim relief where the wider claim concerned a challenge under s 113 to a policy dealing with basements in the Core Strategy. Rejecting the application, Mr Justice Cranston concluded:

> '28 I am afraid that it is at this point that I diverge from the submissions Mr Brown has made. It seems to me that the balance of convenience is against granting interim relief. First, there is the basic point that in terms of individual planning applications, applicants always face the planning policies which operate at the time the application is made. In other words, there is no unfairness to persons making applications. If the claimants are correct and the basements policy is struck down in July, then within a period of 10 to 12 weeks, or slightly longer given the time it will take to produce a judgment, applications can be made in the absence of the basements policy.
>
> 29 Moreover, considerable weight in terms of the public interest must be attached to what I described in the Medical Justice case as the juridical basis of the policy. This is part of the Council's Core Strategy. It was adopted after a lengthy process. It was an intricate process. It involved input from members of the public through consultation and otherwise. Mr Haslam for the second claimant made substantial contributions to that consultation. The plan-making involved in this case all the usual appurtenances, including an Inspector's report. It culminated in the decision of the democratically elected Council in a policy area which is fraught with conflicting interests. In other words, the public interest is strongly in favour of permitting this Council to continue to apply its basements policy until the court has had time to consider in detail whether or not it is a lawful policy.'

---

[144] PCPA 2004, s 115(5).
[145] [1975] AC 396.
[146] [1996] 73 P &CR 446.
[147] [2010] EWHC 1425 (Admin), [2010] ACD 70.
[148] Per Cranston J.
[149] [2015] EWHC 1814 (Admin).

In *IM Properties Development Ltd v Lichfield District Council (No 2)*[150] Holgate
J refused to suspend a local plan. Whilst the claimant contended that a failure to
suspend would prejudice its ongoing planning appeal the Court considered that
there was no prejudice to the claimant if that inquiry was delayed by the section 113
proceedings.[151] Further examples of the weighing up of the balance of convenience
in relation to the suspension of policy/guidance can be found in *Cala Homes (South)
Ltd v Secretary of State for Communities and Local Government*[152] and *Capel Parish
Council v Surrey County Council.*[153] In each case the Court decided against the
granting/continuance of interim relief.

An application for such an interim order may also be made as part of judicial review
proceedings in the form of an interim injunction the principles to be applied by the
Court will be the same as have been considered in the context of s 113.

The hearing of the case

22.35   The Practice Directions require the filing of a trial bundle of the necessary
documents, skeleton submissions and an agreed bundle of authorities. The Practice
Directions require a skeleton argument from the claimant not less than 21 working
days before the hearing and from the defendant and any other party 14 working days
before the hearing[154] although these periods have often been shortened by judges
in directions at the permission stage.[155] Under the Practice Directions skeleton
arguments must contain:[156]

(1)   a time estimate for the complete hearing, including delivery of judgment;

(2)   a list of issues;

(3)   a list of the legal points to be taken (together with any relevant authorities with
       page references to the passages relied on);

(4)   a chronology of events (with page references);

(5)   a list of essential documents for the advance reading of the Court (with page
       references) and a time estimate for that reading; and

(6)   a list of persons referred to.

It may be useful for the parties to agree statement of agreed factual matters, legal
propositions and chronologies.[157] This may save time where the facts are complex
and potentially contentious, such as there being multiple witness statements about
events at a planning inquiry.[158]

---

[150] [2015] EWHC 1982 (Admin).
[151] At paras 52–57.
[152] [2010] EWHC 3278 (Admin), [2011] JPL553.
[153] [2008] EWHC 2364 (Admin).
[154] For statutory reviews, Practice Direction 8C, para 15; judicial review, Practice Direction 54A, paras
       15.1, 15.2.
[155] Periods of three and two or two and one weeks are practical.
[156] In practice the issues and legal points need to be clearly identified, albeit not mechanistically listed.
       Chronologies tend to be useful, but lists of persons are rarely essential in planning cases.
[157] The production of these documents in significant planning cases are encouraged by the Planning
       Court judges Dame Frances Patterson and Sir Ian Dove in their article 'The Planning Court: future
       directions' [2015] JPL 1118.
[158] As was, for example, done in *Anderson v Secretary of State for Communities and Local Government*
       [2015] EWHC 3005 (Admin).

It is conventional for the bundle of authorities to include relevant legislation and published national policy. Parties are not required to file national policy documents as evidence, although it is again conventional to include local policy within evidence, in part because of a need to be satisfied of its relevance, completeness and status.

The case is usually heard by a single judge, either a High Court or Deputy High Court Judge.[159] In the absence of orders for cross-examination of witnesses, the hearing will simply involve submissions, with the usual order being the claimant's advocate, any party supporting the claim, the principal defendant (the Minister or the local planning authority) and any other defendants or interested parties opposing the claim, with the claimant having a final right of reply.

REMEDIES

22.36   Section 113 provides that the High Court may quash the relevant document or remit the relevant document to a person or body with a function relating to its preparation, publication, adoption or approval where it is satisfied that the relevant document is to any extent outside the appropriate power and/or that the interests of the applicant have been substantially prejudiced by a failure to comply with a procedural requirement.[160]

The power to remit the document was the result of an amendment to s 113 by the Planning Act 2008. Previously, s 113 and the earlier provision in s 287 of the Town and Country Planning Act 1990 had merely enabled the Court to quash the plan in whole or in part. With a development plan this conventionally resulted in the deletion of sites or policy text. If the local planning authority wished to fill the hole it would need to commence a partial review of the plan and go through all of the stages again. The inflexibility of this approach was subject to judicial criticism, notably by the Court of Appeal in *First Corporate Shipping Ltd v North Somerset Council.*[161]

Since the 2008 amendment the power to remit has been used on a number of occasions. For example, in *Heard v Broadland District Council*[162] Mr Justice Ouseley ruled that the inclusion of the North East Growth Triangle, involving up to 9,000 houses and commercial development, in the Greater Norwich Joint Core Strategy was unlawful because of a failure to consider reasonable alternatives under SEA. He remitted the relevant parts of the plan on 25 April 2012. Following a further consultation and examination, the Joint Core Strategy was adopted, with various main modifications, on 10 January 2014. The case of *University of Bristol v North Somerset Council*[163] saw the entire housing requirement figure remitted to the decision-maker.

Whilst it is tempting for the Court to provide the shortest process for dealing with major issues, the remissions are complex. Since only part of the plan is remitted,

---

[159] Up to the 1970s, many planning cases were dealt with by the Divisional Court of the High Court, consisting of the Lord Chief Justice or a Lord Justice and one or two High Court judges. The Divisional Court now just deals with criminal appeals by case stated and the most sensitive judicial reviews. A Lord or Lady Justice may occasionally sit as a single judge in the High Court.

[160] PCPA 2004, s113 (6) and (7).

[161] [2001] EWCA Civ 693, [2002] PLCR 7, at para 38 per Buxton LJ.

[162] [2012] EWHC 344 (Admin), [2012] Env LR 23.

[163] [2013] EWHC 231 (Admin), [2013] JPL 940.

it is not possible to modify the surviving adopted parts of the plan in the remitted examination. A further modification process would have to be followed. The *Broadland* remission did in the end lead to a complete adopted plan, and great care needs to be taken to produce such results.

When remitting a document the Court is empowered to 'give directions as to the actions to be taken in relation to the document'.[164] Those directions may:

(a) require the relevant document to be treated (generally or for specified purposes) as not having been approved or adopted;

(b) require specified steps in the process that has resulted in the approval or adoption of the relevant document to be treated (generally or for specified purposes) as having been taken or as not having been taken;

(c) require action to be taken by a person or body with a function relating to the preparation, publication, adoption or approval of the document (whether or not the person or body to which the document is remitted);

(d) require action to be taken by one person or body to depend on what action has been taken by another person or body.[165]

The power to give directions with a remittal are exercisable in relation to the whole or part of the document.[166] In *JJ Gallagher Ltd v Cherwell District Council*[167] the High Court considered that it was so obvious how the error should be corrected that Patterson J directed (i) the Secretary of State appoint a planning inspector who would recommend adoption of the policy subject to a modification deleting the prohibition on built development on the site and (ii) the planning authority adopt the policy subject to the modification recommended by the inspector. The Court of Appeal agreed and commenting on the powers available to the Court under s 113(7)(a)–(c) Lindblom LJ stated:[168]

> '29 The court's powers to grant appropriate relief under section 113(7), (7A), (7B) and (7C) are widely drawn. They afford the court an ample range of remedies to overcome unlawfulness in the various circumstances in which it may occur in a plan-making process. As was recognized by the judge in University of Bristol, the provisions in subsection (7A), (7B) and (7C) were a deliberate expansion of the court's powers to grant relief where a local plan is successfully challenged under section 113. They introduce greater flexibility in the remedies the court may fashion to deal with unlawfulness, having regard to the stage of the process at which it has arisen, and avoiding – when it is possible to do so – uncertainty, expense and delay. They include a broad range of potential requirements in directions given under subsection (7A), all of which go to "the action to be taken in relation to the [relevant] document". The four types of requirement specified in subsection (7B) are stated to be requirements which directions "may in particular" include. None of them, however, would warrant the substitution by the court of its own view as to the issues of substance in a plan-making process, or as to the substantive content of the plan – its policies and text. They do not allow the court to cross the firm boundary separating its proper function in adjudicating on statutory challenges and claims for judicial review in the planning field from the proper exercise of planning judgment by the decision-maker.

---

[164] PCPA 2004, s113(7)(b).
[165] PCPA 2004, s113(7)(b)..
[166] PCPA 2004, s 113(7)(c).
[167] [2016] EWHC 290 (Admin).
[168] *JJ Gallagher Ltd v Cherwell District Council* (sub nom *Woodfield v JJ Gallagher Ltd*) [2016] EWCA Civ 1007, [2016] 1 WLR 5126.

33   ... Such directions are, by their nature, a form of mandatory relief. They enable the court to fit the relief it grants precisely to the particular error of law, in the particular circumstances in which that has occurred. In principle, as I see it, they may be used to require the "person or body" in question to correct some obvious mistake or omission made in the course of the plan-making process, perhaps at a very late stage in the process, without upsetting the whole process by requiring its earlier stages to be gone through again. I cannot see why they should not be used, in an appropriate case, to give proper effect to a planning judgment already exercised by the "person or body" concerned – typically in the formulation of policy or text, or in the allocation of a site for development of a particular kind – or to ensure that a decision taken by that "person or body" in consequence of such an exercise of planning judgment is properly reflected in the outcome of the process. Used in this way, the court's power to give directions can overcome deficiencies in the process without its trespassing into the realm of planning judgment and without arrogating to itself the functions of the inspector who has conducted the examination of a local plan or of the local planning authority in preparing and adopting the plan.

34   There will, I think, be cases where the court can give directions requiring an inspector to recommend a modification in a particular form to reflect the conclusions in his report. In my view Mr Turney was right to accept that. But I think there will also be cases in which the court can properly give a direction under section 113(7A) requiring a local planning authority to adopt a local plan with a particular modification or modifications. Whether a direction of either kind is appropriate in a particular case will always depend on the individual circumstances of that case. In some cases it will be clear that the court can give such directions without transgressing the limits of its jurisdiction under section 113. It may only do so if the relevant planning judgment has already been lawfully exercised within the plan-making process itself, and the relevant consequences of that planning judgment are plain. The directions it gives, if crafted as they should be, will then result in the inspector's or the local planning authority's planning judgment – whichever it is – being given its true and intended effect. The court will have confined itself to rectifying the errors of law it has found, which is its proper remit in proceedings impugning the validity of an adopted local plan. And it will not have ventured into the forbidden realm of planning judgment, or usurped any function of the "person or body" whose error requires to be put right by the "action" prescribed for them under section 113(7A). There is nothing "constitutionally improper" about this, and nothing inconsistent with the ambit of remedies in public law nor with the court's powers to grant relief in claims for judicial review or under other kindred statutory provisions for challenges to planning decisions.'

For judicial review the Court's powers are extremely flexible, encompassing quashing mandatory and prohibitory orders, injunctions, damages and declarations.

COSTS

22.37   Costs are in the Court's discretion. However, the general rule is that the unsuccessful party will be ordered to pay the costs of the successful party'.[169] Consequently, the winner at the final hearing will usually recover its costs. Some exceptions do arise. There is a value in establishing unlawful acts by public authorities even if a substantive remedy is refused in the exercise of the Court's discretion. Lord Toulson JSC held in *R (on the application of Hunt) v North Somerset Council*:[170]

---

[169]   CPR 44.3(2)(a).
[170]   [2015] UKSC 51, [2015] 1 WLR 3575 at para 16.

'If a party who has been given leave to bring a judicial review claim succeeds in establishing after fully contested proceedings that the defendant acted unlawfully, some good reason would have to be shown why he should not recover his reasonable costs.'

In any proceedings some apportionment of costs might also arise. A party who has been ultimately successful but failed on a significant number of its arguments might not recover its full costs.

However, the losing party in judicial review or a statutory application or appeal will not normally be expected to pay more than one set of costs, for example, to both the Secretary of State and the respondent developer, unless this is justified by the case. Following conflicting case law, the House of Lords in *Bolton Metropolitan District Council v Secretary of State for the Environment (Practice Note)*[171] set out tests for these cases. Lord Lloyd said:[172]

'Where there is multiple representation, the losing party will not normally be required to pay more than one set of costs, unless the recovery of further costs is justified in the circumstances of the particular case.'

He continued:

'What then is the proper approach? As in all questions to do with costs, the fundamental rule is that there are no rules. Costs are always in the discretion of the court, and a practice, however widespread and longstanding, must never be allowed to harden into a rule. But the following propositions may be supported

(1)   The Secretary of State, when successful in defending his decision, will normally be entitled to the whole of his costs. He should not be required to share his award of costs by apportionment, whether by agreement with other parties, or by further order of the court. ...

(2)   The developer will not normally be entitled to his costs unless he can show that there was likely to be a separate issue on which he was entitled to be heard, that is to say an issue not covered by counsel for the Secretary of State; or unless he has an interest which requires separate representation. The mere fact that he is the developer will not of itself justify a second set of costs in every case.

(3)   A second set of costs is more likely to be awarded at first instance, than in the Court of Appeal or House of Lords, by which time the issues should have crystallised, and the extent to which there are indeed separate interests should have been clarified.'

The *Bolton* approach has been applied to judicial review and applications to the High Court under planning legislation. The starting point remains a presumption that only one set of costs will be awarded to a successful side. It may be that additional costs may be awarded in part, for example, where the developer helpfully put in evidence on a particular point.

Costs at permission hearings

22.38   In the case of *R (on the application of Mount Cook Land Ltd) v Westminster City Council*[173] Auld LJ laid out guidance as to the payment of costs at the permission stage of judicial review claims. He stated:

---

[171]   [1995] 1 WLR 1176.
[172]   At 1178.
[173]   [2003] EWCA Civ 1346, [2004] CP Rep 12.

'76. Accordingly, I would hold the following to be the proper approach to the award of costs against an unsuccessful claimant, and to the relationship of the obligation in CPR 54.8 on a defendant "who wishes to take part in the judicial review" to file an acknowledgment of service with the general rule in paragraph 8.6 of the Practice Direction that a successful defendant at an oral permission hearing should not generally be awarded costs against the claimant:

1) The effect of Leach, certainly in a case to which the Pre-Action Protocol applies and where a defendant or other interested party has complied with it, is that a successful defendant or other party at the permission stage who has filed an acknowledgment of service pursuant to CPR 54.8 should generally recover the costs of doing so from the claimant, whether or not he attends any permission hearing.

2) The effect of paragraph 8.6, when read with paragraph 8.5, of the Practice Direction, in conformity with the long-established practice of the courts in judicial review and the thinking of the Bowman Report giving rise to the CPR 54 procedure, is that a defendant who attends and successfully resists the grant of permission at a renewal hearing should not generally recover from the claimant his costs of and occasioned by doing so.

3) A court, in considering an award against an unsuccessful claimant of the defendant's and/or any other interested party's costs at a permission hearing, should only depart from the general guidance in the Practice Direction if he considers there are exceptional circumstances for doing so.

4) A court considering costs at the permission stage should be allowed a broad discretion as to whether, on the facts of the case, there are exceptional circumstances justifying the award of costs against an unsuccessful claimant;

5) Exceptional circumstances may consist in the presence of one or more of the features in the following non-exhaustive list:

a) the hopelessness of the claim:

b) the persistence in it by the claimant after having been alerted to facts and/or of the law demonstrating its hopelessness;

c) the extent to which the court considers that the claimant, in the pursuit of his application, has sought to abuse the process of judicial review for collateral ends — a relevant consideration as to costs at the permission stage, as well as when considering discretionary refusal of relief at the stage of substantive hearing, if there is one; and

d) whether, as a result of the deployment of full argument and documentary evidence by both sides at the hearing of a contested application, the unsuccessful claimant has had, in effect, the advantage of an early substantive hearing of the claim.

6) A relevant factor for a court, when considering the exercise of its discretion on the grounds of exceptional circumstances, may be the extent to which the unsuccessful claimant has substantial resources which it has used to pursue the unfounded claim and which are available to meet an order for costs.

7) The Court of Appeal should be slow to interfere with the broad discretion of the court below in its identification of factors constituting exceptional circumstances and in the exercise of its discretion whether to award costs against an unsuccessful claimant.'

In the context of statutory claims, Practice Direction 8C states:

'8.1 Neither the defendant nor any other person need attend a hearing on the question of permission unless the court directs otherwise.

8.2 Where the defendant or any party does attend a hearing, the court will not generally make an order for costs against the claimant.'

Given the content of paras 8.1 and 8.2 of Practice Direction 8C, it is highly likely that courts will apply the *Mount Cook* guidelines to permission hearings in statutory challenges.

Costs protection for parties

22.39 The final hearing of a Planning Court challenge will usually take one or two days. It would be rare for a case to take three or four days to argue and anything more would be exceptional. Parties do not tend to rack up several hundreds of thousands or millions of pounds in costs. Costs are, though, significant in any normal terms and whilst for the developer of a major project such costs may be unwelcome but manageable, for others they may be prohibitive. The greatest concerns tend to be expressed by local resident or pressure group claimants fearing liability for the other parties' costs. Whilst the prospect of paying the developer's costs is slim, those sums are potentially large.

Consequently, in certain circumstances costs protection may be applied, limiting the claimant's liability to adverse costs orders and, in return, restricting the claimant's potential to recover costs (a cross-cap). There are at present three categories of costs protection.

Aarhus Convention claims in judicial review

22.40 The Aarhus Convention on Access to Information, Public Participation in Decision-making and Access to Justice in Environmental Matters provides for access to court proceedings to review access to environmental information (Art 9(1)), environmental impact assessment or consultation on plans under Article 6 of the Convention (Art 9(2)) and acts and omissions which 'contravene provisions of [the Member State's] national law relating to the environment' (Art 9(3)). In all cases the proceedings must 'provide adequate and effective remedies, including injunctive relief as appropriate, and be fair, equitable, timely and not prohibitively expensive' (Art 9(4)).

Cost protection rules for Aarhus Convention claims were introduced into the CPR in April 2013. A claimant who brought judicial review proceedings within Article 9, paras (1)–(3) was able to have the case categorised as an Aarhus Convention claim under CPR 45.41. In such circumstances the claimant's liability was capped to £5,000 where the claimant is claiming only as an individual and not as, or on behalf of, a business or other legal person and in all other cases, £10,000. The defendant's liability in such cases was limited to £35,000.[174] On the CPR as was drafted, Aarhus Convention status could be claimed by any claimant, not just a member of the public and therefore included large local authorities: *R (HS2 Action Alliance, London Borough of Hillingdon) v Secretary of State for Transport.*[175]

Litigation following the introduction of those rules, revealed some issues with regards to their compliance with the Convention. In particular, in *Venn v Secretary of*

---

[174] The figures are in Practice Direction 45, paras 5.1, 5.2.
[175] [2015] EWCA Civ 203, [2015] 2 Costs LR 411.

State for Communities and Local Government[176] the Court of Appeal ruled that the CPR 45.41 procedure applied only to judicial review and not to statutory applications to the High Court, in that case, under the Town and Country Planning Act 1990, s 288[177] and that this omission was in breach of the Aarhus Convention.[178]

The case of *Venn* also identified the breadth of Article 9(3) of the Aarhus Convention in the context of planning cases, as including alleged breaches of planning policies concerned with protecting the environment.[179]

In late 2015, the government consulted on amendments to the rules relating to costs protection in certain environmental challenges. Following that consultation, the government amended section VII of Part 45 of the CPR. Under those amended rules, an 'Aarhus Convention claim' is defined as 'a claim brought by one or more members of the public:

'(i) by judicial review or review under statute which challenges the legality of any decision, act or omission of a body exercising public functions, and which is within the scope of Article 9(1) or 9(2) of the ... Aarhus Convention; or

(ii) by judicial review which challenges the legality of any such decision, act or omission and which is within the scope of Article 9(3) of the Aarhus Convention.'[180]

The rule states that references to a 'member or members of the public' are to be construed in accordance with the Aarhus Convention.[181]

The rules require that to benefit from the costs protection a claimant must state in the claim form that the claim is an 'Aarhus Convention claim' and must file and serve with the claim form a schedule of the claimant's financial resources which takes into account any financial support which any person has provided or is likely to provide to the claimant. The schedule must be verified by a statement of truth.[182]

The general rule is that a claimant who benefits from the costs protection may not be ordered to pay costs exceeding either £5,000 (where claiming as an individual and not on behalf of a business or other legal person) or £10,000 in other cases and that defendants will not be required to pay more than £35,000.[183] In the event that there are multiple claimants or multiple defendants, those amounts apply in relation to each claimant or defendant.[184]

However, the Court now has a discretion whether to vary the amounts stated above or to remove altogether the limits on maximum costs liabilities. CPR 45.44(2) states:

'(2) The court may vary such an amount or remove such a limit only if satisfied that –

(a) to do so would not make the costs of the proceedings prohibitively expensive for the claimant; and

---

[176] [2014] EWCA Civ 1539, [2015] 1 WLR 2328.
[177] At para 33 per Sullivan LJ.
[178] At paras 34, 35 per Sullivan LJ.
[179] At para 18 per Sullivan LJ.
[180] CPR 45.41(2)(a).
[181] CPR 45.41(2)(b). The Aarhus Compliance Committee has held that a Scottish community council is a member of the public for these purposes (ACCC/C/2102/68) but that a London borough council is not (ACCC/C/2014/100).
[182] CPR 45.42(1).
[183] CPR 45.43(2) and (3).
[184] CPR 45.43(4).

(b)   in the case of a variation which would reduce the claimant's maximum costs liability or increase that of a defendant, without the variation the costs of the proceedings would be prohibitively expensive for the claimant.'

The rules provide a list of indicators whereby proceedings are likely to be considered prohibitively expensive for the purposes of CPR 45.44. These are where the likely costs (including court fees) either:

'(a)   exceed the financial resources of the claimant; or

(b)   are objectively unreasonable having regard to –

(i)   the situation of the parties;

(ii)   whether the claimant has a reasonable prospect of success;

(iii)   the importance of what is at stake for the claimant;

(iv)   the importance of what is at stake for the environment;

(v)   the complexity of the relevant law and procedure; and

(vi)   whether the claim is frivolous.'[185]

A defendant may challenge whether a claim is an Aarhus Convention claim. Where a defendant does so, the Court must determine the issue at the earliest opportunity.[186] Where the Court decides that the claim is not an Aarhus Convention claim, it will normally make no order for costs in relation to those proceedings.[187] However, where the Court decides the claim is an Aarhus Convention claim it will normally order that the defendant pays the claimant's costs on the standard basis, even where this would increase the costs payable by the defendant beyond that in rule 45.43(3) (£35,000) or any variation of that amount.[188]

The amendments of the Aarhus cost protection rules were the subject of a High Court challenge brought by ClientEarth, Friends of the Earth and the RSPB.[189] The claimants alleged that the amendments: were a breach of EU law, ought to have provided for hearings into the financial resources of a claimant or their supporters to be in private and that the assessment of what costs were reasonable for a claimant to bear should take into account the claimant's own legal costs.

Dove J rejected the first ground of challenge. He held that when considered within the context of surrounding procedural rules and practices the rules did not breach EU law. In reaching this conclusion the judge noted that key to the requirement of European law that proceedings should not be prohibitively expensive was the principle that the claimant should be provided with reasonable predictability with regards to whether costs would be payable and as to their amount. The judge held that two key questions emerged: (1) would there be a determination as to the variation of the costs cap at an early stage of proceedings, and (2) did the possibility for a later variation of the costs cap conflict with the requirement for reasonable predictability? The judge found that reading the rules as a whole, any dispute regarding the level of costs caps should be raised at the point of the acknowledgement of service and a decision on the costs cap

---

[185]   CPR 45.44(3).

[186]   CPR 45.45(2).

[187]   CPR 45.45(3)(a).

[188]   CPR 45.45(3)(b).

[189]   *R (on the application of Royal Society for the Protection of Birds) v Secretary of State for Justice* [2017] EWHC 2309 (Admin), [2017] 5 Costs LO691.

made at an early stage of proceedings. Were a defendant to seek to vary the costs cap at a later stage this would have to be for good reason which would be either: that the claimant had misled the court when submitting their statement of financial means or the claimant had, subsequent to the filing of the claim, come into some money which affected their ability to pay legal costs.

However, the claim did succeed on the second and third grounds. The judge further found that the rules should have provided for hearings in private both so as to prevent the airing of confidential information and to avoid a chilling effect on claimants and he agreed with the parties (the defendant having conceded the point) that the claimant's own costs should be taken into account when considering what sum was reasonable for a claimant to bear.

Protective costs orders generally

22.41   Where the claim is outside the Aarhus Convention claim rules, for example, where it is not brought by a 'member of the public', then a protective costs order ('PCO') may be applied for.

In August 2016, the Criminal Justice and Courts Act 2015 introduced a costs capping regime which applies in relation to judicial review proceedings. However, that regime does not apply in relation to judicial review proceedings which are Aarhus Convention claims commenced on or after 28 February 2017 or an appeal made against a decision in such a claim.[190]

Where the regime does apply, it prohibits costs capping orders from being made by either the High Court or Court of Appeal in connection with judicial review proceedings except in accordance with ss 88 and 89 of that Act. Section 88 provides that a costs capping order may only be made:

(a)   if leave to apply for judicial review has been granted;

(b)   if an application for such an order has been made by the applicant in accordance with the rules of court;

(c)   if the Court is satisfied that:

(i)   the proceedings are public interest proceedings,

(ii)   in the absence of the order, the applicant for judicial review would withdraw the application for judicial review or cease to participate in the proceedings, and

(iii)   it would be reasonable for the applicant for judicial review to do so.

'Public Interest proceedings' are defined by s 88 as proceedings where:

(a)   an issue that is the subject of the proceedings is of general public importance;

(b)   the public interest requires the issue to be resolved; and

(c)   the proceedings are likely to provide an appropriate means of resolving it.

---

[190]   Criminal Justice and Courts Act 2015, s 91 and the Criminal Justice and Courts Act 2015 (Disapplication of Sections 88 and 89) Regulations 2017, SI 2017/100.

Section 89(1) sets out a range of matters to which the Court must have regard when deciding whether to make a costs capping order in connection with judicial review proceedings. Subsection (2) provides that where a costs capping order removes or limits the liability of the applicant to pay the costs of another party if relief is not granted, it must also limit or remove the liability of the other party to pay the applicant's costs if it is.

In relation to statutory challenges which do not fall within the Aarhus costs provisions the standard criteria to be applied remain those in *R (on the application of Corner House Research) v Secretary of State for Trade and Industry*[191] which as subsequently applied are:

(i)   the issues raised are of general public importance;

(ii)   the public interest requires that those issues be resolved;

(iii)   having regard to the financial resources of the applicant and the respondent(s) and to the amount of costs that are likely to be involved, it is fair and just to make the order;

(iv)   if the order is not made the applicant will probably discontinue the proceedings and will be acting reasonably in so doing.

Protective costs orders in cases falling under certain European Directives

22.42   Some European Directives provide that the public concerned in a decision may apply for a review of its legality. Reflecting the Aarhus Convention, this procedure shall not be prohibitively expensive.[192] In decisions subject to these Directives the public importance and public interest tests under *Corner House* are considered always to be satisfied, whether or not the ground of challenge relates to the Directives.[193]

Appealing to the Court of Appeal in judicial review and section 113 cases

22.43   Where a section 113 application or judicial review proceedings have gone to a final hearing permission to appeal is required and may be sought from the High Court or the Court of Appeal. Whilst there is no requirement to apply for permission from the High Court before an application for permission to appeal can be made to the Court of Appeal, it is conventional to ask the High Court judge who decided the case for permission first. There is little to be lost from making the application and it is possible that permission to appeal will be granted. At the least it provides a first opportunity to think through the grounds of appeal before applying to the Court of Appeal.

The appellants' notice, ground and skeleton submissions must be filed in the Civil Appeals Office within 21 days from the decision on the case in the High Court unless altered by the High Court judge.

---

[191]   [2005] EWCA Civ 192, [2005] 1 WLR 2600.

[192]   See the Environmental Impact Assessment Directive 85/337/EEC, Art 11(4).

[193]   *R (on the application of Garner) v Elmbridge Borough Council* [2010] EWCA Civ 1006, [2012] PTSR 250, at para 39 per Sullivan LJ. For the potential considerations in European law cases, see *R (on the application of Edwards) v Environment Agency* (C-260/11) [2013] 1 WLR 2914 and [2013] UKSC 78, [2014] 1 WLR 55.

Where permission to apply under s 113 or judicial review has been refused either following an oral hearing or by a judge on the papers who has certified the application as totally without merit then permission to appeal can only be sought from the Court of Appeal. In those cases the appellant's notice, ground and skeleton submissions must be filed in the Civil Appeals Office within seven days from the hearing or the receipt of the written decision.[194] These are technically 'applications for permission to appeal the refusal of permission to apply for' planning statutory review or judicial review. Whilst the Court of Appeal can grant permission to appeal and then hold a full hearing to decide whether permission to apply under s 113 or for judicial review should be granted it is common for the Court to simply grant permission to bring the statutory review or judicial review rather than permission to appeal.[195] Such cases will usually be returned to the High Court for a substantive hearing[196] but may be retained in the Court of Appeal, usually if the facts are all in front of the Court and there has been a detailed High Court judgment which has clarified the circumstances and the issues.

In any of these appeals the rule for the grant of permission to appeal is in CPR 52.3(6):

> 'Permission to appeal may be given only where:
>
> (a) the court considers that the appeal would have a real prospect of success; or
>
> (b) there is some other compelling reason why the appeal should be heard.'

Ordinarily the appellant would have taken an active part in the High Court proceedings. However, a person who could have taken part in the lower court but did not do so can appeal.[197]

VALIDITY OF MARINE POLICY STATEMENTS AND MARINE PLANS

22.44   The validity of marine policy statements, marine plans or their amendments cannot be challenged except by way of legal proceedings brought pursuant to s 62 of the Marine and Coastal Access Act 2009 ('MCAA 2009'). The test in subsection 4 states:

> '(4) A person aggrieved by a relevant document may make an application to the appropriate court on any of the following grounds –
>
> (a) that the document is not within the appropriate powers;
>
> (b) that a procedural requirement has not been complied with.'

---

[194] For section 288 applications, see CPR 52.15B(3).

[195] It is empowered to do this for planning reviews by CPR 52.15B(4) and for judicial review by CPR 52.15(3).

[196] See for planning reviews CPR 52.15B(5) and for judicial review CPR 52.15(4).

[197] See *George Wimpey UK Ltd v Tewkesbury Borough Council* [2012] EWCA Civ 12, [2008] 1 WLR 1649 and *JJ Gallagher Ltd v Cherwell District Council* (sub nom *Woodfield v JJ Gallagher Ltd*) [2016] EWCA Civ 1007, [2016] 1 WLR 5126. An example would be a developer leaving the defence of an allocation in the High Court to the local planning authority and seeking to appeal when the authority has been unsuccessful. It would though invariably be better for a party to take part in the High Court rather than to try to salvage the position on appeal.

A challenge under s 62 must be made within six weeks of the publication of the marine policy statement, marine plan or the amendment.[198] Where the impugned document relates to the English inshore region or the Welsh inshore region, the 'appropriate court' will be the High Court. In any other case, the challenge may be brought in any superior court (High Court or the Court of Session) in the UK.[199]

Although CPR Practice Direction 8C does not apply to section 62 challenges, like a section 113 application, a challenge under s 62 of MCAA 2009 is unlikely to involve a substantial dispute of fact and therefore the Part 8 procedure in the CPR is likely to be the most appropriate procedure to be used.[200] However, the permission of the Court is not required to bring the proceedings.

Where an application is brought under s 62 the Court may suspend the operation of a marine policy statement, marine plan (or part thereof) until the challenge has been finally determined.[201] Where the Court is satisfied that the marine policy statement, marine plan or amendment is outside the appropriate powers or that the interests of the applicant have been substantially prejudiced by the failure to comply with a procedural requirement it may quash the relevant document or remit it to a body with a function relating to its preparation, adoption or publication.[202]

JUDICIAL REVIEW IN NORTHERN IRELAND

22.45   Procedures in Northern Ireland are refreshingly straightforward compared to the multitude of different, and often mutually exclusive provisions in England and Wales. All challenges to the making of policy or steps in their processes are subject to judicial review.

Proceedings are governed by Order 53 of the Rules of the Court of Judicature and guidance is given by the Judicial Review Practice Note 1/2008. Pre-action protocol letters are expected.

Applications are made by lodging an ex parte docket, an Order 53 statement and affidavit evidence. The expectation has been that the Order 53 statement will set out the grounds but neither evidence nor arguments. In practice though such statements are becoming fuller and should enable the judge to decide whether the case is arguable. There is no procedure for grounds of resistance to be filed before leave is determined, although the pre-action protocol responses should be put before the Court. Whilst leave applications can be decided on the papers, they have often been referred to oral hearings.

A claim should be brought within three months from the date when the grounds for the application first arose.[203] This time limit has been introduced for proceedings commenced on or after 8 January 2018, replacing the previous 'promptly and within three months' rule. Promptness had been applied quite strictly, but also unpredictably,

---

[198]   MCAA 2009, s 62(5).
[199]   MCAA 2009, s 62(6).
[200]   CPR 8.1(1).
[201]   MCAA 2009, s 63(2).
[202]   MCAA 2009, s 63(3) and (4).
[203]   RCJ Order 53, r 4(1) as amended by Rules of the Court of Judicature (Northern Ireland) (Amendment) 2017, SR 2017/213, r 2.

in planning cases so the removal of the requirement is helpful. Extensions of time can be granted but would need a very considerable justification.

The remedies available to the Court are the same as those in England and Wales, albeit expressed in the traditional language: mandamus (mandatory); certiorari (quashing), prohibition, declaration, injunction and damages. This does give greater flexibility than in statutory reviews in England and Wales but the Court will still refrain from rewriting the decision.[204]

---

[204] See the Belfast Metropolitan Area Plan litigation: *Belfast City Council v Minister of Enterprise, Trade & Investment* [2017] NICA 28 at 16.9 above.

Town and Country Planning Act 1990

PART III CONTROL OVER DEVELOPMENT

[Neighbourhood development orders

61E Neighbourhood development orders

(1)   Any qualifying body is entitled to initiate a process for the purpose of requiring a local planning authority in England to make a neighbourhood development order.

(2)   A 'neighbourhood development order' is an order which grants planning permission in relation to a particular neighbourhood area specified in the order—

    (a)   for development specified in the order, or

    (b)   for development of any class specified in the order.

(3)   Schedule 4B makes provision about the process for the making of neighbourhood development orders, including—

    (a)   provision for independent examination of orders proposed by qualifying bodies, and

    (b)   provision for the holding of referendums on orders proposed by those bodies.

(4)   A local planning authority to whom a proposal for the making of a neighbourhood development order has been made—

    (a)   must make a neighbourhood development order to which the proposal relates if in each applicable referendum under that Schedule more than half of those voting have voted in favour of the order, and

    (b)   if paragraph (a) applies, must make the order as soon as reasonably practicable after the referendum is held [and, in any event, by such date as may be prescribed][1].

(5)   If—

    (a)   there are two applicable referendums under that Schedule (because the order relates to a neighbourhood area designated as a business area under section 61H), and

---

[1]   Inserted by the Housing and Planning Act 2016, s 140(2).

    (b)   in one of those referendums (but not the other) more than half of those voting have voted in favour of the order,

the authority may (but need not) make a neighbourhood development order to which the proposal relates.

(6)   A 'qualifying body' means a parish council, or an organisation or body designated as a neighbourhood forum, authorised for the purposes of a neighbourhood development order to act in relation to a neighbourhood area as a result of section 61F.

(7)   For the meaning of 'neighbourhood area', see sections 61G and 61I(1).

(8)   The authority are not to be subject to the duty under subsection (4)(a) if they consider that the making of the order would breach, or would otherwise be incompatible with, any EU obligation or any of the Convention rights (within the meaning of the Human Rights Act 1998).

(9)   Regulations may make provision as to the procedure to be followed by local planning authorities in cases where they act under subsection (8).

(10)   The regulations may in particular make provision—

    (a)   for the holding of an examination,

    (b)   as to the payment by a local planning authority of remuneration and expenses of the examiner,

    (c)   as to the award of costs by the examiner,

    (d)   as to the giving of notice and publicity,

    (e)   as to the information and documents that are to be made available to the public,

    (f)   as to the making of reasonable charges for anything provided as a result of the regulations,

    (g)   as to consultation with and participation by the public, and

    (h)   as to the making and consideration of representations (including the time by which representations must be made).

(11)   The authority must publish in such manner as may be prescribed—

    (a)   their decision to act under subsection (4) or (8),

    (b)   their reasons for making that decision, and

    (c)   such other matters relating to that decision as may be prescribed.

(12)   The authority must send a copy of the matters required to be published to—

    (a)   the qualifying body that initiated the process for the making of the order, and

    (b)   such other persons as may be prescribed.

(13)   A local planning authority must publish each neighbourhood development order that they make in such manner as may be prescribed.][2]

---

[2]   Inserted by the Localism Act 2011, s 116(1), Sch 9, paras 1, 2.

[61F Authorisation to act in relation to neighbourhood areas

(1)   For the purposes of a neighbourhood development order, a parish council are authorised to act in relation to a neighbourhood area if that area consists of or includes the whole or any part of the area of the council.

(2)   If that neighbourhood area also includes the whole or any part of the area of another parish council, the parish council is authorised for those purposes to act in relation to that neighbourhood area only if the other parish council have given their consent.

(3)   For the purposes of a neighbourhood development order, an organisation or body is authorised to act in relation to a neighbourhood area if it is designated by a local planning authority as a neighbourhood forum for that area.

(4)   An organisation or body may be designated for a neighbourhood area only if that area does not consist of or include the whole or any part of the area of a parish council.

(5)   A local planning authority may designate an organisation or body as a neighbourhood forum if the authority are satisfied that it meets the following conditions—

   (a)   it is established for the express purpose of promoting or improving the social, economic and environmental wellbeing of an area that consists of or includes the neighbourhood area concerned (whether or not it is also established for the express purpose of promoting the carrying on of trades, professions or other businesses in such an area),

   (b)   its membership is open to—

      (i)   individuals who live in the neighbourhood area concerned,

      (ii)   individuals who work there (whether for businesses carried on there or otherwise), and

      (iii)   individuals who are elected members of a county council, district council or London borough council any of whose area falls within the neighbourhood area concerned,

   (c)   its membership includes a minimum of 21 individuals each of whom—

      (i)   lives in the neighbourhood area concerned,

      (ii)   works there (whether for a business carried on there or otherwise), or

      (iii)   is an elected member of a county council, district council or London borough council any of whose area falls within the neighbourhood area concerned,

   (d)   it has a written constitution, and

   (e)   such other conditions as may be prescribed.

(6)   A local planning authority may also designate an organisation or body as a neighbourhood forum if they are satisfied that the organisation or body meets prescribed conditions.

(7) A local planning authority—

    (a) must, in determining under subsection (5) whether to designate an organisation or body as a neighbourhood forum for a neighbourhood area, have regard to the desirability of designating an organisation or body—

        (i) which has secured (or taken reasonable steps to attempt to secure) that its membership includes at least one individual falling within each of sub-paragraphs (i) to (iii) of subsection (5)(b),

        (ii) whose membership is drawn from different places in the neighbourhood area concerned and from different sections of the community in that area, and

        (iii) whose purpose reflects (in general terms) the character of that area,

    (b) may designate only one organisation or body as a neighbourhood forum for each neighbourhood area,

    (c) may designate an organisation or body as a neighbourhood forum only if the organisation or body has made an application to be designated, and

    (d) must give reasons to an organisation or body applying to be designated as a neighbourhood forum where the authority refuse the application.

(8) A designation—

    (a) ceases to have effect at the end of the period of 5 years beginning with the day on which it is made but without affecting the validity of any proposal for a neighbourhood development order made before the end of that period, and

    (b) in the case of the designation of an unincorporated association, is not to be affected merely because of a change in the membership of the association.

(9) A local planning authority may withdraw an organisation or body's designation as a neighbourhood forum if they consider that the organisation or body is no longer meeting—

    (a) the conditions by reference to which it was designated, or

    (b) any other criteria to which the authority were required to have regard in making the designation;

and, where an organisation or body's designation is withdrawn, the authority must give reasons to the organisation or body.

(10) A proposal for a neighbourhood development order by a parish council or neighbourhood forum may not be made at any time in relation to a neighbourhood area if there is at that time another proposal by the council or forum in relation to that area that is outstanding.

(11) Each local planning authority must make such arrangements as they consider appropriate for making people aware as to the times when organisations or bodies could make applications to be designated as neighbourhood forums for neighbourhood areas.

(12) Regulations—

    (a)   may make provision in connection with proposals made by qualifying bodies for neighbourhood development orders, and

    (b)   may make provision in connection with designations (or withdrawals of designations) of organisations or bodies as neighbourhood forums (including provision of a kind mentioned in section 61G(11)(a) to (g)).

(13) The regulations may in particular make provision—

    (a)   as to the consequences of the creation of a new parish council, or a change in the area of a parish council, on any proposal made for a neighbourhood development order,

    (b)   as to the consequences of the dissolution of a neighbourhood forum on any proposal for a neighbourhood development order made by it,

    (c)   suspending the operation of any duty of a local planning authority under paragraph 6 or 7 of Schedule 4B in cases where they are considering the withdrawal of the designation of an organisation or body as a neighbourhood forum,

    (d)   for determining when a proposal for a neighbourhood development order is to be regarded as outstanding, and

    (e)   requiring a local planning authority to have regard (in addition, where relevant, to the matters set out in subsection (7)(a)) to prescribed matters in determining whether to designate an organisation or body as a neighbourhood forum.][3]

[61G Meaning of 'neighbourhood area'

(1)   A 'neighbourhood area' means an area within the area of a local planning authority in England which has been designated by the authority as a neighbourhood area; but that power to designate is exercisable only where—

    (a)   a relevant body has applied to the authority for an area specified in the application to be designated by the authority as a neighbourhood area, and

    (b)   the authority are determining the application (but see subsection (5)).

(2)   A 'relevant body' means—

    (a)   a parish council, or

    (b)   an organisation or body which is, or is capable of being, designated as a neighbourhood forum (on the assumption that, for this purpose, the specified area is designated as a neighbourhood area).

(3)   The specified area—

    (a)   in the case of an application by a parish council, must be one that consists of or includes the whole or any part of the area of the council, and

    (b)   in the case of an application by an organisation or body, must not be one that consists of or includes the whole or any part of the area of a parish council.

---

[3]   Inserted by the Localism Act 2011, s 116(1), Sch 9, paras 1, 2.

(4)   In determining an application the authority must have regard to—

    (a)   the desirability of designating the whole of the area of a parish council as a neighbourhood area, and

    (b)   the desirability of maintaining the existing boundaries of areas already designated as neighbourhood areas.

(5)   If—

    (a)   a valid application is made to the authority,

    (b)   some or all of the specified area has not been designated as a neighbourhood area, and

    (c)   the authority refuse the application because they consider that the specified area is not an appropriate area to be designated as a neighbourhood area,

the authority must exercise their power of designation so as to secure that some or all of the specified area forms part of one or more areas designated (or to be designated) as neighbourhood areas.

(6)   The authority may, in determining any application, modify designations already made; but if a modification relates to any extent to the area of a parish council, the modification may be made only with the council's consent.

(7)   The areas designated as neighbourhood areas must not overlap with each other.

(8)   A local planning authority must publish a map setting out the areas that are for the time being designated as neighbourhood areas.

(9)   If the authority refuse an application, they must give reasons to the applicant for refusing the application.

(10)   In this section 'specified', in relation to an application, means specified in the application.

(11)   Regulations may make provision in connection with the designation of areas as neighbourhood areas; and the regulations may in particular make provision—

    (a)   as to the procedure to be followed in relation to designations,

    (b)   as to the giving of notice and publicity in connection with designations,

    (c)   as to consultation with and participation by the public in relation to designations,

    (d)   as to the making and consideration of representations about designations (including the time by which representations must be made),

    (e)   as to the form and content of applications for designations,

    (f)   requiring an application for a designation to be determined by a prescribed date,

    (g)   entitling or requiring a local planning authority in prescribed circumstances to decline to consider an application for a designation, and

    (h)   about the modification of designations (including provision about the consequences of modification on proposals for neighbourhood development orders, or on neighbourhood development orders, that have already been made).

[(12) Regulations under subsection (11) may provide that where an application under this section—

(a) meets prescribed criteria, or

(b) has not been determined within a prescribed period, the local planning authority must, except in prescribed cases or circumstances, exercise their powers under this section to designate the specified area as a neighbourhood area.

(13) The reference in subsection (12) to the designation of an area as a neighbourhood area includes the modification under subsection (6) of a designation already made.]⁴]⁵

[61H Neighbourhood areas designated as business areas

(1) Whenever a local planning authority exercise their powers under section 61G to designate an area as a neighbourhood area, they must consider whether they should designate the area concerned as a business area.

(2) The reference here to the designation of an area as a neighbourhood area includes the modification under section 61G(6) of a designation already made.

(3) The power of a local planning authority to designate a neighbourhood area as a business area is exercisable by the authority only if, having regard to such matters as may be prescribed, they consider that the area is wholly or predominantly business in nature.

(4) The map published by a local planning authority under section 61G(8) must state which neighbourhood areas (if any) are for the time being designated as business areas.]⁶

[61I Neighbourhood areas in areas of two or more local planning authorities

(1) The power to designate an area as a neighbourhood area under section 61G is exercisable by two or more local planning authorities in England if the area falls within the areas of those authorities.

(2) Regulations may make provision in connection with—

(a) the operation of subsection (1), and

(b) the operation of other provisions relating to neighbourhood development orders (including sections 61F to 61H) in cases where an area is designated as a neighbourhood area as a result of that subsection.

(3) The regulations may in particular make provision—

(a) modifying or supplementing the application of, or disapplying, any of the provisions mentioned in subsection (2)(b),

(b) applying (with or without modifications) any provision of Part 6 of the Local Government Act 1972 (discharge of functions) in cases where the provision would not otherwise apply,

---

⁴   Inserted by the Housing and Planning Act 2016, s 139.
⁵   Inserted by the Localism Act 2011, s 116(1), Sch 9, paras 1, 2.
⁶   Inserted by the Localism Act 2011, s 116(1), Sch 9, paras 1, 2.

(c)   requiring local planning authorities to exercise, or not to exercise, any power conferred by any provision of that Part (including as applied by virtue of paragraph (b)), and

(d)   conferring powers or imposing duties on local planning authorities.][7]

[61J Provision that may be made by neighbourhood development order

(1)   A neighbourhood development order may make provision in relation to—

(a)   all land in the neighbourhood area specified in the order,

(b)   any part of that land, or

(c)   a site in that area specified in the order.

(2)   A neighbourhood development order may not provide for the granting of planning permission for any development that is excluded development.

(3)   For the meaning of 'excluded development', see section 61K.

(4)   A neighbourhood development order may not grant planning permission for any development in any particular case where planning permission is already granted for that development in that case.

(5)   A neighbourhood development order may not relate to more than one neighbourhood area.

(6)   A neighbourhood development order may make different provision for different cases or circumstances.][8]

[61K Meaning of 'excluded development'

The following development is excluded development for the purposes of section 61J—

(a)   development that consists of a county matter within paragraph 1(1)(a) to (h) of Schedule 1,

(b)   development that consists of the carrying out of any operation, or class of operation, prescribed under paragraph 1(j) of that Schedule (waste development) but that does not consist of development of a prescribed description,

(c)   development that falls within Annex 1 to Council Directive 85/337/EEC on the assessment of the effects of certain public and private projects on the environment (as amended from time to time),

(d)   development that consists (whether wholly or partly) of a nationally significant infrastructure project (within the meaning of the Planning Act 2008),

(e)   prescribed development or development of a prescribed description, and

(f)   development in a prescribed area or an area of a prescribed description.][9]

---

[7]   Inserted by the Localism Act 2011, s 116(1), Sch 9, paras 1, 2.
[8]   Inserted by the Localism Act 2011, s 116(1), Sch 9, paras 1, 2.
[9]   Inserted by the Localism Act 2011, s 116(1), Sch 9, paras 1, 2.

[61L Permission granted by neighbourhood development orders

(1) Planning permission granted by a neighbourhood development order may be granted—

    (a) unconditionally, or

    (b) subject to such conditions or limitations as are specified in the order.

(2) The conditions that may be specified include—

    (a) obtaining the approval of the local planning authority who made the order but not of anyone else, and

    (b) provision specifying the period within which applications must be made to a local planning authority for the approval of the authority of any matter specified in the order.

(3) Regulations may make provision entitling a parish council in prescribed circumstances to require any application for approval under subsection (2) of a prescribed description to be determined by them instead of by a local planning authority.

(4) The regulations may in particular make provision—

    (a) as to the procedure to be followed by parish councils in deciding whether to determine applications for approvals (including the time by which the decisions must be made),

    (b) requiring parish councils in prescribed circumstances to cease determining applications for approvals,

    (c) conferring powers or imposing duties on local planning authorities,

    (d) treating parish councils as local planning authorities (instead of, or in addition to, the authorities) for the purposes of the determination of applications for approvals (subject to such exceptions or modifications in the application of any enactment as may be prescribed),

    (e) applying any enactment relating to principal councils within the meaning of section 270 of the Local Government Act 1972 for those purposes (with or without modifications), and

    (f) disapplying, or modifying the application of, any enactment relating to parish councils for those purposes.

(5) A neighbourhood development order may provide for the granting of planning permission to be subject to the condition that the development begins before the end of the period specified in the order.

(6) Regulations may make provision as to the periods that may be specified in neighbourhood development orders under subsection (5).

(7) If—

    (a) planning permission granted by a neighbourhood development order for any development is withdrawn by the revocation of the order under section 61M, and

    (b) the revocation is made after the development has begun but before it has been completed, the development may, despite the withdrawal of the permission, be completed.

(8) But an order under section 61M revoking a neighbourhood development order may provide that subsection (7) is not to apply in relation to development specified in the order under that section.][10]

[61M Revocation or modification of neighbourhood development orders

(1) The Secretary of State may ...[11] revoke a neighbourhood development order.

(2) A local planning authority may, with the consent of the Secretary of State, ...[12] revoke a neighbourhood development order that they have made.

(3) If a neighbourhood development order is revoked, the person revoking the order must state the reasons for the revocation.

(4) A local planning authority may at any time ...[13] modify a neighbourhood development order that they have made for the purpose of correcting errors.

(5) If the qualifying body that initiated the process for the making of that order is still authorised at that time to act for the purposes of a neighbourhood development order in relation to the neighbourhood area concerned, the power under subsection (4) is exercisable only with that body's consent.

(6) A modification of a neighbourhood development order is to be done by replacing the order with a new one containing the modification.

(7) Regulations may make provision in connection with the revocation or modification of a neighbourhood development order.

(8) The regulations may in particular make provision—

(a) for the holding of an examination in relation to a revocation proposed to be made by the authority,

(b) as to the payment by a local planning authority of remuneration and expenses of the examiner,

(c) as to the award of costs by the examiner,

(d) as to the giving of notice and publicity in connection with a revocation or modification,

(e) as to the information and documents relating to a revocation or modification that are to be made available to the public,

(f) as to the making of reasonable charges for anything provided as a result of the regulations,

(g) as to consultation with and participation by the public in relation to a revocation, and

10 Inserted by the Localism Act 2011, s 116(1), Sch 9, paras 1, 2.
11 Repealed (by modification) by the Planning and Compulsory Purchase Act 2004, s 38C(3) (as inserted by the Localism Act 2011, s 116(1), Sch 9, paras 5, 7).
12 Repealed (by modification) by the Planning and Compulsory Purchase Act 2004, s 38C(3) (as inserted by the Localism Act 2011, s 116(1), Sch 9, paras 5, 7).
13 Repealed (by modification) by the Planning and Compulsory Purchase Act 2004, s 38C(3) (as inserted by the Localism Act 2011, s 116(1), Sch 9, paras 5, 7).

(h)   as to the making and consideration of representations about a revocation (including the time by which representations must be made).][14]

[61N Legal challenges in relation to neighbourhood development orders

(1)   A court may entertain proceedings for questioning a decision to act under [section 38A(4) or (6) of the Planning and Compulsory Purchase Act 2004][15] only if—

   (a)   the proceedings are brought by a claim for judicial review, and

   (b)   the claim form is filed before the end of the period of 6 weeks beginning with [the day after][16] the day on which the decision is published.

(2)   A court may entertain proceedings for questioning a decision under paragraph 12 of Schedule 4B (consideration by local planning authority of recommendations made by examiner etc) [or paragraph 13B of that Schedule (intervention powers of Secretary of State)][17] only if—

   (a)   the proceedings are brought by a claim for judicial review, and

   (b)   the claim form is filed before the end of the period of 6 weeks beginning with [the day after][18] the day on which the decision is published.

(3)   A court may entertain proceedings for questioning anything relating to a referendum under paragraph 14 or 15 of Schedule 4B only if—

   (a)   the proceedings are brought by a claim for judicial review, and

   (b)   the claim form is filed [before the end of][19] the period of 6 weeks beginning with [the day after][20] the day on which the result of the referendum is declared.][21]

[61O Guidance

Local planning authorities must have regard to any guidance issued by the Secretary of State in the exercise of any function under any provision relating to neighbourhood development orders (including any function under any of sections 61F to 61H).][22]

[61P Provision as to the making of certain decisions by local planning authorities

(1)   Regulations may make provision regulating the arrangements of a local planning authority for the making of any prescribed decision under any provision relating to neighbourhood development orders (including under any of sections 61F to 61H).

(2)   The provision made by the regulations is to have effect despite provision made by any enactment as to the arrangements of a local planning authority for the

---

[14]   Inserted by the Localism Act 2011, s 116(1), Sch 9, paras 1, 2.
[15]   Substituted (by modification) by the Planning and Compulsory Purchase Act 2004, s 38C(4) (as inserted by the Localism Act 2011, s 116(1), Sch 9, paras 5, 7).
[16]   Inserted by the Criminal Justice and Courts Act 2015, s 92(1)(a), (b)(ii).
[17]   Inserted by the Housing and Planning Act 2016, s 141(3).
[18]   Inserted by the Criminal Justice and Courts Act 2015, s 92(1)(a), (b)(ii).
[19]   Substituted by the Criminal Justice and Courts Act 2015, s 92(1)(b)(i).
[20]   Inserted by the Criminal Justice and Courts Act 2015, s 92(1)(a), (b)(ii).
[21]   Inserted by the Localism Act 2011, s 116(1), Sch 9, paras 1, 2.
[22]   Inserted by the Localism Act 2011, s 116(1), Sch 9, paras 1, 2.

exercise of their functions (such as section 101 of the Local Government Act 1972 or section 13 of the Local Government Act 2000).][23]

[61Q Community right to build orders

Schedule 4C makes provision in relation to a particular type of neighbourhood development order (a community right to build order).][24]

[SCHEDULE 4B PROCESS FOR MAKING OF NEIGHBOURHOOD DEVELOPMENT ORDERS

Proposals for neighbourhood development orders

1

(1) A qualifying body is entitled to submit a proposal to a local planning authority for the making of a neighbourhood development order by the authority in relation to a neighbourhood area within the area of the authority.

(2) The proposal must be accompanied by—

(a) a draft of the order, and

(b) a statement which contains a summary of the proposals and sets out the reasons why an order should be made in the proposed terms.

(3) The proposal must—

(a) be made in the prescribed form, and

(b) be accompanied by other documents and information of a prescribed description.

(4) The qualifying body must send to prescribed persons a copy of—

(a) the proposal,

(b) the draft neighbourhood development order, and

(c) such of the other documents and information accompanying the proposal as may be prescribed.

(5) The Secretary of State may publish a document setting standards for—

(a) the preparation of a draft neighbourhood development order and other documents accompanying the proposal,

(b) the coverage in any document accompanying the proposal of a matter falling to be dealt with in it, and

(c) all or any of the collection, sources, verification, processing and presentation of information accompanying the proposal.

(6) The documents and information accompanying the proposal (including the draft neighbourhood development order) must comply with those standards.][25]

---

23 Inserted by the Localism Act 2011, s 116(1), Sch 9, paras 1, 2.
24 Inserted by the Localism Act 2011, s 116(1), Sch 9, paras 1, 2.
25 Inserted by the Localism Act 2011, s 116(2), Sch 10.

[2

(1) A qualifying body may withdraw a proposal at any time before the local planning authority make a decision under paragraph 12.

(2) If—

    (a) a proposal by a qualifying body is made by an organisation or body designated as a neighbourhood forum, and

    (b) the designation is withdrawn at any time before the proposal is submitted for independent examination under paragraph 7,

the proposal is to be treated as withdrawn by the qualifying body at that time.

(3) If the withdrawal of the designation occurs after the proposal is submitted for independent examination under that paragraph, the withdrawal is not to affect the validity of the proposal.][26]

[Advice and assistance in connection with proposals

3

(1) A local planning authority must give such advice or assistance to qualifying bodies as, in all the circumstances, they consider appropriate for the purpose of, or in connection with, facilitating the making of proposals for neighbourhood development orders in relation to neighbourhood areas within their area.

(2) Nothing in this paragraph is to be read as requiring the giving of financial assistance.][27]

[Requirements to be complied with before proposals made or considered

4

(1) Regulations may make provision as to requirements that must be complied with before proposals for a neighbourhood development order may be submitted to a local planning authority or fall to be considered by a local planning authority.

(2) The regulations may in particular make provision—

    (a) as to the giving of notice and publicity,

    (b) as to the information and documents that are to be made available to the public,

    (c) as to the making of reasonable charges for anything provided as a result of the regulations,

    (d) as to consultation with and participation by the public,

    (e) as to the making and consideration of representations (including the time by which they must be made),

    (f) requiring prescribed steps to be taken before a proposal of a prescribed description falls to be considered by a local planning authority, and

---

[26] Inserted by the Localism Act 2011, s 116(2), Sch 10.
[27] Inserted by the Localism Act 2011, s 116(2), Sch 10.

(g)   conferring powers or imposing duties on local planning authorities, the Secretary of State or other public authorities.

(3)   The power to make regulations under this paragraph must be exercised to secure that—

    (a)   prescribed requirements as to consultation with and participation by the public must be complied with before a proposal for a neighbourhood development order may be submitted to a local planning authority, and

    (b)   a statement containing the following information in relation to that consultation and participation must accompany the proposal submitted to the authority—

        (i)   details of those consulted,

        (ii)   a summary of the main issues raised, and

        (iii)   any other information of a prescribed description.][28]

[Consideration of proposals by authority

5

(1)   A local planning authority may decline to consider a proposal submitted to them if they consider that it is a repeat proposal.

(2)   A proposal ('the proposal in question') is a 'repeat' proposal for the purposes of this paragraph if it meets conditions A and B.

(3)   Condition A is that in the period of two years ending with the date on which the proposal in question is received—

    (a)   the authority have refused a proposal under paragraph 12 or [section 38A(4) of the Planning and Compulsory Purchase Act 2004][29] that is the same as or similar to the proposal in question, or

    (b)   a referendum on an order relating to a proposal under this Schedule that is the same as or similar to the proposal in question has been held under this Schedule and half or less than half of those voting voted in favour of the order.

(4)   Condition B is that the local planning authority consider that there has been no significant change in relevant considerations since the refusal of the proposal or the holding of the referendum.

(5)   For the purposes of this paragraph 'relevant considerations' means—

    (a)   national policies and advice contained in guidance issued by the Secretary of State that are relevant to the draft neighbourhood development order to which the proposal in question relates, and

    (b)   the strategic policies contained in the development plan for the area of the authority (or any part of that area).

---

[28]   Inserted by the Localism Act 2011, s 116(2), Sch 10.
[29]   Substituted (by modification) by the Planning and Compulsory Purchase Act 2004, s 38C(5)(a) (as inserted by the Localism Act 2011, s 116(1), Sch 9, paras 5, 7).

(6)   If the authority decline to consider the proposal, they must notify the qualifying body of that fact and of their reasons for declining to consider it.][30]

[6

(1)   This paragraph applies if—

    (a)   a proposal has been made to a local planning authority, and

    (b)   the authority have not exercised their powers under paragraph 5 to decline to consider it.

(2)   The authority must consider—

    (a)   whether the qualifying body is authorised for the purposes of a neighbourhood development order to act in relation to the neighbourhood area concerned as a result of section 61F,

    (b)   whether the proposal by the body complies with provision made by or under that section,

    (c)   whether the proposal and the documents and information accompanying it (including the draft neighbourhood development order) comply with provision made by or under paragraph 1, and

    (d)   whether the body has complied with the requirements of regulations made under paragraph 4 imposed on it in relation to the proposal.

(3)   The authority must also consider whether the draft neighbourhood development order complies with the provision made by or under [sections 38A and 38B of the Planning and Compulsory Purchase Act 2004][31].

(4)   The authority must—

    (a)   notify the qualifying body as to whether or not they are satisfied that the matters mentioned in sub-paragraphs (2) and (3) have been met or complied with, and

    (b)   in any case where they are not so satisfied, refuse the proposal and notify the body of their reasons for refusing it.][32]

[Independent examination

7

(1)   This paragraph applies if—

    (a)   a local planning authority have considered the matters mentioned in paragraph 6(2) and (3), and

    (b)   they are satisfied that the matters mentioned there have been met or complied with.

(2)   The authority must submit for independent examination—

---

[30]   Inserted by the Localism Act 2011, s 116(2), Sch 10.
[31]   Substituted (by modification) by the Planning and Compulsory Purchase Act 2004, s 38C(5)(b) (as inserted by the Localism Act 2011, s 116(1), Sch 9, paras 5, 7).
[32]   Inserted by the Localism Act 2011, s 116(2), Sch 10.

(a)   the draft neighbourhood development order, and

(b)   such other documents as may be prescribed.

(3)   The authority must make such arrangements as they consider appropriate in connection with the holding of the examination.

(4)   The authority may appoint a person to carry out the examination, but only if the qualifying body consents to the appointment.

(5)   If—

(a)   it appears to the Secretary of State that no person may be appointed under sub-paragraph (4), and

(b)   the Secretary of State considers that it is expedient for an appointment to be made under this sub-paragraph,

the Secretary of State may appoint a person to carry out the examination.

(6)   The person appointed must be someone who, in the opinion of the person making the appointment—

(a)   is independent of the qualifying body and the authority,

(b)   does not have an interest in any land that may be affected by the draft order, and

(c)   has appropriate qualifications and experience.

(7)   The Secretary of State or another local planning authority may enter into arrangements with the authority for the provision of the services of any of their employees as examiners.

(8)   Those arrangements may include—

(a)   provision requiring payments to be made by the authority to the Secretary of State or other local planning authority, and

(b)   other provision in relation to those payments and other financial matters.][33]

[8

(1)   The examiner must consider the following—

(a)   whether the draft neighbourhood development order meets the basic conditions (see sub-paragraph (2)),

(b)   whether the draft order complies with the provision made by or under [sections 38A and 38B of the Planning and Compulsory Purchase Act 2004][34],

(c)   ...[35]

---

[33]   Inserted by the Localism Act 2011, s 116(2), Sch 10.
[34]   Substituted (by modification) by the Planning and Compulsory Purchase Act 2004, s 38C(5)(b) (as inserted by the Localism Act 2011, s 116(1), Sch 9, paras 5, 7).
[35]   Repealed (by modification) by the Planning and Compulsory Purchase Act 2004, s 38C(5)(c), (d) (as inserted by the Localism Act 2011, s 116(1), Sch 9, paras 5, 7).

  (d) whether the area for any referendum should extend beyond the neighbourhood area to which the draft order relates, and

  (e) such other matters as may be prescribed.

(2) A draft order meets the basic conditions if—

  (a) having regard to national policies and advice contained in guidance issued by the Secretary of State, it is appropriate to make the order,

  (b) ...[36]

  (c) ...[37]

  (d) the making of the order contributes to the achievement of sustainable development,

  (e) the making of the order is in general conformity with the strategic policies contained in the development plan for the area of the authority (or any part of that area),

  (f) the making of the order does not breach, and is otherwise compatible with, EU obligations, and

  (g) prescribed conditions are met in relation to the order and prescribed matters have been complied with in connection with the proposal for the order.

(3) ...[38]

(4) ...[39]

(5) ...[40]

(6) The examiner is not to consider any matter that does not fall within sub-paragraph (1) (apart from considering whether the draft order is compatible with the Convention rights).][41]

[9

(1) The general rule is that the examination of the issues by the examiner is to take the form of the consideration of written representations.

(2) But the examiner must cause a hearing to be held for the purpose of receiving oral representations about a particular issue at the hearing—

  (a) in any case where the examiner considers that the consideration of oral representations is necessary to ensure adequate examination of the issue or a person has a fair chance to put a case, or

  (b) in such other cases as may be prescribed.

---

[36] Repealed (by modification) by the Planning and Compulsory Purchase Act 2004, s 38C(5)(c), (d) (as inserted by the Localism Act 2011, s 116(1), Sch 9, paras 5, 7).

[37] Repealed (by modification) by the Planning and Compulsory Purchase Act 2004, s 38C(5)(c), (d) (as inserted by the Localism Act 2011, s 116(1), Sch 9, paras 5, 7).

[38] Repealed (by modification) by the Planning and Compulsory Purchase Act 2004, s 38C(5)(c), (d) (as inserted by the Localism Act 2011, s 116(1), Sch 9, paras 5, 7).

[39] Repealed (by modification) by the Planning and Compulsory Purchase Act 2004, s 38C(5)(c), (d) (as inserted by the Localism Act 2011, s 116(1), Sch 9, paras 5, 7).

[40] Repealed (by modification) by the Planning and Compulsory Purchase Act 2004, s 38C(5)(c), (d) (as inserted by the Localism Act 2011, s 116(1), Sch 9, paras 5, 7).

[41] Inserted by the Localism Act 2011, s 116(2), Sch 10.

(3)   The following persons are entitled to make oral representations about the issue at the hearing—

(a)   the qualifying body,

(b)   the local planning authority,

(c)   where the hearing is held to give a person a fair chance to put a case, that person, and

(d)   such other persons as may be prescribed.

(4)   The hearing must be in public.

(5)   It is for the examiner to decide how the hearing is to be conducted, including—

(a)   whether a person making oral representations may be questioned by another person and, if so, the matters to which the questioning may relate, and

(b)   the amount of time for the making of a person's oral representations or for any questioning by another person.

(6)   In making decisions about the questioning of a person's oral representations by another, the examiner must apply the principle that the questioning should be done by the examiner except where the examiner considers that questioning by another is necessary to ensure—

(a)   adequate examination of a particular issue, or

(b)   a person has a fair chance to put a case.

(7)   Sub-paragraph (5) is subject to regulations under paragraph 11.][42]

[10

(1)   The examiner must make a report on the draft order containing recommendations in accordance with this paragraph (and no other recommendations).

(2)   The report must recommend either—

(a)   that the draft order is submitted to a referendum, or

(b)   that modifications specified in the report are made to the draft order and that the draft order as modified is submitted to a referendum, or

(c)   that the proposal for the order is refused.

(3)   The only modifications that may be recommended are—

(a)   modifications that the examiner considers need to be made to secure that the draft order meets the basic conditions mentioned in paragraph 8(2),

(b)   modifications that the examiner considers need to be made to secure that the draft order is compatible with the Convention rights,

(c)   modifications that the examiner considers need to be made to secure that the draft order complies with the provision made by or under [sections 38A and 38B of the Planning and Compulsory Purchase Act 2004][43],

---

[42]   Inserted by the Localism Act 2011, s 116(2), Sch 10.
[43]   Substituted (by modification) by the Planning and Compulsory Purchase Act 2004, s 38C(5)(b) (as inserted by the Localism Act 2011, s 116(1), Sch 9, paras 5, 7).

(d)   ...[44], and

(e)   modifications for the purpose of correcting errors.

(4)   The report may not recommend that an order (with or without modifications) is submitted to a referendum if the examiner considers that the order does not—

(a)   meet the basic conditions mentioned in paragraph 8(2), or

(b)   comply with the provision made by or under [sections 38A and 38B of the Planning and Compulsory Purchase Act 2004][45].

(5)   If the report recommends that an order (with or without modifications) is submitted to a referendum, the report must also make—

(a)   a recommendation as to whether the area for the referendum should extend beyond the neighbourhood area to which the order relates, and

(b)   if a recommendation is made for an extended area, a recommendation as to what the extended area should be.

(6)   The report must—

(a)   give reasons for each of its recommendations, and

(b)   contain a summary of its main findings.

(7)   The examiner must send a copy of the report to the qualifying body and the local planning authority.

(8)   The local planning authority must then arrange for the publication of the report in such manner as may be prescribed.][46]

[11

(1)   Regulations may make provision in connection with examinations under paragraph 7.

(2)   The regulations may in particular make provision as to—

(a)   the giving of notice and publicity in connection with an examination,

(b)   the information and documents relating to an examination that are to be made available to the public,

(c)   the making of reasonable charges for anything provided as a result of the regulations,

(d)   the making of written or oral representations in relation to draft neighbourhood development orders (including the time by which written representations must be made),

(e)   the written representations which are to be, or which may be or may not be, considered at an examination,

(f)   the refusal to allow oral representations of a prescribed description to be made at a hearing,

---

[44]   Repealed (by modification) by the Planning and Compulsory Purchase Act 2004, s 38C(5)(c) (as inserted by the Localism Act 2011, s 116(1), Sch 9, paras 5, 7).
[45]   Substituted (by modification) by the Planning and Compulsory Purchase Act 2004, s 38C(5)(b) (as inserted by the Localism Act 2011, s 116(1), Sch 9, paras 5, 7).
[46]   Inserted by the Localism Act 2011, s 116(2), Sch 10.

(g)   the procedure to be followed at an examination (including the procedure to be followed at a hearing),

(h)   the payment by a local planning authority of remuneration and expenses of the examiner, and

(i)   the award of costs by the examiner.]⁴⁷

[Consideration by authority of recommendations made by examiner etc

12

(1)   This paragraph applies if an examiner has made a report under paragraph 10.

(2)   The local planning authority must—

(a)   consider each of the recommendations made by the report (and the reasons for them), and

(b)   decide what action to take in response to each recommendation.

(3)   The authority must also consider such other matters as may be prescribed.

(4)   If the authority are satisfied—

(a)   that the draft order meets the basic conditions mentioned in paragraph 8(2), is compatible with the Convention rights and complies with the provision made by or under [sections 38A and 38B of the Planning and Compulsory Purchase Act 2004]⁴⁸, or

(b)   that the draft order would meet those conditions, be compatible with those rights and comply with that provision if modifications were made to the draft order (whether or not recommended by the examiner),

a referendum in accordance with paragraph 14, and (if applicable) an additional referendum in accordance with paragraph 15, must be held on the making by the authority of a neighbourhood development order.

(5)   The order on which the referendum is (or referendums are) to be held is the draft order subject to such modifications (if any) as the authority consider appropriate.

(6)   The only modifications that the authority may make are—

(a)   modifications that the authority consider need to be made to secure that the draft order meets the basic conditions mentioned in paragraph 8(2),

(b)   modifications that the authority consider need to be made to secure that the draft order is compatible with the Convention rights,

(c)   modifications that the authority consider need to be made to secure that the draft order complies with the provision made by or under [sections 38A and 38B of the Planning and Compulsory Purchase Act 2004]⁴⁹,

---

⁴⁷   Inserted by the Localism Act 2011, s 116(2), Sch 10.
⁴⁸   Substituted (by modification) by the Planning and Compulsory Purchase Act 2004, s 38C(5)(b) (as inserted by the Localism Act 2011, s 116(1), Sch 9, paras 5, 7).
⁴⁹   Substituted (by modification) by the Planning and Compulsory Purchase Act 2004, s 38C(5)(b) (as inserted by the Localism Act 2011, s 116(1), Sch 9, paras 5, 7).

(d)   ...⁵⁰, and

(e)   modifications for the purpose of correcting errors.

(7)   The area in which the referendum is (or referendums are) to take place must, as a minimum, be the neighbourhood area to which the proposed order relates.

(8)   If the authority consider it appropriate to do so, they may extend the area in which the referendum is (or referendums are) to take place to include other areas (whether or not those areas fall wholly or partly outside the authority's area).

(9)   If the authority decide to extend the area in which the referendum is (or referendums are) to take place, they must publish a map of that area.

(10)   In any case where the authority are not satisfied as mentioned in sub-paragraph (4), they must refuse the proposal.

(11)   The authority must publish in such manner as may be prescribed—

(a)   the decisions they make under this paragraph,

(b)   their reasons for making those decisions, and

(c)   such other matters relating to those decisions as may be prescribed.

(12)   The authority must send a copy of the matters required to be published to—

(a)   the qualifying body, and

(b)   such other persons as may be prescribed.]⁵¹

[13

(1)   If—

(a)   the local planning authority propose to make a decision which differs from that recommended by the examiner, and

(b)   the reason for the difference is (wholly or partly) as a result of new evidence or a new fact or a different view taken by the authority as to a particular fact,

the authority must notify prescribed persons of their proposed decision (and the reason for it) and invite representations.

(2)   If the authority consider it appropriate to do so, they may refer the issue to independent examination.

(3)   Regulations may make provision about examinations under this paragraph (and the regulations may include any provision of a kind mentioned in paragraph 11(2)).

(4)   This paragraph does not apply in relation to recommendations in relation to the area in which a referendum is to take place.]⁵²

---

⁵⁰ Repealed (by modification) by the Planning and Compulsory Purchase Act 2004, s 38C(5)(c) (as inserted by the Localism Act 2011, s 116(1), Sch 9, paras 5, 7).
⁵¹ Inserted by the Localism Act 2011, s 116(2), Sch 10.
⁵² Inserted by the Localism Act 2011, s 116(2), Sch 10.

[13A

Regulations may make provision—

    (a)   requiring any prescribed action falling to be taken by the local planning authority under paragraph 12 or 13 to be taken by a prescribed date;

    (b)   imposing time limits for the submission of representations invited under paragraph 13(1).][53]

[Intervention powers of Secretary of State

13B

(1)   This paragraph applies where the qualifying body requests the Secretary of State to intervene under this paragraph and—

    (a)   the local planning authority have failed, by the applicable date prescribed under paragraph 13A, to take a decision as to whether a referendum is (or referendums are) to be held on the making of a neighbourhood development order,

    (b)   a recommendation made under paragraph 10(2) is not followed by the authority, or

    (c)   the authority make any modification under paragraph 12(5) that is not—

        (i)   a modification recommended under paragraph 10(2)(b),

        (ii)   a modification that the authority consider needs to be made to secure that the draft order does not breach, and is otherwise compatible with, EU obligations,

        (iii)   a modification that the authority consider needs to be made to secure that the draft order is compatible with the Convention rights, or

        (iv)   a modification for the purpose of correcting an error.

(2)   The Secretary of State may exercise functions of the local planning authority under paragraph 12(2) and (3) and—

    (a)   if satisfied that paragraph (a) or (b) of paragraph 12(4) applies, may direct the authority to make arrangements for a referendum (or referendums) to be held on the making of a neighbourhood development order;

    (b)   if not so satisfied, may direct the authority to refuse the proposal.

(3)   The Secretary of State may direct the authority to take the actions referred to in paragraph 12(8) and (9).

(4)   If by reason (wholly or partly) of new evidence or a new fact, or a different view taken by the Secretary of State as to a particular fact, the Secretary of State proposes to direct the local planning authority to act in a way that is not in accordance with what was recommended by the examiner—

---

[53]   Inserted by the Housing and Planning Act 2016, s 140(1).

(a) the Secretary of State may require the authority to notify prescribed persons of the proposed direction (and the reason for it) and invite representations;

(b) the Secretary of State may also require them to refer the issue to independent examination.

(5) The order on which a referendum is (or referendums are) to be held by virtue of sub-paragraph (2)(a) is the draft order subject to such modification (if any) as the Secretary of State or the local planning authority consider appropriate.

(6) The only modifications the local planning authority may make under sub-paragraph (5) are—

(a) modifications that the authority consider need to be made to secure that the draft order does not breach, and is otherwise compatible with, EU obligations,

(b) modifications that the authority consider need to be made to secure that the draft order is compatible with the Convention rights, and

(c) modifications for the purpose of correcting errors.]⁵⁴

[13C

Regulations may make provision supplementing that made by paragraph 13B; and the regulations may in particular—

(a) prescribe the form and content of a request by the qualifying body under paragraph 13B(1) and the date by which it must be made;

(b) confer power on the Secretary of State to direct a local planning authority to refrain from taking any action specified in the direction that they would otherwise be required or entitled to take under paragraph 12 or 13;

(c) make provision under which decisions falling to be made by the Secretary of State under paragraph 13B may be made instead by a person appointed by the Secretary of State for the purpose (an 'inspector');

(d) prescribe matters that the Secretary of State or an inspector must take into account in making a decision;

(e) require a local planning authority to provide prescribed information to the Secretary of State or to an inspector;

(f) make provision about examinations carried out by virtue of paragraph 13B(4)(b) (including any provision of a kind mentioned in paragraph 11(2));

(g) make provision (in addition to that made by paragraph 13B(4)(b)) for the holding of an examination, and for the payment by a local planning authority of remuneration and expenses of the examiner;

(h) provide for the Secretary of State, or a local planning authority on the direction of the Secretary of State, to notify to prescribed persons and to publish—

---

⁵⁴ Inserted by the Housing and Planning Act 2016, s 141(1).

      (i)   prescribed decisions made by the Secretary of State under paragraph 13B,

      (ii)   the reasons for making those decisions, and

      (iii)   other prescribed matters relating to those decisions.][55]

[Referendum

14

(1)   This paragraph makes provision in relation to a referendum that, as a result of paragraph 12(4) [or a direction under paragraph 13B(2)(a)][56], must be held on the making of a neighbourhood development order.

(2)   A relevant council must make arrangements for the referendum to take place in so much of their area as falls within the area ('the referendum area') in which the referendum is to take place (as determined under paragraph 12(7) and (8)).

This sub-paragraph is subject to regulations under paragraph 16(2)(b).

(3)   A 'relevant council' means—

    (a)   a district council,

    (b)   a London borough council,

    (c)   a metropolitan district council, or

    (d)   a county council in relation to any area in England for which there is no district council.

(4)   A person is entitled to vote in the referendum if on the prescribed date—

    (a)   the person is entitled to vote in an election of any councillors of a relevant council any of whose area is in the referendum area, and

    (b)   the person's qualifying address for the election is in the referendum area.

(5)   Sub-paragraph (4) does not apply in relation to so much of the referendum area as falls within the City of London.

(6)   In that case a person is entitled to vote in the referendum if on the prescribed date—

    (a)   the person is entitled to vote in an Authority election, and

    (b)   the person's qualifying address for the election is in the City of London.

(7)   For the purposes of this paragraph—

    (a)   'Authority election' has the same meaning as in the Representation of the People Act 1983 (see section 203(1)),

    (b)   the Inner Temple and the Middle Temple are to be treated as forming part of the City of London, and

---

[55] Inserted by the Housing and Planning Act 2016, s 141(1).
[56] Inserted by the Housing and Planning Act 2016, s 141(2).

(c)   'qualifying address' has the same meaning as in the Representation of the People Act 1983 (see section 9).][57]

[15

(1)   The additional referendum mentioned in paragraph 12(4) must be held on the making of a neighbourhood development order if the draft order relates to a neighbourhood area that has been designated as a business area under section 61H.

(2)   Sub-paragraph (2) of paragraph 14 is to apply in relation to the additional referendum as it applies in relation to a referendum under that paragraph.

(3)   A person is entitled to vote in the additional referendum if on the prescribed date—

    (a)   the person is a non-domestic ratepayer in the referendum area, or

    (b)   the person meets such other conditions as may be prescribed.

(4)   'Non-domestic ratepayer' has the same meaning as in Part 4 of the Local Government Act 2003 (see section 59(1)).

(5)   Regulations may make provision for excluding a person's entitlement to vote in the additional referendum.][58]

[16

(1)   [The Secretary of State or the [Minister for the Cabinet Office][59] may by regulations][60] make provision about referendums held under paragraph 14 or 15.

(2)   The regulations may in particular make provision—

    (a)   dealing with any case where there are two or more relevant councils any of whose areas fall within the referendum area,

    (b)   for only one relevant council to be subject to the duty to make arrangements for the referendum in a case within paragraph (a),

    (c)   prescribing a date by which the referendum must be held or before which it cannot be held,

    (d)   as to the question to be asked in the referendum and any explanatory material in relation to that question (including provision conferring power on a local planning authority to set the question and provide that material),

    (e)   as to the publicity to be given in connection with the referendum,

    (f)   about the limitation of expenditure in connection with the referendum,

    (g)   as to the conduct of the referendum,

---

[57]   Inserted by the Localism Act 2011, s 116(2), Sch 10.
[58]   Inserted by the Localism Act 2011, s 116(2), Sch 10.
[59]   Substituted by the Transfer of Functions (Elections, Referendums, Third Sector and Information) Order 2016, SI 2016/997, art 13, Sch 2, para 6.
[60]   Substituted by the Transfer of Functions (Elections and Referendums) Order 2013, SI 2013/2597, art 4, Schedule, para 5(a).

(h)   as to when, where and how voting in the referendum is to take place,

(i)   as to how the votes cast are to be counted,

(j)   about certification as to the number of persons voting in the referendum and as to the number of those persons voting in favour of a neighbourhood development order, and

(k)   about the combination of polls at a referendum held under paragraph 14 or 15 with polls at another referendum or at any election.

(3)   The regulations may apply or incorporate, with or without modifications, any provision made by or under any enactment relating to elections or referendums.

(4)   But where the regulations apply or incorporate (with or without modifications) any provision that creates an offence, the regulations may not impose a penalty greater than is provided for in respect of that provision.

(5)   Before making the regulations, the Secretary of State [or the [Minister for the Cabinet Office][61]][62] must consult the Electoral Commission.

(6)   In this paragraph 'enactment' means an enactment, whenever passed or made.][63]

[Interpretation

17

In this Schedule—

'the Convention rights' has the same meaning as in the Human Rights Act 1998, and

'development plan'—

(a)   includes a development plan for the purposes of paragraph 1 of Schedule 8 to the Planning and Compulsory Purchase Act 2004 (transitional provisions), but

(b)   does not include so much of a development plan as consists of a neighbourhood development plan under section 38A of that Act.][64]

---

[61]   Substituted by the Transfer of Functions (Elections, Referendums, Third Sector and Information) Order 2016, SI 2016/997, art 13, Sch 2, para 6.
[62]   Inserted by the Transfer of Functions (Elections and Referendums) Order 2013, SI 2013/2597, art 4, Schedule, para 5(b).
[63]   Inserted by the Localism Act 2011, s 116(2), Sch 10.
[64]   Inserted by the Localism Act 2011, s 116(2), Sch 10.

Planning and Compulsory Purchase Act 2004

PART 2 LOCAL DEVELOPMENT

Survey

13 Survey of area

(1)   The local planning authority must keep under review the matters which may be expected to affect the development of their area or the planning of its development.

(2)   These matters include–

    (a)   the principal physical, economic, social and environmental characteristics of the area of the authority;

    (b)   the principal purposes for which land is used in the area;

    (c)   the size, composition and distribution of the population of the area;

    (d)   the communications, transport system and traffic of the area;

    (e)   any other considerations which may be expected to affect those matters;

    (f)   such other matters as may be prescribed or as the Secretary of State (in a particular case) may direct.

(3)   The matters also include–

    (a)   any changes which the authority think may occur in relation to any other matter;

    (b)   the effect such changes are likely to have on the development of the authority's area or on the planning of such development.

(4)   The local planning authority may also keep under review and examine the matters mentioned in subsections (2) and (3) in relation to any neighbouring area to the extent that those matters may be expected to affect the area of the authority.

(5)   In exercising a function under subsection (4) a local planning authority must consult with the local planning authority for the neighbouring area in question.

(6)   If a neighbouring area is in Wales references to the local planning authority for that area must be construed in accordance with Part 6.

14 Survey of area: county councils

(1)   A county council in respect of so much of their area for which there is a district council must keep under review the matters which may be expected to affect development of that area or the planning of its development in so far as the development relates to a county matter.

(2)   Subsections (2) to (6) of section 13 apply for the purposes of subsection (1) as they apply for the purposes of that section; and references to the local planning authority must be construed as references to the county council.

(3)   The Secretary of State may by regulations require or (in a particular case) may direct a county council to keep under review in relation to so much of their area as is mentioned in subsection (1) such of the matters mentioned in section 13(1) to (4) as he prescribes or directs (as the case may be).

(4)   For the purposes of subsection (3)–

 (a)   it is immaterial whether any development relates to a county matter;

 (b)   if a matter which is prescribed or in respect of which the Secretary of State gives a direction falls within section 13(4) the county council must consult the local planning authority for the area in question.

(5)   The county council must make available the results of their review under subsection (3) to such persons as the Secretary of State prescribes or directs (as the case may be).

(6)   References to a county matter must be construed in accordance with paragraph 1 of Schedule 1 to the principal Act (ignoring sub-paragraph (1)(i)).

[Register

14A Register of land

(1)   The Secretary of State may make regulations requiring a local planning authority in England to prepare, maintain and publish a register of land within (or partly within) the authority's area which—

 (a)   is of a prescribed description, or

 (b)   satisfies prescribed criteria.

(2)   The regulations may require the register to be kept in two or more parts.

A reference to the register in the following subsections includes a reference to a prescribed part of the register.

(3)   The regulations may make provision permitting the local planning authority to enter in the register land within (or partly within) the authority's area which—

 (a)   is of a prescribed description or satisfies prescribed criteria, and

 (b)   is not required by the regulations to be entered in the register.

(4)   The regulations may—

 (a)   require or authorise a local planning authority to carry out consultation and other procedures in relation to entries in the register;

 (b)   specify descriptions of land that are not to be entered in the register;

(c)   confer a discretion on a local planning authority, in prescribed circumstances, not to enter in the register land of a prescribed description that the authority would otherwise be required to enter in it;

(d)   require a local planning authority exercising the discretion referred to in paragraph (c) to explain why they have done so;

(e)   specify information to be included in the register;

(f)   make provision about revising the register.

(5)   The regulations may specify a description of land by reference to a description in national policies and advice.

(6)   The regulations may confer power on the Secretary of State to require a local planning authority—

(a)   to prepare or publish the register, or to bring the register up to date, by a specified date;

(b)   to provide the Secretary of State with specified information, in a specified form and by a specified date, in relation to the register.

In this subsection 'specified' means specified by the Secretary of State.

(7)   In exercising their functions under the regulations, a local planning authority must have regard to—

(a)   the development plan;

(b)   national policies and advice;

(c)   any guidance issued by the Secretary of State for the purposes of the regulations.

(8)   In this section 'national policies and advice' means national policies and advice contained in guidance issued by the Secretary of State (as it has effect from time to time).][1]

Development schemes

15 Local development scheme

(1)   The local planning authority must prepare and maintain a scheme to be known as their local development scheme.

(2)   The scheme must specify–

(a)   ...[2]

[(aa) the local development documents which are to be development plan documents;][3]

(b)   the subject matter and geographical area to which each [development plan document][4] is to relate;

---

[1]   Inserted by the Housing and Planning Act 2016, s 151(1).
[2]   Repealed by the Planning Act 2008, ss 180(1), (2)(a), (d), 238, Sch 13.
[3]   Inserted by the Planning Act 2008, s 180(1), (2)(b).
[4]   Substituted by the Planning Act 2008, s 180(1), (2)(c), (e).

(c) ...⁵

(d) which [development plan documents]⁶ (if any) are to be prepared jointly with one or more other local planning authorities;

(e) any matter or area in respect of which the authority have agreed (or propose to agree) to the constitution of a joint committee under section 29;

(f) the timetable for the preparation and revision of the [development plan documents]⁷;

(g) such other matters as are prescribed.

(3) ...⁸

[(3A) If a local planning authority have not prepared a local development scheme, the Secretary of State or the Mayor of London may—

(a) prepare a local development scheme for the authority, and

(b) direct the authority to bring that scheme into effect.]⁹

(4) The Secretary of State [or the Mayor of London]¹⁰ may direct the local planning authority to make such amendments to the scheme as he thinks appropriate [for the purpose of ensuring [full and effective coverage (both geographically and with regard to subject matter)]¹¹ of the authority's area by the development plan documents (taken as a whole) for that area]¹².

[(4A) The Mayor of London–

(a) may give a direction under subsection [(3A) or]¹³ (4) only if the local planning authority are a London borough, and

(b) in considering whether to give such a direction, and which amendments to include in the direction, must have regard to any guidance issued by the Secretary of State.]¹⁴

(5) [A direction under subsection [(3A) or]¹⁵ (4)]¹⁶ must contain the Secretary of State's[, or (as the case may be) the Mayor of London's,]¹⁷ reasons for giving it.

(6) The local planning authority must comply with a direction given under subsection [(3A) or]¹⁸ (4).

[In the case of a direction given by the Mayor of London, this subsection is subject to subsections (6A) to (6E).]¹⁹

---

⁵ Repealed by the Planning Act 2008, ss 180(1), (2)(a), (d), 238, Sch 13.
⁶ Substituted by the Planning Act 2008, s 180(1), (2)(c), (e).
⁷ Substituted by the Planning Act 2008, s 180(1), (2)(c), (e).
⁸ Repealed by the Localism Act 2011, ss 111(1), (2), 237, Sch 25, Pt 17.
⁹ Inserted by the Housing and Planning Act 2016, s 143(1).
¹⁰ Inserted by the Greater London Authority Act 2007, s 30(1), (4), (5), (6)(b), (7), (8), (9), (10), (11).
¹¹ Substituted by the Housing and Planning Act 2016, s 143(2).
¹² Inserted by the Localism Act 2011, s 111(1), (3), (6), (7).
¹³ Inserted by the Housing and Planning Act 2016, s 143(3).
¹⁴ Inserted by the Greater London Authority Act 2007, s 30(1), (4), (5), (6)(b), (7), (8), (9), (10), (11).
¹⁵ Inserted by the Housing and Planning Act 2016, s 143(3).
¹⁶ Substituted by the Greater London Authority Act 2007, s 30(1), (6)(a).
¹⁷ Inserted by the Greater London Authority Act 2007, s 30(1), (4), (5), (6)(b), (7), (8), (9), (10), (11).
¹⁸ Inserted by the Housing and Planning Act 2016, s 143(3).
¹⁹ Inserted by the Greater London Authority Act 2007, s 30(1), (4), (5), (6)(b), (7), (8), (9), (10), (11).

[(6A) If at any time the Mayor of London gives a direction under subsection [(3A) or][20] (4)–

    (a)   he must at that time send a copy of the direction to the Secretary of State, and

    (b)   [effect is not to be given to the direction][21] until such time as may be prescribed.

(6B)   The Secretary of State may, within such time as may be prescribed, direct the local planning authority–

    (a)   to disregard a direction given under subsection [(3A) or][22] (4) by the Mayor of London, or

    (b)   to give effect to the direction with such modifications as may be specified in the Secretary of State's direction.

(6C)   Such a direction must contain the Secretary of State's reasons for giving it.

(6D)   If at any time the Secretary of State gives a direction under subsection (6B), the Secretary of State must at that time send a copy of the direction to the Mayor of London.

(6E)   The local planning authority must comply with any direction given by the Secretary of State under subsection (6B).][23]

[(7)   To bring the scheme into effect, the local planning authority must resolve that the scheme is to have effect and in the resolution specify the date from which the scheme is to have effect.][24]

(8)   The local planning authority must revise their local development scheme–

    (a)   at such time as they consider appropriate;

    (b)   when directed to do so by the Secretary of State [or the Mayor of London][25].

    [In the case of a direction given by the Mayor of London, paragraph (b) is subject to subsections (8B) to (8F).][26]

[(8A) The Mayor of London–

    (a)   may give a direction under subsection (8) only if the local planning authority are a London borough, and

    (b)   in considering whether to give such a direction, must have regard to any guidance issued by the Secretary of State.

[(8AA) A direction may be given under subsection (8)(b) only if[—

    (a)][27] the person giving the direction thinks that revision of the scheme is necessary for the purpose of ensuring full and effective coverage (both

---

[20]   Inserted by the Housing and Planning Act 2016, s 143(3).
[21]   Substituted by the Localism Act 2011, s 111(1), (4), (5).
[22]   Inserted by the Housing and Planning Act 2016, s 143(3).
[23]   Inserted by the Greater London Authority Act 2007, s 30(1), (4), (5), (6)(b), (7), (8), (9), (10), (11).
[24]   Substituted by the Localism Act 2011, s 111(1), (4), (5).
[25]   Inserted by the Greater London Authority Act 2007, s 30(1), (4), (5), (6)(b), (7), (8), (9), (10), (11).
[26]   Inserted by the Greater London Authority Act 2007, s 30(1), (4), (5), (6)(b), (7), (8), (9), (10), (11).
[27]   Inserted by the Neighbourhood Planning Act 2017, s 11(4).

geographically and with regard to subject matter) of the authority's area by the development plan documents (taken as a whole) for that area[, or

(b) the Secretary of State has published data standards under section 36(3) which apply to the local development scheme and the person giving the direction thinks that the scheme should be revised so that it complies with the standards.]²⁸]²⁹

(8B) If at any time the Mayor of London gives a direction under subsection (8)(b)–

(a) he must at that time send a copy of the direction to the Secretary of State, and

(b) the scheme is not to be revised until such time as may be prescribed.

(8C) The Secretary of State may, within such time as may be prescribed, direct the local planning authority to disregard a direction given under subsection (8)(b) by the Mayor of London.

(8D) Such a direction must contain the Secretary of State's reasons for giving it.

(8E) If at any time the Secretary of State gives a direction under subsection (8C), the Secretary of State must at that time send a copy of the direction to the Mayor of London.

(8F) The local planning authority must comply with any direction given by the Secretary of State under subsection (8C).]³⁰

(9) Subsections (2) to (7) apply to the revision of a scheme as they apply to the preparation of the scheme.

[(9A) The local planning authority must make the following available to the public—

(a) the up-to-date text of the scheme,

(b) a copy of any amendments made to the scheme, and

(c) up-to-date information showing the state of the authority's compliance (or non-compliance) with the timetable mentioned in subsection (2)(f).]³¹

[(10) Section 38(1) of the Greater London Authority Act 1999 (delegation of functions by the Mayor) does not apply to the Mayor of London's functions under this section of giving a direction.]³²

16 Minerals and waste development scheme

(1) A county council in respect of any part of their area for which there is a district council must prepare and maintain a scheme to be known as their minerals and waste development scheme.

(2) Section 15 (ignoring subsections (1) and (2)(e)) applies in relation to a minerals and waste development scheme as it applies in relation to a local development scheme.

---

²⁸ Inserted by the Neighbourhood Planning Act 2017, s 11(4).
²⁹ Inserted by the Localism Act 2011, s 111(1), (3), (6), (7).
³⁰ Inserted by the Greater London Authority Act 2007, s 30(1), (4), (5), (6)(b), (7), (8), (9), (10), (11).
³¹ Inserted by the Localism Act 2011, s 111(1), (3), (6), (7).
³² Inserted by the Greater London Authority Act 2007, s 30(1), (4), (5), (6)(b), (7), (8), (9), (10), (11).

(3)   This Part applies to a minerals and waste development scheme as it applies to a local development scheme and for that purpose–

(a)   references to a local development scheme include references to a minerals and waste development scheme;

(b)   references to a local planning authority include references to a county council.

(4)   But subsection (3) does not apply to–

(a)   section 17(3);

(b)   section 24(1)(b), (4) and (7);

(c)   the references in section 24(5) to subsection (4) and the Mayor;

(d)   sections 29 to 31.

[(5)   Also, subsection (3)(b) does not apply to section 33A(1)(a) and (b).][33]

Documents

17 Local development documents

(1)   …[34]

(2)   …[35]

(3)   [The local planning authority's local development documents][36] must (taken as a whole) set out the authority's policies (however expressed) relating to the development and use of land in their area.

(4)   [Where a county council is required to prepare a minerals and waste development scheme in respect of an area, the council's local development documents must (taken as a whole) set out the council's policies (however expressed) for that area][37] in relation to development which is a county matter within the meaning of paragraph 1 of Schedule 1 to the principal Act (ignoring sub-paragraph (1)(i)).

(5)   If to any extent a policy set out in a local development document conflicts with any other statement or information in the document the conflict must be resolved in favour of the policy.

(6)   The authority must keep under review their local development documents having regard to the results of any review carried out under section 13 or 14.

[(6A) The Secretary of State may by regulations make provision requiring a local planning authority to review a local development document at such times as may be prescribed.

(6B) If regulations under subsection (6A) require a local planning authority to review a local development document—

---

[33]   Inserted by the Localism Act 2011, s 110(2).
[34]   Repealed by the Planning Act 2008, ss 180(1), (3)(a), 238, Sch 13.
[35]   Repealed by the Planning Act 2008, ss 180(1), (3)(a), 238, Sch 13.
[36]   Substituted by the Planning Act 2008, s 180(1), (3)(b), (c).
[37]   Substituted by the Planning Act 2008, s 180(1), (3)(b), (c).

(a)   they must consider whether to revise the document following each review, and

(b)   if they decide not to do so, they must publish their reasons for considering that no revisions are necessary.

(6C) Any duty imposed by virtue of subsection (6A) applies in addition to the duty in subsection (6).][38]

(7)   Regulations under this section may prescribe–

[(za) which descriptions of documents are, or if prepared are, to be prepared as local development documents;][39]

(a)   which descriptions of local development documents are development plan documents;

(b)   the form and content of the local development documents;

(c)   the time at which any step in the preparation of any such document must be taken.

(8)   A document is a local development document only in so far as it or any part of it–

(a)   is adopted by resolution of the local planning authority as a local development document;

(b)   is approved by the Secretary of State under section 21 or 27;

[(c)   is approved by the Mayor of London under paragraph 2 of Schedule A1;

(d)   is approved by a combined authority under paragraph 6 of that Schedule.][40]

18 Statement of community involvement

(1)   The local planning authority must prepare a statement of community involvement.

(2)   The statement of community involvement is a statement of the authority's policy as to the involvement in the exercise of the authority's functions under sections 19, 26 and 28 of this Act and Part 3 of the principal Act of persons who appear to the authority to have an interest in matters relating to development in their area.

[(2A) The reference in subsection (2) to functions under Part 3 of the principal Act does not include functions under any provision of that Act relating to neighbourhood development orders (including any function under any of sections 61F to 61H of that Act).][41]

[(3)   For the purposes of this Part (except sections 19(2) and 24) the statement of community involvement is a local development document.

This is subject to section 17(8).][42]

---

[38]   Inserted by the Neighbourhood Planning Act 2017, s 12.
[39]   Inserted by the Planning Act 2008, s 180(1), (3)(d).
[40]   Inserted by the Housing and Planning Act 2016, s 147(3).
[41]   Inserted by the Localism Act 2011, s 121, Sch 12, paras 27, 28.
[42]   Substituted by the Planning Act 2008, s 180(1), (4)(a).

[(3A) The statement of community involvement must not be specified as a development plan document in the local development scheme.][43]

[(3B) The Secretary of State may by regulations prescribe matters to be addressed by a statement of community involvement in addition to the matters mentioned in subsection (2).][44]

(4)   ...[45]

(5)   ...[46]

(6)   ...[47]

19 Preparation of local development documents

(1)   [Development plan documents][48] must be prepared in accordance with the local development scheme.

[(1A) Development plan documents must (taken as a whole) include policies designed to secure that the development and use of land in the local planning authority's area contribute to the mitigation of, and adaptation to, climate change.][49]

(2)   In preparing a [development plan document or any other][50] local development document the local planning authority must have regard to–

    (a)   national policies and advice contained in guidance issued by the Secretary of State;

    (b)   [the regional strategy][51] for the region in which the area of the authority is situated, if the area is outside Greater London;

    (c)   the spatial development strategy if the authority are a London borough or if any part of the authority's area adjoins Greater London;

    (d)   [the regional strategy][52] for any region which adjoins the area of the authority;

    (e)   the Wales Spatial Plan if any part of the authority's area adjoins Wales;

    (f)   ...[53]

    (g)   ...[54]

    (h)   any other local development document which has been adopted by the authority;

---

[43]   Inserted by the Planning Act 2008, s 180(1), (4)(b).
[44]   Inserted by the Neighbourhood Planning Act 2017, s 13(3) (April 27, 2017 to the extent that they confer power on the Secretary of State to make regulations; not yet in force otherwise).
[45]   Repealed by the Planning Act 2008, ss 180(1), (4)(c), 238, Sch 13.
[46]   Repealed by the Planning Act 2008, ss 180(1), (4)(c), 238, Sch 13.
[47]   Repealed by the Planning Act 2008, ss 180(1), (4)(c), 238, Sch 13.
[48]   Substituted by the Planning Act 2008, s 180(1), (5)(a), (c), (d).
[49]   Inserted by the Planning Act 2008, s 182.
[50]   Inserted by the Planning Act 2008, s 180(1), (5)(b).
[51]   Substituted by the Local Democracy, Economic Development and Construction Act 2009, s 85(1), Sch 5, paras 12, 14.
[52]   Substituted by the Local Democracy, Economic Development and Construction Act 2009, s 85(1), Sch 5, paras 12, 14.
[53]   Repealed by the Deregulation Act 2015, s 100(2)(b).
[54]   Repealed by the Deregulation Act 2015, s 100(2)(b).

> (i)   the resources likely to be available for implementing the proposals in the document;
>
> (j)   such other matters as the Secretary of State prescribes.

(3)   In preparing the [local development documents (other than their statement of community involvement)]⁵⁵ the authority must also comply with their statement of community involvement.

(4)   But subsection (3) does not apply at any time before the authority have adopted their statement of community involvement.

(5)   The local planning authority must also–

> (a)   carry out an appraisal of the sustainability of the proposals in each [development plan document]⁵⁶;
>
> (b)   prepare a report of the findings of the appraisal.

(6)   The Secretary of State may by regulations make provision–

> (a)   as to any further documents which must be prepared by the authority in connection with the preparation of a local development document;
>
> (b)   as to the form and content of such documents.

(7)   …⁵⁷

20 Independent examination

(1)   The local planning authority must submit every development plan document to the Secretary of State for independent examination.

(2)   But the authority must not submit such a document unless–

> (a)   they have complied with any relevant requirements contained in regulations under this Part, and
>
> (b)   they think the document is ready for independent examination.

(3)   The authority must also send to the Secretary of State (in addition to the development plan document) such other documents (or copies of documents) and such information as is prescribed.

(4)   The examination must be carried out by a person appointed by the Secretary of State.

(5)   The purpose of an independent examination is to determine in respect of the development plan document–

> (a)   whether it satisfies the requirements of sections 19 and 24(1), regulations under section 17(7) and any regulations under section 36 relating to the preparation of development plan documents;
>
> (b)   whether it is sound[; and

---

⁵⁵   Substituted by the Planning Act 2008, s 180(1), (5)(a), (c), (d).
⁵⁶   Substituted by the Planning Act 2008, s 180(1), (5)(a), (c), (d).
⁵⁷   Repealed by the Deregulation Act 2015, s 100(2)(b).

      (c)   whether the local planning authority complied with any duty imposed on the authority by section 33A in relation to its preparation.][58]

(6)   Any person who makes representations seeking to change a development plan document must (if he so requests) be given the opportunity to appear before and be heard by the person carrying out the examination.

[(6A) The Secretary of State may by notice to the person appointed to carry out the examination—

      (a)   direct the person not to take any step, or any further step, in connection with the examination of the development plan document, or of a specified part of it, until a specified time or until the direction is withdrawn;

      (b)   require the person—

            (i)   to consider any specified matters;

            (ii)   to give an opportunity, or further opportunity, to specified persons to appear before and be heard by the person;

           (iii)   to take any specified procedural step in connection with the examination.

In this subsection 'specified' means specified in the notice.][59]

[(7)   Where the person appointed to carry out the examination—

      (a)   has carried it out, and

      (b)   considers that, in all the circumstances, it would be reasonable to conclude—

            (i)   that the document satisfies the requirements mentioned in subsection (5)(a) and is sound, and

            (ii)   that the local planning authority complied with any duty imposed on the authority by section 33A in relation to the document's preparation,

the person must recommend that the document is adopted and give reasons for the recommendation.

(7A) Where the person appointed to carry out the examination—

      (a)   has carried it out, and

      (b)   is not required by subsection (7) to recommend that the document is adopted,

the person must recommend non-adoption of the document and give reasons for the recommendation.

(7B) Subsection (7C) applies where the person appointed to carry out the examination—

      (a)   does not consider that, in all the circumstances, it would be reasonable to conclude that the document satisfies the requirements mentioned in subsection (5)(a) and is sound, but

---

[58]   Inserted by the Localism Act 2011, s 110(3).
[59]   Inserted by the Housing and Planning Act 2016, s 144.

(b) does consider that, in all the circumstances, it would be reasonable to conclude that the local planning authority complied with any duty imposed on the authority by section 33A in relation to the document's preparation.

(7C) If asked to do so by the local planning authority, the person appointed to carry out the examination must recommend modifications of the document that would make it one that—

(a) satisfies the requirements mentioned in subsection (5)(a), and

(b) is sound.][60]

(8) The local planning authority must publish the recommendations and the reasons.

21 Intervention by Secretary of State

(1) If the Secretary of State thinks that a local development document is unsatisfactory–

(a) he may at any time before the document is adopted under section 23 direct the local planning authority to modify the document in accordance with the direction;

(b) if he gives such a direction he must state his reasons for doing so.

(2) The authority–

(a) must comply with the direction;

(b) must not adopt the document unless the Secretary of State gives notice that he is satisfied that they have complied with the direction.

(3) But subsection (2) does not apply if [or to the extent that][61] the Secretary of State withdraws the direction.

(4) At any time before a development plan document is adopted by a local planning authority the Secretary of State may direct that the document (or any part of it) is submitted to him for his approval.

(5) The following paragraphs apply if the Secretary of State gives a direction under subsection (4)–

(a) the authority must not take any step in connection with the adoption of the document until the Secretary of State gives his decision[, or withdraws the direction][62];

[(b) if the direction is given, and not withdrawn, before the authority have submitted the document under section 20(1), the Secretary of State must hold an independent examination;][63]

(c) if the direction is given after the authority have submitted the document but before the person appointed to carry out the examination has made his recommendations[, and is not withdrawn before those recommendations

---

[60] Substituted by the Localism Act 2011, s 112(1), (2).
[61] Inserted by the Housing and Planning Act 2016, s 145(1), (2)(a), (3), (4).
[62] Inserted by the Housing and Planning Act 2016, s 145(1), (2)(a), (3), (4).
[63] Substituted by the Housing and Planning Act 2016, s 145(2)(b), (c), (d).

are made, the person][64] must make his recommendations to the Secretary of State;

[(d)   the document has no effect unless the document or (as the case may be) the relevant part of it has been approved by the Secretary of State, or the direction is withdrawn.][65]

[(5A) Subsections (4) to (7C) of section 20 apply to an examination held under subsection (5)(b), the reference to the local planning authority in subsection (7C) of that section being read as a reference to the Secretary of State.

(5B) For the purposes of subsection (5)(d) the 'relevant part' of a development plan document is the part that—

(a)   is covered by a direction under subsection (4) which refers to only part of the document, or

(b)   continues to be covered by a direction under subsection (4) following the partial withdrawal of the direction.][66]

(6)   The Secretary of State must publish the recommendations made to him by virtue of subsection (5)(b) or (c) and the reasons of the person making the recommendations.

(7)   In considering a document or part of a document submitted under subsection (4) the Secretary of State may take account of any matter which he thinks is relevant.

(8)   It is immaterial whether any such matter was taken account of by the authority.

(9)   In relation to a document or part of a document submitted to him under subsection (4) the Secretary of State–

(a)   may approve, approve subject to specified modifications or reject the document or part;

(b)   must give reasons for his decision under paragraph (a).

[(9A) The Secretary of State may at any time—

(a)   after a development plan document has been submitted for independent examination under section 20, but

(b)   before it is adopted under section 23,

direct the local planning authority to withdraw the document.][67]

(10) In the exercise of any function under this section the Secretary of State must have regard to the local development scheme.

[(11) The local planning authority must reimburse the Secretary of State for any expenditure incurred by the Secretary of State under this section that is specified in a notice given to the authority by the Secretary of State.][68]

---

[64] Substituted by the Housing and Planning Act 2016, s 145(2)(b), (c), (d).
[65] Substituted by the Housing and Planning Act 2016, s 145(2)(b), (c), (d).
[66] Inserted by the Housing and Planning Act 2016, s 145(1), (2)(a), (3), (4).
[67] Inserted by the Localism Act 2011, s 112(1), (5).
[68] Inserted by the Localism Act 2011, s 112(1), (5).

[21A Temporary direction pending possible use of intervention powers

(1) If the Secretary of State is considering whether to give a direction to a local planning authority under section 21 in relation to a development plan document or other local development document, he may direct the authority not to take any step in connection with the adoption of the document—

 (a) until the time (if any) specified in the direction, or

 (b) until the direction is withdrawn.

(2) A document to which a direction under this section relates has no effect while the direction is in force.

(3) A direction given under this section in relation to a document ceases to have effect if a direction is given under section 21 in relation to that document.][69]

22 Withdrawal of local development documents

(1) A local planning authority may at any time before a local development document is adopted under section 23 withdraw the document.

(2) ...[70]

23 Adoption of local development documents

(1) The local planning authority may adopt a local development document (other than a development plan document) either as originally prepared or as modified to take account of–

 (a) any representations made in relation to the document;

 (b) any other matter they think is relevant.

[(2) If the person appointed to carry out the independent examination of a development plan document recommends that it is adopted, the authority may adopt the document—

 (a) as it is, or

 (b) with modifications that (taken together) do not materially affect the policies set out in it.

(2A) Subsection (3) applies if the person appointed to carry out the independent examination of a development plan document—

 (a) recommends non-adoption, and

 (b) under section 20(7C) recommends modifications ('the main modifications').

(3) The authority may adopt the document—

 (a) with the main modifications, or

 (b) with the main modifications and additional modifications if the additional modifications (taken together) do not materially affect the policies

---

[69] Inserted by the Housing and Planning Act 2016, s 145(5).
[70] Repealed by the Localism Act 2011, ss 112(1), (4), 237, Sch 25, Pt 17.

> that would be set out in the document if it was adopted with the main modifications but no other modifications.][71]

(4)   The authority must not adopt a development plan document unless they do so in accordance with subsection (2) or (3).

(5)   A document is adopted for the purposes of this section if it is adopted by resolution of the authority.

24 Conformity with regional strategy

(1)   The local development documents must be in general conformity with–

    (a)   [the regional strategy][72] (if the area of the local planning authority is in a region other than London);

    (b)   the spatial development strategy (if the local planning authority are a London borough [or a Mayoral development corporation][73]).

(2)   ...[74]

(3)   ...[75]

(4)   A local planning authority which are a London borough [or a Mayoral development corporation][76]–

    (a)   must request the opinion in writing of the Mayor of London as to the general conformity of a development plan document with the spatial development strategy;

    (b)   may request the opinion in writing of the Mayor as to the general conformity of any other local development document with the spatial development strategy.

(5)   Whether or not the local planning authority make a request mentioned in [subsection (4), the Mayor may give an opinion as to the general conformity of a local development document with the spatial development strategy][77].

(6)   ...[78]

(7)   If in the opinion of the Mayor a document is not in general conformity with the spatial development strategy the Mayor must be taken to have made representations seeking a change to the document.

(8)   ...[79]

---

[71]   Substituted by the Localism Act 2011, s 112(1), (3).
[72]   Substituted by the Local Democracy, Economic Development and Construction Act 2009, s 85(1), Sch 5, paras 12, 15(1), (2), (4).
[73]   Inserted by the Localism Act 2011, s 222, Sch 22, paras 54, 55.
[74]   Repealed by the Local Democracy, Economic Development and Construction Act 2009, ss 85(1), 146(1), Sch 5, Paras 12, 15(1), (3), (5), Sch 7, Pt 4.
[75]   Repealed by the Local Democracy, Economic Development and Construction Act 2009, ss 85(1), 146(1), Sch 5, Paras 12, 15(1), (3), (5), Sch 7, Pt 4.
[76]   Inserted by the Localism Act 2011, s 222, Sch 22, paras 54, 55.
[77]   Substituted by the Local Democracy, Economic Development and Construction Act 2009, s 85(1), Sch 5, paras 12, 15(1), (2), (4).
[78]   Repealed by the Local Democracy, Economic Development and Construction Act 2009, ss 85(1), 146(1), Sch 5, Paras 12, 15(1), (3), (5), Sch 7, Pt 4.
[79]   Repealed by the Local Democracy, Economic Development and Construction Act 2009, ss 85(1), 146(1), Sch 5, Paras 12, 15(1), (3), (5), Sch 7, Pt 4.

(9)   ...[80]

25 Revocation of local development documents

The Secretary of State–

- (a)   may at any time revoke a local development document at the request of the local planning authority;
- (b)   may prescribe descriptions of local development document which may be revoked by the authority themselves.

26 Revision of local development documents

(1)   The local planning authority may at any time prepare a revision of a local development document.

(2)   The authority must prepare a revision of a local development document–

- (a)   if the Secretary of State directs them to do so, and
- (b)   in accordance with such timetable as he directs.

(3)   This Part applies to the revision of a local development document as it applies to the preparation of the document.

(4)   Subsection (5) applies if any part of the area of the local planning authority is an area to which an enterprise zone scheme relates.

(5)   As soon as practicable after the occurrence of a relevant event–

- (a)   the authority must review every local development document in the light of the enterprise zone scheme;
- (b)   if they think that any modifications of the document are required in consequence of the scheme they must prepare a revised document containing the modifications.

(6)   The following are relevant events–

- (a)   the making of an order under paragraph 5 of Schedule 32 to the Local Government, Planning and Land Act 1980 (c. 65) (designation of enterprise zone);
- (b)   the giving of notification under paragraph 11(1) of that Schedule (approval of modification of enterprise zone scheme).

(7)   References to an enterprise zone and an enterprise zone scheme must be construed in accordance with that Act.

[27 Secretary of State's default powers

(1)   This section applies if the Secretary of State thinks that a local planning authority are failing or omitting to do anything it is necessary for them to do in connection with the preparation, revision or adoption of a development plan document.

---

[80]   Repealed by the Local Democracy, Economic Development and Construction Act 2009, ss 85(1), 146(1), Sch 5, Paras 12, 15(1), (3), (5), Sch 7, Pt 4.

(2)   The Secretary of State may—

    (a)   prepare or revise (as the case may be) the document, or

    (b)   give directions to the authority in relation to the preparation or revision of the document.

(3)   The Secretary of State must either—

    (a)   hold an independent examination, or

    (b)   direct the authority to submit the document for independent examination.

(4)   The Secretary of State must either—

    (a)   publish the recommendations and reasons of the person appointed to hold the examination, or

    (b)   give directions to the authority in relation to publication of those recommendations and reasons.

(5)   The Secretary of State may—

    (a)   approve the document, or approve it subject to specified modifications, as a local development document,

    (b)   direct the authority to consider adopting the document by resolution of the authority as a local development document, or

    (c)   (except where it was prepared or revised by the Secretary of State under subsection (2)(a)) reject the document.

(6)   Subsections (4) to (7C) of section 20 apply (subject to subsection (7) below) to an examination held under subsection (3)(a), the reference to the local planning authority in subsection (7C) of that section being read as a reference to the Secretary of State.

(7)   Subsections (5)(c), (7)(b)(ii) and (7B)(b) of section 20 do not apply to an independent examination held—

    (a)   under subsection (3)(a), or

    (b)   in response to a direction under subsection (3)(b),

in respect of a document prepared or revised by the Secretary of State under subsection (2)(a).

(8)   The Secretary of State must give reasons for anything he does in pursuance of subsection (2) or (5).

(9)   The authority must reimburse the Secretary of State for any expenditure he incurs in connection with anything—

    (a)   which is done by him under subsection (2)(a), and

    (b)   which the authority failed or omitted to do as mentioned in subsection (1).][81]

---

[81]   Substituted by the Housing and Planning Act 2016, s 146.

[27A Default powers exercisable by Mayor of London or combined authority

Schedule A1 (default powers exercisable by Mayor of London or combined authority) has effect.][82]

28 Joint local development documents

(1)   Two or more local planning authorities may agree to prepare one or more joint local development documents.

(2)   This Part applies for the purposes of any step which may be or is required to be taken in relation to a joint local development document as it applies for the purposes of any step which may be or is required to be taken in relation to a local development document.

(3)   For the purposes of subsection (2) anything which must be done by or in relation to a local planning authority in connection with a local development document must be done by or in relation to each of the authorities mentioned in subsection (1) in connection with a joint local development document.

(4)   Any requirement of this Part in relation to [regional strategy][83] is a requirement in relation to [regional strategy][84] for the region in which each authority mentioned in subsection (1) is situated.

(5)   If the authorities mentioned in subsection (1) include one or more London boroughs the requirements of this Part in relation to the spatial development strategy also apply.

(6)   Subsections (7) to (9) apply if a local planning authority withdraw from an agreement mentioned in subsection (1).

(7)   Any step taken in relation to the document must be treated as a step taken by–

   (a)   an authority which were a party to the agreement for the purposes of any corresponding document prepared by them;

   (b)   two or more other authorities who were parties to the agreement for the purposes of any corresponding joint local development document.

(8)   Any independent examination of a local development document to which the agreement relates must be suspended.

(9)   If before the end of the period prescribed for the purposes of this subsection an authority which were a party to the agreement request the Secretary of State to do so he may direct that–

   (a)   the examination is resumed in relation to the corresponding document;

   (b)   any step taken for the purposes of the suspended examination has effect for the purposes of the resumed examination.

(10)   A joint local development document is a local development document prepared jointly by two or more local planning authorities.

---

[82]   Inserted by the Housing and Planning Act 2016, s 147(1).
[83]   Substituted by the Local Democracy, Economic Development and Construction Act 2009, s 85(1), Sch 5, paras 12, 16.
[84]   Substituted by the Local Democracy, Economic Development and Construction Act 2009, s 85(1), Sch 5, paras 12, 16.

(11) The Secretary of State may by regulations make provision as to what is a corresponding document.

[28A Power to direct preparation of joint development plan documents

(1) The Secretary of State may direct two or more local planning authorities to prepare a joint development plan document.

(2) The Secretary of State may give a direction under this section in relation to a document whether or not it is specified in the local development schemes of the local planning authorities in question as a document which is to be prepared jointly with one or more other local planning authorities.

(3) The Secretary of State may give a direction under this section only if the Secretary of State considers that to do so will facilitate the more effective planning of the development and use of land in the area of one or more of the local planning authorities in question.

(4) A direction under this section may specify—

    (a) the area to be covered by the joint development plan document to which the direction relates;

    (b) the matters to be covered by that document;

    (c) the timetable for preparation of that document.

(5) The Secretary of State must, when giving a direction under this section, notify the local planning authorities to which it applies of the reasons for giving it.

(6) If the Secretary of State gives a direction under this section, the Secretary of State may direct the local planning authorities to which it is given to amend their local development schemes so that they cover the joint development plan document to which it relates.

(7) A joint development plan document is a development plan document which is, or is required to be, prepared jointly by two or more local planning authorities pursuant to a direction under this section.]⁸⁵

[28B Application of Part to joint development plan documents

(1) This Part applies for the purposes of any step which may be or is required to be taken in relation to a joint development plan document as it applies for the purposes of any step which may be or is required to be taken in relation to a development plan document.

(2) For the purposes of subsection (1) anything which must be done by or in relation to a local planning authority in connection with a development plan document must be done by or in relation to each of the authorities mentioned in section 28A(1) in connection with a joint development plan document.

(3) If the authorities mentioned in section 28A(1) include a London borough council or a Mayoral development corporation, the requirements of this Part in relation to the spatial development strategy also apply.

(4) Those requirements also apply if—

---

⁸⁵ Inserted by the Neighbourhood Planning Act 2017, s 9(1), (2).

(a)   a combined authority established under section 103 of the Local Democracy, Economic Development and Construction Act 2009 has the function of preparing the spatial development strategy for the combined authority's area, and

(b)   the authorities mentioned in section 28A(1) include a local planning authority whose area is within, or is the same as, the area of the combined authority.][86]

[28C Modification or withdrawal of direction under section 28A

(1)   The Secretary of State may modify or withdraw a direction under section 28A by notice in writing to the authorities to which it was given.

(2)   The Secretary of State must, when modifying or withdrawing a direction under section 28A, notify the local planning authorities to which it was given of the reasons for the modification or withdrawal.

(3)   The following provisions of this section apply if—

(a)   the Secretary of State withdraws a direction under section 28A, or

(b)   the Secretary of State modifies a direction under that section so that it ceases to apply to one or more of the local planning authorities to which it was given.

(4)   Any step taken in relation to the joint development plan document to which the direction related is to be treated as a step taken by—

(a)   a local planning authority to which the direction applied for the purposes of any corresponding document prepared by them, or

(b)   two or more local planning authorities to which the direction applied for the purposes of any corresponding joint development plan document prepared by them.

(5)   Any independent examination of a joint development plan document to which the direction related must be suspended.

(6)   If before the end of the period prescribed for the purposes of this subsection a local planning authority to which the direction applied request the Secretary of State to do so, the Secretary of State may direct that—

(a)   the examination is resumed in relation to—

(i)   any corresponding document prepared by a local planning authority to which the direction applied, or

(ii)   any corresponding joint development plan document prepared by two or more local planning authorities to which the direction applied, and

(b)   any step taken for the purposes of the suspended examination has effect for the purposes of the resumed examination.

(7)   The Secretary of State may by regulations make provision as to what is a corresponding document or a corresponding joint development plan document for the purposes of this section.][87]

[86]   Inserted by the Neighbourhood Planning Act 2017, s 9(1), (2).
[87]   Inserted by the Neighbourhood Planning Act 2017, s 9(1), (2).

Joint committees

29 Joint committees

(1)   This section applies if one or more local planning authorities agree with one or more county councils in relation to any area of such a council for which there is also a district council to establish a joint committee to be, for the purposes of this Part, the local planning authority–

    (a)   for the area specified in the agreement;

    (b)   in respect of such matters as are so specified.

(2)   The Secretary of State may by order constitute a joint committee to be the local planning authority–

    (a)   for the area;

    (b)   in respect of those matters.

(3)   Such an order–

    (a)   must specify the authority or authorities and county council or councils (the constituent authorities) which are to constitute the joint committee;

    (b)   may make provision as to such other matters as the Secretary of State thinks are necessary or expedient to facilitate the exercise by the joint committee of its functions.

(4)   Provision under subsection (3)(b)–

    (a)   may include provision corresponding to provisions relating to joint committees in Part 6 of the Local Government Act 1972 (c. 70);

    (b)   may apply (with or without modifications) such enactments relating to local authorities as the Secretary of State thinks appropriate.

(5)   If an order under this section is annulled in pursuance of a resolution of either House of Parliament–

    (a)   with effect from the date of the resolution the joint committee ceases to be the local planning authority as mentioned in subsection (2);

    (b)   anything which the joint committee (as the local planning authority) was required to do for the purposes of this Part must be done for their area by each local planning authority which were a constituent authority of the joint committee;

    (c)   each of those local planning authorities must revise their local development scheme accordingly.

(6)   Nothing in this section or section 30 confers on a local planning authority constituted by virtue of an order under this section any function in relation to section 13 or 14.

(7)   The policies adopted by the joint committee in the exercise of its functions under this Part must be taken for the purposes of the planning Acts to be the policies of each of the constituent authorities which are a local planning authority.

(8)   Subsection (9) applies to any function–

(a)   which is conferred on a local planning authority (within the meaning of the principal Act) under or by virtue of the planning Acts, and

(b)   which relates to the authority's local development scheme or local development documents.

(9)   If the authority is a constituent authority of a joint committee references to the authority's local development scheme or local development documents must be construed as including references to the scheme or documents of the joint committee.

(10)   For the purposes of subsection (4) a local authority is any of the following–

(a)   a county council;

(b)   a district council;

(c)   a London borough council.

30 Joint committees: additional functions

(1)   This section applies if the constituent authorities to a joint committee agree that the joint committee is to be, for the purposes of this Part, the local planning authority for any area or matter which is not the subject of–

(a)   an order under section 29, or

(b)   an earlier agreement under this section.

(2)   Each of the constituent authorities and the joint committee must revise their local development scheme in accordance with the agreement.

(3)   With effect from the date when the last such revision takes effect the joint committee is, for the purposes of this Part, the local planning authority for the area or matter mentioned in subsection (1).

31 Dissolution of joint committee

(1)   This section applies if a constituent authority requests the Secretary of State to revoke an order constituting a joint committee as the local planning authority for any area or in respect of any matter.

(2)   The Secretary of State may revoke the order.

(3)   Any step taken by the joint committee in relation to a local development scheme or a local development document must be treated for the purposes of any corresponding scheme or document as a step taken by a successor authority.

(4)   A successor authority is–

(a)   a local planning authority which were a constituent authority of the joint committee;

(b)   a joint committee constituted by order under section 29 for an area which does not include an area which was not part of the area of the joint committee mentioned in subsection (1).

(5)   If the revocation takes effect at any time when an independent examination is being carried out in relation to a local development document the examination must be suspended.

(6)   But if before the end of the period prescribed for the purposes of this subsection a successor authority falling within subsection (4)(a) requests the Secretary of State to do so he may direct that–

(a)   the examination is resumed in relation to the corresponding document;

(b)   any step taken for the purposes of the suspended examination has effect for the purposes of the resumed examination.

(7)   The Secretary of State may by regulations make provision as to what is a corresponding scheme or document.

Miscellaneous

32 Exclusion of certain representations

(1)   This section applies to any representation or objection in respect of anything which is done or is proposed to be done in pursuance of–

(a)   an order or scheme under section 10, 14, 16, 18, 106(1) or (3) or 108(1) of the Highways Act 1980 (c. 66);

(b)   an order or scheme under section 7, 9, 11, 13 or 20 of the Highways Act 1959 (c. 25), section 3 of the Highways (Miscellaneous Provisions) Act 1961 (c. 63) or section 1 or 10 of the Highways Act 1971 (c. 41) (which provisions were replaced by the provisions mentioned in paragraph (a));

(c)   an order under section 1 of the New Towns Act 1981 (c. 64).

(2)   If the Secretary of State or a local planning authority thinks that a representation made in relation to a local development document is in substance a representation or objection to which this section applies he or they (as the case may be) may disregard it.

33 Urban development corporations

The Secretary of State may direct [that the provisions of—[

(a)   this Part, or

(b)   any particular regulations made under section 14A, do not apply

to the area of an urban development corporation.][88]

[33A Duty to co-operate in relation to planning of sustainable development

(1)   Each person who is—

(a)   a local planning authority,

(b)   a county council in England that is not a local planning authority, or

(c)   a body, or other person, that is prescribed or of a prescribed description,

---

[88]   Substituted by the Housing and Planning Act 2016, s 151(2).

must co-operate with every other person who is within paragraph (a), (b) or (c) or subsection (9) in maximising the effectiveness with which activities within subsection (3) are undertaken.

(2) In particular, the duty imposed on a person by subsection (1) requires the person—

    (a) to engage constructively, actively and on an ongoing basis in any process by means of which activities within subsection (3) are undertaken, and

    (b) to have regard to activities of a person within subsection (9) so far as they are relevant to activities within subsection (3).

(3) The activities within this subsection are—

    (a) the preparation of development plan documents,

    (b) the preparation of other local development documents,

    (c) the preparation of marine plans under the Marine and Coastal Access Act 2009 for the English inshore region, the English offshore region or any part of either of those regions,

    (d) activities that can reasonably be considered to prepare the way for activities within any of paragraphs (a) to (c) that are, or could be, contemplated, and

    (e) activities that support activities within any of paragraphs (a) to (c),

so far as relating to a strategic matter.

(4) For the purposes of subsection (3), each of the following is a 'strategic matter'—

    (a) sustainable development or use of land that has or would have a significant impact on at least two planning areas, including (in particular) sustainable development or use of land for or in connection with infrastructure that is strategic and has or would have a significant impact on at least two planning areas, and

    (b) sustainable development or use of land in a two-tier area if the development or use—

        (i) is a county matter, or

        (ii) has or would have a significant impact on a county matter.

(5) In subsection (4)—

'county matter' has the meaning given by paragraph 1 of Schedule 1 to the principal Act (ignoring sub-paragraph 1(1)(i)),

'planning area' means—

    (a) the area of—

        (i) a district council (including a metropolitan district council),

        (ii) a London borough council, or

        (iii) a county council in England for an area for which there is no district council, but only so far as that area is neither in a National Park nor in the Broads,

(b)   a National Park,

(c)   the Broads,

(d)   the English inshore region, or

(e)   the English offshore region, and

'two-tier area' means an area—

(a)   for which there is a county council and a district council, but

(b)   which is not in a National Park.

(6)   The engagement required of a person by subsection (2)(a) includes, in particular—

(a)   considering whether to consult on and prepare, and enter into and publish, agreements on joint approaches to the undertaking of activities within subsection (3), and

(b)   if the person is a local planning authority, considering whether to agree under section 28 to prepare joint local development documents.

(7)   A person subject to the duty under subsection (1) must have regard to any guidance given by the Secretary of State about how the duty is to be complied with.

(8)   A person, or description of persons, may be prescribed for the purposes of subsection (1)(c) only if the person, or persons of that description, exercise functions for the purposes of an enactment.

(9)   A person is within this subsection if the person is a body, or other person, that is prescribed or of a prescribed description.

(10)   In this section—

'the English inshore region' and 'the English offshore region' have the same meaning as in the Marine and Coastal Access Act 2009, and

'land' includes the waters within those regions and the bed and subsoil of those waters.][89]

34 Guidance

In the exercise of any function conferred under or by virtue of this Part the local planning authority must have regard to any guidance issued by the Secretary of State.

35 [Authorities][90] monitoring [reports][91]

(1)   ...[92]

---

[89]   Inserted by the Localism Act 2011, s 110(1).
[90]   Substituted by the Localism Act 2011, s 113(1), (3), (4), (6).
[91]   Substituted by the Localism Act 2011, s 113(1), (3), (4), (6).
[92]   Repealed by the Localism Act 2011, ss 113(1), (2), 237, Sch 25, Pt 17.

(2) [Every local planning authority must prepare reports containing][93] such information as is prescribed as to–

    (a) the implementation of the local development scheme;

    (b) the extent to which the policies set out in the local development documents are being achieved.

(3) [A report under subsection (2) must—

    (a) be in respect of a period—

        (i) which the authority considers appropriate in the interests of transparency,

        (ii) which begins with the end of the period covered by the authority's most recent report under subsection (2), and

        (iii) which is not longer than 12 months or such shorter period as is prescribed;][94]

    (c) be in such form as is prescribed;

    (d) contain such other matter as is prescribed.

[(4) The authority must make the authority's reports under this section available to the public.][95]

General

36 Regulations [and standards][96]

(1) The Secretary of State may by regulations make provision in connection with the exercise by any person of functions under this Part.

(2) The regulations may in particular make provision as to–

    (a) the procedure to be followed by the local planning authority in carrying out the appraisal under section 19;

    (b) the procedure to be followed in the preparation of local development documents;

    (c) requirements about the giving of notice and publicity;

    (d) requirements about inspection by the public of a local development document or any other document;

    (e) the nature and extent of consultation with and participation by the public in anything done under this Part;

    (f) the making of representations about any matter to be included in a local development document;

    (g) consideration of any such representations;

---

[93] Substituted by the Localism Act 2011, s 113(1), (3), (4), (6).
[94] Substituted by the Localism Act 2011, s 113(1), (3), (4), (6).
[95] Inserted by the Localism Act 2011, s 113(5).
[96] Inserted by the Neighbourhood Planning Act 2017, s 11.

(h)   the remuneration and allowances payable to a person appointed to carry out an independent examination under section 20;

(i)   the determination of the time at which anything must be done for the purposes of this Part;

(j)   the manner of publication of any draft, report or other document published under this Part;

(k)   monitoring the exercise by local planning authorities of their functions under this Part;

(l)   the making of reasonable charges for the provision of copies of documents required by or under this Part.

[(3)   The Secretary of State may from time to time publish data standards for—

(a)   local development schemes,

(b)   local development documents, or

(c)   local development documents of a particular kind.

(4)   For this purpose a 'data standard' is a written standard which contains technical specifications for a scheme or document or the data contained in a scheme or document.

(5)   A local planning authority must comply with the data standards published under subsection (3) in preparing, publishing, maintaining or revising a scheme or document to which the standards apply.]⁹⁷

37 Interpretation

(1)   Local development scheme must be construed in accordance with section 15.

(2)   Local development document must be construed in accordance with [sections 17 and 18(3)]⁹⁸.

[(3)   A development plan document is a local development document which is specified as a development plan document in the local development scheme.]⁹⁹

(4)   Local planning authorities are–

(a)   district councils;

(b)   London borough councils;

(c)   metropolitan district councils;

(d)   county councils in relation to any area in England for which there is no district council;

(e)   the Broads Authority.

(5)   A National Park authority is the local planning authority for the whole of its area and subsection (4) must be construed subject to that.

---

97   Inserted by the Neighbourhood Planning Act 2017, s 11.
98   Substituted by the Planning Act 2008, s 180(1), (6).
99   Substituted by the Planning Act 2008, s 180(1), (6).

[(5ZA) Subsection (4) must also be construed subject to any order under section 198(2) of the Localism Act 2011 so far as providing that a Mayoral development corporation is, as regards an area, to be the local planning authority for some or all of the purposes of this Part in relation to some or all kinds of development.

(5ZB) Where such an order makes such provision, that MDC is, in relation to the kinds of development concerned, the local planning authority for the area and purposes concerned in place of any authority who, in relation to those kinds of development, would otherwise be the local planning authority for that area and those purposes.]¹⁰⁰

[(5A) Subsection (4) must [additionally be construed, and subsection (5ZB) must be construed,]¹⁰¹ subject to any designation order under section 13 of the Housing and Regeneration Act 2008 (power to make designation orders) providing that the Homes and Communities Agency is to be the local planning authority–

    (a)   for an area specified in the order, and

    (b)   for all purposes of this Part or any such purposes so specified.

(5B) Where such an order makes such provision, the Homes and Communities Agency is the local planning authority for the area and the purposes concerned in place of any authority who would otherwise be the local planning authority for that area and those purposes.]¹⁰²

[(6) 'Regional strategy' means a regional strategy under Part 5 of the Local Democracy, Economic Development and Construction Act 2009.

(6A) 'Responsible regional authorities' is to be construed in accordance with Part 5 of the Local Democracy, Economic Development and Construction Act 2009.]¹⁰³

(7)   This section applies for the purposes of this Part.

PART 3 DEVELOPMENT

Development plan

38 Development plan

(1)   A reference to the development plan in any enactment mentioned in subsection (7) must be construed in accordance with subsections (2) to (5).

(2)   For the purposes of any area in Greater London the development plan is–

    (a)   the spatial development strategy, ...¹⁰⁴

    (b)   the development plan documents (taken as a whole) which have been adopted or approved in relation to that area[, and

---

¹⁰⁰ Inserted by the Localism Act 2011, s 222, Sch 22, paras 54, 56(1), (2).
¹⁰¹ Substituted by the Localism Act 2011, s 222, Sch 22, paras 54, 56(1), (3).
¹⁰² Inserted by the Housing and Regeneration Act 2008, s 56, Sch 8, para 81.
¹⁰³ Substituted by the Local Democracy, Economic Development and Construction Act 2009, s 85(1), Sch 5, paras 12, 17.
¹⁰⁴ Repealed by the Localism Act 2011, s 116(1), Sch 9, paras 5, 6(a).

(c)   the neighbourhood development plans which have been made in relation to that area.][105]

(3)   For the purposes of any other area in England the development plan is–

    (a)   the [regional strategy][106] for the region in which the area is situated [(if there is a regional strategy for that region)][107], and

    (b)   the development plan documents (taken as a whole) which have been adopted or approved in relation to that area[, and

    (c)   the neighbourhood development plans which have been made in relation to that area.][108]

[(3A) For the purposes of any area in England (but subject to subsection (3B)) a neighbourhood development plan which relates to that area also forms part of the development plan for that area if—

    (a)   section 38A(4)(a) (approval by referendum) applies in relation to the neighbourhood development plan, but

    (b)   the local planning authority to whom the proposal for the making of the plan has been made have not made the plan.

(3B) The neighbourhood development plan ceases to form part of the development plan if the local planning authority decide under section 38A(6) not to make the plan.][109]

(4)   For the purposes of any area in Wales the development plan is the local development plan adopted or approved in relation to that area.

(5)   If to any extent a policy contained in a development plan for an area conflicts with another policy in the development plan the conflict must be resolved in favour of the policy which is contained in the last document [to become part of the development plan][110].

(6)   If regard is to be had to the development plan for the purpose of any determination to be made under the planning Acts the determination must be made in accordance with the plan unless material considerations indicate otherwise.

(7)   The enactments are–

    (a)   this Act;

    (b)   the planning Acts;

    (c)   any other enactment relating to town and country planning;

    (d)   the Land Compensation Act 1961 (c. 33);

    (e)   the Highways Act 1980 (c. 66).

(8)   In subsection (5) references to a development plan include a development plan for the purposes of paragraph 1 of Schedule 8.

---

[105] Inserted by the Localism Act 2011, s 116(1), Sch 9, paras 5, 6(a), (b), (d).
[106] Substituted by the Local Democracy, Economic Development and Construction Act 2009, s 82(1).
[107] Inserted by the Localism Act 2011, s 109(7), Sch 8, paras 7, 13(1).
[108] Inserted by the Localism Act 2011, s 116(1), Sch 9, paras 5, 6(a), (b), (d).
[109] Inserted by the Neighbourhood Planning Act 2017, s 3.
[110] Substituted by the Localism Act 2011, s 116(1), Sch 9, paras 5, 6(c).

[(9) Development plan document must be construed in accordance with section 37(3).][111]

[(10) Neighbourhood development plan must be construed in accordance with section 38A.][112]

[38A Meaning of 'neighbourhood development plan'

(1) Any qualifying body is entitled to initiate a process for the purpose of requiring a local planning authority in England to make a neighbourhood development plan.

(2) A 'neighbourhood development plan' is a plan which sets out policies (however expressed) in relation to the development and use of land in the whole or any part of a particular neighbourhood area specified in the plan.

(3) Schedule 4B to the principal Act, which makes provision about the process for the making of neighbourhood development orders, including—

   (a) provision for independent examination of orders proposed by qualifying bodies, and

   (b) provision for the holding of referendums on orders proposed by those bodies,

   is to apply in relation to neighbourhood development plans (subject to the modifications set out in section 38C(5) of this Act).

(4) A local planning authority to whom a proposal for the making of a neighbourhood development plan has been made—

   (a) must make a neighbourhood development plan to which the proposal relates if in each applicable referendum under that Schedule (as so applied) more than half of those voting have voted in favour of the plan, and

   (b) if paragraph (a) applies, must make the plan as soon as reasonably practicable after the referendum is held [and, in any event, by such date as may be prescribed][113].

(5) If—

   (a) there are two applicable referendums under that Schedule as so applied (because the plan relates to a neighbourhood area designated as a business area under section 61H of the principal Act), and

   (b) in one of those referendums (but not the other) more than half of those voting have voted in favour of the plan,

   the authority may (but need not) make a neighbourhood development plan to which the proposal relates.

(6) The authority are not to be subject to the duty under subsection (4)(a) if they consider that the making of the plan would breach, or would otherwise be incompatible with, any EU obligation or any of the Convention rights (within the meaning of the Human Rights Act 1998).

---

[111] Substituted by the Localism Act 2011, s 116(1), Sch 9, paras 5, 6(c).
[112] Inserted by the Localism Act 2011, s 116(1), Sch 9, paras 5, 6(a), (b), (d).
[113] Inserted by the Housing and Planning Act 2016, s 140(3).

(7) Regulations made by the Secretary of State may make provision as to the procedure to be followed by local planning authorities in cases where they act under subsection (6).

(8) The regulations may in particular make provision—

    (a) for the holding of an examination,

    (b) as to the payment by a local planning authority of remuneration and expenses of the examiner,

    (c) as to the award of costs by the examiner,

    (d) as to the giving of notice and publicity,

    (e) as to the information and documents that are to be made available to the public,

    (f) as to the making of reasonable charges for anything provided as a result of the regulations,

    (g) as to consultation with and participation by the public, and (h) as to the making and consideration of representations (including the time by which representations must be made).

(9) The authority must publish in such manner as may be prescribed—

    (a) their decision to act under subsection (4) or (6),

    (b) their reasons for making that decision, and

    (c) such other matters relating to that decision as may be prescribed.

(10) The authority must send a copy of the matters required to be published to—

    (a) the qualifying body that initiated the process for the making of the plan, and

    (b) such other persons as may be prescribed.

(11) If a neighbourhood development plan is in force in relation to a neighbourhood area—

    (a) a qualifying body may make a proposal for the existing plan to be replaced by a new one, and

    (b) the process for the making of the replacement plan is the same as the process for the making of the existing plan.

(12) For the purposes of this section—

    'local planning authority' has the same meaning as it has in Part 2 (see section 37), but the Broads Authority are to be the only local planning authority for the Broads,

    'neighbourhood area' has the meaning given by sections 61G and 61I(1) of the principal Act,

    'prescribed' means prescribed by regulations made by the Secretary of State, and

    'qualifying body' means a parish council, or an organisation or body designated as a neighbourhood forum, authorised for the purposes of a neighbourhood development plan to act in relation to a neighbourhood area as a result of section 61F of the principal Act, as applied by section 38C of this Act.][114]

[38B Provision that may be made by neighbourhood development plans

(1)   A neighbourhood development plan—

    (a)   must specify the period for which it is to have effect,

    (b)   may not include provision about development that is excluded development, and

    (c)   may not relate to more than one neighbourhood area.

(2)   Only one neighbourhood development plan may be made for each neighbourhood area.

(3)   If to any extent a policy set out in a neighbourhood development plan conflicts with any other statement or information in the plan, the conflict must be resolved in favour of the policy.

(4)   Regulations made by the Secretary of State may make provision—

    (a)   restricting the provision that may be included in neighbourhood development plans about the use of land,

    (b)   requiring neighbourhood development plans to include such matters as are prescribed in the regulations, and

    (c)   prescribing the form of neighbourhood development plans.

(5)   A local planning authority must publish each neighbourhood development plan that they make in such manner as may be prescribed by regulations made by the Secretary of State.

(6)   Section 61K of the principal Act (meaning of 'excluded development') is to apply for the purposes of subsection (1)(b).][115]

[38C Supplementary provisions

(1)   The following provisions of the principal Act are to apply in relation to neighbourhood development plans.

(2)   The provisions to be applied are—

    (a)   section 61F (authorisation to act in relation to neighbourhood areas),

    (b)   section 61I(2) and (3) (neighbourhood areas in areas of two or more local planning authorities),

    (c)   section 61M (revocation or modification of neighbourhood development orders),

    (d)   section 61N (legal challenges),

    (e)   section 61O (guidance), and

    (f)   section 61P (provision as to the making of certain decisions by local planning authorities).

---

[114]   Inserted by the Localism Act 2011, s 116(1), Sch 9, paras 5, 7.
[115]   Inserted by the Localism Act 2011, s 116(1), Sch 9, paras 5, 7.

(3)   Section 61M of the principal Act is to apply in accordance with subsection (2) of this section as if the words 'by order' (wherever occurring) were omitted.

(4)   Section 61N(1) of the principal Act is to apply in accordance with subsection (2) of this section as if the reference to section 61E(4) or (8) of that Act were a reference to section 38A(4) or (6) of this Act.

(5)   Schedule 4B to the principal Act is to apply in accordance with 38A(3) of this Act with the following modifications—

  (a)   the reference to section 61E(8) of the principal Act is to be read as a reference to section 38A(6) of this Act,

  (b)   references to the provision made by or under sections 61E(2), 61J and 61L of the principal Act are to be read as references to the provision made by or under sections 38A and 38B of this Act,

  (c)   references to section 61L(2)(b) or (5) of the principal Act are to be disregarded, and

  (d)   paragraph 8 is to have effect as if sub-paragraphs (2)(b) and (c) and (3) to (5) were omitted.

(6)   Regulations under section 61G(11) of the principal Act (designation of areas as neighbourhood areas) may include provision about the consequences of the modification of designations on proposals for neighbourhood development plans, or on neighbourhood development plans, that have already been made.

(7)   The fact that the list of applied provisions includes section 61N(2) and (3) of the principal Act is not to affect the operation of section 20(2) of the Interpretation Act 1978 in relation to other references to enactments applied in accordance with this section.][116]

Sustainable development

39 Sustainable development

(1)   This section applies to any person who or body which exercises any function–

  (a)   ...[117]

  (b)   under Part 2 [of this Act][118] in relation to local development documents;

  (c)   ...[119]

(2)   The person or body must exercise the function with the objective of contributing to the achievement of sustainable development.

[(2A) For the purposes of subsection (2) the person or body must (in particular) have regard to the desirability of achieving good design.][120]

---

[116]   Inserted by the Localism Act 2011, s 116(1), Sch 9, paras 5, 7.

[117]   Repealed by the Local Democracy, Economic Development and Construction Act 2009, ss 85(1), 146(1), Sch 5, paras 12, 18(1), (2)(a), Sch 7, Pt 4.

[118]   Inserted by the Local Democracy, Economic Development and Construction Act 2009, s 85(1), Sch 5, paras 12, 18(1), (2)(b).

[119]   Repealed by the Planning (Wales) Act 2015, s 2(6).

[120]   Inserted by the Planning Act 2008, s 183.

(3)   For the purposes of subsection (2) the person or body must have regard to national policies and advice contained in guidance issued by–

(a)   the Secretary of State for the purposes of [subsection (1)(b)][121];

(b)   …[122]

PART 6 WALES

[National Development Framework

60 National Development Framework for Wales

(1)   There must be a plan, prepared and published by the Welsh Ministers, to be known as the National Development Framework for Wales.

(2)   The Framework must set out such of the policies of the Welsh Ministers in relation to the development and use of land in Wales as the Welsh Ministers consider appropriate.

(3)   The Framework may specify that development of a particular description, in a particular area or location, is to constitute development of national significance for the purposes of section 62D of the principal Act (development of national significance: applications to be made to Welsh Ministers).

(4)   The Framework must give reasons for—

(a)   the policies that it sets out, and

(b)   any provision that it makes as mentioned in subsection (3).

(5)   The Framework must explain how, in preparing the Framework, the Welsh Ministers have taken into account relevant policies set out in—

[(za) the national natural resources policy published under section 9 of the Environment (Wales) Act 2016,][123]

(a)   any marine plan adopted and published by them under Part 3 of the Marine and Coastal Access Act 2009, and

(b)   the Wales Transport Strategy published under section 2 of the Transport (Wales) Act 2006.

(6)   The Framework must specify the period for which it is to have effect.

(7)   A plan ceases to be the National Development Framework for Wales on the expiry of the period specified under subsection (6).][124]

[60A Preparation of Framework: statement of public participation

(1)   The Welsh Ministers must prepare and publish a statement of public participation setting out their policies relating to the consultation to be carried out in preparing the National Development Framework for Wales.

---

[121] Substituted by the Local Democracy, Economic Development and Construction Act 2009, s 85(1), Sch 5, paras 12, 18(1), (3).
[122] Repealed by the Planning (Wales) Act 2015, s 2(6).
[123] Inserted by the Environment (Wales) Act 2016, s 27(2), Sch 2, para 8(1), (2).
[124] Substituted by the Planning (Wales) Act 2015, s 3.

(2)   In particular, the statement must include provision about—

    (a)   the form that the consultation will take,

    (b)   when the consultation will take place, and

    (c)   the steps that will be taken to involve members of the public in the preparation of the Framework.

(3)   The statement must provide that, as part of the consultation, the Welsh Ministers will—

    (a)   publish a draft of the Framework, and

    (b)   allow a period of 12 weeks beginning with the publication of the draft Framework during which any person may make representations with regard to the draft.

(4)   The Welsh Ministers may revise the statement, and must publish the statement as revised.][125]

[60B Procedure for preparation and publication of Framework

(1)   Before publishing the National Development Framework for Wales, the Welsh Ministers must—

    (a)   prepare a draft of the Framework,

    (b)   carry out an appraisal of the sustainability of the policies set out in the draft, and

    (c)   carry out consultation in accordance with the statement of public participation.

(2)   The appraisal under subsection (1)(b) must include an assessment of the likely effects of the policies in the draft Framework on the use of the Welsh language.

(3)   If, after complying with subsection (1), the Welsh Ministers wish to proceed with the draft of the Framework (with or without changes), they must lay before the National Assembly for Wales—

    (a)   the draft, and

    (b)   a report which—

        (i)   summarises the representations they received during the consultation carried out under subsection (1)(c), and

        (ii)   explains how they have taken the representations into account.

(4)   The Welsh Ministers must have regard to—

    (a)   any resolution passed by the National Assembly for Wales with regard to the draft Framework during the Assembly consideration period, and

    (b)   any recommendation made by a committee of the National Assembly with regard to the draft during that period.

(5)   After the expiry of the Assembly consideration period, the Welsh Ministers—

---

[125]   Inserted by the Planning (Wales) Act 2015, s 3.

(a)   may publish the National Development Framework for Wales in the terms of the draft laid under subsection (3), or

(b)   if they propose to make changes to that draft, may—

    (i)   lay before the National Assembly for Wales an amended draft of the Framework, and

    (ii)   publish the National Development Framework for Wales in the terms of the amended draft.

(6)   If any resolution was passed or any recommendation was made as mentioned in subsection (4), the Welsh Ministers must also, not later than the day on which the Framework is published, lay before the National Assembly for Wales a statement explaining how they have had regard to the resolution or recommendation.

(7)   In this section, 'the Assembly consideration period' means the period of 60 days beginning with the day on which a draft of the Framework is laid before the National Assembly for Wales under subsection (3), disregarding any time when the National Assembly is dissolved or is in recess for more than four days.][126]

[60C Review and revision of Framework

(1)   The Welsh Ministers must keep the National Development Framework for Wales under review.

(2)   The Welsh Ministers may revise the Framework at any time, and must publish the Framework as revised.

(3)   Sections 60A and 60B apply for the purposes of the revision of the Framework, as if references to the Framework (or a draft of the Framework) were references to the Framework as revised (or a draft of the Framework as revised).

(4)   Subsection (5) applies if the Welsh Ministers, having published a draft of a revised Framework in accordance with the statement of public participation, decide not to proceed with the revision of the Framework.

(5)   The Welsh Ministers must—

(a)   publish notice of their decision and the reasons for it, and

(b)   if a draft of a revised Framework has been laid before the National Assembly for Wales under section 60B(3), lay a copy of the notice before the National Assembly.

(6)   Subsection (7) applies if—

(a)   a review period ends, and

(b)   the Welsh Ministers have not, within that period—

    (i)   published a revised Framework, or

    (ii)   laid a draft revised Framework before the National Assembly for Wales under section 60B(3).

---

[126] Inserted by the Planning (Wales) Act 2015, s 3.

(7)   As soon as reasonably practicable after the end of the review period, the Welsh Ministers must publish and lay before the National Assembly for Wales a statement—

(a)   setting out their assessment of whether the Framework should be revised and giving reasons for that assessment, and

(b)   if they consider that the Framework should be revised, setting out a timetable for its revision.

(8)   For the purposes of subsections (6) and (7)—

(a)   the first review period—

(i)   begins with the day on which the Framework is first published, and

(ii)   ends with the fifth anniversary of the day on which the Framework is first published or, if earlier, with the day on which a revised Framework is published;

(b)   each subsequent review period—

(i)   begins with the day after the last day of the preceding review period, and

(ii)   ends with the fifth anniversary of the last day of the preceding review period or, if earlier, with the day on which a revised Framework is published.][127]

[Strategic planning

60D Power to designate strategic planning area and establish strategic planning panel

(1)   The Welsh Ministers may by regulations—

(a)   designate an area in Wales as a strategic planning area for the purposes of this Part, and

(b)   establish a strategic planning panel for that area.

(2)   A strategic planning area must comprise—

(a)   all of the area of one local planning authority, and

(b)   all or part of the area of at least one other local planning authority.

(3)   The Welsh Ministers must not make regulations under this section unless—

(a)   they have given a direction under section 60E(1) to a local planning authority all or part of whose area is included in the strategic planning area to be designated by the regulations,

(b)   either—

(i)   a proposal for an area to be designated has been submitted in accordance with section 60E(6), or

(ii)   the period for complying with section 60E(6) has ended without a proposal being submitted, and

---

[127] Inserted by the Planning (Wales) Act 2015, s 3.

(c)   they have carried out any consultation required by section 60F(1).

(4)   Paragraphs (a) and (b) of subsection (3) do not apply in relation to regulations that revoke or amend previous regulations under this section.

(5)   Schedule 2A contains provisions about strategic planning panels.]¹²⁸

[60E Preparation and submission of proposal for strategic planning area

(1)   The Welsh Ministers may direct one or more local planning authorities to submit a proposal for an area to be designated as a strategic planning area under section 60D.

(2)   If the Welsh Ministers give a direction under subsection (1), they must state their reasons for doing so.

(3)   In this section, the 'responsible authority' means—

(a)   where a direction under subsection (1) is given to a single local planning authority, that authority;

(b)   where a direction under subsection (1) is given to two or more local planning authorities, those authorities acting jointly.

(4)   The responsible authority must prepare a proposal for an area to be designated as a strategic planning area.

(5)   Before submitting the proposal to the Welsh Ministers, the responsible authority must consult—

(a)   each local planning authority, other than one to which the direction under subsection (1) was given, for an area all or part of which is included in the proposed strategic planning area, and

(b)   any other persons specified in, or of a description specified in, the direction.

(6)   The responsible authority must submit to the Welsh Ministers—

(a)   the proposal, and

(b)   a report about the consultation carried out under subsection (5).

(7)   A proposal submitted under subsection (6)(a) must include—

(a)   a map showing the boundaries of the area which the responsible authority propose should be designated as a strategic planning area,

(b)   a statement of the reasons for proposing that area, and

(c)   any other information specified by the Welsh Ministers in the direction given under subsection (1).

(8)   The responsible authority must comply with subsection (6)—

(a)   before the end of any period specified in the direction;

(b)   if no period is specified in the direction, before the end of six months beginning with the day on which the direction is given.

---

¹²⁸ Inserted by the Planning (Wales) Act 2015, s 4(1).

(9)   The Welsh Ministers may agree to extend the period for complying with subsection (6) in a particular case.

(10)   The responsible authority must comply with any requirements set out in the direction as to—

(a)   how the consultation required by subsection (5) must be carried out;

(b)   the form and content of the report about the consultation;

(c)   how the proposal and the report must be submitted under subsection (6).

(11)   Subsection (12) applies if the Welsh Ministers, having given a direction under subsection (1), decide not to designate a strategic planning area.

(12)   The Welsh Ministers must give notice of their decision and the reasons for it—

(a)   to the responsible authority, and

(b)   if a proposal has been submitted under subsection (6), to each authority within subsection (5)(a).][129]

[60F Consultation by Welsh Ministers before making certain regulations under section 60D

(1)   If the Welsh Ministers propose to make regulations under section 60D to which this section applies, they must consult—

(a)   each relevant local planning authority, and

(b)   any other persons they consider appropriate.

(2)   This section applies to regulations under section 60D if the Welsh Ministers have given a direction under section 60E(1) and—

(a)   the boundaries of the strategic planning area that would be designated by the regulations are different from the boundaries of the area proposed under section 60E(6) pursuant to the direction, or

(b)   the period for complying with section 60E(6) has ended without a proposal being submitted.

(3)   This section also applies to regulations under section 60D revoking or amending previous regulations under that section.

(4)   A local planning authority is a relevant local planning authority in relation to regulations to which this section applies if all or part of the authority's area is included in—

(a)   the strategic planning area that would be designated by the regulations, or

(b)   a strategic planning area designated by previous regulations under section 60D that would be revoked or amended by the regulations.][130]

---

[129]   Inserted by the Planning (Wales) Act 2015, s 4(1).
[130]   Inserted by the Planning (Wales) Act 2015, s 4(1).

[60G Provision of information to Welsh Ministers

A local planning authority must provide the Welsh Ministers with any information that the Welsh Ministers request for the purpose of exercising their functions under sections 60D to 60F.][131]

[60H Strategic planning area: survey

(1)   A strategic planning panel must keep under review the matters which may be expected to affect the development of its strategic planning area or the planning of the development of that area.

(2)   Subsections (2) to (5) of section 61 apply in relation to a strategic planning panel as they apply in relation to a local planning authority.

(3)   In subsections (2) to (5) of section 61 as they apply by virtue of subsection (2)—

    (a)   references to a local planning authority are to be construed as references to a strategic planning panel;

    (b)   references to a neighbouring area are to be construed as references to a neighbouring strategic planning area.][132]

[60I Strategic development plan

(1)   A strategic planning panel must prepare a plan for its strategic planning area, to be known as a strategic development plan.

(2)   The plan must set out—

    (a)   the panel's objectives in relation to the development and use of land in its area;

    (b)   the panel's policies for the implementation of those objectives.

(3)   A strategic development plan must be in general conformity with the National Development Framework for Wales.

(4)   The plan must specify the period for which it is to have effect.

(5)   The Welsh Ministers may by regulations make provision about—

    (a)   the period that may be specified under subsection (4);

    (b)   the form and content of the plan.

(6)   In preparing a strategic development plan, the strategic planning panel must have regard to—

    (a)   current national policies;

    (b)   the National Development Framework for Wales;

    (c)   the strategic development plan for any strategic planning area that adjoins the panel's area;

---

[131]   Inserted by the Planning (Wales) Act 2015, s 4(1).
[132]   Inserted by the Planning (Wales) Act 2015, s 5.

(d)   the local development plan for each area all or part of which is included in the panel's area;

(e)   the resources likely to be available for implementing the strategic development plan;

(f)   any other matters prescribed by the Welsh Ministers in regulations.

(7)   The panel must also—

(a)   carry out an appraisal of the sustainability of the plan;

(b)   prepare a report of the findings of the appraisal.

(8)   The appraisal must include an assessment of the likely effects of the plan on the use of the Welsh language in the strategic planning area.

(9)   A plan is a strategic development plan only in so far as it is—

(a)   adopted by resolution of the strategic planning panel as a strategic development plan, or

(b)   approved by the Welsh Ministers under section 65 or 71 (as they apply by virtue of section 60J).

(10)   The plan ceases to be a strategic development plan on the expiry of the period specified under subsection (4).][133]

[60J Strategic development plan: application of provisions of this Part

(1)   The provisions specified in subsection (3) apply in relation to a strategic development plan as they apply in relation to a local development plan.

(2)   Accordingly, where a provision specified in subsection (3) confers power for the Welsh Ministers to make provision by regulations in respect of a local development plan, that power is also exercisable so as to make provision in respect of a strategic development plan.

(3)   The provisions are sections 63 to 68, 68A(1), 69 to 71, 73 and 75 to 77.

(4)   In those provisions as they apply by virtue of subsection (1)—

(a)   references to a local planning authority are to be construed as references to a strategic planning panel;

(b)   references to a local development plan are to be construed as references to a strategic development plan.

(5)   In section 64(5)(a) as it applies by virtue of this section, the reference to section 62 is to be construed as a reference to section 60I.

(6)   In section 77(2)(a) as it applies by virtue of this section, the reference to section 62(6) is to be construed as a reference to section 60I(7).][134]

---

[133] Inserted by the Planning (Wales) Act 2015, s 6.
[134] Inserted by the Planning (Wales) Act 2015, s 6.

Survey

61 Survey

(1)   The local planning authority must keep under review the matters which may be expected to affect the development of their area or the planning of its development.

(2)   These matters include–

    (a)   the principal physical, economic, social and environmental characteristics of the area of the authority [(including the extent to which the Welsh language is used in the area)][135];

    (b)   the principal purposes for which land is used in the area;

    (c)   the size, composition and distribution of the population of the area;

    (d)   the communications, transport system and traffic of the area;

    (e)   any other considerations which may be expected to affect those matters;

    (f)   such other matters as may be prescribed or as the Assembly in a particular case may direct.

(3)   These matters also include–

    (a)   any changes which the authority think may occur in relation to any other matter;

    (b)   the effect such changes are likely to have on the development of the authority's area or on the planning of such development.

(4)   The local planning authority may also keep under review and examine the matters mentioned in subsections (2) and (3) in relation to any neighbouring area to the extent that those matters may be expected to affect the area of the authority.

(5)   In exercising a function under subsection (4) a local planning authority must consult the local planning authority for the neighbouring area in question.

(6)   If a neighbouring area is in England references to the local planning authority for that area must be construed in accordance with Part 2.

Plans

62 Local development plan

(1)   The local planning authority must prepare a plan for their area to be known as a local development plan.

(2)   The plan must set out–

    (a)   the authority's objectives in relation to the development and use of land in their area;

    (b)   their general policies for the implementation of those objectives.

---

[135]   Inserted by the Planning (Wales) Act 2015, s 11(1), (2).

(3)   The plan may also set out specific policies in relation to any part of the area of the authority.

[(3A) The plan must be in general conformity with—

> (a)   the National Development Framework for Wales, and
>
> (b)   the strategic development plan for any strategic planning area that includes all or part of the area of the authority.][136]

[(3B) The plan must specify the period for which it is to have effect.][137]

(4)   Regulations under this section may[—

> (a)   make provision about the period that may be specified under subsection (3B);
>
> (b)][138]prescribe the form and content of the plan.

(5)   In preparing a local development plan the authority must have regard to–

> (a)   current national policies;
>
> [(b)   the National Development Framework for Wales;
>
> (ba)   the strategic development plan for any strategic planning area that—
>
> > (i)   includes all or part of the area of the authority, or
> >
> > (ii)   adjoins that area;][139]
>
> [(bb)   any area statement published under section 11 of the Environment (Wales) Act 2016 for an area that includes all or part of the area of the authority;][140]
>
> (c)   the RSS for any region which adjoins the area of the authority;
>
> [(d)   any relevant [local well-being plan][141];][142]
>
> (f)   the resources likely to be available for implementing the plan;
>
> (g)   such other matters as the Assembly prescribes.

(6)   The authority must also–

> (a)   carry out an appraisal of the sustainability of the plan;
>
> (b)   prepare a report of the findings of the appraisal.

[(6A) The appraisal must include an assessment of the likely effects of the plan on the use of the Welsh language in the area of the authority.][143]

[(7)   A local well-being plan is relevant if it has been published under section 39 or 44(5) of the Well-being of Future Generations (Wales) Act 2015 (anaw 2) by—

---

[136]   Inserted by the Planning (Wales) Act 2015, s 7(1).
[137]   Inserted by the Planning (Wales) Act 2015, s 12.
[138]   Inserted by the Planning (Wales) Act 2015, s 12.
[139]   Substituted by the Planning (Wales) Act 2015, s 16, Sch 2, paras 23, 25.
[140]   Inserted by the Environment (Wales) Act 2016, s 27(2), Sch 2, para 8(1), (3).
[141]   Substituted by the Well-being of Future Generations (Wales) Act 2015, s 46, Sch 4, paras 8, 9, 10.
[142]   Substituted by the Local Government (Wales) Measure 2009, s 51(2), Sch 2, paras 4, 5.
[143]   Inserted by the Planning (Wales) Act 2015, s 11(1), (3).specified in SI 2015/1987 art.6 otherwise).

(a) in the case of an authority which is a county council or county borough council, the public services board of which that authority is a member;

(b) in the case of an authority which is a National Park Authority, the public services board for an area that includes any part of that authority's area.][144]

(8) A plan is a local development plan only in so far as it–

(a) is adopted by resolution of the local planning authority as a local development plan;

(b) is approved by the Assembly under section 65 or 71.

[(9) A plan ceases to be a local development plan on the expiry of the period specified under subsection (3B).][145]

63 Preparation requirements

(1) A local development plan must be prepared in accordance with–

(a) the local planning authority's community involvement scheme;

(b) the timetable for the preparation and adoption of the authority's local development plan.

(2) The authority's community involvement scheme is a statement of the authority's policy as to the involvement in the exercise of the authority's functions under this Part of the persons to which subsection (3) applies.

(3) The persons mentioned in subsection (2)–

(a) must include such persons as the Assembly prescribes;

(b) may include such other persons as appear to the authority to have an interest in matters relating to development in the area of the authority.

(4) The authority and the Assembly must attempt to agree the terms of the documents mentioned in paragraphs (a) and (b) of subsection (1).

(5) But to the extent that the Assembly and the authority cannot agree the terms the Assembly may direct that the documents must be in the terms specified in the direction.

(6) The authority must comply with the direction.

(7) The Assembly may prescribe–

(a) the procedure in respect of the preparation of the documents mentioned in paragraphs (a) and (b) of subsection (1);

(b) the form and content of the documents;

(c) the time at which any step in the preparation of the documents must be taken;

(d) publicity about the documents;

(e) making the documents available for inspection by the public;

---

[144] Substituted by the Well-being of Future Generations (Wales) Act 2015, s 46, Sch 4, paras 8, 9, 10.
[145] Inserted by the Planning (Wales) Act 2015, s 12.

(f)   circumstances in which the requirements of the documents need not be complied with.

64 Independent examination

(1)   The local planning authority must submit their local development plan to the Assembly for independent examination.

(2)   But the authority must not submit a plan unless–

(a)   they have complied with any relevant requirements contained in regulations under this Part, and

(b)   they think the plan is ready for independent examination.

(3)   The authority must also send to the Assembly (in addition to the local development plan) such other documents (or copies of documents) and such information as is prescribed.

(4)   The examination must be carried out by a person appointed by the Assembly.

(5)   The purpose of the independent examination is to determine in respect of a local development plan–

(a)   whether it satisfies the requirements of sections 62 and 63 and of regulations under section 77;

(b)   whether it is sound.

(6)   Any person who makes representations seeking to change a local development plan must (if he so requests) be given the opportunity to appear before and be heard by the person carrying out the examination.

(7)   The person appointed to carry out the examination must–

(a)   make recommendations;

(b)   give reasons for the recommendations.

(8)   The local planning authority must publish the recommendations and the reasons.

65 Intervention by Assembly

(1)   If the Assembly thinks that a local development plan is unsatisfactory–

(a)   it may at any time before the plan is adopted by the local planning authority direct them to modify the plan in accordance with the direction;

(b)   if it gives such a direction it must state its reasons for doing so.

(2)   The authority–

(a)   must comply with the direction;

(b)   must not adopt the plan unless the Assembly gives notice that it is satisfied that they have complied with the direction.

(3)   But subsection (2) does not apply if the Assembly withdraws the direction.

(4)   At any time before a local development plan is adopted by a local planning authority the Assembly may direct that the plan is submitted to it for its approval.

(5)   The following paragraphs apply if the Assembly gives a direction under subsection (4)–

(a)   the authority must not take any step in connection with the adoption of the plan until the Assembly gives its decision;

(b)   if the direction is given before the authority have submitted the plan under section 64(1) the Assembly must hold an independent examination and section 64(4) to (7) applies accordingly;

(c)   if the direction is given after the authority have submitted the plan the person appointed to carry out the examination must make his recommendations to the Assembly;

(d)   the plan has no effect unless it has been approved by the Assembly.

(6)   The Assembly must publish the recommendations made to it by virtue of subsection (5)(b) or (c) and the reasons of the person making the recommendations.

(7)   In considering a plan submitted under subsection (4) the Assembly may take account of any matter which it thinks is relevant.

(8)   It is immaterial whether any such matter was taken account of by the authority.

(9)   The Assembly–

(a)   may approve, approve subject to specified modifications or reject a plan submitted to it under subsection (4);

(b)   must give reasons for its decision under paragraph (a).

(10)   In the exercise of any function under this section the Assembly must have regard to the documents mentioned in paragraphs (a) and (b) of section 63(1).

[66 Withdrawal of local development plan in accordance with direction

(1)   The Welsh Ministers may, at any time before a local development plan is adopted under section 67, direct the local planning authority to withdraw the plan.

(2)   If the Welsh Ministers give a direction under subsection (1), they must state their reasons for doing so.

(3)   The authority must withdraw the plan in accordance with the direction.]¹⁴⁶

[66A Withdrawal of local development plan in absence of direction

(1)   This section applies where a local planning authority are not required to withdraw their local development plan under section 66.

(2)   Subject to the provisions of this section, the authority may withdraw the plan at any time before adopting it under section 67.

(3)   A local planning authority may not withdraw their local development plan when the Welsh Ministers have—

(a)   directed the authority to submit the plan for approval under section 65(4), or

---

¹⁴⁶ Substituted by the Planning (Wales) Act 2015, s 13.

(b)   taken any step under section 71 in connection with the plan.

(4)   A local planning authority may withdraw a local development plan that has been submitted for independent examination under section 64 only if—

    (a)   the person carrying out the independent examination recommends that the plan is withdrawn, and

    (b)   the recommendation is not overruled by a direction given by the Welsh Ministers.

(5)   A local planning authority may withdraw a local development plan to which subsection (6) applies only if—

    (a)   the authority have given notice to the Welsh Ministers of their intention to withdraw the plan, and

    (b)   the notice period has expired.

(6)   This subsection applies to a local development plan if the local planning authority—

    (a)   have not yet submitted the plan for independent examination under section 64, but

    (b)   have taken steps in connection with the preparation of the plan that are specified in regulations made by the Welsh Ministers.

(7)   Where a local planning authority have given notice under subsection (5)(a), the Welsh Ministers may, by direction to the authority, do either or both of the following—

    (a)   require the authority to provide further information;

    (b)   extend the notice period.

(8)   The Welsh Ministers may by regulations make provision about the giving of notices and directions under this section (including provision about their form and content and how they are to be given).

(9)   Subject to any direction given under subsection (7)(b) in a particular case, the 'notice period' means whatever period, beginning with the giving of notice under subsection (5)(a), is specified in regulations made by the Welsh Ministers.][147]

67 Adoption of local development plan

(1)   The local planning authority may adopt a local development plan as originally prepared if the person appointed to carry out the independent examination of the plan recommends that the plan as originally prepared is adopted.

(2)   The authority may adopt a local development plan with modifications if the person appointed to carry out the independent examination of the plan recommends the modifications.

(3)   A plan is adopted for the purposes of this section if it is adopted by resolution of the authority.

---

[147]   Substituted by the Planning (Wales) Act 2015, s 13.

(4) But the authority must not adopt a local development plan if the Assembly directs them not to do so.

68 Revocation of local development plan

The Assembly may at any time revoke a local development plan at the request of the local planning authority.

[68A Duty to consider whether to review local development plan

(1) Following the publication of the National Development Framework for Wales or a revised Framework, a local planning authority must consider whether to carry out a review of their local development plan.

(2) Following the adoption or approval of a strategic development plan or revised strategic development plan for a strategic planning area, a local planning authority for an area all or part of which is included in the strategic planning area must consider whether to carry out a review of their local development plan.]^{148}

69 Review of local development plan

(1) A local planning authority must carry out a review of their local development plan[—

    (a) if, after consideration under section 68A, they think that the plan should be reviewed, and

    (b) at such other times as the Welsh Ministers prescribe.]^{149}

(2) The authority must report to the Assembly on the findings of their review.

(3) A review must–

    (a) be in such form as is prescribed;

    (b) be published in accordance with such requirements as are prescribed.

70 Revision of local development plan

(1) The local planning authority may at any time prepare a revision of a local development plan.

(2) The authority must prepare a revision of a local development plan–

    (a) if the Assembly directs them to do so;

    (b) if, following a review under section 69, they think that the plan should be revised.

(3) This Part applies to the revision of a local development plan as it applies to the preparation of the plan.

---

148 Inserted by the Planning (Wales) Act 2015, s 8(1).
149 Substituted by the Planning (Wales) Act 2015, s 8(2).

71 Assembly's default power

(1)   This section applies if the Assembly thinks that a local planning authority are failing or omitting to do anything it is necessary for them to do in connection with the preparation, revision or adoption of a local development plan.

(2)   The Assembly must hold an independent examination and section 64(4) to (7) applies accordingly.

(3)   The Assembly must publish the recommendations and reasons of the person appointed to hold the examination.

(4)   The Assembly may–

(a)   prepare or revise (as the case may be) the plan, and

(b)   approve the plan as a local development plan.

(5)   The Assembly must give reasons for anything it does in pursuance of subsection (4).

(6)   The authority must reimburse the Assembly for any expenditure it incurs in connection with anything–

(a)   which is done by it under subsection (4), and

(b)   which the authority failed or omitted to do as mentioned in subsection (1).

72 Joint local development plans

[(A1) The Welsh Ministers may direct two or more local planning authorities to prepare a joint local development plan.

(A2) But a direction under subsection (A1) may not be given to a National Park authority.][150]

(1)   Two or more local planning authorities may[, in the absence of a direction to any of them under subsection (A1),][151] agree to prepare a joint local development plan.

[(1A) If the Welsh Ministers give a direction under subsection (A1), they must state their reasons for doing so.

(1B) The authorities to which a direction is given must, subject to any withdrawal or variation of the direction, act jointly in exercising their functions under this Part relating to local development plans.][152]

(2)   This Part applies for the purposes of the preparation, revision, adoption, withdrawal and revocation of a joint local development plan as it applies for the purposes of the preparation, revision, adoption, withdrawal and revocation of a local development plan.

(3)   For the purposes of subsection (2) anything which must be done by or in relation to a local planning authority in connection with a local development plan must be done by or in relation to each of the authorities mentioned in subsection [(A1) or][153] (1) in connection with a joint local development plan.

---

150   Inserted by the Planning (Wales) Act 2015, s 14(1)-(6), (7)(a), (8)-(10).
151   Inserted by the Planning (Wales) Act 2015, s 14(1)-(6), (7)(a), (8)-(10).
152   Inserted by the Planning (Wales) Act 2015, s 14(1)-(6), (7)(a), (8)-(10).
153   Inserted by the Planning (Wales) Act 2015, s 14(1)-(6), (7)(a), (8)-(10).

(4) Subsections (5) to (7) apply if[—

    (a) the Welsh Ministers withdraw a direction under subsection (A1) or vary such a direction so that it ceases to apply to a local planning authority, or

    (b)]¹⁵⁴a local planning authority withdraw from an agreement mentioned in subsection (1).

(5) Any step taken in relation to the plan must be treated as a step taken by–

    (a) an authority [to which the direction was given or]¹⁵⁵ which was a party to the agreement for the purposes of any corresponding plan prepared by them;

    (b) two or more other authorities [to which the direction was given or which]¹⁵⁶ were parties to the agreement for the purposes of any corresponding joint local development plan.

(6) Any independent examination of a local development plan to which the [direction or]¹⁵⁷ agreement relates must be suspended.

(7) If before the end of the period prescribed for the purposes of this subsection an authority [to which the direction was given or]¹⁵⁸ which was a party to the agreement requests the Assembly to do so it may direct that–

    (a) the examination is resumed in relation to the corresponding plan;

    (b) any step taken for the purposes of the suspended examination has effect for the purposes of the resumed examination.

[(7A) The Welsh Ministers may by regulations—

    (a) specify circumstances in which subsections (5) and (7) are not to apply in relation to an authority;

    (b) make provision as to what is a corresponding plan or corresponding joint local development plan.]¹⁵⁹

(8) A joint local development plan is a local development plan prepared jointly by two or more local planning authorities.

Miscellaneous

73 Exclusion of certain representations

(1) This section applies to any representation or objection in respect of anything which is done or is proposed to be done in pursuance of–

    (a) an order or scheme under section 10, 14, 16, 18, 106(1) or (3) or 108(1) of the Highways Act 1980 (c. 66);

    (b) an order or scheme under section 7, 9, 11, 13 or 20 of the Highways Act 1959 (c. 25), section 3 of the Highways (Miscellaneous Provisions) Act

---

¹⁵⁴ Inserted by the Planning (Wales) Act 2015, s 14(1)-(6), (7)(a), (8)-(10).
¹⁵⁵ Inserted by the Planning (Wales) Act 2015, s 14(1)-(6), (7)(a), (8)-(10).
¹⁵⁶ Substituted by the Planning (Wales) Act 2015, s 14(1), (7)(b).
¹⁵⁷ Inserted by the Planning (Wales) Act 2015, s 14(1)-(6), (7)(a), (8)-(10).
¹⁵⁸ Inserted by the Planning (Wales) Act 2015, s 14(1)-(6), (7)(a), (8)-(10).
¹⁵⁹ Inserted by the Planning (Wales) Act 2015, s 14(1)-(6), (7)(a), (8)-(10).

1961 (c. 63) or section 1 or 10 of the Highways Act 1971 (c. 41) (which provisions were replaced by the provisions mentioned in paragraph (a));

    (c)   an order under section 1 of the New Towns Act 1981 (c. 64).

(2)   If the Assembly or a local planning authority thinks that a representation made in relation to a local development plan is in substance a representation or objection to which this section applies it or they (as the case may be) may disregard it.

74 Urban development corporations

The Assembly may direct that this Part (except section 60) does not apply to the area of an urban development corporation.

75 Guidance

In the exercise of any function conferred under or by virtue of this Part the local planning authority must have regard to any guidance issued by the Assembly.

76 Annual monitoring report

(1)   Every local planning authority must make an annual report to the Assembly.

(2)   The annual report must contain such information as is prescribed as to the extent to which the objectives set out in the local development plan are being achieved.

(3)   The annual report must–

    (a)   be made at such time as is prescribed;

    (b)   be in such form as is prescribed;

    (c)   contain such other matter as is prescribed.

General

77 Regulations

(1)   The Assembly may by regulations make provision in connection with the exercise of functions conferred by this Part on any person.

(2)   The regulations may in particular make provision as to–

    (a)   the procedure to be followed by the local planning authority in carrying out the appraisal under section 62(6);

    (b)   the procedure to be followed in the preparation of local development plans;

    (c)   requirements about the giving of notice and publicity;

    (d)   requirements about inspection by the public of a plan or any other document;

    (e)   the nature and extent of consultation with and participation by the public in anything done under this Part;

(f)   the making of representations about any matter to be included in a local development plan;

(g)   consideration of any such representations;

(h)   the remuneration and allowances payable to the person appointed to carry out an independent examination under section 64;

(i)   the time at which anything must be done for the purposes of this Part;

(j)   the manner of publication of any draft, report or other document published under this Part;

(k)   monitoring the exercise by local planning authorities of their functions under this Part.

78 Interpretation

(1)   Local development plan must be construed in accordance with section 62.

(2)   Local planning authorities are–

(a)   county councils in Wales;

(b)   county borough councils.

[(3)   But—

(a)   a National Park authority is the local planning authority for the whole of its area;

(b)   a joint planning board is the local planning authority for the whole of its united district (and references to the area of a local planning authority are, in relation to such a board, to be construed as references to its united district).]¹⁶⁰

(4)   The Assembly is the National Assembly for Wales.

(5)   RSS must be construed in accordance with Part 1.

(6)   This section applies for the purposes of this Part.

PART 9 MISCELLANEOUS AND GENERAL

Miscellaneous

113 Validity of strategies, plans and documents

(1)   This section applies to–

(a)   a revision of [the regional strategy]¹⁶¹;

(b)   the Wales Spatial Plan;

(c)   a development plan document;

(d)   a local development plan;

---

¹⁶⁰   Substituted by the Planning (Wales) Act 2015, s 15(1), (2).
¹⁶¹   Substituted by the Local Democracy, Economic Development and Construction Act 2009, s 85(1), Sch 5, paras 12, 19(1)-(4).

(e)   a revision of a document mentioned in paragraph (b), (c) or (d);

(f)   the Mayor of London's spatial development strategy;

(g)   an alteration or replacement of the spatial development strategy,

and anything falling within paragraphs (a) to (g) is referred to in this section as a relevant document.

(2)   A relevant document must not be questioned in any legal proceedings except in so far as is provided by the following provisions of this section.

(3)   A person aggrieved by a relevant document may make an application to the High Court on the ground that–

(a)   the document is not within the appropriate power;

(b)   a procedural requirement has not been complied with.

[(3A) An application may not be made under subsection (3) without the leave of the High Court.

(3B)   An application for leave for the purposes of subsection (3A) must be made before the end of the period of six weeks beginning with the day after the relevant date.][162]

(4)   ...[163]

(5)   The High Court may make an interim order suspending the operation of the relevant document–

(a)   wholly or in part;

(b)   generally or as it affects the property of the applicant.

[(5A) An interim order has effect—

(a)   if made on an application for leave, until the final determination of—

(i)   the question of whether leave should be granted, or

(ii)   where leave is granted, the proceedings on any application under this section made with such leave;

(b)   in any other case, until the proceedings are finally determined.][164]

(6)   Subsection (7) applies if the High Court is satisfied–

(a)   that a relevant document is to any extent outside the appropriate power;

(b)   that the interests of the applicant have been substantially prejudiced by a failure to comply with a procedural requirement.

[(7)   The High Court may—

(a)   quash the relevant document;

(b)   remit the relevant document to a person or body with a function relating to its preparation, publication, adoption or approval.

---

[162]   Inserted by the Criminal Justice and Courts Act 2015, s 91, Sch 16, para 8(1), (2), (4).
[163]   Repealed by the Criminal Justice and Courts Act 2015, s 91, Sch 16, para 8(1), (3), (5).
[164]   Inserted by the Criminal Justice and Courts Act 2015, s 91, Sch 16, para 8(1), (2), (4).

(7A) If the High Court remits the relevant document under subsection (7)(b) it may give directions as to the action to be taken in relation to the document.

(7B) Directions under subsection (7A) may in particular—

(a) require the relevant document to be treated (generally or for specified purposes) as not having been approved or adopted;

(b) require specified steps in the process that has resulted in the approval or adoption of the relevant document to be treated (generally or for specified purposes) as having been taken or as not having been taken;

(c) require action to be taken by a person or body with a function relating to the preparation, publication, adoption or approval of the document (whether or not the person or body to which the document is remitted);

(d) require action to be taken by one person or body to depend on what action has been taken by another person or body.

(7C) The High Court's powers under subsections (7) and (7A) are exercisable in relation to the relevant document—

(a) wholly or in part;

(b) generally or as it affects the property of the applicant.][165]

(8)   ...[166]

(9)   The appropriate power is–

[(a) Part 5 of the Local Democracy, Economic Development and Construction Act 2009 in the case of a revision of the regional strategy;][167]

(b) section 60 above in the case of the Wales Spatial Plan or any revision of it;

(c) Part 2 of this Act in the case of a development plan document or any revision of it;

(d) sections 62 to 78 above in the case of a local development plan or any revision of it;

(e) sections 334 to 343 of the Greater London Authority Act 1999 (c. 29) in the case of the spatial development strategy or any alteration or replacement of it.

(10) A procedural requirement is a requirement under the appropriate power or contained in regulations or an order made under that power which relates to the adoption, publication or approval of a relevant document.

(11) References to the relevant date must be construed as follows–

[(a) for the purposes of a revision of the regional strategy, the date when the revision is published by the Secretary of State under Part 5 of Local Democracy, Economic Development and Construction Act 2009;][168]

---

[165] Substituted by the Planning Act 2008, s 185.
[166] Inserted by the Criminal Justice and Courts Act 2015, s 91, Sch 16, para 8(1), (2), (4).
[167] Substituted by the Local Democracy, Economic Development and Construction Act 2009, s 85(1), Sch 5, paras 12, 19(1)-(4).
[168] Substituted by the Local Democracy, Economic Development and Construction Act 2009, s 85(1), Sch 5, paras 12, 19(1)-(4).

(b)   for the purposes of the Wales Spatial Plan (or a revision of it), the date when it is approved by the National Assembly for Wales;

(c)   for the purposes of a development plan document (or a revision of it), the date when it is adopted by the local planning authority or approved by the Secretary of State (as the case may be);

(d)   for the purposes of a local development plan (or a revision of it), the date when it is adopted by a local planning authority in Wales or approved by the National Assembly for Wales (as the case may be);

(e)   for the purposes of the spatial development strategy (or an alteration or replacement of it), the date when the Mayor of London publishes it.

[(12) In this section references to a revision of the regional strategy include a revised strategy under section 79 of the Local Democracy, Economic Development and Construction Act 2009.][169]

114 Examinations

An examination of any document or plan for the purposes of Part 2 or Part 6 of this Act is a statutory inquiry within the meaning of the Tribunals and Inquiries Act 1992 (c. 53).

[SCHEDULE A1 DEFAULT POWERS EXERCISABLE BY MAYOR OF LONDON OR COMBINED AUTHORITY

Default powers exercisable by Mayor of London

1

If the Secretary of State—

(a)   thinks that a London borough council, in their capacity as local planning authority, are failing or omitting to do anything it is necessary for them to do in connection with the preparation, revision or adoption of a development plan document, and

(b)   invites the Mayor of London to prepare or revise the document,

the Mayor of London may prepare or revise (as the case may be) the development plan document.][170]

[2

(1)   This paragraph applies where a development plan document is prepared or revised by the Mayor of London under paragraph 1.

(2)   The Mayor of London must hold an independent examination.

(3)   The Mayor of London—

---

[169] Inserted by the Local Democracy, Economic Development and Construction Act 2009, s 85(1), Sch 5, paras 12, 19(1), (5).

[170] Inserted by the Housing and Planning Act 2016, s 147(2), Sch 11.

(a) must publish the recommendations and reasons of the person appointed to hold the examination, and

(b) may also give directions to the council in relation to publication of those recommendations and reasons.

(4) The Mayor of London may—

(a) approve the document, or approve it subject to specified modifications, as a local development document, or

(b) direct the council to consider adopting the document by resolution of the council as a local development document.]¹⁷¹

[3

(1) Subsections (4) to (7C) of section 20 apply to an examination held under paragraph 2(2)—

(a) with the reference to the local planning authority in subsection (7C) of that section being read as a reference to the Mayor of London, and

(b) with the omission of subsections (5)(c), (7)(b)(ii) and (7B)(b).

(2) The Mayor of London must give reasons for anything he does in pursuance of paragraph 1 or 2(4).

(3) The council must reimburse the Mayor of London—

(a) for any expenditure that the Mayor incurs in connection with anything which is done by him under paragraph 1 and which the council failed or omitted to do as mentioned in that paragraph;

(b) for any expenditure that the Mayor incurs in connection with anything which is done by him under paragraph 2(2).]¹⁷²

[Default powers exercisable by combined authority

4

In this Schedule—

'combined authority' means a combined authority established under section 103 of the Local Democracy, Economic Development and Construction Act 2009;

'constituent planning authority', in relation to a combined authority, means—

(a) a county council, metropolitan district council or non-metropolitan district council which is the local planning authority for an area within the area of the combined authority, or

(b) a joint committee established under section 29 whose area is within, or the same as, the area of the combined authority.]¹⁷³

---

¹⁷¹ Inserted by the Housing and Planning Act 2016, s 147(2), Sch 11.
¹⁷² Inserted by the Housing and Planning Act 2016, s 147(2), Sch 11.
¹⁷³ Inserted by the Housing and Planning Act 2016, s 147(2), Sch 11.

[5

If the Secretary of State—

    (a)   thinks that a constituent planning authority are failing or omitting to do anything it is necessary for them to do in connection with the preparation, revision or adoption of a development plan document, and

    (b)   invites the combined authority to prepare or revise the document,

the combined authority may prepare or revise (as the case may be) the development plan document.][174]

[6

(1)   This paragraph applies where a development plan document is prepared or revised by a combined authority under paragraph 5.

(2)   The combined authority must hold an independent examination.

(3)   The combined authority—

    (a)   must publish the recommendations and reasons of the person appointed to hold the examination, and

    (b)   may also give directions to the constituent planning authority in relation to publication of those recommendations and reasons.

(4)   The combined authority may—

    (a)   approve the document, or approve it subject to specified modifications, as a local development document, or

    (b)   direct the constituent planning authority to consider adopting the document by resolution of the authority as a local development document.][175]

[7

(1)   Subsections (4) to (7C) of section 20 apply to an examination held under paragraph 6(2)—

    (a)   with the reference to the local planning authority in subsection (7C) of that section being read as a reference to the combined authority, and

    (b)   with the omission of subsections (5)(c), (7)(b)(ii) and (7B)(b).

(2)   The combined authority must give reasons for anything they do in pursuance of paragraph 5 or 6(4).

(3)   The constituent planning authority must reimburse the combined authority—

    (a)   for any expenditure that the combined authority incur in connection with anything which is done by them under paragraph 5 and which the constituent planning authority failed or omitted to do as mentioned in that paragraph;

---

[174] Inserted by the Housing and Planning Act 2016, s 147(2), Sch 11.
[175] Inserted by the Housing and Planning Act 2016, s 147(2), Sch 11.

(b)   for any expenditure that the combined authority incur in connection with anything which is done by them under paragraph 6(2).][176]

[Default powers exercisable by county council

7A

In this Schedule—

'upper-tier county council' means a county council for an area for which there is also a district council;

'lower-tier planning authority', in relation to an upper-tier county council, means a district council which is the local planning authority for an area within the area of the upper-tier county council.][177]

[7B

If the Secretary of State—

(a)   thinks that a lower-tier planning authority are failing or omitting to do anything it is necessary for them to do in connection with the preparation, revision or adoption of a development plan document, and

(b)   invites the upper-tier county council to prepare or revise the document,

the upper-tier county council may prepare or revise (as the case may be) the development plan document.][178]

[7C

(1)   This paragraph applies where a development plan document is prepared or revised by an upper-tier county council under paragraph 7B.

(2)   The upper-tier county council must hold an independent examination.

(3)   The upper-tier county council—

(a)   must publish the recommendations and reasons of the person appointed to hold the examination, and

(b)   may also give directions to the lower-tier planning authority in relation to publication of those recommendations and reasons.

(4)   The upper-tier county council may—

(a)   approve the document, or approve it subject to specified modifications, as a local development document, or

(b)   direct the lower-tier planning authority to consider adopting the document by resolution of the authority as a local development document.][179]

---

[176]   Inserted by the Housing and Planning Act 2016, s 147(2), Sch 11.
[177]   Inserted by the Neighbourhood Planning Act 2017, s 10, Sch 2, paras 1, 4.
[178]   Inserted by the Neighbourhood Planning Act 2017, s 10, Sch 2, paras 1, 4.
[179]   Inserted by the Neighbourhood Planning Act 2017, s 10, Sch 2, paras 1, 4.

[7D

(1)   Subsections (4) to (7C) of section 20 apply to an examination held under paragraph 7C(2)—

    (a)   with the reference to the local planning authority in subsection (7C) of that section being read as a reference to the upper-tier county council, and

    (b)   with the omission of subsections (5)(c), (7)(b)(ii) and (7B)(b).

(2)   The upper-tier county council must give reasons for anything they do in pursuance of paragraph 7B or 7C(4).

(3)   The lower-tier planning authority must reimburse the upper-tier county council—

    (a)   for any expenditure that the upper-tier county council incur in connection with anything which is done by them under paragraph 7B and which the lower-tier planning authority failed or omitted to do as mentioned in that paragraph;

    (b)   for any expenditure that the upper-tier county council incur in connection with anything which is done by them under paragraph 7C(2).

(4)   In the case of a joint local development document or a joint development plan document, the upper-tier council may apportion liability for the expenditure on such basis as the council considers just between the authorities for whom the document has been prepared.][180]

[Intervention by Secretary of State

8

(1)   This paragraph applies to a development plan document that has been prepared or revised—

    (a)   under paragraph 1 by the Mayor of London, or

    (b)   under paragraph 5 by a combined authority.

(2)   If the Secretary of State thinks that a development plan document to which this paragraph applies is unsatisfactory—

    (a)   he may at any time before the document is adopted under section 23, or approved under paragraph 2(4)(a) or 6(4)(a), direct the Mayor of London or the combined authority to modify the document in accordance with the direction;

    (b)   if he gives such a direction he must state his reasons for doing so.

(3)   Where a direction is given under sub-paragraph (2)—

    (a)   the Mayor of London or the combined authority must comply with the direction;

    (b)   the document must not be adopted or approved unless the Secretary of State gives notice that the direction has been complied with.

---

[180]   Inserted by the Neighbourhood Planning Act 2017, s 10, Sch 2, paras 1, 4.

(4)   Sub-paragraph (3) does not apply if or to the extent that the direction under sub-paragraph (2) is withdrawn by the Secretary of State.

(5)   At any time before a development plan document to which this paragraph applies is adopted under section 23, or approved under paragraph 2(4)(a) or 6(4)(a), the Secretary of State may direct that the document (or any part of it) is submitted to him for his approval.

(6)   In relation to a document or part of a document submitted to him under sub-paragraph (5) the Secretary of State—

(a)   may approve the document or part;

(b)   may approve it subject to specified modifications;

(c)   may reject it.

The Secretary of State must give reasons for his decision under this sub-paragraph.

(7)   The Secretary of State may at any time-

(a)   after a development plan document to which this paragraph applies has been submitted for independent examination, but

(b)   before it is adopted under section 23 or approved under paragraph 2(4) (a) or 6(4)(a),

direct the Mayor of London or the combined authority to withdraw the document.][181]

[9

(1)   This paragraph applies if the Secretary of State gives a direction under paragraph 8(5).

(2)   No steps are to be taken in connection with the adoption or approval of the document until the Secretary of State gives his decision, or withdraws the direction.

(3)   If the direction is given, and not withdrawn, before the document has been submitted for independent examination, the Secretary of State must hold an independent examination.

(4)   If the direction—

(a)   is given after the document has been submitted for independent examination but before the person appointed to carry out the examination has made his recommendations, and

(b)   is not withdrawn before those recommendations are made, the person must make his recommendations to the Secretary of State.

(5)   The document has no effect unless the document or (as the case may be) the relevant part of it has been approved by the Secretary of State, or the direction is withdrawn.

The 'relevant part' is the part of the document that—

---

[181]   Inserted by the Housing and Planning Act 2016, s 147(2), Sch 11.

(a) is covered by a direction under paragraph 8(5) which refers to only part of the document, or

(b) continues to be covered by a direction under paragraph 8(5) following the partial withdrawal of the direction.

(6) The Secretary of State must publish the recommendations made to him by virtue of sub-paragraph (3) or (4) and the reasons of the person making the recommendations.

(7) In considering a document or part of a document submitted under paragraph 8(5) the Secretary of State may take account of any matter which he thinks is relevant.

(8) It is immaterial whether any such matter was taken account of by the Mayor of London or the combined authority.][182]

[10

Subsections (4) to (7C) of section 20 apply to an examination held under paragraph 9(3)—

(a) with the reference to the local planning authority in subsection (7C) of that section being read as a reference to the Secretary of State, and

(b) with the omission of subsections (5)(c), (7)(b)(ii) and (7B)(b).][183]

[11

In the exercise of any function under paragraph 8 or 9 the Secretary of State must have regard to the local development scheme.][184]

[12

The Mayor of London or the combined authority must reimburse the Secretary of State for any expenditure incurred by the Secretary of State under paragraph 8 or 9 that is specified in a notice given by him to the Mayor or the authority.][185]

[Temporary direction pending possible use of intervention powers

13

(1) If the Secretary of State is considering whether to give a direction to the Mayor of London or a combined authority under paragraph 8 in relation to a development plan document, he may direct the Mayor or the authority not to take any step in connection with the adoption or approval of the document—

(a) until the time (if any) specified in the direction, or

(b) until the direction is withdrawn.

---

[182] Inserted by the Housing and Planning Act 2016, s 147(2), Sch 11.
[183] Inserted by the Housing and Planning Act 2016, s 147(2), Sch 11.
[184] Inserted by the Housing and Planning Act 2016, s 147(2), Sch 11.
[185] Inserted by the Housing and Planning Act 2016, s 147(2), Sch 11.

(2)   A document to which a direction under this paragraph relates has no effect while the direction is in force.

(3)   A direction given under this paragraph in relation to a document ceases to have effect if a direction is given under paragraph 8 in relation to that document.]¹⁸⁶

[SCHEDULE A2 MODIFICATION OF NEIGHBOURHOOD DEVELOPMENT PLANS

Proposals for modification of neighbourhood development plan

1

(1)   This Schedule applies if a neighbourhood development plan has effect for a neighbourhood area within the area of a local planning authority.

(2)   A qualifying body is entitled to submit a proposal to the local planning authority for the modification of the neighbourhood development plan.

(3)   The proposal must be accompanied by—

(a)   a draft of the neighbourhood development plan as proposed to be modified (the 'draft plan'), and

(b)   a statement which contains a summary of the proposals and sets out the reasons why the plan should be modified as proposed.

(4)   The proposal must—

(a)   be made in the prescribed form, and

(b)   be accompanied by other documents and information of a prescribed description.

(5)   The qualifying body must send to prescribed persons a copy of—

(a)   the proposal,

(b)   the draft plan, and

(c)   such of the other documents and information accompanying the proposal as may be prescribed.

(6)   The Secretary of State may publish a document setting standards for—

(a)   the preparation of a draft of a neighbourhood development plan as proposed to be modified and other documents accompanying the proposal,

(b)   the coverage in any document accompanying the proposal of a matter falling to be dealt with in it, and

(c)   all or any of the collection, sources, verification, processing and presentation of information accompanying the proposal.

(7)   The documents and information accompanying the proposal (including the draft plan) must comply with those standards.]¹⁸⁷

---

¹⁸⁶ Inserted by the Housing and Planning Act 2016, s 147(2), Sch 11.
¹⁸⁷ Inserted by the Neighbourhood Planning Act 2017, s 4(10), Sch 1, para 1.

[2

(1)   A qualifying body may withdraw a proposal at any time before the local planning authority act in relation to the proposal under paragraph 14.

(2)   If—

(a)   a proposal by a qualifying body is made by an organisation or body designated as a neighbourhood forum, and

(b)   the designation is withdrawn at any time before the proposal is submitted for independent examination under paragraph 9,

the proposal is to be treated as withdrawn by the qualifying body at that time.

(3)   If the withdrawal of the designation occurs after the proposal is submitted for independent examination under that paragraph, the withdrawal is not to affect the validity of the proposal.]¹⁸⁸

[Advice and assistance in connection with proposals

3

(1)   A local planning authority must give such advice or assistance to a qualifying body as, in all the circumstance, they consider appropriate for the purpose of, or in connection with, facilitating the making of a proposal for the modification of a neighbourhood development plan for a neighbourhood area within their area.

(2)   Nothing in this paragraph is to be read as requiring the giving of financial assistance.]¹⁸⁹

[Requirements to be complied with before proposals made or considered

4

(1)   The Secretary of State may by regulations make provision as to requirements that must be complied with before proposals for the modification of a neighbourhood development plan may be submitted to a local planning authority or fall to be considered by a local planning authority.

(2)   The regulations may in particular make provision—

(a)   as to the giving of notice and publicity,

(b)   as to the information and documents that are to be made available to the public,

(c)   as to the making of reasonable charges for anything provided as a result of the regulations,

(d)   as to consultation with and participation by the public,

(e)   as to the making and consideration of representations (including the time by which they must be made),

---

¹⁸⁸   Inserted by the Neighbourhood Planning Act 2017, s 4(10), Sch 1, para 1.
¹⁸⁹   Inserted by the Neighbourhood Planning Act 2017, s 4(10), Sch 1, para 1.

(f)   requiring prescribed steps to be taken before a proposal of a prescribed description falls to be considered by a local planning authority, and

(g)   conferring powers or imposing duties on local planning authorities, the Secretary of State or other public authorities.

(3)   The power to make regulations under this paragraph must be exercised to secure that—

(a)   prescribed requirements as to consultation with and participation by the public must be complied with before a proposal for the modification of a neighbourhood development plan may be submitted to a local planning authority, and

(b)   a statement containing the following information in relation to that consultation and participation must accompany the proposal submitted to the authority—

(i)   details of those consulted,

(ii) a summary of the main issues raised, and

(iii) any other information of a prescribed description.][190]

[Consideration of proposals by authority

5

(1)   A local planning authority may decline to consider a proposal submitted to them if they consider that it is a repeat proposal.

(2)   A proposal ('the proposal in question') is a 'repeat' proposal for the purposes of this paragraph if it meets conditions A and B.

(3)   Condition A is that—

(a)   in the period of two years ending with the date on which the proposal in question is received, the authority received a proposal under this Schedule ('the earlier proposal'),

(b)   the authority did not make a neighbourhood development plan in response to the earlier proposal as a result of paragraph 8(4) or 14(4) or (8), and

(c)   the earlier proposal was the same as or similar to the proposal in question.

(4)   Condition B is that the local planning authority consider that there has been no significant change in circumstances since the earlier proposal was dealt with as mentioned in sub-paragraph (3)(b).][191]

[6

If a local planning authority decline to consider a proposal under paragraph 5 they must notify the qualifying body of that fact and of their reasons for declining to consider it.][192]

---

[190] Inserted by the Neighbourhood Planning Act 2017, s 4(10), Sch 1, para 1.
[191] Inserted by the Neighbourhood Planning Act 2017, s 4(10), Sch 1, para 1.
[192] Inserted by the Neighbourhood Planning Act 2017, s 4(10), Sch 1, para 1.

[7

(1) This paragraph applies if—

    (a) a proposal has been made to a local planning authority,

    (b) the authority have not exercised their powers under paragraph 5 to decline to consider it, and

    (c) the authority consider that the modifications contained in the draft plan to which it relates are so significant or substantial as to change the nature of the neighbourhood development plan which the draft plan would replace.

(2) The local planning authority must instead consider the proposal under paragraph 6 of Schedule 4B to the principal Act (as applied by sections 38A(3) and 38C(5) of this Act).

(3) That Schedule is to apply in relation to the proposal as if the proposal had been submitted to the local planning authority under that Schedule.]¹⁹³

[8

(1) This paragraph applies if—

    (a) a proposal has been made to a local planning authority,

    (b) the authority have not exercised their power under paragraph 5 to decline to consider it, and

    (c) paragraph 7 does not apply.

(2) The authority must consider—

    (a) whether the qualifying body is authorised for the purposes of a neighbourhood development plan to act in relation to the neighbourhood area concerned as a result of section 61F of the principal Act (as applied by section 38C(2)(a) of this Act),

    (b) whether the proposal by the body complies with provision made by or under that section,

    (c) whether the proposal and the documents and information accompanying it (including the draft plan) comply with provision made by or under paragraph 1, and

    (d) whether the body has complied with the requirements of regulations made under paragraph 4 imposed on it in relation to the proposal.

(3) The authority must also consider whether the draft plan complies with the provision made by or under sections 38A and 38B.

(4) The authority must—

    (a) notify the qualifying body as to whether or not they are satisfied that the matters mentioned in sub-paragraphs (2) and (3) have been met or complied with, and

---

¹⁹³ Inserted by the Neighbourhood Planning Act 2017, s 4(10), Sch 1, para 1.

(b)   in any case where they are not so satisfied, refuse the proposal and notify the body of their reasons for refusing it.]¹⁹⁴

[Requirement to appoint examiner

9

(1)   This paragraph applies if—

    (a)   a local planning authority have considered the matters mentioned in paragraph 8(2) and (3), and

    (b)   they are satisfied that the matters mentioned there have been met or complied with.

(2)   The local planning authority must submit for independent examination—

    (a)   the draft plan, and

    (b)   such other documents as may be prescribed.

(3)   The authority must make such arrangements as they consider appropriate in connection with the holding of the examination.

(4)   The authority may appoint a person to carry out the examination, but only if the qualifying body consents to the appointment.

(5)   If—

    (a)   it appears to the Secretary of State that no person may be appointed under sub-paragraph (4), and

    (b)   the Secretary of State considers that it is expedient for an appointment to be made under this sub-paragraph,

    the Secretary of State may appoint a person to carry out the examination.

(6)   The person appointed must be someone who, in the opinion of the person making the appointment—

    (a)   is independent of the qualifying body and the authority,

    (b)   does not have an interest in any land that may be affected by the draft plan, and

    (c)   has appropriate qualifications and experience.

(7)   The Secretary of State or another local planning authority may enter into arrangements with the authority for the provision of the services of any of their employees as examiners.

(8)   Those arrangements may include—

    (a)   provision requiring payments to be made by the authority to the Secretary of State or other local planning authority, and

    (b)   other provision in relation to those payments and other financial matters.]¹⁹⁵

---

¹⁹⁴ Inserted by the Neighbourhood Planning Act 2017, s 4(10), Sch 1, para 1.
¹⁹⁵ Inserted by the Neighbourhood Planning Act 2017, s 4(10), Sch 1, para 1.

[What examiner must consider

10

(1) The examiner must first determine whether the modifications contained in the draft plan are so significant or substantial as to change the nature of the neighbourhood development plan which the draft plan would replace.

(2) The following provisions of this paragraph apply if the examiner determines that the modifications would have that effect.

(3) The examiner must—

    (a) notify the qualifying body and the local planning authority of the determination, and

    (b) give reasons for the determination.

(4) The qualifying body must decide whether it wishes to proceed with the proposal or withdraw it, and must notify the examiner and the local planning authority of that decision.

(5) If the qualifying body notifies the examiner that it wishes to proceed with the proposal, the examiner must consider the draft plan and the documents submitted with it under paragraph 8 of Schedule 4B to the principal Act (as applied by sections 38A(3) and 38C(5) of this Act).

(6) In that event that Schedule is to apply in relation to the draft plan and the documents submitted with it as if they had been submitted to the examiner under that Schedule.][196]

[11

(1) If paragraph 10(2) does not apply, the examiner must consider the following—

    (a) whether the draft plan meets the basic conditions (see sub-paragraph (2));

    (b) whether the draft plan complies with the provision made by or under sections 38A and 38B;

    (c) such other matters as may be prescribed.

(2) A draft plan meets the basic conditions if—

    (a) having regard to national policies and advice contained in guidance issued by the Secretary of State, it is appropriate to make the plan,

    (b) the making of the plan contributes to the achievement of sustainable development,

    (c) the making of the plan is in general conformity with the strategic policies contained in the development plan for the area of the authority (or any part of that area),

    (d) the making of the plan does not breach, and is otherwise compatible with, EU obligations, and

---

[196] Inserted by the Neighbourhood Planning Act 2017, s 4(10), Sch 1, para 1.

(e)   prescribed conditions are met in relation to the plan and prescribed matters have been complied with in connection with the proposal for the plan.

(3)   The examiner is not to consider any matter that does not fall within sub-paragraph (1) (apart from considering whether the draft plan is compatible with the Convention rights).][197]

[Procedure for examination

12

(1)   The general rule is that the examination of the issues by the examiner under paragraph 10 or 11 is to take the form of the consideration of written representations.

(2)   But the examiner must cause a hearing to be held for the purpose of receiving oral representations about a particular issue at the hearing—

(a)   in any case where the examiner considers that there are exceptional reasons for doing so, or

(b)   in such other cases as may be prescribed.

(3)   The following persons are entitled to make oral representations about the issue at the hearing—

(a)   the qualifying body,

(b)   the local planning authority, and

(c)   such other persons as may be prescribed.

(4)   The hearing must be in public.

(5)   It is for the examiner to decide how the hearing is to be conducted, including—

(a)   whether a person making oral representations may be questioned by another person and, if so, the matters to which the questioning may relate, and

(b)   the amount of time for the making of a person's oral representations or for any questioning by another person.

(6)   In making decisions about the questioning of a person's oral representations by another, the examiner must apply the principle that the questioning should be done by the examiner except where the examiner considers that questioning by another is necessary to ensure—

(a)   adequate examination of a particular issue, or

(b)   a person has a fair chance to put a case.

(7)   Sub-paragraph (5) is subject to regulations under paragraph 15.][198]

---

[197] Inserted by the Neighbourhood Planning Act 2017, s 4(10), Sch 1, para 1.
[198] Inserted by the Neighbourhood Planning Act 2017, s 4(10), Sch 1, para 1.

[Recommendation by examiner

13

(1)   After considering a draft plan under paragraph 11, the examiner must make a report on the draft plan containing recommendations in accordance with this paragraph (and no other recommendations).

(2)   The report must recommend either—

    (a)   that the local planning authority should make the draft plan,

    (b)   that the local planning authority should make the draft plan with the modifications specified in the report, or

    (c)   that the local planning authority should not make the draft plan.

(3)   The only modifications that may be recommended are—

    (a)   modifications that the examiner considers need to be made to secure that the draft plan meets the basic conditions mentioned in paragraph 11(2),

    (b)   modifications that the examiner considers need to be made to secure that the draft plan is compatible with the Convention rights,

    (c)   modifications that the examiner considers need to be made to secure that the draft plan complies with the provision made by or under sections 38A and 38B, and

    (d)   modifications for the purpose of correcting errors.

(4)   The report may not recommend that a plan (with or without modifications) should be made if the examiner considers that the plan does not—

    (a)   meet the basic conditions mentioned in paragraph 11(2), or

    (b)   comply with the provision made by or under sections 38A and 38B.

(5)   The report must—

    (a)   give reasons for each of its recommendations, and

    (b)   contain a summary of its main findings.

(6)   The examiner must send a copy of the report to the qualifying body and the local planning authority.

(7)   The local planning authority must then arrange for the publication of the report in such manner as may be prescribed.][199]

[Functions of authority: modifications proposed by qualifying body

14

(1)   This paragraph applies if an examiner has made a report under paragraph 13.

(2)   If the report recommends that the local planning authority should make the draft plan, the authority must do so (subject as follows).

---

[199] Inserted by the Neighbourhood Planning Act 2017, s 4(10), Sch 1, para 1.

(3) But if the examiner's report recommends that the authority should make the draft plan with the modifications specified in the report, the authority must make the draft plan with those modifications (subject as follows).

(4) Sub-paragraph (2) or (3) does not apply if the authority consider that to make the draft plan or (as the case may be) to do so with those modifications would breach, or would otherwise be incompatible with, any EU obligation or any of the Convention rights.

(5) If the authority do not make the draft plan on that ground, they must give reasons to the qualifying body for doing so.

(6) Where sub-paragraph (2) or (3) applies, the authority may make the draft plan with modifications or (as the case may be) modifications other than those specified in the report if—

    (a) the authority considers the modifications need to be made to secure that the draft plan is compatible with EU obligations and the Convention rights, or

    (b) the modifications are for the purpose of correcting errors.

(7) The authority must make the draft plan or (as the case may be) the draft plan with modifications permitted by this paragraph as soon as reasonably practicable and, in any event, by such date as may be prescribed.

(8) If the examiner's report recommends that the local planning authority should not make the draft plan, the authority must not make the draft plan.][200]

[Regulations about examinations

15

(1) The Secretary of State may by regulations make provision in connection with examinations under paragraph 9.

(2) The regulations may in particular make provision as to—

    (a) the giving of notice and publicity in connection with an examination,

    (b) the information and documents relating to an examination that are to be made available to the public,

    (c) the making of reasonable charges for anything provided as a result of the regulations,

    (d) the making of written or oral representations in relation to draft plans (including the time by which written representations must be made),

    (e) the written representations which are to be, or which may be or may not be, considered at an examination,

    (f) the refusal to allow oral representations of a prescribed description to be made at a hearing,

    (g) the procedure to be followed at an examination (including the procedure to be followed at a hearing),

---

[200] Inserted by the Neighbourhood Planning Act 2017, s 4(10), Sch 1, para 1.

     (h)   the payment by a local planning authority of remuneration and expenses of the examiner, and

     (i)   the award of costs by the examiner.

(3)   The regulations may in particular impose duties on an examiner which are to be complied with by the examiner in considering the draft plan under paragraphs 10 and 11 and which require the examiner—

     (a)   to provide prescribed information to each person within sub-paragraph (4);

     (b)   to publish a draft report containing the recommendations which the examiner is minded to make in the examiner's report under paragraph 13;

     (c)   to invite each person within sub-paragraph (4) or representatives of such a person to one or more meetings at a prescribed stage or prescribed stages of the examination process;

     (d)   to hold a meeting following the issuing of such invitations if such a person requests the examiner to do so.

(4)   Those persons are—

     (a)   the qualifying body,

     (b)   the local planning authority, and

     (c)   such other persons as may be prescribed.

(5)   Where the regulations make provision by virtue of sub-paragraph (3)(c) or (d), they may make further provision about—

     (a)   the procedure for a meeting;

     (b)   the matters to be discussed at a meeting.][201]

[Interpretation

16

In this Schedule—

    'the Convention rights' has the same meaning as in the Human Rights Act 1998;

    'the development plan'—

     (a)   includes a development plan for the purposes of paragraph 1 of Schedule 8 (transitional provisions);

     (b)   does not include so much of a development plan as consists of a neighbourhood development plan under section 38A;

    'draft plan' has the meaning given by paragraph 1(3);

    'prescribed' means prescribed by regulations made by the Secretary of State.][202]

---

[201] Inserted by the Neighbourhood Planning Act 2017, s 4(10), Sch 1, para 1.
[202] Inserted by the Neighbourhood Planning Act 2017, s 4(10), Sch 1, para 1.

[SCHEDULE 2A STRATEGIC PLANNING PANELS

PART 1 STATUS AND MEMBERSHIP

1 Status

(1)   A strategic planning panel is a body corporate.

(2)   The panel has the name specified in the regulations establishing it.]²⁰³

[2 Membership

(1)   A strategic planning panel consists of local planning authority members and nominated members (see paragraphs 3 and 4).

(2)   The regulations establishing the panel must specify—

    (a)   the total number of members of the panel,

    (b)   the number of local planning authority members, and

    (c)   the number of nominated members.

(3)   The number of local planning authority members of the panel—

    (a)   must be equal to or greater than the number of constituent local planning authorities, and

    (b)   must be two thirds of the total membership of the panel, rounded to the nearest whole number.

(4)   The number of nominated members must be one third of the total membership of the panel, rounded to the nearest whole number.

(5)   A person may not be a member of a strategic planning panel if the person is a member of the panel's staff.]²⁰⁴

[3 Appointment of local planning authority members

(1)   Each local planning authority member of a strategic planning panel is to be appointed by a constituent local planning authority from among the authority's eligible members.

(2)   The regulations establishing the panel must specify the number of members to be appointed by each constituent local planning authority, and must ensure that at least one member is to be appointed by each authority.

(3)   A constituent local planning authority, in relation to a strategic planning panel, is a local planning authority all or part of whose area is included in the panel's strategic planning area.

(4)   In the case of a constituent local planning authority which is a county council or a county borough council, the eligible members are—

    (a)   each councillor representing an electoral division all of which is in the panel's strategic planning area, and

---

²⁰³ Inserted by the Planning (Wales) Act 2015, s 4(2), Sch 1, para 1.
²⁰⁴ Inserted by the Planning (Wales) Act 2015, s 4(2), Sch 1, para 1.

(b)   any elected mayor or elected executive member within the meaning of Part 2 of the Local Government Act 2000 (see section 39(1) and (4) of that Act).

(5)   In the case of a constituent local planning authority which is a National Park authority or a joint planning board, the eligible members are each member of that authority or board.]²⁰⁵

[4 Appointment of nominated members

(1)   Each nominated member of a strategic planning panel is to be appointed by the panel, having been nominated in response to a request under this paragraph.

(2)   Before appointing a nominated member, a strategic planning panel must make a request for a nomination to a person chosen by the panel ('the nominating body').

(3)   If the nominating body fails to make a nomination, the panel must make a further request for a nomination to the same person or to another person (who becomes the nominating body for the purposes of this paragraph).

(4)   If the nominating body nominates an individual for appointment to the strategic planning panel, the panel must appoint that individual as a a nominated member of the panel.]²⁰⁶

[5 Composition of strategic planning panels: further provision

(1)   The Welsh Ministers may by regulations make further provision about the composition of strategic planning panels.

(2)   That provision may include (among other things) provision—

(a)   about the gender balance of strategic planning panels;

(b)   about steps to be taken by strategic planning panels and constituent local planning authorities with a view to securing compliance with requirements of the regulations relating to the composition of panels ('composition requirements');

(c)   for exceptions from composition requirements;

(d)   about the effect of failure to comply with composition requirements;

(e)   conferring powers on the Welsh Ministers in respect of such failure.]²⁰⁷

[6 Terms and notice of appointments

(1)   The Welsh Ministers may publish standard terms of appointment for local planning authority members of strategic planning panels and for nominated members of panels.

(2)   The Welsh Ministers may amend any standard terms of appointment, and must publish the standard terms as amended.

---

²⁰⁵ Inserted by the Planning (Wales) Act 2015, s 4(2), Sch 1, para 1.
²⁰⁶ Inserted by the Planning (Wales) Act 2015, s 4(2), Sch 1, para 1.
²⁰⁷ Inserted by the Planning (Wales) Act 2015, s 4(2), Sch 1, para 1.

(3) A member of a strategic planning panel must be appointed on the most recently published standard terms (if any) relevant to the appointment.

(4) A strategic planning panel must give the Welsh Ministers notice of each appointment made to the panel.

(5) Subject to the provisions of this Schedule, the members of a panel hold and vacate office in accordance with their terms of appointment.][208]

[7 Members' allowances

(1) A strategic planning panel may pay allowances to its members in respect of expenses they incur in connection with the exercise of their functions.

(2) A panel may not pay any other remuneration to its members.

(3) For provision about payments that a panel is required or authorised to make in respect of members' allowances, see Part 8 of the Local Government (Wales) Measure 2011.][209]

[8 Termination of membership

(1) A member of a strategic planning panel may resign by giving notice to the panel.

(2) A strategic planning panel may, by giving notice to a member of the panel, remove the member on any of the following grounds—

(a) that the member has been absent from meetings of the panel without its permission for at least 6 months,

(b) that the member has failed to comply with the member's terms of appointment, or

(c) that the member is otherwise unable or unfit to exercise the member's functions.

(3) A notice under sub-paragraph (2) must state the panel's reasons for removing the member.

(4) A strategic planning panel must send a copy of a notice given under this paragraph—

(a) to the Welsh Ministers, and

(b) in the case of a local planning authority member, to the constituent local planning authority that appointed the member.][210]

[9 Termination of membership: further provision about local planning authority members

(1) A constituent local planning authority may at any time remove a local planning authority member of a strategic planning panel appointed by the authority.

(2) If a person who is a local planning authority member of a strategic planning panel ceases to be an eligible member of the constituent local planning authority

---

[208] Inserted by the Planning (Wales) Act 2015, s 4(2), Sch 1, para 1.
[209] Inserted by the Planning (Wales) Act 2015, s 4(2), Sch 1, para 1.
[210] Inserted by the Planning (Wales) Act 2015, s 4(2), Sch 1, para 1.

that appointed the person to the panel, the person ceases to be a member of the panel.

(3)   In the case of a constituent local planning authority which is a county council or a county borough council, a person is not to be treated as ceasing to be a member of the authority by virtue of retiring under section 26 of the Local Government Act 1972 (elections of councillors in Wales) if the person is re-elected to the authority not later than the day the person retires.

(4)   Where a person ceases to be a member of a strategic planning panel by virtue of this paragraph—

    (a)   the constituent local planning authority that appointed the person to the panel must give notice of that fact to the panel, and

    (b)   the panel must send a copy of the notice to the Welsh Ministers.][211]

[10 Chair and deputy chair

(1)   A strategic planning panel must appoint a chair and deputy chair from among its local planning authority members.

(2)   Neither appointment may be for a period of more than one year, but a chair or deputy chair may be re-appointed any number of times.

(3)   A person may resign from the office of chair or deputy chair of a strategic planning panel by giving notice to the panel.

(4)   A person ceases to be the chair or deputy chair of a panel if the person ceases to be a local planning authority member of the panel.][212]

[PART 2 ADMINISTRATION

11 Staff

(1)   A strategic planning panel may employ staff.

(2)   The panel's staff are to be employed on such terms and conditions (including terms and conditions relating to remuneration, allowances and pensions) as the panel may determine.][213]

[12 Delegation

(1)   A strategic planning panel may delegate a function to—

    (a)   a committee of the panel;

    (b)   a member of the panel;

    (c)   a member of the panel's staff.

(2)   But the panel may not delegate—

    (a)   a function under paragraph 4,

---

[211]   Inserted by the Planning (Wales) Act 2015, s 4(2), Sch 1, para 1.
[212]   Inserted by the Planning (Wales) Act 2015, s 4(2), Sch 1, para 1.
[213]   Inserted by the Planning (Wales) Act 2015, s 4(2), Sch 1, para 1.

(b)   the function of deciding whether a strategic development plan (or a revision of such a plan) is ready for independent examination, or

(c)   the function of adopting a strategic development plan (or a revision of such a plan).

(3)   The delegation of a function does not affect—

(a)   the panel's responsibility for the exercise of the function, or

(b)   the panel's ability to exercise the function.]²¹⁴

[13 Voting rights

A nominated member of a strategic planning panel is not entitled to vote at meetings of the panel or any of its committees.]²¹⁵

[14 Procedure

(1)   A strategic planning panel must make standing orders regulating its procedure.

(2)   The standing orders must specify a quorum for meetings of the panel, which must include at least half of the local planning authority members.

(3)   A strategic planning panel—

(a)   may revise its standing orders, and

(b)   must publish the current version of its standing orders.

(4)   The validity of anything done by a strategic planning panel is not affected by—

(a)   a vacancy among its members, or

(b)   a defect in the appointment of a member.]²¹⁶

[15 Access to meetings

(1)   A meeting of a strategic planning panel must be open to the public, except during any item of business from which the panel excludes the public.

(2)   The circumstances (if any) in which the public may be excluded from a meeting must be set out in the panel's standing orders.

(3)   Before each meeting of a strategic planning panel, the panel must publish notice of the meeting.

(4)   The notice must state—

(a)   the time and place of the meeting, and

(b)   the business to be considered at the meeting (other than items during which the public is to be excluded).

(5)   The panel must also publish any reports or other documents to be considered by the panel at the meeting (other than those relating to items during which the public is to be excluded).

---

²¹⁴ Inserted by the Planning (Wales) Act 2015, s 4(2), Sch 1, para 1.
²¹⁵ Inserted by the Planning (Wales) Act 2015, s 4(2), Sch 1, para 1.
²¹⁶ Inserted by the Planning (Wales) Act 2015, s 4(2), Sch 1, para 1.

(6)   As soon as practicable after each meeting of a strategic planning panel, the panel must publish a record of the business at the meeting that was open to the public.][217]

[PART 3 FINANCIAL ARRANGEMENTS

16 Qualifying expenditure

(1)   The qualifying expenditure of a strategic planning panel is to be met by the constituent local planning authorities in accordance with paragraphs 17 to 19.

(2)   'Qualifying expenditure' means expenditure of a description prescribed by regulations made by the Welsh Ministers.][218]

[17 Apportionment of qualifying expenditure

(1)   A strategic planning panel must make a determination specifying the proportion of its qualifying expenditure that is to be met by each constituent local planning authority.

(2)   Not later than 31 December before the start of its second financial year, the panel must send a draft of the determination to each constituent local planning authority and to the Welsh Ministers.

(3)   The panel must have regard to any representations it receives about the draft.

(4)   Not later than 15 February before the start of its second financial year, the panel must send a copy of its determination to each constituent local planning authority and to the Welsh Ministers.

(5)   The panel—

    (a)   may revise the determination, and

    (b)   must send a copy of the determination as revised to each constituent local planning authority and to the Welsh Ministers.

(6)   Before revising its determination, the panel must—

    (a)   send a draft of the revised determination to each constituent local planning authority and to the Welsh Ministers, and

    (b)   have regard to any representations it receives about the draft.

(7)   If the constituent local planning authorities give the panel notice that they have agreed the apportionment between them of the panel's qualifying expenditure, the panel must make or revise its determination so as to give effect to the agreement.

(8)   A determination under this paragraph may be revised only in relation to financial years which have not yet ended.][219]

---

[217]   Inserted by the Planning (Wales) Act 2015, s 4(2), Sch 1, para 1.
[218]   Inserted by the Planning (Wales) Act 2015, s 4(2), Sch 1, para 1.
[219]   Inserted by the Planning (Wales) Act 2015, s 4(2), Sch 1, para 1.

[18 Annual work programme and estimate of qualifying expenditure

(1) A strategic planning panel must, for each financial year other than its first financial year, prepare a work programme which contains—

    (a) a description of the activities which the panel intends to undertake during the year, and

    (b) estimates of—

        (i) the overall expenditure which the panel expects to incur during the year in the exercise of its functions, and

        (ii) the qualifying expenditure which the panel expects to incur during the year.

(2) Not later than 31 December before the start of each financial year for which it is required to prepare a work programme, the panel must send a draft of its work programme for that year to each constituent local planning authority and to the Welsh Ministers.

(3) The panel must have regard to any representations that it receives about the draft.

(4) Not later than 15 February before the start of each financial year for which it is required to prepare a work programme, the panel must—

    (a) publish its work programme for that year, and

    (b) send a copy to each constituent local planning authority and to the Welsh Ministers.

(5) A strategic planning panel may, at any time during a financial year, revise its work programme for that year (including any estimate contained in it).

(6) Before revising a work programme, the panel must—

    (a) send a draft of the revised work programme to each constituent local planning authority and to the Welsh Ministers, and

    (b) have regard to any representations that it receives about the draft.

(7) If the panel revises a work programme, it must—

    (a) publish the work programme as revised, and

    (b) send a copy to each constituent local planning authority and to the Welsh Ministers.][220]

[19 Payments by constituent local planning authorities

(1) Not later than 15 February before the start of each financial year other than its first financial year, a strategic planning panel must give each constituent local planning authority notice of the amount which the authority is required to pay to the panel for that financial year.

(2) The amount is to be calculated as follows—

    (a) take the estimate of the panel's qualifying expenditure set out in its work programme for the year published under paragraph 18;

---

[220] Inserted by the Planning (Wales) Act 2015, s 4(2), Sch 1, para 1.

      (b)   calculate the amount representing the authority's proportion of that expenditure in accordance with the panel's determination under paragraph 17;

      (c)   make any adjustments prescribed by regulations made by the Welsh Ministers.

(3)   The authority must pay the amount to the panel.

(4)   Sub-paragraphs (5) to (7) apply if during a financial year—

      (a)   a strategic planning panel revises its determination under paragraph 17 or the estimate of its qualifying expenditure contained in the work programme published for that financial year under paragraph 18, and

      (b)   making the calculation in sub-paragraph (2) for that financial year in accordance with the revised determination or estimate would give a different amount, for any constituent local planning authority, from that specified in the most recent notice given to the authority under this paragraph.

(5)   The panel must give the authority notice of the revised amount which the authority is required to pay to the panel for the financial year.

(6)   If the authority has not already made a payment to the panel in accordance with this paragraph, it must instead pay the panel the revised amount.

(7)   If the authority has already made a payment to the panel in accordance with this paragraph—

      (a)   where the revised amount is greater than the amount that has been paid, the authority must pay the difference to the panel;

      (b)   where the revised amount is less than the amount that has been paid, the panel must pay the difference to the authority.][221]

[20 Payments by Welsh Ministers

(1)   The Welsh Ministers may make grants, loans or other payments to a strategic planning panel.

(2)   Payments may be made subject to conditions (including conditions as to repayment).

(3)   A strategic planning panel may not borrow money otherwise than from the Welsh Ministers.][222]

[21 Accounts and audit

(1)   A strategic planning panel must for each financial year—

      (a)   keep proper accounts and proper records in relation to them, and

      (b)   prepare a statement of accounts.

(2)   Each statement of accounts must comply with any directions given by the Welsh Ministers as to—

---

[221] Inserted by the Planning (Wales) Act 2015, s 4(2), Sch 1, para 1.
[222] Inserted by the Planning (Wales) Act 2015, s 4(2), Sch 1, para 1.

(a)   the information to be contained in the statement,

(b)   the manner in which the information is to be presented, and

(c)   the methods and principles according to which the statement is to be prepared.

(3)   Not later than 30 November after the end of each financial year, a strategic planning panel must submit its statement of accounts for that year to—

(a)   the Auditor General for Wales,

(b)   the constituent local planning authorities, and

(c)   the Welsh Ministers.

(4)   The Auditor General for Wales must examine, certify and report on each statement of accounts.

(5)   Not later than 4 months after a statement of accounts is submitted, the Auditor General must send copies of the certified statement and the report on it to—

(a)   the constituent local planning authorities, and

(b)   the Welsh Ministers.][223]

[22 Annual report

(1)   A strategic planning panel must, for each financial year, prepare a report on the exercise of its functions during that year.

(2)   Not later than 30 November after the end of each financial year, the panel must—

(a)   publish the report for that year, and

(b)   send copies of the report to—

(i)   the constituent local planning authorities, and

(ii)   the Welsh Ministers.][224]

[23 Financial year

(1)   The first financial year of a strategic planning panel is the period beginning with the day on which the panel is established and ending with the following 31 March.

(2)   But the regulations establishing the panel may provide that the first financial year is instead to end with the second 31 March following the day on which the panel is established.

(3)   After the first financial year, each financial year of the panel is the period of 12 months ending with 31 March.][225]

---

[223]   Inserted by the Planning (Wales) Act 2015, s 4(2), Sch 1, para 1.
[224]   Inserted by the Planning (Wales) Act 2015, s 4(2), Sch 1, para 1.
[225]   Inserted by the Planning (Wales) Act 2015, s 4(2), Sch 1, para 1.

[PART 4 SUPPLEMENTARY

24 Guidance

In exercising functions under this Schedule, a strategic planning panel and a constituent local planning authority must have regard to any guidance issued by the Welsh Ministers.][226]

[25 Default powers of Welsh Ministers

(1)   This paragraph applies if the Welsh Ministers think that a strategic planning panel or a constituent local planning authority is failing or omitting to do anything that it is necessary for it to do for the purpose of complying with a relevant requirement.

(2)   The Welsh Ministers may direct the panel or the authority to take such steps as they think appropriate for the purpose of complying with the relevant requirement.

(3)   A strategic planning panel or constituent local planning authority must comply with a direction given to it under this paragraph.

(4)   If the panel or authority fails to comply with the direction, the Welsh Ministers may themselves do anything that could be done by the panel or the authority (as the case may be) for the purpose of complying with the relevant requirement.

(5)   Before doing anything under sub-paragraph (4), the Welsh Ministers must give the panel or authority notice of their intention to do so.

(6)   The Welsh Ministers may require the panel or authority to reimburse them for any expenditure they incur in connection with anything they do under sub-paragraph (4).

(7)   A relevant requirement is a requirement imposed by any of the following provisions of this Schedule—

(a)   paragraphs 3 and 4 (appointment of members of a strategic planning panel);

(b)   paragraph 10 (appointment of chair and deputy chair);

(c)   paragraph 14(1) (making standing orders);

(d)   paragraphs 17 to 19 (arrangements relating to qualifying expenditure of a panel).][227]

[26 Provision in connection with establishment etc of strategic planning panel

(1)   The regulations establishing a panel may confer power on the Welsh Ministers to give directions—

(a)   requiring a constituent local planning authority to provide the panel with staff or other services for the purpose of enabling the panel to exercise its functions in its first financial year, and

---

[226]   Inserted by the Planning (Wales) Act 2015, s 4(2), Sch 1, para 1.
[227]   Inserted by the Planning (Wales) Act 2015, s 4(2), Sch 1, para 1.

(b)   specifying terms on which the services are to be provided if the authority and the panel cannot agree the terms.

(2)   Regulations under section 60D may include provision for the transfer of property, rights and liabilities—

(a)   from a constituent local planning authority or any other person to a strategic planning panel in connection with the establishment of the panel or the addition of any land to its strategic planning area;

(b)   from a strategic planning panel to a constituent local planning authority or any other person in connection with the abolition of the panel or the removal of any land from its strategic planning area.

(3)   The provision that may be made by virtue of sub-paragraph (2) includes provision for the transfer of rights and liabilities relating to contracts of employment.][228]

[27 Interpretation

In this Schedule—

'constituent local planning authority' has the meaning given by paragraph 3(3);

'eligible member', in relation to a constituent local planning authority, has the meaning given by paragraph 3(4) and (5);

'financial year' and 'first financial year' each have the meaning given by paragraph 23;

'local planning authority member', in relation to a strategic planning panel, means a member appointed under paragraph 3;

'nominated member', in relation to a strategic planning panel, means a member appointed under paragraph 4;

'notice' means notice in writing;

'qualifying expenditure' has the meaning given by paragraph 16(2).][229]

[28 Power to amend provisions about strategic planning panels

The Welsh Ministers may by regulations amend this Schedule.][230]

SCHEDULE 8 TRANSITIONAL PROVISIONS: PARTS 1 AND 2

Development plan

1

(1)   During the transitional period a reference in an enactment mentioned in section 38(7) above to the development plan for an area in England is a reference to—

---

[228] Inserted by the Planning (Wales) Act 2015, s 4(2), Sch 1, para 1.
[229] Inserted by the Planning (Wales) Act 2015, s 4(2), Sch 1, para 1.
[230] Inserted by the Planning (Wales) Act 2015, s 4(2), Sch 1, para 1.

(a)   the RSS for the region in which the area is situated or the spatial development strategy for an area in Greater London, and

(b)   the development plan for the area for the purposes of section 27 or 54 of the principal Act.

(2)   The transitional period is the period starting with the commencement of section 38 and ending on whichever is the earlier of–

(a)   the end of the period of three years;

(b)   the day when in relation to an old policy, a new policy which expressly replaces it is published, adopted or approved.

(3)   But the Secretary of State may direct that for the purposes of such policies as are specified in the direction sub-paragraph (2)(a) does not apply.

(4)   An old policy is a policy which (immediately before the commencement of section 38) forms part of a development plan for the purposes of section 27 or 54 of the principal Act.

(5)   A new policy is a policy which is contained in–

(a)   a revision of an RSS;

(b)   an alteration or replacement of the spatial development strategy;

(c)   a development plan document;

[(d)   a neighbourhood development plan.]²³¹

(6)   But–

(a)   an old policy contained in a structure plan is replaced only by a new policy contained in a revision to an RSS;

(b)   an old policy contained in a waste local plan or a minerals local plan is replaced in relation to any area of a county council for which there is a district council only by a new policy contained in a development plan document which is prepared in accordance with a minerals and waste development scheme.

(7)   A new policy is published if it is contained in–

(a)   a revision of an RSS published by the Secretary of State under section 9(6);

(b)   an alteration or replacement of the Mayor of London's spatial development strategy published in pursuance of section 337 of the Greater London Authority Act 1999 (c. 29);

[(c)   a neighbourhood development plan published under section 38B(5) of the principal Act.]²³²

(8)   A new policy is adopted or approved if it is contained in a development plan document which is adopted or approved for the purposes of Part 2.

---

²³¹ Inserted by the Localism Act 2011 (Consequential Amendments) Order 2012, SI 2012/961, art 4, Sch 3, para 1.
²³² Inserted by the Localism Act 2011 (Consequential Amendments) Order 2012, SI 2012/961, art 4, Sch 3, para 1.

(9)   A minerals and waste development scheme is a scheme prepared in accordance with section 16.

(10)   The development plan mentioned in sub-paragraph (1)(b) does not include a street authorisation map which continued to be treated as having been adopted as a local plan by virtue of paragraph 4 of Part 3 of Schedule 2 to the principal Act.

Structure plans

2

(1)   This paragraph applies to proposals for the alteration or replacement of a structure plan for the area of a local planning authority.

(2)   If before the commencement of Part 1 of this Act the authority have complied with section 33(2) of the principal Act (making copies of proposals and the explanatory memorandum available for inspection) the provisions of Chapter 2 of Part 2 of the principal Act continue to have effect in relation to the proposals.

(3)   In any other case–

(a)   the authority must take no further step in relation to the proposals;

(b)   the proposals have no effect.

(4)   If the proposals are adopted or approved by virtue of sub-paragraph (2) above, paragraph 1 of this Schedule applies to the policies contained in the proposals as if–

(a)   they were policies contained in a development plan within the meaning of section 54 of the principal Act;

(b)   the date of commencement of section 38 is the date when the proposals are adopted or approved (as the case may be).

Unitary development plan

3

(1)   This paragraph applies to proposals for the alteration or replacement of a unitary development plan for the area of a local planning authority.

(2)   If before the relevant date the authority have not complied with section 13(2) of the principal Act (making copies of the proposals available for inspection)–

(a)   they must take no further step in relation to the proposals;

(b)   the proposals have no effect.

(3)   In any other case paragraph 4 or 5 below applies.

4

(1)   This paragraph applies if–

(a)   before the relevant date the local planning authority is not required to cause an inquiry or other hearing to be held by virtue of section 16(1) of the principal Act (inquiry must be held if objections made), or

  (b)   before the commencement of Part 2 of this Act a person is appointed under that section to hold an inquiry or other hearing.

(2)   If this paragraph applies the provisions of Chapter 1 of Part 2 of the principal Act continue to have effect in relation to the proposals.

(3)   The relevant date is whichever is the later of–

  (a)   the end of any period prescribed by regulations under section 26 of the principal Act for the making of objections to the proposals;

  (b)   the commencement of Part 2 of this Act.

5

(1)   If paragraph 4 does not apply the provisions of Chapter 1 of Part 2 of the principal Act continue to have effect in relation to the proposals subject to the modifications in sub-paragraphs (2) to (5) below.

(2)   If before the commencement of Part 2 of this Act the local planning authority have not published revised proposals in pursuance of regulations under section 26 of the principal Act–

  (a)   any provision of the regulations relating to publication of revised proposals must be ignored,

  (b)   the authority must comply again with section 13(2) of the principal Act.

(3)   If before the commencement of Part 2 of this Act the local planning authority have published revised proposals in pursuance of regulations under section 26 of the principal Act the authority must comply again with section 13(2) of that Act.

(4)   Any provision of regulations under section 26 of the principal Act which permits the local planning authority to modify proposals after an inquiry or other hearing has been held under section 16 of that Act must be ignored.

(5)   If such an inquiry or other hearing is held the authority must adopt the proposals in accordance with the recommendations of the person appointed to hold the inquiry or other hearing.

6

If proposals are adopted or approved in pursuance of paragraph 4 or 5 above paragraph 1 of this Schedule applies to the policies contained in the proposals as if–

  (a)   they were policies contained in a development plan for the purposes of section 27 of the principal Act;

  (b)   the date of commencement of section 38 is the date when the proposals are adopted or approved.

7

(1)   This paragraph applies if at the date of commencement of Part 1 a local planning authority have not prepared a unitary development plan in pursuance of section 12 of the principal Act.

(2)   References in paragraphs 3 to 6 to proposals for the alteration or replacement of a plan must be construed as references to the plan.

Local plan

8

(1)   This paragraph applies to proposals for the alteration or replacement of a local plan for the area of a local planning authority.

(2)   If before the commencement of Part 2 of this Act the authority have not complied with section 40(2) of the principal Act (making copies of the proposals available for inspection)–

(a)   they must take no further step in relation to the proposals;

(b)   the proposals have no effect.

(3)   In any other case paragraph 9 or 10 below applies.

9

(1)   This paragraph applies if–

(a)   before the relevant date the local planning authority is not required to cause an inquiry or other hearing to be held by virtue of section 42(1) of the principal Act (inquiry must be held if objections made), or

(b)   before the commencement of Part 2 of this Act a person is appointed under that section to hold an inquiry or other hearing.

(2)   If this paragraph applies the provisions of Chapter 2 of Part 2 of the principal Act continue to have effect in relation to the proposals.

(3)   The relevant date is whichever is the later of–

(a)   the end of any period prescribed by regulations under section 53 of the principal Act for the making of objections to the proposals;

(b)   the commencement of Part 2 of this Act.

10

(1)   If paragraph 9 does not apply the provisions of Chapter 2 of Part 2 of the principal Act continue to have effect in relation to the proposals subject to the modifications in sub-paragraphs (2) to (5) below.

(2)   If before the commencement of Part 2 of this Act the local planning authority have not published revised proposals in pursuance of regulations under section 53 of the principal Act–

(a)   any provision of the regulations relating to publication of revised proposals must be ignored,

(b)   the authority must comply again with section 40(2) of the principal Act.

(3)   If before the commencement of Part 2 of this Act the local planning authority have published revised proposals in pursuance of regulations under section 53 of the principal Act the authority must comply again with section 40(2) of that Act.

(4)   Any provision of regulations under section 53 of the principal Act which permits the local planning authority to modify proposals after an inquiry or other hearing has been held under section 42 of that Act must be ignored.

(5)   If such an inquiry or other hearing is held the authority must adopt the proposals in accordance with the recommendations of the person appointed to hold the inquiry or other hearing.

11

(1)   This paragraph applies if the Secretary of State thinks–

    (a)   that the conformity requirement is likely to give rise to inconsistency between the proposals and relevant policies or guidance, and

    (b)   that it is necessary or expedient to avoid such inconsistency.

(2)   The Secretary of State may direct that to the extent specified in the direction the conformity requirement must be ignored.

(3)   The Secretary of State must give reasons for the direction.

(4)   The conformity requirement is–

    (a)   the requirement under section 36(4) of the principal Act that the local plan is to be in general conformity with the structure plan;

    (b)   the prohibition under section 43(3) of the principal Act on the adoption of proposals for a local plan or for its alteration or replacement which do not conform generally with the structure plan.

(5)   Relevant policies and guidance are–

    (a)   national policies;

    (b)   advice contained in guidance;

    (c)   policies in the RSS.

12

If proposals are adopted or approved in pursuance of paragraphs 9 to 11 above paragraph 1 of this Schedule applies to the policies contained in the proposals as if–

    (a)   they were policies contained in a development plan for the purposes of section 54 of the principal Act;

    (b)   the date of commencement of section 38 is the date when the proposals are adopted or approved.

13

(1)   This paragraph applies if at the date of commencement of Part 1 a local planning authority have not prepared a local plan in pursuance of section 36 of the principal Act.

(2)   References in paragraphs 8 to 12 to proposals for the alteration or replacement of a plan must be construed as references to the plan.

Minerals and waste local plans

14

Paragraphs 8 to 13 above apply to a minerals local plan and a waste local plan as they apply to a local plan and references in those paragraphs to a local planning authority must be construed as including references to a mineral planning authority and an authority who are entitled to prepare a waste local plan.

Schemes

15

(1) This paragraph applies to–

    (a) the local development scheme which a local planning authority are required to prepare and maintain under section 15 of this Act;

    (b) the minerals and waste development scheme which a county council are required to prepare and maintain for any part of their area for which there is a district council.

(2) During the transitional period the local planning authority or county council (as the case may be) must include in the scheme as a development plan document–

    (a) any plan or document which relates to an old policy (for the purposes of paragraph 1 above) which has not been replaced by a new policy;

    (b) any proposals adopted or approved by virtue of paragraphs 3 to 12 above.

Savings

16

(1) The repeal by this Act of paragraphs 1 to 4 of Schedule 13 to the principal Act does not affect anything which is required or permitted to be done for the purposes of Chapter 2 of Part 6 of the principal Act during any time when a plan mentioned in any of those paragraphs continues to form part of the development plan by virtue of–

    (a) paragraph 1 of this Schedule, or

    (b) that paragraph as applied by any other provision of this Schedule.

(2) References to a plan mentioned in any of paragraphs 1 to 4 include any proposal for the alteration or replacement of the plan.

(3) The development plan is the development plan for the purposes of section 27 or 54 of the principal Act.

Regulations and orders

17

(1) The Secretary of State may by regulations make provision for giving full effect to this Schedule.

(2)   The regulations may, in particular–

    (a)   make such provision as he thinks is necessary in consequence of this Schedule;

    (b)   make provision to supplement any modifications of the principal Act required by this Schedule.

(3)   The Secretary of State may by order make such provision as he thinks is necessary in consequence of anything done under or by virtue of this Schedule.

(4)   Provision under sub-paragraph (3) includes provisions corresponding to that which could be made by order under Schedule 2 of the principal Act.

18

The Secretary of State may by regulations make provision–

    (a)   for treating anything done or purported to have been done for the purposes of Part 2 before the commencement of that Part as having been done after that commencement;

    (b)   for disregarding any requirement of section 19 in respect of anything done or purported to have been done for the purposes of any other provision of Part 2.

Interpretation

19

(1)   References to section 27 of the principal Act must be construed subject to section 28(3)(a) and (c) of that Act.

(2)   RSS must be construed in accordance with Part 1 of this Act.

(3)   Development plan document must be construed in accordance with Part 2 of this Act.

Planning Act 2008

PART 2 NATIONAL POLICY STATEMENTS

5 National policy statements

(1) The Secretary of State may designate a statement as a national policy statement for the purposes of this Act if the statement—

    (a) is issued by the Secretary of State, and

    (b) sets out national policy in relation to one or more specified descriptions of development.

(2) In this Act 'national policy statement' means a statement designated under subsection (1) as a national policy statement for the purposes of this Act.

(3) Before designating a statement as a national policy statement for the purposes of this Act the Secretary of State must carry out an appraisal of the sustainability of the policy set out in the statement.

(4) A statement may be designated as a national policy statement for the purposes of this Act only if the consultation and publicity requirements set out in section 7, and the parliamentary requirements set out in section 9 , have been complied with in relation to it [and—

    (a) the consideration period for the statement has expired without the House of Commons resolving during that period that the statement should not be proceeded with, or

    (b) the statement has been approved by resolution of the House of Commons—

        (i) after being laid before Parliament under section 9(8), and

        (ii) before the end of the consideration period.][1]

[(4A) In subsection (4) 'the consideration period', in relation to a statement, means the period of 21 sitting days beginning with the first sitting day after the day on which the statement is laid before Parliament under section 9(8), and here 'sitting day' means a day on which the House of Commons sits.][2]

(5) The policy set out in a national policy statement may in particular—

    (a) set out, in relation to a specified description of development, the amount, type or size of development of that description which is appropriate nationally or for a specified area;

---

[1] Inserted by the Localism Act 2011, s 130(1)-(3).
[2] Inserted by the Localism Act 2011, s 130(1)-(3).

(b)   set out criteria to be applied in deciding whether a location is suitable (or potentially suitable) for a specified description of development;

(c)   set out the relative weight to be given to specified criteria;

(d)   identify one or more locations as suitable (or potentially suitable) or unsuitable for a specified description of development;

(e)   identify one or more statutory undertakers as appropriate persons to carry out a specified description of development;

(f)   set out circumstances in which it is appropriate for a specified type of action to be taken to mitigate the impact of a specified description of development.

(6)   If a national policy statement sets out policy in relation to a particular description of development, the statement must set out criteria to be taken into account in the design of that description of development.

(7)   A national policy statement must give reasons for the policy set out in the statement.

(8)   The reasons must (in particular) include an explanation of how the policy set out in the statement takes account of Government policy relating to the mitigation of, and adaptation to, climate change.

(9)   The Secretary of State must—

(a)   arrange for the publication of a national policy statement; ...[3]

(b)   ...[4]

(10)   In this section 'statutory undertakers' means persons who are, or are deemed to be, statutory undertakers for the purposes of any provision of Part 11 of TCPA 1990.

6 Review

(1)   The Secretary of State must review each national policy statement whenever the Secretary of State thinks it appropriate to do so.

(2)   A review may relate to all or part of a national policy statement.

(3)   In deciding when to review a national policy statement the Secretary of State must consider whether—

(a)   since the time when the statement was first published or (if later) last reviewed, there has been a significant change in any circumstances on the basis of which any of the policy set out in the statement was decided,

(b)   the change was not anticipated at that time, and

(c)   if the change had been anticipated at that time, any of the policy set out in the statement would have been materially different.

(4)   In deciding when to review part of a national policy statement ('the relevant part') the Secretary of State must consider whether—

---

[3]   Repealed by the Localism Act 2011, ss 130(1), (4), 237, Sch 25, Pt 20.
[4]   Repealed by the Localism Act 2011, ss 130(1), (4), 237, Sch 25, Pt 20.

    (a)   since the time when the relevant part was first published or (if later) last reviewed, there has been a significant change in any circumstances on the basis of which any of the policy set out in the relevant part was decided,

    (b)   the change was not anticipated at that time, and

    (c)   if the change had been anticipated at that time, any of the policy set out in the relevant part would have been materially different.

(5)   After completing a review of all or part of a national policy statement the Secretary of State must do one of the following—

    (a)   amend the statement;

    (b)   withdraw the statement's designation as a national policy statement;

    (c)   leave the statement as it is.

(6)   Before amending a national policy statement the Secretary of State must carry out an appraisal of the sustainability of the policy set out in the proposed amendment.

(7)   The Secretary of State may amend a national policy statement only if the consultation and publicity requirements set out in section 7, and the parliamentary requirements set out in section 9 , have been complied with in relation to the proposed amendment [and—

    (a)   the consideration period for the amendment has expired without the House of Commons resolving during that period that the amendment should not be proceeded with, or

    (b)   the amendment has been approved by resolution of the House of Commons—

        (i)   after being laid before Parliament under section 9(8), and

        (ii)   before the end of the consideration period.][5]

[(7A) In subsection (7) 'the consideration period', in relation to an amendment, means the period of 21 sitting days beginning with the first sitting day after the day on which the amendment is laid before Parliament under section 9(8), and here 'sitting day' means a day on which the House of Commons sits.][6]

(8)   Subsections (6) [to (7A)][7] do not apply if the Secretary of State thinks that the proposed amendment (taken with any other proposed amendments) does not materially affect the policy as set out in the national policy statement.

(9)   If the Secretary of State amends a national policy statement, the Secretary of State must—

    (a)   arrange for the amendment, or the statement as amended, to be published, and

    (b)   lay the amendment, or the statement as amended, before Parliament.

---

[5]

[6]   Inserted by the Localism Act 2011, s 130(1), (5), (6).

[7]   Substituted by the Localism Act 2011, s 130(1), (7).

[6A Interpretation of sections 5(4) and 6(7)

(1)　This section applies for the purposes of section 5(4) and 6(7).

(2)　The consultation and publicity requirements set out in section 7 are to be treated as having been complied with in relation to a statement or proposed amendment ('the final proposal') if—

　　(a)　they have been complied with in relation to a different statement or proposed amendment ('the earlier proposal'),

　　(b)　the final proposal is a modified version of the earlier proposal, and

　　(c)　the Secretary of State thinks that the modifications do not materially affect the policy as set out in the earlier proposal.

(3)　The consultation and publicity requirements set out in section 7 are also to be treated as having been complied with in relation to a statement or proposed amendment ('the final proposal') if—

　　(a)　they have been complied with—

　　　　(i)　in relation to a different statement or proposed amendment ('the earlier proposal'), and

　　　　(ii)　in relation to modifications of the earlier proposal ('the main modifications'),

　　(b)　the final proposal is a modified version of the earlier proposal, and

　　(c)　there are no modifications other than the main modifications or, where the modifications include modifications other than the main modifications, the Secretary of State thinks that those other modifications do not materially affect the policy as set out in the earlier proposal modified by the main modifications.

(4)　If section 9(8) has been complied with in relation to a statement or proposed amendment ('the final proposal'), the parliamentary requirements set out in section 9(2) to (7) are to be treated as having been complied with in relation to the final proposal where—

　　(a)　the final proposal is not the same as what was laid under section 9(2), but

　　(b)　those requirements have been complied with in relation to what was laid under section 9(2).

(5)　Ignore any corrections of clerical or typographical errors in what was laid under section 9(8).][8]

[6B Extension of consideration period under section 5(4A) or 6(7A)

(1)　The Secretary of State may—

　　(a)　in relation to a proposed national policy statement, extend the period mentioned in section 5(4A), or

　　(b)　in relation to a proposed amendment of a national policy statement, extend the period mentioned in section 6(7A),

　　by 21 sitting days or less.

---

[8]　Inserted by the Localism Act 2011, s 130(1), (8).

(2) The Secretary of State does that by laying before the House of Commons a statement—

 (a) indicating that the period is to be extended, and

 (b) setting out the length of the extension.

(3) The statement under subsection (2) must be laid before the period would have expired without the extension.

(4) The Secretary of State must publish the statement under subsection (2) in a way the Secretary of State thinks appropriate.

(5) The period may be extended more than once.]⁹

7 Consultation and publicity

(1) This section sets out the consultation and publicity requirements referred to in sections 5(4) and 6(7).

(2) The Secretary of State must carry out such consultation, and arrange for such publicity, as the Secretary of State thinks appropriate in relation to the proposal.

 This is subject to subsections (4) and (5).

(3) In this section 'the proposal' means—

 (a) the statement that the Secretary of State proposes to designate as a national policy statement for the purposes of this Act, or

 (b) (as the case may be) the proposed amendment.

(4) The Secretary of State must consult such persons, and such descriptions of persons, as may be prescribed.

(5) If the policy set out in the proposal identifies one or more locations as suitable (or potentially suitable) for a specified description of development, the Secretary of State must ensure that appropriate steps are taken to publicise the proposal.

(6) The Secretary of State must have regard to the responses to the consultation and publicity in deciding whether to proceed with the proposal.

8 Consultation on publicity requirements

(1) In deciding what steps are appropriate for the purposes of section 7(5), the Secretary of State must consult—

 (a) each local authority that is within subsection (2)[, (3) or (3A)]¹⁰, and

 (b) the Greater London Authority, if any of the locations concerned is in Greater London.

(2) A local authority is within this subsection if any of the locations concerned is in the authority's area.

(3) A local authority ('A') is within this subsection if—

---

⁹   Inserted by the Localism Act 2011, s 130(1), (8).
¹⁰   Substituted by the Localism Act 2011, s 130(1), (9).

    (a)   any of the locations concerned is in the area of another local authority ('B'),

    [(aa) B is a unitary council or a lower-tier district council,][11] and

    (b)   any part of the boundary of A's area is also a part of the boundary of B's area.

[(3A) If any of the locations concerned is in the area of an upper-tier county council ('C'), a local authority ('D') is within this subsection if—

    (a)   D is not a lower-tier district council, and

    (b)   any part of the boundary of D's area is also part of the boundary of C's area.][12]

(4)   In this section 'local authority' means—

    (a)   a county council, or district council, in England;

    (b)   a London borough council;

    (c)   the Common Council of the City of London;

    (d)   the Council of the Isles of Scilly;

    (e)   a county council, or county borough council, in Wales;

    (f)   a council constituted under section 2 of the Local Government etc. (Scotland) Act 1994 (c. 39);

    (g)   a National Park authority;

    (h)   the Broads Authority.

[(5)   In this section—

    'lower-tier district council' means a district council in England for an area for which there is a county council;

    'unitary council' means a local authority that is not an upper-tier county council, a lower-tier district council, a National Park authority or the Broads Authority;

    'upper-tier county council' means a county council in England for each part of whose area there is a district council.][13]

9 Parliamentary requirements

(1)   This section sets out the parliamentary requirements referred to in sections 5(4) and 6(7).

(2)   The Secretary of State must lay the proposal before Parliament.

(3)   In this section 'the proposal' means—

    (a)   the statement that the Secretary of State proposes to designate as a national policy statement for the purposes of this Act, or

---

[11]   Inserted by the Localism Act 2011, s 130(1), (10)-(12).
[12]   Inserted by the Localism Act 2011, s 130(1), (10)-(12).
[13]   Inserted by the Localism Act 2011, s 130(1), (10)-(12).

(b)   (as the case may be) the proposed amendment.

(4)   Subsection (5) applies if, during the relevant period—

(a)   either House of Parliament makes a resolution with regard to the proposal, or

(b)   a committee of either House of Parliament makes recommendations with regard to the proposal.

(5)   The Secretary of State must lay before Parliament a statement setting out the Secretary of State's response to the resolution or recommendations.

(6)   The relevant period is the period specified by the Secretary of State in relation to the proposal.

(7)   The Secretary of State must specify the relevant period in relation to the proposal on or before the day on which the proposal is laid before Parliament under subsection (2).

[(8)   After the end of the relevant period, but not before the Secretary of State complies with subsection (5) if it applies, the Secretary of State must lay the proposal before Parliament.

(9)   If after subsection (8) has been complied with—

(a)   something other than what was laid under subsection (8) becomes the proposal, or

(b)   what was laid under subsection (8) remains the proposal, or again becomes the proposal, despite the condition in section 5(4)(a) not having been met in relation to it,

subsection (8) must be complied with anew.

(10)   For the purposes of subsection (9)(a) and (b) ignore any proposal to correct clerical or typographical errors in what was laid under subsection (8).]¹⁴

10 Sustainable development

(1)   This section applies to the Secretary of State's functions under sections 5 and 6.

(2)   The Secretary of State must, in exercising those functions, do so with the objective of contributing to the achievement of sustainable development.

(3)   For the purposes of subsection (2) the Secretary of State must (in particular) have regard to the desirability of—

(a)   mitigating, and adapting to, climate change;

(b)   achieving good design.

11 Suspension pending review

(1)   This section applies if the Secretary of State thinks that the condition in subsection (2) or (3) is met.

(2)   The condition is that—

---

¹⁴   Inserted by the Localism Act 2011, s 130(1), (13).

> (a) since the time when a national policy statement was first published or (if later) last reviewed, there has been a significant change in any circumstances on the basis of which any of the policy set out in the statement was decided,
>
> (b) the change was not anticipated at that time, and
>
> (c) if the change had been anticipated at that time, any of the policy set out in the statement would have been materially different.

(3) The condition is that—

> (a) since the time when part of a national policy statement ('the relevant part') was first published or (if later) last reviewed, there has been a significant change in any circumstances on the basis of which any of the policy set out in the relevant part was decided,
>
> (b) the change was not anticipated at that time, and
>
> (c) if the change had been anticipated at that time, any of the policy set out in the relevant part would have been materially different.

(4) The Secretary of State may suspend the operation of all or any part of the national policy statement until a review of the statement or the relevant part has been completed.

(5) If the Secretary of State does so, the designation as a national policy statement of the statement or (as the case may be) the part of the statement that has been suspended is treated as having been withdrawn until the day on which the Secretary of State complies with section 6(5) in relation to the review.

12 …[15]

…[16]

13 Legal challenges relating to national policy statements

(1) A court may entertain proceedings for questioning a national policy statement or anything done, or omitted to be done, by the Secretary of State in the course of preparing such a statement only if—

> (a) the proceedings are brought by a claim for judicial review, and
>
> (b) the claim form is filed [before the end of][17] the period of 6 weeks beginning with [the day after][18]—
>
> > (i) the day on which the statement is designated as a national policy statement for the purposes of this Act, or
> >
> > (ii) (if later) the day on which the statement is published.

(2) A court may entertain proceedings for questioning a decision of the Secretary of State not to carry out a review of all or part of a national policy statement only if—

---

[15] Repealed by the Localism Act 2011, ss 130(1), (14), 237, Sch 25, Pt 20.
[16] Repealed by the Localism Act 2011, ss 130(1), (14), 237, Sch 25, Pt 20.
[17] Substituted by the Criminal Justice and Courts Act 2015, s 92(3)(a).
[18] Inserted by the Criminal Justice and Courts Act 2015, s 92(3)(b).

    (a)   the proceedings are brought by a claim for judicial review, and

    (b)   the claim form is filed [before the end of][19] the period of 6 weeks beginning with [the day after][20] the day of the decision not to carry out the review.

(3)   A court may entertain proceedings for questioning a decision of the Secretary of State to carry out a review of all or part of a national policy statement only if—

    (a)   the proceedings are brought by a claim for judicial review, and

    (b)   the claim form is filed [before the end of][21] the period of 6 weeks beginning with [the day after][22] the day on which the Secretary of State complies with section 6(5) in relation to the review concerned.

(4)   A court may entertain proceedings for questioning anything done, or omitted to be done, by the Secretary of State in the course of carrying out a review of all or part of a national policy statement only if—

    (a)   the proceedings are brought by a claim for judicial review, and

    (b)   the claim form is filed [before the end of][23] the period of 6 weeks beginning with [the day after][24] the day on which the Secretary of State complies with section 6(5) in relation to the review concerned.

(5)   A court may entertain proceedings for questioning anything done by the Secretary of State under section 6(5) after completing a review of all or part of a national policy statement only if—

    (a)   the proceedings are brought by a claim for judicial review, and

    (b)   the claim form is filed [before the end of][25] the period of 6 weeks beginning with [the day after][26] the day on which the thing concerned is done.

(6)   A court may entertain proceedings for questioning a decision of the Secretary of State as to whether or not to suspend the operation of all or part of a national policy statement under section 11 only if—

    (a)   the proceedings are brought by a claim for judicial review, and

    (b)   the claim form is filed [before the end of][27] the period of 6 weeks beginning with [the day after][28] the day of the decision.

---

[19]   Substituted by the Criminal Justice and Courts Act 2015, s 92(3)(a).
[20]   Inserted by the Criminal Justice and Courts Act 2015, s 92(3)(b).
[21]   Inserted by the Criminal Justice and Courts Act 2015, s 92(3)(a).
[22]   Inserted by the Criminal Justice and Courts Act 2015, s 92(3)(b).
[23]   Inserted by the Criminal Justice and Courts Act 2015, s 92(3)(a).
[24]   Inserted by the Criminal Justice and Courts Act 2015, s 92(3)(b).
[25]   Inserted by the Criminal Justice and Courts Act 2015, s 92(3)(a).
[26]   Inserted by the Criminal Justice and Courts Act 2015, s 92(3)(b).
[27]   Inserted by the Criminal Justice and Courts Act 2015, s 92(3)(a).
[28]   Inserted by the Criminal Justice and Courts Act 2015, s 92(3)(b).

Environmental Assessment of Plans and Programmes Regulations 2004, SI 2004/1633

PART 1 INTRODUCTORY PROVISIONS

1 Citation and commencement

These Regulations may be cited as the Environmental Assessment of Plans and Programmes Regulations 2004 and shall come into force on 20th July 2004.

2 Interpretation

(1)   In these Regulations–

'consultation body' has the meaning given by regulation 4;

'England' includes the territorial waters of the United Kingdom that are not part of Northern Ireland, Scotland or Wales, and waters in any area for the time being designated under section 17(1) of the Continental Shelf Act 1964;

'the Environmental Assessment of Plans and Programmes Directive' means Directive 2001/42/EC of the European Parliament and of the Council on the assessment of the effects of certain plans and programmes on the environment;

'the Habitats Directive' means Council Directive 92/43/EEC on the conservation of natural habitats and of wild flora and fauna, as last amended by Council Directive 97/62/EC;

'Northern Ireland' has the meaning given by section 98 of the Northern Ireland Act 1998;

'plans and programmes' means plans and programmes, including those co-financed by the European Community, as well as any modifications to them, which–

(a)   are subject to preparation or adoption by an authority at national, regional or local level; or

(b)   are prepared by an authority for adoption, through a legislative procedure by Parliament or Government; and, in either case,

(c)   are required by legislative, regulatory or administrative provisions; and 'responsible authority', in relation to a plan or programme, means–

    (a)   the authority by which or on whose behalf it is prepared; and

    (b)   where, at any particular time, that authority ceases to be responsible, or solely responsible, for taking steps in relation to the plan or programme, the person who, at that time, is responsible (solely or jointly with the authority) for taking those steps;

'Scotland' has the meaning given by section 126 of the Scotland Act 1998; and

'Wales' has the meaning given by section 155 of the Government of Wales Act 1998.

(2)   Other expressions used both in these Regulations and in the Environmental Assessment of Plans and Programmes Directive have the same meaning in these Regulations as they have in that Directive.

3 Application of Regulations

(1)   With the exception of regulations 14 and 15, these Regulations apply as follows.

(2)   These Regulations apply to a plan or programme relating–

    (a)   solely to the whole or any part of England; or

    (b)   to England (whether as to the whole or part) and any other part of the United Kingdom.

(3)   These Regulations apply to a plan or programme relating (whether wholly or in part) to the Isles of Scilly as if the Isles were a county in England.

(4)   These Regulations do not apply to a plan or programme relating solely–

    (a)   to the whole or any part of Northern Ireland;

    (b)   to the whole or any part of Scotland; or

    (c)   to the whole or any part of Wales.

4 Consultation bodies

(1)   Subject to paragraph (5), in relation to every plan or programme to which these Regulations apply, each of the following bodies shall be a consultation body–

    (a)   the Countryside Agency;

    (b)   the Historic Buildings and Monuments Commission for England (English Heritage);

    (c)   English Nature; and

    (d)   the Environment Agency,

but where paragraph (2), (3) or (4) applies, the functions of those bodies under these Regulations shall be exercisable only in relation to so much of the plan or programme as relates to England.

(2)   In relation to such part of a plan or programme to which these Regulations apply as relates to Northern Ireland, the Department of the Environment for Northern Ireland shall be a consultation body for the purposes of these Regulations.

(3)   In relation to such part of a plan or programme to which these Regulations apply as relates to Scotland, each of the following shall be a consultation body for the purposes of these Regulations–

    (a)   the Scottish Ministers;

    (b)   the Scottish Environment Protection Agency; and

    (c)   Scottish Natural Heritage.

(4)   In relation to such part of a plan or programme to which these Regulations apply as relates to Wales, each of the following shall be a consultation body for the purposes of these Regulations–

    (a)   the National Assembly for Wales; and

    (b)   [the Natural Resources Body for Wales][1].

(5)   Where a body mentioned in paragraph (1) is at any time the responsible authority as regards a plan or programme, it shall not at that time exercise the functions under these Regulations of a consultation body in relation to that plan or programme; and references to the consultation bodies in the following provisions of these Regulations shall be construed accordingly.

PART 2 ENVIRONMENTAL ASSESSMENT FOR PLANS AND PROGRAMMES

5 Environmental assessment for plans and programmes: first formal preparatory act on or after 21st July 2004

(1)   Subject to paragraphs (5) and (6) and regulation 7, where–

    (a)   the first formal preparatory act of a plan or programme is on or after 21st July 2004; and

    (b)   the plan or programme is of the description set out in either paragraph (2) or paragraph (3),

the responsible authority shall carry out, or secure the carrying out of, an environmental assessment, in accordance with Part 3 of these Regulations, during the preparation of that plan or programme and before its adoption or submission to the legislative procedure.

(2)   The description is a plan or programme which–

    (a)   is prepared for agriculture, forestry, fisheries, energy, industry, transport, waste management, water management, telecommunications, tourism, town and country planning or land use, and

    (b)   sets the framework for future development consent of projects listed in Annex I or II to Council Directive 85/337/EEC on the assessment of the effects of certain public and private projects on the environment, as amended by Council Directive 97/11/EC.

---

[1]   Substituted by the Natural Resources Body for Wales (Functions) Order 2013, SI 2013/755, art 4(2), Sch 4, para 189.

(3)   The description is a plan or programme which, in view of the likely effect on sites, has been determined to require an assessment pursuant to Article 6 or 7 of the Habitats Directive.

(4)   Subject to paragraph (5) and regulation 7, where–

(a)   the first formal preparatory act of a plan or programme, other than a plan or programme of the description set out in paragraph (2) or (3), is on or after 21st July 2004;

(b)   the plan or programme sets the framework for future development consent of projects; and

(c)   the plan or programme is the subject of a determination under regulation 9(1) or a direction under regulation 10(3) that it is likely to have significant environmental effects,

the responsible authority shall carry out, or secure the carrying out of, an environmental assessment, in accordance with Part 3 of these Regulations, during the preparation of that plan or programme and before its adoption or submission to the legislative procedure.

(5)   Nothing in paragraph (1) or (4) requires the carrying out of an environmental assessment for–

(a)   a plan or programme the sole purpose of which is to serve national defence or civil emergency;

(b)   a financial or budget plan or programme; or

(c)   a plan or programme co-financed under–

(i)   the 2000–2006 programming period for Council Regulation (EC) No. 1260/1999; or

(ii)   the 2000–2006 or 2000–2007 programming period for Council Regulation (EC) No. 1257/1999.

(6)   An environmental assessment need not be carried out–

(a)   for a plan or programme of the description set out in paragraph (2) or (3) which determines the use of a small area at local level; or

(b)   for a minor modification to a plan or programme of the description set out in either of those paragraphs,

unless it has been determined under regulation 9(1) that the plan, programme or modification, as the case may be, is likely to have significant environmental effects, or it is the subject of a direction under regulation 10(3).

6 Environmental assessment for plans and programmes: first formal preparatory act before 21st July 2004

(1)   Subject to paragraph (2) and regulation 7, where–

(a)   a plan or programme of which the first formal preparatory act is before 21st July 2004 has not been adopted or submitted to the legislative procedure for adoption before 22nd July 2006; and

(b) the plan or programme is such that, had the first act in its preparation occurred on 21st July 2004, the plan or programme would have required an environmental assessment by virtue of regulation 5(1); or

(c) the responsible authority is of the opinion that, if a determination under regulation 9(1) in respect of the plan or programme had been made on 21st July 2004, it would have determined that the plan or programme was likely to have significant environmental effects,

the responsible authority shall carry out, or secure the carrying out of, an environmental assessment, in accordance with Part 3 of these Regulations, during the preparation of that plan or programme and before its adoption or submission to the legislative procedure.

(2) Nothing in paragraph (1) shall require the environmental assessment of a particular plan or programme if the responsible authority–

(a) decides that such assessment is not feasible; and

(b) informs the public of its decision.

7 Environmental assessment for plans and programmes co-financed by the European Community

The environmental assessment required by any provision of this Part for a plan or programme co-financed by the European Community shall be carried out by the responsible authority in conformity with the specific provisions in relevant [EU][2] legislation.

8 Restriction on adoption or submission of plans, programmes and modifications

(1) A plan, programme or modification in respect of which a determination under regulation 9(1) is required shall not be adopted or submitted to the legislative procedure for the purpose of its adoption–

(a) where an environmental assessment is required in consequence of the determination or of a direction under regulation 10(3), before the requirements of paragraph (3) below have been met;

(b) in any other case, before the determination has been made under regulation 9(1).

(2) A plan or programme for which an environmental assessment is required by any provision of this Part shall not be adopted or submitted to the legislative procedure for the purpose of its adoption before–

(a) if it is a plan or programme co-financed by the European Community, the environmental assessment has been carried out as mentioned in regulation 7;

(b) in any other case, the requirements of paragraph (3) below, and such requirements of Part 3 as apply in relation to the plan or programme, have been met.

(3) The requirements of this paragraph are that account shall be taken of–

---

[2] Substituted by the Treaty of Lisbon (Changes in Terminology) Order 2011, SI 2011/1043, art 6(2)(b).

(a)   the environmental report for the plan or programme;

(b)   opinions expressed in response to the invitation referred to in regulation 13(2)(d);

(c)   opinions expressed in response to action taken by the responsible authority in accordance with regulation 13(4); and

(d)   the outcome of any consultations under regulation 14(4).

9 Determinations of the responsible authority

(1)   The responsible authority shall determine whether or not a plan, programme or modification of a description referred to in–

(a)   paragraph (4)(a) and (b) of regulation 5;

(b)   paragraph (6)(a) of that regulation; or

(c)   paragraph (6)(b) of that regulation,

is likely to have significant environmental effects.

(2)   Before making a determination under paragraph (1) the responsible authority shall–

(a)   take into account the criteria specified in Schedule 1 to these Regulations; and

(b)   consult the consultation bodies.

(3)   Where the responsible authority determines that the plan, programme or modification is unlikely to have significant environmental effects (and, accordingly, does not require an environmental assessment), it shall prepare a statement of its reasons for the determination.

10 Powers of the Secretary of State

(1)   The Secretary of State may at any time require the responsible authority to send him a copy of–

(a)   any determination under paragraph (1) of regulation 9 with respect to the plan, programme or modification;

(b)   the plan, programme or modification to which the determination relates; and

(c)   where paragraph (3) of that regulation applies, the statement prepared in accordance with that paragraph.

(2)   The responsible authority shall comply with a requirement under paragraph (1) within 7 days.

(3)   The Secretary of State may direct that a plan, programme or modification is likely to have significant environmental effects (whether or not a copy of it has been sent to him in response to a requirement under paragraph (1)).

(4)   Before giving a direction under paragraph (3) the Secretary of State shall–

(a)   take into account the criteria specified in Schedule 1 to these Regulations; and

(b)   consult the consultation bodies.

(5)   The Secretary of State shall, as soon as reasonably practicable after the giving of the direction, send to the responsible authority and to each consultation body–

(a)   a copy of the direction; and

(b)   a statement of his reasons for giving the direction.

(6)   In relation to a plan, programme or modification in respect of which a direction has been given–

(a)   any determination under regulation 9(1) with respect to the plan, programme or modification shall cease to have effect on the giving of the direction; and.

(b)   if no determination has been made under regulation 9(1) with respect to the plan, programme or modification, the responsible authority shall cease to be under any duty imposed by that regulation.

11 Publicity for determinations and directions

(1)   Within 28 days of making a determination under regulation 9(1), the responsible authority shall send to each consultation body–

(a)   a copy of the determination; and

(b)   where the responsible authority has determined that the plan or programme does not require an environmental assessment, a statement of its reasons for the determination.

(2)   The responsible authority shall–

(a)   keep a copy of the determination, and any accompanying statement of reasons, available at its principal office for inspection by the public at all reasonable times and free of charge; and

(b)   within 28 days of the making of the determination, take such steps as it considers appropriate to bring to the attention of the public–

(i)   the title of the plan, programme or modification to which the determination relates;

(ii)   that the responsible authority has determined that the plan, programme or modification is or is not likely to have significant environmental effects (as the case may be) and, accordingly, that an environmental assessment is or is not required in respect of the plan, programme or modification; and

(iii)   the address (which may include a website) at which a copy of the determination and any accompanying statement of reasons may be inspected or from which a copy may be obtained.

(3)   Where the responsible authority receives a direction under regulation 10(3), it shall–

(a)   keep a copy of the direction and of the Secretary of State's statement of his reasons for giving it available at its principal office for inspection by the public at all reasonable times and free of charge; and

(b) within 28 days of the receipt of such a direction, take such steps as it considers appropriate to bring to the attention of the public–

    (i) the title of the plan, programme or modification to which the direction relates;

    (ii) that the Secretary of State has directed that the plan, programme or modification is likely to have significant environmental effects and, accordingly, that an environmental assessment is required in respect of the plan, programme or modification; and

    (iii) the address (which may include a website) at which a copy of the direction and of the Secretary of State's statement of his reasons for giving it may be inspected or from which a copy may be obtained.

(4) The responsible authority shall provide a copy of any document referred to in paragraph (2)(b)(iii) or (3)(b)(iii) free of charge.

PART 3 ENVIRONMENTAL REPORTS AND CONSULTATION PROCEDURES

12 Preparation of environmental report

(1) Where an environmental assessment is required by any provision of Part 2 of these Regulations, the responsible authority shall prepare, or secure the preparation of, an environmental report in accordance with paragraphs (2) and (3) of this regulation.

(2) The report shall identify, describe and evaluate the likely significant effects on the environment of–

(a) implementing the plan or programme; and

(b) reasonable alternatives taking into account the objectives and the geographical scope of the plan or programme.

(3) The report shall include such of the information referred to in Schedule 2 to these Regulations as may reasonably be required, taking account of–

(a) current knowledge and methods of assessment;

(b) the contents and level of detail in the plan or programme;

(c) the stage of the plan or programme in the decision-making process; and

(d) the extent to which certain matters are more appropriately assessed at different levels in that process in order to avoid duplication of the assessment.

(4) Information referred to in Schedule 2 may be provided by reference to relevant information obtained at other levels of decision-making or through other [EU]³ legislation.

(5) When deciding on the scope and level of detail of the information that must be included in the report, the responsible authority shall consult the consultation bodies.

---

³   Substituted by the Treaty of Lisbon (Changes in Terminology) Order 2011, SI 2011/1043, art 6(2)(b).

(6)   Where a consultation body wishes to respond to a consultation under paragraph (5), it shall do so within the period of 5 weeks beginning with the date on which it receives the responsible authority's invitation to engage in the consultation.

13 Consultation procedures

(1)   Every draft plan or programme for which an environmental report has been prepared in accordance with regulation 12 and its accompanying environmental report ('the relevant documents') shall be made available for the purposes of consultation in accordance with the following provisions of this regulation.

(2)   As soon as reasonably practicable after the preparation of the relevant documents, the responsible authority shall–

    (a)   send a copy of those documents to each consultation body;

    (b)   take such steps as it considers appropriate to bring the preparation of the relevant documents to the attention of the persons who, in the authority's opinion, are affected or likely to be affected by, or have an interest in the decisions involved in the assessment and adoption of the plan or programme concerned, required under the Environmental Assessment of Plans and Programmes Directive ('the public consultees');

    (c)   inform the public consultees of the address (which may include a website) at which a copy of the relevant documents may be viewed, or from which a copy may be obtained; and

    (d)   invite the consultation bodies and the public consultees to express their opinion on the relevant documents, specifying the address to which, and the period within which, opinions must be sent.

(3)   The period referred to in paragraph (2)(d) must be of such length as will ensure that the consultation bodies and the public consultees are given an effective opportunity to express their opinion on the relevant documents.

(4)   The responsible authority shall keep a copy of the relevant documents available at its principal office for inspection by the public at all reasonable times and free of charge.

(5)   Nothing in paragraph (2)(c) shall require the responsible authority to provide copies free of charge; but where a charge is made, it shall be of a reasonable amount.

14 Transboundary consultations

(1)   Where a responsible authority, other than the Secretary of State, is of the opinion that a plan or programme for which it is the responsible authority is likely to have significant effects on the environment of another Member State, it shall, as soon as reasonably practicable after forming that opinion–

    (a)   notify the Secretary of State of its opinion and of the reasons for it; and

    (b)   supply the Secretary of State with a copy of the plan or programme concerned, and of the accompanying environmental report.

(2)   Where the Secretary of State has been notified under paragraph (1)(a), the responsible authority shall, within such period as the Secretary of State may

specify by notice in writing to the authority, provide the Secretary of State with such other information about the plan or programme or its accompanying environmental report as he may reasonably require.

(3)   Where–

    (a)   the Secretary of State, whether in consequence of a notice under paragraph (1)(a) or otherwise, considers that the implementation of a plan or programme in any part of the United Kingdom is likely to have significant effects on the environment of another Member State); or

    (b)   a Member State that is likely to be significantly affected by the implementation of a plan or programme so requests,

the Secretary of State shall, before the adoption of the plan or programme or its submission to the legislative procedure for adoption, forward a copy of it and of its accompanying environmental report to the Member State concerned.

(4)   Where the Secretary of State receives from a Member State an indication that it wishes to enter into consultations before the adoption, or submission to the legislative procedure for adoption, of a plan or programme forwarded to it in accordance with paragraph (3), the Secretary of State shall–

    (a)   agree with the Member State–

        (i)   detailed arrangements to ensure that the authorities referred to in paragraph 3 of Article 6 of the Environmental Assessment of Plans and Programmes Directive and the public referred to in paragraph 4 of that Article in the Member State likely to be significantly affected are informed and given an opportunity to forward their opinion within a reasonable time; and

        (ii)   a reasonable time for the duration of the consultations;

    (b)   enter into consultations with the Member State concerning–

        (i)   the likely transboundary environmental effects of implementing the plan or programme; and

        (ii)   the measures envisaged to reduce or eliminate such effects; and

    (c)   where he is not the responsible authority, direct the responsible authority that it shall not adopt the plan or programme, or submit it to the legislative procedure for adoption, until the consultations with the Member State have been concluded.

(5)   Where consultations take place pursuant to paragraph (4), the Secretary of State shall–

    (a)   as soon as reasonably practicable after those consultations begin, notify the consultation bodies of that fact; and

    (b)   notify the consultation bodies and, where he is not the responsible authority, the responsible authority, of the outcome of the consultations.

15 Plans and programmes of other Member States

(1)   This regulation applies where the Secretary of State receives from a Member State (whether or not in response to a request made by the United Kingdom

in that behalf under the Environmental Assessment of Plans and Programmes Directive) a copy of a draft plan or programme–

(a)   that is being prepared in relation to any part of that Member State; and

(b)   whose implementation is likely to have significant effects on the environment of any part of the United Kingdom.

(2)   The Secretary of State shall indicate to the Member State whether, before the adoption of the plan or programme or its submission to the legislative procedure for adoption, the United Kingdom wishes to enter into consultations in respect of that plan or programme concerning–

(a)   the likely transboundary environmental effects of implementing the plan or programme; and

(b)   the measures envisaged to reduce or eliminate such effects.

(3)   Where the Secretary of State so indicates, he shall agree with the Member State concerned–

(a)   detailed arrangements to ensure that the consultation bodies and the public in the United Kingdom or, as the case may be, the part of the United Kingdom that is likely to be significantly affected by the implementation of the plan or programme, are informed and given an opportunity to forward their opinion within a reasonable time; and

(b)   a reasonable time for the duration of the consultations.

(4)   Where such consultations take place under this regulation, the Secretary of State shall–

(a)   inform the consultation bodies of the receipt of the draft plan or programme;

(b)   provide them with a copy of the draft plan or programme and the relevant environmental report provided under Article 7.1 of the Environmental Assessment of Plans and Programmes Directive or specify the address (which may include a website) at which those documents may be inspected;

(c)   take such steps as he considers appropriate to bring the receipt of the draft plan or programme to the attention of such persons as, in his opinion, are affected or likely to be affected by, or have an interest in the decisions involved in the assessment and adoption of the plan or programme concerned, required under the Environmental Assessment of Plans and Programmes Directive ('the transboundary consultees');

(d)   inform the transboundary consultees of the address (which may include a website) at which a copy of the draft plan or programme and the relevant environmental report provided under Article 7.1 of the Environmental Assessment of Plans and Programmes Directive may be inspected, or from which a copy may be obtained; and

(e)   invite the consultation bodies and the transboundary consultees to forward to him their opinions within such period as he may specify.

(5)   The period specified under paragraph (4)(e) shall end not later than 28 days before the end of the period that the Secretary of State has agreed with the

Member State concerned, pursuant to paragraph (3)(b), as reasonable for the duration of their consultations.

(6)   Nothing in paragraph (4)(d) shall require the Secretary of State to provide copies free of charge; but where a charge is made, it shall be of a reasonable amount.

PART 4 POST-ADOPTION PROCEDURES

16 Information as to adoption of plan or programme

(1)   As soon as reasonably practicable after the adoption of a plan or programme for which an environmental assessment has been carried out under these Regulations, the responsible authority shall–

   (a)   make a copy of the plan or programme and its accompanying environmental report available at its principal office for inspection by the public at all reasonable times and free of charge; and

   (b)   take such steps as it considers appropriate to bring to the attention of the public–

      (i)   the title of the plan or programme;

      (ii)   the date on which it was adopted;

      (iii)   the address (which may include a website) at which a copy of it and of its accompanying environmental report, and of a statement containing the particulars specified in paragraph (4), may be viewed or from which a copy may be obtained;

      (iv)   the times at which inspection may be made; and

      (v)   that inspection may be made free of charge.

(2)   As soon as reasonably practicable after the adoption of a plan or programme–

   (a)   the responsible authority shall inform–

      (i)   the consultation bodies;

      (ii)   the persons who, in relation to the plan or programme, were public consultees for the purposes of regulation 13; and

      (iii)   where the responsible authority is not the Secretary of State, the Secretary of State; and

   (b)   the Secretary of State shall inform the Member State with which consultations in relation to the plan or programme have taken place under regulation 14(4),

of the matters referred to in paragraph (3).

(3)   The matters are–

   (a)   that the plan or programme has been adopted;

   (b)   the date on which it was adopted; and

   (c)   the address (which may include a website) at which a copy of–

       (i)   the plan or programme, as adopted,

       (ii)   its accompanying environmental report, and

       (iii) a statement containing the particulars specified in paragraph (4),

       may be viewed, or from which a copy may be obtained.

(4)   The particulars referred to in paragraphs (1)(b)(iii) and (3)(c)(iii) are–

    (a)   how environmental considerations have been integrated into the plan or programme;

    (b)   how the environmental report has been taken into account;

    (c)   how opinions expressed in response to–

       (i)   the invitation referred to in regulation 13(2)(d);

       (ii)   action taken by the responsible authority in accordance with regulation 13(4),

       have been taken into account;

    (d)   how the results of any consultations entered into under regulation 14(4) have been taken into account;

    (e)   the reasons for choosing the plan or programme as adopted, in the light of the other reasonable alternatives dealt with; and

    (f)   the measures that are to be taken to monitor the significant environmental effects of the implementation of the plan or programme.

17 Monitoring of implementation of plans and programmes

(1)   The responsible authority shall monitor the significant environmental effects of the implementation of each plan or programme with the purpose of identifying unforeseen adverse effects at an early stage and being able to undertake appropriate remedial action.

(2)   The responsible authority's monitoring arrangements may comprise or include arrangements established otherwise than for the express purpose of complying with paragraph (1).

SCHEDULE 1 CRITERIA FOR DETERMINING THE LIKELY SIGNIFICANCE OF EFFECTS ON THE ENVIROMMENT

1

The characteristics of plans and programmes, having regard, in particular, to–

    (a)   the degree to which the plan or programme sets a framework for projects and other activities, either with regard to the location, nature, size and operating conditions or by allocating resources;

    (b)   the degree to which the plan or programme influences other plans and programmes including those in a hierarchy;

(c)   the relevance of the plan or programme for the integration of environmental considerations in particular with a view to promoting sustainable development;

(d)   environmental problems relevant to the plan or programme; and

(e)   the relevance of the plan or programme for the implementation of [EU][4] legislation on the environment (for example, plans and programmes linked to waste management or water protection).

2

Characteristics of the effects and of the area likely to be affected, having regard, in particular, to–

(a)   the probability, duration, frequency and reversibility of the effects;

(b)   the cumulative nature of the effects;

(c)   the transboundary nature of the effects;

(d)   the risks to human health or the environment (for example, due to accidents);

(e)   the magnitude and spatial extent of the effects (geographical area and size of the population likely to be affected);

(f)   the value and vulnerability of the area likely to be affected due to–

     (i)   special natural characteristics or cultural heritage;

     (ii)   exceeded environmental quality standards or limit values; or

     (iii)   intensive land-use; and

(g)   the effects on areas or landscapes which have a recognised national, Community or international protection status.

SCHEDULE 2 INFORMATION FOR ENVIRONMENTAL REPORTS

1

An outline of the contents and main objectives of the plan or programme, and of its relationship with other relevant plans and programmes.

2

The relevant aspects of the current state of the environment and the likely evolution thereof without implementation of the plan or programme.

3

The environmental characteristics of areas likely to be significantly affected.

4

Any existing environmental problems which are relevant to the plan or programme including, in particular, those relating to any areas of a particular environmental

---

4   Substituted by the Treaty of Lisbon (Changes in Terminology) Order 2011, SI 2011/1043, art 6(2)(b).

importance, such as areas designated pursuant to Council Directive 79/409/EEC on the conservation of wild birds and the Habitats Directive.

5

The environmental protection objectives, established at international, Community or Member State level, which are relevant to the plan or programme and the way those objectives and any environmental considerations have been taken into account during its preparation.

6

The likely significant effects on the environment, including short, medium and long-term effects, permanent and temporary effects, positive and negative effects, and secondary, cumulative and synergistic effects, on issues such as–

    (a)   biodiversity;

    (b)   population;

    (c)   human health;

    (d)   fauna;

    (e)   flora;

    (f)   soil;

    (g)   water;

    (h)   air;

    (i)   climatic factors;

    (j)   material assets;

    (k)   cultural heritage, including architectural and archaeological heritage;

    (l)   landscape; and

    (m)   the inter-relationship between the issues referred to in sub-paragraphs (a) to (l).

7

The measures envisaged to prevent, reduce and as fully as possible offset any significant adverse effects on the environment of implementing the plan or programme.

8

An outline of the reasons for selecting the alternatives dealt with, and a description of how the assessment was undertaken including any difficulties (such as technical deficiencies or lack of know-how) encountered in compiling the required information.

9

A description of the measures envisaged concerning monitoring in accordance with regulation 17.

10

A non-technical summary of the information provided under paragraphs 1 to 9.

Town and Country Planning (Local Planning) (England) Regulations 2012, SI 2012/767

PART 1 GENERAL

1 Citation, commencement and application

(1)   These Regulations may be cited as the Town and Country Planning (Local Planning) (England) Regulations 2012 and come into force on 6th April 2012.

(2)   These Regulations apply in relation to England only.

2 Interpretation

(1)   In these Regulations—

'the Act' means the Planning and Compulsory Purchase Act 2004;

'address' in relation to electronic communications means any number or address used for the purposes of such communications;

'adopted policies map' means a document of the description referred to in regulation 9;

'electronic communication' has the same meaning as in section 15(1) of the Electronic Communications Act 2000;

'electronic communications apparatus' has the same meaning as in paragraph 1(1) of the electronic communications code;

'electronic communications code' has the same meaning as in section 106(1) of the Communications Act 2003;

'general consultation bodies' means the following—

(a)   voluntary bodies some or all of whose activities benefit any part of the local planning authority's area,

(b)   bodies which represent the interests of different racial, ethnic or national groups in the local planning authority's area,

(c)   bodies which represent the interests of different religious groups in the local planning authority's area,

(d)   bodies which represent the interests of disabled persons in the local planning authority's area,

(e)   bodies which represent the interests of persons carrying on business in the local planning authority's area;

'inspection' means inspection by the public;

'local plan' means any document of the description referred to in regulation 5(1)(a)(i), (ii) or (iv) or 5(2)(a) or (b), and for the purposes of section 17(7)(a) of the Act these documents are prescribed as development plan documents;

'local policing body' means—

(a)   a police and crime commissioner (in relation to a police area listed in Schedule 1 to the Police Act 1996);

(b)   the Mayor's Office for Policing and Crime (in relation to the metropolitan police district);

(c)   the Common Council (in relation to the City of London police area);

['neighbourhood forum' means an organisation or body designated as such under section 61F(3) of the Town and Country Planning Act 1990;][1]

'Ordnance Survey map' means an Ordnance Map or a map on a similar base at a registered scale;

'relevant authority' means—

(a)   a local planning authority ,

(b)   a county council referred to in section 16(1) of the Act,

(c)   a parish council,

(d)   a local policing body;

'site allocation policy' means a policy which allocates a site for a particular use or development;

'specific consultation bodies' means the following—

(a)   the Coal Authority,

(b)   the Environment Agency,

(c)   the Historic Buildings and Monuments Commission for England (known as English Heritage),

(d)   the Marine Management Organisation,

(e)   Natural England,

(f)   Network Rail Infrastructure Limited (company number 2904587),

[(g)   a strategic highways company (for the time being appointed under Part 1 of the Infrastructure Act 2015) any part of whose area is in or adjoins the area of the local planning authority,

---

[1]   Inserted by the Town and Country Planning (Local Planning) (England) (Amendment) Regulations 2016, SI 2016/871, regs 2, 3.

(ga) where the Secretary of State is the highway authority for any highway in the area of the local planning authority, the Secretary of State for Transport,]²

(h) a relevant authority any part of whose area is in or adjoins the local planning authority's area,

[(ha) a neighbourhood forum any part of whose area is in, or adjoins, the local planning authority's area,]³

(i) any person—

    (i) to whom the electronic communications code applies by virtue of a direction given under section 106(3)(a) of the Communications Act 2003, and

    (ii) who owns or controls electronic communications apparatus situated in any part of the local planning authority's area,

(j) if it exercises functions in any part of the local planning authority's area—

    [(i) a clinical commissioning group established under section 14D of the National Health Service Act 2006;

    (ia) the National Health Service Commissioning Board;]⁴

    (ii) a person to whom a licence has been granted under section 6(1)(b) or (c) of the Electricity Act 1989;

    (iii) a person to whom a licence has been granted under section 7(2) of the Gas Act 1986;

    (iv) a sewerage undertaker; and

    (v) a water undertaker;

(k) the Homes and Communities Agency; and

(l) where the local planning authority are a London borough council, the Mayor of London;

'submission policies map' means a map which accompanies a local plan submitted to the Secretary of State under section 20(1) of the Act and which shows how the adopted policies map would be amended by the accompanying local plan, if it were adopted;

'supplementary planning document' means any document of a description referred to in regulation 5 (except an adopted policies map or a statement of community involvement) which is not a local plan; and

'sustainability appraisal report' means the report prepared pursuant to section 19(5)(b) of the Act.

---

² Substituted by the Infrastructure Act 2015 (Strategic Highways Companies) (Consequential, Transitional and Savings Provisions) Regulations 2015, SI 2015/377, reg 3, Schedule, para 54.
³ Inserted by the Town and Country Planning (Local Planning) (England) (Amendment) Regulations 2016, SI 2016/871, regs 2, 3.
⁴ Substituted by the National Treatment Agency (Abolition) and the Health and Social Care Act 2012 (Consequential, Transitional and Saving Provisions) Order 2013, SI 2013/235, art 11, Sch 2, para 169(1), (2).

(2)   These Regulations have effect in relation to the revision of a local plan or a supplementary planning document as they apply to the preparation of a local plan or a supplementary planning document.

(3)   These Regulations have effect in relation to a minerals and waste development scheme as they have effect in relation to a local development scheme and for that purpose—

(a)   references to a local development scheme include references to a minerals and waste development scheme, and

(b)   references to a local planning authority include references to a county council within the meaning of section 16(1) of the Act.

3 Electronic communications

(1)   Where within these Regulations—

(a)   a person is required to—

(i)   send a document, a copy of a document or any notice to another person,

(ii)   notify another person of any matter; and

(b)   that other person has an address for the purposes of electronic communications;

the document, copy, notice or notification may be sent or made by way of electronic communications.

(2)   Where within these Regulations a person may make representations on any matter or document, those representations may be made—

(a)   in writing, or

(b)   by way of electronic communications.

(3)   Where—

(a)   an electronic communication is used as mentioned in paragraphs (1) and (2), and

(b)   the communication is received by the recipient outside the recipient's office hours, it is to be taken to have been received on the next working day, and in this regulation 'working day' means a day which is not a Saturday, Sunday, bank holiday under the Banking and Financial Dealings Act 1971 or other public holiday in England.

PART 2 DUTY TO CO-OPERATE

4 Duty to co-operate

(1)   The bodies prescribed for the purposes of section 33A(1)(c) of the Act are—

(a)   the Environment Agency;

(b)   the Historic Buildings and Monuments Commission for England (known as English Heritage);

(c)   Natural England;

(d)   the Mayor of London;

(e)   the Civil Aviation Authority;

(f)   the Homes and Communities Agency;

[(g)   each clinical commissioning group established under section 14D of the National Health Service Act 2006;

(ga)   the National Health Service Commissioning Board;][5]

(h)   the [Office of Rail and Road][6];

(i)   Transport for London;

(j)   each Integrated Transport Authority;

(k)   each highway authority within the meaning of section 1 of the Highways Act 1980 (including the Secretary of State, where the Secretary of State is the highways authority); and

(l)   the Marine Management Organisation.

[(2)   The bodies prescribed for the purposes of section 33A(9) of the Act are—

(a)   each local enterprise partnership; and

(b)   each local nature partnership.][7]

[(3)   In this regulation—

'local enterprise partnership' means a body, designated by the Secretary of State, which is established for the purpose of creating or improving the conditions for economic growth in an area; and

'local nature partnership' means a body, designated by the Secretary of State, which is established for the purpose of protecting and improving the natural environment in an area and the benefits derived from it.][8]

PART 3 LOCAL DEVELOPMENT DOCUMENTS AND DIRECTIONS BY THE MAYOR OF LONDON

5 Local development documents

(1)   For the purposes of section 17(7)(za) of the Act the documents which are to be prepared as local development documents are—

(a)   any document prepared by a local planning authority individually or in cooperation with one or more other local planning authorities, which contains statements regarding one or more of the following—

---

[5]   Substituted by the National Treatment Agency (Abolition) and the Health and Social Care Act 2012 (Consequential, Transitional and Saving Provisions) Order 2013, SI 2013/235, art 11, Sch 2, para 169(1), (3).

[6]   Substituted by the Office of Rail Regulation (Change of Name) Regulations 2015, SI 2015/1682, reg 2(2), Schedule, para 10(ee).

[7]   Substituted by the Town and Country Planning (Local Planning) (England) (Amendment) Regulations 2012, SI 2012/2613, reg 2.

[8]   Substituted by the Town and Country Planning (Local Planning) (England) (Amendment) Regulations 2012, SI 2012/2613, reg 2.

> (i)   the development and use of land which the local planning authority wish to encourage during any specified period;
>
> (ii) the allocation of sites for a particular type of development or use;
>
> (iii) any environmental, social, design and economic objectives which are relevant to the attainment of the development and use of land mentioned in paragraph (i); and
>
> (iv) development management and site allocation policies, which are intended to guide the determination of applications for planning permission;

(b)   where a document mentioned in sub-paragraph (a) contains policies applying to sites or areas by reference to an Ordnance Survey map, any map which accompanies that document and which shows how the adopted policies map would be amended by the document, if it were adopted.

(2)   For the purposes of section 17(7)(za) of the Act the documents which, if prepared, are to be prepared as local development documents are—

(a)   any document which—

> (i)   relates only to part of the area of the local planning authority;
>
> (ii) identifies that area as an area of significant change or special conservation; and
>
> (iii) contains the local planning authority's policies in relation to the area; and

(b)   any other document which includes a site allocation policy.

6 Local plans

Any document of the description referred to in regulation 5(1)(a)(i), (ii) or (iv) or 5(2)(a) or (b) is a local plan.

7 Direction by the Mayor of London

(1)   Where the Mayor of London has given a direction under section [15(3A), 15(4)][9] or (8) of the Act to a local planning authority they must send a copy of it to the Secretary of State and, notwithstanding regulation 3(1), they must send—

(a)   one copy electronically; and

(b)   two copies in paper form.

(2)   The time prescribed for the purposes of section 15(6B), (8B)(b) and (8C) of the Act is 3 weeks starting on the day the Mayor of London gives the direction in question.

---

[9]   Substituted by the Town and Country Planning (Local Planning) (England) (Amendment) Regulations 2016, SI 2016/871, regs 2, 4.

PART 4 FORM AND CONTENT OF DOCUMENTS AND REGARD TO BE HAD TO CERTAIN MATTERS

8 Form and content of local plans and supplementary planning documents: general

(1) A local plan or a supplementary planning document must—

    (a) contain the date on which the document is adopted; and

    (b) indicate whether the document is a local plan or a supplementary planning document.

(2) A local plan or a supplementary planning document must contain a reasoned justification of the policies contained in it.

(3) Any policies contained in a supplementary planning document must not conflict with the adopted development plan.

(4) Subject to paragraph (5), the policies contained in a local plan must be consistent with the adopted development plan.

(5) Where a local plan contains a policy that is intended to supersede another policy in the adopted development plan, it must state that fact and identify the superseded policy.

9 Form and content of the adopted policies map

(1) The adopted policies map must be comprised of, or contain, a map of the local planning authority's area which must—

    (a) be reproduced from, or be based on, an Ordnance Survey map;

    (b) include an explanation of any symbol or notation which it uses; and

    (c) illustrate geographically the application of the policies in the adopted development plan.

(2) Where the adopted policies map consists of text and maps, the text prevails if the map and text conflict.

10 Local plans and supplementary planning documents: additional matters to which regard is to be had

(1) The matters (additional to those specified in section 19(2)(a) to (i) of the Act) prescribed for the purposes of section 19(2)(j) of the Act are—

    (a) policies developed by a local transport authority in accordance with section 108 of the Transport Act 2000;

    [(b) the objectives of preventing major accidents and limiting the consequences of such accidents for human health and the environment by pursuing those objectives through the controls described in Article 13 of Council Directive 2012/18/EU;][10]

    [(c) the need, in the long term—

---

[10] Substituted by the Planning (Hazardous Substances) Regulations 2015, SI 2015/627, reg 33, Sch 5, para 4.

      (i)   to maintain appropriate safety distances between establishments and residential areas, buildings and areas of public use, recreational areas, and, as far as possible, major transport routes;

      (ii)   to protect areas of particular natural sensitivity or interest in the vicinity of establishments, where appropriate through appropriate safety distances or other relevant measures;

      (ii)   in the case of existing establishments, to take additional technical measures, in accordance with Article 5 of Directive 2012/18/EU of the European Parliament and of the Council on the control of major-accident hazards involving dangerous substances, so as not to increase the risks to human health and the environment;][11]

(d)   the national waste management plan (which has the same meaning as in the Waste (England and Wales) Regulations 2011);

(e)   where a local planning authority's area is adjacent to Wales, the Planning Policy Wales, published by the Welsh Government in February 2011; and

(f)   where a local planning authority's area is adjacent to Scotland, the National Planning Framework for Scotland, published by the Scottish Government in June 2009.

(2)   Expressions appearing both in paragraph (1) and in [Directive 2012/18/EU][12] have the same meaning as in that Directive.

PART 5 SUPPLEMENTARY PLANNING DOCUMENTS

11 Application and interpretation of Part 5

(1)   This Part applies to supplementary planning documents only.

(2)   In this Part—

    'adoption statement' means a statement specifying—

      (a)   the date on which a supplementary planning document was adopted,

      (b)   if applicable, any modifications made pursuant to section 23(1) of the Act,

      (c)   that any person with sufficient interest in the decision to adopt the supplementary planning document may apply to the High Court for permission to apply for judicial review of that decision, and

      (d)   that any such application must be made promptly and in any event not later than 3 months after the date on which the supplementary planning document was adopted; and

    'consultation statement' means the statement prepared under regulation 12(a).

---

[11]   Substituted by the Planning (Hazardous Substances) Regulations 2015, SI 2015/627, reg 33, Sch 5, para 4.

[12]   Substituted by the Planning (Hazardous Substances) Regulations 2015, SI 2015/627, reg 33, Sch 5, para 4.

12 Public participation

Before a local planning authority adopt a supplementary planning document it must—

- (a) prepare a statement setting out—

  - (i) the persons the local planning authority consulted when preparing the supplementary planning document;

  - (ii) a summary of the main issues raised by those persons; and

  - (iii) how those issues have been addressed in the supplementary planning document; and

- (b) for the purpose of seeking representations under regulation 13, make copies of that statement and the supplementary planning document available in accordance with regulation 35 together with details of—

  - (i) the date by which representations must be made (being not less than 4 weeks from the date the local planning authority complies with this paragraph), and

  - (ii) the address to which they must be sent.

13 Representations on supplementary planning documents

- (1) Any person may make representations about a supplementary planning document.

- (2) Any such representations must be received by the local planning authority by the date specified pursuant to regulation 12(b).

14 Adoption of supplementary planning documents

As soon as reasonably practicable after the local planning authority adopt a supplementary planning document they must—

- (a) make available in accordance with regulation 35—

  - (i) the supplementary planning document; and

  - (ii) an adoption statement; and

- (b) send a copy of the adoption statement to any person who has asked to be notified of the adoption of the supplementary planning document.

15 Revocation or withdrawal of a supplementary planning document

- (1) Where a supplementary planning document is withdrawn pursuant to section 22 of the Act the local planning authority must as soon as reasonably practicable—

  - (a) make available a statement of that fact in accordance with regulation 35;

  - (b) send, to each of the bodies or persons which made representations under regulation 13(2) on the supplementary planning document, notification that the supplementary planning document has been withdrawn, and

  - (c) cease to make any documents relating to the withdrawn supplementary planning document (other than the statement mentioned in paragraph (1) (a)) available in accordance with regulation 35.

(2)   A local planning authority may revoke any supplementary planning document.

(3)   Where a supplementary planning document is revoked pursuant to section 25 of the Act the local planning authority must as soon as reasonably practicable—

    (a)   cease to make any documents relating to the revoked supplementary planning document available in accordance with regulation 35; and

    (b)   take such other steps as it considers necessary to draw the revocation of the supplementary planning document to the attention of persons living or working in their area.

16 Direction in respect of a supplementary planning document

(1)   The Secretary of State may at any time direct a local planning authority—

    (a)   not to adopt a supplementary planning document until the Secretary of State decides whether to give a direction under section 21(1) of the Act; and

    (b)   to send to the Secretary of State a copy of the supplementary planning document made available under regulation 12(b).

(2)   A direction made under paragraph (1) is treated as withdrawn on the date on which the local planning authority receive—

    (a)   a statement that the Secretary of State does not intend to give a direction under section 21(1) of the Act; or

    (b)   a direction from the Secretary of State under section 21(1) of the Act.

(3)   If the Secretary of State gives a direction under section 21(1) of the Act in respect of a supplementary planning document, the local planning authority must—

    (a)   make a copy of the direction and the supplementary planning document available in accordance with regulation 35; and

    (b)   at the time they comply with regulation 14, make—

        (i)   the supplementary planning document; and

        (ii)   a statement that the Secretary of State has withdrawn the direction, or a copy of the Secretary of State's notice under section 21(2)(b) of the Act,

    available in accordance with regulation 35.

PART 6 LOCAL PLANS

17 Application and interpretation of Part 6

In this Part—

    'adoption statement' means a statement specifying—

        (a)   the date on which a local plan was adopted,

        (b)   if applicable, any modifications made pursuant to section 23(2) or (3) of the Act,

    (c)   that any person aggrieved by the local plan may make an application to the High Court under section 113 of the Act, and

    (d)   the grounds on which, and the period within which, an application may be made;

'decision statement' means—

    (a)   a statement that the Secretary of State has decided under section 21(9) of the Act to approve, approve subject to specified modifications or reject, a local plan or part of it, and

    (b)   where the Secretary of State decides to approve or approve subject to specified modifications, the local plan or part of it, a statement specifying—

        (i)   the date on which it was approved,

        (ii)   if applicable, any modifications specified in the approval,

        (iii)   that any person aggrieved by it may make an application to the High Court under section 113 of the Act, and

        (iv)   the grounds on which, and the period within which, an application may be made;

'proposed submission documents' means the following documents—

    (a)   the local plan which the local planning authority propose to submit to the Secretary of State,

    (b)   if the adoption of the local plan would result in changes to the adopted policies map, a submission policies map,

    (c)   the sustainability appraisal report of the local plan,

    (d)   a statement setting out—

        (i)   which bodies and persons were invited to make representations under regulation 18,

        (ii)   how those bodies and persons were invited to make such representations,

        (iii)   a summary of the main issues raised by those representations, and

        (iv)   how those main issues have been addressed in the local plan, and

    (e)   such supporting documents as in the opinion of the local planning authority are relevant to the preparation of the local plan; and

'statement of the representations procedure' means a statement specifying—

    (a)   the title of the local plan which the local planning authority propose to submit to the Secretary of State;

    (b)   the subject matter of, and the area covered by, the local plan;

    (c)   the date by which representations about the local plan must be received by the local planning authority, which must be not less than 6 weeks from the day on which the statement is published;

    (d)   the address to which representations about the local plan must be made;

    (e)   that representations may be made in writing or by way of electronic communications; and

    (f)   that representations may be accompanied by a request to be notified at a specified address of any of the following—

        (i)   the submission of the local plan for independent examination under section 20 of the Act,

        (ii)   the publication of the recommendations of the person appointed to carry out an independent examination of the local plan under section 20 of the Act, and

        (iii)   the adoption of the local plan.

18 Preparation of a local plan

(1)   A local planning authority must—

    (a)   notify each of the bodies or persons specified in paragraph (2) of the subject of a local plan which the local planning authority propose to prepare, and

    (b)   invite each of them to make representations to the local planning authority about what a local plan with that subject ought to contain.

(2)   The bodies or persons referred to in paragraph (1) are—

    (a)   such of the specific consultation bodies as the local planning authority consider may have an interest in the subject of the proposed local plan;

    (b)   such of the general consultation bodies as the local planning authority consider appropriate; and

    (c)   such residents or other persons carrying on business in the local planning authority's area from which the local planning authority consider it appropriate to invite representations.

(3)   In preparing the local plan, the local planning authority must take into account any representation made to them in response to invitations under paragraph (1).

19 Publication of a local plan

Before submitting a local plan to the Secretary of State under section 20 of the Act, the local planning authority must—

    (a)   make a copy of each of the proposed submission documents and a statement of the representations procedure available in accordance with regulation 35, and

    (b)   ensure that a statement of the representations procedure and a statement of the fact that the proposed submission documents are available for inspection and of the places and times at which they can be inspected, is sent to each of the general consultation bodies and each of the specific consultation bodies invited to make representations under regulation 18(1).

20 Representations relating to a local plan

(1)   Any person may make representations to a local planning authority about a local plan which the local planning authority propose to submit to the Secretary of State.

(2)   Any such representations must be received by the local planning authority by the date specified in the statement of the representations procedure.

(3)   Nothing in this regulation applies to representations taken to have been made as mentioned in section 24(7) of the Act.

21 Conformity with the London Plan

(1)   A local planning authority which are a London borough council must make a request under section 24(4)(a) of the Act on the day they comply with regulation 19(a).

(2)   Where a request is made under section 24(4)(a) of the Act, the Mayor must send the opinion sought to the Secretary of State and the local planning authority within 6 weeks from the day on which the request is made.

22 Submission of documents and information to the Secretary of State

(1)   The documents prescribed for the purposes of section 20(3) of the Act are—

    (a)   the sustainability appraisal report;

    (b)   a submission policies map if the adoption of the local plan would result in changes to the adopted policies map;

    (c)   a statement setting out—

        (i)   which bodies and persons the local planning authority invited to make representations under regulation 18,

        (ii)   how those bodies and persons were invited to make representations under regulation 18,

        (iii)   a summary of the main issues raised by the representations made pursuant to regulation 18,

        (iv)   how any representations made pursuant to regulation 18 have been taken into account;

        (v)   if representations were made pursuant to regulation 20, the number of representations made and a summary of the main issues raised in those representations; and

        (vi)   if no representations were made in regulation 20, that no such representations were made;

    (d)   copies of any representations made in accordance with regulation 20; and

    (e)   such supporting documents as in the opinion of the local planning authority are relevant to the preparation of the local plan.

(2)   Notwithstanding regulation 3(1), each of the documents referred to in paragraph (1) must be sent in paper form and a copy sent electronically.

(3)   As soon as reasonably practicable after a local planning authority submit a local plan to the Secretary of State they must—

    (a)   make available in accordance with regulation 35—

        (i)   a copy of the local plan;

        (ii)   a copy of each of the documents referred to in paragraph (1)(a), (b) and (c);

        (iii)   any of the documents referred to in paragraph (1)(d) or (e) which it is practicable to so make available, and

        (iv)   a statement of the fact that the documents referred to in sub-paragraphs (i) to (iii) are available for inspection and of the places and times at which they can be inspected;

    (b)   send to each of the general consultation bodies and each of the specific consultation bodies which were invited to make representations under regulation 18(1), notification that the documents referred to in paragraphs (a)(i) to (iii) are available for inspection and of the places and times at which they can be inspected; and

    (c)   give notice to those persons who requested to be notified of the submission of the local plan to the Secretary of State that it has been so submitted.

23 Consideration of representations by appointed person

Before the person appointed to carry out the independent examination under section 20 of the Act makes a recommendation under section 20(7), (7A) or (7C) of the Act the person must consider any representations made in accordance with regulation 20.

24 Independent examination

(1)   At least 6 weeks before the opening of a hearing held for the purpose of giving persons the opportunity to appear before and be heard by the person appointed to carry out the independent examination under section 20 of the Act, the local planning authority must—

    (a)   make the matters mentioned in paragraph (2) available in accordance with regulation 35; and

    (b)   notify any person who has made a representation in accordance with regulation 20 and not withdrawn that representation, of those matters.

(2)   The matters referred to in paragraph (1) are—

    (a)   the date, time and place at which the hearing is to be held, and

    (b)   the name of the person appointed to carry out the independent examination.

25 Publication of the recommendations of the appointed person

(1)   The local planning authority must comply with section 20(8) of the Act—

    (a)   as soon as reasonably practicable after receipt of the report of the person appointed to carry out the independent examination under section 20 of the Act, or

   (b)   if the Secretary of State gives a direction under section 21(1) or (4) of the Act after the person appointed to carry out the independent examination has made a recommendation under section 20(7), (7A) or (7C) of the Act, as soon as reasonably practicable after receipt of the direction.

(2)   When the local planning authority comply with section 20(8) of the Act they must—

   (a)   make the recommendations of the person appointed and the reasons given by that person for those recommendations available in accordance with regulation 35; and

   (b)   give notice, to those persons who requested to be notified of the publication of those recommendations, that the recommendations are available.

26 Adoption of a local plan

As soon as reasonably practicable after the local planning authority adopt a local plan they must—

   (a)   make available in accordance with regulation 35—

       (i)   the local plan;

       (ii)   an adoption statement;

       (iii) the sustainability appraisal report; and

       (iv) details of where the local plan is available for inspection and the places and times at which the document can be inspected;

   (b)   send a copy of the adoption statement to any person who has asked to be notified of the adoption of the local plan; and

   (c)   send a copy of the adoption statement to the Secretary of State.

27 Withdrawal of a local plan

Where a local planning authority withdraw a local plan pursuant to section 22(1) of the Act, the local planning authority must as soon as reasonably practicable after withdrawing it—

   (a)   make available a statement of that fact in accordance with regulation 35;

   (b)   send, to each of the bodies notified under regulation 22(3)(b), notification that the local plan has been withdrawn; and

   (c)   cease to make any documents relating to the withdrawn local plan (other than the statement mentioned in sub-paragraph (a)) available in accordance with regulation 35.

28 Revocation of a local plan

Where a local plan is revoked under section 25 of the Act, the local planning authority must as soon as reasonably practicable after revoking it—

   (a)   make available a statement of that fact in accordance with regulation 35;

    (b)   cease to make any documents relating to the revoked local plan (other than the statement mentioned in sub-paragraph (a)) available in accordance with regulation 35; and

    (c)   take such other steps as they consider necessary to draw the revocation of the local plan to the attention of persons living or working in their area.

[29 Direction in respect of a local plan

(1)   Where the Secretary of State gives a direction under section 21(1), 21A(1) or 27(2)(b), (3)(b), (4)(b) or (5)(b) of the Act in respect of a local plan, or withdraws such a direction, the local planning authority must make—

    (a)   a copy of the direction or a statement that the Secretary of State has withdrawn the direction (as the case may be); and

    (b)   the local plan,

available in accordance with regulation 35.

(2)   Where the Secretary of State gives a direction under paragraph 8(2)(a), 8(5), 8(7) or 13(1) of Schedule A1 to the Act in respect of a local plan, the Mayor of London or the combined authority (as the case may be), as soon as is reasonably practicable after receiving the direction, must provide a copy of the direction to the local planning authority concerned.

(3)   Where a local planning authority receive a copy of a direction under paragraph (2), as soon as is reasonably practicable after receiving the direction, the authority must—

    (a)   make a copy of the direction and the local plan available in accordance with regulation 35; and

    (b)   at the same time as the authority comply with regulation 26, make—

        (i)   the local plan; and

        (ii)   a statement that the Secretary of State has withdrawn the direction, or a copy of the Secretary of State's notice under paragraph 8(3)(b) of Schedule A1 to the Act,

    available in accordance with regulation 35.

(4)   Where—

    (a)   the Mayor of London gives a direction under paragraph 2(4)(b) of Schedule A1 to the Act in respect of a local plan; or

    (b)   a combined authority gives a direction under paragraph 6(4)(b) of Schedule A1 to the Act in respect of a local plan,

the local planning authority must make a copy of the direction and the local plan available in accordance with regulation 35.][13]

---

[13]   Substituted by the Town and Country Planning (Local Planning) (England) (Amendment) Regulations 2016, SI 2016/871, regs 2, 5.

30 Call-in

The provisions in Schedule 1 apply where the Secretary of State gives a direction under section 21(4) of[, or paragraph 8(5) of Schedule A1 to,]¹⁴ the Act.

31 Secretary of State's default power

The provisions of Schedule 2 apply where[—

(a)]¹⁵ the Secretary of State prepares a local plan under section 27 of the Act;

[(b)   the Mayor of London prepares a local plan under paragraph 1 of Schedule A1 to the Act; or

(c)   a combined authority prepares a local plan under paragraph 5 of Schedule A1 to the Act.]¹⁶

PART 7 JOINT LOCAL PLANS OR SUPPLEMENTARY PLANNING DOCUMENTS

32 Joint local plans or supplementary planning documents: corresponding documents

(1)   In relation to an agreement mentioned in section 28(1) of the Act, the period prescribed for the purposes of section 28(9) of the Act is 3 months starting with the day on which any local planning authority which is a party to the agreement withdraw from it.

(2)   A corresponding document for the purposes of section 28(7) of the Act is a document which—

(a)   does not relate to any part of the area of the local planning authority that have withdrawn from the agreement; and

(b)   with respect to the areas of the local planning authorities which prepared it, has substantially the same effect as the original joint document.

(3)   In paragraph (2)(b) 'original joint document' means a joint local plan or supplementary planning document prepared pursuant to the agreement mentioned in paragraph (1).

33 Joint committees: corresponding documents and corresponding schemes

(1)   The period prescribed for the purposes of section 31(6) of the Act is 3 months starting with the day on which, pursuant to section 31(2) of the Act, the Secretary of State revokes the order made under section 29 of the Act.

(2)   Subject to paragraph (5), for the purposes of section 31(3) and (6) of the Act a corresponding document is a document which—

---

¹⁴ Inserted by the Town and Country Planning (Local Planning) (England) (Amendment) Regulations 2016, SI 2016/871, regs 2, 6.
¹⁵ Inserted by the Town and Country Planning (Local Planning) (England) (Amendment) Regulations 2016, SI 2016/871, regs 2, 7.
¹⁶ Inserted by the Town and Country Planning (Local Planning) (England) (Amendment) Regulations 2016, SI 2016/871, regs 2, 7.

(a) does not relate to any part of the area of the constituent authority which requested the revocation of the order made under section 29 of the Act; and

(b) with respect to the area of the successor authority, has substantially the same effect as the original local plan or supplementary planning document.

(3) For the purposes of section 31(3) of the Act, a corresponding scheme is a scheme of a successor authority which—

(a) specifies a document that is a corresponding document for the purposes of section 31(3) of the Act, but

(b) does not specify the original local plan or supplementary planning document,

as a document which is to be a local plan or supplementary planning document.

(4) In paragraph (3)(b) 'original local plan or supplementary planning document' means a local plan or supplementary planning document prepared by the joint committee constituted by the order made under section 29 of the Act.

(5) Paragraph (2)(a) does not apply where the constituent authority is a county council for which there is also a district council.

PART 8 AUTHORITIES' MONITORING REPORTS

34 Authorities' monitoring reports

(1) A local planning authority's monitoring report must contain the following information—

(a) the title of the local plans or supplementary planning documents specified in the local planning authority's local development scheme;

(b) in relation to each of those documents—

(i) the timetable specified in the local planning authority's local development scheme for the document's preparation;

(ii) the stage the document has reached in its preparation; and

(iii) if the document's preparation is behind the timetable mentioned in paragraph (i) the reasons for this; and

(c) where any local plan or supplementary planning document specified in the local planning authority's local development scheme has been adopted or approved within the period in respect of which the report is made, a statement of that fact and of the date of adoption or approval.

(2) Where a local planning authority are not implementing a policy specified in a local plan, the local planning authority's monitoring report must—

(a) identify that policy; and

(b) include a statement of—

(i) the reasons why the local planning authority are not implementing the policy; and

      (ii)   the steps (if any) that the local planning authority intend to take to secure that the policy is implemented.

(3)   Where a policy specified in a local plan specifies an annual number, or a number relating to any other period of net additional dwellings or net additional affordable dwellings in any part of the local planning authority's area, the local planning authority's monitoring report must specify the relevant number for the part of the local planning authority's area concerned—

      (a)   in the period in respect of which the report is made, and

      (b)   since the policy was first published, adopted or approved.

(4)   Where a local planning authority have made a neighbourhood development order or a neighbourhood development plan, the local planning authority's monitoring report must contain details of these documents.

(5)   Where a local planning authority have prepared a report pursuant to regulation 62 of the Community Infrastructure Levy Regulations 2010, the local planning authority's monitoring report must contain the information specified in regulation 62(4) of those Regulations.

(6)   Where a local planning authority have co-operated with another local planning authority, county council, or a body or person prescribed under section 33A of the Act, the local planning authority's monitoring report must give details of what action they have taken during the period covered by the report.

(7)   A local planning authority must make any up-to-date information, which they have collected for monitoring purposes, available in accordance with regulation 35 as soon as possible after the information becomes available.

(8)   In this regulation 'neighbourhood development order' has the meaning given in section 61E of the Town and Country Planning Act 1990.

PART 9 AVAILABILITY OF DOCUMENTS

35 Availability of documents: general

(1)   A document is to be taken to be made available by a local planning authority when—

      (a)   made available for inspection, at their principal office and at such other places within their area as the local planning authority consider appropriate, during normal office hours, and

      (b)   published on the local planning authority's website,

(2)   In relation to any document made available under these Regulations, except a local plan or supplementary planning document which has been adopted or approved, the local planning authority may cease to make the document available once the period specified in paragraph (3) has expired.

(3)   The period mentioned in paragraph (2)—

      (a)   where the document relates to a supplementary planning document or to the local planning authority's statement of community involvement, is 3 months after the day on which the supplementary planning document or statement of community involvement is adopted;

    (b)   where the document relates to a local plan, is the 6 week period referred to in section 113(4) of the Act that applies as regards the local plan concerned.

[(4)   Where—

    (a)   a local planning authority adopt, or the Secretary of State, the Mayor of London or a combined authority approves, a revision to a local plan; or

    (b)   a local planning authority adopt, or the Secretary of State approves, a supplementary planning document,

as soon as reasonably practicable after the adoption or approval, the local planning authority must incorporate the revision into the local plan or make the supplementary planning document available in accordance with this regulation.][17]

36 Copies of documents

(1)   A person may request from the local planning authority a copy of a document made available in accordance with regulation 35.

(2)   The local planning authority must provide a copy of the document to that person as soon as reasonably practicable after receipt of that person's request.

(3)   The local planning authority may make a reasonable charge for a copy of a document—

    (a)   provided in accordance with paragraph (2), or

    (b)   published as required by or under Part 2 of the Act.

PART 10 REVOCATION AND SAVING

37 Revocation

Subject to the saving provision in regulation 38, the following are revoked—

    (a)   the Town and Country Planning (Local Development) (England) Regulations 2004;

    (b)   the Town and Country Planning (Local Development) (England) (Amendment) Regulations 2008;

    (c)   the Town and Country Planning (Local Development) (England) (Amendment) Regulations 2009;

    (d)   article 4 of the Local Democracy, Economic Development and Construction Act 2009 (Consequential Amendments)(England) Order 2010;

    (e)   paragraph 17 of Schedule 4 to the Waste (England and Wales) Regulations 2011; and

    (f)   regulation 20 of Local Policing Bodies (Consequential Amendments) Regulations 2011.

---

[17]   Substituted by the Town and Country Planning (Local Planning) (England) (Amendment) Regulations 2016, SI 2016/871, regs 2, 8.

38 Saving

(1)   Anything done (or having effect as if done) by or in relation to a local planning authority (or the Secretary of State) under a provision of the 2004 Regulations which is revoked and re-enacted, with or without modifications, in these Regulations is to have effect as if done under the corresponding provision of these Regulations by or in relation to that local planning authority (or the Secretary of State) so far as that is required for continuing its effect on and after the commencement date.

(2)   In this Regulation—

'2004 Regulations' means the Town and Country Planning (Local Development) (England) Regulations 2004; and

'commencement date' means the date these Regulations come into force.

SCHEDULE 1 CALL-IN BY THE SECRETARY OF STATE

1

This Schedule applies where the Secretary of State gives a direction under section 21(4)[, or paragraph 8(5) of Schedule A1 to,][18] of the Act.

2 [Making available a direction given under section 21(4)][19]

The local planning authority must make a copy of the direction given under section 21(4) of the Act available in accordance with regulation 35.

[2A Provision of a copy of a direction to the local planning authority concerned

Where the Secretary of State gives a direction under paragraph 8(5) of Schedule A1 to the Act, the Mayor of London or combined authority (as the case may be) must provide a copy of the direction to the local planning authority concerned and that authority must make a copy of the direction available in accordance with regulation 35.][20]

3 [Procedure for pre-submission local plans: direction under paragraph section 21(4)][21]

(1)   If the direction under section 21(4) of the Act is given before the local planning authority submit the local plan to the Secretary of State under section 20 of the Act, the local planning authority must—

(a)   unless they have already complied with section 19(5) of the Act, do so;

---

[18]   Inserted by the Town and Country Planning (Local Planning) (England) (Amendment) Regulations 2016, SI 2016/871, regs 2, 9(1), (2).
[19]   Substituted by the Town and Country Planning (Local Planning) (England) (Amendment) Regulations 2016, SI 2016/871, regs 2, 9(1), (3).
[20]   Inserted by the Town and Country Planning (Local Planning) (England) (Amendment) Regulations 2016, SI 2016/871, regs 2, 9(1), (4).
[21]   Substituted by the Town and Country Planning (Local Planning) (England) (Amendment) Regulations 2016, SI 2016/871, regs 2, 9(1), (5).

(b)   where they are a London borough council, unless they have made a request under section 24(4)(a) of the Act, make such a request;

(c)   before complying with paragraph (d)—

    (i)   make a copy of each of the proposed submission documents and a statement of the representations procedure available in accordance with regulation 35;

    (ii)   ensure that a statement of the representations procedure and a statement of the fact that the proposed submission documents are available for inspection and of the places and times at which they can be inspected, is sent to each of the general consultation bodies and each of the specific consultation bodies which were invited to make representations under regulation 18(1) or this paragraph (as the case may be);

(d)   as soon as reasonably practicable after the period specified pursuant to sub-paragraph (2) has expired send to the Secretary of State—

    (i)   the sustainability appraisal report for the local plan;

    (ii)   a statement of the description referred to in regulation 22(1)(c);

    (iii)   copies of any representations made in accordance with sub-paragraph (2); and

    (iv)   such supporting documents as in the opinion of the local planning authority are relevant to the preparation of the local plan; and

(e)   as soon as reasonably practicable after the period specified pursuant to sub-paragraph (2) has expired—

    (i)   if the adoption or approval of any part of the local plan would result in changes to the adopted policies map, send a map showing those changes to the Secretary of State;

    (ii)   make available in accordance with regulation 35 a copy of the local plan and each of the documents referred to in paragraph (d); and

    (iii)   send to each of the general consultation bodies and each of the specific consultation bodies which were invited to make representations under regulation 18(1), notification that those documents are available for inspection and of the places and times at which they can be inspected.

(2)   Any person may make representations to the local planning authority about a local plan made available pursuant to paragraph 3(1)(c) but they must be received by the local planning authority by the date specified in the statement of the representations procedure made available under that paragraph.

(3)   Nothing in paragraph 3(1)(c), (d) or (e) requires a local planning authority to take any steps if they have taken an equivalent step under regulation 19, 20 or 22 before receipt of the direction under section 21(4) of the Act.

(4)   The following modifications to regulation 17 apply for the purposes of this paragraph—

(a)   the definition of 'proposed submission documents' and the definition of 'statement of the representations procedure' is each to be treated as if 'which the local planning authority propose to submit to the Secretary of State' were omitted;

(b)   paragraph (b) of the definition of 'proposed submission documents' is to be treated as if for 'if the adoption of the local plan' there were substituted 'if the adoption or approval of any part of the local plan';

    (c)   paragraph (f) of the definition of 'statement of the representations procedure' is to be treated as if—(i) sub-paragraph (i) were omitted; and

    (ii)   for the reference to the adoption of the local plan in sub-paragraph (iii) there were a reference to the Secretary of State's decision under section 21(9)(a) of the Act.

[3A Procedure for pre-submission local plans: direction under paragraph 8(5) of Schedule A1

(1)   If the direction under paragraph 8(5) of Schedule A1 to the Act is given before the Mayor of London under paragraph 2(2), or the combined authority under paragraph 6(2), of Schedule A1 to the Act has held an independent examination, the Mayor of London or the combined authority (as the case may be) must—

(a)   unless they have already carried out an appraisal of the sustainability of the proposals in each development plan document, do so;

(b)   before complying with paragraph (c)—

    (i)   provide a copy of each of the proposal documents and a statement of the representations procedure (both as defined in paragraph 2(10) of Schedule 2) to the local planning authority concerned who must make the documents and statement available in accordance with regulation 35;

    (ii)   provide a statement of the representations procedure and a statement of the fact that the proposal documents are available for inspection and of the places and times at which they can be inspected to the local planning authority concerned who must send both statements to each of the general consultation bodies and each of the specific consultation bodies which were invited to make representations under paragraph 2(5)(b) of Schedule 2;

(c)   as soon as reasonably practicable after the period specified pursuant to sub-paragraph (2) has expired send to the Secretary of State—

    (i)   the sustainability appraisal report for the local plan;

    (ii)   the statement of the representations procedure;

    (iii)   copies of any representations made in accordance with sub-paragraph (2); and

    (iv)   such supporting documents as in the opinion of the Mayor of London or the combined authority (as the case may be) are relevant to the preparation of the local plan; and

(d)   as soon as reasonably practicable after the period specified pursuant to sub-paragraph (2) has expired—

      (i)   if the adoption or approval of any part of the local plan would result in changes to the adopted policies map, send a map showing those changes to the Secretary of State;

      (ii)   provide a copy of the local plan and each of the documents referred to in paragraph (c) to the local planning authority concerned who must make the local plan and documents available in accordance with regulation 35; and

      (iii)   provide notification that those documents are available for inspection and of the places at times at which they can be inspected to the local planning authority concerned who must send the notification to each of the general consultation bodies and each of the specific consultation bodies which were invited to make representations under paragraph 2(5)(b) of Schedule 2.

(2)   Any person may make representations to the Mayor of London or the combined authority (as the case may be) about a local plan made available pursuant to sub-paragraph (1)(b) but they must be received by the Mayor of London or the combined authority (as the case may be) before the end of the period specified in the statement of the representations procedure made available under that sub-paragraph.][22]

4 Changes proposed by the Secretary of State to a local plan

(1)   Where the Secretary of State proposes to make a decision under section 21(9) (a) of the Act which proposes changes to the local plan which depart from the recommendations of the person appointed to carry out an independent examination under section 20 of the Act, the Secretary of State must notify the local planning authority of that fact and provide a document containing the proposed changes and the reasons for them.

[(1A) Where the Secretary of State proposes to make a decision under paragraph 8(6) of Schedule A1 to the Act which proposes changes to the local plan which depart from the recommendations of the person appointed to carry out an independent examination under paragraph 2(2) or paragraph 6(2) of Schedule A1 to the Act, the Secretary of State must notify the Mayor of London or the combined authority (as the case may be) of that fact and provide a document containing the proposed changes and the reasons for them.

(1B) Where the Mayor of London or a combined authority receives notice under sub-paragraph (1A), the Mayor of London or the combined authority (as the case may be) must provide the notice and document referred to under sub-paragraph (1A) to the local planning authority concerned.][23]

(2)   As soon as reasonably practicable after receipt of notice under sub-paragraph (1) [or (1B)][24] the local planning authority must—

      (a)   make copies of the proposed changes, the reasons and a statement of the matters in sub-paragraph (3) available in accordance with regulation 35;

---

[22] Inserted by the Town and Country Planning (Local Planning) (England) (Amendment) Regulations 2016, SI 2016/871, regs 2, 9(1), (6).

[23] Inserted by the Town and Country Planning (Local Planning) (England) (Amendment) Regulations 2016, SI 2016/871, regs 2, 9(1), (7), (8).

[24] Inserted by the Town and Country Planning (Local Planning) (England) (Amendment) Regulations 2016, SI 2016/871, regs 2, 9(1), (7), (8).

    (b)   send copies of the proposed changes and the reasons to the bodies in sub-paragraph (4) and notify these bodies of the matters in sub-paragraph (3); and

    (c)   make available in accordance with regulation 35 details of where the proposed changes and the reasons are available for inspection and the places and times at which they can be inspected.

(3)   The matters referred to in sub-paragraph (2) are—

    (a)   the date by which representations on the proposed changes must be made (being not less than 6 weeks from the date on which the local planning authority complies with sub-paragraph (2));

    (b)   the address to which representations must be sent; and

    (c)   a statement that any representations made may be accompanied by a request to be notified of the Secretary of State's decision under section 21(9)(a) of[, or paragraph 8(6) of Schedule A1 to,][25] the Act.

(4)   The bodies referred to in sub-paragraph (2)(b) are—

    (a)   each of the specific consultation bodies to the extent that the Secretary of State thinks the proposed changes affect the body; and

    (b)   such of the general consultation bodies as the Secretary of State considers appropriate.

5 Representations on proposed changes

(1)   Any person may make representations on the proposed changes made available pursuant to paragraph 4(2) of this Schedule.

(2)   Any such representations must be received at the address, and by the date, specified pursuant to paragraph 4(3) of this Schedule.

(3)   Before the Secretary of State approves, approves with specified modifications or rejects a local plan or part of it under section 21(9)(a) of[, or paragraph 8(6) of Schedule A1 to,][26] the Act, the Secretary of State must consider any representations made in accordance with this paragraph.

6 Publication of the recommendations of the person appointed to carry out the independent examination

As soon as reasonably practicable after the Secretary of State publishes the recommendations of the independent examiner in accordance with section 21(6) of[, or paragraph 9(6) of Schedule A1 to,][27] the Act, the local planning authority[, and the Mayor of London or combined authority (as the case may be) where the independent examination is held under paragraph 2(2) or 6(2) of Schedule A1 to the Act,][28] must—

---

[25] Inserted by the Town and Country Planning (Local Planning) (England) (Amendment) Regulations 2016, SI 2016/871, regs 2, 9(1), (7), (8).

[26] Inserted by the Town and Country Planning (Local Planning) (England) (Amendment) Regulations 2016, SI 2016/871, regs 2, 9(1), (7).

[27] Inserted by the Town and Country Planning (Local Planning) (England) (Amendment) Regulations 2016, SI 2016/871, regs 2, 9(1), (9).

[28] Inserted by the Town and Country Planning (Local Planning) (England) (Amendment) Regulations 2016, SI 2016/871, regs 2, 9(1), (9).

(a)   make the recommendations and reasons of the person appointed to carry out the independent examination available in accordance with regulation 35; and

(b)   give notice to those persons who requested to be notified of the publication of those recommendations that they have been published.

7 Secretary of State's decision

As soon as reasonably practicable after the Secretary of State approves, approves subject to specified modifications or rejects a local plan or part of it in accordance with section 21(9)(a) of[, or paragraph 8(6) of Schedule A1 to,][29] the Act, the local planning authority[, and the Mayor of London or combined authority (as the case may be) where the decision in this paragraph is made under paragraph 8(6) of Schedule A1 to the Act,][30] must—

(a)   make available in accordance with regulation 35—

(i)   the local plan and the reasons given by the Secretary of State pursuant to section 21(9)(b) of[, or paragraph 8(6) of Schedule A1 to,][31] the Act,

(ii)   a copy of the decision statement,

(iii) a statement of the fact that the local plan and a copy of the Secretary of State's reasons are available for inspection and the places where and times when the document and reasons can be inspected, and

(b)   send a copy of the decision statement to any person who has asked to be notified of the Secretary of State's decision under section 21(9)(a) of[, or paragraph 8(6) of Schedule A1 to,][32] the Act.

8 Removal of documents after rejection of a local plan

(1)   This paragraph applies where—

(a)   the Secretary of State rejects a local plan under section 21(9)(a) of[, or paragraph 8(6) of Schedule A1 to,][33] the Act; or

(b)   the Secretary of State rejects part of a local plan under section 21(9) (a) of[, or paragraph 8(6) of Schedule A1 to,][34] the Act and the local planning authority decide not to proceed with the remainder.

(2)   The local planning authority must, as soon as reasonably practicable after the end of the period specified in sub-paragraph (3), cease to make available any documents relating to the local plan.

---

[29]   Inserted by the Town and Country Planning (Local Planning) (England) (Amendment) Regulations 2016, SI 2016/871, regs 2, 9(1), (7), (10).
[30]   Inserted by the Town and Country Planning (Local Planning) (England) (Amendment) Regulations 2016, SI 2016/871, regs 2, 9(1), (7), (10).
[31]   Inserted by the Town and Country Planning (Local Planning) (England) (Amendment) Regulations 2016, SI 2016/871, regs 2, 9(1), (7), (10).
[32]   Inserted by the Town and Country Planning (Local Planning) (England) (Amendment) Regulations 2016, SI 2016/871, regs 2, 9(1), (7), (10).
[33]   Inserted by the Town and Country Planning (Local Planning) (England) (Amendment) Regulations 2016, SI 2016/871, regs 2, 9(1), (7).
[34]   Inserted by the Town and Country Planning (Local Planning) (England) (Amendment) Regulations 2016, SI 2016/871, regs 2, 9(1), (7).

(3)   The period mentioned in sub-paragraph (2) is—

    (a)   in the circumstances mentioned in sub-paragraph (1)(a), 3 months from the date of the Secretary of State's rejection of the local plan; or

    (b)   in the circumstances mentioned in sub-paragraph (1)(b), 3 months from the date of the local planning authority's decision.

SCHEDULE 2 [THE RELEVANT AUTHORITY'S][35] DEFAULT POWER

[1

(1)   This Schedule applies where—

    (a)   the Secretary of State prepares a local plan under section 27 of the Act;

    (b)   the Mayor of London prepares a local plan under paragraph 1 of Schedule A1 to the Act; or

    (c)   a combined authority prepares a local plan under paragraph 5 of Schedule A1 to the Act.

(2)   In this Schedule, 'the relevant authority' means a person or body which prepares a local plan in the circumstances mentioned in sub-paragraph (1)(a), (b) or (c).][36]

2

(1)   The [relevant authority][37] must comply with section 19(2) of the Act as if—

    (a)   the duty imposed on the local planning authority were imposed on the [relevant authority][38];

    (b)   references in section 19(2)(b) to (h) to the local planning authority (in whatever terms) were references to the local planning authority in question; and

    (c)   section 19(2)(j) referred to the matters prescribed under regulation 10, treating the references to the local planning authority (in whatever terms) in regulation 10 as references to the local planning authority in question.

(2)   The [relevant authority][39] must comply, to the extent (if any) that the [relevant authority][40] considers appropriate, with section 19(3) of the Act as if the reference to the local planning authority (in whatever terms) were a reference

---

[35] Substituted by the Town and Country Planning (Local Planning) (England) (Amendment) Regulations 2016, SI 2016/871, regs 2, 10(1)-(3).

[36] Substituted by the Town and Country Planning (Local Planning) (England) (Amendment) Regulations 2016, SI 2016/871, regs 2, 10(1)-(3).

[37] Substituted by the Town and Country Planning (Local Planning) (England) (Amendment) Regulations 2016, SI 2016/871, regs 2, 10(1), (4)(a), (c).

[38] Substituted by the Town and Country Planning (Local Planning) (England) (Amendment) Regulations 2016, SI 2016/871, regs 2, 10(1), (4)(a), (c).

[39] Substituted by the Town and Country Planning (Local Planning) (England) (Amendment) Regulations 2016, SI 2016/871, regs 2, 10(1), (4)(a), (c).

[40] Substituted by the Town and Country Planning (Local Planning) (England) (Amendment) Regulations 2016, SI 2016/871, regs 2, 10(1), (4)(a), (c).

to the [relevant authority][41] and the reference to their statement of community involvement were a reference to the statement of community involvement of the local planning authority in question.

(3)   The [relevant authority][42] must comply with section 19(5) of the Act as if the reference to the local planning authority (in whatever terms) were a reference to the [relevant authority][43] and as if the reference to each document were a reference to the local plan.

(4)   [Where the Secretary of State prepares a local plan under section 27 of the Act if][44] the local planning authority in question is a London borough council, the Secretary of State must request the opinion of the Mayor of London as to the general conformity of the local plan with the London spatial development strategy.

(5)   Before holding an independent examination of the local plan under [section 27(2) of, or paragraphs 2(2) or 6(2) of Schedule A1 to, the Act as the case may be][45], the [relevant authority][46] must—

   (a)   notify each of the bodies or persons specified in sub-paragraph (6) of the subject of the local plan which the [relevant authority][47] proposes to prepare;

   (b)   invite each of them to make representations to the [relevant authority][48] about what the local plan with that subject ought to contain;

   (c)   take into account any representation made to the [relevant authority][49] in response to those invitations;

   (d)   make a copy of each of the proposal documents and a statement of the representations procedure available during normal office hours, at such places as the [relevant authority][50] considers appropriate, and

   (e)   ensure that a statement of the representations procedure and a statement of the fact that the proposed submission documents are available for inspection and of the places and times at which they can be inspected, is sent to each of the bodies or persons which are invited to make representations under paragraph (b).

---

[41]   Substituted by the Town and Country Planning (Local Planning) (England) (Amendment) Regulations 2016, SI 2016/871, regs 2, 10(1), (4)(a), (c).

[42]   Substituted by the Town and Country Planning (Local Planning) (England) (Amendment) Regulations 2016, SI 2016/871, regs 2, 10(1), (4)(a), (c).

[43]   Substituted by the Town and Country Planning (Local Planning) (England) (Amendment) Regulations 2016, SI 2016/871, regs 2, 10(1), (4)(a), (c).

[44]   Inserted by the Town and Country Planning (Local Planning) (England) (Amendment) Regulations 2016, SI 2016/871, regs 2, 10(1), (4)(b).

[45]   Substituted by the Town and Country Planning (Local Planning) (England) (Amendment) Regulations 2016, SI 2016/871, regs 2, 10(1), (4)(a), (c).

[46]   Substituted by the Town and Country Planning (Local Planning) (England) (Amendment) Regulations 2016, SI 2016/871, regs 2, 10(1), (4)(a), (c).

[47]   Substituted by the Town and Country Planning (Local Planning) (England) (Amendment) Regulations 2016, SI 2016/871, regs 2, 10(1), (4)(a), (c).

[48]   Substituted by the Town and Country Planning (Local Planning) (England) (Amendment) Regulations 2016, SI 2016/871, regs 2, 10(1), (4)(a), (c).

[49]   Substituted by the Town and Country Planning (Local Planning) (England) (Amendment) Regulations 2016, SI 2016/871, regs 2, 10(1), (4)(a), (c).

[50]   Substituted by the Town and Country Planning (Local Planning) (England) (Amendment) Regulations 2016, SI 2016/871, regs 2, 10(1), (4)(a), (c).

(6) The bodies or persons referred to in sub-paragraph (5)(a) are—

(a) such of the specific consultation bodies (in relation to the area of the local planning authority in question) as the [relevant authority]⁵¹ considers may have an interest in the subject of the proposed local plan;

(b) such of the general consultation bodies (in relation to the area of the local planning authority in question) as the [relevant authority]⁵² considers appropriate; and

(c) such residents or other persons carrying on business in the area of the local planning authority in question from which the [relevant authority]⁵³ considers it appropriate to invite representations.

(7) Where the [relevant authority]⁵⁴ makes available a local plan for the making of representations prior to the holding of an independent examination under [section 27(2) of, or paragraphs 2(2) or 6(2) of Schedule A1 to, the Act as the case may be]⁵⁵, any person may make representations in relation to the local plan but any such representation must be received by the [relevant authority]⁵⁶ by the date specified in the statement of the representations procedure.

(8) Where the [relevant authority]⁵⁷ holds an independent examination under [section 27(2) of, or paragraphs 2(2) or 6(2) of Schedule A1 to, the Act as the case may be]⁵⁸, at least 6 weeks before the opening of a hearing the [relevant authority]⁵⁹ must—

(a) make the matters mentioned in sub-paragraph (9) available in accordance with regulation 35; and

(b) notify any body or person who has made a representation in accordance with sub-paragraph (5) and not withdrawn that representation, of those matters.

(9) The matters referred to in sub-paragraph (8) are—

(a) the date, time and place at which the hearing is to be held, and

(b) the name of the person appointed to carry out the independent examination.

(10) For the purposes of this paragraph—

---

⁵¹ Substituted by the Town and Country Planning (Local Planning) (England) (Amendment) Regulations 2016, SI 2016/871, regs 2, 10(1), (4)(a), (c).
⁵² Substituted by the Town and Country Planning (Local Planning) (England) (Amendment) Regulations 2016, SI 2016/871, regs 2, 10(1), (4)(a), (c).
⁵³ Substituted by the Town and Country Planning (Local Planning) (England) (Amendment) Regulations 2016, SI 2016/871, regs 2, 10(1), (4)(a), (c).
⁵⁴ Substituted by the Town and Country Planning (Local Planning) (England) (Amendment) Regulations 2016, SI 2016/871, regs 2, 10(1), (4)(a), (c).
⁵⁵ Substituted by the Town and Country Planning (Local Planning) (England) (Amendment) Regulations 2016, SI 2016/871, regs 2, 10(1), (4)(a), (c).
⁵⁶ Substituted by the Town and Country Planning (Local Planning) (England) (Amendment) Regulations 2016, SI 2016/871, regs 2, 10(1), (4)(a), (c).
⁵⁷ Substituted by the Town and Country Planning (Local Planning) (England) (Amendment) Regulations 2016, SI 2016/871, regs 2, 10(1), (4)(a), (c).
⁵⁸ Substituted by the Town and Country Planning (Local Planning) (England) (Amendment) Regulations 2016, SI 2016/871, regs 2, 10(1), (4)(a), (c).
⁵⁹ Substituted by the Town and Country Planning (Local Planning) (England) (Amendment) Regulations 2016, SI 2016/871, regs 2, 10(1), (4)(a), (c).

'proposal documents' means the following documents—

(a)   the local plan for which the [relevant authority][60] proposes to hold an independent examination;

(b)   if the approval of the local plan would result in changes to the adopted policies map, a map showing how the adopted policies map of the local planning authority would be amended by the local plan, if it were approved;

(c)   the sustainability appraisal report of the local plan prepared in accordance with section 19(5) of the Act (as modified by sub-paragraph (3));

(d)   a statement setting out—

    (i)   which bodies and persons were invited to make representations under sub-paragraph (5)(b);

    (ii)   how those bodies and persons were invited to make such representations;

    (iii)   a summary of the main issues raised by those representations; and

    (iv)   how those main issues have been addressed in the local plan; and

(e)   such supporting documents as in the opinion of the [relevant authority][61] are relevant to the preparation of the local plan;

'statement of the representations procedure' means a statement specifying—

(a)   the title of the local plan for which the [relevant authority][62] proposes to hold an independent examination;

(b)   the subject matter of, and the area covered by, the local plan;

(c)   the date by which representations about the local plan must be received, by the [relevant authority][63], which must be not less than 6 weeks from the day on which the statement is published;

(d)   the address to which representations about that document must be made;

(e)   that representations may be made in writing or by way of electronic communications; and

(f)   that representations may be accompanied by a request to be notified at a specified address of any of the following—

---

[60]   Substituted by the Town and Country Planning (Local Planning) (England) (Amendment) Regulations 2016, SI 2016/871, regs 2, 10(1), (4)(a), (c).

[61]   Substituted by the Town and Country Planning (Local Planning) (England) (Amendment) Regulations 2016, SI 2016/871, regs 2, 10(1), (4)(a), (c).

[62]   Substituted by the Town and Country Planning (Local Planning) (England) (Amendment) Regulations 2016, SI 2016/871, regs 2, 10(1), (4)(a), (c).

[63]   Substituted by the Town and Country Planning (Local Planning) (England) (Amendment) Regulations 2016, SI 2016/871, regs 2, 10(1), (4)(a), (c).

  (i)   the publication of the recommendations of the person appointed to carry out an independent examination of the local plan, and

  (ii)   the adoption of the local plan.

Neighbourhood Planning (General) Regulations 2012, SI 2012/637

PART 1 GENERAL

1 Citation and commencement

These Regulations may be cited as the Neighbourhood Planning (General) Regulations 2012 and come into force on 6th April 2012.

2 Review

(1)   Before the end of each review period, the Secretary of State must—

    (a)   carry out a review of these Regulations (other than regulations 32 and 33 and Schedules 2 and 3),

    (b)   set out the conclusions of the review in a report, and

    (c)   publish the report.

(2)   The report must in particular—

    (a)   set out the objectives intended to be achieved by the regulatory system established by these Regulations,

    (b)   assess the extent to which those objectives are achieved, and

    (c)   assess whether those objectives remain appropriate and, if so, the extent to which they could be achieved with a system that imposes less regulation.

(3)   'Review period' means—

    (a)   the period of five years beginning with the day on which these Regulations come into force, and

    (b)   subject to paragraph (4), each successive period of five years.

(4)   If a report under this regulation is published before the last day of the review period to which it relates, the following review period is to begin with the day on which that report is published.

3 Interpretation

In these Regulations—

    'the 1990 Act' means the Town and Country Planning Act 1990;

'the 2004 Act' means the Planning and Compulsory Purchase Act 2004;

'address' in relation to electronic communications means any number or address used for the purposes of such communications;

'approvals application' means an application for approval, in relation to a condition or limitation subject to which planning permission is granted by a neighbourhood development order, under section 61L(2) of the 1990 Act;

'area application' means an application for the designation of a neighbourhood area made under section 61G of the 1990 Act;

'consultation body' has the meaning given in Schedule 1;

'contact details' means the name, address and telephone number of the person concerned;

'EIA Regulations' means the [Town and Country Planning (Environmental Impact Assessment) Regulations 2017][1];

'electronic communication' has the meaning given in section 15(1) of the Electronic Communications Act 2000;

'electronic communications apparatus' has the meaning given in paragraph 1(1) of the electronic communications code;

'electronic communications code' has the meaning given in section 106(1) of the Communications Act 2003;

'inspection' means inspection by the public;

'neighbourhood forum application' means an application for designation of a neighbourhood forum made by an organisation or body under section 61F of the 1990 Act;

'order proposal' means a proposal for a neighbourhood development order submitted by a qualifying body under paragraph 1 of Schedule 4B to the 1990 Act or community right to build order submitted by a community organisation under paragraph 1 of Schedule 4B to the 1990 Act, as read with paragraph 2 of Schedule 4C to the 1990 Act; and

'plan proposal' means a proposal for a neighbourhood development plan submitted by a qualifying body under paragraph 1 of Schedule 4B to the 1990 Act (as applied, with modifications, by section 38A of the 2004 Act).

4 Electronic communications

(1) Where within these Regulations—

(a) a person is required to consult or seek representations from another person or body; and

(b) that other person has an address for the purposes of electronic communications;

the document, copy, notice or notification may be sent or made by way of electronic communication.

---

[1] Substituted by the Town and Country Planning (Environmental Impact Assessment) Regulations 2017, SI 2017/571, reg 75(1), (2).

(2)   Where within these Regulations a person may make representations on any matter or document, those representations may be made—

  (a)   in writing, or

  (b)   by way of electronic communication.

(3)   Where—

  (a)   an electronic communication is used as mentioned in paragraphs (1) and (2); and

  (b)   the communication is received by the recipient outside normal working hours;

  it shall be taken to have been received on the next working day.

(4)   In this regulation 'working day' means a day which is not a Saturday, Sunday, bank holiday under the Banking and Financial Dealings Act 1971 or other public holiday in England.

PART 2 NEIGHBOURHOOD AREAS

5 Application for designation of a neighbourhood area

(1)   Where a relevant body submits an area application to the local planning authority it must include—

  (a)   a map which identifies the area to which the area application relates;

  (b)   a statement explaining why this area is considered appropriate to be designated as a neighbourhood area; and

  (c)   a statement that the organisation or body making the area application is a relevant body for the purposes of section 61G of the 1990 Act.

(2)   A local planning authority may decline to consider an area application if the relevant body has already made an area application and a decision has not yet been made on that application.

[5A Designation of the whole of the area of a parish council

(1)   This regulation applies where—

  (a)   a local planning authority receive an area application from a parish council;

  (b)   the area specified in the application consists of the whole of the parish council's area; and

  (c)   if any part of the specified area is part of a neighbourhood area, none of that neighbourhood area extends outside the parish council's area.

(2)   The local planning authority must exercise their powers under section 61G of the 1990 Act to designate the specified area as a neighbourhood area.

(3)   Where this regulation applies, regulations 6 and 6A do not apply.]²

---

²   Inserted by the Neighbourhood Planning (General) and Development Management Procedure (Amendment) Regulations 2016, SI 2016/873, reg 2(1), (2).

6 Publicising an area application

As soon as possible after receiving an area application from a relevant body, a local planning authority must publicise the following on their website and in such other manner as they consider is likely to bring the area application to the attention of people who live, work or carry on business in the area to which the area application relates—

    (a)   a copy of the area application;

    (b)   details of how to make representations; and

    [(c)   the date by which those representations must be received, being ...[3] not less than six weeks from the date on which the area application is first publicised.][4]

[6A Prescribed date for determination of an area application

(1)   Where a local planning authority receive an area application from a relevant body the authority must determine the application by the date prescribed in paragraph (2).

(2)   The date prescribed in this paragraph is—

    (a)   in a case where the area to which the application relates falls within the areas of two or more local planning authorities, the date 20 weeks from the date immediately following that on which the application is first publicised;

    (b)   ...[5]

    (c)   in all other cases, the date 13 weeks from the date immediately following that on which the application is first publicised.

[(3)   Where the application has not been determined by the date prescribed in paragraph (2), the local planning authority must exercise their powers under section 61G of the 1990 Act so as to secure that the whole of the area specified in the application is designated as a neighbourhood area unless on that date—

    (a)   some or all of the specified area has been designated as a neighbourhood area; or

    (b)   some or all of the specified area is specified in another area application and that other area application has not been determined.][6]][7]

7 Publicising a designation of a neighbourhood area etc

(1)   As soon as possible after designating a neighbourhood area, a local planning authority must publish the following on their website and in such other manner

---

[3]   Repealed by the Neighbourhood Planning (General) and Development Management Procedure (Amendment) Regulations 2016, SI 2016/873, reg 2(1), (3).

[4]   Substituted by the Neighbourhood Planning (General) (Amendment) Regulations 2015, SI 2015/20, reg 2(1), (2).

[5]   Repealed by the Neighbourhood Planning (General) and Development Management Procedure (Amendment) Regulations 2016, SI 2016/873, reg 2(1), (4)(a).

[6]   Inserted by the Neighbourhood Planning (General) and Development Management Procedure (Amendment) Regulations 2016, SI 2016/873, reg 2(1), (4)(b).

[7]   Inserted by the Neighbourhood Planning (General) (Amendment) Regulations 2015, SI 2015/20, reg 2(1), (3)..

as they consider is likely to bring the designation to the attention of people who live, work or carry on business in the neighbourhood area—

(a)   the name of the neighbourhood area;

(b)   a map which identifies the area; and

(c)   the name of the relevant body who applied for the designation.

(2)   As soon as possible after deciding to refuse to designate a neighbourhood area, a local planning authority must publish the following on their website and in such other manner as they consider is likely to bring the refusal to the attention of people who live, work or carry on business in the neighbourhood area—

(a)   a document setting out the decision and a statement of their reasons for making that decision ('the decision document'); and

(b)   details of where and when the decision document may be inspected.

PART 3 NEIGHBOURHOOD FORUMS

8 Application for designation of a neighbourhood forum

Where an organisation or body submits a neighbourhood forum application to the local planning authority it must include—

(a)   the name of the proposed neighbourhood forum;

(b)   a copy of the written constitution of the proposed neighbourhood forum;

(c)   the name of the neighbourhood area to which the application relates and a map which identifies the area;

(d)   the contact details of at least one member of the proposed neighbourhood forum to be made public under regulations 9 and 10; and

(e)   a statement which explains how the proposed neighbourhood forum meets the conditions contained in section 61F(5) of the 1990 Act.

9 Publicising a neighbourhood forum application

As soon as possible after receiving a neighbourhood forum application, which the local planning authority do not decline to consider under regulation 11, a local planning authority must publish the following on their website and in such other manner as they consider is likely to bring the application to the attention of people who live, work or carry on business in the area to which the application relates—

(a)   a copy of the application;

(b)   a statement that if a designation is made no other organisation or body may be designated for that neighbourhood area until that designation expires or is withdrawn;

(c)   details of how to make representations; and

(d)   the date by which those representations must be received, being not less than 6 weeks from the date on which the application is first publicised.

[9A Prescribed date for determination of a neighbourhood forum application

(1)   Where a local planning authority receive a neighbourhood forum application, which they do not decline to consider under regulation 11, the authority must determine the application by the date prescribed in paragraph (2).

(2)   The date prescribed in this paragraph is—

(a)   in a case where the neighbourhood area to which the application relates falls within the areas of two or more local planning authorities, the date which is the last day of the period of 20 weeks beginning with the day immediately following that on which the application is first publicised in accordance with regulation 9;

(b)   in all other cases, the date which is the last day of the period of 13 weeks beginning with the day immediately following that on which the application is first publicised in accordance with regulation 9.

(3)   The date prescribed in paragraph (2) does not apply where, on that date, the authority are considering another neighbourhood forum application and that other application relates to an area which consists of or includes some or all of the neighbourhood area to which the application mentioned in paragraph (1) relates.]⁸

10 Publicising a designation of a neighbourhood forum

(1)   As soon as possible after designating a neighbourhood forum, a local planning authority must publish the following on their website and in such other manner as they consider is likely to bring the designation to the attention of people who live, work or carry on business in the neighbourhood area—

(a)   the name of the neighbourhood forum;

(b)   a copy of the written constitution of the neighbourhood forum;

(c)   the name of the neighbourhood area to which the designation relates; and

(d)   contact details for at least one member of the neighbourhood forum.

(2)   As soon as possible after deciding to refuse to designate a neighbourhood forum, a local planning authority must publish the following on their website and in such other manner as they consider is likely to bring the decision to the attention of people who live, work or carry on business in the neighbourhood area—

(a)   a statement setting out the decision and their reasons for making that decision ('the refusal statement'); and

(b)   details of where and when the refusal statement may be inspected.

11 Subsequent applications

Where a neighbourhood forum has been designated in relation to a neighbourhood area under section 61F of the 1990 Act, and that designation has not expired or been withdrawn, a local planning authority may decline to consider any neighbourhood forum application made in relation to that neighbourhood area.

---

8   Inserted by the Neighbourhood Planning (General) and Development Management Procedure (Amendment) Regulations 2016, SI 2016/873, reg 2(1), (5).

12 Voluntary withdrawal of designation

(1)   Where a neighbourhood forum gives notice to a local planning authority that it no longer wishes to be designated as the neighbourhood forum for a neighbourhood area, the local planning authority must withdraw the designation of the neighbourhood forum.

(2)   As soon as possible after withdrawing the designation of a neighbourhood forum under paragraph (1) or under section 61F(9) of the 1990 Act, a local planning authority must publish the following on their website and in such other manner as they consider is likely to bring the withdrawal of the designation to the attention of people who live, work or carry on business in the neighbourhood area—

(a)   a statement setting out details of the withdrawal ('the withdrawal statement'); and

(b)   details of where and when the withdrawal statement may be inspected.

PART 4 COMMUNITY RIGHT TO BUILD ORGANISATIONS

13 Prescribed conditions for community right to build organisations

(1)   For the purposes of paragraph 3(1)(b) of Schedule 4C to the 1990 Act, the following additional conditions are prescribed for any community organisation which is not a parish council—

(a)   individuals who live or work in the particular area for which the community organisation is established ('the particular area') must be entitled to become voting members of the community organisation (whether or not others can also become voting members); and

(b)   the constitution of the community organisation must—

(i)   provide that taken together the individuals who live in the particular area—

(aa)   hold the majority of the voting rights; and

(bb)   have the majority on the board of directors or governing body,

of the community organisation;

(ii)   include a statement—

(aa)   that the community organisation will carry on its activities for the benefit of the community in the particular area or a section of it; and

(bb)   indicating how it is proposed the community organisation's activities will benefit the community in the particular area (or a section of it);

(iii)   provide that any assets of the community organisation may not be disposed of, improved or developed except in a manner which the community organisation consider benefits the community in the particular area or a section of it; and

      (iv)   provide that any profits from its activities may only be used to benefit the community in the particular area or a section of it (the payment of profits directly to members or directors is not to be considered a benefit to the community in the particular area or a section of it);

      (v)   provide that in the event of the winding up of the community organisation or in any other circumstances where the community organisation ceases to exist, its assets must be transferred to another body corporate which has similar objectives; and

      (vi)   provide that the organisation has at least 10 members, living in different dwellings to each other, who live in the particular area.

(2)   For the purposes of this regulation, 'dwelling' has the meaning given in section 3 of the Local Government Finance Act 1992.

PART 5 NEIGHBOURHOOD DEVELOPMENT PLANS

14 Pre-submission consultation and publicity

Before submitting a plan proposal to the local planning authority, a qualifying body must—

    (a)   publicise, in a manner that is likely to bring it to the attention of people who live, work or carry on business in the neighbourhood area—

      (i)   details of the proposals for a neighbourhood development plan;

      (ii)   details of where and when the proposals for a neighbourhood development plan may be inspected;

      (iii)   details of how to make representations; and

      (iv)   the date by which those representations must be received, being not less than 6 weeks from the date on which the draft proposal is first publicised;

    (b)   consult any consultation body referred to in paragraph 1 of Schedule 1 whose interests the qualifying body considers may be affected by the proposals for a neighbourhood development plan; and

    (c)   send a copy of the proposals for a neighbourhood development plan to the local planning authority.

15 Plan proposals

(1)   Where a qualifying body submits a plan proposal to the local planning authority, it must include—

    (a)   a map or statement which identifies the area to which the proposed neighbourhood development plan relates;

    (b)   a consultation statement;

    (c)   the proposed neighbourhood development plan; ...[9]

---

[9]   Word revoked by the Neighbourhood Planning (General) (Amendment) Regulations 2015, SI 2015/20, reg 2(1), (4)(a).

(d)   a statement explaining how the proposed neighbourhood development plan meets the requirements of paragraph 8 of Schedule 4B to the 1990 Act[; and

(e)

> (i)   an environmental report prepared in accordance with paragraphs (2) and (3) of regulation 12 of the Environmental Assessment of Plans and Programmes Regulations 2004; or
>
> (ii)   where it has been determined under regulation 9(1) of those Regulations that the plan proposal is unlikely to have significant environmental effects (and, accordingly, does not require an environmental assessment), a statement of reasons for the determination.][10]

(2)   In this regulation 'consultation statement' means a document which—

(a)   contains details of the persons and bodies who were consulted about the proposed neighbourhood development plan;

(b)   explains how they were consulted;

(c)   summarises the main issues and concerns raised by the persons consulted; and

(d)   describes how these issues and concerns have been considered and, where relevant, addressed in the proposed neighbourhood development plan.

16 Publicising a plan proposal

As soon as possible after receiving a plan proposal which includes each of the documents referred to in regulation 15(1), a local planning authority must—

(a)   publicise the following on their website and in such other manner as they consider is likely to bring the proposal to the attention of people who live, work or carry on business in the neighbourhood area—

> (i)   details of the plan proposal;
>
> (ii)   details of where and when the plan proposal may be inspected;
>
> (iii)   details of how to make representations;
>
> (iv)   a statement that any representations may include a request to be notified of the local planning authority's decision under regulation 19 in relation to the neighbourhood development plan; and
>
> (v)   the date by which those representations must be received, being not less than 6 weeks from the date on which the plan proposal is first publicised; and

(b)   notify any consultation body which is referred to in the consultation statement submitted in accordance with regulation 15, that the plan proposal has been received.

---

[10]   Inserted by the Neighbourhood Planning (General) (Amendment) Regulations 2015, SI 2015/20, reg 2(1), (4)(b).

17 Submission of plan proposal to examination

As soon as possible after the appointment of a person to carry out an examination under paragraph 7 of Schedule 4B to the 1990 Act (as applied by section 38A of the 2004 Act), a local planning authority must send the following to the person appointed—

(a)   the plan proposal;

(b)   the documents referred to in regulation 15(1) and any other document submitted to the local planning authority by the qualifying body in relation to the plan proposal;

(c)   if the order proposal is one to which [the Conservation of Habitats and Species Regulations 2017][11] applies, the information submitted in accordance with [regulation 106][12] of those Regulations; and

(d)   a copy of any representations which have been made in accordance with regulation 16.

[17A Decision on examiner's recommendations

(1)   This regulation applies where an examiner has made a report under paragraph 10 of Schedule 4B to the 1990 Act (applied by section 38A(3) of the 2004 Act) in relation to a plan proposal.

(2)   The persons prescribed for the purposes of paragraph 13(1) of that Schedule are—

(a)   the qualifying body;

(b)   any person whose representation was submitted to the examiner of the plan proposal in accordance with regulation 17(d); and

(c)   any consultation body which is referred to in the consultation statement mentioned in regulation 15.

(3)   Representations invited under paragraph 13(1) must be submitted on or before the date which is the last day of the period of 6 weeks beginning with the day immediately following that on which the local planning authority first invited representations.

(4)   On or after the date prescribed in paragraph (5) the local planning authority must decide what action to take in response to each recommendation made by the report mentioned in paragraph (1).

(5)   The date prescribed in this paragraph is—

(a)   where the local planning authority and the qualifying body agree a date, that date;

(b)   where sub-paragraph (a) does not apply but paragraph 13 of Schedule 4B to the 1990 Act (applied by section 38A(3) of the 2004 Act) applies—

---

[11]   Substituted by the Conservation of Habitats and Species Regulations 2017, SI 2017/1012, reg 139, Sch 6, para 27(1), (2).

[12]   Substituted by the Conservation of Habitats and Species Regulations 2017, SI 2017/1012, reg 139, Sch 6, para 27(1), (2).

(i)   where the authority refer the issue to independent examination, the date which is the last day of the period of 5 weeks beginning with the day immediately following that on which they receive the report of the examiner on that issue;

(ii)   where the authority do not refer the issue to independent examination, the date which is the last day of the period of 5 weeks beginning with the day immediately following the date prescribed in paragraph (3);

(c)   in all other cases, the date which is the last day of the period of 5 weeks beginning with the day immediately following that on which the local planning authority receive the report mentioned in paragraph (1).][13]

18 Publication of the examiner's report and plan proposal decisions

(1)   Paragraph (2) applies where a local planning authority decide—

(a)   to decline to consider a plan proposal under paragraph 5 of Schedule 4B to the 1990 Act (as applied by section 38A of the 2004 Act);

(b)   to refuse a plan proposal under paragraph 6 of Schedule 4B to the 1990 Act (as applied by section 38A of the 2004 Act);

(c)   what action to take in response to the recommendations of an examiner made in a report under paragraph 10 of Schedule 4B to the 1990 Act (as applied by section 38A of the 2004 Act) in relation to a neighbourhood development plan;

(d)   what modifications, if any, they are to make to the draft plan under paragraph 12(6) of Schedule 4B to the 1990 Act (as applied by section 38A of the 2004 Act);

(e)   whether to extend the area to which the referendum is (or referendums are) to take place; or

(f)   that they are not satisfied with the plan proposal under paragraph 12(10) of Schedule 4B to the 1990 Act (as applied by section 38A of the 2004 Act).

(2)   As soon as possible after making a decision referred to in paragraph (1), a local planning authority must publish—

(a)   the decision and their reasons for it ('the decision statement'),

(b)   details of where and when the decision statement may be inspected; and

(c)   in the case of a decision mentioned in paragraph (1)(c), the report made by the examiner under paragraph 10 of Schedule 4B to the 1990 Act (as applied by section 38A of the 2004 Act),

---

[13]   Inserted by the Neighbourhood Planning (General) and Development Management Procedure (Amendment) Regulations 2016, SI 2016/873, reg 2(1), (6).

on their website and in such other manner as they consider is likely to bring the decision statement and, as the case may be, the report to the attention of people who live, work or carry on business in the neighbourhood area.

[18A Prescribed date for making a neighbourhood development plan

(1) The date prescribed for the purposes of section 38A(4)(b) of the 2004 Act is the date which is the last day of the period of 8 weeks beginning with the day immediately following that on which the last applicable referendum is held.

(2) Paragraph (1) does not apply where proceedings for questioning anything relating to an applicable referendum are brought in accordance with section 61N(3) of the 1990 Act (applied by section 38C(2)(d) of the 2004 Act) before the neighbourhood development plan is made.][14]

19 Decision on a plan proposal

As soon as possible after deciding to make a neighbourhood development plan under section 38A(4) of the 2004 Act or refusing to make a plan under section 38A(6) of the 2004 Act, a local planning authority must—

    (a) publish on their website and in such other manner as they consider is likely to bring the decision to the attention of people who live, work or carry on business in the neighbourhood area—

        (i) a statement setting out the decision and their reasons for making that decision ('the decision statement');

        (ii) details of where and when the decision statement may be inspected; and

    (b) send a copy of the decision statement to—

        (i) the qualifying body; and

        (ii) any person who asked to be notified of the decision.

20 Publicising a neighbourhood development plan

As soon as possible after making a neighbourhood development plan under section 38A(4) of the 2004 Act, a local planning authority must—

    (a) publish on their website and in such other manner as they consider is likely to bring the decision to the attention of people who live, work or carry on business in the neighbourhood area—

        (i) the neighbourhood development plan; and

        (ii) details of where and when the neighbourhood development plan may be inspected; and

    (b) notify any person who asked to be notified of the making of the neighbourhood development plan that it has been made and where and when it may be inspected.

---

[14] Inserted by the Neighbourhood Planning (General) and Development Management Procedure (Amendment) Regulations 2016, SI 2016/873, reg 2(1), (7).

PART 6 NEIGHBOURHOOD DEVELOPMENT ORDERS AND COMMUNITY RIGHT TO BUILD ORDERS

21 Pre-submission consultation and publicity

Before submitting an order proposal to the local planning authority, a qualifying body must—

(a) publicise, in a manner that is likely to bring it to the attention of people who live, work or carry on business in the neighbourhood area—

    (i) details of the proposals for a neighbourhood development order or community right to build order;

    (ii) details of where and when the proposals may be inspected;

    (iii) details of how to make representations; and

    (iv) the date by which those representations must be received, being not less than 6 weeks from the date on which details of the proposals are first publicised;

(b) consult—

    (i) any consultation body referred to in paragraph 2(1)(a) to (c) of Schedule 1 whose interests the qualifying body considers may be affected by the proposals for a neighbourhood development order or a community right to build order; and

    (ii) where the qualifying body considers the development to be authorised under the proposed neighbourhood development order or community right to build order which falls within any category set out in the Table in paragraph 2 of Schedule 1, any consultation body mentioned in the Table in relation to each of those categories; and

    (iii) any person who, on the date 21 days before the order proposal is submitted under regulation 22, the qualifying body considers to be—

        (aa) an owner of any of the land which is proposed to be developed under the order proposal; and

        (bb) a tenant of any of that land; and

(c) send a copy of the proposals for a neighbourhood development order or a community right to build order to the local planning authority.

22 Order proposals

(1) Where a qualifying body submits an order proposal to the local planning authority it must include—

(a) a map which identifies the land to which the order proposal relates;

(b) a consultation statement;

(c) the proposed neighbourhood development order or community right to build order;

(d)   where the qualifying body considers it appropriate, following consultation with the Historic Buildings and Monument Commission for England (known as English Heritage), an archaeology statement;

(e)   a statement explaining how the proposed neighbourhood development order or a community right to build order meets the basic conditions in paragraph 8(2) of Schedule 4B to the 1990 Act; and

(f)   in the case of a proposal for a community right to build order, details of the enfranchisement rights, if any, which the qualifying body proposes are not exercisable and the properties, or types of properties, in relation to which to the enfranchisement rights are not exercisable.

(2)   In this regulation—

'archaeology statement' means a document which—

(a)   confirms that the information in relation to archaeology contained in the historic environment record for the neighbourhood area has been reviewed;

(b)   sets out the findings from that review for the area to which the order proposal relates; and

(c)   explains how the findings have been taken into account in preparing the order proposal,

but where no findings relevant to the neighbourhood area were identified in the review the archaeology statement need only—

(i)   confirm that the review mentioned in sub-paragraph (a) took place; and

(ii)   explain there were no findings relevant to the neighbourhood area; and

'consultation statement' means a document which—

(a)   contains details of the persons and bodies who were consulted about the proposed neighbourhood development order or community right to build order;

(b)   explains how they were consulted;

(c)   summarises the main issues and concerns raised by the persons consulted; and

(d)   describes how these issues and concerns have been considered and, where relevant, addressed in the proposed neighbourhood development order or community right to build order.

23 Publicising an order proposal

(1)   As soon as possible after receiving an order proposal which includes each of the documents referred to in regulation 22(1), a local planning authority must—

(a)   publicise the following on their website and in such other manner they consider is likely to bring the proposal to the attention of people who live, work or carry on business in the neighbourhood area—

      (i)   details of the order proposal;

     (ii)   details of where and when the order proposal may be inspected;

    (iii)   details of how to make representations;

    (iv)   a statement that any representations may include a request to be notified of the local planning authority's decision under regulation 26 in relation to the neighbourhood development order or community right to build order; and

     (v)   the date by which those representations must be received, being not less than 6 weeks from the date on which the proposal is first publicised; and

(b)   notify any consultation body which is referred to in the consultation statement submitted in accordance with regulation 22, that the order proposal has been received.

[(2)   As soon as possible after receiving an order proposal to which regulation 33 of the EIA Regulations applies, the local planning authority must, in addition to any publicity required under paragraph (1), publicise the information described in paragraph (1)(a) and the environmental statement submitted in accordance with the EIA Regulations by giving notice—

(a)   by site display in at least one place on or near the land to which the order proposal relates for not less than 30 days;

(b)   by publication of the notice in a newspaper circulating in the locality in which the land to which the order proposal relates is situated; and

(c)   by publication on a website maintained by or on behalf of the authority.]¹⁵

24 Submission of order proposal to examination

As soon as possible after the appointment of a person to carry out an examination under paragraph 7 of Schedule 4B to the 1990 Act, a local planning authority must send the following to the person appointed—

(a)   the order proposal;

(b)   the documents referred to in regulation 22(1);

(c)   if the order proposal is one to which [regulation 33]¹⁶ of the EIA Regulations applies, the environmental statement submitted in accordance with those Regulations;

(d)   if the order proposal is one to which [the Conservation of Habitats and Species Regulations 2017]¹⁷ applies, the information submitted in accordance with [regulation 63(2)]¹⁸ of those Regulations;

---

¹⁵   Substituted by the Town and Country Planning (Environmental Impact Assessment) Regulations 2017, SI 2017/571, reg 75(1), (3).

¹⁶   Substituted by the Town and Country Planning (Environmental Impact Assessment) Regulations 2017, SI 2017/571, reg 75(1), (4).

¹⁷   Substituted by the Conservation of Habitats and Species Regulations 2017, SI 2017/1012, reg 139, Sch 6, para 27(1), (3).

¹⁸   Substituted by the Conservation of Habitats and Species Regulations 2017, SI 2017/1012, reg 139, Sch 6, para 27(1), (3).

    (e)   any other document submitted to the local planning authority by the qualifying body in relation to the order proposal; and

    (f)   a copy of any representations which have been made in accordance with regulation 23.

[24A Decision on examiner's recommendations

(1)   This regulation applies where an examiner has made a report under paragraph 10 of Schedule 4B to the 1990 Act in relation to an order proposal.

(2)   The persons prescribed for the purposes of paragraph 13(1) of that Schedule are—

    (a)   the qualifying body;

    (b)   any person whose representation was submitted to the examiner of the order proposal in accordance with regulation 24(f); and

    (c)   any consultation body which is referred to in the consultation statement mentioned in regulation 22.

(3)   Representations invited under paragraph 13(1) must be submitted on or before the date which is the last day of the period of 6 weeks beginning with the day immediately following that on which the local planning authority first invited representations.

(4)   The local planning authority must decide what action to take in response to each recommendation made by the report mentioned in paragraph (1) by the date prescribed in paragraph (5).

(5)   The date prescribed in this paragraph is—

    (a)   where the local planning authority and the qualifying body agree a date, that date;

    (b)   where sub-paragraph (a) does not apply but paragraph 13 of Schedule 4B to the 1990 Act applies—

        (i)   where the authority refer the issue to independent examination, the date which is the last day of the period of 5 weeks beginning with the day immediately following that on which they receive the report of the examiner on that issue;

        (ii)   where the authority do not refer the issue to independent examination, the date which is the last day of the period of 5 weeks beginning with the day immediately following the date prescribed in paragraph (3);

    (c)   in all other cases, the date which is the last day of the period of 5 weeks beginning with the day immediately following that on which the local planning authority receive the report mentioned in paragraph (1).][19]

25 Publication of the examiner's report and order proposal decisions

(1)   Paragraph (2) applies where a local planning authority decide—

---

[19]   Inserted by the Neighbourhood Planning (General) and Development Management Procedure (Amendment) Regulations 2016, SI 2016/873, reg 2(1), (8).

(a)   to decline to consider an order proposal under paragraph 5 of Schedule 4B to the 1990 Act;

(b)   to refuse an order proposal under paragraph 6 of Schedule 4B to the 1990 Act;

(c)   what action to take in response to the recommendations of an examiner made in a report under paragraph 10 of Schedule 4B to the 1990 Act in relation to a neighbourhood development order or community right to build order (as modified in the case of community right to build orders by paragraphs 7 to 10 of Schedule 4C to the 1990 Act);

(d)   what modifications, if any, they are to make to the draft neighbourhood development order or community right to build order under paragraph 12(6) of Schedule 4B to the 1990 Act (as modified in the case of community right to build orders by paragraphs 7 to 10 of Schedule 4C to the 1990 Act);

(e)   whether to extend the area to which the referendum is (or referendums are) to take place; or

(f)   that they are not satisfied with the proposed neighbourhood development order or community right to build order under paragraph 12(10) of Schedule 4B to the 1990 Act (as modified in the case of community right to build orders by paragraphs 7 to 10 of Schedule 4C to the 1990 Act).

(2)   As soon as possible after making a decision referred to in paragraph (1), a local planning authority must publish—

(a)   the decision and their reasons for it ('the decision statement'),

(b)   details of where and when the decision statement may be inspected, and

(c)   in the case of a decision mentioned in sub-paragraph (c), the report made by the examiner under paragraph 10 of Schedule 4B to the 1990 Act,

on their website and in such other m anner as they consider is likely to bring the decision statement and, as the case may be, the report to the attention of people who live, work or carry on business in the neighbourhood area.

[25A Prescribed date for making a neighbourhood development order

(1)   The date prescribed for the purposes of section 61E(4)(b) of the 1990 Act is the date which is the last day of the period of 8 weeks beginning with the day immediately following that on which the last applicable referendum is held.

(2)   Paragraph (1) does not apply where proceedings for questioning anything relating to an applicable referendum are brought in accordance with section 61N(3) of the 1990 Act before the neighbourhood development order is made.][20]

26 Decision on an order proposal

As soon as possible after deciding to make the neighbourhood development order or community right to build order under section 61E(4) of the 1990 Act or to refuse to

---

[20]   Inserted by the Neighbourhood Planning (General) and Development Management Procedure (Amendment) Regulations 2016, SI 2016/873, reg 2(1), (9).

make it under section 61E(8) of the 1990 Act (as modified in the case of community right to build orders by paragraphs 7 to 10 of Schedule 4C to the 1990 Act), a local planning authority must—

(a) publish on their website and in such other manner as they consider is likely to bring the order to the attention of people who live, work or carry on business in the neighbourhood area—

 (i) a document setting out their decision and their reasons for making that decision ('the decision document');

 (ii) details of where and when the decision document may be inspected;

(b) send a copy of the decision document to—

 (i) the qualifying body or the community organisation, as the case may be; and

 (ii) any person who asked to be notified of the decision.

27 Publicising a neighbourhood development order or a community right to build order

As soon as possible after making a neighbourhood development order or community right to build order under section 61E(4) of the 1990 Act, a local planning authority must—

(a) publish on their website and in such other manner as they consider is likely to bring the order to the attention of people who live, work or carry on business in the neighbourhood area—

 (i) the neighbourhood development order or community right to build order; and

 (ii) details of where and when the order may be inspected;

(b) notify any person who asked to be notified of the making of the neighbourhood development order or community right to build order that it has been made and where and when it may be inspected.

PART 7 COMMUNITY RIGHT TO BUILD ORDERS

28 Enfranchisement rights

(1) Subject to paragraph (2), for the purposes of paragraph 11 of Schedule 4C to the 1990 Act, a community organisation may only provide that an enfranchisement right is not exercisable in relation to a property which is not an existing residential property.

(2) An enfranchisement right is not exercisable in relation to land the development of which is authorised by a community right to build order if the community organisation specified in the order proposal—

(a) the enfranchisement rights which are not exercisable; and

(b) the properties, or types of properties, in relation to which those rights are not exercisable.

(3)   In this regulation—

'existing residential property' means a property (including part of a building)—

(a)   which exists on the date the order proposal was submitted by the community organisation to the local planning authority under regulation 22; and

(b)   in relation to which, on that date, any tenant of the property has an enfranchisement right in respect of the property.

29 Notice

(1)   Where as a result of the making of a community right to build order an enfranchisement right is not exercisable in respect of a property, a landlord who grants a tenancy in relation to the property must give notice to the tenant affected by endorsing a notice on the face of the tenancy stating that the enfranchisement right in question is not exercisable.

(2)   Provided the community organisation complies with regulation 28 a failure to give notice in accordance with paragraph (1) does not cause the enfranchisement right to be exercisable.

PART 8 REVOCATION AND MODIFICATION OF A NEIGHBOURHOOD DEVELOPMENT ORDER, A COMMUNITY RIGHT TO BUILD ORDER OR A NEIGHBOURHOOD DEVELOPMENT PLAN

30 Publicising a modification

As soon as possible after modifying a neighbourhood development plan, a neighbourhood development order or community right to build order under section 61M(4) of the 1990 Act (as applied in the case of neighbourhood development plans by section 38C of the 2004 Act), a local planning authority must—

(a)   publish on their website and in such other manner as they consider is likely to bring the order to the attention of people who live, work or carry on business in the neighbourhood area—

(i)   a document setting out details of the modification ('the modification document'); and

(ii)   details of where and when the modification document may be inspected; and

(b)   give notice of the modification to the following—

(i)   the qualifying body or community organisation, as the case may be; and

(ii)   any person the authority previously notified of the making of the order or plan.

31 Revocation

As soon as possible after revoking a neighbourhood development plan, neighbourhood development order or community right to build order in accordance with section

61M of the 1990 Act (as applied in the case of neighbourhood development plans by section 38C of the 2004 Act), a local planning authority must—

(a) publish on their website and in such other manner as they consider is likely to bring the order to the attention of people who live, work or carry on business in the neighbourhood area—

    (i) a document setting out a statement of the revocation and the reasons for it ('the revocation document'); and

    (ii) details of where and when the revocation document may be inspected;

(b) give notice of the revocation to—

    (i) the qualifying body or community organisation, as the case may be;

    (ii) in the case of the revocation of a neighbourhood development order or community right to build order, any person who the authority knows to be the owner or tenant of any part of the land to which the order applies and whose name and address is known to the local planning authority;

    (iii) any person the local planning authority notified of the making of the neighbourhood development order, community right to build order or neighbourhood development plan; and

    (iv) any other person the local planning authority consider necessary in order to bring the revocation to the attention of people who live, work or carry on business in the area to which the revoked neighbourhood development order, community right to build order or neighbourhood development plan related; and

(c) cease to make the revoked neighbourhood development order, community right to build order or neighbourhood development plan available on their website and at any other place where it was available for inspection.

[PART 8A INTERVENTION BY THE SECRETARY OF STATE

31A Requests to intervene and dealing with requests

(1) This regulation applies where a qualifying body requests the Secretary of State to intervene—

(a) in relation to an order proposal, under paragraph 13B of Schedule 4B to the 1990 Act; or

(b) in relation to a plan proposal, under that paragraph as applied by section 38A(3) of the 2004 Act.

(2) The request must be in writing and give reasons for the request.

(3) In a case where sub-paragraph (1)(b) or (c) of paragraph 13B of Schedule 4B to the 1990 Act applies, the request must be submitted to the Secretary of State by the date prescribed in paragraph (4).

(4) The date prescribed in this paragraph is the last day of the period of 6 weeks beginning with the day immediately following that on which the local planning

authority first publish their decision in accordance with regulation 18(2) (in the case of a plan proposal) or 25(2) (in the case of an order proposal).

(5)   The Secretary of State may appoint an inspector to make any decision falling to be made by the Secretary of State under paragraph 13B of Schedule 4B to the 1990 Act in relation to the proposal.

(6)   The Secretary of State or the inspector may direct the authority to refrain from taking any action that is specified in the direction that the authority would otherwise be required or entitled to take under paragraph 12 or 13 of that Schedule in relation to the proposal.][21]

[31B Information provided to the Secretary of State

Where a qualifying body makes a request in accordance with regulation 31A in relation to an order proposal or a plan proposal, the local planning authority must send to the Secretary of State or the inspector appointed under paragraph (5) of that regulation—

(a)   the report made by the examiner of the proposal under paragraph 10 of Schedule 4B to the 1990 Act;

(b)   in a case where sub-paragraph (1)(b) or (c) of paragraph 13B applies, the decision statement published in accordance with regulation 18(2) (in the case of a plan proposal) or 25(2) (in the case of an order proposal);

(c)   in the case of a plan proposal, each of the documents referred to in regulation 17;

(d)   in the case of an order proposal, each of the documents referred to in regulation 24;

(e)   any representations received by the authority in response to an invitation under paragraph 13(1) of Schedule 4B to the 1990 Act;

(f)   any other document held by the local planning authority that the authority consider to be relevant to the consideration of the request by the Secretary of State or the inspector; and

(g)   any other document held by the local planning authority that is requested by the Secretary of State or the inspector.][22]

[31C Notification where Secretary of State proposes to differ from examiner

The persons prescribed for the purposes of sub-paragraph (4)(a) of paragraph 13B of Schedule 4B to the 1990 Act are—

(a)   the qualifying body; and

(b)   in the case of a plan proposal,

(i)   any person whose representation was submitted to the examiner of the proposal in accordance with regulation 17(d); and

---

[21]   Inserted by the Neighbourhood Planning (General) and Development Management Procedure (Amendment) Regulations 2016, SI 2016/873, reg 2(1), (10).
[22]   Inserted by the Neighbourhood Planning (General) and Development Management Procedure (Amendment) Regulations 2016, SI 2016/873, reg 2(1), (10).

(ii)   any consultation body which is referred to in the consultation statement mentioned in regulation 15;

(c)   in the case of an order proposal,

(i)   any person whose representation was submitted to the examiner of the proposal in accordance with regulation 24(f); and

(ii)   any consultation body which is referred to in the consultation statement mentioned in regulation 22.][23]

[31D Publication of directions

(1)   This regulation applies where the Secretary of State or the inspector appointed under paragraph (5) of regulation 31A gives a direction under sub-paragraph (2) or (3) of paragraph 13B of Schedule 4B to the 1990 Act.

(2)   The direction must be accompanied by a statement setting out the reasons of the Secretary of State or the inspector for making the direction.

(3)   As soon as possible after receiving the direction, the local planning authority must—

(a)   publish—

(i)   the direction and the reasons; and

(ii)   the report made by the examiner under paragraph 10 of Schedule 4B to the 1990 Act (if that report has not been published in accordance with regulation 18(2)(c) (in the case of a plan proposal) or 25(2)(c) (in the case of an order proposal)),

on their website and in such other manner as they consider is likely to bring the direction and, as the case may be, the report to the attention of people who live, work or carry on business in the neighbourhood area; and

(b)   send a copy of the direction and reasons to the qualifying body.][24]

PART 9 EUROPEAN LEGISLATION

32 Habitats

The provisions of Schedule 2 have effect.

33 Environmental impact assessment

The provisions of Schedule 3 have effect.

---

[23]   Inserted by the Neighbourhood Planning (General) and Development Management Procedure (Amendment) Regulations 2016, SI 2016/873, reg 2(1), (10).

[24]   Inserted by the Neighbourhood Planning (General) and Development Management Procedure (Amendment) Regulations 2016, SI 2016/873, reg 2(1), (10).

SCHEDULE 1 CONSULTATION BODIES

1 Neighbourhood development plans

For the purposes of regulations 14 and 16, a 'consultation body' means—

(a) where the local planning authority is a London borough council, the Mayor of London;

(b) a local planning authority, county council or parish council any part of whose area is in or adjoins the area of the local planning authority;

(c) the Coal Authority;

(d) the Homes and Communities Agency;

(e) Natural England;

(f) the Environment Agency;

(g) the Historic Buildings and Monuments Commission for England (known as English Heritage);

(h) Network Rail Infrastructure Limited (company number 2904587);

[(i) a strategic highways company any part of whose area is in or adjoins the neighbourhood area;

(ia) where the Secretary of State is the highway authority for any road in the area of a local planning authority any part of whose area is in or adjoins the neighbourhood area, the Secretary of State for Transport;][25]

(j) the Marine Management Organisation;

(k) any person—

    (i) to whom the electronic communications code applies by virtue of a direction given under section 106(3)(a) of the Communications Act 2003; and

    (ii) who owns or controls electronic communications apparatus situated in any part of the area of the local planning authority;

(l) where it exercises functions in any part of the neighbourhood area—

    [(i) a clinical commissioning group established under section 14D of the National Health Service Act 2006;

    (ia) the National Health Service Commissioning Board;][26]

    (ii) a person to whom a licence has been granted under section 6(1)(b) and (c) of the Electricity Act 1989;

    (iii) a person to whom a licence has been granted under section 7(2) of the Gas Act 1986;

    (iv) a sewerage undertaker; and

    (v) a water undertaker;

(m) voluntary bodies some or all of whose activities benefit all or any part of the neighbourhood area;

---

[25] Substituted by the Infrastructure Act 2015 (Strategic Highways Companies) (Consequential, Transitional and Savings Provisions) Regulations 2015, SI 2015/377, reg 3, Schedule, para 53(1), (2).

[26] Substituted by the National Treatment Agency (Abolition) and the Health and Social Care Act 2012 (Consequential, Transitional and Saving Provisions) Order 2013, SI 2013/235, art 11, Sch 2, para 168.

   (n)   bodies which represent the interests of different racial, ethnic or national groups in the neighbourhood area;

   (o)   bodies which represent the interests of different religious groups in the neighbourhood area;

   (p)   bodies which represent the interests of persons carrying on business in the neighbourhood area; and

   (q)   bodies which represent the interests of disabled persons in the neighbourhood area.

2 Neighbourhood development orders and community right to build orders

(1)   For the purposes of regulations 21 and 23, a 'consultation body' means—

   (a)   any person referred to in paragraph 1(k) and (l);

   (b)   where the neighbourhood area to which the neighbourhood development order or community right to build order relates consists of or includes the whole or any part of the area of a parish council, that parish council;

   (c)   any parish council or, in the case of a neighbourhood development order (but not a community right to build order), a neighbourhood forum for an area which adjoins the neighbourhood area; and

   (d)   where the development to be authorised under the proposed neighbourhood development order or community right to build order falls within any category set out in the following Table, the person mentioned in the Table in relation to each of those categories.

Table

Paragraph	Development	Consultation body
(a)	Any development.	The Historic Buildings and Monument Commission for England (known as English Heritage)
(b)	Development which falls within a category specified in Schedule 5 to the Town and Country Planning (Development Management Procedure) (England) Order 2010.	The person mentioned in relation to that category of development in Schedule 5 to that Order
(c)	Development of land— (i) forming the site of or in the neighbourhood of a civil aerodrome or technical site; or (ii) involving the construction of any building or works extending 91.4 metres or more above ground level.	The Civil Aviation Authority and NATS Holdings Limited

Paragraph	Development	Consultation body
(d)	Development of land— (i) forming the site of or in the neighbourhood of a military aerodrome, technical site or explosives storage area; or (ii) involving the construction of any highway or formation, laying out or alteration of any means of access to a highway, which is planned to run within 300 metres of the perimeter of a military aerodrome.	Secretary of State for Defence
(e)	Development which, in the qualifying body's opinion, is likely to affect any garden or park of special historic interest which is registered in accordance with section 8C of the Historic Buildings and Ancient Monuments Act 1953.	The Garden History Society
(f)	Development in the area of a London borough council to which any of Protected Vista Directions issued by the Secretary of State for Communities and Local Government in July 2010 apply.	Mayor of London and, in relation to the protected vista of the Tower of London from outside City Hall on Queen's Walk, the Historic Royal Palaces Trust
[(g)	Development which consists of or includes the construction , formation or laying out of access to or from a trunk road.	The highway authority for the trunk road.][27]

(2)   In the above Table—

    (a)   in paragraphs (c) and (d) 'aerodrome' means any area of land or water designed, equipped, set apart, commonly used or in prospective use for affording facilities for the landing and departure of aircraft and includes any area of space, whether on the ground, on the roof of a building or elsewhere, which is designed, equipped or set apart for affording facilities for the landing or departure of aircraft capable of descending or climbing vertically, particulars of which have been furnished by the Civil Aviation Authority or the Secretary of State to the local planning authority or authorities for the area in which it is situated;

    (b)   in paragraph (c) 'technical site' means any area within which is sited or is proposed to be sited equipment operated by or on behalf of

---

[27] Substituted by the Infrastructure Act 2015 (Strategic Highways Companies) (Consequential, Transitional and Savings Provisions) Regulations 2015, SI 2015/377, reg 3, Schedule, para 53(1), (3).

NATS Holdings Limited, any of its subsidiaries or such other person who holds a licence under Chapter 1 of Part 1 of the Transport Act 2000(10) for the provision of air traffic services, particulars of which have been furnished by the Civil Aviation Authority to the planning authority or authorities for the area in which it is situated;

(c)   in paragraph (d) 'technical site' means any area within which is sited or is proposed to be sited equipment operated by or on behalf of the Secretary of State for Defence for the provision of air traffic services, particulars of which have been furnished by the Secretary of State for Defence to the planning authority or authorities for the area in which it is situated; and

(d)   in paragraph (g) 'trunk road' and 'special road' have the meanings given in section 329 of the Highways Act 1980.

SCHEDULE 2 HABITATS

Neighbourhood development plans

1 In relation to the examination of neighbourhood development plans the following basic condition is prescribed for the purpose of paragraph 8(2)(g) of Schedule 4B to the 1990 Act—

The making of the neighbourhood development plan is not likely to have a significant effect on a European site (as defined in [the Conservation of Habitats and Species Regulations 2017][28]) or a European offshore marine site (as defined in [the Conservation of Offshore Marine Habitats and Species Regulations 2017][29]) (either alone or in combination with other plans or projects).

SCHEDULE 3 ENVIRONMENTAL IMPACT ASSESSMENTS

1 In this Schedule—

'EIA development' means development which satisfies the definition of 'Schedule 2 development' in regulation 2(1) of the EIA Regulations; and

'environmental information' has the meaning given in regulation 2(1) of the EIA Regulations.

2 Where the development described in an order proposal is EIA development, the following basic condition is prescribed for the purpose of paragraph 8(2)(g) of Schedule 4B to the 1990 Act—

Having regard to all material considerations, it is appropriate that the neighbourhood development order is made.

---

[28]   Substituted by the Conservation of Habitats and Species Regulations 2017, SI 2017/1012, reg 139, Sch 6, para 27(1), (4)(i).
[29]   Substituted by the Conservation of Offshore Marine Habitats and Species Regulations 2017, SI 2017/1013, reg 84, Sch 4, para 12.

Town and Country Planning (Brownfield Land Register) Regulations 2017, SI 2017/403

1 Citation and commencement

These Regulations may be cited as the Town and Country Planning (Brownfield Land Register) Regulations 2017 and come into force on 16th April 2017.

2 Interpretation

In these Regulations—

'the TCPA 1990' means the Town and Country Planning Act 1990;

'development' has the meaning given by section 55 of the TCPA 1990;

'dwelling' includes a flat contained within a building of one or more flats;

'entry date' in relation to any land, means the date on which land is entered in Part 1 of the register;

'flat' means a separate and self-contained set of premises constructed or adapted for use for the purpose of a dwelling and forming part of a building from some other part of which it is divided horizontally;

'hazardous substances' has the meaning given by regulation 3 of the Planning (Hazardous Substances) Regulations 2015;

'housing development' means development for the provision of dwellings;

'infrastructure manager' in relation to relevant railway land means any person who—

    (a)   is responsible for developing or maintaining the land; or

    (b)   manages or uses the land, or permits the land to be used for the operation of a railway;

'maximum net number of dwellings' means the maximum number of dwellings on the land after the proposed development less the number of dwellings on the land immediately prior to the entry of the land on Part 1 or Part 2 of the register, as the case may be;

'minimum net number of dwellings' means the minimum number of dwellings on the land after the proposed development less the number of dwellings on the land immediately prior to the entry of the land on Part 1 or Part 2 of the register, as the case may be;

'neighbourhood forum' means an organisation or body designated by a local planning authority under section 61F of the 1990 Act;

'non-housing development' means development other than housing development;

'operational railway' means a railway which is in use;

'permission in principle' has the same meaning as in section 58A of the TCPA 1990;

'planning permission' means permission under Part 3 of the TCPA 1990 but does not include permission in principle;

'previously developed land' has the same meaning as land of that description in the National Planning Policy Framework issued by the Department for Communities and Local Government, as it has effect from time to time;

'register' means a brownfield land register kept under regulation 3;

'relevant railway land' means land—

    (a)   forming part of any operational railway; or

    (b)   which is authorised to be used for the purposes of an operational railway under—

        (i)   a planning permission granted or deemed to be granted,

        (ii)   a development consent granted by an order made under the Planning Act 2008, or

        (iii)   an Act of Parliament,

including viaducts, tunnels, retaining walls, sidings, shafts, bridges, or other structures used in connection with an operational railway and excluding car parks, offices, shops, hotels or any other land which, by its nature or situation, is comparable with land in general rather than land which is used for the purpose of an operational railway;

'requisite notice' means notice in the form set out in Schedule 1 to these Regulations or in a form substantially to the same effect; and

'residential development' means development the main purpose of which is housing development.

3 Requirement to keep a register

(1)   Each local planning authority must prepare and maintain a register of previously developed land which—

    (a)   is within their area, and

    (b)   meets the criteria in paragraph (1) of regulation 4.

(2)   Each local planning authority must publish their register by 31st December 2017.

(3)   The register to be prepared, maintained and published by each local planning authority in accordance with this regulation is to be known as that local planning authority's 'Brownfield Land Register'.

(4)   The register must be kept in 2 parts.

(5)   In these Regulations, a reference to 'Part 1' or 'Part 2' is a reference to Part 1 or Part 2 of the register.

4 Criteria

(1)   The criteria referred to in paragraph (1)(b) of regulation 3 are, in relation to each parcel of land—

   (a)   the land has an area of at least 0.25 hectares or is capable of supporting at least 5 dwellings;

   (b)   the land is suitable for residential development;

   (c)   the land is available for residential development; and

   (d)   residential development of the land is achievable.

(2)   In this regulation—

   'achievable' in relation to residential development of any land means that, in the opinion of the local planning authority, the development is likely to take place within 15 years of the entry date, having regard to—

      (a)   any information publicly available; and

      (b)   any relevant representations received;

   'available for residential development' in relation to any land means—

      (a)   the relevant owner (or, where there is more than one, all the relevant owners), has expressed an intention to sell or develop the land and at a date not more than 21 days before the entry date there is no evidence indicating a change to that intention, having regard to—

         (i)   any information publicly available on that date; and

         (ii)   any relevant representations received;

      (b)   the developer has expressed an intention to develop the land and at a date not more than 21 days before the entry date there is no evidence indicating a change to that intention, having regard to—

         (i)   any information publicly available on that date; and

         (ii)   any relevant representations received; or

      (c)   in the opinion of the local authority there are no issues relating to the ownership of the land or other legal impediments which might prevent residential development of the land taking place, having regard to—

         (i)   any information publicly available on that date; and

         (ii)   any relevant representations received;

   'the developer' means the developer in control of the land on the prescribed date;

   'heritage asset' means a building, monument, site, place, area or landscape which has been identified by the local planning authority as having heritage interest or is—

      (a)   a property appearing on the World Heritage List kept under article 11(2) of the UNESCO Convention for the Protection of the World Cultural and National Heritage adopted at Paris on 16th November 1972;

(b)   included in the schedule of monuments compiled by the Secretary of State under section 1 of the Ancient Monuments and Archaeological Areas Act 1979 (schedule of monuments);

(c)   a listed building within the meaning of section 1 of the Planning (Listed Buildings and Conservation Areas) Act 1990 (listing of buildings of special architectural or historic interest);

(d)   a garden or other land included in a register compiled by the Historic Buildings and Monuments Commission for England under section 8C of the Historic Buildings and Ancient Monuments Act 1953; or

(e)   an area designated as a conservation area under section 69 of the Planning (Listed Buildings and Conservation Areas) Act 1990 (designation of conservation areas);

'owner' in relation to any land means any person who—

(a)   is the estate owner in fee simple; or

(b)   is entitled to a tenancy granted or extended for a term of years certain of which not less than 15 years remain unexpired;

'the prescribed date' is the day 42 days before the entry date for the land;

'the relevant owner' means in relation to any land, the owner of the land on the prescribed date;

'relevant representations' in relation to the definition of 'achievable', paragraphs (a), (b) and (c) of the definition of 'available for residential development', and paragraph (d) of the definition of 'suitable for residential development', means—

(a)   as regards land to be entered in Part 1, any representations which are—

    (i)   relevant to the definition or paragraph of the definition in question; and

    (ii)   received by the local planning authority—

        (aa)   as a result of any procedures carried out in accordance with paragraph (6)(a) of regulation 5,

        (bb)   before the end of the relevant period specified in accordance with paragraph (6)(b) of regulation 5;

(b)   as regards land to be entered in Part 2, any representations which are—

    (i)   relevant to the definition or paragraph of the definition in question; and

    (ii)   received by the local planning authority—

        (aa)   as a result of any of the procedures carried out in accordance with paragraph (7) of regulation 5,

        (bb)   by the date, or before the end of the relevant period, specified in accordance with regulation 9 or 13, as the case may be; and 'suitable for residential development' in relation to any land means that the land at the entry date—

    (a)   has been allocated in a local development plan document for residential development;

    (b)   has planning permission for residential development;

    (c)   has a grant of permission in principle for residential development; or

    (d)   is, in the opinion of the local planning authority, appropriate for residential development, having regard to—

        (i)   any adverse impact on—

            (aa)   the natural environment;

            (bb)   the local built environment, including in particular on heritage assets;

        (ii)   any adverse impact on the local amenity which such development might cause for intended occupiers of the development or for occupiers of neighbouring properties; and

        (iii)   any relevant representations received.

5 Entry of land in the register

(1)   The local planning authority must enter land in Part 1 where the land falls within the description in paragraph (1)(a) of regulation 3 and meets the criteria in paragraph (1) of regulation 4.

(2)   The local planning authority must also enter land in Part 2 where—

    (a)   the land falls within the description in paragraph (1)(a) of regulation 3,

    (b)   the land meets the criteria in paragraph (1) of regulation 4, and

    (c)   the authority have decided to allocate the land for residential development, having followed the procedures mentioned in paragraph (7).

(3)   The local planning authority may enter land in Part 1 where the land falls within the description in paragraph (1)(a) of regulation 3 and meets the criteria in paragraphs (1)(b) to (d) of regulation 4, but does not meet the criterion in paragraph (1)(a) of regulation 4 (area of site or quantity of development).

(4)   The local planning authority must also enter land in Part 2 where—

    (a)   they have exercised their discretion to enter land in Part 1 in accordance with paragraph (3), and

    (b)   they have decided to allocate the land for residential development, having followed the procedures mentioned in paragraph (7).

(5)   Paragraphs (2) and (4) are subject to regulation 14 (exemptions).

(6)   Before the local planning authority enter land in Part 1 they—

    (a)   may carry out procedures (including consultation) as they see fit; and

    (b)   must take into account any representations received, within such period as the local authority may specify, when carrying out such procedures.

(7)   Before the local planning authority enter land in Part 2, they must follow the applicable procedures in regulations 6 to 9 (publicity and notification) and 10 to 13 (consultation).

6 Publicity of proposal to enter land in Part 2

(1)   A local planning authority must publicise their proposal to enter land in Part 2 by giving requisite notice in at least one place on or near the land for not less than 21 days.

(2)   The requisite notice must be given by posting it by firm fixture to some object and the notice must be sited and displayed in such a way as to be easily visible to and legible by members of the public.

(3)   Where the notice is, without any fault or intention of the local planning authority, removed, obscured or defaced before the period of 21 days referred to in paragraph (1) has elapsed, the authority are to be treated as having complied with the requirement if they have taken reasonable steps for protection of the notice, and, if need be, its replacement.

(4)   The following information must be published on a website maintained by the local planning authority—

(a)   the statement 'If the land is entered in Part 2 of the Brownfield Land Register it will be granted permission in principle, which establishes the suitability, in principle, of land for housing-led development' or a statement to substantially the same effect;

(b)   the information required by paragraphs 1(1)(a), (b), (c), (f), (k), (l), (m)(ii) and (o) of Schedule 2;

(c)   the information required under regulation 26 of the Planning (Hazardous Substances) Regulations 2015 (planning approvals for projects related to hazardous substances) where—

(i)   development of the land would, in the opinion of the local planning authority, be a relevant project for the purpose of that regulation, and

(ii)   the local planning authority are the competent authority for the purpose of that regulation;

(d)   the date by which any representations about the proposed entry of the land in Part 2 must be made, which must not be before the last day of the period of 14 days beginning with the date on which the information is published;

(e)   where and when the information specified in sub-paragraphs (b) and (c) of this paragraph may be inspected; and

(f)   how representations may be made about the proposed entry of the land in Part 2.

7 Land within 10 metres of relevant railway land

(1)   Where the land is situated within 10 metres of relevant railway land, the local planning authority must, except where paragraph (2) applies, publicise their proposal to enter it in Part 2 by serving requisite notice on any infrastructure manager of relevant railway land.

(2)   Where an infrastructure manager has instructed the local planning authority in writing that they do not require notification in relation to any land or geographical areas specified in the instruction, the local planning authority are not required to notify that infrastructure manager.

(3)   The infrastructure manager may withdraw the instruction at any time by notifying the local planning authority in writing.

8 Notification for parish councils and neighbourhood forums of proposal to enter land in Part 2

Where the council of any parish, or a neighbourhood forum, ('the relevant body') in the area of the local planning authority have—

(a)   requested the authority to notify it of a proposed entry of land in Part 2, and

(b)   the land to which the proposed entry relates is within the area of the relevant body,

the local planning authority must notify the relevant body of the proposed entry by serving requisite notice on it.

9 Time periods for representations to be made following publicity or notification

(1)   A local planning authority must, in considering whether to enter land in Part 2, take into account any representations made within the period specified, or the date specified, in paragraphs (2) to (4) as the case may be.

(2)   Where any notice about the proposed entry of land in Part 2 has been given by site display under paragraph (1) of regulation 6, the period specified is 21 days beginning with the date when the notice was first displayed.

(3)   Where any information about the proposed entry of land in Part 2 has been published on a website under paragraph (4) of regulation 6, the date specified is the date given in accordance with paragraph (4)(d) of that regulation.

(4)   Where any notice about the proposed entry of land in Part 2 has been served on an infrastructure manager under paragraph (1) of regulation 7, or on the council of a parish or on a neighbourhood forum under regulation 8, the period specified is—

(a)   42 days beginning with the date when the notice was served on that person or body, where first publication of Part 2, (in accordance with paragraph (2) of regulation 3), has not yet taken place, or

(b)   21 days beginning with the date when the notice was served on that person or body, where first publication of Part 2, (in accordance with paragraph (2) of regulation 3), has taken place.

10 Consultation with county planning authorities before entering land in Part 2

(1)   The local planning authority must consult the county planning authority where—

(a)   they propose to enter land in Part 2;

(b)   there is a county planning authority for the area within which the land is situated; and

(c)   residential development of the land would, in the opinion of the local planning authority, fall within sub-paragraph (4) of paragraph 7 of Schedule 1 to the TCPA 1990 (consultation by a district planning authority with the county planning authority for their area in certain circumstances).

(2)   Paragraph (1) does not apply where—

(a)   the local planning authority is the county planning authority for the area, or

(b)   the county planning authority has advised the local planning authority that they do not wish to be consulted about proposed entries in Part 2 of land situated within a particular area, and the land in question falls within that area.

(3)   In this regulation 'county planning authority' has the same meaning as in section 1 of the TCPA 1990.

11 Consultation with the Mayor of London before entering land in Part 2

(1)   Where the council of a London borough ('the local planning authority') propose to enter land in Part 2 and residential development of the land would, in their opinion, fall within the Schedule to the Town and Country Planning (Mayor of London) Order 2008 (potential strategic importance applications and categories of development), the local planning authority must consult the Mayor of London.

(2)   Paragraph (1) does not apply where—

(a)   the Mayor has advised the local planning authority that the Mayor does not wish to be consulted about proposed entries in Part 2 of land situated within a particular area, and the land in question falls within that area, or

(b)   the land falls within article 3 of that Order (land excluded from the application of section 2A of the TCPA 1990).

12 Consultation with other persons, bodies or authorities before entering land in Part 2

(1)   Where a local planning authority propose to enter land in Part 2 and residential development of the land would, in the opinion of the local planning authority, fall within a category set out in the Table in Schedule 4 to the Town and Country Planning (Development Management Procedure) (England) Order 2015, the local planning authority must consult any person, body or authority mentioned in relation to that category.

(2)   The local planning authority must also consult any person, body or authority with whom they would have been required to consult in relation to an application for planning permission for residential development of the land.

(3)   The duty to consult a particular person, body or authority in accordance with paragraph (1) or (2) does not apply where—

(a)   that authority is the local planning authority;

(b)   that person, body or authority has advised the local planning authority that they do not wish to be consulted about proposed entries in Part 2 situated within a particular area, and the land in question falls within that area; or

(c)   that person, body or authority has published standing advice in relation to a category of development and the potential development falls within that category.

(4)   The exception in paragraph (3)(c) does not apply where the standing advice was published before the period of 2 years ending with the date that requisite notice in relation to that land was given in accordance with paragraph (1) of regulation 6.

13 Time periods for representations to be made by consultees

(1)   Where a local planning authority is required to consult any person, body or authority ('consultee') before entering land in Part 2—

(a)   the local planning authority must give notice to the consultee; and

(b)   subject to paragraph (2), the local planning authority must not enter the land in Part 2—

(i)   until at least 42 days after the date on which notice is given under sub-paragraph (a) where first publication of Part 2, (in accordance with paragraph (2) of regulation 3), has not yet taken place; or

(ii)   until at least 21 days after the date on which notice is given under sub-paragraph (a) where first publication of Part 2, (in accordance with paragraph (2) of regulation 3), has taken place.

(2)   Paragraph (1)(b) does not apply if before the end of the relevant period referred to in that paragraph the local planning authority have received from all consultees—

(a)   representations concerning the proposed entry of land in Part 2, or

(b)   notice that they do not intend to make representations.

(3)   In considering whether to enter land in Part 2, the local planning authority must take into account any representations received from any consultee before the end of the relevant period referred to in paragraph (1)(b).

14 Exemptions for certain types of land

(1)   A local planning authority must not enter land in Part 2, where residential development of that land could be Schedule 1 development.

(2)   A local planning authority must not enter land in Part 2, where residential development of that land could be Schedule 2 development, unless—

(a)   the local planning authority—

(i)   have the information listed in paragraphs (2)(a) and (b) of regulation 5 of the EIA Regulations 2011,

(ii)   have specified the maximum net number of dwellings which in their opinion the land is capable of supporting,

(iii)   are of the view that the information and specified number referred to in paragraphs (i) and (ii) respectively, together with any such other information they may have about residential development of the land, are sufficient for them to adopt a screening opinion under regulation 5 of the EIA Regulations 2011, and

    (iv)   adopt a screening opinion under regulation 5 of the EIA Regulations 2011 that potential residential development up to and including the number of dwellings referred to in paragraph (ii) will not be EIA development;

(b)   the Secretary of State has made a screening direction under paragraph (3) of regulation 4 or paragraph (4) of regulation 6 of the EIA Regulations 2011 that the development is not EIA development; or

(c)   the Secretary of State has made a direction under paragraph (4) of regulation 4 of the EIA Regulations 2011 that the development is exempted from the application of those Regulations.

(3)   For the purposes of paragraph (2)(a), regulation 5 (requests for screening opinions of the local planning authority) of the EIA Regulations 2011 applies with the following modifications—

(a)   as if a person had requested the local planning authority to adopt a screening opinion and had provided them with the information referred to in paragraph (2) of that regulation;

(b)   as if the potential residential development of the land, for the maximum net number of dwellings, were an application for planning permission;

(c)   paragraph (5) were omitted and replaced by—

'(5)   An authority may adopt a screening opinion.'

; and

(d)   paragraphs (3) to (4) and (6) to (8) were omitted.

(4)   A local planning authority must not enter land in Part 2 where residential development of that land could be habitats development, unless—

(a)   they have specified the maximum net number of dwellings which in their opinion the land is capable of supporting; and

(b)   they are satisfied that development up to and including that number would not be habitats development.

(5)   In this regulation—

'EIA development' has the same meaning as in paragraph (1) of regulation 2 of the EIA Regulations 2011;

'the EIA Regulations 2011' means the Town and Country Planning (Environmental Impact Assessment) Regulations 2011;

'habitats development' means development which—

(a)   is likely to have a significant effect on a qualifying European site (either alone or in combination with other plans or projects), and

(b)   is not directly connected with or necessary to the management of the site;

'qualifying European site' means—

637

(a) a European offshore marine site within the meaning of [regulation 18 of the Conservation of Offshore Marine Habitats and Species Regulations 2017][1]; or

(b) a European site within the meaning of regulation 8 of [the Conservation of Habitats and Species Regulations 2017][2]; and

'Schedule 1 development' and 'Schedule 2 development' have the same meaning as in paragraph (1) of regulation 2 of the EIA Regulations 2011.

15 Information to be included in the register

The register must contain the information specified in Schedule 2.

16 Public inspection of the register

(1) The register must be kept available for public inspection at the principal office of the local planning authority.

(2) Where the register kept by a local planning authority under this regulation is kept using electronic storage, the authority may make the register available for inspection by the public on a website maintained by the authority for that purpose.

17 Revision of the register

(1) The local planning authority must review the entries in the register at least once within each register year in accordance with this regulation.

(2) Where the local authority has entered land in the register in accordance with paragraph (1) or (2) of regulation 5 and the land no longer meets the criteria in paragraph (1) of regulation 4, the local planning authority must remove the entry from Part 1, and if applicable Part 2.

(3) Where the local planning authority has entered land in the register in accordance with paragraph (3) or (4) of regulation 5 and the land no longer meets the criteria in paragraphs (1)(b) to (d) of regulation 4, they must remove the entry from Part 1, and if applicable Part 2.

(4) Subject to paragraphs (5) and (6), the local planning authority must update, as necessary, the information required under Schedule 2 in relation to each entry of land in the register.

(5) The local planning authority must not update the information required under paragraph 2 of Schedule 2 in relation to an entry of land in Part 2.

(6) Where—

(a) the local planning authority consider that the information required under paragraph 1(1)(m), (1)(n) or (1)(o) of Schedule 2 in relation to an entry of land in Part 1 should be updated,

(b) there is an entry in Part 2 in relation to that land, and

(c) development of that land has been granted permission in principle by a development order made under section 59A(1)(a) of the TCPA 1990 based on that entry,

---

[1] Substituted by the Conservation of Offshore Marine Habitats and Species Regulations 2017, SI 2017/1013, reg 84, Sch 4, para 19.

[2] Substituted by the Conservation of Habitats and Species Regulations 2017, SI 2017/1012, reg 139, Sch 6, para 75.

the local planning authority must—

    (i)   remove the entry of land from Part 2; and

    (ii)   amend the information in Part 1.

(7)   Before the local planning authority remove entries of land from Parts 1 and 2 under paragraphs (2) or (3), or amend information in Part 1 under paragraph (6) (ii) they—

    (a)   may carry out such procedures (including consultation) as they see fit; and

    (b)   must take into account any representations received, within such period as they may specify, as a result of such procedures.

(8)   Where development of land was granted permission in principle by a development order made under section 59A(1)(a) of the TCPA 1990, and that grant has expired, the local planning authority must remove the relevant entry of land from Part 2.

(9)   The local planning authority must consider in accordance with paragraphs (2) and (3), the criteria mentioned in regulation 4, as if—

    (a)   for 'entry date' in each place that it occurs in the definitions of 'achievable' and 'available for residential development', there were substituted 'review date'; and

    (b)   for the definition of 'relevant representations', there were substituted—

    '"relevant representations" in relation to the definition of 'achievable', paragraphs (a), (b) and (c) of the definition of 'available for residential development', and paragraph (d) of the definition of 'suitable for residential development', means any representations which are—

        (a)   relevant to the definition or paragraph of the definition in question; and

        (b)   received by the local planning authority—

            (i)   as a result of any procedures carried out by the local planning authority in accordance with paragraph (7)(a) of regulation 17;

            (ii)   before the end of the relevant period specified in accordance with paragraph (7)(b) of regulation 17;'.

(10)   In this regulation—

'register year' means—

    (a)   for the first year, the year beginning on the date on which that part of the register is published for the first time;

    (b)   for subsequent years, the year beginning with the anniversary of the date on which that part of the register was published for the first time; and

'review date' in relation to an entry of land in the register means the date on which that entry of land is reviewed under paragraph (1).

18 Information to be given to the Secretary of State

(1)   The Secretary of State may require a local planning authority to bring the register up to date by such date as the Secretary of State may specify.

(2)   The Secretary of State may require a local planning authority to provide the Secretary of State with such information in relation to the register, in such form and by such date, as the Secretary of State may specify.

19 Consequential amendment to the Functions and Responsibilities Regulations 2000

(1)   The Local Authorities (Functions and Responsibilities) Regulations 2000 are amended in accordance with paragraph (2).

(2)   In Schedule 1 (functions not to be the responsibility of an authority's executive), in column (1) (function), in Part A (functions relating to town and country planning and development control), below the entry numbered '31'insert '32. Duty to enter land in Part 2 of the brownfield land register.' and at the corresponding place in column (2) (provision of act or statutory instrument) insert 'Regulation 3 of the Town and Country Planning (Brownfield Land Register) Regulations 2017.'.

SCHEDULE 1 PUBLICITY OF INTENTION TO ENTER LAND IN PART 2 OF THR REGISTER

Town and Country Planning (Brownfield Land Register) Regulations 2017

NOTICE UNDER REGULATION 6(1), 7(1) OR 8(1) OF PROPOSAL TO ENTER LAND IN PART 2 OF THE BROWNFIELD LAND REGISTER AND FOR IT TO BE GRANTED PERMISSION IN PRINCIPLE

(to be displayed by site display on or near the site, or served on infrastructure managers, parish councils or neighbourhood forums)

Land at (a) ………..…… Council gives notice that they propse to include this land in Part 2 of their Brownfield Land Register as land allocated for residential development. If the land is included in Part 2 of that register, it will be granted permission in principle, which establishes the suitability in principle for housing-led development of the land. The net number of dwellings which the Council considers the land is capable of supporting is between ………………………...…….....… (c) and ……………....……………… (d) together with non-housing development of …………………………………………………………. (e)

The land is situated withing 10 metres of relevant railway land*

Members of the public may inspect copies of the proposed entry in the register and associated information at (f) …………………………………………………; during all reasonable hours until (g) ………………………………………………………………

Anyone who wishes to make representations about the proposed entry should write to the council at (h) ……………………………………………………………… ; or (i) …………………………………………………………………………… by (g) ………………………………………………………………………………

Signed …………………………………………… (Council's authorised officer)

On behalf of ……………………………………………………………… Council

Date …………………………………………………………………………

Insert:

(a) address or location of the land

(b) name of the Council

(c) minimum net number of dwellings which the Council considers the land is capable of supporting

(d) maximum net number of dwellings which the Council considers the land is capable of supporting

(e) description of any proposed non-housing development

(f) address at which the proposed entry may be inspected

(g) date giving:

    (i) in the case of a site notice, a period of 21 days, beginning with the date when the notice is first displayed where visible or accessible on or near the site;

    (ii) where the notice is served on an infrastructure manager, parish council or neighbourhood forum and first publication of Part 2 of the register has not yet taken place, a period of 42 days beginning with the date of service of the notice; or

    (iii) where the notice is served on an infrastructure manager, parish council or neighbourhood forum and first publication of Part 2 of the register has taken place, a period of 21 days beginning with the date of service of the notice;

(h) address of the Council

(i) email address of the Council

SCHEDULE 2 INFORMATION TO BE INCLUDED IN THE REGISTER

1 (1)   The register must contain the following information in relation to each entry of land in Part 1—

(a) the local authority's own reference for the land;

(b) the name and address of the land;

(c) a plan which identifies the land;

(d) location co-ordinates to identify a point on the land expressed as an east/west component and a north/south component;

(e) the co-ordinate reference system used for paragraph (d);

(f) the area of the land in hectares;

(g) the name of the local authority;

(h) the uniform resource identifier 'URI' of the local authority expressed in the form http://opendatacommunities.org/id/ followed by the relevant type of authority and name of the local authority;

(i) the ownership status of the land expressed as—

        (i)   where the ownership is known to the local planning authority—

             (aa)   'owned by a public authority',

             (bb)   'not owned by a public authority', or

             (cc)   'mixed ownership';

        (ii)   'unknown ownership' where the ownership is unknown or partly unknown to the local planning authority;

(j)   where the land is 'deliverable' a note to that effect;

(k)   the planning status of the land, expressed as—

        (i)   'permissioned',

        (ii)   'not permissioned', or

        (iii)   'pending decision';

(l)   where the planning status is 'permissioned'—

        (i)   the date that such permission was granted or deemed to have been granted; and

        (ii)   whether the grant of permission is—

             (aa)   'full planning permission',

             (bb)   'outline planning permission',

             (cc)   'reserved matters approval',

             (dd)   'permission in principle',

             (ee)   'technical details consent',

             (ff)   'planning permission granted under a local development order, a mayoral development order or a neighbourhood development order', or

             (gg)   'other';

(m)

        (i)   a description of any proposed housing development; or

        (ii)   the minimum and maximum net number of dwellings, given as a range, which, in the authority's opinion, the land is capable of supporting;

(n)   the minimum net number of dwellings which, in the authority's opinion, the land is capable of supporting;

(o)   where the development includes non-housing development, the scale of any such development and the use to which it is to be put;

(p)   the date that the land was first entered in the register; and

(q)   where applicable, the date that information about the land was last updated in the register.

(2)   Where—

(a)   land has been entered in Part 1,

(b)   first publication of Part 1, (in accordance with paragraph (2) of regulation 3), has taken place, and

(c)   the local planning authority have given requisite notice in accordance with paragraph (1) of regulation 6 of their intention to enter that land in Part 2,

the local planning authority must, within the period of 7 days beginning with the date on which the notice was first displayed, record in Part 1 in relation to that land the statement 'proposed for residential development (permission in principle)'.

2 In relation to each entry of land in Part 2, the register must contain—

(a)   the minimum net number of dwellings, and the maximum net number of dwellings, given as a range, which, in the authority's opinion, the land is capable of supporting; and

(b)   where the development includes non-housing development, the scale of any such development and the use to which it is to be put.

3 In relation to each entry of land in Part 2, the register must contain the information required by paragraph (3) of regulation 26 of the Planning (Hazardous Substances) Regulations 2015 where—

(a)   development of that land would, in the opinion of the local planning authority, be a relevant project for the purpose of that regulation; and

(b)   the local planning authority is the competent authority for the purpose of that regulation.

4 Where land is entered in Part 2, Part 2 of the register must, in relation to that land, contain the statement 'allocated for residential development for the purposes of section 59A of the Town and Country Planning Act 1990 (permission in principle)' and the statement in Part 1, required by paragraph 1(2), if any, must be removed.

5 (1)   In this Schedule—

'co-ordinate reference system' is—

(a)   the world geodetic system (WGS84), expressed as longitude and latitude;

(b)   the ordinance survey national grid reference system (OSGB36), expressed as easting and northing; or

(c)   the European terrestrial reference system 1989 (ETRS89), expressed as longitude and latitude;

'deliverable' means that there is a reasonable prospect that residential development will take place on the land within 5 years beginning with the entry date;

'development' in relation to an unused grant of planning permission, has the meaning given by section 336 of the TCPA 1990;

'full planning permission' means a planning permission, other than a grant of technical details consent, granted by the local planning authority under section 70, 73 or 73A of the TCPA 1990;

'mixed ownership' in relation to land means that the land is partly owned by a public authority;

'other', in relation to land the planning status of which is 'permissioned', means that the land has a grant or deemed grant of planning permission which does not fall within the definitions of the terms mentioned in paragraph 1(1)(l)(ii)(aa) to (ff);

'outline planning permission' means a planning permission for the erection of a building subject to a condition requiring reserved matters approval granted by the local planning authority under section 92 of the TCPA 1990;

'owner' in relation to the ownership status of land has the same meaning as in paragraph (2) of regulation 4;

'pending decision' means that an application for planning permission or permission in principle has been made or is deemed to have been made and has not been finally disposed of;

'permissioned' means that in respect of the land, there is a grant of permission in principle or an unused grant, or unused deemed grant, of planning permission and 'not permissioned' is to be construed accordingly;

'planning permission granted under a local development order, mayoral development order or a neighbourhood development order' means permission granted under an order made under section 61A, 61DA or 61E of the TCPA 1990;

'public authority' in relation to the ownership status of the land means that the land is held by or on behalf of a public authority mentioned in Part 1 of Schedule 19 to the Equality Act 2010;

'reserved matters approval' in relation to an outline planning permission means approval given under section 92 of the TCPA 1990 for any of the following matters in respect of which details have not been given in the application—

    (a)   access;

    (b)   appearance;

    (c)   landscaping;

    (d)   layout; and

    (e)   scale;

'technical details consent' means planning permission granted following an application under section 70(2ZZB) of the TCPA 1990;

'type of authority' means a district council, a London borough council, a metropolitan district council, a county council, the Broads Authority, a National Park authority, a Mayoral development corporation or the Homes and Community Agency; and

'unused', in relation to land, means that development of the land has not been initiated in accordance with section 56 of the TCPA 1990.

(2) For the purposes of the definition in sub-paragraph (1)—

(a)   of the terms mentioned in paragraph 1(l)(l)(ii)(aa) to (ee), such permission, consent or approval may also have been granted or given—

    (i)   by the Secretary of State following an application made to the Secretary of State under section 62A of the TCPA 1990,

    (ii)   by the Secretary of State following the referral of an application under section 77 of that Act,

    (iii)   by the Secretary of State in deciding an appeal under section 78 of that Act, or

    (iv)   by the Secretary of State in deciding an enforcement appeal under section 177(5) of that Act,

as the case may be;

(b)   of 'pending decision', an application has not been finally disposed of unless and until—

    (i)   it has been decided by the authority (or any time prescribed under section 74(1)(d) of the TCPA 1990 for dealing with the application has expired without their giving a decision) and any time prescribed under section 78(3) of the TCPA 1990 has expired without any appeal having been made to the Secretary of State;

    (ii)   if it has been referred to the Secretary of State under section 77 of the TCPA 1990 or an appeal has been made to the Secretary of State under section 78 of the TCPA 1990, the Secretary of State has issued a decision and the period of 6 weeks specified in section 288 of the TCPA 1990 has expired without any application having been made to the High Court under that section;

    (iii)   if an application has been made to the High Court under section 288 of the TCPA 1990, the matter has been finally determined, either by final dismissal of the application by a court or by the quashing of the Secretary of State's decision and the issue of a fresh decision (without a further application under section 288); or

    (iv)   it has been withdrawn before being decided by the authority or the Secretary of State, as the case may be, or an appeal has been withdrawn before the Secretary of State has issued a decision; and

(c)   of 'reserved matters approval', 'layout' and 'scale' have the same meanings as in paragraph (1) of article 2 of the Town and Country Planning (Development Management Procedure) (England) Order 2015.

Conservation of Habitats and Species Regulations 2017, SI 2017/1012

PART 6 ASSESSMENT OF PLANS AND PROJECTS

Chapter 1 General provisions

Introductory provisions

61 Interpretation of Part 6

(1) In this Part—

'the assessment provisions' means regulations 63 and 64;

'the review provisions' means regulations 65 and 66.

(2) In this Part, any reference to—

(a) the giving or granting of any consent, permission or other authorisation (except in the heading to any regulation or in any reference to any such heading), or

(b) directing that planning permission is deemed to be granted,

is to be taken, in relation to any consent, permission or authorisation which is capable of being varied or modified, to include a reference to its variation or modification.

62 Application of provisions of Chapter 1

(1) The requirements of the assessment provisions and the review provisions apply—

(a) subject to and in accordance with the provisions of Chapters 2 to 7, in relation to the matters specified in those provisions; and

(b) subject to regulation 63(7)(c), in relation to all other plans and projects not relating to matters specified in Chapters 2 to 9.

(2) Supplementary provision is made by regulations 67 to 69.

General provisions for protection of European sites and European offshore marine sites

63 Assessment of implications for European sites and European offshore marine sites

(1) A competent authority, before deciding to undertake, or give any consent, permission or other authorisation for, a plan or project which—

(a)   is likely to have a significant effect on a European site or a European offshore marine site (either alone or in combination with other plans or projects), and

(b)   is not directly connected with or necessary to the management of that site,

must make an appropriate assessment of the implications of the plan or project for that site in view of that site's conservation objectives.

(2)   A person applying for any such consent, permission or other authorisation must provide such information as the competent authority may reasonably require for the purposes of the assessment or to enable it to determine whether an appropriate assessment is required.

(3)   The competent authority must for the purposes of the assessment consult the appropriate nature conservation body and have regard to any representations made by that body within such reasonable time as the authority specifies.

(4)   It must also, if it considers it appropriate, take the opinion of the general public, and if it does so, it must take such steps for that purpose as it considers appropriate.

(5)   In the light of the conclusions of the assessment, and subject to regulation 64, the competent authority may agree to the plan or project only after having ascertained that it will not adversely affect the integrity of the European site or the European offshore marine site (as the case may be).

(6)   In considering whether a plan or project will adversely affect the integrity of the site, the competent authority must have regard to the manner in which it is proposed to be carried out or to any conditions or restrictions subject to which it proposes that the consent, permission or other authorisation should be given.

(7)   This regulation does not apply in relation to—

(a)   a site which is a European site by reason of regulation 8(1)(c);

(b)   a site which is a European offshore marine site by reason of regulation 18(c) of the Offshore Marine Conservation Regulations; or

(c)   a plan or project to which any of the following apply—

   (i)   the Offshore Petroleum Activities (Conservation of Habitats) Regulations 2001 (in so far as this regulation is not disapplied by regulation 4 (plans or projects relating to offshore marine area or offshore marine installations) in relation to plans or projects to which those Regulations apply);

   (ii)   the Environmental Impact Assessment (Agriculture) (England) (No. 2) Regulations 2006;

   (iii)   the Environmental Impact Assessment (Agriculture) (Wales) Regulations 2017; or

   (iv)   the Merchant Shipping (Ship-to-Ship Transfers) Regulations 2010.

(8)   Where a plan or project requires an appropriate assessment both under this regulation and under the Offshore Marine Conservation Regulations, the assessment required by this regulation need not identify those effects of the plan or project that are specifically attributable to that part of it that is to be

carried out in the United Kingdom, provided that an assessment made for the purpose of this regulation and the Offshore Marine Conservation Regulations assesses the effects of the plan or project as a whole.

(9)   In paragraph (1) the reference to the competent authority deciding to undertake a plan or project includes the competent authority deciding to vary any plan or project undertaken or to be undertaken.

64 Considerations of overriding public interest

(1)   If the competent authority is satisfied that, there being no alternative solutions, the plan or project must be carried out for imperative reasons of overriding public interest (which, subject to paragraph (2), may be of a social or economic nature), it may agree to the plan or project notwithstanding a negative assessment of the implications for the European site or the European offshore marine site (as the case may be).

(2)   Where the site concerned hosts a priority natural habitat type or a priority species, the reasons referred to in paragraph (1) must be either—

(a)   reasons relating to human health, public safety or beneficial consequences of primary importance to the environment; or

(b)   any other reasons which the competent authority, having due regard to the opinion of the European Commission, considers to be imperative reasons of overriding public interest.

(3)   Where a competent authority other than the Secretary of State or the Welsh Ministers desires to obtain the opinion of the European Commission as to whether reasons are to be considered imperative reasons of overriding public interest, it may submit a written request to the appropriate authority—

(a)   identifying the matter on which an opinion is sought; and

(b)   accompanied by any documents or information which may be required.

(4)   The appropriate authority—

(a)   may seek the opinion of the European Commission concerning the plan or project; and

(b)   where such an opinion is received, must send it to the competent authority.

(5)   Where a competent authority other than the Secretary of State or the Welsh Ministers proposes to agree to a plan or project under this regulation notwithstanding a negative assessment of the implications for the site concerned—

(a)   it must notify the appropriate authority; and

(b)   it must not agree to the plan or project before the end of the period of 21 days beginning with the day notified by the appropriate authority as that on which its notification was received, unless the appropriate authority notifies it that it may do so.

(6)   Without prejudice to any other power, the appropriate authority may give directions to the competent authority in any such case prohibiting it from agreeing to the plan or project, either indefinitely or during such period as may be specified in the direction.

65 Review of existing decisions and consents

(1) Where before the date on which a site becomes a European site or a European offshore marine site a competent authority has decided to undertake, or has given any consent, permission or other authorisation for, a plan or project to which regulation 63(1) would apply if it were to be reconsidered as of that date, the authority must, as soon as reasonably practicable—

    (a) review its decision or, as the case may be, the consent, permission or other authorisation; and

    (b) affirm, modify or revoke it.

(2) The authority must for that purpose make an appropriate assessment of the implications for the site in view of that site's conservation objectives; and the provisions of regulation 63(2) to (4) and (8) apply, with the appropriate modifications, in relation to such a review.

(3) Subject to the provisions of Chapters 2 to 7, any review required by this regulation must be carried out under existing statutory procedures where such procedures exist, and if none exists, the appropriate authority may give directions as to the procedure to be followed.

(4) Nothing in this regulation affects anything done in pursuance of the decision, or the consent, permission or other authorisation, before the date mentioned in paragraph (1).

66 Consideration on review

(1) The following provisions apply where a decision, or a consent, permission or other authorisation, falls to be reviewed under regulation 65.

(2) Subject as follows, the provisions of regulations 63(5) and (6) and 64 apply, with the appropriate modifications, in relation to the decision on the review.

(3) The decision, or the consent, permission or other authorisation, may be affirmed if it appears to the competent authority reviewing it that other action taken or to be taken by it, or by another authority, will secure that the plan or project does not adversely affect the integrity of the site.

(4) Where that object may be attained in a number of ways, the competent authority or authorities concerned must seek to secure that the action taken is the least onerous to those affected.

(5) The appropriate authority may issue guidance to competent authorities for the purposes of paragraph (3) as to the manner of determining which of different ways should be adopted for securing that the plan or project does not have any such effect, and in particular—

    (a) the order of application of different controls; and

    (b) the extent to which account should be taken of the possible exercise of other powers.

(6) The competent authorities concerned must have regard to any such guidance.

(7) Any modification or revocation of a decision, or a consent, permission or other authorisation, must be carried out under existing statutory procedures where such procedures exist, and if none exists, the appropriate authority may give directions as to the procedure to be followed.

67 Co-ordination where more than one competent authority involved

(1)   This regulation applies where a plan or project—

    (a)   is undertaken by more than one competent authority;

    (b)   requires the consent, permission or other authorisation of more than one competent authority; or

    (c)   is undertaken by one or more competent authorities and requires the consent, permission or other authorisation of one or more other competent authorities.

(2)   Nothing in regulation 63(1) or 65(2) requires a competent authority to assess any implications of a plan or project which would be more appropriately assessed under that provision by another competent authority.

(3)   The appropriate authority may issue guidance to competent authorities for the purposes of regulations 63 to 66 as to the circumstances in which a competent authority may or should adopt the reasoning or conclusions of another competent authority as to whether a plan or project—

    (a)   is likely to have a significant effect on a European site or a European offshore marine site; or

    (b)   will adversely affect the integrity of a European site or a European offshore marine site.

(4)   The competent authorities concerned must have regard to any such guidance.

(5)   In determining whether a plan or project should be agreed to under regulation 64, a competent authority other than the Secretary of State or the Welsh Ministers must seek and have regard to the views of the other competent authority or authorities involved.

68 Compensatory measures

Where in accordance with regulation 64—

    (a)   a plan or project is agreed to, notwithstanding a negative assessment of the implications for a European site or a European offshore marine site, or

    (b)   a decision, or a consent, permission or other authorisation, is affirmed on review, notwithstanding such an assessment,

the appropriate authority must secure that any necessary compensatory measures are taken to ensure that the overall coherence of Natura 2000 is protected.

69 Modifications of regulations 63 to 68 in certain cases

(1)   Where any provision of regulations 63 to 68 (a 'general provision') applies in relation to a provision specified in paragraph (2), that general provision applies with the following modifications—

    (a)   any reference to the Welsh Ministers is omitted; and

    (b)   for any reference to the appropriate authority, substitute a reference to the Secretary of State.

(2)   The provisions specified for the purposes of paragraph (1) are—

(a)   regulation 70(1)(e)(i) and (2) (grant of planning permission) in so far as those provisions relate to a direction given by the Secretary of State under section 90 of the TCPA 1990 (development with government authorisation) that planning permission is deemed to be granted; and

(b)   regulations 84 and 85 (development consent under Planning Act 2008).

(3)   Where a general provision applies in relation to a provision specified in paragraph (4), that general provision applies with the following modifications—

(a)   any reference to a competent authority is taken to include the Scottish Ministers;

(b)   for any reference to the Welsh Ministers, substitute a reference to the Scottish Ministers; and

(c)   for any reference to the appropriate authority—

(i)   in a case where the competent authority for the purposes of a provision specified in paragraph (4) is the Scottish Ministers, substitute a reference to the Scottish Ministers; and

(ii)   in any other case, substitute a reference to the Secretary of State.

(4)   The provisions specified for the purposes of paragraph (3) are—

(a)   in regulation 70—

(i)   paragraph (1)(e)(ii) and (iii);

(ii)   paragraph (1)(f), in so far as that paragraph relates to a direction under section 57(2ZA) of the Town and Country Planning (Scotland) Act 1997 (development with government authorisation); and

(iii)   paragraph (2) in so far as that paragraph relates to paragraph (1)(e)(ii) and (iii), and (1)(f) of that regulation;

(b)   Chapter 4 (electricity); and

(c)   Chapter 5 (pipe-lines).

(5)   Where a general provision applies in relation to regulation 103 (marine works), and confers a function on the appropriate authority, that provision applies with the following modifications—

(a)   in a case to which paragraph (6) applies, for any reference to the appropriate authority, substitute a reference to the Welsh Ministers; and

(b)   in any other case, for any reference to the appropriate authority, substitute a reference to the Secretary of State.

(6)   This paragraph applies where the function in question is exercisable in relation to—

(a)   any application to the Welsh Ministers for an authorisation in respect of marine works;

(b)   any application to any other authority for—

(i)   an authorisation in respect of marine works, the refusal of which gives rise to a right of appeal to the Welsh Ministers;

>> (ii) an authorisation in respect of marine works in relation to which the Welsh Ministers exercise any power of direction or call-in; or
>>
>> (iii) an authorisation of harbour works which are, or are to be, carried out in relation to a fishery harbour in Wales under legislation of a kind mentioned in regulation 103(6)(c);
>
> (c) the grant of any application of a kind mentioned in sub-paragraph (a) or (b); or
>
> (d) harbour works which—
>
>> (i) are, or are to be, carried out in relation to a fishery harbour in Wales; and
>>
>> (ii) are authorised by, and are, or are to be, carried out in accordance with, any legislation of a kind mentioned in regulation 103(6)(c).

(7) In paragraph (6)—

'authorisation' means any licence, consent or other approval;

'marine works' and 'harbour works' have the meanings given by regulation 103(5) and (7) respectively.

(8) Where a general provision applies in relation to a plan or project which does not relate to a matter specified in Chapters 2 to 9, to the extent that that general provision applies in relation to Scotland or Northern Ireland, that provision applies with the following modifications—

> (a) any reference to the Welsh Ministers is omitted; and
>
> (b) for any reference to the appropriate authority, substitute a reference to the Secretary of State.

Chapter 8 Land Use Plans

Land use plans

105 Assessment of implications for European sites and European offshore marine sites

(1) Where a land use plan—

> (a) is likely to have a significant effect on a European site or a European offshore marine site (either alone or in combination with other plans or projects), and
>
> (b) is not directly connected with or necessary to the management of the site,

the plan-making authority for that plan must, before the plan is given effect, make an appropriate assessment of the implications for the site in view of that site's conservation objectives.

(2) The plan-making authority must for the purposes of the assessment consult the appropriate nature conservation body and have regard to any representations made by that body within such reasonable time as the authority specifies.

(3) The plan-making authority must also, if it considers it appropriate, take the opinion of the general public, and if it does so, it must take such steps for that purpose as it considers appropriate.

(4)   In the light of the conclusions of the assessment, and subject to regulation 107, the plan-making authority must give effect to the land use plan only after having ascertained that it will not adversely affect the integrity of the European site or the European offshore marine site (as the case may be).

(5)   A plan-making authority must provide such information as the appropriate authority may reasonably require for the purposes of the discharge by the appropriate authority of its obligations under this Chapter.

(6)   This regulation does not apply in relation to a site which is—

    (a)   a European site by reason of regulation 8(1)(c), or

    (b)   a European offshore marine site by reason of regulation 18(c) of the Offshore Marine Conservation Regulations (site protected in accordance with Article 5(4) of the Habitats Directive).

106 Assessment of implications for European site: neighbourhood development plans

(1)   A qualifying body which submits a proposal for a neighbourhood development plan must provide such information as the competent authority may reasonably require for the purposes of the assessment under regulation 105 or to enable it to determine whether that assessment is required.

(2)   In this regulation, 'qualifying body' means a parish council, or an organisation or body designated as a neighbourhood forum, authorised for the purposes of a neighbourhood development plan to act in relation to a neighbourhood area as a result of section 61F of the TCPA 1990 (authorisation to act in relation to neighbourhood areas), as applied by section 38C of the 2004 Planning Act (supplementary provisions).

(3)   Where the competent authority decides to revoke or modify a neighbourhood development plan after it has been made, it must for that purpose make an appropriate assessment of the implications for any European site likely to be significantly affected in view of that site's conservation objectives; and regulation 105 and paragraph (1) apply with the appropriate modifications in relation to such a revocation or modification.

(4)   This regulation applies in relation to England only.

107 Considerations of overriding public interest

(1)   If the plan-making authority is satisfied that, there being no alternative solutions, the land use plan must be given effect for imperative reasons of overriding public interest (which, subject to paragraph (2), may be of a social or economic nature), it may give effect to the land use plan notwithstanding a negative assessment of the implications for the European site or the European offshore marine site (as the case may be).

(2)   Where the site concerned hosts a priority natural habitat type or a priority species, the reasons referred to in paragraph (1) must be either—

    (a)   reasons relating to human health, public safety or beneficial consequences of primary importance to the environment; or

    (b)   any other reasons which the plan-making authority, having due regard to the opinion of the European Commission, considers to be imperative reasons of overriding public interest.

(3)   Where a plan-making authority other than the Secretary of State or the Welsh Ministers desire to obtain the opinion of the European Commission as to whether reasons are to be considered imperative reasons of overriding public interest, it may submit a written request to the appropriate authority—

    (a)   identifying the matter on which an opinion is sought; and

    (b)   accompanied by any documents or information which may be required.

(4)   The appropriate authority—

    (a)   may seek the opinion of the European Commission concerning the plan; and

    (b)   where such an opinion is received, must send it to the plan-making authority.

(5)   Where a plan-making authority other than the Secretary of State or the Welsh Ministers propose to give effect to a land use plan under this regulation notwithstanding a negative assessment of the implications for the site concerned it must—

    (a)   notify the appropriate authority; and

    (b)   not give effect to the land use plan before the end of the period of 21 days beginning with the day notified by the appropriate authority as that on which its notification was received, unless the appropriate authority notify it that it may do so.

(6)   Without prejudice to any other power, the appropriate authority may give directions to the plan-making authority in any such case prohibiting it from giving effect to the land use plan, either indefinitely or during such period as may be specified in the direction.

108 Co-ordination for land use plan prepared by more than one authority

(1)   The following provisions apply where two or more local planning authorities prepare a joint local development document under section 28 (joint local development documents) or a joint local development plan under section 72 (joint local development plans) of the 2004 Planning Act.

(2)   Nothing in paragraph (1) of regulation 105 requires a local planning authority to assess any implications of a joint local development document or plan which would be more appropriately assessed under that provision by another local planning authority.

(3)   The appropriate authority may issue guidance to local planning authorities for the purposes of regulation 105(1) as to the circumstances in which a local planning authority may or should adopt the reasoning or conclusions of another local planning authority as to whether a joint local planning document or plan—

    (a)   is likely to have a significant effect on a European site or a European offshore marine site; or

    (b)   will adversely affect the integrity of a European site or a European offshore marine site.

(4)   The local planning authorities concerned must have regard to any such guidance.

(5)   In determining whether a joint local development document or plan should be adopted under regulation 107, a local planning authority must seek and have regard to the views of the other local planning authorities concerned.

109 Compensatory measures

Where in accordance with regulation 107 a land use plan is given effect notwithstanding a negative assessment of the implications for a European site or a European offshore marine site, the appropriate authority must secure that any necessary compensatory measures are taken to ensure that the overall coherence of Natura 2000 is protected.

Planning Act 2008

110 National policy statements

(1)   This Chapter applies—

    (a)   in relation to a national policy statement under Part 2 of the Planning Act 2008 (national policy statements) as it applies in relation to a land use plan, and

    (b)   in relation to the Secretary of State when exercising powers under Part 2 of that Act as it applies in relation to a plan-making authority,

    with the modifications specified in paragraphs (2) and (3).

(2)   Any reference in this Chapter to giving effect to a land use plan, in relation to a national policy statement, is to be taken to be a reference to the designation of a statement as a national policy statement or an amendment of a national policy statement under Part 2 of the Planning Act 2008.

(3)   Where this Chapter applies by virtue of paragraph (1)—

    (a)   regulations 105(5), 107(3) to (6) and 108 do not apply; and

    (b)   in regulation 109, the reference to the appropriate authority is taken to be a reference to the Secretary of State.

Interpretation of Chapter 8

111 Interpretation of Chapter 8

(1)   In this Chapter—

    'the 1999 Act' means the Greater London Authority Act 1999;

    'the 2004 Planning Act' means the Planning and Compulsory Purchase Act 2004;

    'the 2005 Order' means the Planning and Compulsory Purchase Act 2004 (Commencement No. 3 and Consequential and Transitional Provisions) (Wales) Order 2005;

    'land use plan' means—

        (a)   the spatial development strategy under section 334 of the 1999 Act (the spatial development strategy);

(b)   a local development document as provided for in Part 2 of the 2004 Planning Act (local development) other than a statement of community involvement under section 18 of that Act (statement of community involvement);

(c)   a local development plan as provided for in Part 6 of the 2004 Planning Act (Wales);

(d)   the Wales Spatial Plan under section 60 of the 2004 Planning Act (national development framework for Wales);

(e)   an alteration or replacement of a structure plan, unitary development plan, local plan, minerals local plan, or waste local plan under Part 2 of the TCPA 1990 (development plans) to the extent permitted by Schedule 8 to the 2004 Planning Act (transitional provisions); or

(f)   (in England) a neighbourhood development plan as defined in section 38A of the 2004 Planning Act (neighbourhood development plans).

'plan-making authority' means—

(a)   the Mayor of London when exercising powers under section 341(1) or (2) of the 1999 Act (alteration or replacement);

(b)   an authority which, by virtue of Part 1 of the TCPA 1990 (planning authorities) or an order under section 29(2) of the 2004 Planning Act (joint committees), is a local planning authority;

(c)   the Secretary of State when exercising powers under—

    (i)   section 21 or section 27 of the 2004 Planning Act (intervention by the Secretary of State, Secretary of State's default power, respectively); or

    (ii)   section 19, section 35A(4) or section 45 of the TCPA 1990 (approval of a unitary development plan, calling in of proposal for approval by the Secretary of State, approval of proposals by the Secretary of State, respectively) to the extent permitted by Schedule 8 to the 2004 Planning Act;

(d)   the Welsh Ministers when exercising powers under—

    (i)   section 60(3), section 65 or section 71(4) of the 2004 Planning Act (national development framework for Wales, intervention by Assembly, Assembly's default power, respectively); or

    (ii)   section 19 of the TCPA 1990 to the extent permitted by article 4 of the 2005 Order; or

(e)   (in England) the local planning authority when exercising powers under Schedule 4B to the TCPA 1990 (as applied by section 38A(3) of the 2004 Planning Act).

(2)   References in this Chapter to giving effect to a land use plan are to—

(a)   the approval, under section 21(9) or 27(4) of the 2004 Planning Act, of a local development document;

(b) the adoption, under section 23 of the 2004 Planning Act (adoption of local development documents), of a local development document other than a statement of community involvement under section 18 of that Act;

(c) the publication, under section 341 of the 1999 Act, of alterations of the spatial development strategy or a new spatial development strategy to replace it;

(d) the publication, under section 60 of the 2004 Planning Act, of a revision of the Wales Spatial Plan;

(e) the adoption, under section 67 of the 2004 Planning Act (adoption of local development plan), of a local development plan;

(f) the approval, under section 65(9) or 71(4) of the 2004 Planning Act, of a local development plan;

(g) the adoption, under section 35(1) (adoption of proposals), or approval under section 35A (4) of the TCPA 1990, of an alteration or replacement of a structure plan to the extent permitted by paragraph 2(2) of Schedule 8 to the 2004 Planning Act;

(h) the adoption, under section 15 (adoption of unitary development plans by local planning authority) and that provision as applied by section 21(2) (alteration or replacement of unitary development plans) of the TCPA 1990, of an alteration or replacement of a unitary development plan to the extent permitted by paragraph 4 of Schedule 8 to the 2004 Planning Act;

(i) the approval, under section 19 and that provision as applied by section 21(2) of the TCPA 1990, of an alteration or replacement of a unitary development plan to the extent permitted by paragraph 4 of Schedule 8 to the 2004 Planning Act;

(j) the adoption, under section 43 (adoption of proposals) or approval under section 45 of the TCPA 1990, of an alteration or replacement of a local plan, minerals local plan or waste local plan to the extent permitted by paragraph 9, 10 or 14 of Schedule 8 to the 2004 Planning Act;

(k) the adoption, under section 15 of the TCPA 1990, of a unitary development plan to the extent permitted by article 4 of the 2005 Order;

(l) the approval, under section 19 of the TCPA 1990, of a unitary development plan to the extent permitted by article 4 of the 2005 Order; or

(m) (in England) the holding of a referendum in accordance with paragraph 12(4) of Schedule 4B to the TCPA 1990 (as applied by section 38A(3) of the 2004 Planning Act).

Chapter 9 Marine policy statements and marine plans

112 Marine policy statement

(1) Chapter 8 applies (with the modifications specified in paragraphs (2) and (3))—

(a) in relation to a marine policy statement under Chapter 1 of Part 3 (marine planning) of the Marine Act as it applies in relation to a land use plan; and

    (b)   in relation to a policy authority when exercising powers under Part 3 of that Act as it applies in relation to a plan-making authority.

(2)   Any reference in Chapter 8 to giving effect to a land use plan, in relation to a marine policy statement, is to be taken to be a reference to the adoption and publication of a marine policy statement in accordance with Schedule 5 to the Marine Act or any amendment of a marine policy statement under section 47 of that Act.

(3)   Where Chapter 8 applies by virtue of paragraph (1)—

    (a)   in regulation 105(2), after 'the appropriate nature conservation body' insert 'and the Joint Nature Conservation Committee';

    (b)   regulations 105(5), 107(3) to (6) and 108 do not apply; and

    (c)   in regulation 109, for the reference to the appropriate authority substitute a reference to the policy authority.

(4)   In this regulation 'policy authority' means the Secretary of State or the Welsh Ministers.

113 Marine plan

(1)   Chapter 8 applies (with the modifications specified in paragraphs (2) and (3))—

    (a)   in relation to a marine plan as it applies in relation to a land use plan; and

    (b)   in relation to a marine plan authority when exercising powers under Part 3 of the Marine Act as it applies in relation to a plan-making authority.

(2)   Any reference in Chapter 8 to giving effect to a land use plan, in relation to a marine plan, is to be taken to be a reference to the adoption and publication of a marine plan in accordance with Schedule 6 to the Marine Act or any amendment of a marine plan under section 52 of that Act.

(3)   Where Chapter 8 applies by virtue of paragraph (1), regulations 105(5), 107(3) to (6) and 108 do not apply.

(4)   In this regulation—

'marine plan' means a marine plan under Chapter 2 of Part 3 of the Marine Act;

'marine plan authority' has the meaning given by Part 3 of the Marine Act.

Index

[All references are to paragraph number]

Aarhus Convention claims
 costs, 22.40
 generally, 2.15
Adequate information
 generally, 2.4
Air quality
 air quality plans, 6.50–6.51
 Air Quality Strategy
  generally, 6.45–6.47
  status, 6.48–6.49
 ClientEarth litigation, 6.52–6.51
 domestic law, 6.45–6.6
 EU law, 6.35–6.44
 management areas action plans, 20.34
Airports
 national policy statements, 5.38
Alternatives
 habitats assessments, 3.27
 strategic environmental assessment, 3.15
Anaerobic digestion
 strategy and action plan, 6.33
Area action plans
 generally, 7.2
Area plans
 Northern Ireland, 16.9–16.10
Areas of outstanding natural beauty (AONB)
 generally, 2.23
 management plans
  consultation, 20.25
  establishment of conservation boards, 20.24
  introduction, 20.23
  publicity, 20.25
  requirement to produce, 20.24
 strategic environmental assessment, and, 3.13
Authorisation
 neighbourhood plans, 10.145

Bias
 general prohibition, 2.12
 generally, 2.10
 Localism Act 2011, and, 2.13
 pre-determination, 2.11
 tainting by one member, 2.14
Biodiversity
 generally, 2.26
Birds
 habitats assessments, 3.21

Broads
 generally, 2.22
 plan, 20.22
Brownfield land registers
 achievability of residential development, 8.8
 addition of land to Part 2, 8.12
 area of at least 0.25 ha, 8.5
 available for residential development, 8.7
 background, 8.1
 contents, 8.9
 criteria
  achievability of residential development, 8.8
  area of at least 0.25 ha, 8.5
  available for residential development, 8.7
  introduction, 8.3
  land capable of supporting at least five dwellings, 8.5
  previously developed land, 8.4
  suitable for residential development, 8.6
 decision-making within LPA, 8.11–8.12
 details, 8.9
 environmental impact assessment, 8.16
 environmental regimes, and, 8.13–8.17
 entry of land on, 8.10
 establishment, 8.1
 grant of permission by development order, 8.2
 habitats regulations assessment
  Part 1 entries, 8.15
  Part 2 land, 8.17
 introduction, 8.1
 land capable of supporting at least five dwellings, 8.5
 maintenance, 8.3
 'permission in principle', 8.1
 preparation, 8.3
 previously developed land, 8.4
 publication, 8.3
 registration, 8.3
 review, 8.19
 statutory framework, 8.1
 strategic environmental assessment, 8.14
 structure, 8.1
 suitable for residential development, 8.6
 technical details consent, 8.18

659